I0043340

CALIFORNIA
Probate
Code
2014

California Probate Code 2014

Copyright © 2014 by Snape Legal Publishing

ISBN: 978-1-312-32283-7

Some Rights Reserved. This book contains the laws of the state of California, compiled for easier reference. The laws of this country are in the public domain, but the specific compilation design is copyrighted. You are free to, and encouraged to, take the law listed herein and freely disseminate it to whomever you'd like. We ask that if you are going to do this, please design your own presentation.

First Printing: 2014

Other books available from Snape Legal Publishing:

California Labor Code 2014 .... ISBN # 978-1-304-90622-9
    and an eBook in PDF Format

California Military and Veterans Code 2014................ ISBN # 978-1-304-90050-0
    and an eBook in PDF Format

California Penal Code and Evidence Code 2014
    Book 1 of 2 .... ISBN # 978-1-312-05335-9
    Book 2 of 2 .... ISBN # 978-1-312-05336-6
    and an eBook in PDF Format

California Evidence Code .... ISBN # 978-1-304-87161-9
    and an eBook in PDF Format

California Fish and Game Code .... ISBN # 978-1-304-92522-0
    and an eBook in PDF Format

Snape Legal Publishing
1026 E Washington Ave
El Cajon, CA 92020

Legal Disclaimer: The code in this book is current as of January 1st, 2014. The next compiling of this will be the 2015 edition. Any changes to the law in the meantime will not be reflected in the text. You will need to confirm any text before using it for any legal proceeding.

CALIFORNIA Probate Code 2014

Compiled by

John Snape

Table of Contents

California Probate Code

Division 1. Preliminary Provisions And Definitions

Part 1. Preliminary Provisions

1. This code shall be known as the Probate Code.

2. (a) A provision of this code, insofar as it is substantially the same as a previously existing provision relating to the same subject matter, shall be construed as a restatement and continuation thereof and not as a new enactment.

(b) A provision of this code, insofar as it is the same in substance as a provision of a uniform act, shall be so construed as to effectuate the general purpose to make uniform the law in those states which enact that provision.

3. (a) As used in this section:

(1) "New law" means either of the following, as the case may be:

(A) The act that enacted this code.

(B) The act that makes a change in this code, whether effectuated by amendment, addition, or repeal of any provision of this code.

(2) "Old law" means the applicable law in effect before the operative date of the new law.

(3) "Operative date" means the operative date of the new law.

(b) This section governs the application of a new law except to the extent otherwise expressly provided in the new law.

(c) Subject to the limitations provided in this section, a new law applies on the operative date to all matters governed by the new law, regardless of whether an event occurred or circumstance existed before, on, or after the operative date, including, but not limited to, creation of a fiduciary relationship, death of a person, commencement of a proceeding, making of an order, or taking of an action.

(d) If a petition, account, report, inventory, appraisal, or other document or paper is filed before the operative date, the contents, execution, and notice thereof are governed by the old law and not by the new law; but any subsequent proceedings taken after the operative date concerning the petition, account, report, inventory, appraisal, or other document or paper, including an objection or response, a hearing, an order, or other matter relating thereto is governed by the new law and not by the old law.

(e) If an order is made before the operative date, including an order appointing a personal representative, guardian, conservator, trustee, probate referee, or any other fiduciary or officer, or any action on an order is taken before the operative date, the validity of the order or action is governed by the old law and not by the new law. Nothing in this subdivision precludes proceedings after the operative date to modify an order made, or alter a course of action commenced, before the operative date to the extent proceedings for modification of an order or alteration of a course of action of that type are otherwise provided by statute.

(f) No personal representative, guardian, conservator, trustee, probate referee, or any other fiduciary, officer, or person is liable for any action taken before the operative date that was proper at the time the action was taken, even though the action would be improper if taken on or after the operative date, and such a person has no duty, as a result of the enactment of the new law, to take any step to alter the course of action or its consequences.

(g) If the new law does not apply to a matter that occurred before the operative date, the old law continues to govern the matter notwithstanding its amendment or repeal by the new law.

(h) If a party shows, and the court determines, that application of a particular provision of the new law or of the old law in the manner required by this section or by the new law would substantially interfere with the effective conduct of the proceedings or the rights of the parties or other interested persons in connection with an event that occurred or circumstance that existed before the operative date, the court may, notwithstanding this section or the new law, apply either the new law or the old law to the extent reasonably necessary to mitigate the substantial interference.

4. Division, part, chapter, article, and section headings do not in any manner affect the scope, meaning, or intent of the provisions of this code.

5. If a notice or other communication is required by this code to be mailed by registered mail, the mailing of the notice or other communication by certified mail is deemed to be sufficient compliance with the requirement.

6. Unless the provision or context otherwise requires, the general provisions and rules of construction in this part govern the construction of this code.

7. Whenever a reference is made to any portion of this code or to any other law, the reference applies to all amendments and additions heretofore or hereafter made.

8. Unless otherwise expressly stated:

(a) "Division" means a division of this code.

(b) "Part" means a part of the division in which that term occurs.

(c) "Chapter" means a chapter of the division or part, as the case may be, in which that term occurs.

(d) "Article" means an article of the chapter in which that term occurs.

(e) "Section" means a section of this code.

(f) "Subdivision" means a subdivision of the section in which that term occurs.

(g) "Paragraph" means a paragraph of the subdivision in which that term occurs.

(h) "Subparagraph" means a subparagraph of the paragraph in which that term occurs.

9. The present tense includes the past and future tenses, and the future, the present.

10. The singular number includes the plural, and the plural, the singular.

11. If any provision or clause of this code or application thereof to any person or circumstances is held invalid, the invalidity does not affect other provisions or applications of the code which can be given effect without the invalid provision or application, and to this end the provisions of this code are severable.

12. "Shall" is mandatory and "may" is permissive.

13. (a) The degree of kinship or consanguinity between two persons is determined by counting the number of generations separating those persons, pursuant to subdivision (b) or (c). Each generation is called a degree.

(b) Lineal kinship or consanguinity is the relationship between two persons, one of whom is a direct descendant of the other. The degree of kinship between those persons is determined by counting the generations separating the first person from the second person. In counting the generations, the first person is excluded and the second person is included. For example, parent and child are related in the first degree of lineal kinship or consanguinity, grandchild and grandparent are related in the second degree, and great-grandchild and great-grandparent are related in the third degree.

(c) Collateral kinship or consanguinity is the relationship between two people who spring from a common ancestor, but neither person is the direct descendent of the other. The degree of kinship is determined by counting the generations from the first person up to the common ancestor and from the common ancestor down to the second person. In counting the generations, the first person is excluded, the second person is included, and the common ancestor is counted only once. For example, siblings are related in the second degree of collateral kinship or consanguinity, an aunt or uncle and a niece or nephew are related in the third degree, and first cousins are related in the fourth degree.

Part 2. Definitions

20. Unless the provision or context otherwise requires, the definitions in this part govern the construction of this code.

21. "Account," when used to mean a contract of deposit of funds between a depositor and a financial institution, includes a checking account, savings account, certificate of deposit, share account, mutual capital certificate, and other like arrangements.

22. "Account in an insured credit union" means a share account in a credit union, either federally chartered or state licensed, that is insured under Title II of the Federal Credit Union Act (12 U.S.C. Sec. 1781, et seq.).

23. (a) "Account in an insured savings and loan association" means a savings account or mutual capital certificate of either of the following:

(1) A federal association.

(2) A savings association doing business in this state which is an "insured institution" as defined in Title IV of the National Housing Act (12 U.S.C. Sec. 1724, et seq.).

(b) As used in this section:

(1) "Federal association" has the meaning given that term in subdivision (b) of Section 5102 of the Financial Code.

(2) "Mutual capital certificate" has the meaning given that term in Section 5111 of the Financial Code.

(3) "Savings account" has the meaning given that term in Section 5116 of the Financial Code.

(4) "Savings association" has the meaning given that term in subdivision (a) of Section 5102 of the Financial Code.

24. "Beneficiary" means a person to whom a donative transfer of property is made or that person's successor in interest, and:

(a) As it relates to the intestate estate of a decedent, means an heir.

(b) As it relates to the testate estate of a decedent, means a devisee.

(c) As it relates to a trust, means a person who has any present or future interest, vested or contingent.

(d) As it relates to a charitable trust, includes any person entitled to enforce the trust.

26. "Child" means any individual entitled

to take as a child under this code by intestate succession from the parent whose relationship is involved.

28. "Community property" means:

(a) Community property heretofore or hereafter acquired during marriage by a married person while domiciled in this state.

(b) All personal property wherever situated, and all real property situated in this state, heretofore or hereafter acquired during the marriage by a married person while domiciled elsewhere, that is community property, or a substantially equivalent type of marital property, under the laws of the place where the acquiring spouse was domiciled at the time of its acquisition.

(c) All personal property wherever situated, and all real property situated in this state, heretofore or hereafter acquired during the marriage by a married person in exchange for real or personal property, wherever situated, that is community property, or a substantially equivalent type of marital property, under the laws of the place where the acquiring spouse was domiciled at the time the property so exchanged was acquired.

29. "Conservatee" includes a limited conservatee.

30. "Conservator" includes a limited conservator.

32. "Devise," when used as a noun, means a disposition of real or personal property by will, and, when used as a verb, means to dispose of real or personal property by will.

34. (a) "Devisee" means any person designated in a will to receive a devise.

(b) In the case of a devise to an existing trust or trustee, or to a trustee on trust described by will, the trust or trustee is the devisee and the beneficiaries are not devisees.

36. "Dissolution of marriage" includes divorce.

37. (a) "Domestic partner" means one of two persons who have filed a Declaration of Domestic Partnership with the Secretary of State pursuant to Division 2.5 (commencing with Section 297) of the Family Code, provided that the domestic partnership has not been terminated pursuant to Section 299 of the Family Code.

(b) Notwithstanding Section 299 of the Family Code, if a domestic partnership is terminated by the death of one of the parties and Notice of Termination was not filed by either party prior to the date of death of the decedent, the domestic partner who survives the deceased is a surviving domestic partner, and shall be entitled to the rights of a surviving domestic partner as provided in this code.

38. "Family allowance" means an allowance provided for in Chapter 4 (commencing with Section 6540) of Part 3 of Division 6.

39. "Fiduciary" means personal representative, trustee, guardian, conservator,

attorney-in-fact under a power of attorney, custodian under the California Uniform Transfer To Minors Act (Part 9 (commencing with Section 3900) of Division 4), or other legal representative subject to this code.

40. "Financial institution" means a state or national bank, state or federal savings and loan association or credit union, or like organization.

42. "General personal representative" is defined in subdivision (b) of Section 58.

44. "Heir" means any person, including the surviving spouse, who is entitled to take property of the decedent by intestate succession under this code.

45. "Instrument" means a will, trust, deed, or other writing that designates a beneficiary or makes a donative transfer of property.

46. "Insured account in a financial institution" means an account in a bank, an account in an insured credit union, and an account in an insured savings and loan association, to the extent that the account is insured.

48. (a) Subject to subdivision (b), "interested person" includes any of the following:

(1) An heir, devisee, child, spouse, creditor, beneficiary, and any other person having a property right in or claim against a trust estate or the estate of a decedent which may be affected by the proceeding.

(2) Any person having priority for appointment as personal representative.

(3) A fiduciary representing an interested person.

(b) The meaning of "interested person" as it relates to particular persons may vary from time to time and shall be determined according to the particular purposes of, and matter involved in, any proceeding.

50. "Issue" of a person means all his or her lineal descendants of all generations with the relationship of parent and child at each generation being determined by the definitions of child and parent.

52. "Letters":

(a) As it relates to a personal representative, means letters testamentary, letters of administration, letters of administration with the will annexed, or letters of special administration.

(b) As it relates to a guardian or conservator, means letters of guardianship or conservatorship or temporary guardianship or conservatorship.

54. "Parent" means any individual entitled to take as a parent under this code by intestate succession from the child whose relationship is involved.

55. "Pay-on-death account" or "P.O.D. account" is defined in Section 5140.

56. "Person" means an individual, corporation, government or governmental subdivision or agency, business trust, estate, trust, partnership, limited liability company, association, or other entity.

58. (a) "Personal representative" means executor, administrator, administrator with the will annexed, special administrator, successor personal representative, public administrator acting pursuant to Section 7660, or a person who performs substantially the same function under the law of another jurisdiction governing the person's status.

(b) "General personal representative" excludes a special administrator unless the special administrator has the powers, duties, and obligations of a general personal representative under Section 8545.

59. "Predeceased spouse" means a person who died before the decedent while married to the decedent, except that the term does not include any of the following:

(a) A person who obtains or consents to a final decree or judgment of dissolution of marriage from the decedent or a final decree or judgment of annulment of their marriage, which decree or judgment is not recognized as valid in this state, unless they (1) subsequently participate in a marriage ceremony purporting to marry each to the other or (2) subsequently live together as husband and wife.

(b) A person who, following a decree or judgment of dissolution or annulment of marriage obtained by the decedent, participates in a marriage ceremony to a third person.

(c) A person who was a party to a valid proceeding concluded by an order purporting to terminate all marital property rights.

60. "Probate homestead" means a homestead provided for in Chapter 3 (commencing with Section 6520) of Part 3 of Division 6.

60.1. (a) "Professional fiduciary" means a person who is a professional fiduciary as defined under subdivision (f) of Section 6501 of the Business and Professions Code.

(b) On and after January 1, 2009, no person shall act or hold himself or herself out to the public as a professional fiduciary unless he or she is licensed as a professional fiduciary under Chapter 6 (commencing with Section 6500) of Division 3 of the Business and Professions Code.

62. "Property" means anything that may be the subject of ownership and includes both real and personal property and any interest therein.

66. "Quasi-community property" means the following property, other than community property as defined in Section 28:

(a) All personal property wherever situated, and all real property situated in this state, heretofore or hereafter acquired by a decedent while domiciled elsewhere that would have been the community property of the decedent and the surviving spouse if the decedent had been domiciled in this state at the time of its acquisition.

(b) All personal property wherever situated, and all real property situated in this state, heretofore or hereafter acquired in exchange for real or personal property, wherever situated, that would have been the community property of the decedent and the surviving spouse if the decedent had been domiciled in this state at the time the property so exchanged was acquired.

68. "Real property" includes a leasehold interest in real property.

70. "Security" includes any note, stock, treasury stock, bond, debenture, evidence of indebtedness, certificate of interest or participation in an oil, gas, or mining title or lease or in payments out of production under such a title or lease, collateral trust certificate, transferable share, voting trust certificate or, in general, any interest or instrument commonly known as a security, or any certificate of interest or participation, any temporary or interim certificate, receipt, or certificate of deposit for, or any warrant or right to subscribe to or purchase, any of the foregoing.

74. "State" includes any state of the United States, the District of Columbia, the Commonwealth of Puerto Rico, and any territory or possession subject to the legislative authority of the United States.

76. A "subscribing witness" to a will means a witness who signs the will as provided in Section 6110.

78. "Surviving spouse" does not include any of the following:

(a) A person whose marriage to the decedent has been dissolved or annulled, unless, by virtue of a subsequent marriage, the person is married to the decedent at the time of death.

(b) A person who obtains or consents to a final decree or judgment of dissolution of marriage from the decedent or a final decree or judgment of annulment of their marriage, which decree or judgment is not recognized as valid in this state, unless they (1) subsequently participate in a marriage ceremony purporting to marry each to the other or (2) subsequently live together as husband and wife.

(c) A person who, following a decree or judgment of dissolution or annulment of marriage obtained by the decedent, participates in a marriage ceremony with a third person.

(d) A person who was a party to a valid proceeding concluded by an order purporting to terminate all marital property rights.

80. "Totten trust account" means an account in the name of one or more parties as trustee for one or more beneficiaries where the relationship is established by the form of the account and the deposit agreement with the financial institution and there is no subject of the trust other than the sums on deposit in the account. In a Totten trust account, it is not essential that payment to the beneficiary be mentioned in the deposit agreement. A Totten trust account does not include (1) a regular trust account under a testamentary trust or a trust agreement which has significance apart from the account or (2) a fiduciary account arising from a fiduciary relation such as attorney-client.

81. "Transferor" means the testator, settlor, grantor, owner, or other person who executes an instrument.

81.5. "Transferee" means the beneficiary, donee, or other recipient of an interest transferred by an instrument.

82. (a) "Trust" includes the following:

(1) An express trust, private or charitable, with additions thereto, wherever and however created.

(2) A trust created or determined by a judgment or decree under which the trust is to be administered in the manner of an express trust.

(b) "Trust" excludes the following:

(1) Constructive trusts, other than those described in paragraph (2) of subdivision (a), and resulting trusts.

(2) Guardianships and conservatorships.

(3) Personal representatives.

(4) Totten trust accounts.

(5) Custodial arrangements pursuant to the Uniform Gifts to Minors Act or the Uniform Transfers to Minors Act of any state.

(6) Business trusts that are taxed as partnerships or corporations.

(7) Investment trusts subject to regulation under the laws of this state or any other jurisdiction.

(8) Common trust funds.

(9) Voting trusts.

(10) Security arrangements.

(11) Transfers in trust for purpose of suit or enforcement of a claim or right.

(12) Liquidation trusts.

(13) Trusts for the primary purpose of paying debts, dividends, interest, salaries, wages, profits, pensions, or employee benefits of any kind.

(14) Any arrangement under which a person is nominee or escrowee for another.

83. "Trust company" means an entity that has qualified to engage in and conduct a trust business in this state.

84. "Trustee" includes an original, additional, or successor trustee, whether or not appointed or confirmed by a court.

86. "Undue influence" has the same meaning as defined in Section 15610.70 of the Welfare and Institutions Code. It is the intent of the Legislature that this section supplement the common law meaning of undue influence without superseding or interfering with the operation of that law.

88. "Will" includes codicil and any testamentary instrument which merely appoints an executor or revokes or revises another will.

Division 2. General Provisions

Part 1. Effect Of Death Of Married Person On Community And Quasi-Community Property

100. (a) Upon the death of a married person, one-half of the community property belongs to the surviving spouse and the other half belongs to the decedent.

(b) Notwithstanding subdivision (a), a husband and wife may agree in writing to divide their community property on the basis of a non pro rata division of the aggregate value of the community property or on the basis of a division of each individual item or asset of community property, or partly on each basis. Nothing in this subdivision shall be construed to require this written agreement in order to permit or recognize a non pro rata division of community property.

101. (a) Upon the death of a married person domiciled in this state, one-half of the decedent's quasi-community property belongs to the surviving spouse and the other half belongs to the decedent.

(b) Notwithstanding subdivision (a), a husband and wife may agree in writing to divide their quasi-community property on the basis of a non pro rata division of the aggregate value of the quasi-community property, or on the basis of a division of each individual item or asset of quasi-community property, or partly on each basis. Nothing in this subdivision shall be construed to require this written agreement in order to permit or recognize a non pro rata division of quasi-community property.

102. (a) The decedent's surviving spouse may require the transferee of property in which the surviving spouse had an expectancy under Section 101 at the time of the transfer to restore to the decedent's estate one-half of the property if the transferee retains the property or, if not, one-half of its proceeds or, if none, one-half of its value at the time of transfer, if all of the following requirements are satisfied:

(1) The decedent died domiciled in this state.

(2) The decedent made a transfer of the property to a person other than the surviving spouse without receiving in exchange a consideration of substantial value and without the written consent or joinder of the surviving spouse.

(3) The transfer is any of the following types:

(A) A transfer under which the decedent retained at the time of death the possession or enjoyment of, or the right to income from, the property.

(B) A transfer to the extent that the decedent retained at the time of death a power, either alone or in conjunction with any other person, to revoke or to consume, invade, or dispose of the principal for the decedent's own benefit.

(C) A transfer whereby property is held at the time of the decedent's death by the decedent and another with right of survivorship.

(b) Nothing in this section requires a transferee to restore to the decedent's estate any life insurance, accident insurance, joint annuity, or pension payable to a person other than the surviving spouse.

(c) All property restored to the decedent's estate under this section belongs to the surviving spouse pursuant to Section 101 as though the transfer had not been made.

103. Except as provided by Section 224, if a husband and wife die leaving community or quasi-community property and it cannot be established by clear and convincing evidence that one spouse survived the other:

(a) One-half of the community property and one-half of the quasi-community property shall be administered or distributed, or otherwise dealt with, as if one spouse had survived and as if that half belonged to that spouse.

(b) The other half of the community property and the other half of the quasi-community property shall be administered or distributed, or otherwise dealt with, as if the other spouse had survived and as if that half belonged to that spouse.

104. Notwithstanding Section 100, community property held in a revocable trust described in Section 761 of the Family Code is governed by the provisions, if any, in the trust for disposition in the event of death.

104.5. Transfer of community and quasi-community property to a revocable trust shall be presumed to be an agreement, pursuant to Sections 100 and 101, that those assets retain their character in the aggregate for purposes of any division provided by the trust. This section shall apply to all transfers prior to, on, or after January 1, 2000.

105. This part does not apply where the decedent died before January 1, 1985, and the law applicable prior to January 1, 1985, continues to apply where the decedent died before January 1, 1985.

Part 2. Surviving Spouse's Right In California Real Property Of Nondomiciliary Decedent

120. If a married person dies not domiciled in this state and leaves a valid will disposing of real property in this state which is not the community property of the decedent and the surviving spouse, the surviving spouse has the same right to elect to take a portion of or interest in such property against the will of the decedent as though the property were

located in the decedent's domicile at death.

Part 3. Contractual Arrangements Relating To Rights At Death

Chapter 1. Surviving Spouse's Waiver Of Rights

140. As used in this chapter, "waiver" means a waiver by the surviving spouse of any of the rights listed in subdivision (a) of Section 141, whether signed before or during marriage.

141. (a) The right of a surviving spouse to any of the following may be waived in whole or in part by a waiver under this chapter:

(1) Property that would pass from the decedent by intestate succession.

(2) Property that would pass from the decedent by testamentary disposition in a will executed before the waiver.

(3) A probate homestead.

(4) The right to have exempt property set aside.

(5) Family allowance.

(6) The right to have an estate set aside under Chapter 6 (commencing with Section 6600) of Part 3 of Division 6.

(7) The right to elect to take community or quasi-community property against the decedent's will.

(8) The right to take the statutory share of an omitted spouse.

(9) The right to be appointed as the personal representative of the decedent's estate.

(10) An interest in property that is the subject of a nonprobate transfer on death under Part 1 (commencing with Section 5000) of Division 5.

(b) Nothing in this chapter affects or limits the waiver or manner of waiver of rights other than those referred to in subdivision (a), including, but not limited to, the right to property that would pass from the decedent to the surviving spouse by nonprobate transfer upon the death of the decedent, such as the survivorship interest under a joint tenancy, a Totten trust account, or a pay-on-death account.

142. (a) A waiver under this chapter shall be in writing and shall be signed by the surviving spouse.

(b) Subject to subdivision (c), a waiver under this chapter is enforceable only if it satisfies the requirements of subdivision (a) and is enforceable under either Section 143 or Section 144.

(c) Enforcement of the waiver against the surviving spouse is subject to the same defenses as enforcement of a contract, except that:

(1) Lack of consideration is not a defense to enforcement of the waiver.

(2) A minor intending to marry may make a waiver under this chapter as if married, but the waiver becomes effective only upon

the marriage.

143. (a) Subject to Section 142, a waiver is enforceable under this section unless the surviving spouse proves either of the following:

(1) A fair and reasonable disclosure of the property or financial obligations of the decedent was not provided to the surviving spouse prior to the signing of the waiver unless the surviving spouse waived such a fair and reasonable disclosure after advice by independent legal counsel.

(2) The surviving spouse was not represented by independent legal counsel at the time of signing of the waiver.

(b) Subdivision (b) of Section 721 of the Family Code does not apply if the waiver is enforceable under this section.

144. (a) Except as provided in subdivision (b), subject to Section 142, a waiver is enforceable under this section if the court determines either of the following:

(1) The waiver at the time of signing made a fair and reasonable disposition of the rights of the surviving spouse.

(2) The surviving spouse had, or reasonably should have had, an adequate knowledge of the property and financial obligations of the decedent and the decedent did not violate the duty imposed by subdivision (b) of Section 721 of the Family Code.

(b) If, after considering all relevant facts and circumstances, the court finds that enforcement of the waiver pursuant to subdivision (a) would be unconscionable under the circumstances existing at the time enforcement is sought, the court may refuse to enforce the waiver, enforce the remainder of the waiver without the unconscionable provisions, or limit the application of the unconscionable provisions to avoid an unconscionable result.

(c) Except as provided in paragraph (2) of subdivision (a), subdivision (b) of Section 721 of the Family Code does not apply if the waiver is enforceable under this section.

145. Unless the waiver or property settlement provides to the contrary, a waiver under this chapter of "all rights" (or equivalent language) in the property or estate of a present or prospective spouse, or a complete property settlement entered into after or in anticipation of separation or dissolution or annulment of marriage, is a waiver by the spouse of the rights described in subdivision (a) of Section 141.

146. (a) As used in this section, "agreement" means a written agreement signed by each spouse or prospective spouse altering, amending, or revoking a waiver under this chapter.

(b) Except as provided in subdivisions (c) and (d) of Section 147, unless the waiver specifically otherwise provides, a waiver under this chapter may not be altered, amended, or revoked except by a subsequent written agreement signed by each spouse or prospec-

tive spouse.

(c) Subject to subdivision (d), the agreement is enforceable only if it satisfies the requirements of subdivision (b) and is enforceable under either subdivision (e) or subdivision (f).

(d) Enforcement of the agreement against a party to the agreement is subject to the same defenses as enforcement of any other contract, except that:

(1) Lack of consideration is not a defense to enforcement of the agreement.

(2) A minor intending to marry may enter into the agreement as if married, but the agreement becomes effective only upon the marriage.

(e) Subject to subdivision (d), an agreement is enforceable under this subdivision unless the party to the agreement against whom enforcement is sought proves either of the following:

(1) A fair and reasonable disclosure of the property or financial obligations of the other spouse was not provided to the spouse against whom enforcement is sought prior to the signing of the agreement unless the spouse against whom enforcement is sought waived such a fair and reasonable disclosure after advice by independent legal counsel.

(2) The spouse against whom enforcement is sought was not represented by independent legal counsel at the time of signing of the agreement.

(f) Subject to subdivisions (d) and (g), an agreement is enforceable under this subdivision if the court determines that the agreement at the time of signing made a fair and reasonable disposition of the rights of the spouses.

(g) If, after considering all relevant facts and circumstances, the court finds that enforcement of the agreement pursuant to subdivision (f) would be unconscionable under the circumstances existing at the time enforcement is sought, the court may refuse to enforce the agreement, enforce the remainder of the agreement without the unconscionable provisions, or limit the application of the unconscionable provisions to avoid an unconscionable result.

(h) Subdivision (b) of Section 721 of the Family Code does not apply if the agreement is enforceable under this section.

147. (a) Subject to subdivisions (c) and (d), a waiver, agreement, or property settlement made after December 31, 1984, is invalid insofar as it affects the rights listed in subdivision (a) of Section 141 unless it satisfies the requirements of this chapter.

(b) Nothing in this chapter affects the validity or effect of any waiver, agreement, or property settlement made prior to January 1, 1985, and the validity and effect of such waiver, agreement, or property settlement shall continue to be determined by the law applicable to the waiver, agreement, or settlement prior to January 1, 1985.

(c) Nothing in this chapter affects the validity or effect of any premarital property agreement, whether made prior to, on, or after January 1, 1985, insofar as the premarital property agreement affects the rights listed in subdivision (a) of Section 141, and the validity and effect of such premarital property agreement shall be determined by the law otherwise applicable to the premarital property agreement. Nothing in this subdivision limits the enforceability under this chapter of a waiver made under this chapter by a person intending to marry that is otherwise enforceable under this chapter.

(d) Nothing in this chapter limits any right one spouse otherwise has to revoke a consent or election to disposition of his or her half of the community or quasi-community property under the will of the other spouse.

Part 4. Establishing And Reporting Fact Of Death

Chapter 1. Proceedings To Establish Death

200. If title to or an interest in real or personal property is affected by the death of a person, another person who claims an interest in the property may commence proceedings pursuant to this chapter to establish the fact of the death.

201. (a) Proceedings under this chapter shall be commenced in the superior court of the county of which the decedent was a resident at the time of death or in the superior court of any county in which the property is located.

(b) Proceedings under this chapter shall be commenced by filing a petition that sets forth all of the following information:

(1) The jurisdictional facts.

(2) A particular description of the affected property and of the interest of the petitioner in the property.

202. If proceedings for the administration of the decedent's estate are pending, proceedings under this chapter may be combined with the administration proceedings in the following manner:

(a) The petition shall be filed in the administration proceedings by the person affected or by the personal representative.

(b) The petition shall be filed at any time before the filing of a petition for final distribution. The petition may be included in a petition for probate of the will of the decedent or for letters.

(c) The petition shall be filed without any additional fee.

203. (a) Except as provided in subdivision (b), notice of the hearing shall be given as provided in Section 1220.

(b) If the person who commenced the proceedings files an affidavit with the petition stating that the person has no reason to believe there is any opposition to, or contest of, the petition, the court may act ex parte.

204. (a) The petition and supporting affidavits may be received in evidence and acted upon by the court with the same force and effect as if the petitioner and affiants were personally present and testified to the facts set forth.

(b) The court may render judgment establishing the fact of the death. The judgment is prima facie evidence of the fact of the death. The presumption established by this subdivision is a presumption affecting the burden of producing evidence.

Chapter 2. Recording Evidence Of Death

210. If title to real property is affected by the death of a person, any person may record in the county in which the property is located any of the following documents establishing the fact of the death:

(a) An affidavit of death executed by a person having knowledge of the facts. The affidavit shall include a particular description of the real property and an attested or certified copy of a record of the death made and filed in a designated public office as required by law. For purposes of this subdivision, a certified copy issued in this state shall include any copy issued pursuant to Section 103525 of, subdivision (a) of Section 103526 of, or paragraph (1) of subdivision (b) of Section 103526 of, the Health and Safety Code.

(b) A certified copy of a court order that determines the fact of death made pursuant to Chapter 1 (commencing with Section 200) or pursuant to another statute that provides for a determination of the fact of death.

211. (a) A document establishing the fact of death recorded pursuant to this chapter is subject to all statutory requirements for recorded documents.

(b) The county recorder shall index a document establishing the fact of death recorded pursuant to this chapter in the index of grantors and grantees. The index entry shall be for the grantor, and for the purpose of this index, the person whose death is established shall be deemed to be the grantor.

212. A document establishing the fact of the death of a person recorded pursuant to this chapter is prima facie evidence of the death insofar as the document identifies real property located in the county, title to which is affected by the death. The presumption established by this section is a presumption affecting the burden of producing evidence.

Chapter 3. Reporting Fact Of Death

215. Where a deceased person has received or may have received health care under Chapter 7 (commencing with Section 14000) or Chapter 8 (commencing with Section 14200) of Part 3 of Division 9 of the

Welfare and Institutions Code, or was the surviving spouse of a person who received that health care, the estate attorney, or if there is no estate attorney, the beneficiary, the personal representative, or the person in possession of property of the decedent shall give the Director of Health Services notice of the decedent's death not later than 90 days after the date of death. The notice shall include a copy of the decedent's death certificate. The notice shall be given as provided in Section 1215, addressed to the director at the Sacramento office of the director.

216. When a deceased person has an heir who is confined in a prison or facility under the jurisdiction of the Department of Corrections and Rehabilitation, or its Division of Juvenile Facilities, or confined in any county or city jail, road camp, industrial farm, or other local correctional facility, the estate attorney, or if there is no estate attorney, the beneficiary, the personal representative, or the person in possession of property of the decedent shall give the Director of the California Victim Compensation and Government Claims Board notice of the decedent's death not later than 90 days after the date of death. The notice shall be given as provided in Section 1215 and shall include all of the following:

(a) The name, date of birth, and location of incarceration of the decedent's heir.

(b) The heir's CDCR number if incarcerated in a Department of Corrections and Rehabilitation facility or booking number if incarcerated in a county facility.

(c) A copy of the decedent's death certificate.

(d) The probate case number, and the name of the superior court hearing the case.

217. (a) A business that receives an oral or written request from a family member, attorney, or personal representative of a deceased person to cancel that person's services may not require an in-person cancellation.

(b) For purposes of this section, "services" include, but are not limited to, gas, electrical, water, sewage, cable, satellite, telephone, or cellular telephone service.

Part 5. Simultaneous Death

Chapter 1. General Provisions

220. Except as otherwise provided in this chapter, if the title to property or the devolution of property depends upon priority of death and it cannot be established by clear and convincing evidence that one of the persons survived the other, the property of each person shall be administered or distributed, or otherwise dealt with, as if that person had survived the other.

221. (a) This chapter does not apply in any case where Section 103, 6211, or 6403

applies.

(b) This chapter does not apply in the case of a trust, deed, or contract of insurance, or any other situation, where (1) provision is made dealing explicitly with simultaneous deaths or deaths in a common disaster or otherwise providing for distribution of property different from the provisions of this chapter or (2) provision is made requiring one person to survive another for a stated period in order to take property or providing for a presumption as to survivorship that results in a distribution of property different from that provided by this chapter.

222. (a) If property is so disposed of that the right of a beneficiary to succeed to any interest in the property is conditional upon surviving another person and it cannot be established by clear and convincing evidence that the beneficiary survived the other person, the beneficiary is deemed not to have survived the other person.

(b) If property is so disposed of that one of two or more beneficiaries would have been entitled to the property if he or she had survived the others, and it cannot be established by clear and convincing evidence that any beneficiary survived any other beneficiary, the property shall be divided into as many equal portions as there are beneficiaries and the portion of each beneficiary shall be administered or distributed, or otherwise dealt with, as if that beneficiary had survived the other beneficiaries.

223. (a) As used in this section, "joint tenants" includes owners of property held under circumstances that entitled one or more to the whole of the property on the death of the other or others.

(b) If property is held by two joint tenants and both of them have died and it cannot be established by clear and convincing evidence that one survived the other, the property held in joint tenancy shall be administered or distributed, or otherwise dealt with, one-half as if one joint tenant had survived and one-half as if the other joint tenant had survived.

(c) If property is held by more than two joint tenants and all of them have died and it cannot be established by clear and convincing evidence that any of them survived the others, the property held in joint tenancy shall be divided into as many portions as there are joint tenants and the share of each joint tenant shall be administered or distributed, or otherwise dealt with, as if that joint tenant had survived the other joint tenants.

224. If the insured and a beneficiary under a policy of life or accident insurance have died and it cannot be established by clear and convincing evidence that the beneficiary survived the insured, the proceeds of the policy shall be administered or distributed, or otherwise dealt with, as if the insured had survived the beneficiary, except if the policy is community or quasi-community property of the insured and the spouse of the insured and there is no alternative beneficiary except the estate or personal representative of the insured, the proceeds shall be distributed as community property under Section 103.

226. This chapter does not apply where a person the priority of whose death is in issue died before January 1, 1985, and the law applicable prior to January 1, 1985, continues to apply where none of the persons the priority of whose death is in issue died on or after January 1, 1985.

Chapter 2. Proceedings To Determine Survival

230. A petition may be filed under this chapter for any one or more of the following purposes:

(a) To determine for the purposes of Section 103, 220, 222, 223, 224, 6211, 6242, 6243, 6403, 21109, 21110 or other provision of this code whether one person survived another.

(b) To determine for the purposes of Section 673 whether issue of an appointee survived the donee.

(c) To determine for the purposes of Section 24611 of the Education Code whether a person has survived in order to receive benefits payable under the system.

(d) To determine for the purposes of Section 21509 of the Government Code whether a person has survived in order to receive money payable under the system.

231. A petition may be filed under this chapter by any of the following:

(a) The personal representative of any person the priority of whose death is in issue under the applicable provision referred to in Section 230.

(b) Any other person interested in the estate of any such person.

232. (a) The petition shall be filed in the estate proceeding in which the person filing the petition received his or her appointment or in the estate proceeding for the estate in which the person filing the petition claims an interest.

(b) The court that first acquires jurisdiction under this section has exclusive jurisdiction for the purposes of this chapter.

233. Notice of the hearing on the petition shall be given as provided in Section 1220 to all of the following persons:

(a) The personal representative of each person the priority of whose death is in issue if there is a personal representative for the person.

(b) Each known devisee of each person the priority of whose death is in issue.

(c) Each known heir of each person the priority of whose death is in issue.

(d) All persons (or their attorneys if they have appeared by attorneys) who have requested special notice as provided in Section 1250 in the proceeding in which the petition

is filed or who have given notice of appearance in person or by attorney in that proceeding.

234. If the court determines that the named persons are dead and that it has not been established by clear and convincing evidence that one person survived another, the court shall make an order to that effect. If the court determines that the named persons are dead and that there is clear and convincing evidence that one person survived another, the court shall make an order setting forth the order in which the persons died. The order, when it becomes final, is a binding determination of the facts set forth in the order and is conclusive as against the personal representatives of the deceased persons named in the order and against all persons claiming by, through, or under any of the deceased persons.

Part 6. Distribution Among Heirs Or Beneficiaries

Chapter 1. Intestate Distribution System

240. If a statute calls for property to be distributed or taken in the manner provided in this section, the property shall be divided into as many equal shares as there are living members of the nearest generation of issue then living and deceased members of that generation who leave issue then living, each living member of the nearest generation of issue then living receiving one share and the share of each deceased member of that generation who leaves issue then living being divided in the same manner among his or her then living issue.

241. Section 240 does not apply where the death of the decedent in the case of intestate succession or of the testator, settlor, or other transferor occurred before January 1, 1985, and the law applicable prior to January 1, 1985, shall continue to apply where the death occurred before January 1, 1985.

Chapter 2. Distribution Under A Will, Trust, Or Other Instrument

245. (a) Where a will, trust, or other instrument calls for property to be distributed or taken "in the manner provided in Section 240 of the Probate Code," or where a will, trust, or other instrument that expresses no contrary intention provides for issue or descendants to take without specifying the manner, the property to be distributed shall be distributed in the manner provided in Section 240.

(b) Use of the following words without more, as applied to issue or descendants, is not an expression of contrary intention:

(1) "Per capita" when living members of the designated class are not all of the same

generation.

(2) Contradictory wording, such as "per capita and per stirpes" or "equally and by right of representation."

246. (a) Where a will, trust, or other instrument calls for property to be distributed or taken "in the manner provided in Section 246 of the Probate Code," the property to be distributed shall be divided into as many equal shares as there are living children of the designated ancestor, if any, and deceased children who leave issue then living. Each living child of the designated ancestor is allocated one share, and the share of each deceased child who leaves issue then living is divided in the same manner.

(b) Unless the will, trust, or other instrument expressly provides otherwise, if an instrument executed on or after January 1, 1986, calls for property to be distributed or taken "per stirpes," "by representation," or "by right of representation," the property shall be distributed in the manner provided in subdivision (a).

(c) If a will, trust, or other instrument executed before January 1, 1986, calls for property to be distributed or taken "per stirpes," "by representation," or by "right of representation," the property shall be distributed in the manner provided in subdivision (a), absent a contrary intent of the transferor.

247. (a) Where a will, trust, or other instrument calls for property to be distributed or taken "in the manner provided in Section 247 of the Probate Code," the property to be distributed shall be divided into as many equal shares as there are living members of the nearest generation of issue then living and deceased members of that generation who leave issue then living. Each living member of the nearest generation of issue then living is allocated one share, and the remaining shares, if any, are combined and then divided and allocated in the same manner among the remaining issue as if the issue already allocated a share and their descendants were then deceased.

(b) Unless the will, trust, or other instrument expressly provides otherwise, if an instrument executed on or after January 1, 1986, calls for property to be distributed or taken "per capita at each generation," the property shall be distributed in the manner provided in subdivision (a).

(c) If a will, trust, or other instrument executed before January 1, 1986, calls for property to be distributed or taken "per capita at each generation," the property shall be distributed in the manner provided in subdivision (a), absent a contrary intent of the transferor.

Chapter 3. Identity Of Heirs

248. When title to real or personal property, or any interest therein, vests, other than by laws of succession, on the heirs, heirs of the body, issue, or children of any person, without other description, or means of identification of the persons embraced in the description, any person interested in the property as the heir, heir of the body, issue, or child, or his or her successor in interest, or the personal representative of any interested person or of his or her successor in interest, may file a verified petition in the superior court of the county in which the property or any part thereof is situated, setting forth briefly the deraignment of title of petitioner, a description of the property affected, and so far as known to the petitioner, the names, ages, and residences of the heirs, heirs of the body, issue or children whose identity is sought to be determined, and if any is dead or if the residence of any is unknown, stating the facts, and requesting that a decree be entered determining and establishing the identity of the persons embraced in the general description.

248.5. The clerk shall set the petition for hearing by the court and give notice thereof in the manner provided in Sections 1230 and 1260. The petitioner shall cause notice of the hearing to be given in the manner specified in Sections 1220 and 1260.

249. At any time before the hearing any person interested in the property may answer the petition and deny any of the matters contained therein. The court shall hear the proofs offered by the petitioner and by any person contesting and shall make a decree conformable to the proofs. The decree shall be prima facie evidence of the facts determined thereby, and shall be conclusive in favor of anyone acting thereon in good faith without notice of any conflicting interest.

249.5. For purposes of determining rights to property to be distributed upon the death of a decedent, a child of the decedent conceived and born after the death of the decedent shall be deemed to have been born in the lifetime of the decedent, and after the execution of all of the decedent's testamentary instruments, if the child or his or her representative proves by clear and convincing evidence that all of the following conditions are satisfied:

(a) The decedent, in writing, specifies that his or her genetic material shall be used for the posthumous conception of a child of the decedent, subject to the following:

(1) The specification shall be signed by the decedent and dated.

(2) The specification may be revoked or amended only by a writing, signed by the decedent and dated.

(3) A person is designated by the decedent to control the use of the genetic material.

(b) The person designated by the decedent to control the use of the genetic material has given written notice by certified mail, return receipt requested, that the decedent's genetic material was available for the purpose of posthumous conception. The notice shall have been given to a person who has the power to control the distribution of either the decedent's property or death benefits payable by reason of the decedent's death, within four months of the date of issuance of a certificate of the decedent's death or entry of a judgment determining the fact of the decedent's death, whichever event occurs first.

(c) The child was in utero using the decedent's genetic material and was in utero within two years of the date of issuance of a certificate of the decedent's death or entry of a judgment determining the fact of the decedent's death, whichever event occurs first. This subdivision does not apply to a child who shares all of his or her nuclear genes with the person donating the implanted nucleus as a result of the application of somatic nuclear transfer technology commonly known as human cloning.

249.6. (a) Upon timely receipt of the notice required by Section 249.5 or actual knowledge by a person who has the power to control the distribution of either the decedent's property or death benefits payable by reason of the decedent's death, that person may not make a distribution of property or pay death benefits payable by reason of the decedent's death before two years following the date of issuance of a certificate of the decedent's death or entry of a judgment determining the fact of decedent's death, whichever event occurs first.

(b) Subdivision (a) does not apply to, and the distribution of property or the payment of benefits may proceed in a timely manner as provided by law with respect to, any property if the birth of a child or children of the decedent conceived after the death of the decedent will not have an effect on any of the following:

(1) The proposed distribution of the decedent's property.

(2) The payment of death benefits payable by reason of the decedent's death.

(3) The determination of rights to property to be distributed upon the death of the decedent.

(4) The right of any person to claim a probate homestead or probate family allowance.

(c) Subdivision (a) does not apply to, and the distribution of property or the payment of benefits may proceed in a timely manner as provided by law with respect to, any property if the person named in subdivision (a) of Section 249.5 sends written notice by certified mail, return receipt requested, that the person does not intend to use the genetic material for the posthumous conception of a child of a decedent. This notice shall be signed by the person named in paragraph (3) of subdivision (a) of Section 249.5 and at least one competent witness, and dated.

(d) A person who has the power to control the distribution of either the decedent's property or death benefits payable by reason of the decedent's death, shall incur no liability for making a distribution of property or paying death benefits if that person made a distribution of property or paid death benefits prior to receiving notice or acquiring actual knowledge of the existence of genetic material available for posthumous conception purposes or the written notice required by subdivision (b) of Section 249.5.

(e) Each person to whom payment, delivery, or transfer of the decedent's property is made is personally liable to a person who, pursuant to Section 249.5, has a superior right to the payment, delivery, or transfer of the decedent's property. The aggregate of the personal liability of a person shall not exceed the fair market value, valued as of the time of the transfer, of the property paid, delivered, or transferred to the person under this section, less the amount of any liens and encumbrances on that property at that time.

(f) In addition to any other liability a person may have pursuant to this section, any person who fraudulently secures the payment, delivery, or transfer of the decedent's property pursuant to this section shall be liable to the person having a superior right for three times the fair market value of the property.

(g) An action to impose liability under this section shall be barred three years after the distribution to the holder of the decedent's property, or three years after the discovery of fraud, whichever is later. The three-year period specified in this subdivision may not be tolled for any reason.

249.7. If the written notice required pursuant to Section 249.5 is not given in a timely manner to any person who has the power to control the distribution of either the decedent's property or death benefits payable by reason of the decedent's death, that person may make the distribution in the manner provided by law as if any child of the decedent conceived after the death of the decedent had predeceased the decedent without heirs. Any child of a decedent conceived after the death of the decedent, or that child's representative, shall be barred from making a claim against either the person making the distribution or the recipient of the distribution when the claim is based on wrongful distribution and written notice has not been given in a timely manner pursuant to Section 249.5 to the person making that distribution.

249.8. Notwithstanding Section 249.6, any interested person may file a petition in the manner prescribed in Section 248 or 17200 requesting a distribution of property of the decedent or death benefits payable by reason of decedent's death that are subject to the delayed distribution provisions of Section 249.6. The court may order distribution of all, or a portion of, the property or death benefits, if at the hearing it appears that distribution can be made without any loss to any interested person, including any loss, either actual or contingent, to a decedent's child who is conceived after the death of the decedent. The order for distribution shall be stayed until any bond required by the court is filed.

Part 7. Effect Of Homicide Or Abuse Of An Elder Or Dependent Adult

250. (a) A person who feloniously and intentionally kills the decedent is not entitled to any of the following:

(1) Any property, interest, or benefit under a will of the decedent, or a trust created by or for the benefit of the decedent or in which the decedent has an interest, including any general or special power of appointment conferred by the will or trust on the killer and any nomination of the killer as executor, trustee, guardian, or conservator or custodian made by the will or trust.

(2) Any property of the decedent by intestate succession.

(3) Any of the decedent's quasi-community property the killer would otherwise acquire under Section 101 or 102 upon the death of the decedent.

(4) Any property of the decedent under Part 5 (commencing with Section 5700) of Division 5.

(5) Any property of the decedent under Part 3 (commencing with Section 6500) of Division 6.

(b) In the cases covered by subdivision (a):

(1) The property interest or benefit referred to in paragraph (1) of subdivision (a) passes as if the killer had predeceased the decedent and Section 21110 does not apply.

(2) Any property interest or benefit referred to in paragraph (1) of subdivision (a) which passes under a power of appointment and by reason of the death of the decedent passes as if the killer had predeceased the decedent, and Section 673 not apply.

(3) Any nomination in a will or trust of the killer as executor, trustee, guardian, conservator, or custodian which becomes effective as a result of the death of the decedent shall be interpreted as if the killer had predeceased the decedent.

251. A joint tenant who feloniously and intentionally kills another joint tenant thereby effects a severance of the interest of the decedent so that the share of the decedent passes as the decedent's property and the killer has no rights by survivorship. This section applies to joint tenancies in real and personal property, joint and multiple-party accounts in financial institutions, and any other form of coownership with survivorship incidents.

252. A named beneficiary of a bond, life insurance policy, or other contractual arrangement who feloniously and intentionally kills the principal obligee or the person upon whose life the policy is issued is not entitled to any benefit under the bond, policy, or oth-

er contractual arrangement, and it becomes payable as though the killer had predeceased the decedent.

253. In any case not described in Section 250, 251, or 252 in which one person feloniously and intentionally kills another, any acquisition of property, interest, or benefit by the killer as a result of the killing of the decedent shall be treated in accordance with the principles of this part.

254. (a) A final judgment of conviction of felonious and intentional killing is conclusive for purposes of this part.

(b) In the absence of a final judgment of conviction of felonious and intentional killing, the court may determine by a preponderance of evidence whether the killing was felonious and intentional for purposes of this part. The burden of proof is on the party seeking to establish that the killing was felonious and intentional for the purposes of this part.

255. This part does not affect the rights of any person who, before rights under this part have been adjudicated, purchases from the killer for value and without notice property which the killer would have acquired except for this part, but the killer is liable for the amount of the proceeds or the value of the property.

256. An insurance company, financial institution, or other obligor making payment according to the terms of its policy or obligation is not liable by reason of this part, unless prior to payment it has received at its home office or principal address written notice of a claim under this part.

257. This part does not apply where the decedent was killed before January 1, 1985; and the law applicable prior to January 1, 1985, continues to apply where the decedent was killed before January 1, 1985.

258. A person who feloniously and intentionally kills the decedent is not entitled to bring an action for wrongful death of the decedent or to benefit from the action brought by the decedent's personal representative. The persons who may bring an action for wrongful death of the decedent and to benefit from the action are determined as if the killer had predeceased the decedent.

259. (a) Any person shall be deemed to have predeceased a decedent to the extent provided in subdivision (c) where all of the following apply:

(1) It has been proven by clear and convincing evidence that the person is liable for physical abuse, neglect, or financial abuse of the decedent, who was an elder or dependent adult.

(2) The person is found to have acted in bad faith.

(3) The person has been found to have been reckless, oppressive, fraudulent, or malicious in the commission of any of these acts upon the decedent.

(4) The decedent, at the time those acts occurred and thereafter until the time of his or her death, has been found to have been substantially unable to manage his or her financial resources or to resist fraud or undue influence.

(b) Any person shall be deemed to have predeceased a decedent to the extent provided in subdivision (c) if that person has been convicted of a violation of Section 236 of the Penal Code or any offense described in Section 368 of the Penal Code.

(c) Any person found liable under subdivision (a) or convicted under subdivision (b) shall not (1) receive any property, damages, or costs that are awarded to the decedent's estate in an action described in subdivision (a) or (b), whether that person's entitlement is under a will, a trust, or the laws of intestacy; or (2) serve as a fiduciary as defined in Section 39, if the instrument nominating or appointing that person was executed during the period when the decedent was substantially unable to manage his or her financial resources or resist fraud or undue influence. This section shall not apply to a decedent who, at any time following the act or acts described in paragraph (1) of subdivision (a), or the act or acts described in subdivision (b), was substantially able to manage his or her financial resources and to resist fraud or undue influence within the meaning of subdivision (b) of Section 1801 of the Probate Code and subdivision (b) of Section 39 of the Civil Code.

(d) For purposes of this section, the following definitions shall apply:

(1) "Physical abuse" as defined in Section 15610.63 of the Welfare and Institutions Code.

(2) "Neglect" as defined in Section 15610.57 of the Welfare and Institutions Code.

(3) "False imprisonment" as defined in Section 368 of the Penal Code.

(4) "Financial abuse" as defined in Section 15610.30 of the Welfare and Institutions Code.

(e) Nothing in this section shall be construed to prohibit the severance and transfer of an action or proceeding to a separate civil action pursuant to Section 801.

Part 8. Disclaimer Of Testamentary And Other Interests

Chapter 1. Definitions

260. Unless the provision or context otherwise requires, the definitions in this chapter govern the construction of this part.

262. "Beneficiary" means the person entitled, but for the person's disclaimer, to take an interest.

263. (a) "Creator of the interest" means a person who establishes, declares, creates, or otherwise brings into existence an interest.

(b) "Creator of the interest" includes, but is not limited to, the following:

(1) With respect to an interest created by intestate succession, the person dying intestate.

(2) With respect to an interest created under a will, the testator.

(3) With respect to an interest created under a trust, the settlor.

(4) With respect to an interest created by succession to a disclaimed interest, the disclaimant of the disclaimed interest.

(5) With respect to an interest created by virtue of an election to take against a will, the testator.

(6) With respect to an interest created by creation of a power of appointment, the donor.

(7) With respect to an interest created by exercise or nonexercise of a power of appointment, the donee.

(8) With respect to an interest created by an inter vivos gift, the donor.

(9) With respect to an interest created by surviving the death of a depositor of a Totten trust account or P.O.D. account, the deceased depositor.

(10) With respect to an interest created under an insurance or annuity contract, the owner, the insured, or the annuitant.

(11) With respect to an interest created by surviving the death of another joint tenant, the deceased joint tenant.

(12) With respect to an interest created under an employee benefit plan, the employee or other owner of an interest in the plan.

(13) With respect to an interest created under an individual retirement account, annuity, or bond, the owner.

264. "Disclaimant" means a beneficiary who executes a disclaimer on his or her own behalf or a person who executes a disclaimer on behalf of a beneficiary.

265. "Disclaimer" means any writing which declines, refuses, renounces, or disclaims any interest that would otherwise be taken by a beneficiary.

266. "Employee benefit plan" includes, but is not limited to, any pension, retirement, death benefit, stock bonus, or profit-sharing plan, system, or trust.

267. (a) "Interest" includes the whole of any property, real or personal, legal or equitable, or any fractional part, share, or particular portion or specific assets thereof, or any estate in any such property, or any power to appoint, consume, apply, or expend property, or any other right, power, privilege, or immunity relating to property.

(b) "Interest" includes, but is not limited to, an interest created in any of the following manners:

(1) By intestate succession.

(2) Under a will.

(3) Under a trust.

(4) By succession to a disclaimed interest.

(5) By virtue of an election to take against a will.

(6) By creation of a power of appointment.

(7) By exercise or nonexercise of a power of appointment.

(8) By an inter vivos gift, whether outright or in trust.

(9) By surviving the death of a depositor of a Totten trust account or P.O.D. account.

(10) Under an insurance or annuity contract.

(11) By surviving the death of another joint tenant.

(12) Under an employee benefit plan.

(13) Under an individual retirement account, annuity, or bond.

(14) Any other interest created by any testamentary or inter vivos instrument or by operation of law.

Chapter 2. General Provisions

275. A beneficiary may disclaim any interest, in whole or in part, by filing a disclaimer as provided in this part.

276. A disclaimer on behalf of a conservatee shall be made by the conservator of the estate of the conservatee pursuant to a court order obtained under Article 10 (commencing with Section 2580) of Chapter 6 of Part 4 of Division 4 authorizing or requiring the conservator to execute and file the disclaimer.

277. (a) A disclaimer on behalf of a minor shall be made by the guardian of the estate of the minor if one has been appointed or, if none has been appointed, by a guardian ad litem of the minor. A disclaimer by a guardian is not effective unless made pursuant to a court order obtained under this section.

(b) A disclaimer on behalf of a decedent shall be made by the personal representative of the decedent. Except as provided in Part 6 (commencing with Section 10400) of Division 7, a disclaimer by a guardian or personal representative is not effective unless made pursuant to a court order obtained under this section.

(c) A petition for an order authorizing or requiring a guardian or personal representative to execute and file a disclaimer shall be filed in the superior court in the county in which the estate of the minor or decedent is administered or, if there is no administration, the superior court in any county in which administration would be proper. The petition may be filed by the guardian, personal representative, or other interested person.

(d) The petition shall:

(1) Identify the creator of the interest.

(2) Describe the interest to be disclaimed.

(3) State the extent of the disclaimer.

(4) Identify the person or persons the petitioner believes would take the interest in the event of the disclaimer.

(e) Notice of the hearing on the petition shall be given as follows:

(1) If the petition is for an order authorizing or requiring the guardian of the estate of a minor to execute and file the disclaimer, notice of the hearing on the petition shall be given for the period and in the manner provided in Chapter 3 (commencing with Section 1460) of Part 1 of Division 4 to all of the persons required to be given notice under that chapter.

(2) If the petition is for an order authorizing or requiring the personal representative of a decedent to execute and file the disclaimer, notice of the hearing on the petition shall be given as provided in Section 1220.

(3) If the petition is for an order authorizing or requiring a guardian ad litem of a minor to execute and file the disclaimer, notice of the hearing on the petition shall be given to the persons and in the manner that the court shall by order direct.

(f) After hearing, the court in its discretion may make an order authorizing or requiring the guardian or personal representative to execute and file the disclaimer if the court determines, taking into consideration all of the relevant circumstances, that the minor or decedent as a prudent person would disclaim the interest if he or she had the capacity to do so.

278. The disclaimer shall be in writing, shall be signed by the disclaimant, and shall:

(a) Identify the creator of the interest.

(b) Describe the interest to be disclaimed.

(c) State the disclaimer and the extent of the disclaimer.

279. (a) A disclaimer to be effective shall be filed within a reasonable time after the person able to disclaim acquires knowledge of the interest.

(b) In the case of any of the following interests, a disclaimer is conclusively presumed to have been filed within a reasonable time if it is filed within nine months after the death of the creator of the interest or within nine months after the interest becomes indefeasibly vested, whichever occurs later:

(1) An interest created under a will

(2) An interest created by intestate succession.

(3) An interest created pursuant to the exercise or nonexercise of a testamentary power of appointment.

(4) An interest created by surviving the death of a depositor of a Totten trust account or P.O.D. account.

(5) An interest created under a life insurance or annuity contract.

(6) An interest created by surviving the death of another joint tenant.

(7) An interest created under an employee benefit plan.

(8) An interest created under an individual retirement account, annuity, or bond.

(c) In the case of an interest created by a living trust, an interest created by the exercise of a presently exercisable power of appointment, an outright inter vivos gift, a power of appointment, or an interest created or increased by succession to a disclaimed interest, a disclaimer is conclusively presumed to have been filed within a reasonable time if it is filed within nine months after whichever of the following times occurs latest:

(1) The time of the creation of the trust, the exercise of the power of appointment, the making of the gift, the creation of the power of appointment, or the disclaimer of the disclaimed property.

(2) The time the first knowledge of the interest is acquired by the person able to disclaim.

(3) The time the interest becomes indefeasibly vested.

(d) In case of an interest not described in subdivision (b) or (c), a disclaimer is conclusively presumed to have been filed within a reasonable time if it is filed within nine months after whichever of the following times occurs later:

(1) The time the first knowledge of the interest is acquired by the person able to disclaim.

(2) The time the interest becomes indefeasibly vested.

(e) In the case of a future estate, a disclaimer is conclusively presumed to have been filed within a reasonable time if it is filed within whichever of the following times occurs later:

(1) Nine months after the time the interest becomes an estate in possession.

(2) The time specified in subdivision (b), (c), or (d), whichever is applicable.

(f) If the disclaimer is not filed within the time provided in subdivision (b), (c), (d), or (e), the disclaimant has the burden of establishing that the disclaimer was filed within a reasonable time after the disclaimant acquired knowledge of the interest.

280. (a) A disclaimer shall be filed with any of the following:

(1) The superior court in the county in which the estate of the decedent is administered or, if there is no administration of the decedent's estate, the superior court in any county in which administration of the estate of the decedent would be proper.

(2) The trustee, personal representative, other fiduciary, or person responsible for distributing the interest to the beneficiary.

(3) Any other person having custody or possession of or legal title to the interest.

(4) The creator of the interest.

(b) If a disclaimer made pursuant to this part affects real property or an obligation secured by real property and the disclaimer is acknowledged and proved in like manner as a grant of real property, the disclaimer may be recorded in like manner and with like effect as a grant of real property, and all statutory provisions relating to the recordation or nonrecordation of conveyances of real property and to the effect thereof apply to the disclaimer with like effect, without regard to the date when the disclaimer was filed pursuant to subdivision (a). Failure to file a disclaimer pursuant to subdivision (a) which is recorded pursuant to this subdivision does not affect the validity of any transaction with respect to the real property or the obligation secured thereby, and the general laws on recording and its effect govern any such transaction.

281. A disclaimer, when effective, is irrevocable and binding upon the beneficiary and all persons claiming by, through, or under the beneficiary, including creditors of the beneficiary.

282. (a) Unless the creator of the interest provides for a specific disposition of the interest in the event of a disclaimer, the interest disclaimed shall descend, go, be distributed, or continue to be held (1) as to a present interest, as if the disclaimant had predeceased the creator of the interest or (2) as to a future interest, as if the disclaimant had died before the event determining that the taker of the interest had become finally ascertained and the taker's interest indefeasibly vested. A disclaimer relates back for all purposes to the date of the death of the creator of the disclaimed interest or the determinative event, as the case may be.

(b) Notwithstanding subdivision (a), where the disclaimer is filed on or after January 1, 1985:

(1) The beneficiary is not treated as having predeceased the decedent for the purpose of determining the generation at which the division of the estate is to be made under Part 6 (commencing with Section 240) or other provision of a will, trust, or other instrument.

(2) The beneficiary of a disclaimed interest is not treated as having predeceased the decedent for the purpose of applying subdivision (d) of Section 6409 or subdivision (b) of Section 6410.

283. A disclaimer is not a fraudulent transfer by the beneficiary under Chapter 1 (commencing with Section 3439) of Title 2 of Part 2 of Division 4 of the Civil Code.

284. A person who could file a disclaimer under this part may instead file a written waiver of the right to disclaim. The waiver shall specify the interest to which the waiver applies. Upon being filed as provided in Section 280, the waiver is irrevocable and is binding upon the beneficiary and all persons claiming by, through, or under the beneficiary.

285. (a) A disclaimer may not be made after the beneficiary has accepted the interest sought to be disclaimed.

(b) For the purpose of this section, a beneficiary has accepted an interest if any of the following occurs before a disclaimer is filed with respect to that interest:

(1) The beneficiary, or someone acting

on behalf of the beneficiary, makes a voluntary assignment, conveyance, encumbrance, pledge, or transfer of the interest or part thereof, or contracts to do so; provided, however, that a beneficiary will not have accepted an interest if the beneficiary makes a gratuitous conveyance or transfer of the beneficiary's entire interest in property to the person or persons who would have received the property had the beneficiary made an otherwise qualified disclaimer pursuant to this part.

(2) The beneficiary, or someone acting on behalf of the beneficiary, executes a written waiver under Section 284 of the right to disclaim the interest.

(3) The beneficiary, or someone acting on behalf of the beneficiary, accepts the interest or part thereof or benefit thereunder.

(4) The interest or part thereof is sold at a judicial sale.

(c) An acceptance does not preclude a beneficiary from thereafter disclaiming all or part of an interest if both of the following requirements are met:

(1) The beneficiary became entitled to the interest because another person disclaimed an interest.

(2) The beneficiary or other person acting on behalf of the beneficiary at the time of the acceptance had no knowledge of the interest to which the beneficiary so became entitled.

(d) The acceptance by a joint tenant of the joint tenancy interest created when the joint tenancy is created is not an acceptance by the joint tenant of the interest created when the joint tenant survives the death of another joint tenant.

286. The right to disclaim exists regardless of any limitation imposed on the interest of a beneficiary in the nature of an expressed or implied spendthrift provision or similar restriction.

287. An interest created before January 1, 1984, that has not been accepted may be disclaimed after December 31, 1983, in the manner provided in this part, but no interest that arose before January 1, 1984, in a person other than the beneficiary may be destroyed or diminished by any action of the disclaimant taken pursuant to this part.

288. This part does not limit or abridge any right a person may have under any other law to assign, convey, or release any property or interest, but after December 31, 1983, an interest that would otherwise be taken by a beneficiary may be declined, refused, renounced, or disclaimed only as provided in this part.

Chapter 3. Disclaimers Effective Under Federal Law

295. Notwithstanding any other provision of this part, if as a result of a disclaimer or transfer the disclaimed or transferred interest is treated pursuant to the provisions of Title 26 of the United States Code, as now or hereafter amended, or any successor statute thereto, and the regulations promulgated thereunder, as never having been transferred to the beneficiary, then the disclaimer or transfer is effective as a disclaimer under this part.

Part 9. Trust Company As Fiduciary

300. A trust company may be appointed to act as a personal representative, guardian or conservator of an estate, or trustee, in the same manner as an individual. A trust company may not be appointed guardian or conservator of the person of a ward or conservatee.

301. (a) A trust company appointed to act as a personal representative, or guardian or conservator of an estate, may not be required to give a bond.

(b) The liability of a trust company and the manner of its making of oaths and affidavits are governed by Article 3 (commencing with Section 1540) of Chapter 12 of Division 1 of, and Section 1587 of, the Financial Code.

Part 10. Immediate Steps Concerning Decedent's Tangible Personal Property And Safe Deposit Box

330. (a) Except as provided in subdivision (b), a public administrator, government official, law enforcement agency, the hospital or institution in which a decedent died, or the decedent's employer, may, without the need to wait 40 days after death, deliver the tangible personal property of the decedent in its possession, including keys to the decedent's residence, to the decedent's surviving spouse, relative, or conservator or guardian of the estate acting in that capacity at the time of death.

(b) A person shall not deliver property pursuant to this section if the person knows or has reason to believe that there is a dispute over the right to possession of the property.

(c) A person that delivers property pursuant to this section shall require reasonable proof of the status and identity of the person to whom the property is delivered, and may rely on any document described in subdivision (d) of Section 13104 as proof of identity.

(d) A person that delivers property pursuant to this section shall, for a period of three years after the date of delivery of the property, keep a record of the property delivered and the status and identity of the person to whom the property is delivered.

(e) Delivery of property pursuant to this section does not determine ownership of the property or confer any greater rights in the property than the recipient would otherwise have and does not preclude later proceedings for administration of the decedent's estate. If proceedings for administration of the decedent's estate are commenced, the person holding the property shall deliver it to the personal representative on request by the personal representative.

(f) A person that delivers property pursuant to this section is not liable for loss or damage to the property caused by the person to whom the property is delivered.

331. (a) This section applies only to a safe deposit box in a financial institution held by the decedent in the decedent's sole name, or held by the decedent and others where all are deceased. Nothing in this section affects the rights of a surviving coholder.

(b) A person who has a key to the safe deposit box may, before letters have been issued, obtain access to the safe deposit box only for the purposes specified in this section by providing the financial institution with both of the following:

(1) Proof of the decedent's death. Proof shall be provided by a certified copy of the decedent's death certificate or by a written statement of death from the coroner, treating physician, or hospital or institution where the decedent died.

(2) Reasonable proof of the identity of the person seeking access. Reasonable proof of identity is provided for the purpose of this paragraph if the requirements of Section 13104 are satisfied.

(c) The financial institution has no duty to inquire into the truth of any statement, declaration, certificate, affidavit, or document offered as proof of the decedent's death or proof of identity of the person seeking access.

(d) When the person seeking access has satisfied the requirements of subdivision (b), the financial institution shall do all of the following:

(1) Keep a record of the identity of the person.

(2) Permit the person to open the safe deposit box under the supervision of an officer or employee of the financial institution, and to make an inventory of its contents.

(3) Make a photocopy of all wills and trust instruments removed from the safe deposit box, and keep the photocopy in the safe deposit box until the contents of the box are removed by the personal representative of the estate or other legally authorized person. The financial institution may charge the person given access a reasonable fee for photocopying.

(4) Permit the person given access to remove instructions for the disposition of the decedent's remains, and, after a photocopy is made, to remove the wills and trust instruments.

(e) The person given access shall deliver all wills found in the safe deposit box to the clerk of the superior court and mail or deliver a copy to the person named in the will as executor or beneficiary as provided in Section 8200.

(f) Except as provided in subdivision (d), the person given access shall not remove any of the contents of the decedent's safe deposit box.

Part 11. Fiduciaries' Wartime Substitution Law

Chapter 1. General Provisions

Article 1. Short Title And Definitions

350. This part may be cited as the Fiduciaries' Wartime Substitution Law.

351. Unless the provision or context otherwise requires, the definitions in this article govern the construction of this part.

352. "Consultant" means a person, other than a trustee, designated in a trust to advise or direct the trustee concerning the trust, or whose consent or approval is required for a purchase, sale, exchange, or other transaction by the trustee, and includes a settlor who reserves the power of a consultant.

353. "Estate" means a trust estate, a decedent's estate, a guardianship or conservatorship estate, or other property that is the subject of a donative transfer.

354. "Interested person" means, in addition to the meaning given that term in Section 48, a person having a property right in or claim against a guardianship or conservatorship estate or other estate that may be affected by the proceeding.

355. "Original fiduciary" means a fiduciary who is replaced by a substitute fiduciary or who makes a delegation of power under this part.

356. A fiduciary or consultant is engaged in war service for the purpose of this part in each of the following cases:

(a) Where the person is a member of the armed forces of the United States or like forces of any nation with which the United States is allied or associated in time of war, including all of the following:

(1) Members of the Army, Navy, Marine Corps, Air Force, and Coast Guard.

(2) Members of the Public Health Service detailed by proper authority for duty with the armed forces.

(3) Members of all other organizations or services recognized by the laws of the United States as a part of or auxiliary to the armed forces of the United States.

(b) Where the person has been accepted for and is awaiting induction into the armed forces, or is receiving training or education under government supervision preliminary to induction into any of these forces, in time of war.

(c) Where the person is engaged, outside the 50 states of the United States, in any work in connection with a governmental agency of the United States or with the American Red Cross or any other body with similar objects operating with the approval and sanction of the government of the United States or of any nation with which the United States is allied or associated in time of war.

(d) Where the person is engaged in time of war in service on any ship of United States registry.

(e) Where the person is interned or a prisoner of war in a foreign country or in the United States or any possession or dependency of the United States.

(f) Where the person is absent from the 50 states of the United States and, due to war conditions, is unable to return freely at his or her own volition.

(g) Where the person is engaged in any service in the United States or abroad arising out of or connected with a state of war that the court having jurisdiction of the estate finds prevents the person from giving proper attention to his or her duties.

Article 2. Scope Of Part

360. This part applies to all fiduciaries and consultants, whether appointed or acting before, on, or after July 1, 1989.

361. This part does not apply to the extent an otherwise valid provision in an instrument provides a different or contrary rule or is otherwise inconsistent with this part.

Article 3. Procedural Provisions

365. Proceedings under this part are in the court having jurisdiction over the estate or, if none, any court in which jurisdiction of the estate is proper.

366. Notice of a hearing under this part shall be mailed at least 15 days before the hearing to each fiduciary and consultant and to the following persons:

(a) In the case of a trust, to each known beneficiary, subject to the provisions of Chapter 2 (commencing with Section 15800) of Part 3 of Division 9.

(b) In the case of a decedent's estate, as provided in Section 1220 to both of the following:

(1) Each known heir whose interest in the estate would be affected by the proceedings.

(2) Each known devisee whose interest in the estate would be affected by the proceedings.

(c) In the case of a guardianship or conservatorship estate, as provided in Section 1460.

(d) In other cases, to any additional interested persons required by the court to receive notice.

Chapter 2. Appointment Of Substitute Fiduciary

370. If a fiduciary is engaged in war service, on petition of the fiduciary, a cofiduciary, or an interested person, the court may do any one or more of the following:

(a) Appoint a substitute fiduciary. If there is a qualified and acting cofiduciary, the court is not required to appoint a substitute fiduciary but may vest in the cofiduciary the powers of the original fiduciary engaged in war service.

(b) Order a suspension of the powers and duties of the original fiduciary for the period the original fiduciary is engaged in war service and until further order of the court.

(c) Order an account by the original fiduciary.

371. A substitute fiduciary has all the powers, including discretionary powers, that the original fiduciary had, except powers that the court determines are purely personal to the original fiduciary, and is subject to the same duties as the original fiduciary.

372. Except as otherwise ordered by the court, a substitute fiduciary shall give a bond in the manner and to the extent provided by law for the original fiduciary.

373. After the expiration of an original fiduciary's war service, if the estate has not been closed, the original fiduciary, on petition, is entitled to reinstatement as fiduciary. On reinstatement, the substitute fiduciary may, in the discretion of the court, be removed and may be discharged on conditions prescribed by the court.

374. A substitute fiduciary or an original fiduciary reinstated under Section 373 is not liable for the acts or omissions of the predecessor fiduciary.

Chapter 3. Delegation Of Powers

Article 1. Delegation By Fiduciary

380. (a) A fiduciary who is or will be engaged in war service may delegate the fiduciary's powers, including discretionary powers, to a fiduciary who is not engaged in war service. Delegation may be made for the period during which the original fiduciary is engaged in war service and not to exceed six months following the expiration of that period.

(b) Approval of the court, on petition of the original fiduciary, the delegate, or an interested person, is required for delegation.

381. The right of delegation does not exist to the extent the court determines that powers to be delegated are purely personal to the original fiduciary.

382. After the expiration of the original fiduciary's war service, the court may, on petition of the original fiduciary, authorize the original fiduciary to resume the exercise of the fiduciary functions, and the delegated powers cease.

383. The original fiduciary is not liable for the acts or omissions of the delegate.

Article 2. Delegation By Consultant

385. (a) A consultant who is or will be engaged in war service may delegate the powers of the consultant, including discretionary powers, to a coconsultant who is not engaged in war service, or to the trustee administering the trust. The procedure for delegation by a fiduciary governs delegation by a consultant.

(b) The right of delegation does not exist to the extent the court determines that powers to be delegated are purely personal to the consultant. These powers are suspended until their exercise is resumed pursuant to this article.

386. If a consultant who is engaged in war service does not delegate the consultant's powers, the court, on petition of the trustee or an interested person, may do either of the following:

(a) Suspend the consultant's powers for the period of the consultant's war service and not to exceed six months following the expiration of that period.

(b) Confer the powers, except discretionary powers that the court determines are purely personal to the consultant, on a coconsultant designated in the trust, the trustee, or any other qualified person.

387. If a consultant has delegated or the court has suspended the powers of the consultant, the court may, on petition by the consultant within six months following the expiration of the period of the consultant's war service, authorize the consultant to resume the exercise of the consultant's functions. All powers delegated to or conferred on other persons thereupon cease.

388. A consultant who delegates powers under this article is not liable for the acts or omissions of the delegate.

Part 12. Probate Referees

Chapter 1. Appointment And Revocation

400. (a) The Controller shall appoint at least one person in each county to act as a probate referee for the county.

(b) If there are fewer than three qualified applicants to serve in a county, the Controller may designate a probate referee from another county or make an interim appointment, to serve until the vacancy has been filled by a qualified applicant.

401. (a) Appointment shall be from among persons passing a qualification examination. A person who passes the examination is eligible for appointment for a period of five years from the date of the examination.

(b) Appointment shall be on the basis of merit without regard to sex, race, religious creed, color, national origin, ancestry, marital status, or political affiliation.

402. (a) The qualification examination for applicants for appointment to act as a probate referee shall be held at times and places within the state determined by the Controller.

(b) The Controller may contract with another agency to administer the qualification examination. Administration of the examination shall include:

(1) Development of standards for passage of the examination.

(2) Preparation of examination questions.

(3) Giving the examination.

(4) Scoring the examination.

(c) Each applicant shall pay a fee for taking the qualification examination. The agency administering the examination shall transmit to the Controller a list of candidates who have received a passing score in the examination. The list is a public record.

403. (a) The term of office of a probate referee is four years, expiring June 30. A person may be appointed to complete the unexpired term of office of a probate referee whose appointment is revoked or is otherwise terminated. For a period of five years from the date of expiration of the term of office, a person who had been appointed to act as a probate referee is eligible for reappointment.

(b) If the Controller increases the number of probate referees in a county, the Controller shall stagger the terms of the new appointees so that one-quarter, or as close to one-quarter as possible, of the terms of the probate referees in that county expire on June 30 of each succeeding year.

404. (a) The Controller shall establish and may amend standards of training, performance, and ethics of probate referees. The standards are a public record.

(b) The Controller may revoke the appointment of a person to act as a probate referee for noncompliance with any standard of training, performance, or ethics established under subdivision (a). The Controller may revoke an appointment under this subdivision without notice or a hearing, but the revocation is subject to review by writ of mandate in a court of competent jurisdiction.

405. Notwithstanding Section 404, the Controller may, at the Controller's pleasure, revoke the appointment of a person to act as a probate referee. Under this section, the Controller may revoke the appointment of not more than 10 percent of the probate referees in each county in any one calendar year, but may revoke the appointment of at least one probate referee in each county in any one calendar year.

406. (a) The authority of a person to act as a probate referee ceases immediately upon expiration of the person's term of office, revocation of the person's appointment, or other termination pursuant to law.

(b) Upon cessation of authority of a person to act as a probate referee, the Controller shall notify the superior court of the county for which the probate referee was appointed. Upon receipt of notice, or if it otherwise comes to the attention of the court that the authority of a person to act as a probate referee has ceased, the court shall reassign any estate for which the person had been designated as probate referee to another probate referee.

407. (a) As used in this section, "prohibited political activity" means directly or indirectly soliciting, receiving, or contributing, or being in any manner involved in soliciting, receiving, or contributing, any of the following:

(1) An assessment, subscription, or contribution to any party, incumbent, committee, or candidate exceeding two hundred dollars ($200) in any one calendar year for any partisan public office of this state.

(2) An assessment, subscription, contribution, or political service in any amount for any campaign for the office of Controller.

(b) Upon a person's appointment and thereafter in January of each year during the person's tenure as a probate referee, the person shall file with the Controller a verified statement indicating whether the person has engaged in prohibited political activity during the preceding two calendar years.

(c) The Controller may not appoint or reappoint as a probate referee a person who within the preceding two calendar years has engaged in prohibited political activity, and any such appointment or reappointment is void and shall be revoked. The Controller shall revoke the appointment of a person who, during the person's tenure as a probate referee, engages in prohibited political activity. However, all acts not otherwise invalid, performed by the person before revocation of the person's appointment, are valid.

(d) A person shall not engage in prohibited political activity during the time the person is an applicant for appointment or reappointment, or during the person's tenure as a probate referee. A violation of this subdivision is a misdemeanor.

(e) Subdivisions (a), (c), and (d) do not apply to any prohibited political activity that occurred before July 1, 1989, and the applicable law in effect before July 1, 1989, continues to apply. Subdivision (b) applies on July 1, 1989, to persons who apply for appointment on or after July 1, 1989. A person who applied for appointment or who was appointed before July 1, 1989, shall file the first statement required by subdivision (b) on or before July 1, 1989, and thereafter as prescribed in subdivision (b).

408. The appointment of a probate referee by the Controller before July 1, 1989, is not invalidated by the repeal of the law under which the appointment was made. Appointment of a probate referee before July 1, 1989, may be revoked under this chapter only if revocation would otherwise be proper under this chapter.

Chapter 2. Powers Of Probate Referee

450. Upon designation by the court, the probate referee has all the powers of a referee of the superior court and all other powers provided in this chapter.

451. (a) For the purpose of appraisal of property in the estate, the probate referee may require, and may issue a subpoena to compel, the appearance before the referee of the personal representative, guardian, conservator, or other fiduciary, an interested person, or any other person the referee has reason to believe has knowledge of the property.

(b) A subpoena issued under subdivision (a) is subject to the provisions of Chapter 6 (commencing with Section 2020.010) of Title 4 of Part 4 of the Code of Civil Procedure governing deposition subpoenas.

452. (a) The probate referee may:

(1) Examine and take the testimony under oath of a person appearing before the referee.

(2) Require, and issue a subpoena to compel, the person to produce any document in the person's possession or control, concerning the value of any property in the estate.

(b) A subpoena issued under subdivision (a) is subject to the provisions of Chapter 6 (commencing with Section 2020.010) of Title 4 of Part 4 of the Code of Civil Procedure governing deposition subpoenas.

453. (a) On petition of a person required to appear before the probate referee pursuant to this chapter, the court may make a protective order to protect the person from annoyance, embarrassment, or oppression. The petitioner shall mail notice of the hearing on the petition to the probate referee and to the personal representative, guardian, conservator, or other fiduciary at least 15 days before the date set for the hearing. Any subpoena issued by the probate referee is stayed during the pendency of the petition.

(b) On petition of the probate referee, the court may make an order to show cause why a person who is required, but fails, to appear before the probate referee pursuant to this chapter, should not be compelled to do so. The probate referee shall mail notice of the hearing on the petition to the person at least 15 days before the date set for the hearing.

Part 13. Litigation Involving Decedent

Chapter 1. Liability Of Decedent Covered By insurance

550. (a) Subject to the provisions of this chapter, an action to establish the decedent's liability for which the decedent was protected by insurance may be commenced or continued against the decedent's estate without the need to join as a party the decedent's personal representative or successor in interest.

(b) The remedy provided in this chapter is cumulative and may be pursued concurrently with other remedies.

551. Notwithstanding Section 366.2 of the Code of Civil Procedure, if the limitations period otherwise applicable to the action has not expired at the time of the decedent's death, an action under this chapter may be commenced within one year after the expiration of the limitations period otherwise applicable.

552. (a) An action under this chapter shall name as the defendant, "Estate of (name of decedent), Deceased." Summons shall be served on a person designated in writing by the insurer or, if none, on the insurer. Further proceedings shall be in the name of the estate, but otherwise shall be conducted in the same manner as if the action were against the personal representative.

(b) On motion of an interested person, or on its own motion, the court in which the action is pending may, for good cause, order the appointment and substitution of a personal representative as the defendant.

(c) An action against the estate of the decedent under this chapter may be consolidated with an action against the personal representative.

553. The insurer may deny or otherwise contest its liability in an action under this chapter or by an independent action. Unless the personal representative is joined as a party, a judgment in the action under this chapter or in the independent action does not adjudicate rights by or against the estate.

554. (a) Except as provided in subdivision (b), either the damages sought in an action under this chapter shall be within the limits and coverage of the insurance, or recovery of damages outside the limits or coverage of the insurance shall be waived. A judgment in favor of the plaintiff in the action is enforceable only from the insurance coverage and not against property in the estate.

(b) Where the amount of damages sought in the action exceeds the coverage of the insurance, subdivision (a) does not apply if both of the following conditions are satisfied:

(1) The personal representative is joined as a party to the action.

(2) The plaintiff files a claim in compliance with Section 9390.

555. (a) This chapter does not apply to an action commenced before July 1, 1989.

(b) The applicable law in effect before July 1, 1989, continues to apply to an action commenced before July 1, 1989, notwithstanding its repeal by Chapter 1199 of the Statutes of 1988.

Part 14. Applicability Of Repealed Or Amended Provisions Relating To Compensation Of Estate Attorney And Personal Representative

Part 14. Powers Of Appointment

Chapter 1. General Provisions

600. Except to the extent that the common law rules governing powers of appointment are modified by statute, the common law as to powers of appointment is the law of this state.

601. If the law existing at the time of the creation of a power of appointment and the law existing at the time of the release or exercise of the power of appointment or at the time of the assertion of a right given by this part differ, the law existing at the time of the release, exercise, or assertion of a right controls. Nothing in this section makes invalid a power of appointment created before July 1, 1970, that was valid under the law in existence at the time it was created.

Chapter 2. Definitions; Classification Of Powers Of Appointment

610. As used in this part:

(a) "Appointee" means the person in whose favor a power of appointment is exercised.

(b) "Appointive property" means the property or interest in property that is the subject of the power of appointment.

(c) "Creating instrument" means the deed, will, trust, or other writing or document that creates or reserves the power of appointment.

(d) "Donee" means the person to whom a power of appointment is given or in whose favor a power of appointment is reserved.

(e) "Donor" means the person who creates or reserves a power of appointment.

(f) "Permissible appointee" means a person in whose favor a power of appointment can be exercised.

611. (a) A power of appointment is "general" only to the extent that it is exercisable in favor of the donee, the donee's estate, the donee's creditors, or creditors of the donee's estate, whether or not it is exercisable in favor of others.

(b) A power to consume, invade, or appropriate property for the benefit of a person in discharge of the donee's obligation of support that is limited by an ascertainable standard relating to the person' s health, education, support, or maintenance is not a general power of appointment.

(c) A power exercisable by the donee only in conjunction with a person having a substantial interest in the appointive property that is adverse to the exercise of the power in favor of the donee, the donee's estate, the donee's creditors, or creditors of the donee's estate is not a general power of appointment.

(d) A power of appointment that is not "general" is "special."

(e) A power of appointment may be general as to some appointive property, or an interest in or a specific portion of appointive property, and be special as to other appointive property.

612. (a) A power of appointment is "testamentary" if it is exercisable only by a will.

(b) A power of appointment is "presently exercisable" at the time in question to the extent that an irrevocable appointment can be made.

(c) A power of appointment is "not presently exercisable" if it is "postponed." A power of appointment is "postponed" in either of the following circumstances:

(1) The creating instrument provides that the power of appointment may be exercised only after a specified act or event occurs or a specified condition is met, and the act or event has not occurred or the condition has not been met.

(2) The creating instrument provides that an exercise of the power of appointment is revocable until a specified act or event occurs or a specified condition is met, and the act or event has not occurred or the condition has not been met.

613. A power of appointment is "imperative" where the creating instrument manifests an intent that the permissible appointees be benefited even if the donee fails to exercise the power. An imperative power can exist even though the donee has the privilege of selecting some and excluding others of the designated permissible appointees. All other powers of appointment are "discretionary." The donee of a discretionary power is privileged to exercise, or not to exercise, the power as the donee chooses.

Chapter 3. Creation Of Powers Of Appointment

620. A power of appointment can be created only by a donor having the capacity to transfer the interest in property to which the power relates.

Chapter 4. Exercise Of Powers Of Appointment

Article 1. Donee's Capacity

625. (a) A power of appointment can be exercised only by a donee having the capacity to transfer the interest in property to which the power relates.

(b) Unless the creating instrument otherwise provides, a donee who is a minor may not exercise a power of appointment during minority.

Article 2. Scope Of Donee's Authority

630. (a) Except as otherwise provided in this part, if the creating instrument specifies requirements as to the manner, time, and conditions of the exercise of a power of appointment, the power can be exercised only by complying with those requirements.

(b) Unless expressly prohibited by the creating instrument, a power stated to be exercisable by an inter vivos instrument is also exercisable by a written will.

631. (a) Where an appointment does not satisfy the formal requirements specified in the creating instrument as provided in subdivision (a) of Section 630, the court may excuse compliance with the formal requirements and determine that exercise of the appointment was effective if both of the following requirements are satisfied:

(1) The appointment approximates the manner of appointment prescribed by the donor.

(2) The failure to satisfy the formal requirements does not defeat the accomplishment of a significant purpose of the donor.

(b) This section does not permit a court to excuse compliance with a specific reference requirement under Section 632.

632. If the creating instrument expressly directs that a power of appointment be exercised by an instrument that makes a specific reference to the power or to the instrument that created the power, the power can be exercised only by an instrument containing the required reference.

633. (a) If the creating instrument requires the consent of the donor or other person to exercise a power of appointment, the power can only be exercised when the required consent is contained in the instrument of exercise or in a separate written instrument, signed in each case by the person whose consent is required.

(b) Unless expressly prohibited by the creating instrument:

(1) If a person whose consent is required dies, the power may be exercised by the donee without the consent of that person.

(2) If a person whose consent is required becomes legally incapable of consenting, the person's guardian or conservator may consent to an exercise of the power.

(3) A consent may be given before or after the exercise of the power by the donee.

634. A power of appointment created in favor of two or more donees can only be exercised when all of the donees unite in its exercise. If one or more of the donees dies, becomes legally incapable of exercising the power, or releases the power, the power may be exercised by the others, unless expressly prohibited by the creating instrument.

635. Nothing in this chapter affects the power of a court of competent jurisdiction to remedy a defective exercise of an imperative power of appointment.

Article 3. Donee's Required Intent

640. (a) The exercise of a power of appointment requires a manifestation of the donee's intent to exercise the power.

(b) A manifestation of the donee's intent to exercise a power of appointment exists in any of the following circumstances:

(1) The donee declares, in substance, that the donee exercises specific powers or all the powers the donee has.

(2) The donee purports to transfer an interest in the appointive property that the donee would have no power to transfer except by virtue of the power.

(3) The donee makes a disposition that, when considered with reference to the property owned and the circumstances existing at the time of the disposition, manifests the donee's understanding that the donee was disposing of the appointive property.

(c) The circumstances described in subdivision (b) are illustrative, not exclusive.

641. (a) A general residuary clause in a will, or a will making general disposition of all the testator's property, does not exercise a power of appointment held by the testator unless specific reference is made to the power or there is some other indication of intent to exercise the power.

(b) This section applies in a case where the donee dies on or after July 1, 1982.

642. If a power of appointment existing at the donee's death, but created after the execution of the donee's will, is exercised by the will, the appointment is effective except in either of the following cases:

(a) The creating instrument manifests an intent that the power may not be exercised by a will previously executed.

(b) The will manifests an intent not to exercise a power subsequently acquired.

Article 4. Types Of Appointments

650. (a) The donee of a general power of appointment may make an appointment:

(1) Of all of the appointive property at one time, or several partial appointments at different times, where the power is exercisable inter vivos.

(2) Of present or future interests or both.

(3) Subject to conditions or charges.

(4) Subject to otherwise lawful restraints on the alienation of the appointed interest.

(5) In trust.

(6) Creating a new power of appointment.

(b) The listing in subdivision (a) is illustrative, not exclusive.

651. Subject to the limitations imposed by the creating instrument, the donee of a special power may make any of the types of appointment permissible for the donee of a general power under Section 650.

652. (a) Except as provided in subdivision (b), the donee of a special power of appointment may appoint the whole or any part of the appointive property to any one or more of the permissible appointees and exclude others.

(b) If the donor specifies either a minimum or maximum share or amount to be appointed to one or more of the permissible appointees, the exercise of the power must conform to the specification.

Article 5. Contracts To Appoint; Releases

660. (a) The donee of a power of appointment that is presently exercisable, whether general or special, can contract to make an appointment to the same extent that the donee could make an effective appointment.

(b) The donee of a power of appointment cannot contract to make an appointment while the power of appointment is not presently exercisable. If a promise to make an appointment under such a power is not performed, the promisee cannot obtain either specific performance or damages, but the promisee is not prevented from obtaining restitution of the value given by the promisee for the promise.

(c) Unless the creating instrument expressly provides that the donee may not contract to make an appointment while the power of appointment is not presently exercisable, subdivision (b) does not apply to the case where the donor and the donee are the same person. In this case, the donee can contract to make an appointment to the same extent that the donee could make an effective appointment if the power of appointment were presently exercisable.

661. (a) Unless the creating instrument otherwise provides, a general or special power of appointment that is a discretionary power, whether testamentary or otherwise, may be released, either with or without consideration, by a written instrument signed by the donee and delivered as provided in subdivision (c).

(b) A releasable power may be released with respect to the whole or any part of the appointive property and may also be released in such manner as to reduce or limit the permissible appointees. No partial release of a power shall be deemed to make imperative the remaining power that was not imperative before the release unless the instrument of release expressly so provides. No release of a power that is not presently exercisable is permissible where the donor designated persons or a class to take in default of the donee's exercise of the power unless the release serves to benefit all persons designated as provided by the donor.

(c) A release shall be delivered as follows:

(1) If the creating instrument specifies a person to whom a release is to be delivered, the release shall be delivered to that person, but delivery need not be made as provided in this paragraph if the person cannot with due diligence be found.

(2) In a case where the property to which the power relates is held by a trustee, the release shall be delivered to the trustee.

(3) In a case not covered by paragraph (1) or (2), the release may be delivered to any of the following:

(A) A person, other than the donee, who could be adversely affected by the exercise of the power.

(B) The county recorder of the county in which the donee resides or in which the deed, will, or other instrument creating the power is filed.

(d) A release of a power of appointment that affects real property or obligations secured by real property shall be acknowledged and proved, and may be certified and recorded, in like manner and with like effect as grants of real property, and all statutory provisions relating to the recordation or nonrecordation of conveyances of real property and to the effect thereof apply to a release with like effect, without regard to the date when the release was delivered, if at all, pursuant to subdivision (c). Failure to deliver, pursuant to subdivision (c), a release that is recorded pursuant to this subdivision does not affect the validity of any transaction with respect to the real property or obligation secured thereby, and the general laws of this state on recording and its effect govern the transaction.

(e) This section does not impair the validity of a release made before July 1, 1970.

662. (a) A release on behalf of a minor donee shall be made by the guardian of the estate of the minor pursuant to an order of court obtained under this section.

(b) The guardian or other interested person may file a petition with the court in which the guardianship of the estate proceeding is pending for an order of the court authorizing or requiring the guardian to release the ward's powers as a donee or a power of appointment in whole or in part.

(c) Notice of the hearing on the petition shall be given for the period and in the manner provided in Chapter 3 (commencing with Section 1460) of Part 1 of Division 4 to all of the following (other than the petitioner or persons joining in the petition):

(1) The persons required to be given notice under Chapter 3 (commencing with Section 1460) of Part 1 of Division 4.

(2) The donor of the power, if alive.

(3) The trustee, if the property to which the power relates is held by a trustee.

(4) Other persons as ordered by the court.

(d) After hearing, the court in its discretion may make an order authorizing or requiring the guardian to release on behalf of the ward a general or special power of appointment as permitted under Section 661, if the court determines, taking into consideration all the relevant circumstances, that the ward as a prudent person would make the release of the power of appointment if the ward had the capacity to do so.

(e) Nothing in this section imposes any duty on the guardian to file a petition under this section, and the guardian is not liable for failure to file a petition under this section.

Chapter 5. Effect Of Failure To Make Effective Appointment

670. An exercise of a power of appointment is not void solely because it is more extensive than authorized by the power, but is valid to the extent that the exercise was permissible under the terms of the power.

671. (a) Unless the creating instrument or the donee, in writing, manifests a contrary intent, where the donee dies without having exercised an imperative power of appointment either in whole or in part, the persons designated as permissible appointees take equally of the property not already appointed. Where the creating instrument establishes a minimum distribution requirement that is not satisfied by an equal division of the property not already appointed, the appointees who have received a partial appointment are required to return a pro rata portion of the property they would otherwise be entitled to receive in an amount sufficient to meet the minimum distribution requirement.

(b) Where an imperative power of appointment has been exercised defectively, either in whole or in part, its proper execution may be adjudged in favor of the person intended to be benefited by the defective exercise.

(c) Where an imperative power of appointment has been created so that it confers on a person a right to have the power exercised in the person's favor, the proper exercise of the power can be compelled in favor of the person, or the person's assigns, creditors, guardian, or conservator.

672. (a) Except as provided in subdivision (b), if the donee of a discretionary power of appointment fails to appoint the property, releases the entire power, or makes an ineffective appointment, in whole or in part, the appointive property not effectively appointed passes to the person named by the donor as taker in default or, if there is none, reverts to the donor.

(b) If the donee of a general power of appointment makes an ineffective appointment, an implied alternative appointment to the donee's estate may be found if the donee has manifested an intent that the appointive property be disposed of as property of the donee rather than as in default of appointment.

673. (a) Except as provided in subdivision (b), if an appointment by will or by instrument effective only at the death of the donee is ineffective because of the death of an appointee before the appointment becomes effective and the appointee leaves issue surviving the donee, the surviving issue of the appointee take the appointed property in the same manner as the appointee would have taken had the appointee survived the donee, except that the property passes only to persons who are permissible appointees, including appointees permitted under Section 674. If the surviving issue are all of the same degree of kinship to the deceased appointee, they take equally, but if of unequal degree, then those of more remote degree take in the manner provided in Section 240.

(b) This section does not apply if either the donor or donee manifests an intent that some other disposition of the appointive property shall be made.

674. (a) Unless the creating instrument expressly provides otherwise, if a permissible appointee dies before the exercise of a special power of appointment, the donee has the power to appoint to the issue of the deceased permissible appointee, whether or not the issue was included within the description of the permissible appointees, if the deceased permissible appointee was alive at the time of the execution of the creating instrument or was born thereafter.

(b) This section applies whether the special power of appointment is exercisable by inter vivos instrument, by will, or otherwise.

(c) This section applies to a case where the power of appointment is exercised on or after July 1, 1982, but does not affect the validity of any exercise of a power of appointment made before July 1, 1982.

Chapter 6. Rights Of Creditors

680. The donor of a power of appointment cannot nullify or alter the rights given creditors of the donee by Sections 682, 683, and 684 by any language in the instrument creating the power.

681. Property covered by a special power of appointment is not subject to the claims of creditors of the donee or of the donee's estate or to the expenses of the administration of the donee's estate.

682. (a) To the extent that the property owned by the donee is inadequate to satisfy the claims of the donee's creditors, property subject to a general power of appointment that is presently exercisable is subject to the claims to the same extent that it would be subject to the claims if the property were owned by the donee.

(b) Upon the death of the donee, to the extent that the donee's estate is inadequate to satisfy the claims of creditors of the estate and the expenses of administration of the estate, property subject to a general testamentary power of appointment or to a general power of appointment that was presently exercisable at the time of the donee's death is subject to the claims and expenses to the same extent that it would be subject to the claims and expenses if the property had been owned by the donee.

(c) This section applies whether or not the power of appointment has been exercised.

683. Property subject to an unexercised general power of appointment created by the donor in the donor's favor, whether or not presently exercisable, is subject to the claims of the donor's creditors or the donor's estate and to the expenses of the administration of the donor's estate.

684. For the purposes of Sections 682 and 683, a person to whom the donee owes an obligation of support shall be considered a creditor of the donee to the extent that a legal obligation exists for the donee to provide the support.

Chapter 7. Rule Against Perpetuities

690. The statutory rule against perpetuities provided by Part 2 (commencing with Section 21200) of Division 11 applies to powers of appointment governed by this part.

Chapter 8. Revocability Of Creation, Exercise, Or Release Of Power Of Appointment

695. (a) Unless the power to revoke is in the creating instrument or exists pursuant to Section 15400, the creation of a power of appointment is irrevocable.

(b) Unless made expressly irrevocable by the creating instrument or the instrument of exercise, an exercise of a power of appointment is revocable if the power to revoke exists pursuant to Section 15400 or so long as the interest in the appointive property, whether present or future, has not been transferred or become distributable pursuant to the appointment.

(c) Unless the power to revoke is reserved in the instrument releasing the power, a release of a power of appointment is irrevocable.

Part 15. Deposit Of Estate Planning Documents With Attorney

Chapter 1. Definitions

700. Unless the provision or context otherwise requires, the definitions in this chapter govern the construction of this part.

701. "Attorney" means an individual licensed to practice law in this state.

702. "Deposit" means delivery of a document by a depositor to an attorney for safekeeping or authorization by a depositor for an attorney to retain a document for safekeeping.

703. "Depositor" means a natural person who deposits the person's document with an attorney.

704. "Document" means any of the following:

(a) A signed original will, declaration of trust, trust amendment, or other document modifying a will or trust.

(b) A signed original power of attorney.

(c) A signed original nomination of conservator.

(d) Any other signed original instrument that the attorney and depositor agree in writing to make subject to this part.

Chapter 2. Duties And Liabilities Of Attorney

710. If a document is deposited with an attorney, the attorney, and a successor attorney that accepts transfer of the document, shall use ordinary care for preservation of the document on and after July 1, 1994, whether or not consideration is given, and shall hold the document in a safe, vault, safe deposit box, or other secure place where it will be reasonably protected against loss or destruction.

711. If a document deposited with an attorney is lost or destroyed, the attorney shall give notice of the loss or destruction to the depositor by one of the following methods:

(a) By mailing the notice to the depositor's last known address.

(b) By the method most likely to give the depositor actual notice.

712. Notwithstanding failure of an attorney to satisfy the standard of care required by Section 710 or 716, the attorney is not liable for loss or destruction of the document if the depositor has actual notice of the loss or destruction and a reasonable opportunity to replace the document, and the attorney offers without charge either to assist the depositor in replacing the document, or to prepare a substantially similar document and assist in its execution.

713. The acceptance by an attorney of a document for deposit imposes no duty on the attorney to do either of the following:

(a) Inquire into the content, validity, invalidity, or completeness of the document, or the correctness of any information in the document.

(b) Provide continuing legal services to the depositor or to any beneficiary under the document. This subdivision does not affect the duty, if any, of the drafter of the document to provide continuing legal services to any person.

714. (a) If so provided in a written agreement signed by the depositor, an attorney may charge the depositor for compensation and expenses incurred in safekeeping or delivery of a document deposited with the attorney.

(b) No lien arises for the benefit of an attorney on a document deposited with the attorney, whether before or after its transfer, even if provided by agreement.

715. An attorney may give written notice to a depositor, and obtain written acknowledgment from the depositor, in the following form:

> PLEASE SEE THE APPENDIX

716. Notwithstanding Section 710, if an attorney has given written notice to the depositor, and has obtained written acknowledgment from the depositor, in substantially the form provided in Section 715, and the requirements of subdivision (a) of Section 732 are satisfied, the attorney, and a successor attorney that accepts transfer of a document, shall use at least slight care for preservation of a document deposited with the attorney.

Chapter 3. Termination Of Deposit

Article 1. Termination By Depositor

720. A depositor may terminate a deposit on demand, in which case the attorney shall deliver the document to the depositor.

Article 2. Termination By Attorney

730. An attorney with whom a document has been deposited, or to whom a document has been transferred pursuant to this article, may terminate the deposit only as provided in this article.

731. An attorney may terminate the deposit by one of the following methods:

(a) Personal delivery of the document to the depositor.

(b) Mailing the document to the depositor's last known address, by registered or certified mail with return receipt requested, and receiving a signed receipt.

(c) The method agreed on by the depositor and attorney.

732. (a) An attorney may terminate a deposit under this section if the attorney has mailed notice to reclaim the document to the depositor's last known address and the depositor has failed to reclaim the document within 90 days after the mailing.

(b) Subject to subdivision (f), an attorney may terminate a deposit under this section by transferring the document to another attorney. All documents transferred under this subdivision shall be transferred to the same attorney.

(c) Subject to subdivision (f), if an attorney is deceased, lacks legal capacity, or is no longer an active member of the State Bar, a deposit may be terminated under this section by transferring the document to the clerk of the superior court of the county of the depositor's last known domicile. The attorney shall advise the clerk that the document is being transferred pursuant to Section 732.

(d) An attorney may not accept a fee or compensation from a transferee for transferring a document under this section. An attorney may charge a fee for receiving a document under this section.

(e) Transfer of a document by an attorney under this section is not a waiver or breach of any privilege or confidentiality associated with the document, and is not a violation of the rules of professional conduct. If the document is privileged under Article 3 (commencing with Section 950) of Chapter 4 of Division 8 of the Evidence Code, the document remains privileged after the transfer.

(f) If the document is a will and the attorney has actual notice that the depositor has died, the attorney may terminate a deposit only as provided in Section 734.

733. (a) An attorney transferring one or more documents under Section 732 shall mail notice of the transfer to the State Bar of California. The notice shall contain all of the following information:

(1) The name of the depositor.

(2) The date of the transfer.

(3) The name, address, and State Bar number of the transferring attorney.

(4) Whether any documents are transferred to an attorney, and the name, address, and State Bar number of the attorney to whom the documents are transferred.

(5) Whether any documents are transferred to a superior court clerk.

(b) The State Bar shall record only one notice of transfer for each transferring attorney. The State Bar shall prescribe the form for the notice of transfer. On request by any person, the State Bar shall give that person information in the notice of transfer. At its sole election, the State Bar may give the information orally or in writing.

734. (a) In cases not governed by subdivision (b) or (c), after the death of the depositor an attorney may terminate a deposit by personal delivery of the document to the depositor's personal representative.

(b) If the document is a will and the attorney has actual notice that the depositor has died but does not have actual notice that a personal representative has been appointed for the depositor, an attorney may terminate a deposit only as provided in Section 8200.

(c) If the document is a trust, after the death of the depositor an attorney may terminate a deposit by personal delivery of the document either to the depositor's personal representative or to the trustee named in the document.

735. (a) If the attorney is deceased or lacks legal capacity, a deposit may be terminated as provided in this article by the attorney's law partner, by a shareholder of the attorney's law corporation, or by a lawyer or nonlawyer employee of the attorney's firm, partnership, or corporation.

(b) If the attorney lacks legal capacity and there is no person to act under subdivision (a), a deposit may be terminated by the conservator of the attorney's estate or by an attorney in fact acting under a durable power of attorney. A conservator of the attorney's estate may act without court approval.

(c) If the attorney is deceased and there is no person to act under subdivision (a), a deposit may be terminated by the attorney's personal representative.

(d) If a person authorized under this section terminates a deposit as provided in Section 732, the person shall give the notice required by Section 733.

Part 16. Jurisdiction

800. The court in proceedings under this code is a court of general jurisdiction and the court, or a judge of the court, has the same power and authority with respect to the proceedings as otherwise provided by law for a superior court, or a judge of the superior court, including, but not limited to, the matters authorized by Section 128 of the Code of Civil Procedure.

801. The court, on its own motion or on the motion of any interested party, may order that an action or proceeding not specifically provided in this code be determined in a separate civil action. Upon the payment of the appropriate filing fees, the court may order transfer of the severed action or proceeding to the separate civil action.

Part 17. Legal Mental Capacity

810. The Legislature finds and declares the following:

(a) For purposes of this part, there shall exist a rebuttable presumption affecting the burden of proof that all persons have the capacity to make decisions and to be responsible for their acts or decisions.

(b) A person who has a mental or physical disorder may still be capable of contracting, conveying, marrying, making medical decisions, executing wills or trusts, and performing other actions.

(c) A judicial determination that a person is totally without understanding, or is of unsound mind, or suffers from one or more mental deficits so substantial that, under the circumstances, the person should be deemed to lack the legal capacity to perform a specific act, should be based on evidence of a deficit in one or more of the person's mental functions rather than on a diagnosis of a person's mental or physical disorder.

811. (a) A determination that a person is of unsound mind or lacks the capacity to make a decision or do a certain act, including, but not limited to, the incapacity to contract, to make a conveyance, to marry, to make medical decisions, to execute wills, or to execute trusts, shall be supported by evidence of a deficit in at least one of the following mental functions, subject to subdivision (b), and evidence of a correlation between the deficit or deficits and the decision or acts in question:

(1) Alertness and attention, including, but not limited to, the following:

(A) Level of arousal or consciousness.

(B) Orientation to time, place, person, and situation.

(C) Ability to attend and concentrate.

(2) Information processing, including, but not limited to, the following:

(A) Short- and long-term memory, including immediate recall.

(B) Ability to understand or communicate with others, either verbally or otherwise.

(C) Recognition of familiar objects and familiar persons.

(D) Ability to understand and appreciate quantities.

(E) Ability to reason using abstract concepts.

(F) Ability to plan, organize, and carry out actions in one's own rational self-interest.

(G) Ability to reason logically.

(3) Thought processes. Deficits in these functions may be demonstrated by the presence of the following:

(A) Severely disorganized thinking.

(B) Hallucinations.

(C) Delusions.

(D) Uncontrollable, repetitive, or intrusive thoughts.

(4) Ability to modulate mood and affect. Deficits in this ability may be demonstrated by the presence of a pervasive and persistent or recurrent state of euphoria, anger, anxiety, fear, panic, depression, hopelessness or despair, helplessness, apathy or indifference, that is inappropriate in degree to the individual's circumstances.

(b) A deficit in the mental functions listed above may be considered only if the deficit, by itself or in combination with one or more other mental function deficits, significantly impairs the person's ability to understand and appreciate the consequences of his or her actions with regard to the type of act or decision in question.

(c) In determining whether a person suffers from a deficit in mental function so substantial that the person lacks the capacity to do a certain act, the court may take into consideration the frequency, severity, and duration of periods of impairment.

(d) The mere diagnosis of a mental or physical disorder shall not be sufficient in and of itself to support a determination that a person is of unsound mind or lacks the capacity to do a certain act.

(e) This part applies only to the evidence that is presented to, and the findings that are made by, a court determining the capacity of a person to do a certain act or make a decision, including, but not limited to, making medical decisions. Nothing in this part shall affect the decisionmaking process set forth in Section 1418.8 of the Health and Safety Code, nor increase or decrease the burdens of documentation on, or potential liability of, health care providers who, outside the judicial context, determine the capacity of patients to make a medical decision.

812. Except where otherwise provided by law, including, but not limited to, Section 813 and the statutory and decisional law of testamentary capacity, a person lacks the capacity to make a decision unless the person has the ability to communicate verbally, or by any other means, the decision, and to understand and appreciate, to the extent relevant, all of the following:

(a) The rights, duties, and responsibilities created by, or affected by the decision.

(b) The probable consequences for the decisionmaker and, where appropriate, the persons affected by the decision.

(c) The significant risks, benefits, and reasonable alternatives involved in the decision.

813. (a) For purposes of a judicial determination, a person has the capacity to give informed consent to a proposed medical treatment if the person is able to do all of the following:

(1) Respond knowingly and intelligently to queries about that medical treatment.

(2) Participate in that treatment decision by means of a rational thought process.

(3) Understand all of the following items of minimum basic medical treatment information with respect to that treatment:

(A) The nature and seriousness of the illness, disorder, or defect that the person has.

(B) The nature of the medical treatment that is being recommended by the person's health care providers.

(C) The probable degree and duration of any benefits and risks of any medical intervention that is being recommended by the person's health care providers, and the consequences of lack of treatment.

(D) The nature, risks, and benefits of any reasonable alternatives.

(b) A person who has the capacity to give informed consent to a proposed medical treatment also has the capacity to refuse consent to that treatment.

Part 18. Right To Trial

825. Except as otherwise expressly provided in this code, there is no right to a jury trial in proceedings under this code.

Part 19. Conveyance Or Transfer Of Property Claimed To Belong To Decedent Or Other Person

850. (a) The following persons may file a petition requesting that the court make an order under this part:

(1) A guardian, conservator, or any claimant, in the following cases:

(A) Where the conservatee is bound by a contract in writing to convey real property or to transfer personal property, executed by the conservatee while competent or executed by the conservatee's predecessor in interest, and the contract is one that can be specifically enforced.

(B) Where the minor has succeeded to the interest of a person bound by a contract in writing to convey real property or to transfer personal property, and the contract is one that can be specifically enforced.

(C) Where the guardian or conservator or the minor or conservatee is in possession of, or holds title to, real or personal property, and the property or some interest therein is claimed to belong to another.

(D) Where the minor or conservatee has a claim to real or personal property title to or possession of which is held by another.

(2) The personal representative or any interested person in any of the following cases:

(A) Where the decedent while living is bound by a contract in writing to convey real property or to transfer personal property and dies before making the conveyance or transfer and the decedent, if living, could have been compelled to make the conveyance or transfer.

(B) Where the decedent while living binds himself or herself or his or her personal representative by a contract in writing to convey real property or to transfer personal property upon or after his or her death and the contract is one which can be specifically enforced.

(C) Where the decedent died in possession of, or holding title to, real or personal property, and the property or some interest therein is claimed to belong to another.

(D) Where the decedent died having a claim to real or personal property, title to or possession of which is held by another.

(3) The trustee or any interested person in any of the following cases:

(A) Where the trustee is in possession of, or holds title to, real or personal property, and the property, or some interest, is claimed to belong to another.

(B) Where the trustee has a claim to real or personal property, title to or possession of which is held by another.

(C) Where the property of the trust is claimed to be subject to a creditor of the settlor of the trust.

(b) The petition shall set forth facts upon which the claim is based.

851. (a) At least 30 days prior to the day of the hearing, the petitioner shall cause notice of the hearing and a copy of the petition to be served in the manner provided in Chapter 4 (commencing with Section 413.10) of Title 5 of Part 2 of the Code of Civil Procedure on all of the following persons where applicable:

(1) The personal representative, conservator, guardian, or trustee as appropriate.

(2) Each person claiming an interest in, or having title to or possession of, the property.

(b) Except for those persons given notice pursuant to subdivision (a), notice of the hearing, together with a copy of the petition, shall be given as provided in Section 1220 if the matter concerns a decedent estate, as provided in Section 1460 if the matter concerns a conservatorship or guardianship, or as provided in Section 17203 if the matter concerns a trust to all of the following persons:

(1) Each person listed in Section 1220 along with any heir or devisee whose interest in the property may be affected by the petition if the matter concerns a decedent estate.

(2) Each person listed in Section 1460 if the matter concerns a conservatorship or guardianship.

(3) Each person listed in Section 17203 if the matter concerns a trust.

(c) The court may not shorten the time for giving the notice of hearing under this section.

852. An interested person may request time for filing a response to the petition for discovery proceedings, or for other preparation for the hearing, and the court shall grant a continuance for a reasonable time for any of these purposes.

853. A person having or claiming title to or an interest in the property which is the subject of the petition may, at or prior to the hearing, object to the hearing of the petition if the petition is filed in a court which is not the proper court under any other provision of law for the trial of a civil action seeking the same relief and, if the objection is established, the court shall not grant the petition.

854. If a civil action is pending with respect to the subject matter of a petition filed pursuant to this chapter and jurisdiction has been obtained in the court where the civil action is pending prior to the filing of the petition, upon request of any party to the civil action, the court shall abate the petition until the conclusion of the civil action. This section shall not apply if the court finds that the civil action was filed for the purpose of delay.

855. An action brought under this part may include claims, causes of action, or matters that are normally raised in a civil action to the extent that the matters are related factually to the subject matter of a petition filed under this part.

856. Except as provided in Sections 853 and 854, if the court is satisfied that a conveyance, transfer, or other order should be made, the court shall make an order authorizing and directing the personal representative or other fiduciary, or the person having title to or possession of the property, to execute a conveyance or transfer to the person entitled thereto, or granting other appropriate relief.

856.5. The court may not grant a petition under this chapter if the court determines that the matter should be determined by a civil action.

857. (a) The order is prima facie evidence of the correctness of the proceedings and of the authority of the personal representative or other fiduciary or other person to make the conveyance or transfer.

(b) After entry of an order that the personal representative, other fiduciary, or other person execute a conveyance or transfer, the person entitled thereunder has the right to the possession of the property, and the right to hold the property, according to the terms of the order as if the property had been conveyed or transferred in accordance with the terms of the order.

858. If a proceeding has been brought under this part by a conservator on behalf of a conservatee, or by a guardian on behalf of a minor, and the conservatee or minor dies during the pendency of the proceeding, the personal representative of the conservatee or minor's estate or other successor in interest may proceed with the matter and the existing proceeding shall not be dismissed on account of the death of the conservatee or minor.

859. If a court finds that a person has in bad faith wrongfully taken, concealed, or disposed of property belonging to a conservatee, a minor, an elder, a dependent adult, a trust, or the estate of a decedent, or has taken, concealed, or disposed of the property by the use of undue influence in bad faith or through the commission of elder or dependent adult financial abuse, as defined in Section 15610.30 of the Welfare and Institutions Code, the person shall be liable for twice the value of the property recovered by an action under this part. In addition, except as otherwise required by law, including Section 15657.5 of the Welfare and Institutions Code, the person may, in the court's discretion, be liable for reasonable attorney's fees and costs. The remedies provided in this section shall be in addition to any other remedies available in law to a person authorized to bring an action pursuant to this part.

Division 3. General Provisions Of A Procedural Nature

Part 1. General Provisions

Chapter 1. Rules Of Practice

1000. Except to the extent that this code provides applicable rules, the rules of practice applicable to civil actions, including discovery proceedings and proceedings under Title 3a (commencing with Section 391) of Part 2 of the Code of Civil Procedure, apply to, and constitute the rules of practice in, proceedings under this code. All issues of fact joined in probate proceedings shall be tried in conformity with the rules of practice in civil actions.

1001. (a) The Judicial Council may provide by rule for the practice and procedure under this code. Unless disapproved by the Judicial Council, a court may provide by local rule for the practice and procedure under this code. Judicial Council and local court rules shall be consistent with the applicable statutes.

(b) The Judicial Council may prescribe the form of the applications, notices, orders, and other documents required by this code. Any form prescribed by the Judicial Council is deemed to comply with this code.

1002. Unless it is otherwise provided by this code or by rules adopted by the Judicial Council, either the superior court or the court on appeal may, in its discretion, order costs to be paid by any party to the proceedings, or out of the assets of the estate, as justice may require.

1003. (a) The court may, on its own motion or on request of a personal representative, guardian, conservator, trustee, or other interested person, appoint a guardian ad litem at any stage of a proceeding under this code to represent the interest of any of the following persons, if the court determines that representation of the interest otherwise would be inadequate:

(1) A minor.

(2) An incapacitated person.

(3) An unborn person.

(4) An unascertained person.

(5) A person whose identity or address is unknown.

(6) A designated class of persons who are not ascertained or are not in being.

(b) If not precluded by a conflict of interest, a guardian ad litem may be appointed to represent several persons or interests.

(c) The reasonable expenses of the guardian ad litem, including compensation and attorney's fees, shall be determined by the court and paid as the court orders, either out of the property of the estate involved or by the petitioner or from such other source as the court orders.

1003.5. The public guardian shall not be appointed as a guardian ad litem pursuant to Section 1003 unless the court, after reasonable notice and inquiry, finds that no other qualified person is willing to act as a guardian ad litem.

1004. If a proceeding under this code affects the title to or the right of possession of real property, notice of the pendency of the proceeding may be filed pursuant to Title 4.5 (commencing with Section 405) of Part 2 of the Code of Civil Procedure.

Chapter 2. Petitions And Other Papers

1020. Except as provided in Section 1023, a petition, objection, response, report, or account filed pursuant to this code shall be in writing, signed by all of the petitioners, objectors, or respondents or by all of the persons making the report or account, and filed with the court clerk. Verification of a document shall constitute signature of that document, unless expressly provided to the contrary.

1021. (a) All of the following shall be verified:

(1) A petition, report, or account filed pursuant to this code.

(2) An objection or response filed pursuant to this code to a petition, report, or account.

(b) Except as provided in Section 1023, the verification shall be made as follows:

(1) A petition shall be verified by the petitioner or, if there are two or more parties joining in the petition, by any of them.

(2) A report or account shall be verified by the person who has the duty to make the report or account or, if there are two or more persons having a duty to make the report or account, by any of them.

(3) An objection or response shall be verified by the objector or respondent or, if there are two or more parties joining in the objection or response, by any of them.

1022. An affidavit or verified petition shall be received as evidence when offered in an uncontested proceeding under this code.

1023. If a petitioner, objector, or respondent is absent from the county or for some other cause is unable to sign or verify a petition, objection, or response filed pursuant to this code, the person's attorney may sign or verify the petition, objection, or response unless the person is a fiduciary appointed in the proceeding.

Chapter 3. Hearings And Orders

1040. This chapter governs the hearing of all matters under this code, except where the statute that provides for the hearing of the matter prescribes a different procedure.

1041. When a petition, report, account, or other matter that requires a hearing is filed with the court clerk, the clerk shall set the matter for hearing.

1042. A hearing under this code shall be on notice unless the statute that provides for the hearing dispenses with notice.

1043. (a) An interested person may appear and make a response or objection in writing at or before the hearing.

(b) An interested person may appear and make a response or objection orally at the hearing. The court in its discretion shall either hear and determine the response or objection at the hearing, or grant a continuance for the purpose of allowing a response or objection to be made in writing.

(c) A request for a continuance for the purpose of making a written response or objection shall not itself be considered as a response or objection, nor shall the failure to make a response or objection during the time allowed be considered as a response or objection.

1044. The petitioner or other party affirming is the plaintiff and the party objecting or responding is the defendant.

1045. The court may continue or postpone any hearing, from time to time, in the interest of justice.

1046. The court shall hear and determine any matter at issue and any response or objection presented, consider evidence presented, and make appropriate orders.

1047. Except as otherwise provided in this code, an order made in a proceeding under this code need not recite the existence of facts, or the performance of acts, upon which jurisdiction depends, but need only contain the matters ordered.

1048. (a) Except as provided in subdivision (b), orders shall be either entered at length in the minute book of the court or signed by the judge and filed.

(b) An order for distribution shall be entered at length in a judgment book or other permanent record of the court.

1049. An order may be enforced as provided in Title 9 (commencing with Section 680.010) of Part 2 of the Code of Civil Procedure.

1050. The judgment roll in a proceeding under this code consists of the following papers, where applicable:

(a) In all cases:

(1) The petition, application, report, or account that initiates a particular proceeding.

(2) Any order directing notice of the hearing to be given.

(3) Any notice of the hearing, and any order to show cause made in the proceeding, with the affidavits showing publication, posting, mailing, or personal delivery of the notice or order as may be required by law or court order.

(4) Any citation, in case no answer or written opposition is filed by a party entitled, by law or court order, to notice of the proceeding by citation, with the affidavit or proof of service and, if service of the citation is made by publication, the affidavit of publication and the order directing publication.

(5) Any finding of the court or referee in the proceeding.

(6) The order or statement of decision made in the proceeding.

(7) Any letters (as defined in Section 52).

(b) If an answer, demurrer, written opposition, or counter petition is filed in a proceeding:

(1) Pleadings and papers in the nature of pleadings.

(2) Any orders striking out a pleading in whole or in part.

(3) Any order made on demurrer, or relating to a change of parties, in the proceeding.

(4) The verdict of the jury, if any.

(c) If the proceeding is for the probate of a will, the will.

(d) If the proceeding is a contest of a will, for the revocation of the probate of a will, or for a preliminary or final distribution of the estate under a will:

(1) The will.

(2) The order admitting the will to probate.

(e) If the proceeding is for the settlement of the final account of a personal representative or for the final distribution of an estate, the affidavit showing publication of notice to creditors.

1051. (a) In the absence of a stipulation to the contrary between parties who have filed pleadings in a proceeding under this code, there shall be no ex parte communications between any party, or attorney for the party, and the court concerning a subject raised in those pleadings, except as permitted or required by law.

(b) Notwithstanding subdivision (a), in any case upon which the court has exercised its jurisdiction, the court may refer to the court investigator or take other appropriate action in response to an ex parte communication regarding either or both of the following: (1) a fiduciary, as defined in Section 39, about the fiduciary's performance of his or her duties and responsibilities, and (2) a person who is the subject of a conservatorship or guardianship proceeding under Division 4 (commencing with Section 1400). Any action by the court pursuant to this subdivision shall be consistent with due process and the requirements of this code. The court shall disclose the ex parte communication to all parties and counsel. The court may, for good cause, dispense with the disclosure if necessary to protect the ward or conservatee from harm.

(c) The Judicial Council shall, on or before January 1, 2008, adopt a rule of court to implement this section.

(d) Subdivisions (a) and (b) of this section shall become operative on January 1, 2008.

(e) A superior court shall not be required

to perform any duties imposed by this section until the Legislature makes an appropriation identified for this purpose.

Chapter 4. Accounts

1060. This chapter governs all accounts to be filed with the court. Except as specifically provided elsewhere in this code, or unless good cause is shown therefore, no information in addition to that required in this chapter need be in an account.

1060.5. This chapter shall be operative on and after July 1, 1997.

1061. (a) All accounts shall state the period covered by the account and contain a summary showing all of the following, to the extent applicable:

(1) The property on hand at the beginning of the period covered by the account, which shall be the value of the property initially received by the fiduciary if this is the first account, and shall be the property on hand at the end of the prior account if this is a subsequent account.

(2) The value of any assets received during the period of the accounting which are not assets on hand as of the commencement of the administration of an estate.

(3) The amount of any receipts of income or principal, excluding items listed under paragraphs (1) and (2) or receipts from a trade or business.

(4) Net income from a trade or business.

(5) Gains on sales.

(6) The amount of disbursements, excluding disbursements for a trade or business or distributions.

(7) Loss on sales.

(8) Net loss from trade or business.

(9) Distributions to beneficiaries, the ward or conservatee.

(10) Property on hand at the end of the accounting period, stated at its carry value.

(b) The summary shall be in a format substantially the same as the following, except that inapplicable categories need not be shown:

> PLEASE SEE THE APPENDIX

(c) Total charges shall equal total credits.

(d) For purposes of this section, the terms "net income" and "net loss" shall be utilized in accordance with general accounting principles. Nothing in this section is intended to require that the preparation of the summary must include "net income" and "net loss" as reflected in the tax returns governing the period of the account.

1062. The summary shall be supported by detailed schedules showing the following:

(a) Receipts, showing the nature or purpose of each item, the source of the receipt, and the date thereof.

(b) Disbursement, including the nature or purpose of each item, the name of the payee, and the date thereof.

(c) Net income or loss from a trade or business, which shall be sufficient if it provides the information disclosed on Schedule C or F of the federal income tax return.

(d) Calculation of gains or losses on sale or other disposition.

(e) Distributions of cash or property to beneficiaries, ward or conservatee, showing the date and amount of each, with the distribution of property shown at its carry value.

(f) Itemized list of property on hand, describing each item at its carry value.

1063. (a) In all accounts, there shall be an additional schedule showing the estimated market value of the assets on hand as of the end of the accounting period, and a schedule of the estimated market value of the assets on hand as of the beginning of the accounting period for all accounts subsequent to the initial account. The requirement of an estimated value of real estate, a closely held business, or other assets without a ready market, may be satisfied by a good faith estimate by the fiduciary.

(b) If there were purchases or other changes in the form of assets occurring during the period of the account, there shall be a schedule showing these transactions. However, no reporting is required for transfers between cash or accounts in a financial institution or money market mutual funds as defined in subdivision (d) of Section 8901.

(c) If an estate of a decedent or a trust will be distributed to an income beneficiary, there shall be a schedule showing an allocation of receipts and disbursements between principal and income.

(d) If there is specifically devised property, there shall be an additional schedule accounting for income, disbursements, and proceeds of sale pursuant to Section 12002 and subdivision (a) of Section 16340.

(e) If any interest has been paid or is to be paid under Section 12003, 12004, or 12005, or subdivision (b) of Section 16340, there shall be a schedule showing the calculation of the interest.

(f) If the accounting contemplates a proposed distribution, there shall be a schedule setting forth the proposed distribution, including the allocation of income required under Section 12006. If the distribution requires an allocation between trusts, the allocation shall be set forth on the schedule, unless the allocation is to be made by a trustee after receipt of the assets. If the distribution requires valuation of assets as of the date of distribution, the schedule shall set forth the fair market value of those assets.

(g) If, at the end of the accounting period, there are liabilities of the estate or trust, except current or future periodic payments, including rent, salaries, utilities, or other recurring expenses, there shall be a schedule showing all of the following:

(1) All liabilities which are a lien on es-

tate or trust assets.

(2) Taxes due but unpaid as shown on filed returns or assessments received subsequent to filing of returns.

(3) All notes payable.

(4) Any judgments for which the estate or trust is liable.

(5) Any other material liability.

(h) If the guardian or conservator has knowledge of any real property of the conservatee or ward located in a foreign jurisdiction, the guardian or conservator shall include an additional schedule that identifies the real property, provides a good faith estimate of the fair market value of the real property, and states what action, if any, will or has been taken to preserve and protect the real property, including a recommendation whether an ancillary proceeding is necessary to preserve and protect the real property.

1064. (a) The petition for approval of the account or a report accompanying the petition shall contain all of the following:

(1) A description of all sales, purchases, changes in the form of assets, or other transactions occurring during the period of the account that are not otherwise readily understandable from the schedule.

(2) An explanation of any unusual items appearing in the account.

(3) A statement of all compensation paid from the assets subject to the account to the fiduciary or to the attorneys for the fiduciary other than pursuant to a prior court order.

(4) A statement disclosing any family or affiliate relationship between the fiduciary and any agent hired by the fiduciary during the accounting period.

(5) An allegation disclosing whether all of the cash has been invested and maintained in interest bearing accounts or in investments authorized by law or the governing instrument, except for an amount of cash that is reasonably necessary for the orderly administration of the estate.

(b) The filing of an account shall be deemed to include a petition requesting its approval, and may include additional petitions for authorization, instruction or confirmation authorized by the code, including, but not limited to, a request for an order for compensation of the fiduciary and the attorney for the fiduciary.

(c) For purposes of this section, "family" means a relationship created by blood or marriage. For purposes of this section, "affiliate" means an entity that directly or indirectly through one or more intermediaries controls, is controlled by, or is under common control with, the fiduciary.

Part 2. Notices And Citations

Chapter 1. General Notice Provisions

1200. (a) Except as otherwise provided in this code, this part governs notice required or permitted under this code.

(b) This part does not apply to notice under a particular provision to the extent that the particular provision is inconsistent with this part.

(c) This part does not apply to the giving of a particular notice where the notice was delivered, mailed, posted, or first published before July 1, 1991. The applicable law in effect before July 1, 1991, continues to apply to the giving of that notice, notwithstanding its repeal.

1201. If a person is required to give notice, the person required to give the notice need not give the notice to himself or herself or to any other person who joins in the petition.

1202. Where the court determines that the notice otherwise required is insufficient in the particular circumstances, the court may require that further or additional notice, including a longer period of notice, be given.

1203. (a) Subject to subdivision (b), unless the particular provision governing the notice of hearing provides that the time for giving notice may not be shortened, the court may, for good cause, shorten the time for giving a notice of hearing.

(b) Unless the particular provision governing the publication of notice of hearing otherwise provides, the court may not shorten the time for publication of notice of hearing.

1204. A person, including a guardian ad litem, guardian, conservator, trustee, or other fiduciary, may waive notice by a writing signed by the person or the person's attorney and filed in the proceeding.

1205. If a hearing is continued or postponed, no further notice of the continued or postponed hearing is required unless ordered by the court.

1206. (a) Subject to subdivision (b), where notice is required to be given to known heirs or known devisees, notice shall be given to the following persons:

(1) If the estate is an intestate estate, to the heirs named in the petition for letters of administration and to any additional heirs who become known to the person giving the notice prior to the giving of the notice.

(2) If the estate is a testate estate, to the devisees named in the petition for probate of the will and to any additional devisees who become known to the person giving the notice prior to the giving of the notice.

(b) Notice need not be given to a person

under subdivision (a) if the person's interest has been satisfied pursuant to court order or as evidenced by the person's written receipt.

1207. (a) Subject to subdivision (b), where notice is required to be given to a decedent's beneficiaries, devisees, or heirs, notice need not be given to a person who, because of a possible parent-child relationship between a stepchild and a stepparent or between a foster child and a foster parent, may be (1) an heir of the decedent or (2) a member of a class to which a devise is made.

(b) Subdivision (a) does not apply where the person required to give the notice has actual knowledge of facts that a person would reasonably believe give rise under Section 6454 to the parent-child relationship between the stepchild and the stepparent or between the foster child and the foster parent.

1208. (a) Except as provided in subdivision (b), if notice is required to be given to a trust or trustee, notice to trust beneficiaries is not required.

(b) Subject to subdivision (c), where the personal representative and the trustee are the same person, or where no trustee has been appointed, notice shall be given to (1) each person to whom income or principal would be required or authorized in the trustee's discretion to be currently distributed if the trust were in effect, or (2) if there are no such persons, to each person who, under the terms of the trust, would be entitled to any distribution if the trust were terminated at the time the notice is required to be given.

(c) Notice to trust beneficiaries is not required under subdivision (b) where the trust has more than one trustee and notice is given to a cotrustee who is not a personal representative.

1209. (a) Where notice is required to be given to the State of California, the notice shall be given to the Attorney General.

(b) Where notice is required to be given to the Attorney General, the notice shall be mailed to the Attorney General at the office of the Attorney General at Sacramento, California.

1210. If an interested person has a guardian or conservator of the estate who resides in this state, personal service on the guardian or conservator of any process, notice, or court order concerning a decedent's estate is equivalent to service on the ward or conservatee, and it is the duty of the guardian or conservator to attend to the interests of the ward or conservatee in the matter. The guardian or conservator may appear for the ward or conservatee and waive any process, notice, or order to show cause that a person not under legal disability might waive.

1211. If a notice is required by this code and no other type of notice is prescribed by law, by the Judicial Council, or by the court or judge, the notice shall be in substantially the following form:

PLEASE SEE THE APPENDIX

1212. Unless the court dispenses with the notice, if the address of the person to whom a notice or other paper is required to be mailed or delivered is not known, notice shall be given as the court may require in the manner provided in Section 413.30 of the Code of Civil Procedure.

1213. (a) The following persons shall mail a notice, as described in Section 1211, to a surety who has filed a court bond in a proceeding:

(1) A person who files a petition to surcharge.

(2) A person who files an objection to an account.

(3) A person who files a petition to suspend or remove a guardian, conservator, or personal representative.

(4) An attorney who files a motion to withdraw from representation of a guardian, conservator, or personal representative.

(b) Within five days after entry of an order to suspend or remove a guardian, conservator, or personal representative, the person who filed a petition to suspend or remove a guardian or, if the order to suspend or remove a guardian, conservator, or personal representative was issued upon a motion by the court, the court, shall notify the surety who has filed a court bond of the order by first-class mail, postage prepaid.

(c) The notice required by this section shall be mailed to the address listed on the surety bond.

(d) Notwithstanding subdivisions (a) and (b), notice is not required to a surety pursuant to this section if the surety bond is for a guardian, conservator, or personal representative who is not the subject of the petition, motion, or order described in this section.

1214. If a notice or other paper is required or permitted to be mailed, delivered, served, or otherwise given to a person who is represented by an attorney of record, the notice or other paper shall also be mailed to this attorney, unless otherwise specified in a request for special notice.

Chapter 2. Mailing In General

1215. Unless otherwise expressly provided:

(a) If a notice or other paper is required or permitted to be mailed to a person, the notice or other paper shall be mailed as provided in this section or personally delivered as provided in Section 1216.

(b) The notice or other paper shall be sent by:

(1) First-class mail if the person's address is within the United States. First-class mail includes certified, registered, and express mail.

(2) Airmail if the person's address is not within the United States.

(c) The notice or other paper shall be deposited for collection in the United States mail, in a sealed envelope, with postage paid, addressed to the person to whom it is mailed.

(d) Subject to Section 1212, the notice or other paper shall be addressed to the person at the person's place of business or place of residence.

(e) When the notice or other paper is deposited in the mail, mailing is complete and the period of notice is not extended.

1216. (a) If a notice or other paper is required or permitted to be mailed to a person, it may be delivered personally to that person. Personal delivery as provided in this section satisfies a provision that requires or permits a notice or other paper to be mailed.

(b) Personal delivery pursuant to this section is complete when the notice or other paper is delivered personally to the person who is to receive it.

1217. If a notice or other paper is required to be served or otherwise given and no other manner of giving the notice or other paper is specified by statute, the notice or other paper shall be mailed or personally delivered as provided in this chapter.

Chapter 3. Mailing Notice Of Hearing

1220. (a) When notice of hearing is required to be given as provided in this section:

(1) At least 15 days before the time set for the hearing, the petitioner or the person filing the report, account, or other paper shall cause notice of the time and place of the hearing to be mailed to the persons required to be given notice.

(2) Unless the statute requiring notice specifies the persons to be given notice, notice shall be mailed to all of the following:

(A) The personal representative.

(B) All persons who have requested special notice in the estate proceeding pursuant to Section 1250.

(3) Subject to Section 1212, the notice shall be addressed to the person required to be given notice at the person's place of business or place of residence.

(b) Subject to subdivision (c), nothing in this section excuses compliance with the requirements for notice to a person who has requested special notice pursuant to Chapter 6 (commencing with Section 1250).

(c) The court for good cause may dispense with the notice otherwise required to be given to a person as provided in this section.

1221. Where notice of hearing is required but no other period or manner is prescribed by statute, unless the period or manner of giving the notice is ordered by the court or judge, the notice of hearing shall be given for the period and in the manner provided in Section 1220.

Chapter 4. Posting Notice Of Hearing

1230. Where notice of hearing is required to be posted as provided in this section:

(a) At least 15 days before the time set for the hearing, the court clerk shall cause a notice of the time and place of the hearing to be posted at the courthouse of the county where the proceedings are pending. If court is held at a place other than the county seat, the notice may be posted either at the courthouse of the county where the proceedings are pending or at the building where the court is held.

(b) The posted notice of hearing shall state all of the following:

(1) The name of the estate.

(2) The name of the petitioner.

(3) The nature of the petition, referring to the petition for further particulars.

(4) The time and place of the hearing of the petition.

Chapter 5. Citations

1240. Where use of a citation is authorized or required by statute, a citation may be issued by the court clerk on the application of any party, without a court order, except in cases where an order is expressly required by law.

1241. The citation shall be directed to the person to be cited, signed by the court clerk, and issued under the seal of the court. The citation shall contain the title of the proceeding, a brief statement of the nature of the proceeding, and a direction that the person cited appear at a time and place specified.

1242. The citation shall be served on the person cited in the manner provided in Chapter 4 (commencing with Section 413.10) of Title 5 of Part 2 of the Code of Civil Procedure. Except as otherwise provided by statute, the citation shall be served at least five days before its return day.

Chapter 6. Request For Special Notice

1250. (a) At any time after the issuance of letters in a proceeding under this code for the administration of a decedent's estate, any person interested in the estate, whether as devisee, heir, creditor, beneficiary under a trust, or as otherwise interested, may in person or by attorney, file with the court clerk a written request for special notice.

(b) The request for special notice shall be so entitled and shall set forth the name of the person and the address to which notices shall be sent.

(c) Special notice may be requested of one or more of the following matters:

(1) Petitions filed in the administration proceeding.

(2) Inventories and appraisals of property in the estate, including any supplemental inventories and appraisals.

(3) Objections to an appraisal.

(4) Accounts of a personal representative.

(5) Reports of status of administration.

(d) Special notice may be requested of any matter in subdivision (c) by describing it, or of all the matters in subdivision (c) by referring generally to "the matters described in subdivision (c) of Section 1250 of the Probate Code" or by using words of similar meaning.

(e) A copy of the request shall be personally delivered or mailed to the personal representative or to the attorney for the personal representative. If personally delivered, the request is effective when it is delivered. If mailed, the request is effective when it is received.

(f) When the original of the request is filed with the court clerk, it shall be accompanied by a written admission or proof of service.

1251. A request for special notice under this chapter may be modified or withdrawn in the same manner as provided for the making of the initial request.

1252. (a) Unless the court makes an order dispensing with the notice, if a request has been made pursuant to Section 1250 for special notice of a hearing, the person filing the petition, report, account, or other paper shall give written notice of the filing, together with a copy of the petition, report, account, or other paper, and the time and place set for the hearing, by mail to the person named in the request at the address set forth in the request, at least 15 days before the time set for the hearing.

(b) If a request has been made pursuant to Section 1250 for special notice of the filing of an inventory and appraisal of the estate or of the filing of any other paper that does not require a hearing, the inventory and appraisal or other paper shall be mailed not later than 15 days after the inventory and appraisal or other paper is filed with the court.

Chapter 7. Proof Of Giving Notice

1260. (a) If notice of a hearing is required, proof of giving notice of the hearing shall be made to the satisfaction of the court at or before the hearing.

(b) If it appears to the satisfaction of the court that notice has been regularly given or that the party entitled to notice has waived it, the court shall so find in its order.

(c) The finding described in subdivision (b), when the order becomes final, is conclusive on all persons.

1261. Proof of mailing may be made in the manner prescribed in Section 1013a of the Code of Civil Procedure.

1262. Proof of publication may be made by the affidavit of the publisher or printer, or the foreman or principal clerk of the publisher or printer, showing the time and place of publication.

1263. Proof of posting may be made by the affidavit of the person who posted the notice.

1264. Proof of notice by personal delivery may be made by the affidavit of the person making the delivery showing the time and place of delivery and the name of the person to whom delivery was made.

1265. Proof of notice, however given, may be made by evidence presented at the hearing.

Part 3. Appeals

Chapter 1. General

1300. In all proceedings governed by this code, an appeal may be taken from the making of, or the refusal to make, any of the following orders:

(a) Directing, authorizing, approving, or confirming the sale, lease, encumbrance, grant of an option, purchase, conveyance, or exchange of property.

(b) Settling an account of a fiduciary.

(c) Authorizing, instructing, or directing a fiduciary, or approving or confirming the acts of a fiduciary.

(d) Directing or allowing payment of a debt, claim, or cost.

(e) Fixing, authorizing, allowing, or directing payment of compensation or expenses of an attorney.

(f) Fixing, directing, authorizing, or allowing payment of the compensation or expenses of a fiduciary.

(g) Surcharging, removing, or discharging a fiduciary.

(h) Transferring the property of the estate to a fiduciary in another jurisdiction.

(i) Allowing or denying a petition of the fiduciary to resign.

(j) Discharging a surety on the bond of a fiduciary.

(k) Adjudicating the merits of a claim made under Part 19 (commencing with Section 850) of Division 2.

1301. With respect to guardianships, conservatorships, and other protective proceedings, the grant or refusal to grant the following orders is appealable:

(a) Granting or revoking of letters of guardianship or conservatorship, except letters of temporary guardianship or temporary conservatorship.

(b) Granting permission to the guardian or conservator to fix the residence of the ward or conservatee at a place not within this state.

(c) Directing, authorizing, approving, or modifying payments, whether for support, maintenance, or education of the ward or conservatee or for a person legally entitled to support, maintenance, or education from the ward or conservatee.

(d) Granting or denying a petition under Section 2423 or under Article 10 (commencing with Section 2580) of Chapter 6 of Part 4 of Division 4.

(e) Affecting the legal capacity of the conservatee pursuant to Chapter 4 (commencing with Section 1870) of Part 3 of Division 4.

(f) Adjudicating the merits of a claim under Article 5 (commencing with Section 2500) of Chapter 6 of Part 4 of Division 4.

(g) Granting or denying a petition under Chapter 3 (commencing with Section 3100) of Part 6 of Division 4.

1302. With respect to a power of attorney governed by the Power of Attorney Law (Division 4.5 (commencing with Section 4000)), an appeal may be taken from any of the following:

(a) Any final order under Section 4541, except an order pursuant to subdivision (c) of Section 4541.

(b) An order dismissing the petition or denying a motion to dismiss under Section 4543.

1302.5. With respect to an advance health care directive governed by the Health Care Decisions Law (Division 4.7 (commencing with Section 4600)), an appeal may be taken from any of the following:

(a) Any final order under Section 4766.

(b) An order dismissing the petition or denying a motion to dismiss under Section 4768.

1303. With respect to a decedent's estate, the grant or refusal to grant the following orders is appealable:

(a) Granting or revoking letters to a personal representative, except letters of special administration or letters of special administration with general powers.

(b) Admitting a will to probate or revoking the probate of a will.

(c) Setting aside a small estate under Section 6609.

(d) Setting apart a probate homestead or property claimed to be exempt from enforcement of a money judgment.

(e) Granting, modifying, or terminating a family allowance.

(f) Determining heirship, succession, entitlement, or the persons to whom distribution should be made.

(g) Directing distribution of property.

(h) Determining that property passes to, or confirming that property belongs to, the surviving spouse under Section 13656.

(i) Authorizing a personal representative to invest or reinvest surplus money under Section 9732.

(j) Determining whether an action constitutes a contest under former Chapter 2 (commencing with Section 21320) of Part 3 of Division 11, as that chapter read prior to its repeal by Chapter 174 of the Statutes of 2008.

(k) Determining the priority of debts under Chapter 3 (commencing with Section 11440) of Part 9 of Division 7.

(l) Any final order under Chapter 1 (commencing with Section 20100) or Chapter 2 (commencing with Section 20200) of Division 10.

1304. With respect to a trust, the grant or denial of the following orders is appealable:

(a) Any final order under Chapter 3 (commencing with Section 17200) of Part 5 of Division 9, except the following:

(1) Compelling the trustee to submit an account or report acts as trustee.

(2) Accepting the resignation of the trustee.

(b) Any final order under Chapter 2 (commencing with Section 19020) of Part 8 of Division 9.

(c) Any final order under Part 1 (commencing with Section 20100) and Part 2 (commencing with Section 20200) of Division 10.

(d) Determining whether an action constitutes a contest under former Chapter 2 (commencing with Section 21320) of Part 3 of Division 11, as that chapter read prior to its repeal by Chapter 174 of the Statutes of 2008.

Chapter 2. Effect Of An Appeal

1310. (a) Except as provided in subdivisions (b), (c), (d), and (e), an appeal pursuant to Chapter 1 (commencing with Section 1300) stays the operation and effect of the judgment or order.

(b) Notwithstanding that an appeal is taken from the judgment or order, for the purpose of preventing injury or loss to a person or property, the trial court may direct the exercise of the powers of the fiduciary, or may appoint a temporary guardian or conservator of the person or estate, or both, or a special administrator or temporary trustee, to exercise the powers, from time to time, as if no appeal were pending. All acts of the fiduciary pursuant to the directions of the court made under this subdivision are valid, irrespective of the result of the appeal. An appeal of the directions made by the court under this subdivision shall not stay these directions.

(c) In proceedings for guardianship of the person, Section 917.7 of the Code of Civil Procedure shall apply.

(d) An appeal shall not stay the operation and effect of the judgment or order if the court requires an undertaking, as provided in Section 917.9 of the Code of Civil Procedure, and the undertaking is not given.

(e) An appeal shall not stay the operation and effect of a judgment for money or an order directing payment of money, unless one of the following applies:

(1) A bond is posted as provided in Section 917.1 of the Code of Civil Procedure.

(2) The payment is to be made from a decedent's estate being administered under Division 7 (commencing with Section 7000) or from the estate of a person who is subject to a guardianship or conservatorship of the estate under Division 4 (commencing with

Section 1400). However, a court may require a bond as provided in subdivision (d).

1311. If an order appointing a fiduciary is reversed on appeal for error, all acts of the fiduciary performed after issuance of letters and prior to the reversal are as valid as though the order were affirmed and the person appointed is not liable for any otherwise proper act done in good faith before the reversal, nor is any transaction void by reason of the reversal if entered into with a third person dealing in good faith and for value.

1312. Notwithstanding the repeal of former Section 1297 by Chapter 1199 of the Statutes of 1988, an appeal may be taken from an order or the refusal to make an order fixing an inheritance tax or determining that none is due.

Division 4. Guardianship, Conservatorship, And Other Protective Proceedings

Part 1. Definitions And General Provisions

Chapter 1. Short Title And Definitions

1400. The portion of this division consisting of Part 1 (commencing with Section 1400), Part 2 (commencing with Section 1500), Part 3 (commencing with Section 1800), and Part 4 (commencing with Section 2100) may be cited as the Guardianship-Conservatorship Law.

1401. Unless the provision or context otherwise requires, the definitions in this chapter govern the construction of this division.

1403. "Absentee" means either of the following:

(a) A member of a uniformed service covered by United States Code, Title 37, Chapter 10, who is determined thereunder by the secretary concerned, or by the authorized delegate thereof, to be in missing status as missing status is defined therein.

(b) An employee of the United States government or an agency thereof covered by United States Code, Title 5, Chapter 55, Subchapter VII, who is determined thereunder by the head of the department or agency concerned, or by the authorized delegate thereof, to be in missing status as missing status is defined therein.

1418. "Court," when used in connection with matters in the guardianship or conservatorship proceeding, means the court in which such proceeding is pending.

1419. "Court investigator" means the person referred to in Section 1454.

1419.5. "Custodial parent" means the parent who either (a) has been awarded sole legal and physical custody of the child in another proceeding, or (b) with whom the child resides if there is currently no operative custody order. If the child resides with both parents, then they are jointly the custodial parent.

1420. "Developmental disability" means a disability that originates before an individual attains 18 years of age, continues, or can be expected to continue, indefinitely, and constitutes a substantial handicap for the individual. As defined by the Director of Developmental Services, in consultation with the Superintendent of Public Instruction, this term includes intellectual disability, cerebral palsy, epilepsy, and autism. This term also includes handicapping conditions found to be closely related to intellectual disability or to require treatment similar to that required for individuals with an intellectual disability, but does not include other handicapping conditions that are solely physical in nature.

1424. "Interested person" includes, but is not limited to:

(a) Any interested state, local, or federal entity or agency.

(b) Any interested public officer or employee of this state or of a local public entity of this state or of the federal government.

1430. "Petition" includes an application or request in the nature of a petition.

1431. "Proceedings to establish a limited conservatorship" include proceedings to modify or revoke the powers or duties of a limited conservator.

1440. "Secretary concerned" has the same meaning as provided in United States Code, Title 37, Section 101.

1446. "Single-premium deferred annuity" means an annuity offered by an admitted life insurer for the payment of a one-time lump-sum premium and for which the insurer neither assesses any initial charges or administrative fees against the premium paid nor exacts or assesses any penalty for withdrawal of any funds by the annuitant after a period of five years.

1449. (a) As used in this division, unless the context otherwise requires, the terms "Indian," "Indian child," "Indian child's tribe," "Indian custodian," "Indian tribe," "reservation," and "tribal court" shall be defined as provided in Section 1903 of the Indian Child Welfare Act (25 U.S.C. Sec. 1901 et seq.).

(b) When used in connection with an Indian child custody proceeding, the terms "extended family member" and "parent" shall be defined as provided in Section 1903 of the Indian Child Welfare Act (25 U.S.C. Sec. 1901 et seq.).

(c) "Indian child custody proceeding" means a "child custody proceeding" within the meaning of Section 1903 of the Indian Child Welfare Act (25 U.S.C. Sec. 1901 et seq.), including a voluntary or involuntary proceeding that may result in an Indian child's temporary or long-term foster care or guardianship placement if the parent or Indian custodian cannot have the child returned upon demand, termination of parental rights or adoptive placement.

(d) When an Indian child is a member of more than one tribe or is eligible for membership in more than one tribe, the court shall make a determination, in writing together with the reasons for it, as to which tribe is the Indian child's tribe for purposes of the Indian child custody proceeding. The court shall make that determination as follows:

(1) If the Indian child is or becomes a member of only one tribe, that tribe shall be designated as the Indian child's tribe, even though the child is eligible for membership in another tribe.

(2) If an Indian child is or becomes a member of more than one tribe, or is not a member of any tribe but is eligible for membership in more than one tribe, the tribe with which the child has the more significant contacts shall be designated as the Indian child's tribe. In determining which tribe the child has the more significant contacts with, the court shall consider, among other things, the following factors:

(A) The length of residence on or near the reservation of each tribe and frequency of contact with each tribe.

(B) The child's participation in activities of each tribe.

(C) The child's fluency in the language of each tribe.

(D) Whether there has been a previous adjudication with respect to the child by a court of one of the tribes.

(E) The residence on or near one of the tribes' reservations by the child parents, Indian custodian, or extended family members.

(F) Tribal membership of custodial parent or Indian custodian.

(G) Interest asserted by each tribe in response to the notice specified in Section 1460.2.

(H) The child's self-identification.

(3) If an Indian child becomes a member of a tribe other than the one designated by the court as the Indian child's tribe under paragraph (2), actions taken based on the court's determination prior to the child's becoming a tribal member shall continue to be valid.

Chapter 2. General Provisions

1452. Except as otherwise specifically provided in this division, there is no right to trial by jury in proceedings under this division.

1453. A motion for a new trial may be made only in cases in which, under the provisions of this division, a right to jury trial is expressly granted, whether or not the case was tried by a jury.

1454. (a) The court shall appoint a court investigator when one is required for the purposes of a proceeding under this division. The person appointed as the court investigator shall be an officer or special appointee of the court with no personal or other beneficial interest in the proceeding.

(b) The person appointed as the court investigator shall have the following qualifications:

(1) The training or experience, or both, necessary (i) to make the investigations required under this division, (ii) to communicate with, assess, and deal with persons who are or may be the subject of proceedings under this division, and (iii) to perform the

other duties required of a court investigator.

(2) A demonstrated sufficient knowledge of law so as to be able to inform conservatees and proposed conservatees of the nature and effect of a conservatorship proceeding and of their rights, to answer their questions, and to inform conservators concerning their powers and duties.

1455. Any petition for instructions or to grant a guardian or a conservator any power or authority under this division, which may be filed by a guardian or conservator, may also be filed by a person who petitions for the appointment of a guardian or conservator.

1456. (a) In addition to any other requirements that are part of the judicial branch education program, on or before January 1, 2008, the Judicial Council shall adopt a rule of court that shall do all of the following:

(1) Specifies the qualifications of a court-employed staff attorney, examiner, and investigator, and any attorney appointed pursuant to Sections 1470 and 1471.

(2) Specifies the number of hours of education in classes related to conservatorships or guardianships that a judge who is regularly assigned to hear probate matters shall complete, upon assuming the probate assignment, and then over a three-year period on an ongoing basis.

(3) Specifies the number of hours of education in classes related to conservatorships or guardianships that a court-employed staff attorney, examiner, and investigator, and any attorney appointed pursuant to Sections 1470 and 1471 shall complete each year.

(4) Specifies the particular subject matter that shall be included in the education required each year.

(5) Specifies reporting requirements to ensure compliance with this section.

(b) In formulating the rule required by this section, the Judicial Council shall consult with interested parties, including, but not limited to, the California Judges Association, the California Association of Superior Court Investigators, the California Public Defenders Association, the County Counsels' Association of California, the State Bar of California, the National Guardianship Association, the Professional Fiduciary Association of California, the California Association of Public Administrators, Public Guardians and Public Conservators, a disability rights organization, and the Association of Professional Geriatric Care Managers.

1456.2. On or before January 1, 2010, the public conservator shall comply with the continuing education requirements that are established by the California State Association of Public Administrators, Public Guardians, and Public Conservators.

1456.5. Each court shall ensure compliance with the requirements of filing the inventory and appraisal and the accountings required by this division. Courts may comply with this section in either of the following ways:

(a) By placing on the court's calendar, at the time of the appointment of the guardian or conservator and at the time of approval of each accounting, a future hearing date to enable the court to confirm timely compliance with these requirements.

(b) By establishing and maintaining internal procedures to generate an order for appearance and consideration of appropriate sanctions or other actions if the guardian or conservator fails to comply with the requirements of this section.

1457. In order to assist relatives and friends who may seek appointment as a nonprofessional conservator or guardian the Judicial Council shall, on or before January 1, 2008, develop a short educational program of no more than three hours that is user-friendly and shall make that program available free of charge to each proposed conservator and guardian and each court-appointed conservator and guardian who is not required to be licensed as a professional conservator or guardian pursuant to Chapter 6 (commencing with Section 6500) of Division 3 of the Business and Professions Code. The program may be available by video presentation or Internet access.

1459. (a) The Legislature finds and declares the following:

(1) There is no resource that is more vital to the continued existence and integrity of recognized Indian tribes than their children, and the State of California has an interest in protecting Indian children who are members of, or are eligible for membership in, an Indian tribe. The state is committed to protecting the essential tribal relations and best interest of an Indian child by promoting practices, in accordance with the Indian Child Welfare Act (25 U.S.C. Sec. 1901 et seq.) and other applicable law, designed to prevent the child's involuntary out-of-home placement and, whenever such placement is necessary or ordered, by placing the child, whenever possible, in a placement that reflects the unique values of the child's tribal culture and is best able to assist the child in establishing, developing, and maintaining a political, cultural, and social relationship with the child's tribe and tribal community.

(2) It is in the interest of an Indian child that the child's membership in the child's Indian tribe and connection to the tribal community be encouraged and protected, regardless of whether or not the child is in the physical custody of an Indian parent or Indian custodian at the commencement of a child custody proceeding, the parental rights of the child's parents have been terminated, or where the child has resided or been domiciled.

(b) In all Indian child custody proceedings, as defined in the federal Indian Child Welfare Act, the court shall consider all of the findings contained in subdivision (a), strive to promote the stability and security of Indian tribes and families, comply with the federal Indian Child Welfare Act, and seek to protect the best interest of the child. Whenever an Indian child is removed from a foster care home or institution, guardianship, or adoptive placement for the purpose of further foster care, guardianship, or adoptive placement, placement of the child shall be in accordance with the Indian Child Welfare Act.

(c) A determination by an Indian tribe that an unmarried person, who is under the age of 18 years, is either (1) a member of an Indian tribe or (2) eligible for membership in an Indian tribe and a biological child of a member of an Indian tribe shall constitute a significant political affiliation with the tribe and shall require the application of the federal Indian Child Welfare Act to the proceedings.

(d) In any case in which this code or other applicable state or federal law provides a higher standard of protection to the rights of the parent or Indian custodian of an Indian child, or the Indian child's tribe, than the rights provided under the Indian Child Welfare Act, the court shall apply the higher state or federal standard.

(e) Any Indian child, the Indian child's tribe, or the parent or Indian custodian from whose custody the child has been removed, may petition the court to invalidate an action in an Indian child custody proceeding for foster care or guardianship placement or termination of parental rights if the action violated Sections 1911, 1912, and 1913 of the Indian Child Welfare Act.

1459.5. (a) The Indian Child Welfare Act (25 U.S.C. Sec. 1901 et seq.) shall apply to the following guardianship or conservatorship proceedings under this division when the proposed ward or conservatee is an Indian child:

(1) In any case in which the petition is a petition for guardianship of the person and the proposed guardian is not the natural parent or Indian custodian of the proposed ward, unless the proposed guardian has been nominated by the natural parents pursuant to Section 1500 and the parents retain the right to have custody of the child returned to them upon demand.

(2) To a proceeding to have an Indian child declared free from the custody and control of one or both parents brought in a guardianship proceeding.

(3) In any case in which the petition is a petition for conservatorship of the person of a minor whose marriage has been dissolved, the proposed conservator is seeking physical custody of the minor, the proposed conservator is not the natural parent or Indian custodian of the proposed conservatee and the natural parent or Indian custodian does not retain the right to have custody of the child

returned to them upon demand.

(b) When the Indian Child Welfare Act applies to a proceeding under this division, the court shall apply Sections 224.3 to 224.6, inclusive, and Sections 305.5, 361.31, and 361.7 of the Welfare and Institutions Code, and the following rules from the California Rules of Court, as they read on January 1, 2005:

(1) Paragraph (7) of subdivision (b) of Rule 1410.

(2) Subdivision (i) of Rule 1412.

(c) In the provisions cited in subdivision (b), references to social workers, probation officers, county welfare department, or probation department shall be construed as meaning the party seeking a foster care placement, guardianship, or adoption.

Chapter 3. Notices

1460. (a) Subject to Sections 1202 and 1203, if notice of hearing is required under this division but the applicable provision does not fix the manner of giving notice of hearing, the notice of the time and place of the hearing shall be given at least 15 days before the day of the hearing as provided in this section.

(b) Subject to subdivision (e), the petitioner, who includes for the purposes of this section a person filing a petition, report, or account, shall cause the notice of hearing to be mailed to each of the following persons:

(1) The guardian or conservator.

(2) The ward or the conservatee.

(3) The spouse of the ward or conservatee, if the ward or conservatee has a spouse, or the domestic partner of the conservatee, if the conservatee has a domestic partner.

(4) Any person who has requested special notice of the matter, as provided in Section 2700.

(5) For any hearing on a petition to terminate a guardianship, to accept the resignation of, or to remove the guardian, the persons described in subdivision (c) of Section 1510.

(6) For any hearing on a petition to terminate a conservatorship, to accept the resignation of, or to remove the conservator, the persons described in subdivision (b) of Section 1821.

(c) The clerk of the court shall cause the notice of the hearing to be posted as provided in Section 1230 if the posting is required by subdivision (c) of Section 2543.

(d) Except as provided in subdivision (e), nothing in this section excuses compliance with the requirements for notice to a person who has requested special notice pursuant to Chapter 10 (commencing with Section 2700) of Part 4.

(e) The court for good cause may dispense with the notice otherwise required to be given to a person as provided in this section.

1460.1. Notwithstanding any other provision of this division, no notice is required to be given to any child under the age of 12 years if the court determines either of the following:

(a) Notice was properly given to a parent, guardian, or other person having legal custody of the minor, with whom the minor resides.

(b) The petition is brought by a parent, guardian, or other person having legal custody of the minor, with whom the minor resides.

1460.2. (a) If the court or petitioner knows or has reason to know that the proposed ward or conservatee may be an Indian child, notice shall comply with subdivision (b) in any case in which the Indian Child Welfare Act (25 U.S.C. Sec. 1901 et seq.) applies, as specified in Section 1459.5.

(b) Any notice sent under this section shall be sent to the minor' s parent or legal guardian, Indian custodian, if any, and the Indian child's tribe, and shall comply with all of the following requirements:

(1) Notice shall be sent by registered or certified mail with return receipt requested. Additional notice by first-class mail is recommended, but not required.

(2) Notice to the tribe shall be to the tribal chairperson, unless the tribe has designated another agent for service.

(3) Notice shall be sent to all tribes of which the child may be a member or eligible for membership until the court makes a determination as to which tribe is the Indian child's tribe in accordance with subdivision (d) of Section 1449, after which notice need only be sent to the tribe determined to be the Indian child's tribe.

(4) Notice, to the extent required by federal law, shall be sent to the Secretary of the Interior's designated agent, the Sacramento Area Director, Bureau of Indian Affairs. If the identity or location of the Indian child's tribe is known, a copy of the notice shall also be sent directly to the Secretary of the Interior, unless the Secretary of the Interior has waived the notice in writing and the person responsible for giving notice under this section has filed proof of the waiver with the court.

(5) The notice shall include all of the following information:

(A) The name, birthdate, and birthplace of the Indian child, if known.

(B) The name of any Indian tribe in which the child is a member or may be eligible for membership, if known.

(C) All names known of the Indian child's biological parents, grandparents and great-grandparents or Indian custodians, including maiden, married, and former names or aliases, as well as their current and former addresses, birthdates, places of birth and death, tribal enrollment numbers, and any other identifying information, if known.

(D) A copy of the petition.

(E) A copy of the child's birth certificate, if available.

(F) The location, mailing address, and telephone number of the court and all parties notified pursuant to this section.

(G) A statement of the following:

(i) The absolute right of the child's parents, Indian custodians, and tribe to intervene in the proceeding.

(ii) The right of the child's parents, Indian custodians, and tribe to petition the court to transfer the proceeding to the tribal court of the Indian child's tribe, absent objection by either parent and subject to declination by the tribal court.

(iii) The right of the child's parents, Indian custodians, and tribe to, upon request, be granted up to an additional 20 days from the receipt of the notice to prepare for the proceeding.

(iv) The potential legal consequences of the proceedings on the future custodial rights of the child's parents or Indian custodians.

(v) That if the parents or Indian custodians are unable to afford counsel, counsel shall be appointed to represent the parents or Indian custodians pursuant to Section 1912 of the Indian Child Welfare Act (25 U.S.C. Sec. 1901 et seq.).

(vi) That the information contained in the notice, petition, pleading, and other court documents is confidential, so any person or entity notified shall maintain the confidentiality of the information contained in the notice concerning the particular proceeding and not reveal it to anyone who does not need the information in order to exercise the tribe's rights under the Indian Child Welfare Act (25 U.S.C. Sec. 1901 et seq.).

(c) Notice shall be sent whenever it is known or there is reason to know that an Indian child is involved, and for every hearing thereafter, including, but not limited to, the hearing at which a final adoption order is to be granted. After a tribe acknowledges that the child is a member or eligible for membership in the tribe, or after the Indian child's tribe intervenes in a proceeding, the information set out in subparagraphs (C), (D), (E), and (G) of paragraph (5) of subdivision (b) need not be included with the notice.

(d) Proof of the notice, including copies of notices sent and all return receipts and responses received, shall be filed with the court in advance of the hearing except as permitted under subdivision (e).

(e) No proceeding shall be held until at least 10 days after receipt of notice by the parent, Indian custodian, the tribe or the Bureau of Indian Affairs. The parent, Indian custodian, or the tribe shall, upon request, be granted up to 20 additional days to prepare for the proceeding. Nothing herein shall be construed as limiting the rights of the parent, Indian custodian, or tribe to 10 days' notice when a lengthier notice period is required by statute.

(f) With respect to giving notice to Indian tribes, a party shall be subject to court sanctions if that person knowingly and willfully falsifies or conceals a material fact concerning whether the child is an Indian child, or counsels a party to do so.

(g) The inclusion of contact information of any adult or child that would otherwise be required to be included in the notification pursuant to this section, shall not be required if that person is at risk of harm as a result of domestic violence, child abuse, sexual abuse, or stalking.

1461. (a) As used in this section, "director" means:

(1) The Director of State Hospitals when the state hospital referred to in subdivision (b) is under the jurisdiction of the State Department of State Hospitals.

(2) The Director of Developmental Services when the state hospital referred to in subdivision (b) is under the jurisdiction of the State Department of Developmental Services.

(b) Notice of the time and place of hearing on the petition, report, or account, and a copy of the petition, report, or account, shall be mailed to the director at the director's office in Sacramento at least 15 days before the hearing if both of the following conditions exist:

(1) The ward or conservatee is or has been during the guardianship or conservatorship proceeding a patient in, or on leave from, a state hospital under the jurisdiction of the State Department of State Hospitals or the State Department of Developmental Services.

(2) The petition, report, or account is filed under any one or more of the following provisions: Section 1510, 1820, 1861, 2212, 2403, 2421, 2422, or 2423; Article 7 (commencing with Section 2540) of Chapter 6 of Part 4; Section 2580, 2592, or 2620; Chapter 9.5 (commencing with Section 2670) of Part 4; Section 3080 or 3088; or Chapter 3 (commencing with Section 3100) of Part 6. Notice under this section is not required in the case of an account pursuant to Section 2620 if the total guardianship or conservatorship assets are less than one thousand five hundred dollars ($1,500) and the gross annual income, exclusive of any public assistance income, is less than six thousand dollars ($6,000), and the ward or conservatee is not a patient in, or on leave or on outpatient status from, a state hospital at the time of the filing of the petition.

(c) If the ward or conservatee has been discharged from the state hospital, the director, upon ascertaining the facts, may file with the court a certificate stating that the ward or conservatee is not indebted to the state and waive the giving of further notices under this section. Upon the filing of the certificate of the director, compliance with this section thereafter is not required unless the certificate is revoked by the director and notice of the revocation is filed with the court.

(d) The statute of limitations does not run against any claim of the State Department of State Hospitals or the State Department of Developmental Services against the estate of the ward or conservatee for board, care, maintenance, or transportation with respect to an account that is settled without giving the notice required by this section.

1461.4. (a) The petitioner shall mail or personally serve a notice of the hearing and a copy of the petition to the director of the regional center for the developmentally disabled at least 30 days before the day of the hearing on a petition for appointment in any case in which all of the following conditions exist:

(1) The proposed ward or conservatee has developmental disabilities.

(2) The proposed guardian or conservator is not the natural parent of the proposed ward or conservatee.

(3) The proposed guardian or conservator is a provider of board and care, treatment, habilitation, or other services to persons with developmental disabilities or is a spouse or employee of a provider.

(4) The proposed guardian or conservator is not a public entity.

(b) The regional center shall file a written report and recommendation with the court regarding the suitability of the petitioners to meet the needs of the proposed ward or conservatee in any case described in subdivision (a).

1461.5. Notice of the time and place of hearing on a petition, report, or account, and a notice of the filing of an inventory, together with a copy of the petition, report, inventory, or account, shall be mailed to the office of the Veterans Administration having jurisdiction over the area in which the court is located at least 15 days before the hearing, or within 15 days after the inventory is filed, if both of the following conditions exist:

(a) The guardianship or conservatorship estate consists or will consist wholly or in part of any of the following:

(1) Money received from the Veterans Administration.

(2) Revenue or profit from such money or from property acquired wholly or in part from such money.

(3) Property acquired wholly or in part with such money or from such property.

(b) The petition, report, inventory, or account is filed under any one or more of the following provisions: Section 1510, 1601, 1820, 1861, 1874, 2422, or 2423; Article 7 (commencing with Section 2540) of Chapter 6 of Part 4; Section 2570, 2571, 2580, 2592, 2610, 2613, or 2620; Chapter 8 (commencing with Section 2640) of Part 4; Chapter 9.5 (commencing with Section 2670) of Part 4; Section 3080 or 3088; or Chapter 3 (commencing with Section 3100) of Part 6.

1461.7. Unless the court for good cause dispenses with such notice, notice of the time and place of the hearing on a petition, report, or account, together with a copy of the petition, report, or account, shall be given to the same persons who are required to be given notice under Section 2581 for the period and in the manner provided in this chapter if both of the following conditions exist:

(a) A conservator of the estate has been appointed under Article 5 (commencing with Section 1845) of Chapter 1 of Part 3 for a person who is missing and whose whereabouts is unknown.

(b) The petition, report, or account is filed in the conservatorship proceeding under any one or more of the following provisions:

(1) Section 1861 or 2423.

(2) Article 7 (commencing with Section 2540) of Chapter 6 of Part 4.

(3) Section 2570, 2571, 2580, 2592, or 2620.

(4) Chapter 8 (commencing with Section 2640) of Part 4.

(5) Chapter 9.5 (commencing with Section 2670) of Part 4.

(6) Chapter 3 (commencing with Section 3100) of Part 6.

1467. If service is made by mail pursuant to this division in the manner authorized in Section 415.30 of the Code of Civil Procedure, the service is complete on the date a written acknowledgment of receipt is executed.

1469. Where a provision of this division applies the provisions of this code applicable to personal representatives to proceedings under this division, a reference to Section 1220 in the provisions applicable to personal representatives shall be deemed to be a reference to this chapter.

Chapter 4. Appointment Of Legal Counsel

1470. (a) The court may appoint private legal counsel for a ward, a proposed ward, a conservatee, or a proposed conservatee in any proceeding under this division if the court determines the person is not otherwise represented by legal counsel and that the appointment would be helpful to the resolution of the matter or is necessary to protect the person's interests.

(b) If a person is furnished legal counsel under this section, the court shall, upon conclusion of the matter, fix a reasonable sum for compensation and expenses of counsel. The sum may, in the discretion of the court, include compensation for services rendered, and expenses incurred, before the date of the order appointing counsel.

(c) The court shall order the sum fixed under subdivision (b) to be paid:

(1) If the person for whom legal counsel is appointed is an adult, from the estate of that person.

(2) If the person for whom legal counsel is appointed is a minor, by a parent or the parents of the minor or from the minor's estate, or any combination thereof, in any proportions the court deems just.

(3) If a ward or proposed ward is furnished legal counsel for a guardianship proceeding, upon its own motion or that of a party, the court shall determine whether a parent or parents of the ward or proposed ward or the estate of the ward or proposed ward is financially unable to pay all or a portion of the cost of counsel appointed pursuant to this section. Any portion of the cost of that counsel that the court finds the parent or parents or the estate of the ward or proposed ward is unable to pay shall be paid by the county. The Judicial Council shall adopt guidelines to assist in determining financial eligibility for county payment of counsel appointed by the court pursuant to this chapter.

(d) The court may make an order under subdivision (c) requiring payment by a parent or parents of the minor only after the parent or parents, as the case may be, have been given notice and the opportunity to be heard on whether the order would be just under the circumstances of the particular case.

1471. (a) If a conservatee, proposed conservatee, or person alleged to lack legal capacity is unable to retain legal counsel and requests the appointment of counsel to assist in the particular matter, whether or not such person lacks or appears to lack legal capacity, the court shall, at or before the time of the hearing, appoint the public defender or private counsel to represent the interest of such person in the following proceedings under this division:

(1) A proceeding to establish a conservatorship or to appoint a proposed conservator.

(2) A proceeding to terminate the conservatorship.

(3) A proceeding to remove the conservator.

(4) A proceeding for a court order affecting the legal capacity of the conservatee.

(5) A proceeding to obtain an order authorizing removal of a temporary conservatee from the temporary conservatee's place of residence.

(b) If a conservatee or proposed conservatee does not plan to retain legal counsel and has not requested the court to appoint legal counsel, whether or not such person lacks or appears to lack legal capacity, the court shall, at or before the time of the hearing, appoint the public defender or private counsel to represent the interests of such person in any proceeding listed in subdivision (a) if, based on information contained in the court investigator's report or obtained from any other source, the court determines that the appointment would be helpful to the resolution of the matter or is necessary to protect the interests of the conservatee or proposed conservatee.

(c) In any proceeding to establish a limited conservatorship, if the proposed limited conservatee has not retained legal counsel and does not plan to retain legal counsel, the court shall immediately appoint the public defender or private counsel to represent the proposed limited conservatee. The proposed limited conservatee shall pay the cost for such legal service if he or she is able. This subdivision applies irrespective of any medical or psychological inability to attend the hearing on the part of the proposed limited conservatee as allowed in Section 1825.

1472. (a) If a person is furnished legal counsel under Section 1471:

(1) The court shall, upon conclusion of the matter, fix a reasonable sum for compensation and expenses of counsel and shall make a determination of the person's ability to pay all or a portion of that sum. The sum may, in the discretion of the court, include compensation for services rendered, and expenses incurred, before the date of the order appointing counsel.

(2) If the court determines that the person has the ability to pay all or a portion of the sum, the court shall order the conservator of the estate or, if none, the person, to pay in any installments and in any manner the court determines to be reasonable and compatible with the person's financial ability.

(3) In a proceeding under Chapter 3 (commencing with Section 3100) of Part 6 for court authorization of a proposed transaction involving community property, the court may order payment out of the proceeds of the transaction.

(4) If a conservator is not appointed for the person furnished legal counsel, the order for payment may be enforced in the same manner as a money judgment.

(b) If the court determines that a person furnished private counsel under Section 1471 lacks the ability to pay all or a portion of the sum determined under paragraph (1) of subdivision (a), the county shall pay the sum to the private counsel to the extent the court determines the person is unable to pay.

(c) The payment ordered by the court under subdivision (a) shall be made to the county if the public defender has been appointed or if private counsel has been appointed to perform the duties of the public defender and the county has compensated that counsel. In the case of other court-appointed counsel, the payment shall be made to that counsel.

1474. If an Indian custodian or biological parent of an Indian child lacks the financial ability to retain counsel and requests the appointment of counsel in proceedings described in Section 1459.5, the provisions of subsection (b) of Section 1912 of the Indian Child Welfare Act (25 U.S.C. Sec. 1901 et seq.) and Section 23.13 of Title 25 of the Code of Federal Regulations are applicable.

Chapter 5. Transitional Provisions

1488. If before January 1, 1981, an adult has in a signed writing nominated a person to serve as guardian if a guardian is in the future appointed for such adult, such nomination shall be deemed to be a nomination of a conservator. This section applies whether or not the signed writing was executed in the same manner as a witnessed will so long as the person signing the writing had at the time the writing was signed sufficient capacity to form an intelligent preference.

1489. If, before January 1, 1981, a parent or other person has in a signed writing appointed a person to serve as the guardian of the person or estate or both of a minor, or as the guardian of the property the minor receives from or by designation of the person making the appointment, such appointment shall be deemed to be a nomination of a guardian if the requirements of Section 1500 or 1501 are satisfied and, in such case, shall be given the same effect it would have under Section 1500 or 1501, as the case may be, if made on or after January 1, 1981. This section applies whether or not the signed writing is a will or deed so long as the person signing the writing had at the time the writing was signed sufficient capacity to form an intelligent preference.

1490. When used in any statute of this state with reference to an adult or to the person of a married minor, "guardian" means the conservator of that adult or the conservator of the person in case of the married minor.

Part 2. Guardianship

Chapter 1. Establishment Of Guardianship

Article 1. Nomination Of Guardian

1500. Subject to Section 1502, a parent may nominate a guardian of the person or estate, or both, of a minor child in either of the following cases:

(a) Where the other parent nominates, or consents in writing to the nomination of, the same guardian for the same child.

(b) Where, at the time the petition for appointment of the guardian is filed, either (1) the other parent is dead or lacks legal capacity to consent to the nomination or (2) consent of the other parent would not be required for an adoption of the child.

1500.1. (a) Notwithstanding any other section in this part, and in accordance with Section 1913 of the Indian Child Welfare Act (25 U.S.C. Sec. 1901 et seq.), consent to nomination of a guardian of the person or of a guardian of the person and the estate given by an Indian child's parent is not valid unless both of the following occur:

(1) The consent is executed in writing at least 10 days after the child's birth and recorded before a judge.

(2) The judge certifies that the terms and consequences of the consent were fully explained in detail in English and were fully understood by the parent or that they were interpreted into a language that the parent understood.

(b) The parent of an Indian child may withdraw his or her consent to guardianship for any reason at any time prior to the issuance of letters of guardianship and the child shall be returned to the parent.

1501. Subject to Section 1502, a parent or any other person may nominate a guardian for property that a minor receives from or by designation of the nominator (whether before, at the time of, or after the nomination) including, but not limited to, property received by the minor by virtue of a gift, deed, trust, will, succession, insurance, or benefits of any kind.

1502. (a) A nomination of a guardian under this article may be made in the petition for the appointment of the guardian or at the hearing on the petition or in a writing signed either before or after the petition for the appointment of the guardian is filed.

(b) The nomination of a guardian under this article is effective when made except that a writing nominating a guardian under this article may provide that the nomination becomes effective only upon the occurrence of such specified condition or conditions as are stated in the writing, including but not limited to such conditions as the subsequent legal incapacity or death of the person making the nomination.

(c) Unless the writing making the nomination expressly otherwise provides, a nomination made under this article remains effective notwithstanding the subsequent legal incapacity or death of the person making the nomination.

Article 2. Appointment Of Guardian Generally

1510. (a) A relative or other person on behalf of the minor, or the minor if 12 years of age or older, may file a petition for the appointment of a guardian of the minor. A relative may file a petition for the appointment of a guardian under this section regardless of the relative's immigration status.

(b) The petition shall request that a guardian of the person or estate of the minor, or both, be appointed, shall specify the name and address of the proposed guardian and the name and date of birth of the proposed ward, and shall state that the appointment is necessary or convenient.

(c) The petition shall set forth, so far as is known to the petitioner, the names and addresses of all of the following:

(1) The parents of the proposed ward.

(2) The person having legal custody of the proposed ward and, if that person does not have the care of the proposed ward, the person having the care of the proposed ward.

(3) The relatives of the proposed ward within the second degree.

(4) In the case of a guardianship of the estate, the spouse of the proposed ward.

(5) Any person nominated as guardian for the proposed ward under Section 1500 or 1501.

(6) In the case of a guardianship of the person involving an Indian child, any Indian custodian and the Indian child's tribe.

(d) If the petitioner or proposed guardian is a professional fiduciary, as described in Section 2340, who is required to be licensed under the Professional Fiduciaries Act (Chapter 6 (commencing with Section 6500) of Division 3 of the Business and Professions Code), the petition shall include the following:

(1) The petitioner's or proposed guardian's proposed hourly fee schedule or another statement of his or her proposed compensation from the estate of the proposed ward for services performed as a guardian. The petitioner's or proposed guardian's provision of a proposed hourly fee schedule or another statement of his or her proposed compensation, as required by this paragraph, shall not preclude a court from later reducing the petitioner's or proposed guardian's fees or other compensation.

(2) Unless a petition for appointment of a temporary guardian that contains the statements required by this paragraph is filed together with a petition for appointment of a guardian, both of the following:

(A) A statement of the petitioner's or proposed guardian's license information.

(B) A statement explaining who engaged the petitioner or proposed guardian or how the petitioner or proposed guardian was engaged to file the petition for appointment of a guardian or to agree to accept the appointment as guardian and what prior relationship the petitioner or proposed guardian had with the proposed ward or the proposed ward's family or friends.

(e) If the proposed ward is a patient in or on leave of absence from a state institution under the jurisdiction of the State Department of State Hospitals or the State Department of Developmental Services and that fact is known to the petitioner or proposed guardian, the petition shall state that fact and name the institution.

(f) The petition shall state, so far as is known to the petitioner or proposed guardian, whether or not the proposed ward is receiving or is entitled to receive benefits from the Veterans Administration and the estimated amount of the monthly benefit payable by the Veterans Administration for the proposed ward.

(g) If the petitioner or proposed guardian has knowledge of any pending adoption, juvenile court, marriage dissolution, domestic relations, custody, or other similar proceeding affecting the proposed ward, the petition shall disclose the pending proceeding.

(h) If the petitioners or proposed guardians have accepted or intend to accept physical care or custody of the child with intent to adopt, whether formed at the time of placement or formed subsequent to placement, the petitioners or proposed guardians shall so state in the guardianship petition, whether or not an adoption petition has been filed.

(i) If the proposed ward is or becomes the subject of an adoption petition, the court shall order the guardianship petition consolidated with the adoption petition, and the consolidated case shall be heard and decided in the court in which the adoption is pending.

(j) If the proposed ward is or may be an Indian child, the petition shall state that fact.

1511. (a) Except as provided in subdivisions (f) and (g), at least 15 days before the hearing on the petition for the appointment of a guardian, notice of the time and place of the hearing shall be given as provided in subdivisions (b), (c), (d), and (e) of this section. The notice shall be accompanied by a copy of the petition. The court may not shorten the time for giving the notice of hearing under this section.

(b) Notice shall be served in the manner provided in Section 415.10 or 415.30 of the Code of Civil Procedure, or in any manner authorized by the court, on all of the following persons:

(1) The proposed ward if 12 years of age or older.

(2) Any person having legal custody of the proposed ward, or serving as guardian of the estate of the proposed ward.

(3) The parents of the proposed ward.

(4) Any person nominated as a guardian for the proposed ward under Section 1500 or 1501.

(c) Notice shall be given by mail sent to their addresses stated in the petition, or in any manner authorized by the court, to all of the following:

(1) The spouse named in the petition.

(2) The relatives named in the petition, except that if the petition is for the appointment of a guardian of the estate only the court may dispense with the giving of notice to any one or more or all of the relatives.

(3) The person having the care of the proposed ward if other than the person having legal custody of the proposed ward.

(d) If notice is required by Section 1461 or Section 1542 to be given to the Director of State Hospitals or the Director of Developmental Services or the Director of Social Services, notice shall be mailed as so required.

(e) If the petition states that the proposed ward is receiving or is entitled to receive benefits from the Veterans Administration, notice shall be mailed to the office of the Veterans Administration referred to in Section 1461.5.

(f) Unless the court orders otherwise, notice shall not be given to any of the following:

(1) The parents or other relatives of a proposed ward who has been relinquished to a licensed adoption agency.

(2) The parents of a proposed ward who has been judicially declared free from their custody and control.

(g) Notice need not be given to any person if the court so orders upon a determination of either of the following:

(1) The person cannot with reasonable diligence be given the notice.

(2) The giving of the notice would be contrary to the interest of justice.

(h) Before the appointment of a guardian is made, proof shall be made to the court that each person entitled to notice under this section either:

(1) Has been given notice as required by this section.

(2) Has not been given notice as required by this section because the person cannot with reasonable diligence be given the notice or because the giving of notice to that person would be contrary to the interest of justice.

(i) If notice is required by Section 1460.2 to be given to an Indian custodian or tribe, notice shall be mailed as so required.

1512. Within 10 days after the petitioner in the guardianship proceeding becomes aware of any proceeding not disclosed in the guardianship petition affecting the custody of the proposed ward (including any adoption, juvenile court, marriage dissolution, domestic relations, or other similar proceeding affecting the proposed ward), the petitioner shall amend the guardianship petition to disclose the other proceeding.

1513. (a) Unless waived by the court, a court investigator, probation officer, or domestic relations investigator shall make an investigation and file with the court a report and recommendation concerning each proposed guardianship of the person or guardianship of the estate. Investigations where the proposed guardian is a relative shall be made by a court investigator. Investigations where the proposed guardian is a nonrelative shall be made by the county agency designated to investigate potential dependency. The report for the guardianship of the person shall include, but need not be limited to, an investigation and discussion of all of the following:

(1) A social history of the guardian.

(2) A social history of the proposed ward, including, to the extent feasible, an assessment of any identified developmental, emotional, psychological, or educational needs of the proposed ward and the capability of the petitioner to meet those needs.

(3) The relationship of the proposed ward

to the guardian, including the duration and character of the relationship, where applicable, the circumstances whereby physical custody of the proposed ward was acquired by the guardian, and a statement of the proposed ward's attitude concerning the proposed guardianship, unless the statement of the attitude is affected by the proposed ward's developmental, physical, or emotional condition.

(4) The anticipated duration of the guardianship and the plans of both natural parents and the proposed guardian for the stable and permanent home for the child. The court may waive this requirement for cases involving relative guardians.

(b) If the proposed ward is or may be described by Section 300 of the Welfare and Institutions Code, the court may refer the matter to the local child welfare services agency to initiate an investigation of the referral pursuant to Sections 328 and 329 of the Welfare and Institutions Code and to report the findings of that investigation to the court. Pending completion of the investigation, the court may take any reasonable steps it deems appropriate to protect the child's safety, including, but not limited to, appointment of a temporary guardian or issuance of a temporary restraining order. If dependency proceedings are initiated, the guardianship proceedings shall be stayed in accordance with Section 304 of the Welfare and Institutions Code. Nothing in this section shall affect the applicability of Section 16504 or 16506 of the Welfare and Institutions Code. If a dependency proceeding is not initiated, the probate court shall retain jurisdiction to hear the guardianship matter.

(c) Prior to ruling on the petition for guardianship, the court shall read and consider all reports submitted pursuant to this section, which shall be reflected in the minutes or stated on the record. Any person who reports to the court pursuant to this section may be called and examined by any party to the proceeding.

(d) All reports authorized by this section are confidential and shall only be made available to persons who have been served in the proceedings or their attorneys. The clerk of the court shall make provisions to limit access to the reports exclusively to persons entitled to receipt. The reports shall be made available to all parties entitled to receipt no less than three court days before the hearing on the guardianship petition.

(e) For the purpose of writing either report authorized by this section, the person making the investigation and report shall have access to the proposed ward's school records, probation records, and public and private social services records, and to an oral or written summary of the proposed ward's medical records and psychological records prepared by any physician, psychologist, or psychiatrist who made or who is maintain-

ing those records. The physician, psychologist, or psychiatrist shall be available to clarify information regarding these records pursuant to the investigator's responsibility to gather and provide information for the court.

(f) This section does not apply to guardianships resulting from a permanency plan for a dependent child pursuant to Section 366.26 of the Welfare and Institutions Code.

(g) For purposes of this section, a "relative" means a person who is a spouse, parent, stepparent, brother, sister, stepbrother, stepsister, half-brother, half-sister, uncle, aunt, niece, nephew, first cousin, or any person denoted by the prefix "grand" or "great," or the spouse of any of these persons, even after the marriage has been terminated by death or dissolution.

(h) In an Indian child custody proceeding, any person making an investigation and report shall consult with the Indian child's tribe and include in the report information provided by the tribe.

1513.1. (a) Each court or county shall assess (1) the parent, parents, or other person charged with the support and maintenance of the ward or proposed ward, and (2) the guardian, proposed guardian, or the estate of the ward or proposed ward, for court or county expenses incurred for any investigation or review conducted by the court investigator, probation officer, or domestic relations investigator. The court may order reimbursement to the court or to the county in the amount of the assessment, unless the court finds that all or any part of the assessment would impose a hardship on the ward or the ward's estate. A county may waive any or all of an assessment against the guardianship on the basis of hardship. There shall be a rebuttable presumption that the assessment would impose a hardship if the ward is receiving Medi-Cal benefits.

(b) Any amount chargeable as state-mandated local costs incurred by a county for the cost of the investigation or review shall be reduced by any assessments actually collected by the county pursuant to subdivision (a) during that fiscal year.

1513.2. (a) To the extent resources are available, the court shall implement procedures, as described in this section, to ensure that every guardian annually completes and returns to the court a status report, including the statement described in subdivision (b). A guardian who willfully submits any material information required by the form which he or she knows to be false shall be guilty of a misdemeanor. Not later than one month prior to the date the status report is required to be returned, the clerk of the court shall mail to the guardian by first-class mail a notice informing the guardian that he or she is required to complete and return the status report to the court. The clerk shall enclose with the letter a blank status report form for the guardian to complete and return by mail. If the status report is not completed and returned as required, or if the court finds, after a status report has been completed and returned, that further information is needed, the court shall attempt to obtain the information required in the report from the guardian or other sources. If the court is unable to obtain this information within 30 days after the date the status report is due, the court shall either order the guardian to make himself or herself available to the investigator for purposes of investigation of the guardianship, or to show cause why the guardian should not be removed.

(b) The Judicial Council shall develop a form for the status report. The form shall include the following statement: "A guardian who willfully submits any material information required by this form which he or she knows to be false is guilty of a misdemeanor." The form shall request information the Judicial Council deems necessary to determine the status of the guardianship, including, but not limited to, the following:

(1) The guardian's present address.

(2) The name and birth date of the child under guardianship.

(3) The name of the school in which the child is enrolled, if any.

(4) If the child is not in the guardian's home, the name, relationship, address, and telephone number of the person or persons with whom the child resides.

(5) If the child is not in the guardian's home, why the child was moved.

(c) The report authorized by this section is confidential and shall only be made available to persons who have been served in the proceedings or their attorneys. The clerk of the court shall implement procedures for the limitation of the report exclusively to persons entitled to its receipt.

(d) The Judicial Council shall report to the Legislature no later than December 31, 2004, regarding the costs and benefits of utilizing the annual status report.

1514. (a) Upon hearing of the petition, if it appears necessary or convenient, the court may appoint a guardian of the person or estate of the proposed ward or both.

(b) (1) In appointing a guardian of the person, the court is governed by Chapter 1 (commencing with Section 3020) and Chapter 2 (commencing with Section 3040) of Part 2 of Division 8 of the Family Code, relating to custody of a minor.

(2) Except as provided in Section 2105, a minor's parent may not be appointed as a guardian of the person of the minor.

(c) The court shall appoint a guardian nominated under Section 1500 insofar as the nomination relates to the guardianship of the estate unless the court determines that the nominee is unsuitable. If the nominee is a relative, the nominee's immigration status alone shall not constitute unsuitability.

(d) The court shall appoint the person nominated under Section 1501 as guardian of the property covered by the nomination unless the court determines that the nominee is unsuitable. If the person so appointed is appointed only as guardian of the property covered by the nomination, the letters of guardianship shall so indicate.

(e) Subject to subdivisions (c) and (d), in appointing a guardian of the estate:

(1) The court is to be guided by what appears to be in the best interest of the proposed ward, taking into account the proposed guardian's ability to manage and to preserve the estate as well as the proposed guardian's concern for and interest in the welfare of the proposed ward.

(2) If the proposed ward is of sufficient age to form an intelligent preference as to the person to be appointed as guardian, the court shall give consideration to that preference in determining the person to be so appointed.

1514.5. Notwithstanding any other provision of law, except provisions of law governing the retention and storage of data, a family law court shall, upon request from the court in any county hearing a probate guardianship matter proceeding before the court pursuant to this part, provide to the court all available information the court deems necessary to make a determination regarding the best interest of a child, as described in Section 3011 of the Family Code, who is the subject of the proceeding. The information shall also be released to a guardianship investigator, as provided in subdivision (a) of Section 1513, acting within the scope of his or her duties in that proceeding. Any information released pursuant to this section that is confidential pursuant to any other provision of law shall remain confidential and may not be released, except to the extent necessary to comply with this section. No records shared pursuant to this section may be disclosed to any party in a case unless the party requests the agency or court that originates the record to release these records and the request is granted. In counties that provide confidential family law mediation, or confidential dependency mediation, those mediations are not covered by this section.

1515. Notwithstanding any other provision of this part, no guardian of the person may be appointed for a minor who is married or whose marriage has been dissolved. This section does not apply in the case of a minor whose marriage has been adjudged a nullity.

1516. (a) In each case involving a petition for guardianship of the person, the petitioner shall mail a notice of the hearing and a copy of the petition, at least 15 days prior to the hearing, to the local agency designated by the board of supervisors to investigate guardianships for the court. The local social services agency providing child protection services shall screen the name of the guardian for prior referrals of neglect or abuse of minors. The results of this screening shall be provided to the court.

(b) This section does not apply to guardianships resulting from a permanency plan for a dependent child pursuant to Section 366.25 of the Welfare and Institutions Code.

1516.5. (a) A proceeding to have a child declared free from the custody and control of one or both parents may be brought in accordance with the procedures specified in Part 4 (commencing with Section 7800) of Division 12 of the Family Code within an existing guardianship proceeding, in an adoption action, or in a separate action filed for that purpose, if all of the following requirements are satisfied:

(1) One or both parents do not have the legal custody of the child.

(2) The child has been in the physical custody of the guardian for a period of not less than two years.

(3) The court finds that the child would benefit from being adopted by his or her guardian. In making this determination, the court shall consider all factors relating to the best interest of the child, including, but not limited to, the nature and extent of the relationship between all of the following:

(A) The child and the birth parent.

(B) The child and the guardian, including family members of the guardian.

(C) The child and any siblings or half siblings.

(b) The court shall appoint a court investigator or other qualified professional to investigate all factors enumerated in subdivision (a). The findings of the investigator or professional regarding those issues shall be included in the written report required pursuant to Section 7851 of the Family Code.

(c) The rights of the parent, including the rights to notice and counsel provided in Part 4 (commencing with Section 7800) of Division 12 of the Family Code, shall apply to actions brought pursuant to this section.

(d) This section does not apply to any child who is a dependent of the juvenile court or to any Indian child.

1517. (a) This part does not apply to guardianships resulting from the selection and implementation of a permanent plan pursuant to Section 366.26 of the Welfare and Institutions Code. For those minors, Section 366.26 of the Welfare and Institutions Code and Division 3 (commencing with Rule 5.500) of Title Five of the California Rules of Court specify the exclusive procedures for establishing, modifying, and terminating legal guardianships. If no specific provision of the Welfare and Institutions Code or the California Rules of Court is applicable, the provisions applicable to the administration of estates under Part 4 (commencing with Section 2100) govern so far as they are applicable to like situations.

(b) This chapter shall not be construed to prevent a court that assumes jurisdiction of a minor child pursuant to Section 300 of the Welfare and Institutions Code, or a probate court, as appropriate, from issuing orders or making appointments, on motion of the child's counsel, consistent with Division 2 of the Welfare and Institutions Code or Divisions 4 to 6, inclusive, of the Probate Code necessary to ensure the appropriate administration of funds for the benefit of the child. Orders or appointments regarding those funds may continue after the court's jurisdiction is terminated pursuant to Section 391 of the Welfare and Institutions Code.

Article 3. Nonrelative Guardianships

1540. This article does not apply in any of the following cases:

(a) Where the petition is for guardianship of the estate exclusively.

(b) Where the proposed guardian is a relative of the proposed ward.

(c) Where the Director of Developmental Services is appointed guardian pursuant to Article 7.5 (commencing with Section 416) of Chapter 2 of Part 1 of Division 1 of the Health and Safety Code.

(d) Where the director of the department designated by the board of supervisors to provide social services is appointed guardian.

(e) Where the public guardian is appointed guardian.

(f) Where the guardianship results from a permanency plan for a dependent child pursuant to Section 366.25 of the Welfare and Institutions Code.

1541. In addition to the other required contents of the petition for appointment of a guardian, the petition shall include both of the following:

(a) A statement by the proposed guardian that, upon request by an agency referred to in Section 1543 for information relating to the investigation referred to in that section, the proposed guardian will promptly submit the information required.

(b) A disclosure of any petition for adoption by the proposed guardian of the minor who is the subject of the guardianship petition regardless of when or where filed.

(c) A statement whether or not the home of the proposed guardian is licensed as a foster family home.

1542. In each case involving a petition for guardianship of the person, the petitioner shall mail a notice of the hearing and a copy of the petition, at least 15 days prior to the hearing, to the Director of Social Services at the director's office in Sacramento and to the local agency designated by the board of supervisors to investigate guardianships for the court.

1543. (a) If the petition as filed or as

amended states that an adoption petition has been filed, a report with respect to the suitability of the proposed guardian for guardianship shall be filed with the court by the agency investigating the adoption. In other cases, the local agency designated by the board of supervisors to provide public social services shall file a report with the court with respect to the proposed guardian of the same character required to be made with regard to an applicant for foster family home licensure.

(b) The report filed with the court pursuant to this section is confidential. The report may be considered by the court and shall be made available only to the persons who have been served in the proceeding and the persons who have appeared in the proceeding or their attorneys. The report may be received in evidence upon stipulation of counsel for all such persons who are present at the hearing or, if such person is present at the hearing but is not represented by counsel, upon consent of such person.

Chapter 2. Termination

1600. (a) A guardianship of the person or estate or both terminates when the ward attains majority or dies.

(b) A guardianship of the person terminates upon the adoption of the ward or upon the emancipation of the ward under Section7002 of the Family Code.

1601. Upon petition of the guardian, a parent, the ward, or, in the case of an Indian child custody proceeding, an Indian custodian or the ward's tribe, the court may make an order terminating the guardianship if the court determines that it is in the ward's best interest to terminate the guardianship. Notice of the hearing on the petition shall be given for the period and in the manner provided in Chapter 3 (commencing with Section 1460) of Part 1.

1602. (a) The Legislature hereby finds and declares that guardians perform a critical and important role in the lives of minors, frequently assuming a parental role and caring for a child when the child's parent or parents are unable or unwilling to do so.

(b) Upon making a determination that a guardianship should be terminated pursuant to Section 1601, the court may consider whether continued visitation between the ward and the guardian is in the ward's best interest. As part of the order of termination, the court shall have jurisdiction to issue an order providing for ongoing visitation between a former guardian and his or her former minor ward after the termination of the guardianship. The order granting or denying visitation may not be modified unless the court determines, based upon evidence presented, that there has been a significant change of circumstances since the court issued the order and that modification of the order is in the best interest of the child.

(c) A copy of the visitation order shall be filed in any court proceeding relating to custody of the minor. If a prior order has not been filed, and a proceeding is not pending relating to the custody of the minor in the court of any county, the visitation order may be used as the sole basis for opening a file in the court of the county in which the custodial parent resides. While a parent of the child has custody of the child, proceedings for modification of the visitation order shall be determined in a proceeding under the Family Code.

Chapter 3. Permanent And Stable Home

1610. (a) The Legislature finds and declares that it is in the best interests of children to be raised in a permanent, safe, stable, and loving environment.

(b) Unwarranted petitions, applications, or motions other than discovery motions after the guardianship has been established create an environment that can be harmful to children and are inconsistent with the goals of permanency, safety, and stability.

1611. If a person files a petition for visitation, termination of the guardianship, or instruction to the guardian that is unmeritorious, or intended to harass or annoy the guardian, and the person has previously filed pleadings in the guardianship proceedings that were unmeritorious, or intended to harass or annoy the guardian, this petition shall be grounds for the court to determine that the person is a vexatious litigant for the purposes of Title 3a (commencing with Section 391) of Part 2 of the Code of Civil Procedure. For these purposes, the term "new litigation" shall include petitions for visitation, termination of the guardianship, or instruction to the guardian.

Part 3. Conservatorship

Chapter 1. Establishment Of Conservatorship

Article 1. Persons For Whom Conservator May Be Appointed

1800. It is the intent of the Legislature in enacting this chapter to do the following:

(a) Protect the rights of persons who are placed under conservatorship.

(b) Provide that an assessment of the needs of the person is performed in order to determine the appropriateness and extent of a conservatorship and to set goals for increasing the conservatee's functional abilities to whatever extent possible.

(c) Provide that the health and psychosocial needs of the proposed conservatee are met.

(d) Provide that community-based services are used to the greatest extent in order to allow the conservatee to remain as independent and in the least restrictive setting as possible.

(e) Provide that the periodic review of the conservatorship by the court investigator shall consider the best interests of the conservatee.

(f) Ensure that the conservatee's basic needs for physical health, food, clothing, and shelter are met.

(g) Provide for the proper management and protection of the conservatee's real and personal property.

1800.3. (a) If the need therefor is established to the satisfaction of the court and the other requirements of this chapter are satisfied, the court may appoint:

(1) A conservator of the person or estate of an adult, or both.

(2) A conservator of the person of a minor who is married or whose marriage has been dissolved.

(b) No conservatorship of the person or of the estate shall be granted by the court unless the court makes an express finding that the granting of the conservatorship is the least restrictive alternative needed for the protection of the conservatee.

1801. Subject to Section 1800.3:

(a) A conservator of the person may be appointed for a person who is unable to provide properly for his or her personal needs for physical health, food, clothing, or shelter, except as provided for the person as described in subdivision (b) or (c) of Section 1828.5.

(b) A conservator of the estate may be appointed for a person who is substantially unable to manage his or her own financial resources or resist fraud or undue influence, except as provided for that person as described in subdivision (b) or (c) of Section 1828.5. Substantial inability may not be proved solely by isolated incidents of negligence or improvidence.

(c) A conservator of the person and estate may be appointed for a person described in subdivisions (a) and (b).

(d) A limited conservator of the person or of the estate, or both, may be appointed for a developmentally disabled adult. A limited conservatorship may be utilized only as necessary to promote and protect the well-being of the individual, shall be designed to encourage the development of maximum self-reliance and independence of the individual, and shall be ordered only to the extent necessitated by the individual's proven mental and adaptive limitations. The conservatee of the limited conservator shall not be presumed to be incompetent and shall retain all legal and civil rights except those which by court order have been designated as legal disabilities and have been specifically granted to the limited conservator. The intent of the Legislature, as expressed in Section 4501 of the Welfare and Institutions Code, that developmentally disabled citizens of this state receive services resulting in more independent, productive, and normal lives is the underlying mandate of this division in its application to adults alleged to be developmentally disabled.

(e) The standard of proof for the appointment of a conservator pursuant to this section shall be clear and convincing evidence.

1802. Subject to Section 1800.3, a conservator of the person or estate, or both, may be appointed for a person who voluntarily requests the appointment and who, to the satisfaction of the court, establishes good cause for the appointment.

1803. A conservator of the estate may be appointed for a person who is an absentee as defined in Section 1403.

1804. Subject to Section 1800.3, a conservator of the estate may be appointed for a person who is missing and whose whereabouts is unknown.

Article 2. Order Of Preference For Appointment Of Conservator

1810. If the proposed conservatee has sufficient capacity at the time to form an intelligent preference, the proposed conservatee may nominate a conservator in the petition or in a writing signed either before or after the petition is filed. The court shall appoint the nominee as conservator unless the court finds that the appointment of the nominee is not in the best interests of the proposed conservatee.

1811. (a) Subject to Section 1813, the spouse, domestic partner, or an adult child, parent, brother, or sister of the proposed conservatee may nominate a conservator in the petition or at the hearing on the petition.

(b) Subject to Section 1813, the spouse, domestic partner, or a parent of the proposed conservatee may nominate a conservator in a writing signed either before or after the petition is filed and that nomination remains effective notwithstanding the subsequent legal incapacity or death of the spouse, domestic partner, or parent.

1812. (a) Subject to Sections 1810 and 1813, the selection of a conservator of the person or estate, or both, is solely in the discretion of the court and, in making the selection, the court is to be guided by what appears to be for the best interests of the proposed conservatee.

(b) Subject to Sections 1810 and 1813, of persons equally qualified in the opinion of the court to appointment as conservator of the person or estate or both, preference is to be given in the following order:

(1) The spouse or domestic partner of the proposed conservatee or the person nominated by the spouse or domestic partner pursuant to Section 1811.

(2) An adult child of the proposed conservatee or the person nominated by the child pursuant to Section 1811.

(3) A parent of the proposed conservatee

or the person nominated by the parent pursuant to Section 1811.

(4) A brother or sister of the proposed conservatee or the person nominated by the brother or sister pursuant to Section 1811.

(5) Any other person or entity eligible for appointment as a conservator under this code or, if there is no person or entity willing to act as a conservator, under the Welfare and Institutions Code.

(c) The preference for any nominee for appointment under paragraphs (2), (3), and (4) of subdivision (b) is subordinate to the preference for any other parent, child, brother, or sister in that class.

1813. (a) The spouse of a proposed conservatee may not petition for the appointment of a conservator for a spouse or be appointed as conservator of the person or estate of the proposed conservatee unless the petitioner alleges in the petition for appointment as conservator, and the court finds, that the spouse is not a party to any action or proceeding against the proposed conservatee for legal separation of the parties, dissolution of marriage, or adjudication of nullity of their marriage. However, if the court finds by clear and convincing evidence that the appointment of the spouse, who is a party to an action or proceeding against the proposed conservatee for legal separation of the parties, dissolution of marriage, or adjudication of nullity of their marriage, or has obtained a judgment in any of these proceedings, is in the best interests of the proposed conservatee, the court may appoint the spouse.

Prior to making this appointment, the court shall appoint counsel to consult with and advise the conservatee, and to report to the court his or her findings concerning the suitability of appointing the spouse as conservator.

(b) The spouse of a conservatee shall disclose to the conservator, or if the spouse is the conservator, shall disclose to the court, the filing of any action or proceeding against the conservatee for legal separation of the parties, dissolution of marriage, or adjudication of nullity of the marriage, within 10 days of the filing of the action or proceeding by filing a notice with the court and serving the notice according to the notice procedures under this title. The court may, upon receipt of the notice, set the matter for hearing on an order to show cause why the appointment of the spouse as conservator, if the spouse is the conservator, should not be terminated and a new conservator appointed by the court.

1813.1. (a) (1) The domestic partner of a proposed conservatee may not petition for the appointment of a conservator for a domestic partner or be appointed as conservator of the person or estate of the proposed conservatee unless the petitioner alleges in the petition for appointment as conservator, and the court finds, that the domestic part-

ner has not terminated and is not intending to terminate the domestic partnership as provided in Section 299 of the Family Code. However, if the court finds by clear and convincing evidence that the appointment of a domestic partner who has terminated or is intending to terminate the domestic partnership is in the best interests of the proposed conservatee, the court may appoint the domestic partner.

(2) Prior to making this appointment, the court shall appoint counsel to consult with and advise the conservatee, and to report to the court his or her findings concerning the suitability of appointing the domestic partner as conservator.

(b) The domestic partner of a conservatee shall disclose to the conservator, or if the domestic partner is the conservator, shall notify the court, of the termination of a domestic partnership as provided in Section 299 of the Family Code within 10 days of its occurrence. The court may, upon receipt of the notice, set the matter for hearing on an order to show cause why the appointment of the domestic partner as conservator, if the domestic partner is the conservator, should not be terminated and a new conservator appointed by the court.

Article 3. Establishment Of Conservatorship

1820. (a) A petition for the appointment of a conservator may be filed by any of the following:

(1) The proposed conservatee.

(2) The spouse or domestic partner of the proposed conservatee.

(3) A relative of the proposed conservatee.

(4) Any interested state or local entity or agency of this state or any interested public officer or employee of this state or of a local public entity of this state.

(5) Any other interested person or friend of the proposed conservatee.

(b) If the proposed conservatee is a minor, the petition may be filed during his or her minority so that the appointment of a conservator may be made effective immediately upon the minor's attaining the age of majority. An existing guardian of the minor may be appointed as conservator under this part upon the minor's attaining the age of majority, whether or not the guardian's accounts have been settled.

(c) A creditor of the proposed conservatee may not file a petition for appointment of a conservator unless the creditor is a person described in paragraph (2), (3), or (4) of subdivision (a).

1821. (a) The petition shall request that a conservator be appointed for the person or estate, or both, shall specify the name, address, and telephone number of the proposed conservator and the name, address, and telephone number of the proposed conservatee, and state the reasons why a conservatorship is necessary. Unless the petitioner or proposed conservator is a bank or other entity authorized to conduct the business of a trust company, the petitioner or proposed conservator shall also file supplemental information as to why the appointment of a conservator is required. The supplemental information to be submitted shall include a brief statement of facts addressed to each of the following categories:

(1) The inability of the proposed conservatee to properly provide for his or her needs for physical health, food, clothing, and shelter.

(2) The location of the proposed conservatee's residence and the ability of the proposed conservatee to live in the residence while under conservatorship.

(3) Alternatives to conservatorship considered by the petitioner or proposed conservator and reasons why those alternatives are not available.

(4) Health or social services provided to the proposed conservatee during the year preceding the filing of the petition, when the petitioner or proposed conservator has information as to those services.

(5) The inability of the proposed conservatee to substantially manage his or her own financial resources, or to resist fraud or undue influence.

The facts required to address the categories set forth in paragraphs (1) to (5), inclusive, shall be set forth by the petitioner or proposed conservator if he or she has knowledge of the facts or by the declarations or affidavits of other persons having knowledge of those facts.

If any of the categories set forth in paragraphs (1) to (5), inclusive, are not applicable to the proposed conservatorship, the petitioner or proposed conservator shall so indicate and state on the supplemental information form the reasons therefor.

The Judicial Council shall develop a supplemental information form for the information required pursuant to paragraphs (1) to (5), inclusive, after consultation with individuals or organizations approved by the Judicial Council, who represent public conservators, court investigators, the State Bar, specialists with experience in performing assessments and coordinating community-based services, and legal services for the elderly and disabled.

The supplemental information form shall be separate and distinct from the form for the petition. The supplemental information shall be confidential and shall be made available only to parties, persons given notice of the petition who have requested this supplemental information or who have appeared in the proceedings, their attorneys, and the court. The court shall have discretion at any other time to release the supplemental information to other persons if it would serve the interests of the conservatee. The clerk of the court shall make provision for limiting disclosure of the supplemental information exclusively to persons entitled thereto under this section.

(b) The petition shall set forth, so far as they are known to the petitioner or proposed conservator, the names and addresses of the spouse or domestic partner, and of the relatives of the proposed conservatee within the second degree. If no spouse or domestic partner of the proposed conservatee or relatives of the proposed conservatee within the second degree are known to the petitioner or proposed conservator, the petition shall set forth, so far as they are known to the petitioner or proposed conservator, the names and addresses of the following persons who, for the purposes of Section 1822, shall all be deemed to be relatives:

(1) A spouse or domestic partner of a predeceased parent of a proposed conservatee.

(2) The children of a predeceased spouse or domestic partner of a proposed conservatee.

(3) The siblings of the proposed conservatee's parents, if any, but if none, then the natural and adoptive children of the proposed conservatee's parents' siblings.

(4) The natural and adoptive children of the proposed conservatee' s siblings.

(c) If the petitioner or proposed conservator is a professional fiduciary, as described in Section 2340, who is required to be licensed under the Professional Fiduciaries Act (Chapter 6 (commencing with Section 6500) of Division 3 of the Business and Professions Code), the petition shall include the following:

(1) The petitioner's or proposed conservator's proposed hourly fee schedule or another statement of his or her proposed compensation from the estate of the proposed conservatee for services performed as a conservator. The petitioner's or proposed conservator's provision of a proposed hourly fee schedule or another statement of his or her proposed compensation, as required by this paragraph, shall not preclude a court from later reducing the petitioner's or proposed conservator's fees or other compensation.

(2) Unless a petition for appointment of a temporary conservator that contains the statements required by this paragraph is filed together with a petition for appointment of a conservator, both of the following:

(A) A statement of the petitioner's or proposed conservator's license information.

(B) A statement explaining who engaged the petitioner or proposed conservator or how the petitioner or proposed conservator was engaged to file the petition for appointment of a conservator or to agree to accept the appointment as conservator and what prior relationship the petitioner or proposed conservator had with the proposed conservatee or the proposed conservatee's family or friends.

(d) If the petition is filed by a person other than the proposed conservatee, the petition shall include a declaration of due diligence showing both of the following:

(1) Either the efforts to find the proposed conservatee's relatives or why it was not feasible to contact any of them.

(2) Either the preferences of the proposed conservatee concerning the appointment of a conservator and the appointment of the proposed conservator or why it was not feasible to ascertain those preferences.

(e) If the petition is filed by a person other than the proposed conservatee, the petition shall state whether or not the petitioner is a creditor or debtor, or the agent of a creditor or debtor, of the proposed conservatee.

(f) If the proposed conservatee is a patient in or on leave of absence from a state institution under the jurisdiction of the State Department of State Hospitals or the State Department of Developmental Services and that fact is known to the petitioner or proposed conservator, the petition shall state that fact and name the institution.

(g) The petition shall state, so far as is known to the petitioner or proposed conservator, whether or not the proposed conservatee is receiving or is entitled to receive benefits from the Veterans Administration and the estimated amount of the monthly benefit payable by the Veterans Administration for the proposed conservatee.

(h) The petition may include an application for any order or orders authorized under this division, including, but not limited to, orders under Chapter 4 (commencing with Section 1870).

(i) The petition may include a further statement that the proposed conservatee is not willing to attend the hearing on the petition, does not wish to contest the establishment of the conservatorship, and does not object to the proposed conservator or prefer that another person act as conservator.

(j) In the case of an allegedly developmentally disabled adult, the petition shall set forth the following:

(1) The nature and degree of the alleged disability, the specific duties and powers requested by or for the limited conservator, and the limitations of civil and legal rights requested to be included in the court's order of appointment.

(2) Whether or not the proposed limited conservatee is or is alleged to be developmentally disabled.

Reports submitted pursuant to Section 416.8 of the Health and Safety Code meet the requirements of this section, and conservatorships filed pursuant to Article 7.5 (commencing with Section 416) of Part 1 of Division 1 of the Health and Safety Code are exempt from providing the supplemental information required by this section, so long as the guidelines adopted by the State Department of Developmental Services for regional centers require the same information that is required pursuant to this section.

1822. (a) At least 15 days before the hearing on the petition for appointment of a conservator, notice of the time and place of the hearing shall be given as provided in this section. The notice shall be accompanied by a copy of the petition. The court may not shorten the time for giving the notice of hearing under this section.

(b) Notice shall be mailed to the following persons:

(1) The spouse, if any, or registered domestic partner, if any, of the proposed conservatee at the address stated in the petition.

(2) The relatives named in the petition at their addresses stated in the petition.

(c) If notice is required by Section 1461 to be given to the Director of State Hospitals or the Director of Developmental Services, notice shall be mailed as so required.

(d) If the petition states that the proposed conservatee is receiving or is entitled to receive benefits from the Veterans Administration, notice shall be mailed to the Office of the Veterans Administration referred to in Section 1461.5.

(e) If the proposed conservatee is a person with developmental disabilities, at least 30 days before the day of the hearing on the petition, the petitioner shall mail a notice of the hearing and a copy of the petition to the regional center identified in Section 1827.5.

(f) If the petition states that the petitioner and the proposed conservator have no prior relationship with the proposed conservatee and are not nominated by a family member, friend, or other person with a relationship to the proposed conservatee, notice shall be mailed to the public guardian of the county in which the petition is filed.

1823. (a) If the petition is filed by a person other than the proposed conservatee, the clerk shall issue a citation directed to the proposed conservatee setting forth the time and place of hearing.

(b) The citation shall include a statement of the legal standards by which the need for a conservatorship is adjudged as stated in Section 1801 and shall state the substance of all of the following:

(1) The proposed conservatee may be adjudged unable to provide for personal needs or to manage financial resources and, by reason thereof, a conservator may be appointed for the person or estate or both.

(2) Such adjudication may affect or transfer to the conservator the proposed conservatee's right to contract, in whole or in part, to manage and control property, to give informed consent for medical treatment, and to fix a residence.

(3) The proposed conservatee may be disqualified from voting if not capable of completing an affidavit of voter registration.

(4) The court or a court investigator will explain the nature, purpose, and effect of the proceeding to the proposed conservatee and will answer questions concerning the expla-

nation.

(5) The proposed conservatee has the right to appear at the hearing and to oppose the petition, and in the case of an alleged developmentally disabled adult, to oppose the petition in part, by objecting to any or all of the requested duties or powers of the limited conservator.

(6) The proposed conservatee has the right to choose and be represented by legal counsel and has the right to have legal counsel appointed by the court if unable to retain legal counsel.

(7) The proposed conservatee has the right to a jury trial if desired.

1824. The citation and a copy of the petition shall be served on the proposed conservatee at least 15 days before the hearing. Service shall be made in the manner provided in Section 415.10 or 415.30 of the Code of Civil Procedure or in such manner as may be authorized by the court. If the proposed conservatee is outside this state, service may also be made in the manner provided in Section 415.40 of the Code of Civil Procedure.

1825. (a) The proposed conservatee shall be produced at the hearing except in the following cases:

(1) Where the proposed conservatee is out of the state when served and is not the petitioner.

(2) Where the proposed conservatee is unable to attend the hearing by reason of medical inability.

(3) Where the court investigator has reported to the court that the proposed conservatee has expressly communicated that the proposed conservatee (i) is not willing to attend the hearing, (ii) does not wish to contest the establishment of the conservatorship, and (iii) does not object to the proposed conservator or prefer that another person act as conservator, and the court makes an order that the proposed conservatee need not attend the hearing.

(b) If the proposed conservatee is unable to attend the hearing because of medical inability, such inability shall be established (1) by the affidavit or certificate of a licensed medical practitioner or (2) if the proposed conservatee is an adherent of a religion whose tenets and practices call for reliance on prayer alone for healing and is under treatment by an accredited practitioner of that religion, by the affidavit of the practitioner. The affidavit or certificate is evidence only of the proposed conservatee's inability to attend the hearing and shall not be considered in determining the issue of need for the establishment of a conservatorship.

(c) Emotional or psychological instability is not good cause for the absence of the proposed conservatee from the hearing unless, by reason of such instability, attendance at the hearing is likely to cause serious and immediate physiological damage to the proposed conservatee.

1826. Regardless of whether the proposed conservatee attends the hearing, the court investigator shall do all of the following:

(a) Conduct the following interviews:

(1) The proposed conservatee personally.

(2) All petitioners and all proposed conservators who are not petitioners.

(3) The proposed conservatee's spouse or registered domestic partner and relatives within the first degree. If the proposed conservatee does not have a spouse, registered domestic partner, or relatives within the first degree, to the greatest extent possible, the proposed conservatee's relatives within the second degree.

(4) To the greatest extent practical and taking into account the proposed conservatee's wishes, the proposed conservatee's relatives within the second degree not required to be interviewed under paragraph (3), neighbors, and, if known, close friends.

(b) Inform the proposed conservatee of the contents of the citation, of the nature, purpose, and effect of the proceeding, and of the right of the proposed conservatee to oppose the proceeding, to attend the hearing, to have the matter of the establishment of the conservatorship tried by jury, to be represented by legal counsel if the proposed conservatee so chooses, and to have legal counsel appointed by the court if unable to retain legal counsel.

(c) Determine whether it appears that the proposed conservatee is unable to attend the hearing and, if able to attend, whether the proposed conservatee is willing to attend the hearing.

(d) Review the allegations of the petition as to why the appointment of the conservator is required and, in making his or her determination, do the following:

(1) Refer to the supplemental information form submitted by the petitioner and consider the facts set forth in the form that address each of the categories specified in paragraphs (1) to (5), inclusive, of subdivision (a) of Section 1821.

(2) Consider, to the extent practicable, whether he or she believes the proposed conservatee suffers from any of the mental function deficits listed in subdivision (a) of Section 811 that significantly impairs the proposed conservatee's ability to understand and appreciate the consequences of his or her actions in connection with any of the functions described in subdivision (a) or (b) of Section 1801 and identify the observations that support that belief.

(e) Determine whether the proposed conservatee wishes to contest the establishment of the conservatorship.

(f) Determine whether the proposed conservatee objects to the proposed conservator or prefers another person to act as conservator.

(g) Determine whether the proposed conservatee wishes to be represented by legal counsel and, if so, whether the proposed conservatee has retained legal counsel and, if not, the name of an attorney the proposed conservatee wishes to retain.

(h) Determine whether the proposed conservatee is capable of completing an affidavit of voter registration.

(i) If the proposed conservatee has not retained legal counsel, determine whether the proposed conservatee desires the court to appoint legal counsel.

(j) Determine whether the appointment of legal counsel would be helpful to the resolution of the matter or is necessary to protect the interests of the proposed conservatee in any case where the proposed conservatee does not plan to retain legal counsel and has not requested the appointment of legal counsel by the court.

(k) Report to the court in writing, at least five days before the hearing, concerning all of the foregoing, including the proposed conservatee's express communications concerning both of the following:

(1) Representation by legal counsel.

(2) Whether the proposed conservatee is not willing to attend the hearing, does not wish to contest the establishment of the conservatorship, and does not object to the proposed conservator or prefer that another person act as conservator.

(l) Mail, at least five days before the hearing, a copy of the report referred to in subdivision (k) to all of the following:

(1) The attorney, if any, for the petitioner.

(2) The attorney, if any, for the proposed conservatee.

(3) The proposed conservatee.

(4) The spouse, registered domestic partner, and relatives within the first degree of the proposed conservatee who are required to be named in the petition for appointment of the conservator, unless the court determines that the mailing will result in harm to the conservatee.

(5) Any other persons as the court orders.

(m) The court investigator has discretion to release the report required by this section to the public conservator, interested public agencies, and the long-term care ombudsman.

(n) The report required by this section is confidential and shall be made available only to parties, persons described in subdivision (l), persons given notice of the petition who have requested this report or who have appeared in the proceedings, their attorneys, and the court. The court has discretion at any other time to release the report, if it would serve the interests of the conservatee. The clerk of the court shall provide for the limitation of the report exclusively to persons entitled to its receipt.

(o) This section does not apply to a proposed conservatee who has personally executed the petition for conservatorship, or one who has nominated his or her own conserva-

tor, if he or she attends the hearing.

(p) If the court investigator has performed an investigation within the preceding six months and furnished a report thereon to the court, the court may order, upon good cause shown, that another investigation is not necessary or that a more limited investigation may be performed.

(q) Any investigation by the court investigator related to a temporary conservatorship also may be a part of the investigation for the general petition for conservatorship, but the court investigator shall make a second visit to the proposed conservatee and the report required by this section shall include the effect of the temporary conservatorship on the proposed conservatee.

(r) The Judicial Council shall, on or before January 1, 2009, adopt rules of court and Judicial Council forms as necessary to implement an expedited procedure to authorize, by court order, a proposed conservatee's health care provider to disclose confidential medical information about the proposed conservatee to a court investigator pursuant to federal medical information privacy regulations promulgated under the Health Insurance Portability and Accountability Act of 1996.

(s) A superior court shall not be required to perform any duties imposed pursuant to the amendments to this section enacted by Chapter 493 of the Statutes 2006 until the Legislature makes an appropriation identified for this purpose.

1827. The court shall hear and determine the matter of the establishment of the conservatorship according to the law and procedure relating to the trial of civil actions, including trial by jury if demanded by the proposed conservatee.

1827.5. (a) In the case of any proceeding to establish a limited conservatorship for a person with developmental disabilities, within 30 days after the filing of a petition for limited conservatorship, a proposed limited conservatee, with his or her consent, shall be assessed at a regional center as provided in Chapter 5 (commencing with Section 4620) of Division 4.5 of the Welfare and Institutions Code. The regional center shall submit a written report of its findings and recommendations to the court.

(b) In the case of any proceeding to establish a general conservatorship for a person with developmental disabilities, the regional center, with the consent of the proposed conservatee, may prepare an assessment as provided in Chapter 5 (commencing with Section 4620) of Division 4.5 of the Welfare and Institutions Code. If an assessment is prepared, the regional center shall submit its findings and recommendations to the court.

(c) A report prepared under subdivision (a) or (b) shall include a description of the specific areas, nature, and degree of disability of the proposed conservatee or proposed limited conservatee. The findings and recommendations of the regional center are not binding upon the court.

In a proceeding where the petitioner is a provider of board and care, treatment, habilitation, or other services to persons with developmental disabilities or a spouse or employee of a provider, is not the natural parent of the proposed conservatee or proposed limited conservatee, and is not a public entity, the regional center shall include a recommendation in its report concerning the suitability of the petitioners to meet the needs of the proposed conservatee or proposed limited conservatee.

(d) At least five days before the hearing on the petition, the regional center shall mail a copy of the report referred to in subdivision (a) to all of the following:

(1) The proposed limited conservatee.

(2) The attorney, if any, for the proposed limited conservatee.

(3) If the petitioner is not the proposed limited conservatee, the attorney for the petitioner or the petitioner if the petitioner does not have an attorney.

(4) Such other persons as the court orders.

(e) The report referred to in subdivisions (a) and (b) shall be confidential and shall be made available only to parties listed in subdivision (d) unless the court, in its discretion, determines that the release of the report would serve the interests of the conservatee who is developmentally disabled. The clerk of the court shall make provision for limiting disclosure of the report exclusively to persons entitled thereto under this section.

1828. (a) Except as provided in subdivision (c), prior to the establishment of a conservatorship of the person or estate, or both, the court shall inform the proposed conservatee of all of the following:

(1) The nature and purpose of the proceeding.

(2) The establishment of a conservatorship is a legal adjudication of the conservatee's inability properly to provide for the conservatee's personal needs or to manage the conservatee's own financial resources, or both, depending on the allegations made and the determinations requested in the petition, and the effect of such an adjudication on the conservatee's basic rights.

(3) The proposed conservatee may be disqualified from voting if not capable of completing an affidavit of voter registration.

(4) The identity of the proposed conservator.

(5) The nature and effect on the conservatee's basic rights of any order requested under Chapter 4 (commencing with Section 1870), and in the case of an allegedly developmentally disabled adult, the specific effects of each limitation requested in such order.

(6) The proposed conservatee has the right to oppose the proceeding, to have the matter of the establishment of the conservatorship tried by jury, to be represented by legal counsel if the proposed conservatee so chooses, and to have legal counsel appointed by the court if unable to retain legal counsel.

(b) After the court so informs the proposed conservatee and prior to the establishment of the conservatorship, the court shall consult the proposed conservatee to determine the proposed conservatee's opinion concerning all of the following:

(1) The establishment of the conservatorship.

(2) The appointment of the proposed conservator.

(3) Any order requested under Chapter 4 (commencing with Section 1870), and in the case of an allegedly developmentally disabled adult, of each limitation requested in such order.

(c) This section does not apply where both of the following conditions are satisfied:

(1) The proposed conservatee is absent from the hearing and is not required to attend the hearing under the provisions of subdivision (a) of Section 1825.

(2) Any showing required by Section 1825 has been made.

1828.5. (a) At the hearing on the petition for appointment of a limited conservator for an allegedly developmentally disabled adult, the court shall do each of the following:

(1) Inquire into the nature and extent of the general intellectual functioning of the individual alleged to be developmentally disabled.

(2) Evaluate the extent of the impairment of his or her adaptive behavior.

(3) Ascertain his or her capacity to care for himself or herself and his or her property.

(4) Inquire into the qualifications, abilities, and capabilities of the person seeking appointment as limited conservator.

(5) If a report by the regional center, in accordance with Section 1827.5, has not been filed in court because the proposed limited conservatee withheld his or her consent to assessment by the regional center, the court shall determine the reason for withholding such consent.

(b) If the court finds that the proposed limited conservatee possesses the capacity to care for himself or herself and to manage his or her property as a reasonably prudent person, the court shall dismiss the petition for appointment of a limited conservator.

(c) If the court finds that the proposed limited conservatee lacks the capacity to perform some, but not all, of the tasks necessary to provide properly for his or her own personal needs for physical health, food, clothing, or shelter, or to manage his or her own financial resources, the court shall appoint a limited conservator for the person or the estate or the person and the estate.

(d) If the court finds that the proposed limited conservatee lacks the capacity to perform all of the tasks necessary to provide properly for his or her own personal needs for physical health, food, clothing, or shelter, or to manage his or her own financial resources, the court shall appoint either a conservator or a limited conservator for the person or the estate, or the person and the estate.

(e) The court shall define the powers and duties of the limited conservator so as to permit the developmentally disabled adult to care for himself or herself or to manage his or her financial resources commensurate with his or her ability to do so.

(f) Prior to the appointment of a limited conservator for the person or estate or person and estate of a developmentally disabled adult, the court shall inform the proposed limited conservatee of the nature and purpose of the limited conservatorship proceeding, that the appointment of a limited conservator for his or her person or estate or person and estate will result in the transfer of certain rights set forth in the petition and the effect of such transfer, the identity of the person who has been nominated as his or her limited conservator, that he or she has a right to oppose such proceeding, and that he or she has a right to have the matter tried by jury. After communicating such information to the person and prior to the appointment of a limited conservator, the court shall consult the person to determine his or her opinion concerning the appointment.

1829. Any of the following persons may appear at the hearing to support or oppose the petition:

(a) The proposed conservatee.

(b) The spouse or registered domestic partner of the proposed conservatee.

(c) A relative of the proposed conservatee.

(d) Any interested person or friend of the proposed conservatee.

1830. (a) The order appointing the conservator shall contain, among other things, the names, addresses, and telephone numbers of:

(1) The conservator.

(2) The conservatee's attorney, if any.

(3) The court investigator, if any.

(b) In the case of a limited conservator for a developmentally disabled adult, any order the court may make shall include the findings of the court specified in Section 1828.5. The order shall specify the powers granted to and duties imposed upon the limited conservator, which powers and duties may not exceed the powers and duties applicable to a conservator under this code. The order shall also specify the following:

(1) The properties of the limited conservatee to which the limited conservator is entitled to possession and management, giving a description of the properties that will be sufficient to identify them.

(2) The debts, rentals, wages, or other claims due to the limited conservatee which the limited conservator is entitled to collect, or file suit with respect to, if necessary, and thereafter to possess and manage.

(3) The contractual or other obligations which the limited conservator may incur on behalf of the limited conservatee.

(4) The claims against the limited conservatee which the limited conservator may pay, compromise, or defend, if necessary.

(5) Any other powers, limitations, or duties with respect to the care of the limited conservatee or the management of the property specified in this subdivision by the limited conservator which the court shall specifically and expressly grant.

(c) An information notice of the rights of conservatees shall be attached to the order. The conservator shall mail the order and the attached information notice to the conservatee and the conservatee's relatives, as set forth in subdivision (b) of Section 1821, within 30 days of the issuance of the order. By January 1, 2008, the Judicial Council shall develop the notice required by this subdivision.

1834. (a) Before letters are issued, the conservator (other than a trust company or a public conservator) shall file an acknowledgment of receipt of (1) a statement of duties and liabilities of the office of conservator, and (2) a copy of the conservatorship information required under Section 1835. The acknowledgment and the statement shall be in the form prescribed by the Judicial Council.

(b) The court may by local rules require the acknowledgment of receipt to include the conservator's birth date and driver's license number, if any, provided that the court ensures their confidentiality.

(c) The statement of duties and liabilities prescribed by the Judicial Council shall not supersede the law on which the statement is based.

1835. (a) Every superior court shall provide all private conservators with written information concerning a conservator's rights, duties, limitations, and responsibilities under this division.

(b) The information to be provided shall include, but need not be limited to, the following:

(1) The rights, duties, limitations, and responsibilities of a conservator.

(2) The rights of a conservatee.

(3) How to assess the needs of the conservatee.

(4) How to use community-based services to meet the needs of the conservatee.

(5) How to ensure that the conservatee is provided with the least restrictive possible environment.

(6) The court procedures and processes relevant to conservatorships.

(7) The procedures for inventory and appraisal, and the filing of accounts.

(c) An information package shall be developed by the Judicial Council, after consultation with the following organizations or individuals:

(1) The California State Association of Public Administrators, Public Guardians, and Public Conservators, or other comparable organizations.

(2) The State Bar.

(3) Individuals or organizations, approved by the Judicial Council, who represent court investigators, specialists with experience in performing assessments and coordinating community-based services, and legal services programs for the elderly.

(d) The failure of any court or any employee or agent thereof, to provide information to a conservator as required by this section does not:

(1) Relieve the conservator of any of the conservator's duties as required by this division.

(2) Make the court or the employee or agent thereof, liable, in either a personal or official capacity, for damages to a conservatee, conservator, the conservatorship of a person or an estate, or any other person or entity.

(e) The information package shall be made available to individual courts. The Judicial Council shall periodically update the information package when changes in the law warrant revision. The revisions shall be provided to individual courts.

(f) To cover the costs of providing the written information required by this section, a court may charge each private conservator a fee of twenty dollars ($20) which shall be distributed to the court in which it was collected.

Article 4. Special Provisions Applicable Where Proposed Conservatee Is An Absentee

1840. Except as otherwise provided in this article, a conservator for an absentee (Section 1403) shall be appointed as provided in Article 3 (commencing with Section 1820).

1841. In addition to the other required contents of the petition, if the proposed conservatee is an absentee:

(a) The petition, and any notice required by Section 1822 or any other law, shall set forth the last known military rank or grade and the social security account number of the proposed conservatee.

(b) The petition shall state whether the absentee's spouse has commenced any action or proceeding against the absentee for judicial or legal separation, dissolution of marriage, annulment, or adjudication of nullity of their marriage.

1842. In addition to the persons and entities to whom notice of hearing is required under Section 1822, if the proposed conservatee is an absentee, a copy of the petition

and notice of the time and place of the hearing shall be mailed at least 15 days before the hearing to the secretary concerned or to the head of the United States department or agency concerned, as the case may be. In such case, notice shall also be published pursuant to Section 6061 of the Government Code in a newspaper of general circulation in the county in which the hearing will be held.

1843. No citation is required under Section 1823 to the proposed conservatee if the proposed conservatee is an absentee.

1844. (a) An official written report or record complying with Section 1283 of the Evidence Code that a proposed conservatee is an absentee shall be received as evidence of that fact and the court shall not determine the status of the proposed conservatee inconsistent with the status determined as shown by the written report or record.

(b) The inability of the proposed conservatee to attend the hearing is established by the official written report or record referred to in subdivision (a).

Article 5. Special Provisions Applicable Where Proposed Conservatee Is A Missing Person

1845. (a) Except as otherwise provided in this article, a conservator of the estate of a person who is missing and whose whereabouts is unknown shall be appointed as provided in Article 3 (commencing with Section 1820).

(b) This article does not apply where the proposed conservatee is an absentee as defined in Section 1403.

1846. In addition to the other required contents of the petition, if the proposed conservatee is a person who is missing and whose whereabouts is unknown, the petition shall state all of the following:

(a) The proposed conservatee owns or is entitled to the possession of real or personal property located in this state.

(b) The time and circumstance of the person's disappearance and that the missing person has not been heard from by the persons most likely to hear (naming them and their relationship to the missing person) since the time of disappearance and that the whereabouts of the missing person is unknown to those persons and to the petitioner.

(c) The last known residence of the missing person.

(d) A description of any search or inquiry made concerning the whereabouts of the missing person.

(e) A description of the estate of the proposed conservatee which requires attention, supervision, and care.

1847. In addition to the persons and entities to whom notice of hearing is required under Section 1822, if the proposed conservatee is a person who is missing and whose whereabouts is unknown:

(a) A copy of the petition for appointment of a conservator and notice of the time and place of the hearing on the petition shall be mailed at least 15 days before the hearing to the proposed conservatee at the last known address of the proposed conservatee.

(b) Notice of the time and place of the hearing shall also be published pursuant to Section 6061 of the Government Code in a newspaper of general circulation in the county in which the proposed conservatee was last known to reside if the proposed conservatee's last known address is in this state.

(c) Pursuant to Section 1202, the court may require that further or additional notice of the hearing be given.

1848. In a proceeding to appoint a conservator of the estate of a person who is missing and whose whereabouts is unknown, the following acts are not required:

(a) Issuance of a citation to the proposed conservatee pursuant to Section 1823.

(b) Service of a citation and petition pursuant to Section 1824.

(c) Production of the proposed conservatee at the hearing pursuant to Section 1825.

(d) Performance of the duties of the court investigator pursuant to Section 1826.

(e) Performance of any other act that depends upon knowledge of the location of the proposed conservatee.

1849. A conservator of the estate of a person who is missing and whose whereabouts is unknown may be appointed only if the court finds all of the following:

(a) The proposed conservatee owns or is entitled to the possession of real or personal property located in this state.

(b) The proposed conservatee remains missing and his or her whereabouts remains unknown.

(c) The estate of the proposed conservatee requires attention, supervision, and care.

1849.5. (a) A petition may be filed under this article regardless of when the proposed conservatee became missing or how long the proposed conservatee has been missing.

(b) If a trustee was appointed pursuant to former Section 262, repealed by Chapter 201 of the Statutes of 1983, the provisions of former Sections 260 to 272, inclusive, repealed by Chapter 201 of the Statutes of 1983, continue to apply to the case after December 31, 1983, unless, upon a petition filed under this article after December 31, 1983, the trustee is replaced by a conservator.

Chapter 2. Periodic Review Of Conservatorship

1850. (a) Except as provided in subdivision (b), each conservatorship initiated pursuant to this part shall be reviewed by the court as follows:

(1) At the expiration of six months after the initial appointment of the conservator, the court investigator shall visit the conservatee, conduct an investigation in accordance with the provisions of subdivision (a) of Section 1851, and report to the court regarding the appropriateness of the conservatorship and whether the conservator is acting in the best interests of the conservatee regarding the conservatee's placement, quality of care, including physical and mental treatment, and finances. The court may, in response to the investigator's report, take appropriate action including, but not limited to:

(A) Ordering a review of the conservatorship pursuant to subdivision (b).

(B) Ordering the conservator to submit an accounting pursuant to subdivision (a) of Section 2620.

(2) One year after the appointment of the conservator and annually thereafter. However, at the review that occurs one year after the appointment of the conservator, and every subsequent review conducted pursuant to this paragraph, the court may set the next review in two years if the court determines that the conservator is acting in the best interest interests of the conservatee. In these cases, the court shall require the investigator to conduct an investigation pursuant to subdivision (a) of Section 1851 one year before the next review and file a status report in the conservatee's court file regarding whether the conservatorship still appears to be warranted and whether the conservator is acting in the best interests of the conservatee. If the investigator determines pursuant to this investigation that the conservatorship still appears to be warranted and that the conservator is acting in the best interests of the conservatee regarding the conservatee's placement, quality of care, including physical and mental treatment, and finances, no hearing or court action in response to the investigator's report is required.

(b) The court may, on its own motion or upon request by any interested person, take appropriate action including, but not limited to, ordering a review of the conservatorship, including at a noticed hearing, and ordering the conservator to present an accounting of the assets of the estate pursuant to Section 2620.

(c) Notice of a hearing pursuant to subdivision (b) shall be provided to all persons listed in subdivision (b) of Section 1822.

(d) This chapter does not apply to either of the following:

(1) A conservatorship for an absentee as defined in Section 1403.

(2) A conservatorship of the estate for a nonresident of this state where the conservatee is not present in this state.

(e) The amendments made to this section by the act adding this subdivision shall become operative on July 1, 2007.

(f) A superior court shall not be required to perform any duties imposed pursuant to the amendments to this section enacted by

Chapter 493 of the Statutes 2006 until the Legislature makes an appropriation identified for this purpose.

1850.5. (a) Notwithstanding Section 1850, each limited conservatorship for a developmentally disabled adult, as defined in subdivision (d) of Section 1801, shall be reviewed by the court one year after the appointment of the conservator and biennially thereafter.

(b) The court may, on its own motion or upon request by any interested person, take appropriate action, including, but not limited to, ordering a review of the limited conservatorship, including at a noticed hearing, at any time.

(c) A superior court shall not be required to perform any duties imposed by this section until the Legislature makes an appropriation identified for this purpose.

1851. (a) When court review is required pursuant to Section 1850, the court investigator shall, without prior notice to the conservator except as ordered by the court for necessity or to prevent harm to the conservatee, visit the conservatee. The court investigator shall inform the conservatee personally that the conservatee is under a conservatorship and shall give the name of the conservator to the conservatee. The court investigator shall determine whether the conservatee wishes to petition the court for termination of the conservatorship, whether the conservatee is still in need of the conservatorship, whether the present conservator is acting in the best interests of the conservatee, and whether the conservatee is capable of completing an affidavit of voter registration. In determining whether the conservator is acting in the best interests of the conservatee, the court investigator's evaluation shall include an examination of the conservatee's placement, the quality of care, including physical and mental treatment, and the conservatee's finances. To the extent practicable, the investigator shall review the accounting with a conservatee who has sufficient capacity. To the greatest extent possible, the court investigator shall interview individuals set forth in subdivision (a) of Section 1826, in order to determine if the conservator is acting in the best interests of the conservatee. If the court has made an order under Chapter 4 (commencing with Section 1870), the court investigator shall determine whether the present condition of the conservatee is such that the terms of the order should be modified or the order revoked. Upon request of the court investigator, the conservator shall make available to the court investigator during the investigation for inspection and copying all books and records, including receipts and any expenditures, of the conservatorship.

(b) (1) The findings of the court investigator, including the facts upon which the findings are based, shall be certified in writing to the court not less than 15 days prior to the date of review. A copy of the report shall be mailed to the conservator and to the attorneys of record for the conservator and conservatee at the same time it is certified to the court. A copy of the report, modified as set forth in paragraph (2), also shall be mailed to the conservatee's spouse or registered domestic partner, the conservatee's relatives in the first degree, and if there are no such relatives, to the next closest relative, unless the court determines that the mailing will result in harm to the conservatee.

(2) Confidential medical information and confidential information from the California Law Enforcement Telecommunications System shall be in a separate attachment to the report and shall not be provided in copies sent to the conservatee's spouse or registered domestic partner, the conservatee's relatives in the first degree, and if there are no such relatives, to the next closest relative.

(c) In the case of a limited conservatee, the court investigator shall make a recommendation regarding the continuation or termination of the limited conservatorship.

(d) The court investigator may personally visit the conservator and other persons as may be necessary to determine whether the present conservator is acting in the best interests of the conservatee.

(e) The report required by this section shall be confidential and shall be made available only to parties, persons described in subdivision (b), persons given notice of the petition who have requested the report or who have appeared in the proceeding, their attorneys, and the court. The court shall have discretion at any other time to release the report if it would serve the interests of the conservatee. The clerk of the court shall make provision for limiting disclosure of the report exclusively to persons entitled thereto under this section.

(f) The amendments made to this section by the act adding this subdivision shall become operative on July 1, 2007.

(g) A superior court shall not be required to perform any duties imposed pursuant to the amendments to this section enacted by Chapter 493 of the Statutes 2006 until the Legislature makes an appropriation identified for this purpose.

1851.2. Each court shall coordinate investigations with the filing of accountings, so that investigators may review accountings before visiting conservatees, if feasible.

1851.5. Each court shall assess each conservatee in the county for any investigation or review conducted by a court investigator with respect to that person. The court may order reimbursement to the court for the amount of the assessment, unless the court finds that all or any part of the assessment would impose a hardship on conservatee or the conservatee's estate. There shall be a rebuttable presumption that the assessment would impose a hardship if the conservatee is receiving Medi-Cal benefits.

1852. If the conservatee wishes to petition the court for termination of the conservatorship or for removal of the existing conservator or for the making, modification, or revocation of a court order under Chapter 4 (commencing with Section 1870) or for restoration of the right to register to vote, or if, based on information contained in the court investigator's report or obtained from any other source, the court determines that a trial or hearing for termination of the conservatorship or removal of the existing conservator is in the best interests of the conservatee, the court shall notify the attorney of record for the conservatee, if any, or shall appoint the public defender or private counsel under Section 1471, to file the petition and represent the conservatee at the trial or hearing and, if such appointment is made, Section 1472 applies.

1853. (a) If the court investigator is unable to locate the conservatee, the court shall order the court investigator to serve notice upon the conservator of the person, or upon the conservator of the estate if there is no conservator of the person, in the manner provided in Section 415.10 or 415.30 of the Code of Civil Procedure or in such other manner as is ordered by the court, to make the conservatee available for the purposes of Section 1851 to the court investigator within 15 days of the receipt of such notice or to show cause why the conservatorship should not be terminated.

(b) If the conservatee is not made available within the time prescribed, unless good cause is shown for not doing so, the court shall make such a finding and shall enter judgment terminating the conservatorship and, in case of a conservatorship of the estate, shall order the conservator to file an account and to surrender the estate to the person legally entitled thereto. At the hearing, or thereafter on further notice and hearing, the conservator may be discharged and the bond given by the conservator may be exonerated upon the settlement and approval of the conservator's final account by the court.

(c) Termination of the conservatorship under this section does not preclude institution of new proceedings for the appointment of a conservator. Nothing in this section limits the power of a court to appoint a temporary conservator under Chapter 3 (commencing with Section 2250) of Part 4.

Chapter 3. Termination

1860. (a) A conservatorship continues until terminated by the death of the conservatee or by order of the court.

(b) If a conservatorship is established for the person of a married minor, the conservatorship does not terminate if the marriage is dissolved or is adjudged a nullity.

(c) This section does not apply to limited conservatorships.

1860.5. (a) A limited conservatorship continues until the authority of the conservator is terminated by one of the following:

(1) The death of the limited conservator.

(2) The death of the limited conservatee.

(3) By an order appointing a conservator of the former limited conservatee.

(4) By an order of the court stating that the limited conservatorship is no longer necessary for the limited conservatee and terminating the limited conservatorship.

(b) A petition for the termination of a limited conservatorship may be filed by any of the following:

(1) The limited conservator.

(2) The limited conservatee.

(3) Any relative or friend of the limited conservatee.

(c) The petition shall state facts showing that the limited conservatorship is no longer required.

(d) The petition shall be set for hearing and notice thereof shall be given to the persons in the same manner as provided for a petition for the appointment of a limited conservator. The limited conservator in such case, if he or she is not the petitioner or has not joined in the petition, shall be served with a notice of the time and place of the hearing accompanied by a copy of the petition at least five days prior to the hearing. Such service shall be made in the same manner provided for in Section 415.10 or 415.30 of the Code of Civil Procedure or in such other manner as may be authorized by the court. If the limited conservator cannot, with reasonable diligence, be so served with notice, the court may dispense with notice.

(e) The limited conservator or any relative or friend of the limited conservatee may appear and oppose the petition. The court shall hear and determine the matter according to the laws and procedures relating to the trial of civil actions, including trial by jury if demanded. If it is determined that the limited conservatorship is no longer required, the limited conservatorship shall cease. If the petition alleges and if it is determined that the limited conservatee is able to properly care for himself or herself and for his or her property, the court shall make such finding and enter judgment accordingly. The limited conservator may at the hearing, or thereafter on further notice and hearing, be discharged and his or her bond exonerated upon the settlement and approval of the final account by the court.

1861. (a) A petition for the termination of the conservatorship may be filed by any of the following:

(1) The conservator.

(2) The conservatee.

(3) The spouse, or domestic partner, or any relative or friend of the conservatee or other interested person.

(b) The petition shall state facts showing that the conservatorship is no longer required.

1862. Notice of the hearing on the petition shall be given for the period and in the manner provided in Chapter 3 (commencing with Section 1460) of Part 1.

1863. (a) The court shall hear and determine the matter according to the law and procedure relating to the trial of civil actions, including trial by jury if demanded by the conservatee. The conservator, the conservatee, or the spouse, or domestic partner, or any relative or friend of the conservatee or other interested person may appear and support or oppose the petition.

(b) If the court determines that the conservatorship is no longer required or that grounds for establishment of a conservatorship of the person or estate, or both, no longer exist, the court shall make this finding and shall enter judgment terminating the conservatorship accordingly.

(c) At the hearing, or thereafter on further notice and hearing, the conservator may be discharged and the bond given by the conservator may be exonerated upon the settlement and approval of the conservator's final account by the court.

(d) Termination of conservatorship does not preclude a new proceeding for appointment of a conservator on the same or other grounds.

1864. (a) In the case of the conservatorship of an absentee as defined in Section 1403, the petition to terminate the conservatorship may also be filed by any officer or agency of this state or of the United States or the authorized delegate thereof.

(b) If the petition states and the court determines that the absentee has returned to the controllable jurisdiction of the military department or civilian department or agency concerned, or is deceased, as determined under 37 United States Code, Section 556, or 5 United States Code, Section 5566, as the case may be, the court shall order the conservatorship terminated. An official written report or record of such military department or civilian department or agency that the absentee has returned to such controllable jurisdiction or is deceased shall be received as evidence of such fact.

1865. If the conservatee has been disqualified from voting pursuant to Section 2208 or 2209 of the Elections Code, upon termination of the conservatorship, the court shall notify the county elections official of the county of residence of the former conservatee that the former conservatee's right to register to vote is restored.

Chapter 4. Legal Capacity Of Conservatee

Article 1. Capacity To Bind Or Obligate Conservatorship Estate

1870. As used in this article, unless the context otherwise requires, "transaction" includes, but is not limited to, making a contract, sale, transfer, or conveyance, incurring a debt or encumbering property, making a gift, delegating a power, and waiving a right.

1871. Nothing in this article shall be construed to deny a conservatee any of the following:

(a) The right to control an allowance provided under Section 2421.

(b) The right to control wages or salary to the extent provided in Section 2601.

(c) The right to make a will.

(d) The right to enter into transactions to the extent reasonable to provide the necessaries of life to the conservatee and the spouse and minor children of the conservatee and to provide the basic living expenses, as defined in Section 297 of the Family Code, to the domestic partner of the conservatee.

1872. (a) Except as otherwise provided in this article, the appointment of a conservator of the estate is an adjudication that the conservatee lacks the legal capacity to enter into or make any transaction that binds or obligates the conservatorship estate.

(b) Except as otherwise provided in the order of the court appointing a limited conservator, the appointment does not limit the legal capacity of the limited conservatee to enter into transactions or types of transactions.

1873. (a) In the order appointing the conservator or upon a petition filed under Section 1874, the court may, by order, authorize the conservatee, subject to Section 1876, to enter into transactions or types of transactions as may be appropriate in the circumstances of the particular conservatee and conservatorship estate. The court, by order, may modify the legal capacity a conservatee would otherwise have under Section 1872 by broadening or restricting the power of the conservatee to enter into transactions or types of transactions as may be appropriate in the circumstances of the particular conservatee and conservatorship estate.

(b) In an order made under this section, the court may include limitations or conditions on the exercise of the authority granted to the conservatee as the court determines to be appropriate including, but not limited to, the following:

(1) A requirement that for specific types of transactions or for all transactions authorized by the order, the conservatee obtain prior approval of the transaction by the court or conservator before exercising the authority granted by the order.

(2) A provision that the conservator has the right to avoid any transaction made by the conservatee pursuant to the authority of the order if the transaction is not one into which a reasonably prudent person might enter.

(c) The court, in its discretion, may provide in the order that, unless extended by subsequent order of the court, the order or specific provisions of the order terminate at a time specified in the order.

(d) An order under this section continues in effect until the earliest of the following times:

(1) The time specified in the order, if any.

(2) The time the order is modified or revoked.

(3) The time the conservatorship of the estate is terminated.

(e) An order under this section may be modified or revoked upon petition filed by the conservator, conservatee, the spouse or domestic partner of the conservatee, or any relative or friend of the conservatee, or any interested person. Notice of the hearing on the petition shall be given for the period and in the manner provided in Chapter 3 (commencing with Section 1460) of Part 1.

1874. (a) After a conservator has been appointed, a petition requesting an order under Section 1873 may be filed by any of the following:

(1) The conservator.

(2) The conservatee.

(3) The spouse, domestic partner, or any relative or friend of the conservatee.

(b) Notice of the hearing on the petition shall be given for the period and in the manner provided in Chapter 3 (commencing with Section 1460) of Part 1.

1875. A transaction that affects real property of the conservatorship estate, entered into by a person acting in good faith and for a valuable consideration and without knowledge of the establishment of the conservatorship, is not affected by any provision of this article or any order made under this article unless a notice of the establishment of the conservatorship or temporary conservatorship has been recorded prior to the transaction in the county in which the property is located.

1876. The provisions of this article relating to the legal capacity of a conservatee to bind or obligate the conservatorship estate, and the provisions of any order of the court broadening such capacity, do not displace but are supplemented by general principles of law and equity relating to transactions including, but not limited to, capacity to contract, joinder or consent requirements, estoppel, fraud, misrepresentation, duress, coercion, mistake, or other validating or invalidating cause.

Article 2. Capacity To Give Informed Consent For Medical Treatment

1880. If the court determines that there is no form of medical treatment for which the conservatee has the capacity to give an informed consent, the court shall (1) adjudge that the conservatee lacks the capacity to give informed consent for medical treatment and (2) by order give the conservator of the person the powers specified in Section 2355. If an order is made under this section, the letters shall include a statement that the conservator has the powers specified in Section 2355.

1881. (a) A conservatee shall be deemed unable to give informed consent to any form of medical treatment pursuant to Section 1880 if, for all medical treatments, the conservatee is unable to respond knowingly and intelligently to queries about medical treatment or is unable to participate in a treatment decision by means of a rational thought process.

(b) In order for a court to determine that a conservatee is unable to respond knowingly and intelligently to queries about his or her medical treatment or is unable to participate in treatment decisions by means of a rational thought process, a court shall do both of the following:

(1) Determine that, for all medical treatments, the conservatee is unable to understand at least one of the following items of minimum basic medical treatment information:

(A) The nature and seriousness of any illness, disorder, or defect that the conservatee has or may develop.

(B) The nature of any medical treatment that is being or may be recommended by the conservatee's health care providers.

(C) The probable degree and duration of any benefits and risks of any medical intervention that is being or may be recommended by the conservatee's health care providers, and the consequences of lack of treatment.

(D) The nature, risks, and benefits of any reasonable alternatives.

(2) Determine that one or more of the mental functions of the conservatee described in subdivision (a) of Section 811 is impaired and that there is a link between the deficit or deficits and the conservatee's inability to give informed consent.

(c) A deficit in the mental functions listed in subdivision (a) of Section 811 may be considered only if the deficit by itself, or in combination with one or more other mental function deficits, significantly impairs the conservatee's ability to understand the consequences of his or her decisions regarding medical care.

(d) In determining whether a conservatee's mental functioning is so severely impaired that the conservatee lacks the capacity to give informed consent to any form of medical treatment, the court may take into consideration the frequency, severity, and duration of periods of impairment.

(e) In the interest of minimizing unnecessary expense to the parties to a proceeding, paragraph (2) of subdivision (b) shall not apply to a petition pursuant to Section 1880 wherein the conservatee, after notice by the court of his or her right to object which, at least, shall include an interview by a court investigator pursuant to Section 1826 prior to the hearing on the petition, does not object to the proposed finding of incapacity, or waives any objections.

1890. (a) An order of the court under Section 1880 may be included in the order of appointment of the conservator if the order was requested in the petition for the appointment of the conservator or, except in the case of a limited conservator, may be made subsequently upon a petition made, noticed, and heard by the court in the manner provided in this article.

(b) In the case of a petition filed under this chapter requesting that the court make an order under this chapter or that the court modify or revoke an order made under this chapter, when the order applies to a limited conservatee, the order may only be made upon a petition made, noticed, and heard by the court in the manner provided by Article 3 (commencing with Section 1820) of Chapter 1.

(c) No court order under Section 1880, whether issued as part of an order granting the original petition for appointment of a conservator or issued subsequent thereto, may be granted unless supported by a declaration, filed at or before the hearing on the request, executed by a licensed physician, or a licensed psychologist within the scope of his or her licensure, and stating that the proposed conservatee or the conservatee, as the case may be, lacks the capacity to give an informed consent for any form of medical treatment and the reasons therefor. Nothing in this section shall be construed to expand the scope of practice of psychologists as set forth in the Business and Professions Code.

1891. (a) A petition may be filed under this article requesting that the court make an order under Section 1880 or that the court modify or revoke an order made under Section 1880. The petition shall state facts showing that the order requested is appropriate.

(b) The petition may be filed by any of the following:

(1) The conservator.

(2) The conservatee.

(3) The spouse, domestic partner, or any relative or friend of the conservatee.

(c) The petition shall set forth, so far as they are known to the petitioner, the names and addresses of the spouse or domestic partner and of the relatives of the conservatee within the second degree.

1892. Notice of the hearing on the petition shall be given for the period and in the manner provided in Chapter 3 (commencing with Section 1460) of Part 1.

1893. The conservatee shall be produced at the hearing except in the following cases:

(a) Where the conservatee is out of state when served and is not the petitioner.

(b) Where the conservatee is unable to attend the hearing by reason of medical inability established (1) by the affidavit or certificate of a licensed medical practitioner or (2) if the conservatee is an adherent of a religion whose tenets and practices call for reliance on prayer alone for healing and is under treatment by an accredited practitioner of that religion, by the affidavit of the practitioner. The affidavit or certificate is evidence only of the conservatee's inability to attend the hearing and shall not be considered in determining the issue of the legal capacity of the conservatee. Emotional or psychological instability is not good cause for the absence of the conservatee from the hearing unless, by reason of such instability, attendance at the hearing is likely to cause serious and immediate physiological damage to the conservatee.

(c) Where the court investigator has reported to the court that the conservatee has expressly communicated that the conservatee (1) is not willing to attend the hearing and (2) does not wish to contest the petition, and the court makes an order that the conservatee need not attend the hearing.

1894. If the petition alleges that the conservatee is not willing to attend the hearing or upon receipt of an affidavit or certificate attesting to the medical inability of the conservatee to attend the hearing, the court investigator shall do all of the following:

(a) Interview the conservatee personally.

(b) Inform the conservatee of the contents of the petition, of the nature, purpose, and effect of the proceeding, and of the right of the conservatee to oppose the petition, attend the hearing, and be represented by legal counsel.

(c) Determine whether it appears that the conservatee is unable to attend the hearing and, if able to attend, whether the conservatee is willing to attend the hearing.

(d) Determine whether the conservatee wishes to contest the petition.

(e) Determine whether the conservatee wishes to be represented by legal counsel and, if so, whether the conservatee has retained legal counsel and, if not, the name of an attorney the conservatee wishes to retain.

(f) If the conservatee has not retained counsel, determine whether the conservatee desires the court to appoint legal counsel.

(g) Determine whether the appointment of legal counsel would be helpful to the resolution of the matter or is necessary to protect the interests of the conservatee in any case where the conservatee does not plan to retain legal counsel and has not requested the court to appoint legal counsel.

(h) Report to the court in writing, at least five days before the hearing, concerning all of the foregoing, including the conservatee's express communications concerning both (1) representation by legal counsel and (2) whether the conservatee is not willing to attend the hearing and does not wish to contest the petition.

1895. (a) The conservatee, the spouse, the domestic partner, any relative, or any friend of the conservatee, the conservator, or any other interested person may appear at the hearing to support or oppose the petition.

(b) Except where the conservatee is absent from the hearing and is not required to attend the hearing under the provisions of Section 1893 and any showing required by Section 1893 has been made, the court shall, prior to granting the petition, inform the conservatee of all of the following:

(1) The nature and purpose of the proceeding.

(2) The nature and effect on the conservatee's basic rights of the order requested.

(3) The conservatee has the right to oppose the petition, to be represented by legal counsel if the conservatee so chooses, and to have legal counsel appointed by the court if unable to retain legal counsel.

(c) After the court informs the conservatee of the matters listed in subdivision (b) and prior to granting the petition, the court shall consult the conservatee to determine the conservatee's opinion concerning the order requested in the petition.

1896. (a) If the court determines that the order requested in the petition is proper, the court shall make the order.

(b) The court, in its discretion, may provide in the order that, unless extended by subsequent order of the court, the order or specific provisions of the order terminate at a time specified in the order.

1897. An order of the court under Section 1880 continues in effect until the earliest of the following times:

(1) The time specified in the order, if any.

(2) The time the order is modified or revoked.

(3) The time the conservatorship is terminated.

1898. An order of the court under Section 1880 may be modified or revoked upon a petition made, noticed, and heard by the court in the manner provided in this article.

Article 3. Capacity Of Conservatee To Marry

1900. The appointment of a conservator of the person or estate or both does not affect the capacity of the conservatee to marry or to enter into a registered domestic partnership.

1901. (a) The court may by order determine whether the conservatee has the capacity to enter into a valid marriage, as provided in Part 1 (commencing with Section 300) of Division 3 of the Family Code, or to enter into a registered domestic partnership, as provided in Section 297 of the Family Code, at the time the order is made.

(b) A petition for an order under this section may be filed by the conservator of the person or estate or both, the conservatee, any relative or friend of the conservatee, or any interested person.

(c) Notice of the hearing on the petition shall be given for the period and in the manner provided in Chapter 3 (commencing with Section 1460) of Part 1.

Chapter 5. Disqualification From Voting

1910. If the court determines the conservatee is not capable of completing an affidavit of voter registration in accordance with Section 2150 of the Elections Code, the court shall by order disqualify the conservatee from voting pursuant to Section 2208 or 2209 of the Elections Code.

Chapter 6. Sterilization

1950. The Legislature recognizes that the right to exercise choice over matters of procreation is fundamental and may not be denied to an individual on the basis of disability. This chapter is enacted for the benefit of those persons with developmental disabilities who, despite those disabilities, are capable of engaging in sexual activity yet who, because of those disabilities, are unable to give the informed, voluntary consent necessary to their fully exercising the right to procreative choice, which includes the right to choose sterilization.

However, the Legislature further recognizes that the power to sterilize is subject to abuse and, historically, has been abused. It is the intent of the Legislature that no individual shall be sterilized solely by reason of a developmental disability and that no individual who knowingly opposes sterilization be sterilized involuntarily. It is further the intent of the Legislature that this chapter shall be applied in accord with the overall intent of Division 4.5 (commencing with Section 4500) of the Welfare and Institutions Code that persons with developmental disabilities be provided with those services needed to enable them to live more normal, independent, and productive lives, including assistance and training that might obviate the need for sterilization.

1951. (a) No person who has the ability to consent to his or her sterilization shall be sterilized pursuant to this chapter.

(b) For the purposes of this chapter, the following terms have the meanings given:

(1) "Consent to sterilization" means making a voluntary decision to undergo steril-

ization after being fully informed about, and after fully understanding the nature and consequences of, sterilization.

(2) "Voluntary" means performed while competent to make the decision, and as a matter of free choice and will and not in response to coercion, duress, or undue influence.

(3) "Fully understanding the nature and consequences of sterilization," includes, but is not limited to, the ability to understand each of the following:

(A) That the individual is free to withhold or withdraw consent to the procedure at any time before the sterilization without affecting the right to future care or treatment and without loss or withdrawal of any publicly funded program benefits to which the individual might be otherwise entitled.

(B) Available alternative methods of family planning and birth control.

(C) That the sterilization procedure is considered to be irreversible.

(D) The specific sterilization procedure to be performed.

(E) The discomforts and risks that may accompany or follow the performing of the procedure, including an explanation of the type and possible effects of any anesthetic to be used.

(F) The benefits or advantages that may be expected as a result of the sterilization.

(G) The approximate length of the hospital stay.

(H) The approximate length of time for recovery.

(c) The court shall appoint a facilitator or interpreter if such a person's assistance would enable the person named in the petition to understand any of these factors.

1952. The conservator of an adult, or any person authorized to file a petition for the appointment of a conservator under paragraphs (2) to (5), inclusive, of subdivision (a) of Section 1820, may file a petition under this chapter for appointment of a limited conservator authorized to consent to the sterilization of an adult with a developmental disability. The content of the petition under this chapter shall conform to the provisions of Section 1821 and in addition allege that the person for whom sterilization is proposed has a developmental disability as defined in Section 1420 and shall allege specific reasons why court-authorized sterilization is deemed necessary. A petition under this chapter shall be considered separately from any contemporaneous petition for appointment of a conservator under this division.

1953. At least 90 days before the hearing on the petition under this chapter, notice of the time and place of the hearing and a copy of the petition shall be served on the person named in the petition and, if the petitioner is not the conservator of the person, on the conservator, if any. Service shall be made in the manner provided in Section 415.10 or Section 415.30 of the Code of Civil Procedure or in such manner as may be authorized by the court.

1954. In any proceeding under this chapter, if the person named in the petition for court authorization to consent to sterilization has not retained legal counsel and does not plan to retain legal counsel, the court shall immediately appoint the public defender or private counsel to represent the individual for whom sterilization is proposed. Counsel shall undertake the representation with the presumption that the individual opposes the petition.

1954.5. (a) The court shall appoint a facilitator for the person named in the petition, who shall assist the person named in the petition to do all of the following:

(1) Understand the nature of the proceedings.

(2) Understand the evaluation process required by Section 1955.

(3) Communicate his or her views.

(4) Participate as fully as possible in the proceedings.

(b) All of the following factors shall be considered by the court in appointing a facilitator:

(1) The preference of the person named in the petition.

(2) The proposed facilitator's personal knowledge of the person named in the petition.

(3) The proposed facilitator's ability to communicate with the person named in the petition, when that person is nonverbal, has limited verbal skills, or relies on alternative modes of communication.

(4) The proposed facilitator's knowledge of the developmental disabilities service system.

(c) The petitioner may not be appointed as the facilitator.

1955. (a) The court shall request the director of the appropriate regional center for the developmentally disabled to coordinate an investigation and prepare and file a written report thereon. The appropriate regional center for purposes of this section is (1) the regional center of which the person named in the petition is a client, (2) if the individual named in the petition is not a client of any regional center, the regional center responsible for the area in which the individual is then living, or (3) such other regional center as may be in the best interests of the individual. The report shall be based upon comprehensive medical, psychological, and sociosexual evaluations of the individual conducted pursuant to subdivisions (b) and (c), and shall address, but shall not be limited to, each of the factors listed in Section 1958. A copy of the report shall be provided to each of the parties at least 15 days prior to the hearing.

(b) Prior to the hearing on the issue of

sterilization, the person who is proposed to be sterilized shall be personally examined by two physicians, one of whom shall be a surgeon competent to perform the procedure, and one psychologist or clinical social worker, each of whom has been mutually agreed to by the petitioner and counsel for the person named in the petition or, if agreement is not reached, appointed by the court from a panel of qualified professionals. At the request of counsel for the person named in the petition, the court shall appoint one additional psychologist, clinical social worker, or physician named by counsel. Any psychologist or clinical social worker and, to the extent feasible, any physicians conducting an examination shall have had experience with persons who have developmental disabilities. To the extent feasible, each of the examiners shall also have knowledge and experience relating to sociosexual skills and behavior. The examinations shall be at county expense subject to Section 1963.

(c) The examiners shall consider all available alternatives to sterilization and shall recommend sterilization only if no suitable alternative is available. Each examiner shall prepare a written, comprehensive report containing all relevant aspects of the person's medical, psychological, family, and sociosexual conditions. Each examiner shall address those factors specified in Section 1958 related to his or her particular area of expertise. In considering the factors in subdivision (a) of, and paragraph (1) of subdivision (d) of, Section 1958, each examiner shall include information regarding the intensity, extent, and recentness of the person's education and training, if any, regarding human sexuality, including birth control methods and parenting skills, and in addition, shall consider whether the individual would benefit from training provided by persons competent in education and training of persons with comparable intellectual impairments. If an examiner recommends against sterilization, the examiner shall set forth in his or her report available alternatives, including, as warranted, recommendations for sex education, parent training, or training in the use of alternative methods of contraception. Copies of each report shall be furnished at least 30 days prior to the hearing on the petition to the person or persons who filed the petition, the conservator, if any, and counsel for the person proposed to be sterilized, the regional center responsible for the investigation and report required under this section, and such other persons as the court may direct. The court may receive these reports in evidence.

(d) The contents of the reports prepared pursuant to this section shall be confidential. Upon judgment in the action or the proceeding becoming final, the court shall order the contents of the reports sealed.

(e) Regional centers for the developmentally disabled shall compile and maintain lists of persons competent to perform the examinations required by this section. These lists shall be provided to the court. If the person named in the petition resides at a state hospital or other residential care facility, no person conducting an examination pursuant to subdivision (b) shall be an employee of the facility.

(f) Any party to the proceedings has the right to submit additional reports from qualified experts.

(g) Any person who has written a report received in evidence may be subpoenaed and questioned by any party to the proceedings or by the court and when so called is subject to all rules of evidence including those of legal objections as to the qualification of expert witnesses.

(h) No regional center or person acting in his or her capacity as a regional center employee may file a petition under Section 1952.

1956. The person to whom the petition applies shall be present at the hearing except for reason of medical inability. Emotional or psychological instability is not good cause for the absence of the proposed conservatee from the hearing unless, by reason of the instability, attendance at the hearing is likely to cause serious and immediate physiological damage to the proposed conservatee.

1957. To the greatest extent possible, the court shall elicit and take into account the views of the individual for whom sterilization is proposed in determining whether sterilization is to be authorized.

1958. The court may authorize the conservator of a person proposed to be sterilized to consent to the sterilization of that person only if the court finds that the petitioner has established all of the following beyond a reasonable doubt:

(a) The person named in the petition is incapable of giving consent to sterilization, as defined in Section 1951, and the incapacity is in all likelihood permanent.

(b) Based on reasonable medical evidence, the individual is fertile and capable of procreation.

(c) The individual is capable of engaging in, and is likely to engage in sexual activity at the present or in the near future under circumstances likely to result in pregnancy.

(d) Either of the following:

(1) The nature and extent of the individual's disability as determined by empirical evidence and not solely on the basis of any standardized test, renders him or her permanently incapable of caring for a child, even with appropriate training and reasonable assistance.

(2) Due to a medical condition, pregnancy or childbirth would pose a substantially elevated risk to the life of the individual to such a degree that, in the absence of other appropriate methods of contraception, sterilization would be deemed medically neces-

sary for an otherwise nondisabled woman under similar circumstances.

(e) All less invasive contraceptive methods including supervision are unworkable even with training and assistance, inapplicable, or medically contraindicated. Isolation and segregation shall not be considered as less invasive means of contraception.

(f) The proposed method of sterilization entails the least invasion of the body of the individual.

(g) The current state of scientific and medical knowledge does not suggest either (1) that a reversible sterilization procedure or other less drastic contraceptive method will shortly be available, or (2) that science is on the threshold of an advance in the treatment of the individual's disability.

(h) The person named in the petition has not made a knowing objection to his or her sterilization. For purposes of this subdivision, an individual may be found to have knowingly objected to his or her sterilization notwithstanding his or her inability to give consent to sterilization as defined in Section 1951. In the case of persons who are nonverbal, have limited verbal ability to communicate, or who rely on alternative modes of communication, the court shall ensure that adequate effort has been made to elicit the actual views of the individual by the facilitator appointed pursuant to Section 1954.5, or by any other person with experience in communicating with developmentally disabled persons who communicate using similar means.

1959. The fact that, due to the nature or severity of his or her disability, a person for whom an authorization to consent to sterilization is sought may be vulnerable to sexual conduct by others that would be deemed unlawful, shall not be considered by the court in determining whether sterilization is to be authorized under this chapter.

1960. If the person named in the petition already has a conservator, the court may authorize that person to consent to sterilization or may appoint another person as limited conservator under the provisions of this chapter. The court shall ensure that the person or agency designated as conservator under this chapter is capable of adequately representing and safeguarding the interests of the conservatee.

1961. A sterilization procedure authorized under this chapter shall not include hysterectomy or castration. However, if the report prepared under Section 1955 indicates that hysterectomy or castration is a medically necessary treatment, regardless of the need for sterilization, the court shall proceed pursuant to Section 2357.

1962. (a) Any court order granting a petition under this chapter shall be accompanied by a written statement of decision pursuant to Section 632 of the Code of Civil Procedure detailing the factual and legal bases for the court's determination on each of the findings required under Section 1958.

(b) When a judgment authorizing the conservator of a person to consent to the sterilization is rendered, an appeal is automatically taken by the person proposed to be sterilized without any action by that person, or by his or her counsel. The Judicial Council shall provide by rule for notice of and procedure for the appeal. The appeal shall have precedence over other cases in the court in which the appeal is pending.

1963. (a) At the conclusion of the hearing, the court, after inquiring into financial ability, may make an order based upon their ability that any one or more of the following persons pay court costs and fees in whole or in part as in the opinion of the court is proper and in any installments and manner which is both reasonable and compatible with ability to pay:

(1) The person to whom the petition applies.

(2) The petitioner.

(3) Any person liable for the support and maintenance of the person to whom the petition applies.

(b) An order under subdivision (a) may be enforced in the same manner as a money judgment.

(c) For the purposes of this section, court costs and fees include the costs of any examination or investigation ordered by the court, expert witnesses' fees, and the costs and fees of the court-appointed public defender or private counsel representing the person to whom the petition applies.

(d) Any fees and costs not ordered to be paid by persons under subdivision (a) are a charge against and paid out of the treasury of the county on order of the court.

1964. An order of the court authorizing a conservator to consent to sterilization which is upheld on appeal automatically expires in one year from the final determination on appeal unless earlier terminated by the court. A conservatorship established for the sole purpose of authorizing a conservator to consent to sterilization under this chapter shall automatically terminate upon completion of the sterilization procedure or upon expiration of the court's order authorizing the conservator to consent to sterilization, whichever occurs first. If, upon the expiration of the court's order under this chapter, the person named as conservator determines that the conservatorship is still required for the purpose of this chapter, he or she may petition the court for reappointment as conservator for a succeeding six-month period upon a showing of good cause as to why any sterilization authorized by the court has not been completed.

1965. Any court order made pursuant to this chapter granting authority to consent to sterilization shall be stayed pending a final determination on appeal.

1966. After the filing of a first petition for sterilization pursuant to this chapter and a determination by the court that any one or more of the conditions required in Section 1958 has not been proven beyond a reasonable doubt, and that therefore authorization for the proposed sterilization should not be given by the court, a subsequent petition may be filed only on the showing of a material change in circumstances.

1967. (a) The sterilization of a person in accordance with this chapter does not render the petitioner or any person participating in the conservatorship proceedings or sterilization liable, either civilly or criminally, except for any injury caused by negligent or willful misconduct in the performance of the sterilization.

(b) Notwithstanding the provisions of subdivision (a), any individual who petitions for authorization to consent to sterilization knowing that the person to whom the petition relates is capable of giving consent to sterilization as defined in Section 1951 is guilty of a misdemeanor, and may be civilly liable to the person concerning whom sterilization was sought.

1968. This chapter does not prohibit medical treatment or surgery required for other medical reasons and in which sterilization is an unavoidable or medically probable consequence, but is not the object of the treatment or surgery.

1969. Nothing in this chapter shall infringe on the right of persons with developmental disabilities who are capable of giving consent to sterilization to give that consent without the necessity of a court order or substitute decisionmaker.

Chapter 7. Unwarranted Petitions

1970. (a) The Legislature finds that unwarranted petitions, applications, or motions other than discovery motions after a conservatorship has been established create an environment that can be harmful to the conservatee and are inconsistent with the goal of protecting the conservatee.

(b) Notwithstanding Section 391 of the Code of Civil Procedure, if a person other than the conservatee files a petition for termination of the conservatorship, or instruction to the conservator, that is unmeritorious or intended to harass or annoy the conservator, and the person has previously filed pleadings in the conservatorship proceedings that were unmeritorious or intended to harass or annoy the conservator, the petition shall be grounds for the court to determine that the person is a vexatious litigant for the purposes of Title 3A (commencing with Section 391) of Part 2 of the Code of Civil Procedure. For these purposes, the term "new litigation" shall include petitions for visitation, termination of the conservatorship, or instruction to the conservator.

Part 4. Provisions Common To Guardianship And Conservatorship

Chapter 1. General Provisions

2100. Guardianships and conservatorships are governed by Division 3 (commencing with Section 1000), except to the extent otherwise expressly provided by statute, and by this division. If no specific provision of this division is applicable, the provisions applicable to administration of estates of decedents govern so far as they are applicable to like situations.

2101. The relationship of guardian and ward and of conservator and conservatee is a fiduciary relationship that is governed by the law of trusts, except as provided in this division.

2102. A guardian or conservator is subject to the regulation and control of the court in the performance of the duties of the office.

2103. (a) When a judgment or order made pursuant to this division becomes final, it releases the guardian or conservator and the sureties from all claims of the ward or conservatee and of any persons affected thereby based upon any act or omission directly authorized, approved, or confirmed in the judgment or order. For the purposes of this section, "order" includes an order settling an account of the guardian or conservator, whether an intermediate or final account.

(b) This section does not apply where the judgment or order is obtained by fraud or conspiracy or by misrepresentation contained in the petition or account or in the judgment or order as to any material fact. For the purposes of this subdivision, misrepresentation includes, but is not limited to, the omission of a material fact.

2104. (a) A nonprofit charitable corporation may be appointed as a guardian or conservator of the person or estate, or both, if all of the following requirements are met:

(1) The corporation is incorporated in this state.

(2) The articles of incorporation specifically authorize the corporation to accept appointments as guardian or conservator, as the case may be.

(3) The corporation has been providing, at the time of appointment, care, counseling, or financial assistance to the proposed ward or conservatee under the supervision of a registered social worker certified by the Board of Behavioral Science Examiners of this state.

(b) The petition for appointment of a nonprofit charitable corporation described in this section as a guardian or conservator shall include in the caption the name of a responsible corporate officer who shall act for the corporation for the purposes of this division. If, for any reason, the officer so named ceases to act as the responsible corporate officer for the purposes of this section, the corporation shall file with the court a notice containing (1) the name of the successor responsible corporate officer and (2) the date the successor becomes the responsible corporate officer.

(c) If a nonprofit charitable corporation described in this section is appointed as a guardian or conservator:

(1) The corporation's compensation as guardian or conservator shall be allowed only for services actually rendered.

(2) Any fee allowed for an attorney for the corporation shall be for services actually rendered.

2105. (a) The court, in its discretion, may appoint for a ward or conservatee:

(1) Two or more joint guardians or conservators of the person.

(2) Two or more joint guardians or conservators of the estate.

(3) Two or more joint guardians or conservators of the person and estate.

(b) When joint guardians or conservators are appointed, each shall qualify in the same manner as a sole guardian or conservator.

(c) Subject to subdivisions (d) and (e):

(1) Where there are two guardians or conservators, both must concur to exercise a power.

(2) Where there are more than two guardians or conservators, a majority must concur to exercise a power.

(d) If one of the joint guardians or conservators dies or is removed or resigns, the powers and duties continue in the remaining joint guardians or conservators until further appointment is made by the court.

(e) Where joint guardians or conservators have been appointed and one or more are (1) absent from the state and unable to act, (2) otherwise unable to act, or (3) legally disqualified from serving, the court may, by order made with or without notice, authorize the remaining joint guardians or conservators to act as to all matters embraced within its order.

(f) If a custodial parent has been diagnosed as having a terminal condition, as evidenced by a declaration executed by a licensed physician, the court, in its discretion, may appoint the custodial parent and a person nominated by the custodial parent as joint guardians of the person of the minor. However, this appointment shall not be made over the objection of a noncustodial parent without a finding that the noncustodial parent's custody would be detrimental to the minor, as provided in Section 3041 of the Family Code. It is the intent of the Legislature in enacting the amendments to this subdivision adopted during the 1995-96 Regular Session for a parent with a terminal condition to be able to make arrangements for the joint care, custody, and control of his or her minor children so as to minimize the emotional stress of, and disruption for, the minor children whenever the parent is incapacitated or upon the parent's death, and to avoid the need to provide a temporary guardian or place the minor children in foster care, pending appointment of a guardian, as might otherwise be required.

"Terminal condition," for purposes of this subdivision, means an incurable and irreversible condition that, without the administration of life-sustaining treatment, will, within reasonable medical judgment, result in death.

2105.5. (a) Except as provided in subdivision (b), where there is more than one guardian or conservator of the estate, one guardian or conservator is not liable for a breach of fiduciary duty committed by another guardian or conservator.

(b) Where there is more than one guardian or conservator of the estate, one guardian or conservator is liable for a breach of fiduciary duty committed by another guardian or conservator of the same estate under any of the following circumstances:

(1) Where the guardian or conservator participates in a breach of fiduciary duty committed by the other guardian or conservator.

(2) Where the guardian or conservator improperly delegates the administration of the estate to the other guardian or conservator.

(3) Where the guardian or conservator approves, knowingly acquiesces in, or conceals a breach of fiduciary duty committed by the other guardian or conservator.

(4) Where the guardian or conservator negligently enables the other guardian or conservator to commit a breach of fiduciary duty.

(5) Where the guardian or conservator knows or has information from which the guardian or conservator reasonably should have known of the breach of fiduciary duty by the other guardian or conservator and fails to take reasonable steps to compel the other guardian or conservator to redress the breach.

(c) The liability of a guardian or conservator for a breach of fiduciary duty committed by another guardian or conservator that occurred before July 1, 1988, is governed by prior law and not by this section.

2106. (a) The court, in its discretion, may appoint one guardian or conservator for several wards or conservatees.

(b) The appointment of one guardian or conservator for several wards or conservatees may be requested in the initial petition filed in the proceeding or may be requested subsequently upon a petition filed in the same proceeding and noticed and heard with respect to the newly proposed ward or conservatee in the same manner as an initial petition for appointment of a guardian or conservator.

2107. (a) Unless limited by court order, a guardian or conservator of the person of a nonresident has the same powers and duties as a guardian or conservator of the person of a resident while the nonresident is in this state.

(b) A guardian or conservator of the estate of a nonresident has, with respect to the property of the nonresident within this state, the same powers and duties as a guardian or conservator of the estate of a resident. The responsibility of such a guardian or conservator with regard to inventory, accounting, and disposal of the estate is confined to the property that comes into the hands of the guardian or conservator in this state.

2108. (a) Except to the extent the court for good cause determines otherwise, if a guardian of the person is nominated as provided in Article 1 (commencing with Section 1500) of Chapter 1 of Part 2 and is appointed by the court, the guardian shall be granted in the order of appointment, to the extent provided in the nomination, the same authority with respect to the person of the ward as a parent having legal custody of a child and may exercise such authority without notice, hearing, or court authorization, instructions, approval, or confirmation in the same manner as if such authority were exercised by a parent having legal custody of a child.

(b) Except to the extent the court for good cause determines otherwise and subject to Sections 2593, 2594, and 2595, if a guardian of the estate is nominated under Section 1500 or a guardian for property is nominated under Section 1501 and the guardian is appointed by the court, the guardian shall be granted in the order of appointment, to the extent provided in the nomination, the right to exercise any one or more of the powers listed in Section 2591 without notice, hearing, or court authorization, instructions, approval, or confirmation in the same manner as if such authority were granted by order of the court under Section 2590. In the case of a guardian nominated under Section 1501, such additional authority shall be limited to the property covered by the nomination.

(c) The terms of any order made under this section shall be included in the letters.

2109. (a) Subject to Section 2108, a guardian appointed under subdivision (d) of Section 1514 for particular property upon a nomination made under Section 1501 has, with respect to that property, the same powers and duties as a guardian of the estate. The responsibility of such a guardian with regard to inventory, accounting, and disposal of the estate is confined to the property covered by the nomination.

(b) When a guardian is appointed under subdivision (d) of Section 1514 for particular property upon a nomination made under Section 1501 and there is a guardian of the estate appointed under any other provision of Part 2 (commencing with Section 1500):

(1) The guardian appointed for the property covered by the nomination manages and controls that property and the guardian of the estate manages and controls the balance of the guardianship estate.

(2) Either guardian may petition under Section 2403 to the court in which the guardianship of the estate proceeding is pending for instructions concerning how the duties that are imposed by law upon the guardian of the estate are to be allocated between the two guardians.

2110. Unless otherwise provided in the instrument or in this division, a guardian or conservator is not personally liable on an instrument, including but not limited to a note, mortgage, deed of trust, or other contract, properly entered into in the guardian's or conservator's fiduciary capacity in the course of the guardianship or conservatorship unless the guardian or conservator fails to reveal the guardian's or conservator's representative capacity or identify the guardianship or conservatorship estate in the instrument.

2111. (a) As used in this section, "transaction" means any of the following:

(1) A conveyance or lease of real property of the guardianship or conservatorship estate.

(2) The creation of a mortgage or deed of trust on real property of the guardianship or conservatorship estate.

(3) A transfer of personal property of the guardianship or conservatorship estate.

(4) The creation of a security interest or other lien in personal property of the guardianship or conservatorship estate.

(b) Whenever the court authorizes or directs a transaction, the transaction shall be carried out by the guardian or conservator of the estate in accordance with the terms of the order.

(c) A conveyance, lease, or mortgage of, or deed of trust on, real property executed by a guardian or conservator shall set forth therein that it is made by authority of the order authorizing or directing the transaction and shall give the date of the order. A certified copy of the order shall be recorded in the office of the county recorder in each county in which any portion of the real property is located.

(d) A transaction carried out by a guardian or conservator in accordance with an order authorizing or directing the transaction has the same effect as if the ward or conservatee had carried out the transaction while having legal capacity to do so.

2111.5. (a) Except as provided in subdivision (b), every court official or employee who has duties or responsibilities related to the appointment of a guardian or conservator, or the processing of any document related to a guardian or conservator, and every person who is related by blood or marriage to a court official or employee who has these duties, is prohibited from purchasing, leasing, or renting any real or personal property from the estate of the ward or conservatee whom the guardian or conservator represents. For purposes of this subdivision, a "person related by blood or marriage" means any of the following:

(1) A person's spouse or domestic partner.

(2) Relatives within the second degree of lineal or collateral consanguinity of a person or a person's spouse.

(b) A person described in subdivision (a) is not prohibited from purchasing real or personal property from the estate of the ward or conservatee whom the guardian or conservator represents where the purchase is made under terms and conditions of a public sale of the property.

(c) A violation of this section shall result in the rescission of the purchase, lease, or rental of the property. Any losses incurred by the estate of the ward or conservatee because the property was sold or leased at less than fair market value shall be deemed as charges against the guardian or conservator under the provisions of Sections 2401.3 and 2401.5. The court shall assess a civil penalty equal to three times the charges against the guardian, conservator, or other person in violation of this section, and may assess punitive damages as it deems proper. If the estate does not incur losses as a result of the violation, the court shall order the guardian, conservator, or other person in violation of this section to pay a fine of up to five thousand dollars ($5,000) for each violation. The fines and penalties provided in this section are in addition to any other rights and remedies provided by law.

2113. A conservator shall accommodate the desires of the conservatee, except to the extent that doing so would violate the conservator's fiduciary duties to the conservatee or impose an unreasonable expense on the conservatorship estate.

Chapter 2. Jurisdiction And Venue

Article 1. Jurisdiction And Venue

2200. The superior court has jurisdiction of guardianship and conservatorship proceedings.

2201. The proper county for the commencement of a guardianship or conservatorship proceeding for a resident of this state is either of the following:

(a) The county in which the proposed ward or proposed conservatee resides.

(b) Such other county as may be in the best interests of the proposed ward or proposed conservatee.

2202. (a) The proper county for the commencement of a proceeding for the guardianship or conservatorship of the person of a nonresident of this state is either of the following:

(1) The county in which the proposed ward or conservatee is temporarily living.

(2) Such other county as may be in the best interests of the proposed ward or proposed conservatee.

(b) The proper county for the commencement of a proceeding for the guardianship or conservatorship of the estate for a nonresident of this state is any of the following:

(1) The county in which the proposed ward or proposed conservatee is temporarily living.

(2) Any county in which the proposed ward or proposed conservatee has property.

(3) Such other county as may be in the best interests of the proposed ward or proposed conservatee.

2203. (a) If proceedings for the guardianship or conservatorship of the estate are commenced in more than one county, the guardianship or conservatorship of the estate first granted, including a temporary guardianship or conservatorship of the estate, governs and extends to all the property of the ward or conservatee within this state and the other proceeding shall be dismissed.

(b) If proceedings for the guardianship or conservatorship of the person are commenced in more than one county, the guardianship or conservatorship of the person first granted, including a temporary guardianship or conservatorship of the person, governs and the other proceeding shall be dismissed.

(c) If a proceeding for the guardianship or conservatorship of the person is commenced in one county and a proceeding for the guardianship or conservatorship of the estate is commenced in a different county, the court first granting the guardianship or conservatorship, whether of the person or of the estate, may find that it is in the best interests of the ward or conservatee that the guardianship or conservatorship of both the person and the estate be maintained in that county or in such other county as the court shall determine. Thereupon, the guardianship or conservatorship proceeding in the court of the county found by the court to be in the best interests of the ward or conservatee shall govern and shall extend to all property of the ward or conservatee within this state, and the other proceeding shall be dismissed.

2204. (a) If a proceeding for the guardianship of the person of the minor is filed in one county and a custody or visitation proceeding has already been filed in one or more other counties, the following shall apply:

(1) If the guardianship proceeding is filed in a county where the proposed ward and the proposed guardian have resided for six or more consecutive months immediately prior to the commencement of the proceeding, or, in the case of a minor less than six months of

age, since the minor's birth, the court in that county is the proper court to hear and determine the guardianship proceeding, unless that court determines that the best interests of the minor require that the proceeding be transferred to one of the other courts. A period of temporary absence no longer than 30 days from the county of the minor or the proposed guardian shall not be considered an interruption of the six-month period.

(2) If the guardianship proceeding is filed in a county where the proposed ward and the proposed guardian have resided for less than six consecutive months immediately prior to the commencement of the proceeding, or, in the case of a minor less than six months of age, a period less than the minor's life, the court shall transfer the case to one of the other courts, unless the court determines that the best interests of the minor require that the guardianship proceeding be maintained in the court where it was filed.

(3) If a petitioner or respondent in a custody or visitation proceeding who is an authorized petitioner under Section 2212 petitions the court where the guardianship proceeding is filed for transfer of the guardianship proceeding to the court where the custody or visitation proceeding is on file at any time before the appointment of a guardian, including a temporary guardian, the provisions of this subdivision shall apply to the court's determination of the petition for transfer. Except as provided in this paragraph, the petition for transfer shall be determined as provided in Sections 2212 to 2217, inclusive.

(b) The following shall apply concerning communications between the courts:

(1) The court where the guardianship proceeding is commenced shall communicate concerning the proceedings with each court where a custody or visitation proceeding is on file prior to making a determination authorized in subdivision (a), including a determination of a petition to transfer.

(2) If a petitioner or respondent, who is authorized to petition to transfer under Section 2212, petitions the court where the guardianship proceeding is filed for transfer of the guardianship after the appointment of a guardian, including a temporary guardian, the court in the guardianship proceeding may communicate with each court where a custody or visitation proceeding is on file before determining the petition for transfer.

(3) If the court in the guardianship proceeding appoints a guardian of the person of the minor, including a temporary guardian, the court shall transmit a copy of the order appointing a guardian to each court where a custody or visitation proceeding is on file, and each of those courts shall file the order in the case file for its custody or visitation proceeding.

(4) The provisions of subdivisions (b) to (e), inclusive, of Section 3410 of the Family Code shall apply to communications between courts under this subdivision.

(5) The Judicial Council shall, on or before January 1, 2013, adopt rules of court to implement the provisions of this subdivision.

(c) For purposes of this section, "custody or visitation proceeding" means a proceeding described in Section 3021 of the Family Code that relates to the rights to custody or visitation of the minor under Part 2 (commencing with Section 3020) of Division 8 of the Family Code.

2205. (a) Except as provided in Section 304 of the Welfare and Institutions Code, and subject to the provisions specified in subdivision (b), upon the filing of an order appointing a guardian of the person of a minor in a guardianship proceeding, including an order appointing a temporary guardian of the person of the minor, the court in the guardianship proceeding shall have exclusive jurisdiction to determine all issues of custody or visitation of the minor until the guardianship proceeding is terminated

(b) This section is subject to the provisions of Sections 1510 of this code, and 8714, 8714.5, and 8802 of the Family Code, relating to consolidation of guardianship and adoption proceedings and the court where the consolidated case is to be heard and decided.

Article 2. Change Of Venue

2210. As used in this article:

(a) "Guardian or conservator" includes a proposed guardian or proposed conservator.

(b) "Ward or conservatee" includes a proposed ward or proposed conservatee.

2211. The court in which a guardianship or conservatorship proceeding is pending may, upon petition therefor, transfer the proceeding to another county within this state.

2212. The petition for transfer may be filed only by one or more of the following:

(a) The guardian or conservator.

(b) The ward or conservatee.

(c) The spouse of the ward or the spouse or domestic partner of the conservatee.

(d) A relative or friend of the ward or conservatee.

(e) Any other interested person.

2213. The petition for transfer shall set forth all of the following:

(a) The county to which the proceeding is to be transferred.

(b) The name and address of the ward or conservatee.

(c) A brief description of the character, value, and location of the property of the ward or conservatee.

(d) The reasons for the transfer.

(e) The names and addresses, so far as they are known to the petitioner, of the spouse and of the relatives of the ward within the second degree, or of the spouse or domestic partner and of the relatives of the conservatee within the second degree.

(f) The name and address of the guardian

or conservator if other than the petitioner.

2214. Notice of the hearing shall be given for the period and in the manner provided in Chapter 3 (commencing with Section 1460) of Part 1. In addition, the petitioner shall mail a notice of the time and place of the hearing and a copy of the petition to all persons required to be listed in the petition at least 15 days before the date set for the hearing.

2215. (a) Any of the following persons may appear at the hearing to support or oppose the petition and may file written objections to the petition:

(1) Any person required to be listed in the petition.

(2) Any creditor of the ward or conservatee or of the estate.

(3) Any other interested person.

(b) (1) If the court determines that the transfer requested in the petition will be for the best interests of the ward or conservatee, it shall make an order transferring the proceeding to the other county.

(2) In those cases in which the court has approved a change of residence of the conservatee, it shall be presumed to be in the best interests of the conservatee to transfer the proceedings if the ward or conservatee has moved his or her residence to another county within the state in which any person set forth in subdivision (b) of Section 1821 also resides. The presumption that the transfer is in the best interests of the ward or conservatee, may be rebutted by clear and convincing evidence that the transfer will harm the ward or conservatee.

2216. (a) Upon the order of transfer, the clerk shall transmit to the clerk of the court to which the proceeding is transferred a certified or exemplified copy of the order, together with all papers in the proceeding on file with the clerk.

(b) The clerk of the court from which the removal is made shall receive no fee therefor but shall be paid out of the estate all expenses incurred by the clerk in the removal. The clerk of the court to which the proceeding is transferred is entitled to such fees as are payable on the filing of a like original proceeding.

2217. (a) When an order has been made transferring venue to another county, the court transferring the matter shall set a hearing within two months to confirm receipt of the notification described in subdivision (b). If the notification has not been made, the transferring court shall make reasonable inquiry into the status of the matter.

(b) When a court receives the file of a transferred guardianship or conservatorship, the court:

(1) Shall send written notification of the receipt to the court that transferred the matter.

(2) Shall take proper action pursuant to ensure compliance by the guardian or conservator with the matters provided in Section 1456.5.

(3) If the case is a conservatorship, may conduct a review, including an investigation, as described in Sections 1851 to 1853, inclusive.

Chapter 3. Temporary Guardians And Conservators

2250. (a) On or after the filing of a petition for appointment of a guardian or conservator, any person entitled to petition for appointment of the guardian or conservator may file a petition for appointment of:

(1) A temporary guardian of the person or estate, or both.

(2) A temporary conservator of the person or estate, or both.

(b) The petition shall state facts which establish good cause for appointment of the temporary guardian or temporary conservator. The court, upon that petition or other showing as it may require, may appoint a temporary guardian of the person or estate, or both, or a temporary conservator of the person or estate, or both, to serve pending the final determination of the court upon the petition for the appointment of the guardian or conservator.

(c) If the petitioner, proposed guardian, or proposed conservator is a professional fiduciary, as described in Section 2340, who is required to be licensed under the Professional Fiduciaries Act (Chapter 6 (commencing with Section 6500) of Division 3 of the Business and Professions Code), the petition for appointment of a temporary guardian or temporary conservator shall include the following:

(1) The petitioner's, proposed guardian's, or proposed conservator' s proposed hourly fee schedule or another statement of his or her proposed compensation from the estate of the proposed ward or proposed conservatee for services performed as a guardian or conservator. The petitioner's, proposed guardian's, or proposed conservator's provision of a proposed hourly fee schedule or another statement of his or her proposed compensation, as required by this paragraph, shall not preclude a court from later reducing the petitioner's, proposed guardian's, or proposed conservator's fees or other compensation.

(2) Unless a petition for appointment of a guardian or conservator that contains the statements required by this paragraph is filed together with a petition for appointment of a temporary guardian or temporary conservator, both of the following:

(A) A statement of the petitioner's, proposed guardian's, or proposed conservator's registration or license information.

(B) A statement explaining who engaged the petitioner, proposed guardian, or proposed conservator or how the petitioner, proposed guardian, or proposed conservator was engaged to file the petition for appointment of a temporary guardian or temporary conservator or to agree to accept the appointment as temporary guardian or temporary conservator and what prior relationship the petitioner, proposed guardian, or proposed conservator had with the proposed ward or proposed conservatee or the proposed ward's or proposed conservatee's family or friends.

(d) If the petition is filed by a party other than the proposed conservatee, the petition shall include a declaration of due diligence showing both of the following:

(1) Either the efforts to find the proposed conservatee's relatives named in the petition for appointment of a general conservator or why it was not feasible to contact any of them.

(2) Either the preferences of the proposed conservatee concerning the appointment of a temporary conservator and the appointment of the proposed temporary conservator or why it was not feasible to ascertain those preferences.

(e) Unless the court for good cause otherwise orders, at least five court days before the hearing on the petition, notice of the hearing shall be given as follows:

(1) Notice of the hearing shall be personally delivered to the proposed ward if he or she is 12 years of age or older, to the parent or parents of the proposed ward, and to any person having a valid visitation order with the proposed ward that was effective at the time of the filing of the petition. Notice of the hearing shall not be delivered to the proposed ward if he or she is under 12 years of age. In a proceeding for temporary guardianship of the person, evidence that a custodial parent has died or become incapacitated, and that the petitioner or proposed guardian is the nominee of the custodial parent, may constitute good cause for the court to order that this notice not be delivered.

(2) Notice of the hearing shall be personally delivered to the proposed conservatee, and notice of the hearing shall be served on the persons required to be named in the petition for appointment of conservator. If the petition states that the petitioner and the proposed conservator have no prior relationship with the proposed conservatee and has not been nominated by a family member, friend, or other person with a relationship to the proposed conservatee, notice of hearing shall be served on the public guardian of the county in which the petition is filed.

(3) A copy of the petition for temporary appointment shall be served with the notice of hearing.

(f) If a temporary guardianship is granted ex parte and the hearing on the general guardianship petition is not to be held within 30 days of the granting of the temporary guardianship, the court shall set a hearing within 30 days to reconsider the temporary guardianship. Notice of the hearing for reconsideration of the temporary guardian-

ship shall be provided pursuant to Section 1511, except that the court may for good cause shorten the time for the notice of the hearing.

(g) Visitation orders with the proposed ward granted prior to the filing of a petition for temporary guardianship shall remain in effect, unless for good cause the court orders otherwise.

(h) (1) If a temporary conservatorship is granted ex parte, and a petition to terminate the temporary conservatorship is filed more than 15 days before the first hearing on the general petition for appointment of conservator, the court shall set a hearing within 15 days of the filing of the petition for termination of the temporary conservatorship to reconsider the temporary conservatorship. Unless the court otherwise orders, notice of the hearing on the petition to terminate the temporary conservatorship shall be given at least 10 days prior to the hearing.

(2) If a petition to terminate the temporary conservatorship is filed within 15 days before the first hearing on the general petition for appointment of conservator, the court shall set the hearing at the same time that the hearing on the general petition is set. Unless the court otherwise orders, notice of the hearing on the petition to terminate the temporary conservatorship pursuant to this section shall be given at least five court days prior to the hearing.

(i) If the court suspends powers of the guardian or conservator under Section 2334 or 2654 or under any other provision of this division, the court may appoint a temporary guardian or conservator to exercise those powers until the powers are restored to the guardian or conservator or a new guardian or conservator is appointed.

(j) If for any reason a vacancy occurs in the office of guardian or conservator, the court, on a petition filed under subdivision (a) or on its own motion, may appoint a temporary guardian or conservator to exercise the powers of the guardian or conservator until a new guardian or conservator is appointed.

(k) On or before January 1, 2008, the Judicial Council shall adopt a rule of court that establishes uniform standards for good cause exceptions to the notice required by subdivision (e), limiting those exceptions to only cases when waiver of the notice is essential to protect the proposed conservatee or ward, or the estate of the proposed conservatee or ward, from substantial harm.

(l) A superior court shall not be required to perform any duties imposed pursuant to the amendments to this section enacted by Chapter 493 of the Statutes 2006 until the Legislature makes an appropriation identified for this purpose.

2250.2. (a) On or after the filing of a petition for appointment of a conservator, any person entitled to petition for appointment of the conservator may file a petition for appointment of a temporary conservator of the person or estate or both.

(b) The petition shall state facts that establish good cause for appointment of the temporary conservator. The court, upon that petition or any other showing as it may require, may appoint a temporary conservator of the person or estate or both, to serve pending the final determination of the court upon the petition for the appointment of the conservator.

(c) Unless the court for good cause otherwise orders, not less than five days before the appointment of the temporary conservator, notice of the proposed appointment shall be personally delivered to the proposed conservatee.

(d) If the court suspends powers of the conservator under Section 2334 or 2654 or under any other provision of this division, the court may appoint a temporary conservator to exercise those powers until the powers are restored to the conservator or a new conservator is appointed.

(e) If for any reason a vacancy occurs in the office of conservator, the court, on a petition filed under subdivision (a) or on its own motion, may appoint a temporary conservator to exercise the powers of the conservator until a new conservator is appointed.

(f) This section shall only apply to proceedings under Chapter 3 (commencing with Section 5350) of Part 1 of Division 5 of the Welfare and Institutions Code.

2250.4. The proposed temporary conservatee shall attend the hearing except in the following cases:

(a) If the proposed temporary conservatee is out of the state when served and is not the petitioner.

(b) If the proposed temporary conservatee is unable to attend the hearing by reason of medical inability.

(c) If the court investigator has visited the proposed conservatee prior to the hearing and the court investigator has reported to the court that the proposed temporary conservatee has expressly communicated that all of the following apply:

(1) The proposed conservatee is not willing to attend the hearing.

(2) The proposed conservatee does not wish to contest the establishment of the temporary conservatorship.

(3) The proposed conservatee does not object to the proposed temporary conservator or prefer that another person act as temporary conservator.

(d) If the court determines that the proposed conservatee is unable or unwilling to attend the hearing, and holding the hearing in the absence of the proposed conservatee is necessary to protect the conservatee from substantial harm.

(e) A superior court shall not be required to perform any duties imposed by this section until the Legislature makes an appropriation identified for this purpose.

2250.6. (a) Regardless of whether the proposed temporary conservatee attends the hearing, the court investigator shall do all of the following prior to the hearing, unless it is not feasible to do so, in which case the court investigator shall comply with the requirements set forth in subdivision (b):

(1) Interview the proposed conservatee personally. The court investigator also shall do all of the following:

(A) Interview the petitioner and the proposed conservator, if different from the petitioner.

(B) To the greatest extent possible, interview the proposed conservatee's spouse or registered domestic partner, relatives within the first degree, neighbors and, if known, close friends.

(C) To the extent possible, interview the proposed conservatee's relatives within the second degree as set forth in subdivision (b) of Section 1821 before the hearing.

(2) Inform the proposed conservatee of the contents of the citation, of the nature, purpose, and effect of the temporary conservatorship, and of the right of the proposed conservatee to oppose the proceeding, to attend the hearing, to have the matter of the establishment of the conservatorship tried by jury, to be represented by legal counsel if the proposed conservatee so chooses, and to have legal counsel appointed by the court if unable to retain legal counsel.

(3) Determine whether it appears that the proposed conservatee is unable to attend the hearing and, if able to attend, whether the proposed conservatee is willing to attend the hearing.

(4) Determine whether the proposed conservatee wishes to contest the establishment of the conservatorship.

(5) Determine whether the proposed conservatee objects to the proposed conservator or prefers another person to act as conservator.

(6) Report to the court, in writing, concerning all of the foregoing.

(b) If not feasible before the hearing, the court investigator shall do all of the following within two court days after the hearing:

(1) Interview the conservatee personally. The court investigator also shall do all of the following:

(A) Interview the petitioner and the proposed conservator, if different from the petitioner.

(B) To the greatest extent possible, interview the proposed conservatee's spouse or registered domestic partner, relatives within the first degree, neighbors and, if known, close friends.

(C) To the extent possible, interview the proposed conservatee's relatives within the second degree as set forth in subdivision (b) of Section 1821.

(2) Inform the conservatee of the nature, purpose, and effect of the temporary conservatorship, as well as the right of the conservatee to oppose the proposed general conservatorship, to attend the hearing, to have the matter of the establishment of the conservatorship tried by jury, to be represented by legal counsel if the proposed conservatee so chooses, and to have legal counsel appointed by the court if unable to retain legal counsel.

(c) If the investigator does not visit the conservatee until after the hearing at which a temporary conservator was appointed, and the conservatee objects to the appointment of the temporary conservator, or requests an attorney, the court investigator shall report this information promptly, and in no event more than three court days later, to the court. Upon receipt of that information, the court may proceed with appointment of an attorney as provided in Chapter 4 (commencing with Section 1470) of Part 1.

(d) If it appears to the court investigator that the temporary conservatorship is inappropriate, the court investigator shall immediately, and in no event more than two court days later, provide a written report to the court so the court can consider taking appropriate action on its own motion.

(e) A superior court shall not be required to perform any duties imposed by this section until the Legislature makes an appropriation identified for this purpose.

2250.8. Sections 2250, 2250.4, and 2250.6 shall not apply to proceedings under Chapter 3 (commencing with Section 5350) of Part 1 of Division 5 of the Welfare and Institutions Code.

2251. A temporary guardian or temporary conservator shall be issued letters of temporary guardianship or conservatorship upon taking the oath and filing the bond as in the case of a guardian or conservator. The letters shall indicate the termination date of the temporary appointment.

2252. (a) Except as otherwise provided in subdivisions (b) and (c), a temporary guardian or temporary conservator has only those powers and duties of a guardian or conservator that are necessary to provide for the temporary care, maintenance, and support of the ward or conservatee and that are necessary to conserve and protect the property of the ward or conservatee from loss or injury.

(b) Unless the court otherwise orders:

(1) A temporary guardian of the person has the powers and duties specified in Section 2353 (medical treatment).

(2) A temporary conservator of the person has the powers and duties specified in Section 2354 (medical treatment).

(3) A temporary guardian of the estate or temporary conservator of the estate may marshal assets and establish accounts at financial institutions.

(c) The temporary guardian or temporary conservator has the additional powers and duties as may be ordered by the court (1) in the order of appointment or (2) by subsequent order made with or without notice as the court may require. Notwithstanding subdivision (e), those additional powers and duties may include relief granted pursuant to Article 10 (commencing with Section 2580) of Chapter 6 if this relief is not requested in a petition for the appointment of a temporary conservator but is requested in a separate petition.

(d) The terms of any order made under subdivision (b) or (c) shall be included in the letters of temporary guardianship or conservatorship.

(e) A temporary conservator is not permitted to sell or relinquish, on the conservatee's behalf, any lease or estate in real or personal property used as or within the conservatee's place of residence without the specific approval of the court. This approval may be granted only if the conservatee has been served with notice of the hearing, the notice to be personally delivered to the temporary conservatee unless the court for good cause otherwise orders, and only if the court finds that the conservatee will be unable to return to the residence and exercise dominion over it and that the action is necessary to avert irreparable harm to the conservatee. The temporary conservator is not permitted to sell or relinquish on the conservatee's behalf any estate or interest in other real or personal property without specific approval of the court, which may be granted only upon a finding that the action is necessary to avert irreparable harm to the conservatee. A finding of irreparable harm as to real property may be based upon a reasonable showing that the real property is vacant, that it cannot reasonably be rented, and that it is impossible or impractical to obtain fire or liability insurance on the property.

2253. (a) If a temporary conservator of the person proposes to fix the residence of the conservatee at a place other than that where the conservatee resided prior to the commencement of the proceedings, that power shall be requested of the court in writing, unless the change of residence is required of the conservatee by a prior court order. The request shall be filed with the petition for temporary conservatorship or, if a temporary conservatorship has already been established, separately. The request shall specify in particular the place to which the temporary conservator proposes to move the conservatee, and the precise reasons why it is believed that the conservatee will suffer irreparable harm if the change of residence is not permitted, and why no means less restrictive of the conservatee's liberty will suffice to prevent that harm.

(b) Unless the court for good cause orders otherwise, the court investigator shall do all of the following:

(1) Interview the conservatee personally.

(2) Inform the conservatee of the nature, purpose, and effect of the request made under subdivision (a), and of the right of the conservatee to oppose the request, attend the hearing, be represented by legal counsel if the conservatee so chooses, and to have legal counsel appointed by the court if unable to obtain legal counsel.

(3) Determine whether the conservatee is unable to attend the hearing because of medical inability and, if able to attend, whether the conservatee is willing to attend the hearing.

(4) Determine whether the conservatee wishes to oppose the request.

(5) Determine whether the conservatee wishes to be represented by legal counsel at the hearing and, if so, whether the conservatee has retained legal counsel and, if not, the name of an attorney the proposed conservatee wishes to retain or whether the conservatee desires the court to appoint legal counsel.

(6) If the conservatee does not plan to retain legal counsel and has not requested the appointment of legal counsel by the court, determine whether the appointment of legal counsel would be helpful to the resolution of the matter or is necessary to protect the interests of the conservatee.

(7) Determine whether the proposed change of place of residence is required to prevent irreparable harm to the conservatee and whether no means less restrictive of the conservatee's liberty will suffice to prevent that harm.

(8) Report to the court in writing, at least two days before the hearing, concerning all of the foregoing, including the conservatee's express communications concerning representation by legal counsel and whether the conservatee is not willing to attend the hearing and does not wish to oppose the request.

(c) Within seven days of the date of filing of a temporary conservator's request to remove the conservatee from his or her previous place of residence, the court shall hold a hearing on the request.

(d) The conservatee shall be present at the hearing except in the following cases:

(1) Where the conservatee is unable to attend the hearing by reason of medical inability. Emotional or psychological instability is not good cause for the absence of the conservatee from the hearing unless, by reason of that instability, attendance at the hearing is likely to cause serious and immediate physiological damage to the conservatee.

(2) Where the court investigator has reported to the court that the conservatee has expressly communicated that the conservatee is not willing to attend the hearing and does not wish to oppose the request, and the court makes an order that the conservatee need not attend the hearing.

(e) If the conservatee is unable to attend the hearing because of medical inability, that inability shall be established (1) by the affidavit or certificate of a licensed medical practitioner or (2) if the conservatee is an adherent of a religion whose tenets and practices call for reliance on prayer alone for healing and is under treatment by an accredited practitioner of that religion, by the affidavit of the practitioner. The affidavit or certificate is evidence only of the conservatee's inability to attend the hearing and shall not be considered in determining the issue of need for the establishment of a conservatorship.

(f) At the hearing, the conservatee has the right to be represented by counsel and the right to confront and cross-examine any witness presented by or on behalf of the temporary conservator and to present evidence on his or her own behalf.

(g) The court may approve the request to remove the conservatee from the previous place of residence only if the court finds (1) that change of residence is required to prevent irreparable harm to the conservatee and (2) that no means less restrictive of the conservatee's liberty will suffice to prevent that harm. If an order is made authorizing the temporary conservator to remove the conservatee from the previous place of residence, the order shall specify the specific place wherein the temporary conservator is authorized to place the conservatee. The temporary conservator may not be authorized to remove the conservatee from this state unless it is additionally shown that such removal is required to permit the performance of specified nonpsychiatric medical treatment, consented to by the conservatee, which is essential to the conservatee's physical survival. A temporary conservator who willfully removes a temporary conservatee from this state without authorization of the court is guilty of a felony.

(h) Subject to subdivision (e) of Section 2252, the court shall also order the temporary conservator to take all reasonable steps to preserve the status quo concerning the conservatee's previous place of residence.

(i) A superior court shall not be required to perform any duties imposed pursuant to the amendments to this section enacted by Chapter 493 of the Statutes 2006 until the Legislature makes an appropriation identified for this purpose.

2254. (a) Notwithstanding Section 2253, a temporary conservator may remove a temporary conservatee from the temporary conservatee's place of residence without court authorization if an emergency exists. For the purposes of this section, an emergency exists if the temporary conservatee's place of residence is unfit for habitation or if the temporary conservator determines in good faith based upon medical advice that the case is an emergency case in which removal from the place of residence is required (1) to provide medical treatment needed to alleviate severe pain or (2) to diagnose or treat a medical condition which, if not immediately diagnosed and treated, will lead to serious disability or death.

(b) No later than one judicial day after the emergency removal of the temporary conservatee, the temporary conservator shall file a written request pursuant to Section 2253 for authorization to fix the residence of the temporary conservatee at a place other than the temporary conservatee's previous place of residence.

(c) Nothing in this chapter prevents a temporary conservator from removing a temporary conservatee from the place of residence to a health facility for treatment without court authorization when the temporary conservatee has given informed consent to the removal.

(d) Nothing in this chapter prevents a temporary conservator from removing a temporary conservatee without court authorization from one health facility where the conservatee is receiving medical care to another health facility where the conservatee will receive medical care.

2255. (a) Except as provided in subdivision (b), an inventory and appraisal of the estate shall be filed by the temporary guardian or temporary conservator of the estate as required by Article 2 (commencing with Section 2610) of Chapter 7.

(b) A temporary guardian or temporary conservator of the estate may inventory the estate in the final account, without the necessity for an appraisal of the estate, if the final account is filed within 90 days after the appointment of the temporary guardian or temporary conservator.

2256. (a) Except as provided in subdivision (b), the temporary guardian or temporary conservator of the estate shall present his or her account to the court for settlement and allowance within 90 days after the appointment of a guardian or conservator of the estate or within such other time as the court may fix.

(b) If the temporary guardian or temporary conservator of the estate is appointed guardian or conservator of the estate, the guardian or conservator may account for the administration as temporary guardian or temporary conservator in his or her first regular account.

(c) Accounts are subject to Sections 2621 to 2626, inclusive, Sections 2630 to 2633, inclusive, and Sections 2640 to 2642, inclusive.

2257. (a) Except as provided in subdivision (b), the powers of a temporary guardian or temporary conservator terminate, except for the rendering of the account, at the earliest of the following times:

(1) The time the temporary guardian or conservator acquires notice that a guardian or conservator is appointed and qualified.

(2) Thirty days after the appointment of the temporary guardian or temporary conservator or such earlier time as the court may specify in the order of appointment.

(b) With or without notice as the court may require, the court may for good cause order that the time for the termination of the powers of the temporary guardian or temporary conservator be extended or shortened pending final determination by the court of the petition for appointment of a guardian or conservator or pending the final decision on appeal therefrom or for other cause. The order which extends the time for termination shall fix the time when the powers of the temporary guardian or temporary conservator terminate except for the rendering of the account.

2258. A temporary guardian or temporary conservator is subject to the provisions of this division governing the suspension, removal, resignation, and discharge of a guardian or conservator.

Chapter 4. Oath, Letters, And Bond

Article 1. Requirement Of Oath And Bond

2300. Before the appointment of a guardian or conservator is effective, the guardian or conservator shall:

(a) Take an oath to perform the duties of the office according to law, which oath shall be attached to or endorsed upon the letters.

(b) File the required bond if a bond is required.

Article 2. Letters

2310. (a) The appointment, the taking of the oath, and the filing of the bond, if required, shall thereafter be evidenced by the issuance of letters by the clerk of the court.

(b) The order appointing a guardian or conservator shall state in capital letters on the first page of the order, in at least 12-point type, the following:
"WARNING: THIS APPOINTMENT IS NOT EFFECTIVE UNTIL LETTERS HAVE ISSUED."

2311. Except as otherwise required by the order of appointment, the letters of guardianship or conservatorship shall be in substantially the same form as letters of administration.

2313. Except in temporary conservatorships, a conservator of the estate shall record a certified copy of the letters with the county recorder's office in each county in which the conservatee owns an interest in real property, including a security interest. The conservator shall record the letters as soon as practicable after they are issued, but no later than 90 days after the conservator is appointed. A temporary conservator of the estate may record the letters if the conservator deems it appropriate.

Article 3. Bonds Of Guardians And Conservators

2320. (a) Except as otherwise provided by statute, every person appointed as guardian or conservator shall, before letters are issued, give a bond approved by the court.

(b) The bond shall be for the benefit of the ward or conservatee and all persons interested in the guardianship or conservatorship estate and shall be conditioned upon the faithful execution of the duties of the office, according to law, by the guardian or conservator.

(c) Except as otherwise provided by statute, unless the court increases or decreases the amount upon a showing of good cause, the amount of a bond given by an admitted surety insurer shall be the sum of all of the following:

(1) The value of the personal property of the estate.

(2) The probable annual gross income of all of the property of the estate.

(3) The sum of the probable annual gross payments from the following:

(A) Part 3 (commencing with Section 11000) of, Part 4 (commencing with Section 16000) of, or Part 5 (commencing with Section 17000) of, Division 9 of the Welfare and Institutions Code.

(B) Subchapter II (commencing with Section 401) of, or Part A of Subchapter XVI (commencing with Section 1382) of, Chapter 7 of Title 42 of the United States Code.

(C) Any other public entitlements of the ward or conservatee.

(4) On or after January 1, 2008, a reasonable amount for the cost of recovery to collect on the bond, including attorney's fees and costs. The attorney's fees and costs incurred in a successful action for surcharge against a conservator or guardian for breach of his or her duty under this code shall be a surcharge against the conservator or guardian and, if unpaid, shall be recovered against the surety on the bond. The Judicial Council shall, on or before January 1, 2008, adopt a rule of court to implement this paragraph.

(d) If the bond is given by personal sureties, the amount of the bond shall be twice the amount required for a bond given by an admitted surety insurer.

(e) The Bond and Undertaking Law (Chapter 2 (commencing with Section 995.010) of Title 14 of Part 2 of the Code of Civil Procedure) applies to a bond given under this article, except to the extent inconsistent with this article.

2320.1. When the conservator or guardian has knowledge of facts from which the guardian or conservator knows or should know that the bond posted is less than the amount required under Section 2320, the conservator or guardian, and the attorney, if any, shall make an ex parte application for an order increasing the bond to the amount required under Section 2320.

2320.2. If additional bond is required by the court when the account is heard, the order approving the account and related matters, including fees, is not effective and the court shall not file the order until the additional bond is filed.

2321. (a) Notwithstanding any other provision of law, the court in a conservatorship proceeding may not waive the filing of a bond or reduce the amount of bond required, without a good cause determination by the court which shall include a determination by the court that the conservatee will not suffer harm as a result of the waiver or reduction of the bond. Good cause may not be established merely by the conservator having filed a bond in another or prior proceeding.

(b) In a conservatorship proceeding, where the conservatee, having sufficient capacity to do so, has waived the filing of a bond, the court in its discretion may permit the filing of a bond in an amount less than would otherwise be required under Section 2320.

2322. One appointed only as guardian of the person or conservator of the person need not file a bond unless required by the court.

2323. (a) The court may dispense with the requirement of a bond if it appears likely that the estate will satisfy the conditions of subdivision (a) of Section 2628 for its duration.

(b) If at any time it appears that the estate does not satisfy the conditions of subdivision (a) of Section 2628, the court shall require the filing of a bond unless the court determines that good cause exists, as provided in Section 2321.

2324. If the person making the nomination has waived the filing of the bond, a guardian nominated under Section 1500 or 1501 need not file a bond unless required by the court.

2325. The surety on the bond of a nonprofit charitable corporation described in Section 2104 shall be an admitted surety insurer.

2326. (a) If joint guardians or conservators are appointed, the court may order that separate bonds or a joint bond or a combination thereof be furnished.

(b) If a joint bond is furnished, the liability on the bond is joint and several.

2327. (a) In a conservatorship proceeding, the court shall order a separate bond for each conservatee, except where the assets of the conservatees are commingled in which case a combined bond that covers all assets may be provided.

(b) If a guardianship proceeding involves more than one ward, the court may order separate bonds, or a single bond which is for the benefit of two or more wards in that proceeding, or a combination thereof.

2328. (a) In any proceeding to determine the amount of the bond of the guardian or conservator (whether at the time of appointment or subsequently), if the estate includes property which has been or will be deposited with a trust company or financial institution pursuant to Sections 2453 to 2456, inclusive, upon the condition that the property, including any earnings thereon, will not be withdrawn except on authorization of the court, the court, in its discretion, with or without notice, may so order and may do either of the following:

(1) Exclude the property deposited in determining the amount of the required bond or reduce the amount of the bond to be required in respect to the property deposited to such an amount as the court determines is reasonable.

(2) If a bond has already been furnished or the amount fixed, reduce the amount to such an amount as the court determines is reasonable.

(b) The petitioner for letters, or the proposed guardian or conservator in advance of appointment of a guardian or conservator, may do any one or more of the following:

(1) Deliver personal property in the person's possession to a trust company.

(2) Deliver money in the person's possession for deposit in an insured account in a financial institution in this state.

(3) Allow a trust company to retain personal property already in its possession.

(4) Allow a financial institution in this state to retain money already invested in an insured account in a financial institution.

(c) In the cases described in subdivision (b), the petitioner or proposed guardian or conservator shall obtain and file with the court a written receipt including the agreement of the trust company or financial institution that the property deposited, including any earnings thereon, shall not be allowed to be withdrawn except upon authorization of the court.

(d) In receiving and retaining property on deposit pursuant to subdivisions (b) and (c), the trust company or financial institution is protected to the same extent as though it received the property on deposit from a person to whom letters had been issued.

2329. (a) If a guardian or conservator moves the court for reduction in the amount of the bond, the motion shall include an affidavit setting forth the condition of the estate.

(b) Except upon a showing of good cause, the amount of the bond shall not be reduced below the amount determined pursuant to Section 2320.

(c) Nothing in this section limits the authority of the court to reduce the amount of the bond with or without notice under Section 2328.

2330. Upon the confirmation of the sale of any real property of the estate, or upon the authorization of the borrowing of money secured by a mortgage or deed of trust on real property of the estate, the guardian or conservator shall furnish an additional bond as is required by the court in order to make the sum of the bonds furnished by the guardian or conservator equal to the amount determined pursuant to Section 2320, taking into account the proceeds of the sale or mortgage or deed of trust, unless the court makes an express finding stating the reason why the bond should not be increased. If a bond or additional bond is required under this section, the order confirming the sale of real property of the estate or authorizing the borrowing of money secured by a mortgage or deed of trust on real property of the estate is not effective and the court shall not file the order until the additional bond is filed.

2333. (a) In case of a breach of a condition of the bond, an action may be brought against the sureties on the bond for the use and benefit of the ward or conservatee or of any person interested in the estate.

(b) No action may be maintained against the sureties on the bond unless commenced within four years from the discharge or removal of the guardian or conservator or within four years from the date the order surcharging the guardian or conservator becomes final, whichever is later.

(c) In any case, and notwithstanding subdivision (b) of Section 2103, no action may be maintained against the sureties on the bond unless the action commences within six years from the date the judgment under Section 2103 or the later of the orders under subdivision (b) of this section becomes final.

2334. Where a petition is filed requesting an order that a guardian or conservator be required to give a bond where no bond was originally required, or an objection is made to the sufficiency of the bond, and the petition or affidavit supporting the objection alleges facts showing that the guardian or conservator is failing to use ordinary care and diligence in the management of the estate, the court, by order, may suspend the powers of the guardian or conservator until the matter can be heard and determined.

2335. A guardian or conservator who applies for a substitution and release of a surety shall file an account with the application. The court shall not order a substitution unless the account is approved.

Article 4. Professional Fiduciaries

2340. A superior court may not appoint a person to carry out the duties of a professional fiduciary, or permit a person to continue those duties, unless he or she holds a valid, unexpired, unsuspended license as a professional fiduciary under Chapter 6 (commencing with Section 6500) of Division 3 of the Business and Professions Code, is exempt from the definition of "professional fiduciary" under Section 6501 of the Business and Professions Code, or is exempt from the licensing requirements of Section 6530 of the Business and Professions Code.

2341. This article shall become operative on July 1, 2008.

Chapter 5. Powers And Duties Of Guardian Or Conservator Of The Person

2350. As used in this chapter:

(a) "Conservator" means the conservator of the person.

(b) "Guardian" means the guardian of the person.

(c) "Residence" does not include a regional center established pursuant to Chapter 5 (commencing with Section 4620) of Division 4.5 of the Welfare and Institutions Code.

2351. (a) Subject to subdivision (b), the guardian or conservator, but not a limited conservator, has the care, custody, and control of, and has charge of the education of, the ward or conservatee. This control shall not extend to personal rights retained by the conservatee, including, but not limited to, the right to receive visitors, telephone calls, and personal mail, unless specifically limited by court order.

(b) Where the court determines that it is appropriate in the circumstances of the particular conservatee, the court, in its discretion, may limit the powers and duties that the conservator would otherwise have under subdivision (a) by an order stating either of the following:

(1) The specific powers that the conservator does not have with respect to the conservatee's person and reserving the powers so specified to the conservatee.

(2) The specific powers and duties the conservator has with respect to the conservatee's person and reserving to the conservatee all other rights with respect to the conservatee's person that the conservator otherwise would have under subdivision (a).

(c) An order under this section (1) may be included in the order appointing a conservator of the person or (2) may be made, modified, or revoked upon a petition subsequently filed, notice of the hearing on the petition having been given for the period and in the manner provided in Chapter 3 (commencing with Section 1460) of Part 1.

(d) The guardian or conservator, in exercising his or her powers, may not hire or refer any business to an entity in which he or she has a financial interest except upon authorization of the court. Prior to authorization from the court, the guardian or conservator shall disclose to the court in writing his or her financial interest in the entity. For the purposes of this subdivision, "financial interest" shall mean (1) an ownership interest in a sole proprietorship, a partnership, or a closely held corporation, or (2) an ownership interest of greater than 1 percent of the outstanding shares in a publicly traded corporation, or (3) being an officer or a director of a corporation. This subdivision shall apply only to conservators and guardians required to register with the Statewide Registry under Chapter 13 (commencing with Section 2850).

2351.5. (a) Subject to subdivision (b):

(1) The limited conservator has the care, custody, and control of the limited conservatee.

(2) The limited conservator shall secure for the limited conservatee those habilitation or treatment, training, education, medical and psychological services, and social and vocational opportunity as appropriate and as will assist the limited conservatee in the development of maximum self-reliance and independence.

(b) A limited conservator does not have any of the following powers or controls over the limited conservatee unless those powers or controls are specifically requested in the petition for appointment of a limited conservator and granted by the court in its order appointing the limited conservator:

(1) To fix the residence or specific dwelling of the limited conservatee.

(2) Access to the confidential records and papers of the limited conservatee.

(3) To consent or withhold consent to the marriage of, or the entrance into a registered domestic partnership by, the limited conservatee.

(4) The right of the limited conservatee to contract.

(5) The power of the limited conservatee to give or withhold medical consent.

(6) The limited conservatee's right to control his or her own social and sexual contacts and relationships.

(7) Decisions concerning the education of the limited conservatee.

(c) Any limited conservator, the limited conservatee, or any relative or friend of the limited conservatee may apply by petition to the superior court of the county in which the proceedings are pending to have the limited conservatorship modified by the elimination or addition of any of the powers which must be specifically granted to the limited conservator pursuant to subdivision (b). The petition shall state the facts alleged to establish that the limited conservatorship should be modified. The granting or elimination of those powers is discretionary with the court. Notice of the hearing on the petition shall be given for the period and in the manner provided in Chapter 3 (commencing with Section 1460) of Part 1.

(d) The limited conservator or any relative or friend of the limited conservatee may appear and oppose the petition. The court shall hear and determine the matter according to the laws and procedures relating to the trial of civil actions, including trial by jury if demanded. If any of the powers which must be specifically granted to the limited conservator pursuant to subdivision (b) are granted or eliminated, new letters of limited conservatorship shall be issued reflecting the change in the limited conservator's powers.

2352. (a) The guardian may establish the residence of the ward at any place within this state without the permission of the court. The guardian shall select the least restrictive appropriate residence that is available and necessary to meet the needs of the ward, and that is in the best interests of the ward.

(b) The conservator may establish the residence of the conservatee at any place within this state without the permission of the court. The conservator shall select the least restrictive appropriate residence, as described in Section 2352.5, that is available and necessary to meet the needs of the conservatee, and that is in the best interests of the conservatee.

(c) If permission of the court is first obtained, a guardian or conservator may establish the residence of a ward or conservatee at a place not within this state. Notice of the hearing on the petition to establish the residence of the ward or conservatee out of state, together with a copy of the petition, shall be given in the manner required by subdivision (a) of Section 1460 to all persons entitled to notice under subdivision (b) of Section 1511 or subdivision (b) of Section 1822.

(d) An order under subdivision (c) shall require the guardian or conservator either to return the ward or conservatee to this state, or to cause a guardianship or conservatorship proceeding or its equivalent to be commenced in the place of the new residence, when the ward or conservatee has resided in the place of new residence for a period of four months or a longer or shorter period specified in the order.

(e) (1) The guardian or conservator shall file a notice of change of residence with the court within 30 days of the date of the change. The guardian or conservator shall include in the notice of change of residence a declaration stating that the ward's or conservatee's change of residence is consistent with the standard described in subdivision (b).

(2) The guardian or conservator shall mail a copy of the notice to all persons entitled to notice under subdivision (b) of Section 1511 or subdivision (b) of Section 1822 and shall file proof of service of the notice with the court. The court may, for good cause, waive the mailing requirement pursuant to this paragraph in order to prevent harm to the conservatee or ward.

(3) If the guardian or conservator proposes to remove the ward or conservatee from his or her personal residence, except as provided by subdivision (c), the guardian or conservator shall mail a notice of his or her intention to change the residence of the ward

or conservatee to all persons entitled to notice under subdivision (b) of Section 1511 and subdivision (b) of Section 1822. In the absence of an emergency, that notice shall be mailed at least 15 days before the proposed removal of the ward or conservatee from his or her personal residence. If the notice is served less than 15 days prior to the proposed removal of the ward or conservatee, the guardian or conservatee shall set forth the basis for the emergency in the notice. The guardian or conservator shall file proof of service of that notice with the court.

(f) This section does not apply where the court has made an order under Section 2351 pursuant to which the conservatee retains the right to establish his or her own residence.

(g) As used in this section, "guardian" or "conservator" includes a proposed guardian or proposed conservator and "ward" or "conservatee" includes a proposed ward or proposed conservatee.

(h) This section does not apply to a person with developmental disabilities for whom the Director of the Department of Developmental Services or a regional center, established pursuant to Chapter 5 (commencing with Section 4620) of Division 4.5 of the Welfare and Institutions Code, acts as the conservator.

2352.5. (a) It shall be presumed that the personal residence of the conservatee at the time of commencement of the proceeding is the least restrictive appropriate residence for the conservatee. In any hearing to determine if removal of the conservatee from his or her personal residence is appropriate, that presumption may be overcome by a preponderance of the evidence.

(b) Upon appointment, the conservator shall determine the appropriate level of care for the conservatee.

(1) That determination shall include an evaluation of the level of care existing at the time of commencement of the proceeding and the measures that would be necessary to keep the conservatee in his or her personal residence.

(2) If the conservatee is living at a location other than his or her personal residence at the commencement of the proceeding, that determination shall either include a plan to return the conservatee to his or her personal residence or an explanation of the limitations or restrictions on a return of the conservatee to his or her personal residence in the foreseeable future.

(c) The determination made by the conservator pursuant to subdivision (b) shall be in writing, signed under penalty of perjury, and submitted to the court within 60 days of appointment as conservator.

(d) The conservator shall evaluate the conservatee's placement and level of care if there is a material change in circumstances affecting the conservatee's needs for placement and care.

(e) (1) This section shall not apply to a conservatee with developmental disabilities for whom the Director of Developmental Services or a regional center for the developmentally disabled, established pursuant to Chapter 5 (commencing with Section 4620) of Division 4.5 of the Welfare and Institutions Code, acts as the conservator and who receives services from a regional center pursuant to the Lanterman Developmental Disabilities Act (Division 4.5 (commencing with Section 4500) of the Welfare and Institutions Code).

(2) Services, including residential placement, for a conservatee described in paragraph (1) who is a consumer, as defined in Section 4512 of the Welfare and Institutions Code, shall be identified, delivered, and evaluated consistent with the individual program plan process described in Article 2 (commencing with Section 4640) of Chapter 5 of Division 4.5 of the Welfare and Institutions Code.

2353. (a) Subject to subdivision (b), the guardian has the same right as a parent having legal custody of a child to give consent to medical treatment performed upon the ward and to require the ward to receive medical treatment.

(b) Except as provided in subdivision (c), if the ward is 14 years of age or older, no surgery may be performed upon the ward without either (1) the consent of both the ward and the guardian or (2) a court order obtained pursuant to Section 2357 specifically authorizing such treatment.

(c) The guardian may consent to surgery to be performed upon the ward, and may require the ward to receive the surgery, in any case where the guardian determines in good faith based upon medical advice that the case is an emergency case in which the ward faces loss of life or serious bodily injury if the surgery is not performed. In such a case, the consent of the guardian alone is sufficient and no person is liable because the surgery is performed upon the ward without the ward's consent.

(d) Nothing in this section requires the consent of the guardian for medical or surgical treatment for the ward in any case where the ward alone may consent to such treatment under other provisions of law.

2354. (a) If the conservatee has not been adjudicated to lack the capacity to give informed consent for medical treatment, the conservatee may consent to his or her medical treatment. The conservator may also give consent to the medical treatment, but the consent of the conservator is not required if the conservatee has the capacity to give informed consent to the medical treatment, and the consent of the conservator alone is not sufficient under this subdivision if the conservatee objects to the medical treatment.

(b) The conservator may require the conservatee to receive medical treatment, whether or not the conservatee consents to the treatment, if a court order specifically authorizing the medical treatment has been obtained pursuant to Section 2357.

(c) The conservator may consent to medical treatment to be performed upon the conservatee, and may require the conservatee to receive the medical treatment, in any case where the conservator determines in good faith based upon medical advice that the case is an emergency case in which the medical treatment is required because (1) the treatment is required for the alleviation of severe pain or (2) the conservatee has a medical condition which, if not immediately diagnosed and treated, will lead to serious disability or death. In such a case, the consent of the conservator alone is sufficient and no person is liable because the medical treatment is performed upon the conservatee without the conservatee's consent.

2355. (a) If the conservatee has been adjudicated to lack the capacity to make health care decisions, the conservator has the exclusive authority to make health care decisions for the conservatee that the conservator in good faith based on medical advice determines to be necessary. The conservator shall make health care decisions for the conservatee in accordance with the conservatee's individual health care instructions, if any, and other wishes to the extent known to the conservator. Otherwise, the conservator shall make the decision in accordance with the conservator's determination of the conservatee's best interest. In determining the conservatee's best interest, the conservator shall consider the conservatee's personal values to the extent known to the conservator. The conservator may require the conservatee to receive the health care, whether or not the conservatee objects. In this case, the health care decision of the conservator alone is sufficient and no person is liable because the health care is administered to the conservatee without the conservatee's consent. For the purposes of this subdivision, "health care" and "health care decision" have the meanings provided in Sections 4615 and 4617, respectively.

(b) If prior to the establishment of the conservatorship the conservatee was an adherent of a religion whose tenets and practices call for reliance on prayer alone for healing, the treatment required by the conservator under the provisions of this section shall be by an accredited practitioner of that religion.

2356. (a) No ward or conservatee may be placed in a mental health treatment facility under this division against the will of the ward or conservatee. Involuntary civil placement of a ward or conservatee in a mental health treatment facility may be obtained only pursuant to Chapter 2 (commencing with Section 5150) or Chapter 3 (commencing with Section 5350) of Part 1 of Division 5 of the Welfare and Institutions Code. Nothing in this subdivision precludes the placing of a ward in a state hospital under Section 6000 of the Welfare and Institutions Code upon application of the guardian as provided in that section. The Director of Mental Health shall adopt and issue regulations defining "mental health treatment facility" for the purposes of this subdivision.

(b) No experimental drug as defined in Section 111515 of the Health and Safety Code may be prescribed for or administered to a ward or conservatee under this division. Such an experimental drug may be prescribed for or administered to a ward or conservatee only as provided in Article 4 (commencing with Section 111515) of Chapter 6 of Part 5 of Division 104 of the Health and Safety Code.

(c) No convulsive treatment as defined in Section 5325 of the Welfare and Institutions Code may be performed on a ward or conservatee under this division. Convulsive treatment may be performed on a ward or conservatee only as provided in Article 7 (commencing with Section 5325) of Chapter 2 of Part 1 of Division 5 of the Welfare and Institutions Code.

(d) No minor may be sterilized under this division.

(e) This chapter is subject to a valid and effective advance health care directive under the Health Care Decisions Law (Division 4.7 (commencing with Section 4600)).

2356.5. (a) The Legislature hereby finds and declares:

(1) That people with dementia, as defined in the last published edition of the "Diagnostic and Statistical Manual of Mental Disorders," should have a conservatorship to serve their unique and special needs.

(2) That, by adding powers to the probate conservatorship for people with dementia, their unique and special needs can be met. This will reduce costs to the conservatee and the family of the conservatee, reduce costly administration by state and county government, and safeguard the basic dignity and rights of the conservatee.

(3) That it is the intent of the Legislature to recognize that the administration of psychotropic medications has been, and can be, abused by caregivers and, therefore, granting powers to a conservator to authorize these medications for the treatment of dementia requires the protections specified in this section.

(b) Notwithstanding any other provision of law, a conservator may authorize the placement of a conservatee in a secured perimeter residential care facility for the elderly operated pursuant to Section 1569.698 of the Health and Safety Code, or a locked and secured nursing facility which specializes in the care and treatment of people with de-

mentia pursuant to subdivision (c) of Section 1569.691 of the Health and Safety Code, and which has a care plan that meets the requirements of Section 87724 of Title 22 of the California Code of Regulations, upon a court's finding, by clear and convincing evidence, of all of the following:

(1) The conservatee has dementia, as defined in the last published edition of the "Diagnostic and Statistical Manual of Mental Disorders."

(2) The conservatee lacks the capacity to give informed consent to this placement and has at least one mental function deficit pursuant to subdivision (a) of Section 811, and this deficit significantly impairs the person's ability to understand and appreciate the consequences of his or her actions pursuant to subdivision (b) of Section 811.

(3) The conservatee needs or would benefit from a restricted and secure environment, as demonstrated by evidence presented by the physician or psychologist referred to in paragraph (3) of subdivision (f).

(4) The court finds that the proposed placement in a locked facility is the least restrictive placement appropriate to the needs of the conservatee.

(c) Notwithstanding any other provision of law, a conservator of a person may authorize the administration of medications appropriate for the care and treatment of dementia, upon a court's finding, by clear and convincing evidence, of all of the following:

(1) The conservatee has dementia, as defined in the last published edition of the "Diagnostic and Statistical Manual of Mental Disorders."

(2) The conservatee lacks the capacity to give informed consent to the administration of medications appropriate to the care of dementia, and has at least one mental function deficit pursuant to subdivision (a) of Section 811, and this deficit or deficits significantly impairs the person's ability to understand and appreciate the consequences of his or her actions pursuant to subdivision (b) of Section 811.

(3) The conservatee needs or would benefit from appropriate medication as demonstrated by evidence presented by the physician or psychologist referred to in paragraph (3) of subdivision (f).

(d) Pursuant to subdivision (b) of Section 2355, in the case of a person who is an adherent of a religion whose tenets and practices call for a reliance on prayer alone for healing, the treatment required by the conservator under subdivision (c) shall be by an accredited practitioner of that religion in lieu of the administration of medications.

(e) A conservatee who is to be placed in a facility pursuant to this section shall not be placed in a mental health rehabilitation center as described in Section 5675 of the Welfare and Institutions Code, or in an institution for mental disease as described in Section 5900 of the Welfare and Institutions

Code.

(f) A petition for authority to act under this section shall be governed by Section 2357, except:

(1) The conservatee shall be represented by an attorney pursuant to Chapter 4 (commencing with Section 1470) of Part 1.

(2) The conservatee shall be produced at the hearing, unless excused pursuant to Section 1893.

(3) The petition shall be supported by a declaration of a licensed physician, or a licensed psychologist within the scope of his or her licensure, regarding each of the findings required to be made under this section for any power requested, except that the psychologist has at least two years of experience in diagnosing dementia.

(4) The petition may be filed by any of the persons designated in Section 1891.

(g) The court investigator shall annually investigate and report to the court every two years pursuant to Sections 1850 and 1851 if the conservator is authorized to act under this section. In addition to the other matters provided in Section 1851, the conservatee shall be specifically advised by the investigator that the conservatee has the right to object to the conservator's powers granted under this section, and the report shall also include whether powers granted under this section are warranted. If the conservatee objects to the conservator's powers granted under this section, or the investigator determines that some change in the powers granted under this section is warranted, the court shall provide a copy of the report to the attorney of record for the conservatee. If no attorney has been appointed for the conservatee, one shall be appointed pursuant to Chapter 4 (commencing with Section 1470) of Part 1. The attorney shall, within 30 days after receiving this report, do one of the following:

(1) File a petition with the court regarding the status of the conservatee.

(2) File a written report with the court stating that the attorney has met with the conservatee and determined that the petition would be inappropriate.

(h) A petition to terminate authority granted under this section shall be governed by Section 2359.

(i) Nothing in this section shall be construed to affect a conservatorship of the estate of a person who has dementia.

(j) Nothing in this section shall affect the laws that would otherwise apply in emergency situations.

(k) Nothing in this section shall affect current law regarding the power of a probate court to fix the residence of a conservatee or to authorize medical treatment for any conservatee who has not been determined to have dementia.

(l) (1) Until such time as the conservatorship becomes subject to review pursuant to Section 1850, this section shall not apply to a conservatorship established on or before the effective date of the adoption of Judicial Council forms that reflect the procedures authorized by this section, or January 1, 1998, whichever occurs first.

(2) Upon the adoption of Judicial Council forms that reflect the procedures authorized by this section or January 1, 1998, whichever occurs first, this section shall apply to any conservatorships established after that date.

2357. (a) As used in this section:

(1) "Guardian or conservator" includes a temporary guardian of the person or a temporary conservator of the person.

(2) "Ward or conservatee" includes a person for whom a temporary guardian of the person or temporary conservator of the person has been appointed.

(b) If the ward or conservatee requires medical treatment for an existing or continuing medical condition which is not authorized to be performed upon the ward or conservatee under Section 2252, 2353, 2354, or 2355, and the ward or conservatee is unable to give an informed consent to this medical treatment, the guardian or conservator may petition the court under this section for an order authorizing the medical treatment and authorizing the guardian or conservator to consent on behalf of the ward or conservatee to the medical treatment.

(c) The petition shall state, or set forth by medical affidavit attached thereto, all of the following so far as is known to the petitioner at the time the petition is filed:

(1) The nature of the medical condition of the ward or conservatee which requires treatment.

(2) The recommended course of medical treatment which is considered to be medically appropriate.

(3) The threat to the health of the ward or conservatee if authorization to consent to the recommended course of treatment is delayed or denied by the court.

(4) The predictable or probable outcome of the recommended course of treatment.

(5) The medically available alternatives, if any, to the course of treatment recommended.

(6) The efforts made to obtain an informed consent from the ward or conservatee.

(7) The name and addresses, so far as they are known to the petitioner, of the persons specified in subdivision (c) of Section 1510 in a guardianship proceeding or subdivision (b) of Section 1821 in a conservatorship proceeding.

(d) Upon the filing of the petition, unless an attorney is already appointed the court shall appoint the public defender or private counsel under Section 1471, to consult with and represent the ward or conservatee at the hearing on the petition and, if that appointment is made, Section 1472 applies.

(e) Notice of the petition shall be given as follows:

(1) Not less than 15 days before the hearing, notice of the time and place of the hearing, and a copy of the petition shall be personally served on the ward, if 12 years of age or older, or the conservatee, and on the attorney for the ward or conservatee.

(2) Not less than 15 days before the hearing, notice of the time and place of the hearing, and a copy of the petition shall be mailed to the following persons:

(A) The spouse or domestic partner, if any, of the proposed conservatee at the address stated in the petition.

(B) The relatives named in the petition at their addresses stated in the petition.

(f) For good cause, the court may shorten or waive notice of the hearing as provided by this section. In determining the period of notice to be required, the court shall take into account both of the following:

(1) The existing medical facts and circumstances set forth in the petition or in a medical affidavit attached to the petition or in a medical affidavit presented to the court.

(2) The desirability, where the condition of the ward or conservatee permits, of giving adequate notice to all interested persons.

(g) Notwithstanding subdivisions (e) and (f), the matter may be submitted for the determination of the court upon proper and sufficient medical affidavits or declarations if the attorney for the petitioner and the attorney for the ward or conservatee so stipulate and further stipulate that there remains no issue of fact to be determined.

(h) The court may make an order authorizing the recommended course of medical treatment of the ward or conservatee and authorizing the guardian or conservator to consent on behalf of the ward or conservatee to the recommended course of medical treatment for the ward or conservatee if the court determines from the evidence all of the following:

(1) The existing or continuing medical condition of the ward or conservatee requires the recommended course of medical treatment.

(2) If untreated, there is a probability that the condition will become life-endangering or result in a serious threat to the physical or mental health of the ward or conservatee.

(3) The ward or conservatee is unable to give an informed consent to the recommended course of treatment.

(i) Upon petition of the ward or conservatee or other interested person, the court may order that the guardian or conservator obtain or consent to, or obtain and consent to, specified medical treatment to be performed upon the ward or conservatee. Notice of the hearing on the petition under this subdivision shall be given for the period and in the manner provided in Chapter 3 (commencing with Section 1460) of Part 1.

2358. When a guardian or conservator is appointed, the court may, with the consent of the guardian or conservator, insert in the order of appointment conditions not otherwise obligatory providing for the care, treatment, education, and welfare of the ward or conservatee. Any such conditions shall be included in the letters. The performance of such conditions is a part of the duties of the guardian or conservator for the faithful performance of which the guardian or conservator and the sureties on the bond are responsible.

2359. (a) Upon petition of the guardian or conservator or ward or conservatee or other interested person, the court may authorize and instruct the guardian or conservator or approve and confirm the acts of the guardian or conservator.

(b) Notice of the hearing on the petition shall be given for the period and in the manner provided in Chapter 3 (commencing with Section 1460) of Part 1.

(c) (1) When a guardian or conservator petitions for the approval of a purchase, lease, or rental of real or personal property from the estate of a ward or conservatee, the guardian or conservator shall provide a statement disclosing the family or affiliate relationship between the guardian and conservator and the purchaser, lessee, or renter of the property, and the family or affiliate relationship between the guardian or conservator and any agent hired by the guardian or conservator.

(2) For the purposes of this subdivision, "family" means a person' s spouse, domestic partner, or relatives within the second degree of lineal or collateral consanguinity of a person or a person's spouse. For the purposes of this subdivision, "affiliate" means an entity that is under the direct control, indirect control, or common control of the guardian or conservator.

(3) A violation of this section shall result in the rescission of the purchase, lease, or rental of the property. Any losses incurred by the estate of the ward or conservatee because the property was sold or leased at less than fair market value shall be deemed as charges against the guardian or conservator under the provisions of Sections 2401.3 and 2401.5. The court shall assess a civil penalty equal to three times the charges against the guardian, conservator, or other person in violation of this section, and may assess punitive damages as it deems proper. If the estate does not incur losses as a result of the violation, the court shall order the guardian, conservator, or other person in violation of this section to pay a fine of up to five thousand dollars ($5,000) for each violation. The fines and penalties provided in this section are in addition to any other rights and remedies provided by law.

2360. Upon the establishment of a conservatorship by the court and annually thereafter, the conservator shall ensure that a clear photograph of the conservatee is taken and preserved for the purpose of identifying the conservatee if he or she becomes missing.

Chapter 6. Powers And Duties Of Guardian Or Conservator Of The Estate

Article 1. Definitions And General Provisions

2400. As used in this chapter:

(a) "Conservator" means the conservator of the estate, or the limited conservator of the estate to the extent that the powers and duties of the limited conservator are specifically and expressly provided by the order appointing the limited conservator.

(b) "Estate" means all of the conservatee's or ward's personal property, wherever located, and real property located in this state.

(c) "Guardian" means the guardian of the estate.

2401. (a) The guardian or conservator, or limited conservator to the extent specifically and expressly provided in the appointing court's order, has the management and control of the estate and, in managing and controlling the estate, shall use ordinary care and diligence. What constitutes use of ordinary care and diligence is determined by all the circumstances of the particular estate.

(b) The guardian or conservator:

(1) Shall exercise a power to the extent that ordinary care and diligence requires that the power be exercised.

(2) Shall not exercise a power to the extent that ordinary care and diligence requires that the power not be exercised.

(c) Notwithstanding any other law, a guardian or conservator who is not a trust company, in exercising his or her powers, may not hire or refer any business to an entity in which he or she has a financial interest except upon authorization of the court. Prior to authorization from the court, the guardian or conservator shall disclose to the court in writing his or her financial interest in the entity. For the purposes of this subdivision, "financial interest" shall mean (1) an ownership interest in a sole proprietorship, a partnership, or a closely held corporation, or (2) an ownership interest of greater than 1 percent of the outstanding shares in a publicly held corporation, or (3) being an officer or a director of a corporation.

(d) Notwithstanding any other law, a guardian or conservator who is a trust company, in exercising its powers may not, except upon authorization of the court, invest in securities of the trust company or an affiliate or subsidiary, or other securities from which the trust company or affiliate or subsidiary receives a financial benefit or in a mutual fund, other than a mutual fund authorized in paragraph (5) of subdivision (a) of Section 2574, registered under the Investment Company Act of 1940 (Subchapter 1 (commencing with Sec. 80a-1) of Chapter 2D of Title 15 of the United States Code), to which the trust company or its affiliate provides services, including, but not limited to, services as an investment adviser, sponsor, distributor, custodian, agent, registrar, administrator, servicer, or manager, and for which the trust company or its affiliate receives compensation.

Prior to authorization from the court, the guardian or conservator shall disclose to the court in writing the trust company's financial interest.

2401.1. The guardian or conservator shall use ordinary care and diligence to determine whether the ward or conservatee owns real property in a foreign jurisdiction and to preserve and protect that property. What constitutes use of ordinary care and diligence shall be determined by all the facts and circumstances known, or that become known, to the guardian or conservator, the value of the real property located in the foreign jurisdiction, and the needs of the ward or conservatee. The guardian or conservator, except as provided in subdivision (a) of Section 1061 and in Section 1062, is not charged with, and shall have no duty to inventory or account for the real property located in a foreign jurisdiction, but the guardian or conservator shall, when presenting the inventory and appraisal and accounting to the court, include the schedule set forth in subdivision (h) of Section 1063.

2401.3. (a) If the guardian or conservator breaches a fiduciary duty, the guardian or conservator is chargeable with any of the following that is appropriate under the circumstances:

(1) Any loss or depreciation in value of the estate resulting from the breach of duty, with interest.

(2) Any profit made by the guardian or conservator through the breach of duty, with interest.

(3) Any profit that would have accrued to the estate if the loss of profit is the result of the breach of duty.

(b) If the guardian or conservator has acted reasonably and in good faith under the circumstances as known to the guardian or conservator, the court, in its discretion, may excuse the guardian or conservator in whole or in part from liability under subdivision (a) if it would be equitable to do so.

2401.5. (a) If the guardian or conservator is liable for interest pursuant to Section 2401.3, the guardian or conservator is liable for the greater of the following amounts:

(1) The amount of interest that accrues at the legal rate on judgments.

(2) The amount of interest actually received.

(b) If the guardian or conservator has acted reasonably and in good faith under the circumstances as known to the guardian or conservator, the court, in its discretion, may excuse the guardian or conservator in whole or in part from liability under subdivision (a) if it would be equitable to do so.

2401.6. Any surcharge that a guardian or conservator incurs under the provisions of Sections 2401.3 or 2401.5 may not be paid by or offset against future fees or wages to be provided by the estate to the guardian or conservator.

2401.7. The provisions of Sections 2401.3 and 2401.5 for liability of a guardian or conservator for breach of a fiduciary duty do not prevent resort to any other remedy available against the guardian or conservator under the statutory or common law.

2402. When a guardian or conservator is appointed, the court may, with the consent of the guardian or conservator, insert in the order of appointment conditions not otherwise obligatory providing for the care and custody of the property of the ward or conservatee. Any such conditions shall be included in the letters. The performance of such conditions is a part of the duties of the guardian or conservator for the faithful performance of which the guardian or conservator and the sureties on the bond are responsible.

2403. (a) Upon petition of the guardian or conservator, the ward or conservatee, a creditor, or other interested person, the court may authorize and instruct the guardian or conservator, or approve and confirm the acts of the guardian or conservator, in the administration, management, investment, disposition, care, protection, operation, or preservation of the estate, or the incurring or payment of costs, fees, or expenses in connection therewith.

(b) Notice of the hearing on the petition shall be given for the period and in the manner provided in Chapter 3 (commencing with Section 1460) of Part 1.

(c) (1) When a guardian or conservator petitions for the approval of a purchase, lease, or rental of real or personal property from the estate of a ward or conservatee, the guardian or conservator shall provide a statement disclosing the family or affiliate relationship between the guardian and conservator and the purchaser, lessee, or renter of the property, and the family or affiliate relationship between the guardian or conservator and any agent hired by the guardian or conservator.

(2) For the purposes of this subdivision, "family" means a person's spouse, domestic partner, or relatives within the second degree of lineal or collateral consanguinity of a person or a person's spouse. For the purposes of this subdivision, "affiliate" means an entity that is under the direct control, indirect control, or common control of the guardian or conservator.

(3) A violation of this section shall result in the rescission of the purchase, lease, or rental of the property. Any losses incurred by the estate of the ward or conservatee because the property was sold or leased at less than fair market value shall be deemed as

charges against the guardian or conservator under the provisions of Sections 2401.3 and 2401.5. The court shall assess a civil penalty equal to three times the charges against the guardian, conservator, or other person in violation of this section, and may assess punitive damages as it deems proper. If the estate does not incur losses as a result of the violation, the court shall order the guardian, conservator, or other person in violation of this section to pay a fine of up to five thousand dollars ($5,000) for each violation. The fines and penalties provided in this section are in addition to any other rights and remedies provided by law.

2404. (a) If the guardian or conservator fails, neglects, or refuses to furnish comfortable and suitable support, maintenance, or education for the ward or conservatee as required by this division, or to pay a debt, expense, or charge lawfully due and payable by the ward or conservatee or the estate as provided in this division, the court shall, upon petition or upon its own motion, order the guardian or conservator to do so from the estate.

(b) The petition may be filed by the ward or conservatee or by the creditor or any other interested person. Notice of the hearing on the petition shall be given for the period and in the manner provided in Chapter 3 (commencing with Section 1460) of Part 1.

2405. If there is a dispute relating to the estate between the guardian or conservator and a third person, the guardian or conservator, or the limited conservator to the extent specifically and expressly provided in the order appointing the limited conservator, may do either of the following:

(a) Enter into an agreement in writing with the third person to refer the dispute to a temporary judge designated in the agreement. The agreement shall be filed with the clerk, who shall thereupon, with the approval of the court, enter an order referring the matter to the designated person. The temporary judge shall proceed promptly to hear and determine the matter in controversy by summary procedure, without any pleadings, discovery, or jury trial. The decision of the temporary judge is subject to Section 632 of the Code of Civil Procedure. Judgment shall be entered on the decision and is as valid and effective as if rendered by a judge of the court in an action against the guardian or conservator or the third person commenced by ordinary process.

(b) Enter into an agreement in writing with the third person that a judge of the court, pursuant to the agreement and with the written consent of the judge, both filed with the clerk within the time for bringing an independent action on the matter in dispute, may hear and determine the dispute pursuant to the procedure provided in subdivision (a).

2406. If there is a dispute relating to the

estate between the guardian or conservator and a third person, the guardian or conservator may enter into an agreement in writing with the third person to submit the dispute to arbitration under Title 9 (commencing with Section 1280) of Part 3 of the Code of Civil Procedure. The agreement is not effective unless it has first been approved by the court and a copy of the approved agreement is filed with the court.

2407. This chapter applies to property owned by husband and wife as community property only to the extent authorized by Part 6 (commencing with Section 3000).

2408. Nothing in this chapter limits or restricts any authority granted to a guardian or conservator pursuant to Article 11 (commencing with Section 2590) to administer the estate under that article.

2410. On or before January 1, 2008, the Judicial Council, in consultation with the California Judges Association, the California Association of Superior Court Investigators, the California State Association of Public Administrators, Public Guardians, and Public Conservators, the State Bar of California, the National Guardianship Association, and the Association of Professional Geriatric Care Managers, shall adopt a rule of court that shall require uniform standards of conduct for actions that conservators and guardians may take under this chapter on behalf of conservatees and wards to ensure that the estate of conservatees or wards are maintained and conserved as appropriate and to prevent risk of loss or harm to the conservatees or wards. This rule shall include at a minimum standards for determining the fees that may be charged to conservatees or wards and standards for asset management.

Article 2. Support And Maintenance Of Ward Or Conservatee And Dependents

2420. (a) Subject to Section 2422, the guardian or conservator shall apply the income from the estate, so far as necessary, to the comfortable and suitable support, maintenance, and education of the ward or conservatee (including care, treatment, and support of a ward or conservatee who is a patient in a state hospital under the jurisdiction of the State Department of State Hospitals or the State Department of Developmental Services) and of those legally entitled to support, maintenance, or education from the ward or conservatee, taking into account the value of the estate and the condition of life of the persons required to be furnished such support, maintenance, or education.

(b) If the income from the estate is insufficient for the purpose described in subdivision (a), the guardian or conservator may sell or give a security interest in or other lien on any personal property of the estate, or sell or mortgage or give a deed of trust on any real property of the estate, as provided in this part.

(c) When the amount paid by the guardian or conservator for the purpose described in subdivision (a) satisfies the standard set out in that subdivision, and the payments are supported by proper vouchers or other proof satisfactory to the court, the guardian or conservator shall be allowed credit for such payments when the accounts of the guardian or conservator are settled.

(d) Nothing in this section requires the guardian or conservator to obtain court authorization before making the payments authorized by this section, but nothing in this section dispenses with the need to obtain any court authorization otherwise required for a particular transaction.

(e) Nothing in this section precludes the guardian or conservator from seeking court authorization or instructions or approval and confirmation pursuant to Section 2403.

2421. (a) Upon petition of the guardian or conservator or the ward or conservatee, the court may authorize the guardian or conservator to pay to the ward or conservatee out of the estate a reasonable allowance for the personal use of the ward or conservatee. The allowance shall be in such amount as the court may determine to be for the best interests of the ward or conservatee.

(b) Notice of the hearing on the petition shall be given for the period and in the manner provided in Chapter 3 (commencing with Section 1460) of Part 1.

(c) The guardian or conservator is not required to account for such allowance other than to establish that it has been paid to the ward or conservatee. The funds so paid are subject to the sole control of the ward or conservatee.

2422. (a) Upon petition of the guardian or conservator, the ward or conservatee, or any other interested person, the court may for good cause order the ward or conservatee to be wholly or partially supported, maintained, or educated out of the estate notwithstanding the existence of a third party legally obligated to provide such support, maintenance, or education. Such order may be made for a limited period of time. If not so limited, it continues in effect until modified or revoked.

(b) Notice of the hearing on the petition shall be given for the period and in the manner provided in Chapter 3 (commencing with Section 1460) of Part 1.

2423. (a) Upon petition of the conservator, the conservatee, the spouse or domestic partner of the conservatee, or a relative within the second degree of the conservatee, the court may by order authorize or direct the conservator to pay and distribute surplus income of the estate or any part of the surplus income (not used for the support, maintenance, and education of the conservatee and of those legally entitled to support, maintenance, or education from the conservatee) to the spouse or domestic partner of the conservatee and to relatives within the second degree of the conservatee whom the conservatee would, in the judgment of the court, have aided but for the existence of the conservatorship. The court in ordering payments under this section may impose conditions if the court determines that the conservatee would have imposed the conditions if the conservatee had the capacity to act.

(b) The granting of the order and the amounts and proportions of the payments are discretionary with the court, but the court shall consider all of the following:

(1) The amount of surplus income available after adequate provision has been made for the comfortable and suitable support, maintenance, and education of the conservatee and of those legally entitled to support, maintenance, or education from the conservatee.

(2) The circumstances and condition of life to which the conservatee and the spouse or domestic partner and relatives have been accustomed.

(3) The amount that the conservatee would in the judgment of the court have allowed the spouse or domestic partner and relatives but for the existence of the conservatorship.

(c) Notice of the hearing on the petition shall be given for the period and in the manner provided in Chapter 3 (commencing with Section 1460) of Part 1.

Article 3. Payment Of Debts And Expenses

2430. (a) Subject to subdivisions (b) and (c), the guardian or conservator shall pay the following from any principal and income of the estate:

(1) The debts incurred by the ward or conservatee before creation of the guardianship or conservatorship, giving priority to the debts described in Section 2431 to the extent required by that section.

(2) The debts incurred by the ward or conservatee during the guardianship or conservatorship to provide the necessaries of life to the ward or conservatee, and to the spouse and minor children of the ward or conservatee, to the extent the debt is reasonable. Also, the debts reasonably incurred by the conservatee during the conservatorship to provide the basic living expenses, as defined in Section 297 of the Family Code, to the domestic partner of the conservatee. The guardian or conservator may deduct the amount of any payments for these debts from any allowance otherwise payable to the ward or conservatee.

(3) In the case of a conservatorship, any other debt incurred by the conservatee during the conservatorship only if the debt

satisfies the requirements of any order made under Chapter 4 (commencing with Section 1870) of Part 3.

(4) The reasonable expenses incurred in the collection, care, and administration of the estate, but court authorization is required for payment of compensation to any of the following:

(A) The guardian or conservator of the person or estate or both.

(B) An attorney for the guardian or conservator of the person or estate or both.

(C) An attorney for the ward or conservatee.

(D) An attorney for the estate.

(E) The public guardian for the costs and fee under Section 2902.

(b) The payments provided for by paragraph (3) of subdivision (a) are not required to be made to the extent the payments would impair the ability to provide the necessaries of life to the conservatee and the spouse and minor children of the conservatee and to provide the basic living expenses, as defined in Section 297 of the Family Code, of the domestic partner of the conservatee.

(c) The guardian or conservator may petition the court under Section 2403 for instructions when there is doubt whether a debt should be paid under this section.

2431. (a) Subject to subdivision (d), the guardian or conservator may petition the court under Section 2403 for instructions when there is doubt whether a wage claim should be paid under this section.

(b) The guardian or conservator shall promptly pay wage claims for work done or services rendered for the ward or conservatee within 30 days prior to the date the petition for appointment of the guardian or conservator was filed. The payments made pursuant to this subdivision shall not exceed nine hundred dollars ($900) to each claimant. If there is insufficient money to pay all the claims described in this subdivision up to nine hundred dollars ($900), the money available shall be distributed among such claimants in proportion to the amount of their respective claims.

(c) After the payments referred to in subdivision (b) have been made, the guardian or conservator shall pay wage claims for work done or services rendered for the ward or conservatee within 90 days prior to the date the petition for appointment of the guardian or conservator was filed, excluding the claims described in subdivision (b). The payments made pursuant to this subdivision shall not exceed one thousand one hundred dollars ($1,100) to each claimant. If there is insufficient money to pay all the claims described in this subdivision up to one thousand one hundred dollars ($1,100), the money available shall be distributed among such claimants in proportion to the amounts of their respective claims.

(d) The guardian or conservator may require sworn claims to be presented. If there is reasonable cause to believe that the claim is not valid, the guardian or conservator may refuse to pay the claim in whole or in part but shall pay any part thereof that is not disputed without prejudice to the claimant's rights as to the balance of the claim. The guardian or conservator shall withhold sufficient money to cover the disputed portion until the claimant has had a reasonable opportunity to establish the validity of the claim by bringing an action, either in the claimant's own name or through an assignee, against the guardian or conservator.

(e) If the guardian or conservator neglects or refuses to pay all or any portion of a claim which is not in dispute, the court shall order the guardian or conservator to do so upon the informal application of any wage claimant or the assignee or legal representative of such claimant.

Article 4. Estate Management Powers Generally

2450. (a) Unless this article specifically provides a proceeding to obtain court authorization or requires court authorization, the powers and duties set forth in this article may be exercised or performed by the guardian or conservator without court authorization, instruction, approval, or confirmation. Nothing in this subdivision precludes the guardian or conservator from seeking court authorization, instructions, approval, or confirmation pursuant to Section 2403.

(b) Upon petition of the ward or conservatee, a creditor, or any other interested person, or upon the court's own motion, the court may limit the authority of the guardian or conservator under subdivision (a) as to a particular power or duty or as to particular powers or duties. Notice of the hearing on a petition under this subdivision shall be given for the period and in the manner provided in Chapter 3 (commencing with Section 1460) of Part 1.

2451. The guardian or conservator may collect debts and benefits due to the ward or conservatee and the estate.

2451.5. The guardian or conservator may do any of the following:

(a) Contract for the guardianship or conservatorship, perform outstanding contracts, and, thereby, bind the estate.

(b) Purchase tangible personal property.

(c) Subject to the provisions of Chapter 8 (commencing with Section 2640), employ an attorney to advise and represent the guardian or conservator in all matters, including the conservatorship proceeding and all other actions or proceedings.

(d) Employ and pay the expense of accountants, investment advisers, agents, depositaries, and employees.

(e) Operate for a period of 45 days after the issuance of the letters of guardianship or conservatorship, at the risk of the estate, a business, farm, or enterprise constituting an asset of the estate.

2452. (a) The guardian or conservator may endorse and cash or deposit any checks, warrants, or drafts payable to the ward or conservatee which constitute property of the estate.

(b) If it appears likely that the estate will satisfy the conditions of subdivision (b) of Section 2628, the court may order that the guardian or conservator be the designated payee for public assistance payments received pursuant to Part 3 (commencing with Section 11000) or Part 4 (commencing with Section 16000) of Division 9 of the Welfare and Institutions Code.

2453. The guardian or conservator may deposit money belonging to the estate in an insured account in a financial institution in this state. Unless otherwise provided by court order, the money deposited under this section may be withdrawn without order of court.

2453.5. (a) Subject to subdivision (b), where a trust company is a guardian or conservator and in the exercise of reasonable judgment deposits money of the estate in an account in any department of the corporation or association of which it is a part, it is chargeable with interest thereon at the rate of interest prevailing among banks of the locality on such deposits.

(b) Where it is to the advantage of the estate, the amount of cash that is reasonably necessary for orderly administration of the estate may be deposited in a checking account that does not bear interest which is maintained in a department of the corporation or association of which the trust company is a party.

2454. The guardian or conservator may deposit personal property of the estate with a trust company for safekeeping. Unless otherwise provided by court order, the personal property may be withdrawn without order of court.

2455. (a) A trust company serving as guardian or conservator may deposit securities that constitute all or part of the estate in a securities depository as provided in Section 775 of the Financial Code.

(b) If the securities have been deposited with a trust company pursuant to Section 2328 or Section 2454, the trust company may deposit the securities in a securities depository as provided in Section 775 of the Financial Code.

(c) The securities depository may hold securities deposited with it in the manner authorized by Section 775 of the Financial Code.

2456. (a) Upon application of the guardian or conservator, the court may, with or without notice, order that money or other personal property be deposited pursuant to Section 2453 or 2454, and be subject to withdrawal only upon authorization of the court.

(b) The guardian or conservator shall deliver a copy of the court order to the financial institution or trust company at the time the deposit is made.

(c) No financial institution or trust company accepting a deposit pursuant to Section 2453 or 2454 is on notice of the existence of an order that the money or other property is subject to withdrawal only upon authorization of the court unless it has actual notice of the order.

2457. The guardian or conservator may maintain in good condition and repair the home or other dwelling of either or both of the following:

(a) The ward or conservatee.

(b) The persons legally entitled to such maintenance and repair from the ward or conservatee.

2458. With respect to a share of stock of a domestic or foreign corporation held in the estate, a membership in a nonprofit corporation held in the estate, or other property held in the estate, a guardian or conservator may do any one or more of the following:

(a) Vote in person, and give proxies to exercise, any voting rights with respect to the share, membership, or other property.

(b) Waive notice of a meeting or give consent to the holding of a meeting.

(c) Authorize, ratify, approve, or confirm any action which could be taken by shareholders, members, or property owners.

2459. (a) The guardian or conservator may obtain, continue, renew, modify, terminate, or otherwise deal in any of the following for the purpose of providing protection to the ward or conservatee or a person legally entitled to support from the ward or conservatee:

(1) Medical, hospital, and other health care policies, plans, or benefits.

(2) Disability policies, plans, or benefits.

(b) The conservator may continue in force any of the following in which the conservatee, or a person legally entitled to support, maintenance, or education from the conservatee, has or will have an interest:

(1) Life insurance policies, plans, or benefits.

(2) Annuity policies, plans, or benefits.

(3) Mutual fund and other dividend reinvestment plans.

(4) Retirement, profit-sharing, and employee welfare plans or benefits.

(c) The right to elect benefit or payment options, to terminate, to change beneficiaries or ownership, to assign rights, to borrow, or to receive cash value in return for a surrender of rights, or to take similar actions under any of the policies, plans, or benefits described in subdivision (b) may be exercised by the conservator only after authorization or direction by order of the court, except as permitted in Section 2544.5. To obtain such an order, the conservator or

other interested person shall petition under Article 10 (commencing with Section 2580).

(d) Notwithstanding subdivision (c), unless the court otherwise orders, the conservator without authorization of the court may borrow on the loan value of an insurance policy to pay the current premiums to keep the policy in force if the conservatee followed that practice prior to the establishment of the conservatorship.

(e) The guardian may give the consent provided in Section 10112 of the Insurance Code without authorization of the court, but the guardian may use funds of the guardianship estate to effect or maintain in force a contract entered into by the ward under Section 10112 of the Insurance Code only after authorization by order of the court. To obtain such an order, the guardian, the ward, or any other interested person shall file a petition showing that it is in the best interest of the ward or of the guardianship estate to do so. Notice of the hearing on the petition shall be given for the period and in the manner provided in Chapter 3 (commencing with Section 1460) of Part 1.

(f) Nothing in this section limits the power of the guardian or conservator to make investments as otherwise authorized by this division.

2460. The guardian or conservator may insure:

(a) Property of the estate against loss or damage.

(b) The ward or conservatee, the guardian or conservator, and all or any part of the estate against liability to third persons.

2461. (a) The guardian or conservator may prepare, execute, and file tax returns for the ward or conservatee and for the estate and may exercise options and elections and claim exemptions for the ward or conservatee and for the estate under the applicable tax laws.

(b) Notwithstanding Section 2502, the guardian or conservator may pay, contest, and compromise taxes, penalties, and assessments upon the property of the estate and income and other taxes payable or claimed to be payable by the ward or conservatee or the estate.

2462. Subject to Section 2463, unless another person is appointed for that purpose, the guardian or conservator may:

(a) Commence and maintain actions and proceedings for the benefit of the ward or conservatee or the estate.

(b) Defend actions and proceedings against the ward or conservatee, the guardian or conservator, or the estate.

(c) File a petition commencing a case under Title 11 of the United States Code (Bankruptcy) on behalf of the ward or conservatee.

2463. (a) The guardian or conservator may bring an action against the other cotenants for partition of any property in which the ward or conservatee has an undivided interest if the court has first made an order authorizing the guardian or conservator to do so. The court may make such an order ex parte on a petition filed by the guardian or conservator.

(b) The guardian or conservator may consent and agree, without an action, to a partition of the property and to the part to be set off to the estate, and may execute deeds or conveyances to the owners of the remaining interests of the parts to which they may be respectively entitled, if the court has made an order under Article 5 (commencing with Section 2500) authorizing the guardian or conservator to do so.

(c) If the ward or conservatee, or the guardian or conservator as such, is made a defendant in a partition action, the guardian or conservator may defend the action without authorization of the court.

2464. (a) If it is to the advantage of the estate to accept a deed to property which is subject to a mortgage or deed of trust in lieu of foreclosure of the mortgage or sale under the deed of trust, the guardian or conservator may, after authorization by order of the court and upon such terms and conditions as may be imposed by the court, accept a deed conveying the property to the ward or conservatee.

(b) To obtain an order under this section, the guardian or conservator shall file a petition showing the advantage to the estate of accepting the deed. Notice of the hearing on the petition shall be given for the period and in the manner provided in Chapter 3 (commencing with Section 1460) of Part 1.

(c) The court shall make an order under this section only if the advantage to the estate of accepting the deed is shown by clear and convincing evidence.

2465. The guardian or conservator may dispose of or abandon valueless property.

2466. The guardian or conservator may advance the guardian's or conservator's own funds for the benefit of the ward or conservatee or the estate and may reimburse the advance out of the income and principal of the estate first available. With court authorization or approval, interest on the amount advanced may be allowed at the legal rate payable on judgments.

2467. (a) The guardian or conservator continues to have the duty of custody and conservation of the estate after the death of the ward or conservatee pending the delivery thereof to the personal representative of the ward's or conservatee's estate or other disposition according to law.

(b) The guardian or conservator has such powers as are granted to a guardian or conservator under this division as are necessary for the performance of the duty imposed by subdivision (a).

2468. (a) The conservator of the estate of a disabled attorney who was engaged in the practice of law at the time of his or her disability, or other person interested in the estate, may bring a petition seeking the appointment of an active member of the State Bar of California to take control of the files and assets of the practice of the disabled member.

(b) The petition may be filed and heard on such notice that the court determines is in the best interests of the persons interested in the estate of the disabled member. If the petition alleges that the immediate appointment of a practice administrator is required to safeguard the interests of the estate, the court may dispense with notice provided that the conservator is the petitioner or has joined in the petition or has otherwise waived notice of hearing on the petition.

(c) The petition shall indicate the powers sought for the practice administrator from the list of powers set forth in Section 6185 of the Business and Professions Code. These powers shall be specifically listed in the order appointing the practice administrator.

(d) The petition shall allege the value of the assets that are to come under the control of the practice administrator, including but not limited by the amount of funds in all accounts used by the disabled member. The court shall require the filing of a surety bond in the amount of the value of the personal property to be filed with the court by the practice administrator. No action may be taken by the practice administrator unless a bond has been duly filed with the court.

(e) The practice administrator shall not be the attorney representing the conservator.

(f) The court shall appoint the attorney nominated by the disabled member in a writing, including but not limited to the disabled member's will, unless the court concludes that the appointment of the nominated person would be contrary to the best interests of the estate or would create a conflict of interest with any of the clients of the disabled member.

(g) The practice administrator shall be compensated only upon order of the court making the appointment for his or her reasonable and necessary services. The law practice shall be the source of the compensation for the practice administrator unless the assets are insufficient, in which case, the compensation of the practice administrator shall be charged against the assets of the estate as a cost of administration. The practice administrator shall also be entitled to reimbursement of his or her costs.

(h) Upon conclusion of the services of the practice administrator, the practice administrator shall render an accounting and petition for its approval by the superior court making the appointment. Upon settlement of the accounting, the practice administrator shall be discharged and the surety on his or her bond exonerated.

(i) If the court appointing the practice administrator determines upon petition that the disabled attorney has recovered his or her capacity to resume his or her law practice, the appointment of a practice administrator shall forthwith terminate and the disabled attorney shall be restored to his or her practice.

(j) For purposes of this section, the person appointed to take control of the practice of the disabled member shall be referred to as the "practice administrator" and the conservatee shall be referred to as the "disabled member."

Article 5. Compromise Of Claims And Actions; Extension, Renewal, Or Modification Of Obligations

2500. (a) Unless this article or some other applicable statute requires court authorization or approval, if it is to the advantage of the estate, the guardian or conservator may do any of the following without court authorization, instruction, approval, or confirmation:

(1) Compromise or settle a claim, action, or proceeding by or for the benefit of, or against, the ward or conservatee, the guardian or conservator, or the estate, including the giving of a covenant not to sue.

(2) Extend, renew, or in any manner modify the terms of an obligation owing to or running in favor of the ward or conservatee or the estate.

(b) Nothing in this section precludes the guardian or conservator from seeking court authorization, instructions, approval, or confirmation pursuant to Section 2403.

(c) Upon petition of the ward or conservatee, a creditor, or any interested person, or upon the court's own motion, the court may limit the authority of the guardian or conservator under subdivision (a). Notice of the hearing on the petition shall be given for the period and in the manner provided in Chapter 3 (commencing with Section 1460) of Part 1.

2501. (a) Except as provided in subdivision (b), court approval is required for a compromise, settlement, extension, renewal, or modification which affects any of the following:

(1) Title to real property.

(2) An interest in real property or a lien or encumbrance on real property.

(3) An option to purchase real property or an interest in real property.

(b) If it is to the advantage of the estate, the guardian or conservator without prior court approval may extend, renew, or modify a lease of real property in either of the following cases:

(1) Where under the lease as extended, renewed, or modified the rental does not exceed five thousand dollars ($5,000) a month and the term does not exceed two years.

(2) Where the lease is from month to month, regardless of the amount of the rental.

(c) For the purposes of subdivision (b), if the lease as extended, renewed, or modified gives the lessee the right to extend the term of the lease, the length of the term shall be considered as though the right to extend had been exercised.

2502. Court approval is required for a compromise or settlement of a matter when the transaction requires the transfer or encumbrance of property of the estate, or the creation of an unsecured liability of the estate, or both, in an amount or value in excess of twenty-five thousand dollars ($25,000).

2503. Court approval is required for any of the following:

(a) A compromise or settlement of a claim by the ward or conservatee against the guardian or conservator or against the attorney for the guardian or conservator, whether or not the claim arises out of the administration of the estate.

(b) An extension, renewal, or modification of the terms of a debt or similar obligation of the guardian or conservator, or of the attorney for the guardian or conservator, owing to or running in favor of the ward or conservatee or the estate.

2504. Court approval is required for the compromise or settlement of any of the following:

(a) A claim for the support, maintenance, or education of (1) the ward or conservatee, or (2) a person whom the ward or conservatee is legally obligated to support, maintain, or educate, against any other person (including, but not limited to, the spouse or parent of the ward or the spouse, domestic partner, parent, or adult child of the conservatee).

(b) A claim of the ward or conservatee for wrongful death.

(c) A claim of the ward or conservatee for physical or nonphysical harm to the person.

2505. (a) Subject to subdivision (c), where the claim or matter is the subject of a pending action or proceeding, the court approval required by this article shall be obtained from the court in which the action or proceeding is pending.

(b) Where the claim or matter is not the subject of a pending action or proceeding, the court approval required by this article shall be obtained from one of the following:

(1) The court in which the guardianship or conservatorship proceeding is pending.

(2) The superior court of the county where the ward or conservatee or guardian or conservator resides at the time the petition for approval is filed.

(3) The superior court of any county where a suit on the claim or matter properly could be brought.

(c) Where the claim or matter is the subject of a pending action or proceeding that is not brought in a court of this state, court approval required by this article shall be obtained from either of the following:

(1) The court in which the action or proceeding is pending.

(2) The court in which the guardianship or conservatorship proceeding is pending.

2506. Where approval of the court in which the guardianship or conservatorship proceeding is pending is required under this article, the guardian or conservator shall file a petition with the court showing the advantage of the compromise, settlement, extension, renewal, or modification to the ward or conservatee and the estate. Notice of the hearing on the petition shall be given for the period and in the manner provided in Chapter 3 (commencing with Section 1460) of Part 1.

2507. Notwithstanding Sections 2500 to 2506, inclusive:

(a) Whenever another statute requires, provides a procedure for, or dispenses with court approval of a compromise, settlement, extension, renewal, or modification, the provisions of that statute govern any case to which that statute applies.

(b) Whenever another statute provides that a compromise or settlement of an administrative proceeding is not valid unless approved in such proceeding, the approval is governed by that statute, and approval in the guardianship or conservatorship proceeding is not required.

Article 7. Sales

2540. (a) Except as otherwise provided in Sections 2544 and 2545, and except for the sale of a conservatee's present or former personal residence as set forth in subdivision (b), sales of real or personal property of the estate under this article are subject to authorization, confirmation, or direction of the court, as provided in this article.

(b) In seeking authorization to sell a conservatee's present or former personal residence, the conservator shall notify the court that the present or former personal residence is proposed to be sold and that the conservator has discussed the proposed sale with the conservatee. The conservator shall inform the court whether the conservatee supports or is opposed to the proposed sale and shall describe the circumstances that necessitate the proposed sale, including whether the conservatee has the ability to live in the personal residence and why other alternatives, including, but not limited to, in-home care services, are not available. The court, in its discretion, may require the court investigator to discuss the proposed sale with the conservatee. This subdivision shall not apply when the conservator is granted the power to sell real property of the estate pursuant to Article 11 (commencing with Section 2590).

2541. The guardian or conservator may sell real or personal property of the estate in any of the following cases:

(a) If the income of the estate is insufficient for the comfortable and suitable support, maintenance, and education of the ward or conservatee (including care, treatment, and support of the ward or conservatee if a patient in a state hospital under the jurisdiction of the State Department of State Hospitals or the State Department of Developmental Services) or of those legally entitled to support, maintenance, or education from the ward or conservatee.

(b) If the sale is necessary to pay the debts referred to in Sections 2430 and 2431.

(c) If the sale is for the advantage, benefit, and best interest of (1) the ward or conservatee, (2) the estate, or (3) the ward or conservatee and those legally entitled to support, maintenance, or education from the ward or conservatee.

2542. (a) All sales shall be for cash or for part cash and part deferred payments. Except as otherwise provided in Sections 2544 and 2545, the terms of sale are subject to the approval of the court.

(b) If real property is sold for part deferred payments, the guardian or conservator shall take the note of the purchaser for the unpaid portion of the purchase money, with a mortgage or deed of trust on the property to secure payment of the note. The mortgage or deed of trust shall be subject only to encumbrances existing at the date of sale and such other encumbrances as the court may approve.

(c) If real or personal property of the estate sold for part deferred payments consists of an undivided interest, a joint tenancy interest, or any other interest less than the entire ownership, and the owner or owners of the remaining interests in the property join in the sale, the note and deed of trust or mortgage may be made to the ward or conservatee and the other owner or owners.

2543. (a) If estate property is required or permitted to be sold, the guardian or conservator may:

(1) Use discretion as to which property to sell first.

(2) Sell the entire interest of the estate in the property or any lesser interest therein.

(3) Sell the property either at public auction or private sale.

(b) Subject to Section 1469, unless otherwise specifically provided in this article, all proceedings concerning sales by guardians or conservators, publishing and posting notice of sale, reappraisal for sale, minimum offer price for the property, reselling the property, report of sale and petition for confirmation of sale, and notice and hearing of that petition, making orders authorizing sales, rejecting or confirming sales and reports of sales, ordering and making conveyances of property sold, and allowance of commissions, shall conform, as nearly as may be, to the provisions of this code concerning sales by a personal representative, including, but not limited to, Articles 6 (commencing with

Section 10300), 7 (commencing with Section 10350), 8 (commencing with Section 10360), and 9 (commencing with Section 10380) of Chapter 18 of Part 5 of Division 7. The provisions concerning sales by a personal representative as described in the Independent Administration of Estates Act, Part 6 (commencing with Section 10400) of Division 7 shall not apply to this subdivision.

(c) Notwithstanding Section 10309, if the last appraisal of the conservatee's personal residence was conducted more than six months prior to the confirmation hearing, a new appraisal shall be required prior to the confirmation hearing, unless the court finds that it is in the best interests of the conservatee to rely on an appraisal of the personal residence that was conducted not more than one year prior to the confirmation hearing.

(d) The clerk of the court shall cause notice to be posted pursuant to subdivision (b) only in the following cases:

(1) If posting of notice of hearing is required on a petition for the confirmation of a sale of real or personal property of the estate.

(2) If posting of notice of a sale governed by Section 10250 (sales of personal property) is required or authorized.

(3) If posting of notice is ordered by the court.

2544. (a) Except as specifically limited by order of the court, subject to Section 2541, the guardian or conservator may sell securities without authorization, confirmation, or direction of the court if any of the following conditions is satisfied:

(1) The securities are to be sold on an established stock or bond exchange.

(2) The securities to be sold are securities designated as a national market system security on an interdealer quotation system or subsystem thereof, by the National Association of Securities Dealers, Inc., sold through a broker-dealer registered under the Securities Exchange Act of 1934 during the regular course of business of the broker-dealer.

(3) The securities are to be directly redeemed by the issuer thereof.

(b) Section 2543 does not apply to sales under this section.

2544.5. Except as specifically limited by the court, subject to Section 2541, the guardian or conservator may sell mutual funds held without designation of a beneficiary without authorization, confirmation, or direction of the court. Section 2543 does not apply to sales under this section.

2545. (a) Subject to subdivisions (b) and (c) and to Section 2541, the guardian or conservator may sell or exchange tangible personal property of the estate without authorization, confirmation, or direction of the court.

(b) The aggregate of the sales or exchanges made during any calendar year under this section may not exceed five thousand dollars ($5,000).

(c) A sale or exchange of personal effects or of furniture or furnishings used for personal, family, or household purposes may be made under this section only if:

(1) In the case of a guardianship, the ward is under the age of 14 or, if 14 years of age or over, consents to the sale or exchange.

(2) In the case of a conservatorship, the conservatee either (i) consents to the sale or exchange or (ii) the conservatee does not have legal capacity to give such consent.

(d) Failure of the guardian or conservator to observe the limitations of subdivision (b) or (c) does not invalidate the title of, or impose any liability upon, a third person who acts in good faith and without actual notice of the lack of authority of the guardian or conservator.

(e) Subdivision (b) of Section 2543 does not apply to sales under this section.

2547. The guardian or conservator shall apply the proceeds of the sale to the purposes for which it was made, as far as necessary, and the residue, if any, shall be managed as the other property of the estate.

2548. No action for the recovery of any property sold by a guardian or conservator may be maintained by the ward or conservatee or by any person claiming under the ward or conservatee unless commenced within the later of the following times:

(a) Three years after the termination of the guardianship or conservatorship.

(b) When a legal disability to sue exists by reason of minority or otherwise at the time the cause of action accrues, within three years after the removal thereof.

Article 8. Notes, Mortgages, Leases, Conveyances, And Exchanges

2550. Except as otherwise provided by statute, a guardian or conservator may borrow money, lend money, give security, lease, convey, or exchange property of the estate, or engage in any other transaction under this article only after authorization by order of the court. Such an order may be obtained in the manner provided in this article.

2551. (a) In any case described in Section 2541 or Section 2552, the guardian or conservator, after authorization by order of the court, may borrow money upon a note, either unsecured or to be secured by a security interest or other lien on the personal property of the estate or any part thereof or to be secured by a mortgage or deed of trust on the real property of the estate or any part thereof. The guardian or conservator shall apply the money to the purpose specified in the order.

(b) To obtain an order under this section, the guardian or conservator, the ward or conservatee, or any other interested person may file a petition with the court. The petition shall state the purpose for which the order is sought, the necessity for or advantage to accrue from the order, the amount of money proposed to be borrowed, the rate of interest to be paid, the length of time the note is to run, and a general description of the property proposed to be mortgaged or subjected to a deed of trust or other lien. Notice of the hearing on the petition shall be given for the period and in the manner provided in Chapter 3 (commencing with Section 1460) of Part 1.

(c) The court may require such additional proof of the fairness and feasibility of the transaction as the court determines is necessary. If the required showing is made, the court may make an order authorizing the transaction.

The court in its order may do any one or more of the following:

(1) Order that the amount specified in the petition, or a lesser amount, be borrowed.

(2) Prescribe the maximum rate of interest and the period of the loan.

(3) Require that the interest and the whole or any part of the principal be paid from time to time out of the estate or any part thereof.

(4) Require that the personal property used as security or any buildings on real property to be mortgaged or subjected to the deed of trust be insured for the further security of the lender and that the premiums be paid out of the estate.

(5) Specify the purpose for which the money to be borrowed is to be applied.

(6) Prescribe such other terms and conditions concerning the transaction as the court determines to be to the advantage of the estate.

(d) The note and the mortgage or deed of trust, if any, shall be signed by the guardian or conservator.

(e) Jurisdiction of the court to administer the estate of the ward or conservatee is effectual to vest the court with jurisdiction to make the order for the note and for the security interest, lien, mortgage, or deed of trust. This jurisdiction shall conclusively inure to the benefit of the owner of the security interest or lien, mortgagee named in the mortgage, or the trustee and beneficiary named in the deed of trust, and their heirs and assigns. No omission, error, or irregularity in the proceedings shall impair or invalidate the proceedings or the note, security interest, lien, mortgage, or deed of trust given pursuant to an order under this section.

(f) Upon any foreclosure or sale under a security interest, lien, mortgage, or deed of trust described in subdivision (a), if the proceeds of the sale of the encumbered property are insufficient to pay the note, the security interest, lien, mortgage, or deed of trust, and the costs or expenses of sale, no judgment or claim for any deficiency may be had or allowed against the ward or conservatee or the estate.

2552. (a) The guardian or conservator may give a security interest or other lien upon the personal property of the estate or any part thereof or a mortgage or deed of trust upon the real property of the estate or any part thereof, after authorization by order of the court as provided in Section 2551, for any of the following purposes:

(1) To pay, reduce, extend, or renew a security interest, lien, mortgage, or deed of trust already existing on property of the estate.

(2) To improve, use, operate, or preserve the property proposed to be mortgaged or subjected to a deed of trust, or some part thereof.

(b) If property of the estate consists of an undivided interest in real or personal property, or any other interest therein less than the entire ownership, upon a showing that it would be to the advantage of the estate to borrow money to improve, use, operate, or preserve the property jointly with the owners of the other interests therein, or to pay, reduce, extend, or renew a security interest, lien, mortgage, or deed of trust already existing on all of the property, the guardian or conservator, after authorization by order of the court as provided in Section 2551, may join with the owners of the other interests in the borrowing of money and the execution of a joint and several note and such security interest, lien, mortgage, or deed of trust as may be required to secure the payment of the note. The note may be for such sum as is required for the purpose.

(c) No omission, error, or irregularity in the proceedings under this section shall impair or invalidate the proceedings or the note, security interest, lien, mortgage, or deed of trust given pursuant to an order made under this section.

2552.5. For the purpose of this article, if a lease gives the lessee the right to extend the term of the lease, the length of the term shall be considered as though the right to extend had been exercised.

2553. (a) Except as provided in Section 2555, leases may be executed by the guardian or conservator with respect to the property of the estate only after authorization by order of the court.

(b) To obtain an order under this section, the guardian or conservator or any interested person may file a petition with the court. The petition shall state (1) a general description of the property proposed to be leased, (2) the term, rental, and general conditions of the proposed lease, and (3) the advantage to the estate to accrue from giving the lease. If the lease is proposed to be for a term longer than 10 years, the petition shall also state facts showing the need for the longer lease and its advantage to the estate. Notice of the hearing on the petition shall be given for the period and in the manner provided in Chapter 3 (commencing with Section 1460) of Part 1.

(c) At the hearing, the court shall entertain and consider any other offer made in good faith at the hearing to lease the same property on more favorable terms. If the court is satisfied that it will be to the advantage of the estate, the court shall make an order authorizing the guardian or conservator to make the lease to the person and on the terms and conditions stated in the order. The court shall not make an order authorizing the guardian or conservator to make the lease to any person other than the lessee named in the petition unless the offer made at the hearing is acceptable to the guardian or conservator.

(d) Jurisdiction of the court to administer the estate of the ward or conservatee is effectual to vest the court with jurisdiction to make the order for the lease. This jurisdiction shall conclusively inure to the benefit of the lessee and the lessee's heirs and assigns. No omission, error, or irregularity in the proceedings shall impair or invalidate the proceedings or the lease made pursuant to an order made under this article.

2554. (a) An order authorizing the execution of a lease shall set forth the minimum rental or royalty or both and the period of the lease, which shall be for such time as the court may authorize.

(b) The order may authorize other terms and conditions, including, with respect to a lease for the purpose of exploration for or production or removal of minerals, oil, gas, or other hydrocarbon substances, or geothermal energy, any one or more of the following:

(1) A provision for the payment of rental and royalty to a depositary.

(2) A provision for the appointment of a common agent to represent the interests of all the lessors.

(3) A provision for the payment of a compensatory royalty in lieu of rental and in lieu of drilling and producing operations on the land covered by the lease.

(4) A provision empowering the lessee to enter into any agreement authorized by Section 3301 of the Public Resources Code with respect to the land covered by the lease.

(5) A provision for a community oil lease or pooling or unitization by the lessee.

(c) If the lease covers additional property owned by other persons or an undivided or other interest of the ward or conservatee less than the entire ownership in the property, the order may authorize the lease to provide for division of rental and royalty in the proportion that the land or interest of each owner bears to the total area of the land or total interests covered by such lease.

(d) If the lease is for the purpose of exploration for or production or removal of minerals, oil, gas, or other hydrocarbon substances, or geothermal energy, the court may authorize that the lease be for a fixed period and any of the following:

(1) So long thereafter as minerals, oil, gas, or other hydrocarbon substances or geothermal energy are produced in paying quantities from the property leased or mining or drilling operations are conducted thereon.

(2) If the lease provides for the payment of a compensatory royalty, so long thereafter as such compensatory royalty is paid.

(3) If the land covered by the lease is included in an agreement authorized by Section 3301 of the Public Resources Code, so long thereafter as oil, gas, or other hydrocarbon substances are produced in paying quantities from any of the lands included in any such agreement or drilling operations are conducted thereon.

2555. If it is to the advantage of the estate, the guardian or conservator may lease, as lessor, real property of the estate without authorization of the court in either of the following cases:

(a) Where the rental does not exceed five thousand dollars ($5,000) a month and the term does not exceed two years.

(b) Where the lease is from month to month, regardless of the amount of the rental.

2556. (a) If it is for the advantage, benefit, and best interests of the estate and those interested therein, the guardian or conservator, after authorization by order of the court, may do any of the following either with or without consideration:

(1) Dedicate or convey real property of the estate for any purpose to any of the following:

(A) This state or any public entity in this state.

(B) The United States or any agency or instrumentality of the United States.

(2) Dedicate or convey an easement over any real property of the estate to any person for any purpose.

(3) Convey, release, or relinquish to this state or any public entity in this state any access rights to any street, highway, or freeway from any real property of the estate.

(4) Consent as a lienholder to a dedication, conveyance, release, or relinquishment under paragraph (1), (2), or (3) by the owner of property subject to the lien.

(b) To obtain an order under this section, the guardian or conservator or any other interested person shall file a petition with the court. Notice of the hearing on the petition shall be given for the period and in the manner provided in Chapter 3 (commencing with Section 1460) of Part 1.

2557. (a) Whenever it is for the advantage, benefit, and best interests of the ward or conservatee and those legally entitled to support, maintenance, or education from the ward or conservatee, the guardian or conservator, after authorization by order of the court, may exchange any property of the estate for other property upon such terms and conditions as may be prescribed by the court.

The terms and conditions prescribed by the court may include the payment or receipt of part cash by the guardian or conservator.

(b) To obtain an order under this section, the guardian or conservator or any interested person shall file a petition containing all of the following:

(1) A description of the property.

(2) The terms and conditions of the proposed exchange.

(3) A showing that the proposed exchange is for the advantage, benefit, and best interests of the ward or conservatee and those legally entitled to support, maintenance, or education from the ward or conservatee.

(c) Except as provided in subdivision (d), notice of the hearing on the petition shall be given for the period and in the manner provided in Chapter 3 (commencing with Section 1460) of Part 1.

(d) If the petition is for authorization to exchange stocks, bonds, or other securities as defined in Section 10200 for different stocks, bonds, or other securities, the court, upon a showing of good cause, may order that the notice be given for a shorter period or be dispensed with.

(e) After authorization by order of the court, the guardian or conservator may execute the conveyance or transfer to the person with whom the exchange is made to effectuate the exchange.

(f) No omission, error, or irregularity in the proceedings under this section shall impair or invalidate the proceedings or the exchange made pursuant to an order made under this section.

Article 9. Investments And Purchase Of Property

2570. (a) The guardian or conservator, after authorization by order of the court, may invest the proceeds of sales and any other money of the estate as provided in the order.

(b) To obtain an order of the court authorizing a transaction under subdivision (a) of this section, the guardian or conservator, the ward or conservatee, or any other interested person may file a petition with the court.

(c) Notice of the hearing on the petition shall be given for the period and in the manner provided in Chapter 3 (commencing with Section 1460) of Part 1. The court may order that the notice be dispensed with.

(d) The court may require such proof of the fairness and feasibility of the transaction as the court determines is necessary.

(e) If the required showing is made, the court may make an order authorizing the transaction and may prescribe in the order the terms and conditions upon which the transaction shall be made.

2571. When authorized by order of the court under Section 2570, the guardian or conservator may purchase:

(a) Real property in this state as a home for the ward or conservatee if such purchase is for the advantage, benefit, and best interest of the ward or conservatee.

(b) Real property as a home for those legally entitled to support and maintenance from the ward or conservatee if such purchase is for the advantage, benefit, and best interest of the ward or conservatee and of those legally entitled to support and maintenance from the ward or conservatee.

2572. An order authorizing the guardian or conservator to purchase real property may authorize the guardian or conservator to join with the spouse of the ward or the spouse or domestic partner of the conservatee or with any other person or persons in the purchase of the real property, or an interest, equity, or estate therein, in severalty, in common, in community, or in joint tenancy, for cash or upon a credit or for part cash and part credit. When the court authorizes the purchase of real property, the court may order the guardian or conservator to execute all necessary instruments and commitments to complete the transaction.

2573. An order authorizing investment in bonds issued by any state or of any city, county, city and county, political subdivision, public corporation, district, or special district of any state may authorize the guardian or conservator to select from among bonds issued by any such issuer, without specifying any particular issuer or issue of bonds, if the type of issuer is designated in general terms and the order specifies as to such bonds a minimum quality rating as shown in a recognized investment service, a minimum interest coupon rate, a minimum yield to maturity, and the date of maturity within a five-year range.

2574. (a) Subject to subdivision (b), the guardian or conservator, without authorization of the court, may invest funds of the estate pursuant to this section in:

(1) Direct obligations of the United States, or of the State of California, maturing not later than five years from the date of making the investment.

(2) United States Treasury bonds redeemable at par value on the death of the holder for payment of federal estate taxes, regardless of maturity date.

(3) Securities listed on an established stock or bond exchange in the United States which are purchased on such exchange.

(4) Eligible securities for the investment of surplus state moneys as provided for in Section 16430 of the Government Code.

(5) An interest in a money market mutual fund registered under the Investment Company Act of 1940 (15 U.S.C. Sec. 80a-1, et seq.) or an investment vehicle authorized for the collective investment of trust funds pursuant to Section 9.18 of Part 9 of Title 12 of the Code of Federal Regulations, the portfolios of which are limited to United States government obligations maturing not later than five years from the date of investment

and to repurchase agreements fully collateralized by United States government obligations.

(6) Units of a common trust fund described in Section 1564 of the Financial Code. The common trust fund shall have as its objective investment primarily in short-term fixed income obligations and shall be permitted to value investments at cost pursuant to regulations of the appropriate regulatory authority.

(b) In making and retaining investments made under this section, the guardian or conservator shall take into consideration the circumstances of the estate, indicated cash needs, and, if reasonably ascertainable, the date of the prospective termination of the guardianship or conservatorship.

(c) Nothing in this section limits the authority of the guardian or conservator to seek court authorization for any investment, or to make other investments with court authorization, as provided in this division.

Article 10. Substituted Judgment

2580. (a) The conservator or other interested person may file a petition under this article for an order of the court authorizing or requiring the conservator to take a proposed action for any one or more of the following purposes:

(1) Benefiting the conservatee or the estate.

(2) Minimizing current or prospective taxes or expenses of administration of the conservatorship estate or of the estate upon the death of the conservatee.

(3) Providing gifts for any purposes, and to any charities, relatives (including the other spouse or domestic partner), friends, or other objects of bounty, as would be likely beneficiaries of gifts from the conservatee.

(b) The action proposed in the petition may include, but is not limited to, the following:

(1) Making gifts of principal or income, or both, of the estate, outright or in trust.

(2) Conveying or releasing the conservatee's contingent and expectant interests in property, including marital property rights and any right of survivorship incident to joint tenancy or tenancy by the entirety.

(3) Exercising or releasing the conservatee's powers as donee of a power of appointment.

(4) Entering into contracts.

(5) Creating for the benefit of the conservatee or others, revocable or irrevocable trusts of the property of the estate, which trusts may extend beyond the conservatee's disability or life. A special needs trust for money paid pursuant to a compromise or judgment for a conservatee may be established only under Chapter 4 (commencing with Section 3600) of Part 8, and not under this article.

(6) Transferring to a trust created by the conservator or conservatee any property unintentionally omitted from the trust.

(7) Exercising options of the conservatee to purchase or exchange securities or other property.

(8) Exercising the rights of the conservatee to elect benefit or payment options, to terminate, to change beneficiaries or ownership, to assign rights, to borrow, or to receive cash value in return for a surrender of rights under any of the following:

(A) Life insurance policies, plans, or benefits.

(B) Annuity policies, plans, or benefits.

(C) Mutual fund and other dividend investment plans.

(D) Retirement, profit sharing, and employee welfare plans and benefits.

(9) Exercising the right of the conservatee to elect to take under or against a will.

(10) Exercising the right of the conservatee to disclaim any interest that may be disclaimed under Part 8 (commencing with Section 260) of Division 2.

(11) Exercising the right of the conservatee (A) to revoke or modify a revocable trust or (B) to surrender the right to revoke or modify a revocable trust, but the court shall not authorize or require the conservator to exercise the right to revoke or modify a revocable trust if the instrument governing the trust (A) evidences an intent to reserve the right of revocation or modification exclusively to the conservatee, (B) provides expressly that a conservator may not revoke or modify the trust, or (C) otherwise evidences an intent that would be inconsistent with authorizing or requiring the conservator to exercise the right to revoke or modify the trust.

(12) Making an election referred to in Section 13502 or an election and agreement referred to in Section 13503.

(13) Making a will.

2581. Notice of the hearing of the petition shall be given, regardless of age, for the period and in the manner provided in Chapter 3 (commencing with Section 1460) or Part 1 to all of the following:

(a) The persons required to be given notice under Chapter 3 (commencing with Section 1460) of Part 1.

(b) The persons required to be named in a petition for the appointment of a conservator.

(c) So far as is known to the petitioner, beneficiaries under any document executed by the conservatee which may have testamentary effect unless the court for good cause dispenses with such notice.

(d) So far as is known to the petitioner, the persons who, if the conservatee were to die immediately, would be the conservatee's heirs under the laws of intestate succession unless the court for good cause dispenses with such notice.

(e) Such other persons as the court may

order.

2582. The court may make an order authorizing or requiring the proposed action under this article only if the court determines all of the following:

(a) The conservatee either (1) is not opposed to the proposed action or (2) if opposed to the proposed action, lacks legal capacity for the proposed action.

(b) Either the proposed action will have no adverse effect on the estate or the estate remaining after the proposed action is taken will be adequate to provide for the needs of the conservatee and for the support of those legally entitled to support, maintenance, and education from the conservatee, taking into account the age, physical condition, standards of living, and all other relevant circumstances of the conservatee and those legally entitled to support, maintenance, and education from the conservatee.

2583. In determining whether to authorize or require a proposed action under this article, the court shall take into consideration all the relevant circumstances, which may include, but are not limited to, the following:

(a) Whether the conservatee has legal capacity for the proposed transaction and, if not, the probability of the conservatee's recovery of legal capacity.

(b) The past donative declarations, practices, and conduct of the conservatee.

(c) The traits of the conservatee.

(d) The relationship and intimacy of the prospective donees with the conservatee, their standards of living, and the extent to which they would be natural objects of the conservatee's bounty by any objective test based on such relationship, intimacy, and standards of living.

(e) The wishes of the conservatee.

(f) Any known estate plan of the conservatee (including, but not limited to, the conservatee's will, any trust of which the conservatee is the settlor or beneficiary, any power of appointment created by or exercisable by the conservatee, and any contract, transfer, or joint ownership arrangement with provisions for payment or transfer of benefits or interests at the conservatee's death to another or others which the conservatee may have originated).

(g) The manner in which the estate would devolve upon the conservatee's death, giving consideration to the age and the mental and physical condition of the conservatee, the prospective devisees or heirs of the conservatee, and the prospective donees.

(h) The value, liquidity, and productiveness of the estate.

(i) The minimization of current or prospective income, estate, inheritance, or other taxes or expenses of administration.

(j) Changes of tax laws and other laws which would likely have motivated the conservatee to alter the conservatee's estate plan.

(k) The likelihood from all the circumstances that the conservatee as a reasonably prudent person would take the proposed action if the conservatee had the capacity to do so.

(l) Whether any beneficiary is the spouse or domestic partner of the conservatee.

(m) Whether a beneficiary has committed physical abuse, neglect, false imprisonment, or financial abuse against the conservatee after the conservatee was substantially unable to manage his or her financial resources, or resist fraud or undue influence, and the conservatee's disability persisted throughout the time of the hearing on the proposed substituted judgment.

2584. After hearing, the court, in its discretion, may approve, modify and approve, or disapprove the proposed action and may authorize or direct the conservator to transfer or dispose of assets or take other action as provided in the court's order.

2585. Nothing in this article imposes any duty on the conservator to propose any action under this article, and the conservator is not liable for failure to propose any action under this article.

2586. (a) As used in this section, "estate plan of the conservatee" includes, but is not limited to, the conservatee's will, any trust of which the conservatee is the settlor or beneficiary, any power of appointment created by or exercisable by the conservatee, and any contract, transfer, or joint ownership arrangement with provisions for payment or transfer of benefits or interests at the conservatee's death to another or others which the conservatee may have originated.

(b) Notwithstanding Article 3 (commencing with Section 950) of Chapter 4 of Division 8 of the Evidence Code (lawyer-client privilege), the court, in its discretion, may order that any person having possession of any document constituting all or part of the estate plan of the conservatee shall deliver the document to the court for examination by the court, and, in the discretion of the court, by the attorneys for the persons who have appeared in the proceedings under this article, in connection with the petition filed under this article.

(c) Unless the court otherwise orders, no person who examines any document produced pursuant to an order under this section shall disclose the contents of the document to any other person. If that disclosure is made, the court may adjudge the person making the disclosure to be in contempt of court.

(d) For good cause, the court may order that a document constituting all or part of the estate plan of the conservatee, whether or not produced pursuant to an order under this section, shall be delivered for safekeeping to the custodian designated by the court. The court may impose those conditions it determines are appropriate for holding and safeguarding the document. The court may authorize the conservator to take any action a depositor may take under Part 15 (commencing with Section 700) of Division 2.

Article 11. Independent Exercise Of Powers

2590. (a) The court may, in its discretion, make an order granting the guardian or conservator any one or more or all of the powers specified in Section 2591 if the court determines that, under the circumstances of the particular guardianship or conservatorship, it would be to the advantage, benefit, and best interest of the estate to do so. Subject only to the requirements, conditions, or limitations as are specifically and expressly provided, either directly or by reference, in the order granting the power or powers, and if consistent with Section 2591, the guardian or conservator may exercise the granted power or powers without notice, hearing, or court authorization, instructions, approval, or confirmation in the same manner as the ward or conservatee could do if possessed of legal capacity.

(b) The guardian or conservator does not have a power specified in Section 2591 without authorization by a court under this article or other express provisions of this code.

2591. The powers referred to in Section 2590 are:

(a) The power to operate, for a period longer than 45 days, at the risk of the estate a business, farm, or enterprise constituting an asset of the estate.

(b) The power to grant and take options.

(c) (1) The power to sell at public or private sale real or personal property of the estate without confirmation of the court of the sale, other than the personal residence of a conservatee.

(2) The power to sell at public or private sale the personal residence of the conservatee as described in Section 2591.5 without confirmation of the court of the sale. The power granted pursuant to this paragraph is subject to the requirements of Sections 2352.5 and 2541.

(3) For purposes of this subdivision, authority to sell property includes authority to contract for the sale and fulfill the terms and conditions of the contract, including conveyance of the property.

(d) The power to create by grant or otherwise easements and servitudes.

(e) The power to borrow money.

(f) The power to give security for the repayment of a loan.

(g) The power to purchase real or personal property.

(h) The power to alter, improve, raze, replace, and rebuild property of the estate.

(i) The power to let or lease property of the estate, or extend, renew, or modify a lease of real property, for which the monthly rental or lease term exceeds the maximum specified in Sections 2501 and 2555 for any purpose (including exploration for and removal of gas, oil, and other minerals and natural resources) and for any period, including a term commencing at a future time.

(j) The power to lend money on adequate security.

(k) The power to exchange property of the estate.

(l) The power to sell property of the estate on credit if any unpaid portion of the selling price is adequately secured.

(m) The power to commence and maintain an action for partition.

(n) The power to exercise stock rights and stock options.

(o) The power to participate in and become subject to and to consent to the provisions of a voting trust and of a reorganization, consolidation, merger, dissolution, liquidation, or other modification or adjustment affecting estate property.

(p) The power to pay, collect, compromise, or otherwise adjust claims, debts, or demands upon the guardianship or conservatorship described in subdivision (a) of Section 2501, Section 2502 or 2504, or to arbitrate any dispute described in Section 2406.

2591.5. (a) Notwithstanding any other provisions of this article, a conservator seeking an order under Section 2590 authorizing a sale of the conservatee's personal residence shall demonstrate to the court that the terms of sale, including the price for which the property is to be sold and the commissions to be paid from the estate, are in all respects in the best interests of the conservatee.

(b) A conservator authorized to sell the conservatee's personal residence pursuant to Section 2590 shall comply with the provisions of Section 10309 concerning appraisal or new appraisal of the property for sale and sale at a minimum offer price. Notwithstanding Section 10309, if the last appraisal of the conservatee's personal residence was conducted more than six months prior to the proposed sale of the property, a new appraisal shall be required prior to the sale of the property, unless the court finds that it is in the best interests of the conservatee to rely on an appraisal of the personal residence that was conducted not more than one year prior to the proposed sale of the property. For purposes of this section, the date of sale is the date of the contract for sale of the property.

(c) Within 15 days of the close of escrow, the conservator shall serve a copy of the final escrow settlement statement on all persons entitled to notice of the petition for appointment for a conservator and all persons who have filed and served a request for special notice and shall file a copy of the final escrow statement along with a proof of service with the court.

(d) The court may, for good cause, waive any of the requirements of this section.

2592. (a) The guardian or conservator may apply by petition for an order under Section 2590.

(b) The application for the order may be included in the petition for the appointment of the guardian or conservator. In such case, the notice of hearing on the petition shall include a statement that the petition includes an application for the grant of one or more powers under this article and shall list the specific power or powers applied for.

(c) If the application for the order is made by petition filed after the filing of the petition for the appointment of the guardian or conservator, notice of the hearing on the petition shall be given for the period and in the manner provided in Chapter 3 (commencing with Section 1460) of Part 1.

2593. (a) The court, on its own motion or on petition of any interested person, when it appears to be for the best interests of the ward or conservatee or the estate, may withdraw any or all of the powers previously granted pursuant to this article or may impose restrictions, conditions, and limitations on the exercise of such powers by the guardian or conservator.

(b) Notice of the hearing on a petition under this section shall be given for the period and in the manner provided in Chapter 3 (commencing with Section 1460) of Part 1.

2594. (a) When a power or powers are granted pursuant to this article, the letters of guardianship or conservatorship shall state the power or powers so granted and the restrictions, conditions, or limitations, if any, prescribed in the order and shall refer to this article.

(b) When a power or powers are granted by a subsequent order, new letters shall be issued in the form described in subdivision (a).

(c) If the powers are withdrawn, or if the powers are restricted, conditioned, or limited by a subsequent order after they are granted, new letters shall be issued accordingly.

2595. (a) The grant of a power or powers pursuant to this article does not affect the right of the guardian or conservator to petition the court as provided in Section 2403 or to petition the court under other provisions of this code, as to a particular transaction or matter, in the same manner as if the power or powers had not been granted pursuant to this article.

(b) Where authority exists under other provisions of law, either general or specific, for the guardian or conservator to do any act or to enter into any transaction described in Section 2591, the guardian or conservator may proceed under such other provisions of law and is not required to obtain authority under this article.

Chapter 7. Inventory And Accounts

Article 1. Definitions And General Provisions

2600. As used in this chapter, unless the context otherwise requires:

(a) "Conservator" means (1) the conservator of the estate or (2) the limited conservator of the estate to the extent that the powers and duties of the limited conservator are specifically and expressly provided by the order appointing the limited conservator.

(b) "Estate" means all of the conservatee's or ward's personal property, wherever located, and real property located in this state.

(c) "Guardian" means the guardian of the estate.

2601. (a) Unless otherwise ordered by the court, if the ward or conservatee is employed at any time during the continuance of the guardianship or conservatorship:

(1) The wages or salaries for such employment are not a part of the estate and the guardian or conservator is not accountable for such wages or salaries.

(2) The wages or salaries for such employment shall be paid to the ward or conservatee and are subject to his or her control to the same extent as if the guardianship or conservatorship did not exist.

(b) Any court order referred to in subdivision (a) is binding upon the employer only after notice of the order has been received by the employer.

Article 2. Inventory And Appraisal Of Estate

2610. (a) Within 90 days after appointment, or within any further time as the court for reasonable cause upon ex parte petition of the guardian or conservator may allow, the guardian or conservator shall file with the clerk of the court and mail to the conservatee and to the attorneys of record for the ward or conservatee, along with notice of how to file an objection, an inventory and appraisal of the estate, made as of the date of the appointment of the guardian or conservator. A copy of this inventory and appraisal, along with notice of how to file an objection, also shall be mailed to the conservatee's spouse or registered domestic partner, the conservatee's relatives in the first degree, and, if there are no such relatives, to the next closest relative, unless the court determines that the mailing will result in harm to the conservatee.

(b) The guardian or conservator shall take and subscribe to an oath that the inventory contains a true statement of all of the estate of the ward or conservatee of which the guardian or conservator has possession or knowledge. The oath shall be endorsed upon or annexed to the inventory.

(c) The property described in the inventory shall be appraised in the manner provided for the inventory and appraisal of estates of decedents. The guardian or conservator may appraise the assets that a personal representative could appraise under Section 8901.

(d) If a conservatorship is initiated pursuant to the Lanterman-Petris-Short Act (Part 1 (commencing with Section 5000) of Division 5 of the Welfare and Institutions Code), and no sale of the estate will occur:

(1) The inventory and appraisal required by subdivision (a) shall be filed within 90 days after appointment of the conservator.

(2) The property described in the inventory may be appraised by the conservator and need not be appraised by a probate referee.

(e) By January 1, 2008, the Judicial Council shall develop a form to effectuate the notice required in subdivision (a).

2611. If the ward or conservatee is or has been during the guardianship or conservatorship a patient in a state hospital under the jurisdiction of the State Department of State Hospitals or the State Department of Developmental Services, the guardian or conservator shall mail a copy of the inventory and appraisal filed under Section 2610 to the director of the appropriate department at the director's office in Sacramento not later than 15 days after the inventory and appraisal is filed with the court. Compliance with this section is not required if an unrevoked certificate described in subdivision (c) of Section 1461 is on file with the court with respect to the ward or conservatee.

2612. If a timely request is made, the clerk of court shall mail a copy of the inventory and appraisal filed under Section 2610 to the county assessor.

2613. Whenever any property of the ward or conservatee is discovered that was not included in the inventory, or whenever any other property is received by the ward or conservatee or by the guardian or conservator on behalf of the ward or conservatee (other than by the actions of the guardian or conservator in the investment and management of the estate), the guardian or conservator shall file a supplemental inventory and appraisal for that property and like proceedings shall be followed with respect thereto as in the case of an original inventory, but the appraisal shall be made as of the date the property was so discovered or received.

2614. (a) Within 30 days after the inventory and appraisal is filed, the guardian or conservator or any creditor or other interested person may file written objections to any or all appraisals. The clerk shall set the objections for hearing not less than 15 days after their filing.

(b) Notice of the hearing, together with a copy of the objections, shall be given for the period and in the manner provided in Chapter 3 (commencing with Section 1460) of Part 1. If the appraisal was made by a probate referee, the person objecting shall also mail notice of the hearing and a copy of the objection to the probate referee at least 15 days before the time set for the hearing.

(c) The court shall determine the objections and may fix the true value of any asset to which objection has been filed. For the purpose of this subdivision, the court may cause an independent appraisal or appraisals to be made by at least one additional appraiser at the expense of the estate or, if the objecting party is not the guardian or conservator and the objection is rejected by the court, the court may assess the cost of any such additional appraisal or appraisals against the objecting party.

2614.5. (a) If the guardian or conservator fails to file an inventory and appraisal within the time allowed by law or by court order, upon request of the ward or conservatee, the spouse of the ward or the spouse or domestic partner of the conservatee, any relative or friend of the ward or conservatee, or any interested person, the court shall order the guardian or conservator to file the inventory and appraisal within the time prescribed in the order or to show cause why the guardian or conservator should not be removed. The person who requested the order shall serve it upon the guardian or conservator in the manner provided in Section 415.10 or 415.30 of the Code of Civil Procedure or in a manner as is ordered by the court.

(b) If the guardian or conservator fails to file the inventory and appraisal as required by the order within the time prescribed in the order, unless good cause is shown for not doing so, the court, on its own motion or on petition, may remove the guardian or conservator, revoke the letters of guardianship or conservatorship, and enter judgment accordingly, and order the guardian or conservator to file an account and to surrender the estate to the person legally entitled thereto.

(c) The procedure provided in this section is optional and does not preclude the use of any other remedy or sanction when an inventory and appraisal is not timely filed.

2614.7. If a guardian or conservator of the person or estate, or both, is a professional fiduciary, as described in Section 2340, who is required to be licensed under the Professional Fiduciaries Act (Chapter 6 (commencing with Section 6500) of Division 3 of the Business and Professions Code), the guardian or conservator shall file, concurrently with the inventory and appraisal required by Section 2610, a proposed hourly fee schedule or another statement of his or her proposed compensation from the estate of the ward or conservatee for services performed as a guardian or conservator. The filing of a proposed hourly fee schedule or another statement of the guardian's or conservator's proposed compensation, as required by this section, shall not preclude a court from later reducing the guardian's, conservator's, or his or her attorney's fees or other compensation.

2614.8. At any time on or after one year from the submission of an hourly fee schedule or another statement of proposed compensation under this section or under Section 1510, 1821, 2250, or 2614.7, a guardian or conservator who is a professional fiduciary may submit a new proposed hourly fee schedule or another statement of his or her proposed compensation from the estate of the proposed ward or proposed conservatee. The submittal of a new hourly fee schedule or another statement of the guardian's or conservator's proposed compensation, as authorized by this section, shall not preclude a court from later reducing the guardian's or conservator's hourly fees or other compensation, or his or her attorney's fees or other compensation.

2615. If a guardian or conservator fails to file any inventory required by this article within the time prescribed by law or by court order, the guardian or conservator is liable for damages for any injury to the estate, or to any interested person, directly resulting from the failure timely to file the inventory. Damages awarded pursuant to this section are a personal liability of the guardian or conservator and a liability on the bond, if any.

Article 2.5. Examination Concerning Assets Of Estate

2616. (a) A petition may be filed under this article by any one or more of the following:

(1) The guardian or conservator.

(2) The ward or conservatee.

(3) A creditor or other interested person, including persons having only an expectancy or prospective interest in the estate.

(b) Upon the filing of a petition under this article, the court may order that a citation be issued to a person to answer interrogatories, or to appear before the court and be examined under oath, or both, concerning any of the following allegations made in the petition:

(1) The person has wrongfully taken, concealed, or disposed of property of the ward or conservatee.

(2) The person has knowledge or possession of any of the following:

(A) A deed, conveyance, bond, contract, or other writing that contains evidence of or tends to disclose the right, title, interest, or claim of the ward or conservatee to property.

(B) An instrument in writing belonging to the ward or conservatee.

(3) The person asserts a claim against the ward or conservatee or the estate.

(4) The estate asserts a claim against the person.

(c) If the citation requires the person to appear before the court, the court and the petitioner may examine the person under oath upon the matters recited in the petition. The citation may include a requirement for this person to produce documents and other personal property specified in the citation.

(d) Disobedience of a citation issued pursuant to this section may be punished as a contempt of the court issuing the citation.

2617. Interrogatories may be put to a person cited to answer interrogatories under Section 2616. The interrogatories and answers shall be in writing. The answers shall be signed under penalty of perjury by the person cited. The interrogatories and answers shall be filed with the court.

2618. (a) At an examination, witnesses may be produced and examined on either side.

(b) If upon the examination it appears that the allegations of the petition are true, the court may order the person to disclose the person's knowledge of the facts.

(c) If upon the examination it appears that the allegations of the petition are not true, the person's necessary expenses, including reasonable attorney's fees, shall be charged against the petitioner or allowed out of the estate, in the discretion of the court.

2619. (a) On petition of the guardian or conservator, the court may issue a citation to a person who has possession or control of property in the estate of the ward or conservatee to appear before the court and make an account under oath of the property and the person's actions with respect to the property.

(b) Disobedience of a citation issued pursuant to this section may be punished as a contempt of the court issuing the citation.

Article 3. Accounts

2620. (a) At the expiration of one year from the time of appointment and thereafter not less frequently than biennially, unless otherwise ordered by the court to be more frequent, the guardian or conservator shall present the accounting of the assets of the estate of the ward or conservatee to the court for settlement and allowance in the manner provided in Chapter 4 (commencing with Section 1060) of Part 1 of Division 3. By January 1, 2008, the Judicial Council, in consultation with the California Judges Association, the California Association of Superior Court Investigators, the California State Association of Public Administrators, Public Guardians, and Public Conservators, the State Bar of California, and the California Society of Certified Public Accountants, shall develop a standard accounting form, a simplified accounting form, and rules for when the simplified accounting form may be used. After January 1, 2008, all accountings submitted pursuant to this section shall be submitted on the Judicial Council form.

(b) The final court accounting of the guardian or conservator following the death of the ward or conservatee shall include a court accounting for the period that ended on the date of death and a separate accounting for the period subsequent to the date of death.

(c) Along with each court accounting, the guardian or conservator shall file supporting documents, as provided in this section.

(1) For purposes of this subdivision, the term "account statement" shall include any original account statement from any institution, as defined in Section 2890, or any financial institution, as defined in Section 2892, in which money or other assets of the estate are held or deposited.

(2) The filing shall include all account statements showing the account balance as of the closing date of the accounting period of the court accounting. If the court accounting is the first court accounting of the guardianship or conservatorship, the guardian or conservator shall provide to the court all account statements showing the account balance immediately preceding the date the conservator or guardian was appointed and all account statements showing the account balance as of the closing date of the first court accounting.

(3) If the guardian or conservator is a private professional or licensed guardian or conservator, the guardian or conservator shall also file all original account statements, as described above, showing the balance as of all periods covered by the accounting.

(4) The filing shall include the original closing escrow statement received showing the charges and credits for any sale of real property of the estate.

(5) If the ward or conservatee is in a residential care facility or a long-term care facility, the filing shall include the original bill statements for the facility.

(6) This subdivision shall not apply to the public guardian if the money belonging to the estate is pooled with money belonging to other estates pursuant to Section 2940 and Article 3 (commencing with Section 7640) of Chapter 4 of Part 1 of Division 7. Nothing in this section shall affect any other duty or responsibility of the public guardian with regard to managing money belonging to the estate or filing accountings with the court.

(7) If any document to be filed or lodged with the court under this section contains the ward's or conservatee's social security number or any other personal information regarding the ward or conservatee that would not ordinarily be disclosed in a court accounting, an inventory and appraisal, or other nonconfidential pleadings filed in the action, the account statement or other document shall be attached to a separate affidavit describing the character of the document, captioned "CONFIDENTIAL FINANCIAL STATEMENT" in capital letters. Except as otherwise ordered by the court, the clerk of the court shall keep the document confidential except to the court and subject to disclosure only upon an order of the court. The guardian or conservator may redact the

ward's or conservatee's social security number from any document lodged with the court under this section.

(8) Courts may provide by local rule that the court shall retain all documents lodged with it under this subdivision until the court's determination of the guardian's or conservator's account has become final, at which time the supporting documents shall be returned to the depositing guardian or conservator or delivered to any successor appointed by the court.

(d) Each accounting is subject to random or discretionary, full or partial review by the court. The review may include consideration of any information necessary to determine the accuracy of the accounting. If the accounting has any material error, the court shall make an express finding as to the severity of the error and what further action is appropriate in response to the error, if any. Among the actions available to the court is immediate suspension of the guardian or conservator without further notice or proceedings and appointment of a temporary guardian or conservator or removal of the guardian or conservator pursuant to Section 2650 and appointment of a temporary guardian or conservator.

(e) The guardian or conservator shall make available for inspection and copying, upon reasonable notice, to any person designated by the court to verify the accuracy of the accounting, all books and records, including receipts for any expenditures, of the guardianship or conservatorship.

(f) A superior court shall not be required to perform any duties imposed pursuant to the amendments to this section enacted by Chapter 493 of the Statutes 2006 until the Legislature makes an appropriation identified for this purpose.

2620.1. The Judicial Council shall, by January 1, 2009, develop guidelines to assist investigators and examiners in reviewing accountings and detecting fraud.

2620.2. (a) Whenever the conservator or guardian has failed to file an accounting as required by Section 2620, the court shall require that written notice be given to the conservator or guardian and the attorney of record for the conservatorship or guardianship directing the conservator or guardian to file an accounting and to set the accounting for hearing before the court within 30 days of the date of the notice or, if the conservator or guardian is a public agency, within 45 days of the date of the notice. The court may, upon cause shown, grant an additional 30 days to file the accounting.

(b) Failure to file the accounting within the time specified under subdivision (a), or within 45 days of actual receipt of the notice, whichever is later, shall constitute a contempt of the authority of the court as described in Section 1209 of the Code of Civil Procedure.

(c) If the conservator or guardian does not file an accounting with all appropriate supporting documentation and set the accounting for hearing as required by Section 2620, the court shall do one or more of the following and shall report that action to the bureau established pursuant to Section 6510 of the Business and Professions Code:

(1) Remove the conservator or guardian as provided under Article 1 (commencing with Section 2650) of Chapter 9 of Part 4 of Division 4.

(2) Issue and serve a citation requiring a guardian or conservator who does not file a required accounting to appear and show cause why the guardian or conservator should not be punished for contempt. If the guardian or conservator purposely evades personal service of the citation, the guardian or conservator shall be immediately removed from office.

(3) Suspend the powers of the conservator or guardian and appoint a temporary conservator or guardian, who shall take possession of the assets of the conservatorship or guardianship, investigate the actions of the conservator or guardian, and petition for surcharge if this is in the best interests of the ward or conservatee. Compensation for the temporary conservator or guardian, and counsel for the temporary conservator or guardian, shall be treated as a surcharge against the conservator or guardian, and if unpaid shall be considered a breach of condition of the bond.

(4) (A) Appoint legal counsel to represent the ward or conservatee if the court has not suspended the powers of the conservator or guardian and appoint a temporary conservator or guardian pursuant to paragraph (3). Compensation for the counsel appointed for the ward or conservatee shall be treated as a surcharge against the conservator or guardian, and if unpaid shall be considered a breach of a condition on the bond, unless for good cause shown the court finds that counsel for the ward or conservatee shall be compensated according to Section 1470. The court shall order the legal counsel to do one or more of the following:

(i) Investigate the actions of the conservator or guardian, and petition for surcharge if this is in the best interests of the ward or conservatee.

(ii) Recommend to the court whether the conservator or guardian should be removed.

(iii) Recommend to the court whether money or other property in the estate should be deposited pursuant to Section 2453, 2453.5, 2454, or 2455, to be subject to withdrawal only upon authorization of the court.

(B) After resolution of the matters for which legal counsel was appointed in subparagraph (A), the court shall terminate the appointment of legal counsel, unless the court determines that continued representation of the ward or conservatee and the estate is necessary and reasonable.

(5) If the conservator or guardian is exempt from the licensure requirements of Chapter 6 (commencing with Section 6500) of Division 3 of the Business and Professions Code, upon ex parte application or any notice as the court may require, extend the time to file the accounting, not to exceed an additional 30 days after the expiration of the deadline described in subdivision (a), where the court finds there is good cause and that the estate is adequately bonded. After expiration of any extensions, if the accounting has not been filed, the court shall take action as described in paragraphs (1) to (3), inclusive.

(d) Subdivision (c) does not preclude the court from additionally taking any other appropriate action in response to a failure to file a proper accounting in a timely manner.

2621. Notice of the hearing on the account of the guardian or conservator shall be given for the period and in the manner provided in Chapter 3 (commencing with Section 1460) of Part 1. If notice is required to be given to the Director of State Hospitals or the Director of Developmental Services under Section 1461, the account shall not be settled or allowed unless notice has been given as provided in Section 1461.

2622. The ward or conservatee, the spouse of the ward or the spouse or domestic partner of the conservatee, any relative or friend of the ward or conservatee, or any creditor or other interested person may file written objections to the account of the guardian or conservator, stating the items of the account to which objection is made and the basis for the objection.

2622.5. (a) If the court determines that the objections were without reasonable cause and in bad faith, the court may order the objector to pay the compensation and costs of the conservator or guardian and other expenses and costs of litigation, including attorney's fees, incurred to defend the account. The objector shall be personally liable to the guardianship or conservatorship estate for the amount ordered.

(b) If the court determines that the opposition to the objections was without reasonable cause and in bad faith, the court may award the objector the costs of the objector and other expenses and costs of litigation, including attorney's fees, incurred to contest the account. The amount awarded is a charge against the compensation of the guardian or conservator, and the guardian or conservator is liable personally and on the bond, if any, for any amount that remains unsatisfied.

2623. (a) Except as provided in subdivision (b) of this section, the guardian or conservator shall be allowed all of the following:

(1) The amount of the reasonable expenses incurred in the exercise of the powers and the performance of the duties of the guardian or conservator (including, but not limit-

ed to, the cost of any surety bond furnished, reasonable attorney's fees, and such compensation for services rendered by the guardian or conservator of the person as the court determines is just and reasonable).

(2) Such compensation for services rendered by the guardian or conservator as the court determines is just and reasonable.

(3) All reasonable disbursements made before appointment as guardian or conservator.

(4) In the case of termination other than by the death of the ward or conservatee, all reasonable disbursements made after the termination of the guardianship or conservatorship but prior to the discharge of the guardian or conservator by the court.

(5) In the case of termination by the death of the ward or conservatee, all reasonable expenses incurred prior to the discharge of the guardian or conservator by the court for the custody and conservation of the estate and its delivery to the personal representative of the estate of the deceased ward or conservatee or in making other disposition of the estate as provided for by law.

(b) The guardian or conservator shall not be compensated from the estate for any costs or fees that the guardian or conservator incurred in unsuccessfully opposing a petition, or other request or action, made by or on behalf of the ward or conservatee, unless the court determines that the opposition was made in good faith, based on the best interests of the ward or conservatee.

2625. Any sale or purchase of property or other transaction not previously authorized, approved, or confirmed by the court is subject to review by the court upon the next succeeding account of the guardian or conservator occurring after the transaction. Upon such account and review, the court may hold the guardian or conservator liable for any violation of duties in connection with the sale, purchase, or other transaction. Nothing in this section shall be construed to affect the validity of any sale or purchase or other transaction.

2626. If it appears upon the settlement of any account that the estate has been entirely exhausted through expenditures or disbursements which are approved by the court, the court, upon settlement of the account, shall order the proceeding terminated and the guardian or conservator forthwith discharged unless the court determines that there is reason to continue the proceeding.

2627. (a) After a ward has reached majority, the ward may settle accounts with the guardian and give the guardian a release which is valid if obtained fairly and without undue influence.

(b) Except as otherwise provided by this code, a guardian is not entitled to a discharge until one year after the ward has attained majority.

2628. (a) The court may make an order

that the guardian or conservator need not present the accounts otherwise required by this chapter so long as all of the following conditions are satisfied:

(1) The estate at the beginning and end of the accounting period for which an account is otherwise required consisted of property, exclusive of the residence of the ward or conservatee, of a total net value of less than fifteen thousand dollars ($15,000).

(2) The income of the estate for each month of the accounting period, exclusive of public benefit payments, was less than two thousand dollars ($2,000).

(3) All income of the estate during the accounting period, if not retained, was spent for the benefit of the ward or conservatee.

(b) Notwithstanding that the court has made an order under subdivision (a), the ward or conservatee or any interested person may petition the court for an order requiring the guardian or conservator to present an account as otherwise required by this chapter or the court on its own motion may make that an order. An order under this subdivision may be made ex parte or on such notice of hearing as the court in its discretion requires.

(c) For any accounting period during which all of the conditions of subdivision (a) are not satisfied, the guardian or conservator shall present the account as otherwise required by this chapter.

Article 4. Accounts On Termination Of Relationship

2630. The termination of the relationship of guardian and ward or conservator and conservatee by the death of either, by the ward attaining majority, by the determination of the court that the guardianship or conservatorship is no longer necessary, by the removal or resignation of the guardian or conservator, or for any other reason, does not cause the court to lose jurisdiction of the proceeding for the purpose of settling the accounts of the guardian or conservator or for any other purpose incident to the enforcement of the judgments and orders of the court upon such accounts or upon the termination of the relationship.

2631. (a) Upon the death of the ward or conservatee, the guardian or conservator may contract for and pay a reasonable sum for the expenses of the last illness and the disposition of the remains of the deceased ward or conservatee, and for unpaid court-approved attorney's fees, and may pay the unpaid expenses of the guardianship or conservatorship accruing before or after the death of the ward or conservatee, in full or in part, to the extent reasonable, from any personal property of the deceased ward or conservatee which is under the control of the guardian or conservator.

(b) If after payment of expenses under subdivision (a), the total market value of the remaining estate of the decedent does not exceed the amount determined under Section 13100, the guardian or conservator may petition the court for an order permitting the guardian or conservator to liquidate the decedent's estate. The guardian or conservator may petition even though there is a will of the decedent in existence if the will does not appoint an executor or if the named executor refuses to act. No notice of the petition need be given. If the order is granted, the guardian or conservator may sell personal property of the decedent, withdraw money of the decedent in an account in a financial institution, and collect a debt, claim, or insurance proceeds owed to the decedent or the decedent's estate, and a person having possession or control shall pay or deliver the money or property to the guardian or conservator.

(c) After payment of expenses, the guardian or conservator may transfer any remaining property as provided in Division 8 (commencing with Section 13000). For this purpose, the value of the property of the deceased ward or conservatee shall be determined after the deduction of the expenses so paid.

2632. (a) As used in this section:

(1) "Incapacitated" means lack of capacity to serve as guardian or conservator.

(2) "Legal representative" means the personal representative of a deceased guardian or conservator or the conservator of the estate of an incapacitated guardian or conservator.

(b) If a guardian or conservator dies or becomes incapacitated and a legal representative is appointed for the deceased or incapacitated guardian or conservator, the legal representative shall, not later than 60 days after appointment unless the court extends the time, file an account of the administration of the deceased or incapacitated guardian or conservator.

(c) If a guardian or conservator dies or becomes incapacitated and no legal representative is appointed for the deceased or incapacitated guardian or conservator, or if the guardian or conservator absconds, the court may compel the attorney for the deceased, incapacitated, or absconding guardian or conservator or the attorney of record in the guardianship or conservatorship proceeding to file an account of the administration of the deceased, incapacitated, or absconding guardian or conservator.

(d) The legal representative or attorney shall exercise reasonable diligence in preparing an account under this section. Verification of the account may be made on information and belief. The court shall settle the account as in other cases. The court shall allow reasonable compensation to the legal representative or the attorney for preparing the account. The amount allowed shall be a charge against the estate that was being administered by the deceased, incapacitated, or absconding guardian or conservator. Legal services for which compensation shall be allowed to the attorney under this subdivision include those services rendered by any paralegal performing the services under the direction and supervision of an attorney. The petition or application for compensation shall set forth the hours spent and services performed by the paralegal.

2633. Subject to Section 2630, where the guardianship or conservatorship terminates before the inventory of the estate has been filed, the court, in its discretion and upon such notice as the court may require, may make an order that the guardian or conservator need not file the inventory and appraisal and that the guardian or conservator shall file an account covering only those assets of the estate of which the guardian or conservator has possession or control.

Chapter 8. Compensation Of Guardian, Conservator, And Attorney

2640. (a) At any time after the filing of the inventory and appraisal, but not before the expiration of 90 days from the issuance of letters or any other period of time as the court for good cause orders, the guardian or conservator of the estate may petition the court for an order fixing and allowing compensation to any one or more of the following:

(1) The guardian or conservator of the estate for services rendered to that time.

(2) The guardian or conservator of the person for services rendered to that time.

(3) The attorney for services rendered to that time by the attorney to the guardian or conservator of the person or estate or both.

(b) Notice of the hearing shall be given for the period and in the manner provided for in Chapter 3 (commencing with Section 1460) of Part 1.

(c) Upon the hearing, the court shall make an order allowing (1) any compensation requested in the petition the court determines is just and reasonable to the guardian or conservator of the estate for services rendered or to the guardian or conservator of the person for services rendered, or to both, and (2) any compensation requested in the petition the court determines is reasonable to the attorney for services rendered to the guardian or conservator of the person or estate or both. The compensation allowed to the guardian or conservator of the person, the guardian or conservator of the estate, and to the attorney may, in the discretion of the court, include compensation for services rendered before the date of the order appointing the guardian or conservator. The compensation allowed shall thereupon be charged to the estate. Legal services for which the attorney may be compensated include those services rendered by any paralegal performing legal services under the direction and supervision of an attorney. The petition or application for compensation shall set forth the hours spent and services performed by the paralegal.

(d) Notwithstanding the provisions of subdivision (c), the guardian or conservator shall not be compensated from the estate for any costs or fees that the guardian or conservator incurred in unsuccessfully opposing a petition, or other request or action, made by or on behalf of the ward or conservatee, unless the court determines that the opposition was made in good faith, based on the best interests of the ward or conservatee.

2640.1. (a) If a person has petitioned for the appointment of a particular conservator and another conservator was appointed while the petition was pending, but not before the expiration of 90 days from the issuance of letters, the person who petitioned for the appointment of a conservator but was not appointed and that person's attorney may petition the court for an order fixing and allowing compensation and reimbursement of costs, provided that the court determines that the petition was filed in the best interests of the conservatee.

(b) Notice of the hearing shall be given for the period and in the manner provided in Chapter 3 (commencing with Section 1460) of Part 1.

(c) Upon the hearing, the court shall make an order to allow both of the following:

(1) Any compensation or costs requested in the petition the court determines is just and reasonable to the person who petitioned for the appointment of a conservator but was not appointed, for his or her services rendered in connection with and to facilitate the appointment of a conservator, and costs incurred in connection therewith.

(2) Any compensation or costs requested in the petition the court determines is just and reasonable to the attorney for that person, for his or her services rendered in connection with and to facilitate the appointment of a conservator, and costs incurred in connection therewith.

Any compensation and costs allowed shall be charged to the estate of the conservatee. If a conservator of the estate is not appointed, but a conservator of the person is appointed, the compensation and costs allowed shall be ordered by the court to be paid from property belonging to the conservatee, whether held outright, in trust, or otherwise.

(d) It is the intent of the Legislature for this section to have retroactive effect.

2641. (a) At any time permitted by Section 2640 and upon the notice therein prescribed, the guardian or conservator of the person may petition the court for an order fixing and allowing compensation for services rendered to that time.

(b) Upon the hearing, the court shall make an order allowing any compensation the court determines is just and reasonable

to the guardian or conservator of the person for services rendered. The compensation allowed to the guardian or conservator of the person may, in the discretion of the court, include compensation for services rendered before the date of the order appointing the guardian or conservator. The compensation allowed shall thereupon be charged against the estate.

(c) The guardian or conservator shall not be compensated from the estate for any costs or fees that the guardian or conservator incurred in unsuccessfully opposing a petition, or other request or action, made by or on behalf of the ward or conservatee, unless the court determines that the opposition was made in good faith, based on the best interests of the ward or conservatee.

2642. (a) At any time permitted by Section 2640 and upon the notice therein prescribed, an attorney who has rendered legal services to the guardian or conservator of the person or estate or both, including services rendered under Section 2632, may petition the court for an order fixing and allowing compensation for such services rendered to that time. Legal services for which the attorney may petition the court for an order fixing and allowing compensation under this subdivision include those services rendered by any paralegal performing the legal services under the direction and supervision of an attorney. The petition or application for compensation shall set forth the hours spent and services performed by the paralegal.

(b) Upon the hearing, the court shall make an order allowing such compensation as the court determines reasonable to the attorney for services rendered to the guardian or conservator. The compensation so allowed shall thereupon be charged against the estate.

2643. (a) Except as provided in Section 2643.1, on petition by the guardian or conservator of the person or estate, or both, the court may by order authorize periodic payments on account to any one or more of the following persons for the services rendered by that person during the period covered by each payment:

(1) The guardian of the person.

(2) The guardian of the estate.

(3) The conservator of the person.

(4) The conservator of the estate.

(5) The attorney for the guardian or conservator of the person or estate, or both.

(b) Notice of the hearing on the petition shall be given for the period and in the manner provided in Chapter 3 (commencing with Section 1460) of Part 1.

(c) The petition shall describe the services to be rendered on a periodic basis and the reason why authority to make periodic payments is requested. In fixing the amount of the periodic payment, the court shall take into account the services to be rendered on a periodic basis and the reasonable value of those services. The guardian or conservator of the estate may make the periodic payments authorized by the order only if the services described in the petition are actually rendered. The payments made pursuant to the order are subject to review by the court upon the next succeeding account of the guardian or conservator of the estate to determine that the services were actually rendered and that the amount paid on account was not unreasonable, and the court shall make an appropriate order if the court determines that the amount paid on account was either excessive or inadequate in view of the services actually rendered.

2643.1. (a) On petition by a guardian or conservator of the person or estate, or both, who is a professional fiduciary, as described in Section 2340 and who is required to be licensed under the Professional Fiduciaries Act (Chapter 6 (commencing with Section 6500) of Division 3 of the Business and Professions Code), the court may by order authorize periodic payments on account to a person described in subdivision (a) of Section 2643 for the services rendered by that person during the period covered by each payment only if that person has filed a proposed hourly fee schedule or another statement of his or her proposed compensation from the estate of the ward or conservatee for services performed as a guardian or conservator, as required by Section 2614.7, and only after the court has addressed any objections filed pursuant to subdivision (d).

(b) The petition shall describe the services to be rendered on a periodic basis, the reason why authority to make periodic payments is requested, and a good faith estimate of the fees to be charged by the professional fiduciary from the date the petition is filed up to, and including, the date of the next succeeding account required by Section 2620 or, if the next succeeding account required by Section 2620 is due in less than one year, a good faith estimate of the fees to be charged by the professional fiduciary from the date the petition is filed through the next succeeding 12 months, inclusive. Prior to ordering periodic payments or fixing the amount of the periodic payment, the court shall determine whether making periodic payments is in the best interest of the ward or conservatee, taking into consideration the needs of the ward or conservatee and the need to preserve and protect the estate. If the court determines that making periodic payments is not in the best interest of the ward or conservatee, the court shall deny the petition to authorize periodic payments. If the court determines that making periodic payments is in the best interest of the ward or conservatee, the court shall fix the amount of the periodic payment. In fixing the amount of the periodic payment, the court shall take into account the services to be rendered on a periodic basis and the reasonable value of those services.

(c) (1) Notice of the hearing on the petition and notice of how to file an objection to the petition shall be given for the period and in the manner provided in Chapter 3 (commencing with Section 1460) of Part 1.

(2) The notices required by paragraph (1) shall be made to the court investigator for the period and in the manner provided in Chapter 3 (commencing with Section 1460) of Part 1.

(d) (1) Any person entitled to notice under paragraph (1) of subdivision (c) may file with the court a written objection to the authorization of periodic payments on account. The court clerk shall set any objections for a hearing no fewer than 15 days after the date the objections are filed.

(2) If an objection is filed pursuant to paragraph (1), the guardian or conservator shall have the burden of establishing the necessity for and amount, if any, of periodic payments.

(e) The guardian or conservator of the estate may make the periodic payments authorized by the order only if the services described in the petition are actually rendered. The payments made pursuant to the order shall be reviewed by the court upon the next succeeding account of the guardian or conservator of the estate to determine that the services were actually rendered and that the amount paid on account was reasonable and in the best interest of the ward or conservatee, taking into consideration the needs of the ward or conservatee and the need to preserve and protect the estate. The court shall make an appropriate order reducing the guardian or conservator's compensation if the court determines that the amount paid on account was either unreasonable or not in the best interest of the ward or conservatee in view of the services actually rendered.

(f) The authorization for periodic payments granted pursuant to this section shall terminate on a date determined by the court, but not later than the due date of the next succeeding account required by Section 2620. Nothing in this section shall preclude a guardian or conservator from filing a subsequent petition to receive periodic payments pursuant to this section.

2644. (a) Where it is to the advantage, benefit, and best interest of the ward or conservatee or the estate, the guardian or conservator of the estate may contract with an attorney for a contingent fee for the attorney's services in representing the ward or conservatee or the estate in connection with a matter that is of a type that is customarily the subject of a contingent fee contract, but such a contract is valid only if (1) the contract is made pursuant to an order of the court authorizing the guardian or conservator to execute the contract or (2) the contract is approved by order of the court.

(b) To obtain an order under this section,

the guardian or conservator shall file a petition with the court showing the advantage, benefit, and best interest of the ward or conservatee or the estate of the contingent fee contract. A copy of the contingent fee contract shall be attached to the petition.

(c) Notice of the hearing on the petition shall be given for the period and in the manner provided in Chapter 3 (commencing with Section 1460) of Part 1.

(d) As used in this section, "court" includes either of the following:

(1) The court in which the guardianship or conservatorship proceeding is pending.

(2) Where the contract is in connection with a matter in litigation, the court in which the litigation is pending.

2645. (a) No attorney who is a guardian or conservator shall receive any compensation from the guardianship or conservatorship estate for legal services performed for the guardian or conservator unless the court specifically approves the right to the compensation and finds that it is to the advantage, benefit, and best interests of the ward or conservatee.

(b) No parent, child, sibling, or spouse of a person who is a guardian or conservator, and no law partnership or corporation whose partner, shareholder, or employee is serving as a guardian or conservator shall receive any compensation for legal services performed for the guardian or conservator unless the court specifically approves the right to the compensation and finds that it is to the advantage, benefit, and best interests of the ward or conservatee.

(c) This section shall not apply if the guardian or conservator is related by blood or marriage to, or is a cohabitant with, the ward or conservatee.

(d) After full disclosure of the relationships of all persons to receive compensation for legal services under this section, the court may, in its discretion and at any time, approve the right to that compensation, including any time during the pendency of any of the following orders:

(1) An order appointing the guardian or conservator.

(2) An order approving the general plan under Section 1831.

(3) An order settling any account of the guardian or conservator.

(4) An order approving a separate petition, with notice given under Section 2581.

2646. In proceedings under this chapter, the court shall only determine fees that are payable from the estate of the ward or conservatee and not limit fees payable from other sources.

2647. No attorney fees may be paid from the estate of the ward or conservatee without prior court order. The estate of the ward or conservatee is not obligated to pay attorney fees established by any engagement agreement or other contract until it has been approved by the court. This does not preclude an award of fees by the court pursuant to this chapter even if the contractual obligations are unenforceable pursuant to this section.

Chapter 9. Removal Or Resignation

Article 1. Removal Of Guardian Or Conservator

2650. A guardian or conservator may be removed for any of the following causes:

(a) Failure to use ordinary care and diligence in the management of the estate

(b) Failure to file an inventory or an account within the time allowed by law or by court order.

(c) Continued failure to perform duties or incapacity to perform duties suitably.

(d) Conviction of a felony, whether before or after appointment as guardian or conservator.

(e) Gross immorality.

(f) Having such an interest adverse to the faithful performance of duties that there is an unreasonable risk that the guardian or conservator will fail faithfully to perform duties.

(g) In the case of a guardian of the person or a conservator of the person, acting in violation of any provision of Section 2356.

(h) In the case of a guardian of the estate or a conservator of the estate, insolvency or bankruptcy of the guardian or conservator.

(i) In any other case in which the court in its discretion determines that removal is in the best interests of the ward or conservatee; but, in considering the best interests of the ward, if the guardian was nominated under Section 1500 or 1501, the court shall take that fact into consideration.

2651. The ward or conservatee, the spouse of the ward or the spouse or domestic partner of the conservatee, any relative or friend of the ward or conservatee, or any interested person may apply by petition to the court to have the guardian or conservator removed. The petition shall state facts showing cause for removal.

2652. Notice of the hearing on the petition shall be given for the period and in the manner provided in Chapter 3 (commencing with Section 1460) of Part 1.

2653. (a) The guardian or conservator, the ward or conservatee, the spouse of the ward or the spouse or registered domestic partner of the conservatee, any relative or friend of the ward or conservatee, and any interested person may appear at the hearing and support or oppose the petition.

(b) If the court determines that cause for removal of the guardian or conservator exists, the court may remove the guardian or conservator, revoke the letters of guardianship or conservatorship, and enter judgment accordingly and, in the case of a guardianship or conservatorship of the estate, order the guardian or conservator to file an accounting and to surrender the estate to the person legally entitled thereto. If the guardian or conservator fails to file the accounting as ordered, the court may compel the accounting pursuant to Section 2620.2.

(c) If the court removes the guardian or conservator for cause, as described in subdivisions (a) to (g), inclusive, of Section 2650 or Section 2655, both of the following shall apply:

(1) The court shall award the petitioner the costs of the petition and other expenses and costs of litigation, including attorney's fees, incurred under this article, unless the court determines that the guardian or conservator has acted in good faith, based on the best interests of the ward or conservatee.

(2) The guardian or conservator may not deduct from, or charge to, the estate his or her costs of litigation, and is personally liable for those costs and expenses.

2654. Whenever it appears that the ward or conservatee or the estate may suffer loss or injury during the time required for notice and hearing under this article, the court, on its own motion or on petition, may do either or both of the following:

(a) Suspend the powers of the guardian or conservator pending notice and hearing to such extent as the court deems necessary.

(b) Compel the guardian or conservator to surrender the estate to a custodian designated by the court.

2655. (a) A guardian or conservator may be removed from office if the guardian or conservator is found in contempt for disobeying an order of the court.

(b) Notwithstanding any other provision of this article, a guardian or conservator may be removed from office under subdivision (a) by a court order reciting the facts and without further showing or notice.

Article 2. Resignation Of Guardian Or Conservator

2660. A guardian or conservator may at any time file with the court a petition tendering the resignation of the guardian or conservator. Notice of the hearing on the petition shall be given for the period and in the manner provided in Chapter 3 (commencing with Section 1460) of Part 1. The court shall allow such resignation when it appears proper, to take effect at such time as the court shall fix, and may make any order as may be necessary to deal with the guardianship or conservatorship during the period prior to the appointment of a new guardian or conservator and the settlement of the accounts of the resigning guardian or conservator.

2662. Whenever the court grants a petition removing the guardian or conservator of a minor ward or conservatee or tendering the resignation of the guardian or conser-

vator of a minor ward or conservatee, if the court does not immediately appoint a successor guardian or conservator, the court shall at the same time appoint a responsible adult to make educational decisions for the minor until a successor guardian or conservator is appointed. Whenever the court suspends or limits the powers of the guardian or conservator to make educational decisions for a minor ward or conservatee, the court shall at the same time appoint a responsible adult to make educational decisions for the minor ward or conservatee until the guardian or conservator is again authorized to make educational decisions for the minor ward or conservatee. An individual who would have a conflict of interest in representing the child may not be appointed to make educational decisions. For purposes of this section, "an individual who would have a conflict of interest," means a person having any interests that might restrict or bias his or her ability to make educational decisions, including, but not limited to, those conflicts of interest prohibited by Section 1126 of the Government Code, and the receipt of compensation or attorneys' fees for the provision of services pursuant to this section. A foster parent may not be deemed to have a conflict of interest solely because he or she receives compensation for the provision of services pursuant to this section.

Chapter 9.5. Appointment Of Successor Guardian Or Conservator

Article 1. Appointment Of Successor Guardian

2670. When for any reason a vacancy occurs in the office of guardian, the court may appoint a successor guardian, after notice and hearing as in the case of an original appointment of a guardian.

Article 2. Appointment Of Successor Conservator

2680. When for any reason a vacancy occurs in the office of conservator, the court may appoint a successor conservator in the manner provided in this article.

2681. A petition for appointment of a successor conservator may be filed by any of the following:

(a) The conservatee.

(b) The spouse or domestic partner of the conservatee.

(c) A relative of the conservatee.

(d) Any interested state or local entity or agency of this state or any interested public officer or employee of this state or of a local public entity of this state.

(e) Any other interested person or friend of the conservatee.

2682. (a) The petition shall request that a successor conservator be appointed for the person or estate, or both, and shall specify the name and address of the proposed successor conservator and the name and address of the conservatee.

(b) The petition shall set forth, so far as they are known to the petitioner, the names and addresses of the spouse or domestic partner and of the relatives of the conservatee within the second degree.

(c) If the petition is filed by one other than the conservatee, the petition shall state whether or not the petitioner is a creditor or debtor of the conservatee.

(d) If the conservatee is a patient in or on leave of absence from a state institution under the jurisdiction of the State Department of State Hospitals or the State Department of Developmental Services and that fact is known to the petitioner, the petition shall state that fact and name the institution.

(e) The petition shall state, so far as is known to the petitioner, whether or not the conservatee is receiving or is entitled to receive benefits from the Veterans Administration and the estimated amount of the monthly benefit payable by the Veterans Administration for the conservatee.

(f) The petition shall state whether or not the conservatee will be present at the hearing.

2683. (a) At least 15 days before the hearing on the petition for appointment of a successor conservator, notice of the time and place of the hearing shall be given as provided in this section. The notice shall be accompanied by a copy of the petition.

(b) Notice shall be mailed to the persons designated in Section 1460 and to the relatives named in the petition.

(c) If notice is required by Section 1461 to be given to the Director of State Hospitals or the Director of Developmental Services, notice shall be mailed as so required.

(d) If notice is required by Section 1461.5 to be given to the Veterans Administration, notice shall be mailed as so required.

2684. Unless the petition states that the conservatee will be present at the hearing, the court investigator shall do all of the following:

(a) Interview the conservatee personally.

(b) Inform the conservatee of the nature of the proceeding to appoint a successor conservator, the name of the person proposed as successor conservator, and the conservatee's right to appear personally at the hearing, to object to the person proposed as successor conservator, to nominate a person to be appointed as successor conservator, to be represented by legal counsel if the conservatee so chooses, and to have legal counsel appointed by the court if unable to retain legal counsel.

(c) Determine whether the conservatee objects to the person proposed as successor conservator or prefers another person to be appointed.

(d) If the conservatee is not represented by legal counsel, determine whether the conservatee wishes to be represented by legal counsel and, if so, determine the name of an attorney the conservatee wishes to retain or whether the conservatee desires the court to appoint legal counsel.

(e) Determine whether the appointment of legal counsel would be helpful to the resolution of the matter or is necessary to protect the interests of the conservatee in any case where the conservatee does not plan to retain legal counsel and has not requested the appointment of legal counsel by the court.

(f) Report to the court in writing, at least five days before the hearing, concerning all of the foregoing, including the conservatee's express communications concerning representation by legal counsel and whether the conservatee objects to the person proposed as successor conservator or prefers that some other person be appointed.

(g) Mail, at least five days before the hearing, a copy of the report referred to in subdivision (f) to all of the following:

(1) The attorney, if any, for the petitioner.

(2) The attorney, if any, for the conservatee.

(3) Such other persons as the court orders.

2685. If the conservatee is present at the hearing, prior to making an order appointing a successor conservator the court shall do all of the following:

(a) Inform the conservatee of the nature and purpose of the proceeding.

(b) Inform the conservatee that the conservatee has the right to object to the person proposed as successor conservator, to nominate a person to be appointed as successor conservator, and, if not represented by legal counsel, to be represented by legal counsel if the conservatee so chooses and to have legal counsel appointed by the court if unable to retain legal counsel.

(c) After the court so informs the conservatee, the court shall consult the conservatee to determine the conservatee's opinion concerning the question of who should be appointed as successor conservator.

2686. If the petition states that the conservatee will be present at the hearing and the conservatee fails to appear at the hearing, the court shall continue the hearing and direct the court investigator to perform the duties set forth in Section 2684.

2687. The conservatee, the spouse, the domestic partner, or any relative or friend of the conservatee, or any other interested person may appear at the hearing to support or oppose the petition.

2688. (a) The court shall determine the question of who should be appointed as successor conservator according to the provisions of Article 2 (commencing with Section 1810) of Chapter 1 of Part 3.

(b) The order appointing the successor conservator shall contain, among other things, the names, addresses and telephone numbers of the successor conservator, the conservatee's attorney, if any, and the court investigator, if any.

2689. If the conservatee is an "absentee" as defined in Section 1403:

(a) The petition for appointment of a successor conservator shall contain the matters required by Section 1841 in addition to the matters required by Section 2682.

(b) Notice of the hearing shall be given as provided by Section 1842 in addition to the requirements of Section 2683, except that notice need not be given to the conservatee.

(c) An interview and report by the court investigator is not required.

Chapter 10. Requests For Special Notice

2700. (a) At any time after the issuance of letters of guardianship or conservatorship, the ward, if over 14 years of age or the conservatee, the spouse of the ward or the spouse or domestic partner of the conservatee, any relative or creditor of the ward or conservatee, or any other interested person, in person or by attorney, may file with the court clerk a written request for special notice.

(b) The request for special notice shall be so entitled and shall set forth the name of the person and the address to which notices shall be sent.

(c) Special notice may be requested of any one or more of the following matters:

(1) Petitions filed in the guardianship or conservatorship proceeding.

(2) Inventories and appraisals of property in the estate, including any supplemental inventories and appraisals.

(3) Accounts of the guardian or conservator.

(4) Proceedings for the final termination of the guardianship or conservatorship proceeding.

(d) Special notice may be requested of:

(1) Any one or more of the matters in subdivision (c) by describing the matter or matters.

(2) All the matters in subdivision (c) by referring generally to "the matters described in subdivision (c) of Section 2700 of the Probate Code" or by using words of similar meaning.

(e) A copy of the request shall be personally delivered or mailed to the guardian or conservator or to the attorney for the guardian or conservator. If personally delivered, the request is effective when it is delivered. If mailed, the request is effective when it is received.

(f) When the original of the request is filed with the court clerk, it shall be accompanied by a written admission or proof of service.

2701. (a) A request for special notice may be modified or withdrawn in the same man-

ner as provided for the making of the initial request.

(b) A new request for special notice may be served and filed at any time as provided in the case of an initial request.

2702. (a) Unless the court makes an order dispensing with the notice, if a request has been made pursuant to this chapter for special notice of a hearing, the person filing the petition, account, or other paper shall give written notice of the filing, together with a copy of the petition, account, or other paper, and the time and place set for the hearing, by mail to the person named in the request at the address set forth in the request, at least 15 days before the time set for the hearing.

(b) If a request has been made pursuant to this chapter for special notice of the filing of an inventory and appraisal of the estate or of the filing of any other paper that does not require a hearing, the inventory and appraisal or other paper shall be mailed not later than 15 days after the inventory and appraisal or other paper is filed with the court.

Chapter 12. Transfer Of Personal Property Out Of State

2800. As used in this chapter, "foreign guardian or conservator" means a guardian, conservator, committee, or comparable fiduciary in another jurisdiction.

2801. Subject to the limitations and requirements of this chapter, the court in which the guardianship of the estate or conservatorship of the estate is pending may order the transfer of some or all of the personal property of the estate to a foreign guardian or conservator in another jurisdiction outside this state where the ward or conservatee resides at the time the petition for the order authorizing the transfer is filed.

2802. A petition for an order authorizing a transfer may be filed by any of the following:

(a) The guardian of the estate or the conservator of the estate.

(b) The ward or conservatee.

(c) A foreign guardian or conservator.

2803. The petition shall set forth all of the following:

(a) The name and address of:

(1) The foreign guardian or conservator, who may but need not be the guardian or conservator appointed in this state.

(2) The ward or conservatee.

(3) The guardian or conservator, so far as is known to the petitioner.

(b) The names, ages, and addresses, so far as they are known to the petitioner, of the spouse of the ward or the spouse or domestic partner of the conservatee and of relatives of the ward or conservatee within the second degree.

(c) A brief description of the character, condition, value, and location of the personal property sought to be transferred.

(d) A statement whether the foreign guardian or conservator has agreed to accept the transfer of the property. If the foreign guardian or conservator has so agreed, the acceptance shall be attached as an exhibit to the petition or otherwise filed with the court.

(e) A statement of the manner in which and by whom the foreign guardian or conservator was appointed.

(f) A general statement of the qualifications of the foreign guardian or conservator.

(g) The amount of bond, if any, of the foreign guardian or conservator.

(h) A general statement of the nature and value of the property of the ward or conservatee already under the management or control of the foreign guardian or conservator.

(i) The name of the court having jurisdiction of the foreign guardian or conservator or of the accounts of the foreign guardian or conservator or, if none, the court in which a proceeding may be had with respect to the guardianship or conservatorship if the property is transferred.

(j) Whether there is any pending civil action in this state against the guardian or conservator, the ward or conservatee, or the estate.

(k) A statement of the reasons for the transfer.

2804. At least 30 days before the hearing, the petitioner shall mail a notice of the time and place of the hearing and a copy of the petition to each person required to be listed in the petition at the address stated in the petition.

2805. Any of the following may appear and file written objections to the petition:

(a) Any person required to be listed in the petition.

(b) Any creditor of the ward or conservatee or of the estate.

(c) The spouse of the ward or the spouse or domestic partner of the conservatee or any relative or friend of the ward or conservatee.

(d) Any other interested person.

2806. The court may grant the petition and order the guardian or conservator to transfer some or all of the personal property of the estate to the foreign guardian or conservator if the court determines all of the following:

(a) The transfer will promote the best interests of the ward or conservatee and the estate.

(b) The substantial rights of creditors or claimants in this state will not be materially impaired by the transfer.

(c) The foreign guardian or conservator is qualified, willing, and able to administer the property to be transferred.

2807. If a transfer is ordered, the court may direct the manner of transfer and impose such terms and conditions as may be just.

2808. (a) If the court's order provides for the transfer of all of the property of the estate to the foreign guardian or conservator, the court, upon settlement of the final account, shall order the guardianship of the estate or the conservatorship of the estate terminated upon the filing with the clerk of the court of a receipt for the property executed by the foreign guardian or conservator.

(b) Unless notice is waived, a copy of the final account of the guardian or conservator and of the petition for discharge, together with a notice of the hearing thereon, shall be mailed at least 30 days before the date of the hearing to all persons required to be listed in the petition for transfer, including the foreign guardian or conservator.

Chapter 14. Notification To Court By Institutions

2890. (a) When a guardian or conservator, pursuant to letters of guardianship or conservatorship of the estate, takes possession or control of any asset of the ward or conservatee held by an institution, as defined in subdivision (c), the institution shall file with the court having jurisdiction of the guardianship or conservatorship a statement containing the following information:

(1) The name of the ward or conservatee.

(2) The name of the guardian or joint guardians or conservator or joint conservators.

(3) The court case number.

(4) The name of the institution.

(5) The address of the institution.

(6) The account number of the account, if any, in which the asset was held by the ward or conservatee.

(7) A description of the asset or assets held by the institution. If an asset is a life insurance policy or annuity, the description shall include the policy number, if available. If the asset is a security listed on a public exchange, the description shall include the name and reference number, if available.

(8) The value, if known, or the estimated value otherwise, of the asset on the date the letters were issued by the court to the guardian or conservator, to the extent this value is routinely provided in the statements from the institution to the owner.

(b) Taking possession or control of an asset includes, for purposes of this chapter, changing title to the asset, withdrawing all or any portion of the asset, or transferring all or any portion of an asset from the institution.

(c) For purposes of this chapter, "institution" means an insurance company, insurance broker, insurance agent, investment company, investment bank, securities broker-dealer, investment adviser, financial planner, financial adviser, or any other person who takes, holds, or controls an asset subject to a conservatorship or guardianship that is not a "financial institution" as defined in Section 2892.

2891. (a) The statement filed pursuant to Section 2890 shall be an affidavit by a person having authority to make the statement on behalf of the institution, as defined in Section 2890, and shall include that fact in the statement.

(b) If the affidavit and any accompanying information to be filed pursuant to this section also contains the ward or conservatee's social security number or any other personal information, including financial information regarding the ward or conservatee which would not be disclosed in an accounting, an inventory and appraisal, or any other non-confidential pleading filed in the action, the information shall be kept confidential and subject to disclosure to any person only upon order of the court.

(c) This chapter does not apply to any trust arrangement described in subdivision (b) of Section 82 except paragraph (4) of that subdivision relating to assets held in Totten trust.

(d) No fee shall be charged by the court for the filing of the affidavit or related information as required by this section.

(e) The affidavit required by Section 2890 is not required to be filed in a proceeding more than once for each asset. However, all assets held by institutions may be listed in a single affidavit filed with the court.

(f) When a guardian or conservator takes possession or control of an asset in an institution, as defined in Section 2890, the institution may then file with the court the statement required by Section 2890 as to any or all other assets of the ward or conservatee held in the institution.

2892. (a) When a guardian or conservator, pursuant to letters of guardianship or conservatorship of the estate, opens or changes the name to an account or safe-deposit box in a financial institution, as defined in subdivision (b), the financial institution shall send to the court identified in the letters of guardianship or conservatorship a statement containing the following information:

(1) The name of the person with whom the account or safe-deposit box is opened or changed.

(2) The account number or reference number.

(3) The date the account or safe-deposit box was opened or changed ownership pursuant to letters of guardianship or conservatorship.

(4) If the asset is held in an account in a financial institution, the balance as of the date the account was opened or changed.

(5) If the asset is held in a safe-deposit box, and the financial institution has been given access to the safe-deposit box, a list of the contents, including, for example, currency, coins, jewelry, tableware, insurance policies or certificates, stock certificates, bonds, deeds, and wills.

(6) The name and address of the financial institution in which the asset is maintained.

(b) For purposes of this chapter, "financial institution" means a bank, trust, savings and loan association, savings bank, industrial bank, or credit union.

2893. (a) The written statement provided pursuant to Section 2892 by the financial institution shall be in the form of an affidavit signed by an officer of the financial institution and the officer shall provide his or her name and title in the affidavit.

(b) The affidavit required by this section is subject to disclosure under the circumstances described in subdivision (l) of Section 7480 of the Government Code under the California Right to Financial Privacy Act (Chapter 20 (commencing with Section 7460) of Division 7 of Title 1 of the Government Code).

(c) This chapter does not apply to any trust arrangement described in subdivision (b) of Section 82 except paragraph (4) of that subdivision relating to assets held in a Totten trust.

(d) The affidavit described in Section 2892 is not required to be filed in a proceeding more than once for each asset. However, all assets held by the financial institution may be listed in a single affidavit filed with the court.

(e) If the affidavit and any accompanying information to be filed pursuant to this section also contains the ward or conservatee's social security number or any other personal information, including financial information regarding the ward or conservatee which would not be disclosed in an accounting, an inventory and appraisal, or other nonconfidential pleading filed in the action, the information shall be kept confidential and subject to disclosure to any person only upon order of the court.

Part 5. Public Guardian

Chapter 1. Taking Temporary Possession Or Control Of Property

2900. (a) (1) If the public guardian or public conservator determines that the requirements for appointment of a guardian or conservator of the estate are satisfied and the public guardian or public conservator intends to apply for appointment, the public guardian or public conservator may take possession or control of real or personal property of a person domiciled in the county that is subject to loss, injury, waste, or misappropriation, and, subject to subdivision (b), may deny use of, access to, or prohibit residency in, the real or personal property, by anyone who does not have a written rental agreement or other legal right to the use of, or access to, the property.

(2) (A) Except as provided in subparagraph (C), if the public guardian or public

122

conservator determines that the requirements for appointment of a guardian or conservator of the estate are satisfied and the public guardian or public conservator intends to apply for appointment as the guardian or conservator of a person domiciled in the county, the public guardian or public conservator may restrain any person from transferring, encumbering, or in any way disposing of any real or personal property held in a trust, provided all of the following requirements are met:

(i) The real or personal property held in the trust is subject to loss, injury, waste, or misappropriation.

(ii) The proposed ward or conservatee is a settlor of the trust.

(iii) The proposed ward or conservatee has a beneficial interest in the trust to currently receive income or principal from the trust.

(iv) The proposed ward or conservatee holds a power to revoke the trust.

(B) During the period of any restraint under this paragraph, the property subject to the restraint shall continue to be retained as property of the trust pending termination of the restraint or further court order. The public guardian or public conservator shall provide notice of any action taken under this paragraph to all of the persons required to be noticed pursuant to Section 17203, to the extent the public guardian or public conservator has access to the trust documents or is otherwise able to determine the persons entitled to receive notice. Any settlor, trustee, or beneficiary may petition the court for relief from any action taken by the public guardian or public conservator under this paragraph.

(C) This paragraph shall not apply if a current trustee or cotrustee is a spouse of the proposed ward or conservatee and that spouse is also a settlor of the trust, unless the public guardian or public conservator determines that the real or personal property held in the trust is subject to substantial loss, injury, waste, or misappropriation.

(b) The authority provided to the public guardian and public conservator in subdivision (a) includes the authority to terminate immediately the occupancy of anyone living in the home of an intended ward or conservatee, other than the intended ward or conservatee, and the authority to remove any such occupant residing therein, subject to the following requirements:

(1) The public guardian or public conservator shall first determine that the person whose occupancy is to be terminated has no written rental agreement or other legal right to occupancy, and has caused, contributed to, enabled, or threatened loss, injury, waste, or misappropriation of the home or its contents. In making this determination, the public guardian or public conservator shall contact the intended ward or conservatee and the occupant, advise them of the pro-

posed removal and the grounds therefor, and consider whatever information they provide.

(2) At the time of the removal, the public guardian or public conservator shall advise the intended ward or conservatee and the occupant that a hearing will be held as provided in paragraph (3).

(3) The public guardian or public conservator shall file a petition regarding removal, showing the grounds therefor, to be set for hearing within 10 days of the filing of the petition and within 15 days of the removal. The person removed and the intended ward or conservatee shall be personally served with a notice of hearing and a copy of the petition at least five days prior to the hearing, subject to Part 2 (commencing with Section 1200) of Division 3. The right of the public guardian or public conservator to deny occupancy by the removed person to the premises shall terminate 15 days after removal, unless extended by the court at the hearing on the petition. The court shall not grant an extension unless the public guardian or public conservator has filed a petition for appointment as guardian or conservator of the estate.

(c) If the public guardian or public conservator takes possession of the residence of an intended ward or conservatee under this section, then for purposes of Section 602.3 of the Penal Code, the public guardian or public conservator shall be the owner's representative.

2901. (a) A public guardian who is authorized to take possession or control of property under this chapter may issue a written certification of that fact. The written certification is effective for 30 days after the date of issuance.

(b) The written recordable certification shall substantially comply with the following form:

PLEASE SEE THE APPENDIX

(c) The public guardian may record a copy of the written certification in any county in which is located real property of which the public guardian is authorized to take possession or control under this chapter.

(d) A financial institution or other person shall, without the necessity of inquiring into the truth of the written certification and without court order or letters being issued:

(1) Provide the public guardian information concerning property held in the sole name of the proposed ward or conservatee.

(2) Surrender to the public guardian property of the proposed ward or conservatee that is subject to loss, injury, waste, or misappropriation.

(e) Receipt of the written certification:

(1) Constitutes sufficient acquittance for providing information and for surrendering property of the proposed ward or conservatee.

(2) Fully discharges the financial insti-

tution or other person from any liability for any act or omission of the public guardian with respect to the property.

2901.5. (a) A public guardian or public conservator, who is authorized to restrain any person from transferring, encumbering, or in any way disposing of any real or personal property held in a trust in accordance with paragraph (2) of subdivision (a) of Section 2900, may issue a written certification of that fact. The written certification is effective for 30 days after the date of issuance.

(b) The written recordable certification shall substantially comply with the following form:

PLEASE SEE THE APPENDIX

(c) The public guardian or public conservator may record a copy of the written certification in any county in which is located real property held in a trust as to which the public guardian or public conservator has determined it has authority to issue the written certification.

(d) A financial institution or other person who is provided with the written certification by the public guardian or public conservator shall, without the necessity of inquiring into the truth of the written certification and without court order or letters being issued:

(1) Provide the public guardian or public conservator information concerning any real or personal property held in the trust identified in the written certification.

(2) Restrain any person from transferring, encumbering, or in any way disposing of any real or personal property, held in the trust identified in the written certification.

(e) Receipt of the written certification:

(1) Constitutes sufficient acquittance for providing information and for restraining any person from transferring, encumbering, or in any way disposing of any real or personal property held in the trust identified in the written certification.

(2) Fully discharges the financial institution or other person from any liability for any act or omission of the public guardian or public conservator with respect to the property.

2902. A public guardian who takes possession or control of property pursuant to this chapter is entitled to reasonable costs incurred for the preservation of the property, together with reasonable compensation for services, in case of the subsequent appointment of another person as guardian or conservator of the estate. The costs and compensation are a proper and legal charge against the estate of the ward or conservatee.

2903. This chapter applies only to possession or control of property by a public guardian on or after July 1, 1989. Possession or control of property by a public guardian before July 1, 1989, is governed by the applicable law in effect before July 1, 1989, notwithstanding its repeal by Chapter 1199 of the Statutes of 1988.

Chapter 2. Prefiling Investigation By Public Guardian

2910. (a) Upon a showing of probable cause to believe that a person is in substantial danger of abuse or neglect and needs a conservator of the person, the estate, or the person and estate for his or her own protection, the public guardian or the county's adult protective services agency may petition for either or both of the orders of the court provided in subdivision (b) in connection with his or her investigation to determine whether a petition for the appointment of the public guardian as conservator of the person, estate, or the person and estate of the person would be necessary or appropriate.

(b) The petition may request either or both of the following orders for the limited purposes of the investigation concerning a person:

(1) An order authorizing identified health care providers or organizations to provide private medical information about the person to the public guardian's authorized representatives.

(2) An order authorizing identified financial institutions or advisers, accountants, and others with financial information about the person to provide the information to the public guardian's authorized representatives.

(c) Notice of the hearing and a copy of the petition shall be served on the person who is the subject of the investigation in the manner and for the period required by Section 1460 or, on application of the public guardian contained in or accompanying the petition, on an expedited basis in the manner and for the period ordered by the court. The court may dispense with notice of the hearing only on a showing of facts demonstrating an immediate threat of substantial harm to the person if notice is given.

2911. A court order issued in response to a public guardian's petition pursuant to Section 2910 shall do all of the following:

(a) Authorize health care providers to disclose a person's confidential medical information as permitted under California law, and also authorize disclosure of the information under federal medical privacy regulations enacted pursuant to the Health Insurance Portability and Accountability Act of 1996.

(b) Direct the public guardian or the adult protective services agency to keep the information acquired under the order confidential, except as disclosed in a judicial proceeding or as required by law enforcement or an authorized regulatory agency.

(c) Direct the public guardian or the adult protective services agency to destroy all copies of written information obtained under the order or give them to the person who was the subject of the investigation if a conservatorship proceeding is not commenced within 60 days after the date of the order. The court may extend this time period as the court finds to be in the subject's best interest.

Chapter 3. Appointment Of Public Guardian

2920. (a) If any person domiciled in the county requires a guardian or conservator and there is no one else who is qualified and willing to act and whose appointment would be in the best interests of the person, then either of the following shall apply:

(1) The public guardian shall apply for appointment as guardian or conservator of the person, the estate, or the person and estate, if there is an imminent threat to the person's health or safety or the person's estate.

(2) The public guardian may apply for appointment as guardian or conservator of the person, the estate, or the person and estate in all other cases.

(b) The public guardian shall apply for appointment as guardian or conservator of the person, the estate, or the person and estate, if the court so orders. The court may make an order under this subdivision on motion of an interested person or on the court's own motion in a pending proceeding or in a proceeding commenced for that purpose. The court shall order the public guardian to apply for appointment as guardian or conservator of the person, the estate, or the person and estate, on behalf of any person domiciled in the county who appears to require a guardian or conservator, if it appears that there is no one else who is qualified and willing to act, and if that appointment as guardian or conservator appears to be in the best interests of the person. However, if prior to the filing of the petition for appointment it is discovered that there is someone else who is qualified and willing to act as guardian or conservator, the public guardian shall be relieved of the duty under the order. The court shall not make an order under this subdivision except after notice to the public guardian for the period and in the manner provided for in Chapter 3 (commencing with Section 1460) of Part 1, consideration of the alternatives, and a determination by the court that the appointment is necessary. The notice and hearing under this subdivision may be combined with the notice and hearing required for appointment of a guardian or conservator.

(c) The public guardian shall begin an investigation within two business days of receiving a referral for conservatorship or guardianship.

2921. An application of the public guardian for guardianship or conservatorship of the person, the estate, or the person and es-

tate, of a person who is under the jurisdiction of the State Department of State Hospitals or the State Department of Developmental Services shall not be granted without the written consent of the department having jurisdiction of the person.

2922. If the public guardian is appointed as guardian or conservator:

(a) Letters shall be issued in the same manner and by the same proceedings as letters are issued to other persons. Letters may be issued to "the public guardian" of the county without naming the public guardian.

(b) The official bond and oath of the public guardian are in lieu of the guardian or conservator's bond and oath on the grant of letters.

2923. On or before January 1, 2008, the public guardian shall comply with the continuing education requirements that are established by the California State Association of Public Administrators, Public Guardians, and Public Conservators.

Chapter 4. Administration By Public Guardian

2940. All funds coming into the custody of the public guardian shall be deposited or invested in the same manner and subject to the same terms and conditions as deposit or investment by the public administrator of money in an estate pursuant to Article 3 (commencing with Section 7640) of Chapter 4 of Part 1 of Division 7.

2941. The public guardian may, if necessary and in the public guardian's discretion, employ private attorneys where the cost of employment can be defrayed out of estate funds or where satisfactory pro bono or contingency fee arrangements can be made.

2942. The public guardian shall be paid from the estate of the ward or conservatee for all of the following:

(a) Reasonable expenses incurred in the execution of the guardianship or conservatorship.

(b) Compensation for services of the public guardian and the attorney of the public guardian, and for the filing and processing services of the county clerk or the clerk of the superior court, in the amount the court determines is just and reasonable. In determining what constitutes just and reasonable compensation, the court shall, among other factors, take into consideration the actual costs of the services provided, the amount of the estate involved, the special value of services provided in relation to the estate, and whether the compensation requested might impose an economic hardship on the estate. Nothing in this section shall require a public guardian to base a request for compensation upon an hourly rate of service.

(c) An annual bond fee in the amount of twenty-five dollars ($25) plus one-fourth of 1 percent of the amount of an estate greater than ten thousand dollars ($10,000). The amount charged shall be deposited in the county treasury. This subdivision does not apply if the ward or conservatee is eligible for Social Security Supplemental Income benefits.

2943. (a) Notwithstanding subdivision (c) of Section 2610, the property described in the inventory may be appraised by the public guardian and need not be appraised by a probate referee if the public guardian files with the inventory an appraisal showing that the estimated value of the property in the estate does not exceed the amount prescribed in Section 13100.

(b) If the conservator seeks authority pursuant to subdivision (b) of Section 2540 to sell the conservatee's personal residence, whether or not it is real property, or if the conservator seeks authority pursuant to Section 2590 to sell the conservatee's real property, valued in excess of ten thousand dollars ($10,000), or an item of personal property valued in excess of ten thousand dollars ($10,000) that is not a security sold pursuant to subdivision (a) of Section 2544, that property shall be appraised by a probate referee.

2944. The public guardian is not liable for failing to take possession or control of property that is beyond the ability of the public guardian to possess or control.

Chapter 5. Financial Abuse Of Mentally Impaired Elders

Article 1. General

2950. (a) It is the intent of the Legislature to do all of the following:

(1) Reduce the incidence of financial abuse perpetrated against mentally impaired elder adults.

(2) Minimize monetary losses to mentally impaired elder adults as a result of financial abuse.

(3) Facilitate timely intervention by law enforcement, in collaboration with the public guardian, to effectively protect mentally impaired elder adult victims of financial abuse, and to recover their assets.

(b) Any peace officer or public guardian of a county that has both of the following, as determined by the public guardian of that county, may take the actions authorized by this chapter:

(1) The existence of sufficient law enforcement personnel with expertise in the assessment of competence.

(2) The existence of a law enforcement unit devoted to investigating elder financial abuse and the enforcement of laws applicable to elder abuse.

(c) This chapter shall be coordinated with existing mandated programs affecting financial abuse of mentally impaired elders that are administered by the adult protective services agency of the county.

2951. The definitions contained in this section shall govern the construction of this chapter, unless the context requires otherwise.

(a) "Declaration" means a document that substantially complies with the requirements of Section 2954, and is signed by both a peace officer and a supervisor from the county's adult protective services agency and provided to the public guardian in accordance with subdivision (b) of Section 2952.

(b) "Elder person" means any person residing in this state, 65 years of age or older.

(c) "Financial abuse" means a situation described in Section 15610.30 of the Welfare and Institutions Code.

(d) "Financial abuse POST training" means an elder financial abuse training course certified by the Commission on Peace Officer Standards and Training.

(e) "Financial institution" means any bank, savings and loan, thrift, industrial loan company, credit union, or any branch of any of these institutions doing business in the state, as defined by provisions of the Financial Code.

(f) "Peace officer" means a sheriff, deputy sheriff, municipal police officer, or a peace officer authorized under subdivision (b) of Section 830.1 of the Penal Code, duly sworn under the requirements of state law, who satisfies any of the following requirements:

(1) The sheriff, deputy sheriff, municipal police officer, or peace officer authorized under subdivision (b) of Section 830.1 of the Penal Code has completed or participated as a lecturer in a financial abuse POST training program within the last 36 months. The completion of the course may be satisfied by telecourse, video training tape, or other instruction. The training shall, at a minimum, address relevant elder abuse laws, recognition of financial abuse and fraud, assessment of mental competence in accordance with the standards set forth in Part 17 (commencing with Section 810) of the Probate Code, reporting requirements and procedures for the investigation of financial abuse and related crimes, including neglect, and civil and criminal procedures for the protection of victims. The course may be presented as part of a training program that includes other subjects or courses.

(2) The sheriff, deputy sheriff, municipal police officer, or peace officer authorized under subdivision (b) of Section 830.1 of the Penal Code, has consulted with a sheriff, deputy sheriff, municipal police officer, or peace officer authorized under subdivision (b) of Section 830.1 of the Penal Code, who satisfies the requirements of paragraph (1) concerning the declaration defined in subdivision (a) and obtained the signature of that sheriff, deputy sheriff, municipal police officer, or peace officer authorized under subdivision (b) of Section 830.1 of the Penal Code on a declaration that substantially complies with the form described in Section 2954.

(g) "Property" means all personal property and real property of every kind belonging to, or alleged to belong to, the elder.

Article 2. Estate Protection

2952. (a) A peace officer may issue a declaration, as provided in Section 2954, concerning an elder person if all of the following conditions are satisfied:

(1) There is probable cause to believe that the elder person is substantially unable to manage his or her financial resources or to resist fraud or undue influence.

(2) There exists a significant danger that the elder person will lose all or a portion of his or her property as a result of fraud or misrepresentations or the mental incapacity of the elder person.

(3) There is probable cause to believe that a crime is being committed against the elder person.

(4) The crime is connected to the inability of the elder person to manage his or her financial resources or to resist fraud or undue influence, and that inability is the result of deficits in the elder person's mental functions.

(5) The peace officer has consulted with an individual qualified to perform a mental status examination.

(b) If the requirements of subdivision (a) are satisfied, the peace officer may provide a signed declaration to the public guardian of the county. The declaration provided by the peace officer under this subdivision shall be signed by both the peace officer and a supervisor from the county's adult protective services agency. The declaration shall be transmitted to the public guardian within 24 hours of its being signed, and may be transmitted by facsimile.

(c) (1) Upon receiving a signed declaration from a peace officer, the public guardian is authorized to rely on the information contained in the declaration to take immediate possession or control of any real or personal property belonging to the elder person referred to in the declaration, including any property that is held jointly between the elder person and a third party that is subject to loss, injury, waste, or misappropriation, and may issue a written recordable certification of that fact pursuant to this section. The written recordable certification shall substantially comply with the following form:

PLEASE SEE THE APPENDIX

(2) The mere issuance of the declaration provided by this section shall not require the public guardian to take possession or control of property and shall not require the public guardian to make a determination that the requirements for the appointment of a conservator are satisfied.

(3) The authority provided to the public guardian in paragraph (1) includes the authority to deny use of, access to, or prohibit residency in the home of the elder, by anyone who does not have a written rental agreement or other legal right to the use of, or access to, the residence, and, subject to the requirements of subdivision (b) of Section 2900, the authority to terminate the occupancy of anyone living in the home of the elder person, and the authority to remove that occupant residing therein.

(4) The public guardian shall serve, or cause to be served, a copy of the certification issued pursuant to this section on the elder person by mail within 24 hours of the execution of the certification, or as soon thereafter as is practical, in the manner provided in Chapter 4 (commencing with Section 413.10) of Title 5 of Part 2 of the Code of Civil Procedure.

(5) Receipt of a certification issued under this section constitutes sufficient acquittance to financial institutions and others in possession of an elder person's property to provide information and surrender property of the elder person to the public guardian. Any financial institution or other person who provides information or surrenders property pursuant to this section shall be discharged from any liability for any act or omission of the public guardian with respect to the property.

(6) A public guardian acting in good faith is not liable when taking possession or control of property pursuant to this section.

(7) A certification issued pursuant to this section is valid for 15 days after the date of issuance. Upon ex parte petition to the superior court, the public guardian may seek additional 15-day certifications. The court shall grant that petition only if it determines that the additional certification is necessary to protect the elder from financial abuse and the elder's property from loss, injury, waste, or misappropriation.

(d) (1) If the public guardian takes possession of an elder person' s property pursuant to this section, the public guardian shall attempt to find agents pursuant to the use of durable powers of attorney or successor trustees nominated in trust instruments, or other persons having legal authority under existing legal instruments, to manage the elder person's estate.

(2) If the public guardian is unable to find any appropriate person to manage the elder person's estate pursuant to paragraph (1), the public guardian shall attempt to find appropriate family members willing to manage the elder person's estate. If no documents exist appointing appropriate fiduciaries, the public guardian shall follow the priorities set forth in Article 2 (commencing with Section 1810) of Chapter 1 of Part 3.

(3) The public guardian shall take the steps described in paragraphs (1) and (2) within 15 days of taking possession of an elder person's property pursuant to this section.

(e) Nothing in this section prevents the

county's adult protective services agency from conducting an investigation regarding the elder person named in the declaration and providing appropriate services, in co-ordination with any actions taken with the public guardian under this section or an investigation conducted by law enforcement regarding the elder person.

2953. (a) (1) A public guardian who has taken possession or control of the property of an elder person pursuant to this chapter is entitled to petition a court of competent jurisdiction for the reasonable costs incurred by the public guardian for the protection of the person or the property, together with reasonable fees for services, including, but not limited to, reasonable attorneys' fees. These fees shall be payable from the estate of the elder person if the person is not deemed competent by the court and if any of the following apply:

(A) The public guardian or someone else is appointed as the temporary or general conservator of the estate.

(B) An attorney-in-fact, under a durable power of attorney, or a trustee, takes steps, or is notified of the need to take steps, to protect the estate of the elder person.

(C) An action is brought against the alleged financial abuser by the elder person, his or her conservator, a trustee, a fiduciary, or a successor in interest of the elder person, arising from a harm that the public guardian taking charge was intended to prevent or minimize.

(2) Any costs incurred by the public guardian pursuant to paragraph (1) shall be compensable as provided in Section 2902. Fees collected by the public guardian pursuant to this chapter shall be used for the activities described in this chapter.

(b) When a public guardian has taken possession or control of the property of an elder person pursuant to this chapter, the public guardian shall exercise reasonable care to ensure that the reasonable living expenses and legitimate debts of the elder person are addressed as well as is practical under the circumstances.

(c) Any person identified as a victim in a declaration described in Section 2954 may bring an ex parte petition in the superior court for an order quashing the certification issued by the public guardian as provided in subdivision (c) of Section 2952.

(1) Upon request by the petitioner, the court may defer filing fees related to the petition, and order the public guardian to authorize the release of funds from a financial institution to reimburse the petitioner the filing fees from assets belonging to the petitioner, but shall waive filing fees if the petitioner meets the standards of eligibility established by subparagraph (A) or (B) of paragraph (6) of subdivision (a) of Section 68511.3 of the Government Code for the waiver of a filing fee.

(2) The court shall quash the certification if the court determines that there is insufficient evidence to justify the imposition on the alleged victim's civil liberties caused by the certification.

(3) If the court determines that there is sufficient evidence to justify the imposition on the alleged victim's civil liberties caused by the certification, the court may, in its discretion, do one or more of the following:

(A) Order disbursements from the alleged victim's assets, as are reasonably needed to address the alleged victim's needs.

(B) Appoint a temporary conservator of the alleged victim's estate, where the facts before the court would be sufficient for the appointment of a temporary conservator under Section 2250.

(C) Deny the petition.

(D) Award reasonable attorney's fees to the respondent's attorney from the victim's estate.

2954. A declaration issued by a peace officer under this chapter shall not be valid unless it substantially complies with the following form:

| PLEASE SEE THE APPENDIX |

2955. Nothing in this chapter shall prohibit or restrict a public guardian from undertaking any other proceeding authorized by law.

Part 6. Management Or Disposition Of Community Property Where Spouse Lacks Legal Capacity

Chapter 1. Definitions And General Provisions

Article 1. Definitions

3000. Unless the provision or context otherwise requires, the definitions contained in this article govern the construction of this part.

3002. "Community property" means community real property and community personal property, including, but not limited to, a community property business that is or was under the primary management and control of one of the spouses.

3004. "Conservator" means conservator of the estate, or limited conservator of the estate to the extent that the powers and duties of the limited conservator are specifically and expressly provided by the order appointing the limited conservator, and includes the guardian of the estate of a married minor.

3006. "Conservatorship estate" includes the guardianship estate of a married minor.

3008. "Conservatorship proceeding" means conservatorship of the estate proceeding and includes a guardianship of the estate proceeding of a married minor.

3012. (a) Unless the spouse lacks legal capacity under the applicable standard prescribed in subdivision (b), a spouse has legal capacity to:

(1) Manage and control community property, including legal capacity to dispose of community property.

(2) Join in or consent to a transaction involving community property.

(b) A spouse lacks legal capacity to:

(1) Manage and control, including legal capacity to dispose of, community property if the spouse is substantially unable to manage or control the community property.

(2) Join in or consent to a transaction involving community property if the spouse does not have legal capacity for the particular transaction measured by principles of law otherwise applicable to the particular transaction.

(3) Do any act, or engage in any activity, described in paragraph (1) or (2) if the spouse has a conservator.

(c) Nothing in this section shall be construed to deny a spouse, whether or not lacking legal capacity, any of the following:

(1) The right to control an allowance provided under Section 2421.

(2) The right to control wages or salary to the extent provided in Section 2601.

(3) The right to make a will.

(4) The right to enter into transactions to the extent reasonable to provide the necessities of life to the spouse, the other spouse, and the minor children of the spouses.

Article 2. General Provisions

3020. (a) The proceeds, rents, issues, and profits of community property dealt with or disposed of under this division, and any property taken in exchange for the community property or acquired with the proceeds, are community property.

(b) Except as provided in this part for the management, control, and disposition of community property, nothing in this division alters the rights of the spouses in community property or in the proceeds, rents, issues, or profits of community property.

3023. (a) Except as provided in subdivisions (b) and (c), where one or both of the spouses has a conservator, the court in which any of the conservatorship proceedings is pending may hear and determine whether property is community property or the separate property of either spouse when the issue is raised in any proceeding under this division.

(b) Any person having or claiming title to or an interest in the property, at or prior to the hearing on the issue, may object to the hearing if the court is not the proper court under any other provision of law for the trial of an action to determine the issue. If the objection is established, the court shall not hear and determine the issue.

(c) Except as provided in subdivision (d), if a civil action is pending with respect to the issue and jurisdiction has been obtained in the court in which the civil action is pending, upon request of any party to the civil action, the court shall abate the hearing until the conclusion of the civil action.

(d) The court need not abate the hearing if the court determines that the civil action was filed for the purpose of delay.

Chapter 2. Management, Control, And Disposition

Article 1. Management, Control, And Disposition Generally

3051. (a) Subject to Section 3071, the right of a spouse to manage and control community property, including the right to dispose of community property, is not affected by the lack or alleged lack of legal capacity of the other spouse.

(b) Except as provided in subdivision (c), if one spouse has legal capacity and the other has a conservator:

(1) The spouse who has legal capacity has the exclusive management and control of the community property including, subject to Section 3071, the exclusive power to dispose of the community property.

(2) The community property is not part of the conservatorship estate.

(c) If one spouse has legal capacity and the other has a conservator, the spouse having legal capacity may consent, by a writing filed in the proceeding, that all or part of the community property be included in and, subject to Section 3071, be managed, controlled, and disposed of as a part of the conservatorship estate.

(d) Except as provided in subdivision (e), if both spouses have conservators, an undivided one-half interest in the community property shall be included in and, subject to Section 3071, be managed, controlled, and disposed of as a part of the conservatorship estate of each spouse.

(e) If both spouses have conservators, when authorized by order of the court in which any of the conservatorship proceedings is pending, the conservators may agree in writing that all or specific parts of the community property shall be included in the conservatorship estate of one or the other of the spouses and, subject to Section 3071, be managed, controlled, and disposed of as a part of the conservatorship estate of that spouse.

3054. When community property is included or proposed to be included in the conservatorship estate of a spouse, the court in which the conservatorship proceeding is pending, upon its own motion or upon petition of a spouse having legal capacity or the conservator of either spouse and upon such notice to such persons as the court prescribes, may do any of the following:

(a) Determine that the inclusion of some or all of the community property that is proposed to be included in the conservatorship estate would not be in the best interest of the spouses or their estates and order that such property not be included.

(b) Permit revocation of a written consent for inclusion of property in the conservatorship estate, with or without terms or conditions.

(c) Determine that the continued inclusion of some or all of the community property in the conservatorship estate is not in the best interest of the spouses or their estates and order that the inclusion of such property in the conservatorship estate be terminated, with or without terms or conditions.

(d) Make such other orders as may be appropriate for the orderly administration of the conservatorship estate or to protect the interests of the spouses.

3055. (a) If consent is given under this article that community property be included in the conservatorship estate of a spouse, the death of either spouse terminates the consent.

(b) If a spouse consents under this article that community property be included in the conservatorship estate of the other spouse:

(1) Subject to paragraph (2), the subsequent lack of legal capacity of the spouse giving the consent has no effect on the inclusion of the property in the conservatorship estate of the other spouse.

(2) The appointment of a conservator for the spouse giving the consent terminates the consent.

3056. Except as otherwise provided in this part and subject to Section 3071, when community property is included in a conservatorship estate under this article for the purpose of management, control, and disposition, the conservator has the same powers and duties with respect to such property as the conservator has with respect to other property of the conservatorship estate.

3057. (a) Where a spouse lacks legal capacity and does not have a conservator, any interested person who has knowledge or reason to believe that the rights of such spouse in the community property are being prejudiced may bring an action on behalf of such spouse to enforce the duty imposed by Sections 721 and 1100 of the Family Code with respect to the management and control of the community property and to obtain such relief as may be appropriate.

(b) If one spouse has a conservator and the other spouse is managing or controlling community property, the conservator has the duty to keep reasonably informed concerning the management and control, including the disposition, of the community property. If the conservator has knowledge or reason to believe that the rights of the conservatee in the community property are being prejudiced, the conservator may bring an action on behalf of the conservatee to enforce the duty imposed by Sections 721 and 1100 of the Family Code with respect to the management and control of the community property and to obtain such relief as may be appropriate.

Article 2. Substitute For Joinder Or Consent Requirements

3070. If the requirements of this article are satisfied with respect to a transaction described in Section 3071, the transaction is deemed to satisfy the joinder or consent requirements of the statute referred to in that section.

3071. (a) In case of a transaction for which the joinder or consent of both spouses is required by Section 1100 or 1102 of the Family Code or by any other statute, if one or both spouses lacks legal capacity for the transaction, the requirement of joinder or consent shall be satisfied as provided in this section.

(b) Where one spouse has legal capacity for the transaction and the other spouse has a conservator, the requirement of joinder or consent is satisfied if both of the following are obtained:

(1) The joinder or consent of the spouse having legal capacity.

(2) The joinder or consent of the conservator of the other spouse given in compliance with Section 3072.

(c) Where both spouses have conservators, the joinder or consent requirement is satisfied by the joinder or consent of each such conservator given in compliance with Section 3072.

(d) In any case, the requirement of joinder or consent is satisfied if the transaction is authorized by an order of court obtained in a proceeding pursuant to Chapter 3 (commencing with Section 3100).

3072. (a) Except as provided in subdivision (b), a conservator may join in or consent to a transaction under Section 3071 only after authorization by either of the following:

(1) An order of the court obtained in the conservatorship proceeding upon a petition filed pursuant to Section 2403 or under Article 7 (commencing with Section 2540) or 10 (commencing with Section 2580) of Chapter 6 of Part 4.

(2) An order of the court made in a proceeding pursuant to Chapter 3 (commencing with Section 3100).

(b) A conservator may consent without court authorization to a sale, conveyance, or encumbrance of community personal property requiring consent under subdivision (c) of Section 1100 of the Family Code if the conservator could sell or transfer the property under Section 2545 without court authorization if the property were a part of the conservatorship estate.

3073. (a) The joinder or consent under Section 3071 of a spouse having legal capacity shall be in a manner that complies with

Section 1100 or 1102 of the Family Code or other statute that applies to the transaction.

(b) The joinder or consent under Section 3071 of a conservator shall be in the same manner as a spouse would join in or consent to the transaction under the statute that applies to the transaction except that the joinder or consent shall be executed by the conservator and shall refer to the court order, if one is required, authorizing the conservator to join in or consent to the transaction.

3074. Notwithstanding any other provision of this article, a transaction that affects real property, entered into by a person acting in good faith and for a valuable consideration, is not affected by the fact that one or both spouses have conservators unless a notice of the establishment of the conservatorship or conservatorships, as the case may be, has been recorded prior to the transaction in the county in which the property is located.

Article 3. Enforcement Of Support Of Spouse Who Has Conservator

3080. If one spouse has a conservator and the other spouse has the management or control of community property, the conservator or conservatee, a relative or friend of the conservatee, or any interested person may file a petition under this article in the court in which the conservatorship proceeding is pending for an order requiring the spouse who has the management or control of community property to apply the income or principal, or both, of the community property to the support and maintenance of the conservatee as ordered by the court.

3081. (a) Notice of the hearing on the petition shall be given for the period and in the manner provided in Chapter 3 (commencing with Section 1460) of Part 1.

(b) If the spouse who has the management or control of community property is not the conservator, the petitioner shall also cause notice of the hearing and a copy of the petition to be served on that spouse in accordance with Title 5 (commencing with Section 410.10) of Part 2 of the Code of Civil Procedure.

3082. Upon the filing of a petition under this article, the court may cite the spouse who has the management or control of community property to appear before the court, and the court and the petitioner may examine the spouse under oath concerning the community property and other matters relevant to the petition filed under this article. If the person so cited refuses to appear and submit to an examination, the court may proceed against the person as provided in Article 2 (commencing with Section 8870) of Chapter 2 of Part 3 of Division 7. Upon such examination, the court may make an order requiring the person cited to disclose his or her knowledge of the community property and other matters relevant to the petition filed under this article, and if the order is not complied with, the court may proceed against the person as provided in Article 2 (commencing with Section 8870) of Chapter 2 of Part 3 of Division 7.

3083. In any proceeding under this article, the court may, after notice and hearing, order the spouse who has the management or control of community property to pay from the community property such amount as the court determines is necessary to the support and maintenance of the conservatee spouse pending the determination of the petition under this article. An order made pursuant to this section does not prejudice the rights of the spouses or other interested parties with respect to any subsequent order which may be made under this article. Any order made under this section may be modified or revoked at any time except as to any amount that may have accrued prior to the date of filing of the petition to modify or revoke the order.

3084. When a petition is filed under this article, the spouse having the management or control of community property shall serve and file a current income and expense declaration and a current property declaration on the forms prescribed by the Judicial Council for use in family law proceedings.

3085. During the pendency of any proceeding under this article, the court, upon the application of the petitioner, may issue ex parte orders:

(a) Restraining the spouse having the management or control of community property from transferring, encumbering, hypothecating, concealing, or in any way disposing of any property, real or personal, whether community, quasi-community, or separate, except in the usual course of business or for the necessities of life.

(b) Requiring the spouse having the management or control of the community property to notify the petitioner of any proposed extraordinary expenditures and to account to the court for all such extraordinary expenditures.

3086. Any person interested in the proceeding under this article may request time for filing a response to the petition, for discovery proceedings, or for other preparation for the hearing, and the court shall grant a continuance for a reasonable time for any of such purposes.

3087. In a proceeding under this article, the court may hear and determine whether property is community property or the separate property of either spouse if that issue is raised in the proceeding.

3088. (a) The court may order the spouse who has the management or control of community property to apply the income or principal, or both, of the community property to the support and maintenance of the conservatee, including care, treatment, and support of a conservatee who is a patient in a state hospital under the jurisdiction of the State Department of State Hospitals or the State Department of Developmental Services, as ordered by the court.

(b) In determining the amount ordered for support and maintenance, the court shall consider the following circumstances of the spouses:

(1) The earning capacity and needs of each spouse.

(2) The obligations and assets, including the separate property, of each spouse.

(3) The duration of the marriage.

(4) The age and health of the spouses.

(5) The standard of living of the spouses.

(6) Any other relevant factors which it considers just and equitable.

(c) At the request of any interested person, the court shall make appropriate findings with respect to the circumstances.

(d) The court may order the spouse who has the management or control of community property to make a specified monthly or other periodic payment to the conservator of the person of the conservatee or to any other person designated in the order. The court may order the spouse required to make the periodic payments to give reasonable security therefor.

(e) (1) The court may order the spouse required to make the periodic payments to assign, to the person designated in the order to receive the payments, that portion of the earnings of the spouse due or to be due in the future as will be sufficient to pay the amount ordered by the court for the support and maintenance of the conservatee. The order operates as an assignment and is binding upon any existing or future employer upon whom a copy of the order is served. The order shall be in the form of an earnings assignment order for support prescribed by the Judicial Council for use in family law proceedings. The employer may deduct the sum of one dollar and fifty cents ($1.50) for each payment made pursuant to the order. Any such assignment made pursuant to court order shall have priority as against any execution or other assignment unless otherwise ordered by the court or unless the other assignment is made pursuant to Chapter 8 (commencing with Section 5200) of Part 5 of Division 9 of the Family Code. No employer shall use any assignment authorized by this subdivision as grounds for the dismissal of that employee.

(2) As used in this subdivision, "employer" includes the United States government and any public entity as defined in Section 811.2 of the Government Code. This subdivision applies to the money and benefits described in Sections 704.110 and 704.113 of the Code of Civil Procedure to the extent that those moneys and benefits are subject to a wage assignment for support under Chapter 4 (commencing with Section 703.010) of Division 2 of Title 9 of Part 2 of the Code of Civil Procedure.

(f) The court retains jurisdiction to modify or to vacate an order made under this section where justice requires, except as to any amount that may have accrued prior to the date of the filing of the petition to modify or revoke the order. At the request of any interested person, the order of modification or revocation shall include findings of fact and may be made retroactive to the date of the filing of the petition to revoke or modify, or to any date subsequent thereto. At least 15 days before the hearing on the petition to modify or vacate the order, the petitioner shall mail a notice of the time and place of the hearing on the petition, accompanied by a copy of the petition, to the spouse who has the management or control of the community property. Notice shall be given for the period and in the manner provided in Chapter 3 (commencing with Section 1460) of Part 1 to any other persons entitled to notice of the hearing under that chapter.

(g) In a proceeding for dissolution of the marriage or for legal separation, the court has jurisdiction to modify or vacate an order made under this section to the same extent as it may modify or vacate an order made in the proceeding for dissolution of the marriage or for legal separation.

3089. If the spouse who has the management or control of the community property refuses to comply with any order made under this article or an order made in a separate action to provide support for the conservatee spouse, upon request of the petitioner or other interested person, the court may, in its discretion, divide the community property and the quasi-community property of the spouses, as it exists at the time of division, equally in the same manner as where a marriage is dissolved. If the property is so divided, the property awarded to each spouse is the separate property of that spouse and the court shall order that the property awarded to the conservatee spouse be transferred or paid over to the conservator of the estate of that spouse to be included in the conservatorship estate and be managed, controlled, and disposed of as a part of the conservatorship estate. The fact that property has been divided pursuant to this section has no effect on the nature of property thereafter acquired by the spouses, and the determination whether the thereafter-acquired property is community or separate property shall be made without regard to the fact that property has been divided pursuant to this section.

3090. Any order of the court made under this article may be enforced by the court by execution, the appointment of a receiver, contempt, or by such other order or orders as the court in its discretion may from time to time deem necessary.

3091. Notwithstanding any other provision of law, the Judicial Council may provide by rule for the practice and procedure in proceedings under this article.

3092. Nothing in this article affects or limits the right of the conservator or any interested person to institute an action against any person to enforce the duty otherwise imposed by law to support the spouse having a conservator. This article is permissive and in addition to any other procedure otherwise available to enforce the obligation of support.

Chapter 3. Proceeding For Particular Transaction

Article 1. General Provisions

3100. (a) As used in this chapter, "transaction" means a transaction that involves community real or personal property, tangible or intangible, or an interest therein or a lien or encumbrance thereon, including, but not limited to, those transactions with respect thereto as are listed in Section 3102.

(b) However, if a proposed transaction involves property in which a spouse also has a separate property interest, for good cause the court may include that separate property in the transaction.

3101. (a) A proceeding may be brought under this chapter for a court order authorizing a proposed transaction, whether or not the proposed transaction is one that otherwise would require the joinder or consent of both spouses, if both of the following conditions are satisfied:

(1) One of the spouses is alleged to lack legal capacity for the proposed transaction, whether or not that spouse has a conservator.

(2) The other spouse either has legal capacity for the proposed transaction or has a conservator.

(b) A proceeding may be brought under this chapter for a court order declaring that one or both spouses has legal capacity for a proposed transaction.

(c) One proceeding may be brought under this chapter under both subdivision (a) and subdivision (b).

(d) In a proceeding under this chapter, the court may determine whether the property that is the subject of the proposed transaction is community property or the separate property of either spouse, but such determination shall not be made in the proceeding under this chapter if the court determines that the interest of justice requires that the determination be made in a civil action.

(e) This chapter is permissive and cumulative for the transactions to which it applies.

3102. The transactions that may be the subject of a proceeding under this chapter include, but are not limited to:

(a) Sale, conveyance, assignment, transfer, exchange, conveyance pursuant to a pre-existing contract, encumbrance by security interest, deed of trust, mortgage, or other-

wise, lease, including but not limited to a lease for the exploration for and production of oil, gas, minerals, or other substances, or unitization or pooling with other property for or in connection with such exploration and production.

(b) Assignment, transfer, or conveyance, in whole or in part, in compromise or settlement of an indebtedness, demand, or proceeding to which the property may be subject.

(c) Dedication or conveyance, with or without consideration, of any of the following:

(1) The property to this state or any public entity in this state, or to the United States or any agency or instrumentality of the United States, for any purpose.

(2) An easement over the property to any person for any purpose.

(d) Conveyance, release, or relinquishment to this state or any public entity in this state, with or without consideration, of any access rights to a street, highway, or freeway from the property.

(e) Consent as a lienholder to a dedication, conveyance, release, or relinquishment under subdivision (c) or (d) by the owner of property subject to the lien.

(f) Conveyance or transfer, without consideration, to provide gifts for such purposes, and to such charities, relatives (including one of the spouses), friends, or other objects of bounty, as would be likely beneficiaries of gifts from the spouses.

Article 2. Commencement Of Proceeding

3110. (a) A proceeding under this chapter shall be brought by a petition filed in the superior court.

(b) The proper county for commencement of the proceeding is the county in which a conservatorship proceeding of one of the spouses is pending. If a conservatorship proceeding is not pending, then in either of the following:

(1) The county in which one or both of the spouses resides.

(2) Any other county as may be in the best interests of the spouses.

3111. (a) Except as provided in subdivision (b), any of the following persons may file, or join in, a petition under this chapter:

(1) Either spouse, whether or not the spouse has legal capacity.

(2) The conservator of either spouse.

(b) If the petition requests approval of a proposed transaction, at least one of the petitioners shall be either a conservator or a spouse having legal capacity for the transaction.

3112. (a) If a petitioning spouse is one whose legal capacity for the proposed transaction is to be determined in the proceeding, the court may do any of the following:

(1) Permit the spouse to appear without a

representative.

(2) Appoint a guardian ad litem for the spouse.

(3) Take such other action as the circumstances warrant.

(b) If a petitioning spouse lacks legal capacity for the proposed transaction, the court may do either of the following:

(1) Require the spouse to be represented by the conservator of the spouse.

(2) Appoint a guardian ad litem for the spouse.

3113. A proceeding may be brought under this chapter by the conservator of a spouse, or by a spouse having legal capacity for the proposed transaction, without the necessity of appointing a conservator for the other spouse.

Article 3. Petition

3120. (a) Several proposed transactions may be included in one petition and proceeding under this chapter.

(b) The petition may contain inconsistent allegations and may request relief in the alternative.

3121. The petition shall set forth all of the following information:

(a) The name, age, and residence of each spouse.

(b) If one or both spouses is alleged to lack legal capacity for the proposed transaction, a statement that the spouse has a conservator or a statement of the facts upon which the allegation is based.

(c) If there is a conservator of a spouse, the name and address of the conservator, the county in which the conservatorship proceeding is pending, and the court number of the proceeding.

(d) If a spouse alleged to lack legal capacity for the proposed transaction is a patient in or on leave of absence from a state institution under the jurisdiction of the State Department of State Hospitals or the State Department of Developmental Services, the name and address of the institution.

(e) The names and addresses of all of the following persons:

(1) Relatives within the second degree of each spouse alleged to lack legal capacity for the proposed transaction.

(2) If the petition is to provide gifts or otherwise affect estate planning of the spouse who is alleged to lack capacity, as would be properly the subject of a petition under Article 10 (commencing with Section 2580) of Chapter 6 of Part 4 (substituted judgment) in the case of a conservatorship, the names and addresses of the persons identified in Section 2581.

(f) A sufficient description of the property that is the subject of the proposed transaction.

(g) An allegation that the property is community property, and, if the proposed transaction involves property in which a spouse also has a separate property interest, an allegation of good cause to include that separate property in the transaction.

(h) The estimated value of the property.

(i) The terms and conditions of the proposed transaction, including the names of all parties thereto.

(j) The relief requested.

3122. If the proceeding is brought for a court order authorizing a proposed transaction, the petition shall set forth, in addition to the information required by Section 3121, all of the following:

(a) An allegation that one of the spouses has a conservator or facts establishing lack of legal capacity of the spouse for the proposed transaction.

(b) An allegation that the other spouse has legal capacity for the proposed transaction or has a conservator.

(c) An allegation that each spouse either: (1) joins in or consents to the proposed transaction, (2) has a conservator, or (3) is substantially unable to manage his or her financial resources or resist fraud or undue influence.

(d) Facts that may be relied upon to show that the authorization sought is for one or more of the following purposes:

(1) The advantage, benefit, or best interests of the spouses or their estates.

(2) The care and support of either spouse or of such persons as either spouse may be legally obligated to support.

(3) The payment of taxes, interest, or other encumbrances or charges for the protection and preservation of the community property.

(4) The providing of gifts for such purposes, and to such charities, relatives (including one of the spouses), friends, or other objects of bounty, as would be likely beneficiaries of gifts from the spouses.

3123. If the proceeding is brought for a court order declaring that one or both spouses has legal capacity for a proposed transaction, the petition shall set forth, in addition to the information required by Section 3121, an allegation of the legal capacity of such spouse or spouses for the proposed transaction.

Article 4. Citation And Notice Of Hearing

3130. (a) Except as provided in subdivision (b), upon the filing of the petition, the clerk shall issue a citation to each nonpetitioning spouse alleged to lack legal capacity for the proposed transaction, setting forth the time and place of hearing. The citation and a copy of the petition shall be served upon the spouse at least 15 days before the hearing.

(b) Unless the court otherwise orders, if a spouse alleged to lack legal capacity for the proposed transaction has a conservator, no citation to the spouse need be issued, and the petitioner shall cause a notice of the time and place of the hearing on the petition, accompanied by a copy of the petition, to be served on the conservator at least 15 days before the hearing.

(c) Service under this section shall be made in the manner provided in Section 415.10 or 415.30 of the Code of Civil Procedure or in such other manner as may be authorized by the court. If the person to be served is outside this state, service may also be made in the manner provided in Section 415.40 of the Code of Civil Procedure.

3131. (a) At least 15 days before the hearing on the petition, the petitioner shall cause a notice of the time and place of the hearing and a copy of the petition to be served upon any nonpetitioning spouse not alleged to lack legal capacity for the proposed transaction.

(b) Service under subdivision (a) shall be made in the manner provided in Section 415.10 or 415.30 of the Code of Civil Procedure or in such other manner as may be authorized by the court. If the person to be served is outside this state, service may also be made in the manner provided in Section 415.40 of the Code of Civil Procedure.

(c) At least 15 days before the hearing on the petition, the petitioner shall mail a notice of the time and place of the hearing on the petition to those persons required to be named in the petition at the addresses set forth in the petition.

Article 5. Hearing And Order

3140. (a) A conservator served pursuant to this article shall, and the Director of State Hospitals or the Director of Developmental Services given notice pursuant to Section 1461 may, appear at the hearing and represent a spouse alleged to lack legal capacity for the proposed transaction.

(b) The court may, in its discretion and if necessary, appoint an investigator to review the proposed transaction and report to the court regarding its advisability.

(c) If the court determines that a spouse alleged to lack legal capacity has not competently retained independent counsel, the court may in its discretion appoint the public guardian, public administrator, or a guardian ad litem to represent the interests of the spouse.

(d) (1) If a spouse alleged to lack legal capacity is unable to retain legal counsel, upon request of the spouse, the court shall appoint the public defender or private counsel under Section 1471 to represent the spouse and, if that appointment is made, Section 1472 applies.

(2) If the petition proposes a transfer of substantial assets to the petitioner from the other spouse and the court determines that the spouse has not competently retained independent counsel for the proceeding, the court may, in its discretion, appoint counsel for the other spouse if the court determines

that appointment would be helpful to resolve the matter or necessary to protect the interests of the other spouse.

(e) Except as provided in paragraph (1) of subdivision (d), the court may fix a reasonable fee, to be paid out of the proceeds of the transaction or otherwise as the court may direct, for all services rendered by privately engaged counsel, the public guardian, public administrator, or guardian ad litem, and by counsel for such persons.

(f) The court may order the cost of the review and report by a court investigator pursuant to subdivision (b) to be paid out of the proceeds of the transaction or otherwise as the court may direct, if the court determines that its order would not cause a hardship.

3141. (a) If a spouse is alleged to lack legal capacity for the proposed transaction and has no conservator, the spouse shall be produced at the hearing unless unable to attend the hearing.

(b) If the spouse is not able to attend the hearing because of medical inability, such inability shall be established (1) by the affidavit or certificate of a licensed medical practitioner or (2) if the spouse is an adherent of a religion whose tenets and practices call for reliance upon prayer alone for healing and is under treatment by an accredited practitioner of the religion, by the affidavit of the practitioner.

(c) Emotional or psychological instability is not good cause for absence of the spouse from the hearing unless, by reason of such instability, attendance at the hearing is likely to cause serious and immediate physiological damage.

3142. (a) If a spouse is alleged to lack legal capacity for the proposed transaction and has no conservator, the court, before commencement of the hearing on the merits, shall inform the spouse of all of the following:

(1) A determination of lack of legal capacity for the proposed transaction may result in approval of the proposed transaction.

(2) The spouse has the right to legal counsel of the spouse's own choosing, including the right to have legal counsel appointed by the court if unable to retain legal counsel.

(b) This section does not apply if the spouse is absent from the hearing and is not required to attend the hearing under the provisions of subdivision (a) of Section 3141 and any showing required by Section 3141 has been made.

3143. (a) If the petition requests that the court make an order declaring a spouse to have legal capacity for the proposed transaction and the court determines that the spouse has legal capacity for the proposed transaction, the court shall so order.

(b) If the petition alleges that a spouse having no conservator lacks legal capacity for the proposed transaction and the court determines that the spouse has legal capacity for the transaction, the court shall make an order so declaring.

3144. (a) The court may authorize the proposed transaction if the court determines all of the following:

(1) The property that is the subject of the proposed transaction is community property of the spouses, and, if the proposed transaction involves property in which a spouse also has a separate property interest, that there is good cause to include that separate property in the transaction.

(2) One of the spouses then has a conservator or otherwise lacks legal capacity for the proposed transaction.

(3) The other spouse either has legal capacity for the proposed transaction or has a conservator.

(4) Each of the spouses either (i) joins in or consents to the proposed transaction, (ii) has a conservator, or (iii) is substantially unable to manage his or her own financial resources or resist fraud or undue influence. Substantial inability may not be proved by isolated incidents of negligence or improvidence.

(5) The proposed transaction is one that should be authorized under this chapter.

(b) If the proposed transaction is to provide gifts or otherwise affect estate planning of the spouse who is alleged to lack capacity, as would be properly the subject of a petition under Article 10 (commencing with Section 2580) of Chapter 6 of Part 4 (substituted judgment) in the case of a conservatorship, the court may authorize the transaction under this chapter only if the transaction is one that the court would authorize under that article.

(c) If the court determines under subdivision (a) that the transaction should be authorized, the court shall so order and may authorize the petitioner to do and perform all acts and to execute and deliver all papers, documents, and instruments necessary to effectuate the order.

(d) In an order authorizing a transaction, the court may prescribe any terms and conditions as the court in its discretion determines appropriate, including, but not limited to, requiring joinder or consent of another person.

3145. A court determination pursuant to this chapter that a spouse lacks legal capacity for the proposed transaction affects the legal capacity of the spouse for that transaction alone and has no effect on the legal capacity of the spouse for any other purpose.

Article 6. Consummation Of Transaction

3150. (a) Unless the court for good cause dispenses with the bond, the court shall require the petitioner to give a bond, in the amount fixed by the court, conditioned on the duty of the petitioner to account for and apply the proceeds of the transaction to be received by the petitioner only as the court may by order direct.

(b) Unless the court for good cause fixes the amount of the bond in a lesser amount, if given by an admitted surety insurer, the bond shall be in an amount not less than the value of the personal property (including cash and any notes) to be received by the petitioner, as determined by the court.

(c) If the sureties on the bond are personal sureties, the bond shall be approved by the court and shall be for twice the amount required for a bond given by an admitted surety insurer.

(d) Section 2328 is applicable to the bond of the petitioner under this chapter.

3151. (a) The petitioner shall, upon receipt of the consideration therefor, execute, acknowledge, and deliver any necessary instruments or documents as directed by the court, setting forth therein that they are made by authority of the order.

(b) The petitioner shall cause a certified copy of the order to be recorded in the office of the recorder of each county in which is located any real property affected by the order or any real property upon which there is a lien or encumbrance affected by the order.

(c) If a sale is made upon a credit pursuant to the order, the petitioner shall take the note of the person to whom the sale is made for the amount of the unpaid balance of the purchase money, with such security for the payment thereof as the court shall by order approve. The note shall be made payable to the petitioner or, if the petition was made by a conservator, to the petitioner as conservator.

3152. A sale, conveyance, assignment, transfer, exchange, encumbrance, security interest, mortgage, deed of trust, lease, dedication, release, or relinquishment, and any instrument or document, made pursuant to the court's order, is as valid and effectual as if the property affected thereby were the sole and absolute property of the person making it.

3153. Notes, encumbrances, security interests, mortgages, leases, or deeds of trust, executed as provided in this chapter by a petitioning conservator create no personal liability against the conservator so executing, unless the conservator is one of the spouses and then only to the extent that personal liability would have resulted had both spouses had legal capacity for the transaction and joined in the execution.

3154. (a) If any party to the transaction, other than the petitioner, does not consummate a transaction authorized by the court, the court, on application of the petitioner, after such notice to the parties to the transaction as the court directs, may vacate the order authorizing the transaction.

(b) If the order authorized the sale or encumbrance of property, the petitioner may by supplemental petition apply to the court for an order authorizing any other sale or encumbrance of the property to the advantage, benefit, or best interests of the spouses or their estates. The supplemental petition and a notice of the time and place of the hearing shall be served and mailed as provided in Article 4 (commencing with Section 3130) except that (1) no further citation shall be issued and (2) a copy of the supplemental petition and a notice of the time and place of the hearing shall be served upon any person who has appeared as representative of a nonpetitioning spouse or upon counsel of record for a nonpetitioning spouse or as the court may otherwise direct.

(c) If it appears to the court that the other sale or encumbrance is to the advantage, benefit, or best interests of the spouses or their estates and that the request in the supplemental petition that the transaction be authorized should be granted, the court may so order and may authorize the petitioner to do and perform acts and to execute and deliver all papers, documents, and instruments necessary to effectuate the order.

Part 7. Capacity Determinations And Health Care Decisions For Adult Without Conservator

3200. As used in this part:

(a) "Health care" means any care, treatment, service, or procedure to maintain, diagnose, or otherwise affect a patient's physical or mental condition.

(b) "Health care decision" means a decision regarding the patient' s health care, including the following:

(1) Selection and discharge of health care providers and institutions.

(2) Approval or disapproval of diagnostic tests, surgical procedures, programs of medication.

(3) Directions to provide, withhold, or withdraw artificial nutrition and hydration and all other forms of health care, including cardiopulmonary resuscitation.

(c) "Health care institution" means an institution, facility, or agency licensed, certified, or otherwise authorized or permitted by law to provide health care in the ordinary course of business.

(d) "Patient" means an adult who does not have a conservator of the person and for whom a health care decision needs to be made.

3201. (a) A petition may be filed to determine that a patient has the capacity to make a health care decision concerning an existing or continuing condition.

(b) A petition may be filed to determine that a patient lacks the capacity to make a health care decision concerning specified treatment for an existing or continuing condition, and further for an order authorizing a designated person to make a health care decision on behalf of the patient.

(c) One proceeding may be brought under this part under both subdivisions (a) and (b).

3202. The petition may be filed in the superior court of any of the following counties:

(a) The county in which the patient resides.

(b) The county in which the patient is temporarily living.

(c) Such other county as may be in the best interests of the patient.

3203. A petition may be filed by any of the following:

(a) The patient.

(b) The patient's spouse.

(c) A relative or friend of the patient, or other interested person, including the patient's agent under a power of attorney for health care.

(d) The patient's physician.

(e) A person acting on behalf of the health care institution in which the patient is located if the patient is in a health care institution.

(f) The public guardian or other county officer designated by the board of supervisors of the county in which the patient is located or resides or is temporarily living.

3204. The petition shall state, or set forth by a medical declaration attached to the petition, all of the following known to the petitioner at the time the petition is filed:

(a) The condition of the patient's health that requires treatment.

(b) The recommended health care that is considered to be medically appropriate.

(c) The threat to the patient's condition if authorization for the recommended health care is delayed or denied by the court.

(d) The predictable or probable outcome of the recommended health care.

(e) The medically available alternatives, if any, to the recommended health care.

(f) The efforts made to obtain consent from the patient.

(g) If the petition is filed by a person on behalf of a health care institution, the name of the person to be designated to give consent to the recommended health care on behalf of the patient.

(h) The deficit or deficits in the patient's mental functions listed in subdivision (a) of Section 811 that are impaired, and an identification of a link between the deficit or deficits and the patient's inability to respond knowingly and intelligently to queries about the recommended health care or inability to participate in a decision about the recommended health care by means of a rational thought process.

(i) The names and addresses, so far as they are known to the petitioner, of the persons specified in subdivision (b) of Section 1821.

3205. Upon the filing of the petition, the court shall determine the name of the attorney the patient has retained to represent the patient in the proceeding under this part or the name of the attorney the patient plans to retain for that purpose. If the patient has not retained an attorney and does not plan to retain one, the court shall appoint the public defender or private counsel under Section 1471 to consult with and represent the patient at the hearing on the petition and, if such appointment is made, Section 1472 applies.

3206. (a) Not less than 15 days before the hearing, notice of the time and place of the hearing and a copy of the petition shall be personally served on the patient, the patient's attorney, and the agent under the patient's power of attorney for health care, if any.

(b) Not less than 15 days before the hearing, notice of the time and place of the hearing and a copy of the petition shall be mailed to the following persons:

(1) The patient's spouse, if any, at the address stated in the petition.

(2) The patient's relatives named in the petition at their addresses stated in the petition.

(c) For good cause, the court may shorten or waive notice of the hearing as provided by this section. In determining the period of notice to be required, the court shall take into account both of the following:

(1) The existing medical facts and circumstances set forth in the petition or in a medical declaration attached to the petition or in a medical declaration presented to the court.

(2) The desirability, where the condition of the patient permits, of giving adequate notice to all interested persons.

3207. Notwithstanding Section 3206, the matter presented by the petition may be submitted for the determination of the court upon proper and sufficient medical declarations if the attorney for the petitioner and the attorney for the patient so stipulate and further stipulate that there remains no issue of fact to be determined.

3208. (a) Except as provided in subdivision (b), the court may make an order authorizing the recommended health care for the patient and designating a person to give consent to the recommended health care on behalf of the patient if the court determines from the evidence all of the following:

(1) The existing or continuing condition of the patient's health requires the recommended health care.

(2) If untreated, there is a probability that the condition will become life-endangering or result in a serious threat to the physical or mental health of the patient.

(3) The patient is unable to consent to the recommended health care.

(b) In determining whether the patient's mental functioning is so severely impaired that the patient lacks the capacity to make any health care decision, the court may take into consideration the frequency, severity, and duration of periods of impairment.

(c) The court may make an order authorizing withholding or withdrawing artificial nutrition and hydration and all other forms of health care and designating a person to give or withhold consent to the recommended health care on behalf of the patient if the court determines from the evidence all of the following:

(1) The recommended health care is in accordance with the patient's best interest, taking into consideration the patient's personal values to the extent known to the petitioner.

(2) The patient is unable to consent to the recommended health care.

3208.5. In a proceeding under this part:

(a) Where the patient has the capacity to consent to the recommended health care, the court shall so find in its order.

(b) Where the court has determined that the patient has the capacity to consent to the recommended health care, the court shall, if requested, determine whether the patient has accepted or refused the recommended health care, and whether the patient's consent to the recommended health care is an informed consent.

(c) Where the court finds that the patient has the capacity to consent to the recommended health care, but that the patient refuses consent, the court shall not make an order authorizing the recommended health care or designating a person to give consent to the recommended health care. If an order has been made authorizing the recommended health care and designating a person to give consent to the recommended health care, the order shall be revoked if the court determines that the patient has recovered the capacity to consent to the recommended health care. Until revoked or modified, the order is effective authorization for the recommended health care.

3209. The court in which the petition is filed has continuing jurisdiction to revoke or modify an order made under this part upon a petition filed, noticed, and heard in the same manner as an original petition filed under this part.

3210. (a) This part is supplemental and alternative to other procedures or methods for obtaining consent to health care or making health care decisions, and is permissive and cumulative for the relief to which it applies.

(b) Nothing in this part limits the providing of health care in an emergency case in which the health care is required because (1) the health care is required for the alleviation of severe pain or (2) the patient has a medical condition that, if not immediately diagnosed and treated, will lead to serious disability or death.

(c) Nothing in this part supersedes the right that any person may have under existing law to make health care decisions on behalf of a patient, or affects the decision-making process of a health care institution.

3211. (a) No person may be placed in a mental health treatment facility under the provisions of this part.

(b) No experimental drug as defined in Section 111515 of the Health and Safety Code may be prescribed for or administered to any person under this part.

(c) No convulsive treatment as defined in Section 5325 of the Welfare and Institutions Code may be performed on any person under this part.

(d) No person may be sterilized under this part.

(e) The provisions of this part are subject to a valid advance health care directive under the Health Care Decisions Law, Division 4.7 (commencing with Section 4600).

3212. Nothing in this part shall be construed to supersede or impair the right of any individual to choose treatment by spiritual means in lieu of medical treatment, nor shall any individual choosing treatment by spiritual means, in accordance with the tenets and practices of that individual's established religious tradition, be required to submit to medical testing of any kind pursuant to a determination of capacity.

Part 8. Other Protective Proceedings

Chapter 1. General Provisions

3300. A parent who receives any money or property belonging to a minor under any provision of this part shall account to the minor for the money or other property when the minor reaches the age of majority.

3303. Nothing in this part limits the provisions of the California Uniform Transfers to Minors Act, Part 9 (commencing with Section 3900).

Chapter 2. Money Or Property Belonging To Minor

Article 1. Total Estate Not In Excess Of $5,000

3400. (a) As used in this article, "total estate of the minor" includes both the money and other property belonging to the minor and the money and other property belonging to the guardianship estate, if any, of the minor.

(b) In computing the "total estate of the minor" for the purposes of this article, all of the following shall be deducted:

(1) "Custodial property" held pursuant to the California Uniform Transfers to Minors Act, Part 9 (commencing with Section 3900).

(2) Any money or property subject to court order pursuant to subdivision (c) of Section 3602 or Article 2 (commencing with Section

3610) of Chapter 4.

3401. (a) Where a minor does not have a guardian of the estate, money or other property belonging to the minor may be paid or delivered to a parent of the minor entitled to the custody of the minor to be held in trust for the minor until the minor reaches majority if the requirements of subdivision (c) are satisfied.

(b) Where the minor has a guardian of the estate, all the money and other property belonging to the guardianship estate may be paid or delivered to a parent entitled to the custody of the minor to be held in trust for the minor until the minor reaches majority if the requirements of subdivision (c) are satisfied.

(c) This section applies only if both of the following requirements are satisfied:

(1) The total estate of the minor, including the money and other property to be paid or delivered to the parent, does not exceed five thousand dollars ($5,000) in value.

(2) The parent to whom the money or other property is to be paid or delivered gives the person making the payment or delivery written assurance, verified by the oath of such parent, that the total estate of the minor, including the money or other property to be paid or delivered to the parent, does not exceed five thousand dollars ($5,000) in value.

3402. The written receipt of the parent giving the written assurance under Section 3401 shall be an acquittance of the person making the payment of money or delivery of other property pursuant to this article.

Article 2. Property In The Form Of Money

3410. (a) This article applies to both of the following cases:

(1) Where the minor has a guardian of the estate and the sole asset of the guardianship estate is money.

(2) Where the minor has no guardian of the estate and there is money belonging to the minor.

(b) This article does not apply to, and there shall be excluded in computing "money belonging to the minor" for the purpose of this article, all of the following:

(1) Money or property which is or will be held as "custodial property" pursuant to the California Uniform Transfers to Minors Act, Part 9 (commencing with Section 3900).

(2) Any money or property subject to court order pursuant to subdivision (c) of Section 3602 or Article 2 (commencing with Section 3610) of Chapter 4.

3411. (a) A parent of a minor entitled to custody of the minor, the guardian of the estate of the minor, or the person holding the money belonging to the minor may file a petition requesting that the court make an order under this article.

(b) The petition shall be filed in the superior court of:

(1) The county where the minor resides if the minor has no guardian of the estate.

(2) The county having jurisdiction of the guardianship estate if the minor has a guardian of the estate.

3412. If the minor has a guardian of the estate and the sole asset of the guardianship estate is money, the court may order that the guardianship of the estate be terminated and, if the court so orders, the court in its discretion shall also order any one or more of the following:

(a) That the money be deposited in an insured account in a financial institution in this state, or in a single-premium deferred annuity, subject to withdrawal only upon authorization of the court.

(b) That all or any part of the money be transferred to a custodian for the benefit of the minor under the California Uniform Transfers to Minors Act, Part 9 (commencing with Section 3900).

(c) If the money of the guardianship estate does not exceed twenty thousand dollars ($20,000), that the money be held on any other condition that the court in its discretion determines to be in the best interests of the minor.

(d) If the money of the guardianship estate does not exceed five thousand dollars ($5,000), that all or any part of the money be paid to a parent of the minor, without bond, upon the terms and under the conditions specified in Article 1 (commencing with Section 3400).

(e) That the remaining balance of any money paid or to be paid be deposited with the county treasurer, if all of the following conditions are met:

(1) The county treasurer has been authorized by the county board of supervisors to handle the deposits.

(2) The county treasurer shall receive and safely keep all money deposited with the county treasurer pursuant to this subdivision, shall pay the money out only upon the order of the court, and shall credit each estate with the interest earned by the funds deposited less the county treasurer's actual cost authorized to be recovered under Section 27013 of the Government Code.

(3) The county treasurer and sureties on the official bond of the county treasurer are responsible for the safekeeping and payment of the money.

(4) The county treasurer shall ensure that the money deposited is to earn interest or dividends, or both, at the highest rate which the county can reasonably obtain as a prudent investor.

(5) Funds so deposited with the county treasurer shall only be invested or deposited in compliance with the provisions governing the investment or deposit of state funds set forth in Chapter 5 (commencing with Section 16640) of Part 2 of Division 4 of Title 2 of the Government Code, the investment or deposit of county funds set forth in Chapter 4 (commencing with Section 53600) of Part 1 of Division 2 of Title 5 of the Government Code, or as authorized under Chapter 6 (commencing with Section 2400) of Part 4.

3413. If the minor has no guardian of the estate and there is money belonging to the minor, the court may order that a guardian of the estate be appointed and that the money be paid to the guardian or the court may order any one or more of the following:

(a) That the money be deposited in an insured account in a financial institution in this state, or in a single-premium deferred annuity, subject to withdrawal only upon authorization of the court.

(b) That all or any part of the money be transferred to a custodian for the benefit of the minor under the California Uniform Transfers to Minors Act, Part 9 (commencing with Section 3900).

(c) If the money belonging to the minor does not exceed twenty thousand dollars ($20,000), that the money be held on any other condition that the court in its discretion determines to be in the best interests of the minor.

(d) If the money belonging to the minor does not exceed five thousand dollars ($5,000), that all or any part of the money be paid to a parent of the minor, without bond, upon the terms and under the conditions specified in Article 1 (commencing with Section 3400).

(e) That the remaining balance of any money paid or to be paid be deposited with the county treasurer, if all of the following conditions are met:

(1) The county treasurer has been authorized by the county board of supervisors to handle the deposits.

(2) The county treasurer shall receive and safely keep all money deposited with the county treasurer pursuant to this subdivision, shall pay the money out only upon the order of the court, and shall credit each estate with the interest earned by the funds deposited less the county treasurer's actual cost authorized to be recovered under Section 27013 of the Government Code.

(3) The county treasurer and sureties on the official bond of the county treasurer are responsible for the safekeeping and payment of the money.

(4) The county treasurer shall ensure that the money deposited is to earn interest or dividends, or both, at the highest rate which the county can reasonably obtain as a prudent investor.

(5) Funds so deposited with the county treasurer shall only be invested or deposited in compliance with the provisions governing the investment or deposit of state funds set forth in Chapter 5 (commencing with Section 16640) of Part 2 of Division 4 of Title 2 of the Government Code, the investment or deposit

of county funds set forth in Chapter 4 (commencing with Section 53600) of Part 1 of Division 2 of Title 5 of the Government Code, or as authorized under Chapter 6 (commencing with Section 2400) of Part 4.

Chapter 3. Compromise By Parent Of Minor's Disputed Claim

3500. (a) When a minor has a disputed claim for damages, money, or other property and does not have a guardian of the estate, the following persons have the right to compromise, or to execute a covenant not to sue on or a covenant not to enforce judgment on, the claim, unless the claim is against such person or persons:

(1) Either parent if the parents of the minor are not living separate and apart.

(2) The parent having the care, custody, or control of the minor if the parents of the minor are living separate and apart.

(b) The compromise or covenant is valid only after it has been approved, upon the filing of a petition, by the superior court of either of the following counties:

(1) The county where the minor resides when the petition is filed.

(2) Any county where suit on the claim or matter properly could be brought.

(c) Any money or other property to be paid or delivered for the benefit of the minor pursuant to the compromise or covenant shall be paid and delivered in the manner and upon the terms and conditions specified in Chapter 4 (commencing with Section 3600).

(d) A parent having the right to compromise the disputed claim of the minor under this section may execute a full release and satisfaction, or execute a covenant not to sue on or a covenant not to enforce judgment on the disputed claim, after the money or other property to be paid or delivered has been paid or delivered as provided in subdivision (c). If the court orders that all or any part of the money to be paid under the compromise or covenant be deposited in an insured account in a financial institution in this state, or in a single-premium deferred annuity, the release and satisfaction or covenant is not effective for any purpose until the money has been deposited as directed in the order of the court.

Chapter 4. Money Or Property Paid Or Delivered Pursuant To Compromise Or Judgment For Minor Or Incompetent Person

Article 1. General Provisions

3600. This chapter applies whenever both of the following conditions exist:

(a) A court (1) approves a compromise of, or the execution of a covenant not to sue on or a covenant not to enforce judgment on, a minor's disputed claim, (2) approves a compromise of a pending action or proceeding to which a minor or person with a disability is a party, or (3) gives judgment for a minor or person with a disability.

(b) The compromise, covenant, or judgment provides for the payment or delivery of money or other property for the benefit of the minor or person with a disability.

3601. (a) The court making the order or giving the judgment referred to in Section 3600, as a part thereof, shall make a further order authorizing and directing that reasonable expenses, medical or otherwise and including reimbursement to a parent, guardian, or conservator, costs, and attorney's fees, as the court shall approve and allow therein, shall be paid from the money or other property to be paid or delivered for the benefit of the minor or person with a disability.

(b) The order required by subdivision (a) may be directed to the following:

(1) A parent of the minor, the guardian ad litem, or the guardian of the estate of the minor or the conservator of the estate of the person with a disability.

(2) The payer of any money to be paid pursuant to the compromise, covenant, or judgment for the benefit of the minor or person with a disability.

3602. (a) If there is no guardianship of the estate of the minor or conservatorship of the estate of the person with a disability, the remaining balance of the money and other property, after payment of all expenses, costs, and fees as approved and allowed by the court under Section 3601, shall be paid, delivered, deposited, or invested as provided in Article 2 (commencing with Section 3610).

(b) Except as provided in subdivisions (c) and (d), if there is a guardianship of the estate of the minor or conservatorship of the estate of the person with a disability, the remaining balance of the money and other property, after payment of all expenses, costs, and fees as approved and allowed by the court under Section 3601, shall be paid or delivered to the guardian or conservator of the estate. Upon application of the guardian or conservator, the court making the order or giving the judgment referred to in Section 3600 or the court in which the guardianship or conservatorship proceeding is pending may, with or without notice, make an order that all or part of the money paid or to be paid to the guardian or conservator under this subdivision be deposited or invested as provided in Section 2456.

(c) Upon ex parte petition of the guardian or conservator or upon petition of any person interested in the guardianship or conservatorship estate, the court making the order or giving the judgment referred to in Section 3600 may for good cause shown order one or more of the following:

(1) That all or part of the remaining

balance of money not become a part of the guardianship or conservatorship estate and instead be deposited in an insured account in a financial institution in this state, or in a single-premium deferred annuity, subject to withdrawal only upon authorization of the court.

(2) If there is a guardianship of the estate of the minor, that all or part of the remaining balance of money and other property not become a part of the guardianship estate and instead be transferred to a custodian for the benefit of the minor under the California Uniform Transfers to Minors Act, Part 9 (commencing with Section 3900).

(3) That all or part of the remaining balance of money and other property not become a part of the guardianship estate and, instead, be transferred to the trustee of a trust which is either created by, or approved of, in the order or judgment described in Section 3600. This trust shall be revocable by the minor upon attaining 18 years of age, and shall contain other terms and conditions, including, but not limited to, terms and conditions concerning trustee's accounts and trustee's bond, as the court determines to be necessary to protect the minor's interests.

(d) Upon petition of the guardian, conservator, or any person interested in the guardianship or conservatorship estate, the court making the order or giving the judgment referred to in Section 3600 may order that all or part of the remaining balance of money not become a part of the guardianship or conservatorship estate and instead be paid to a special needs trust established under Section 3604 for the benefit of the minor or person with a disability.

(e) If the petition is by a person other than the guardian or conservator, notice of hearing on a petition under subdivision (c) shall be given for the period and in the manner provided in Chapter 3 (commencing with Section 1460) of Part 1.

(f) Notice of the time and place of hearing on a petition under subdivision (d), and a copy of the petition, shall be mailed to the State Director of Health Care Services, the Director of State Hospitals, and the Director of Developmental Services at the office of each director in Sacramento at least 15 days before the hearing.

3603. Where reference is made in this chapter to a "person with a disability," the reference shall be deemed to include the following:

(a) A person for whom a conservator may be appointed.

(b) Any of the following persons, subject to the provisions of Section 3613:

(1) A person who meets the definition of disability as defined in Section 1382c(a)(3) of Title 42 of the United States Code, or as defined in Section 416(i)(1) of Title II of the federal Social Security Act (42 U.S.C. Sec. 401 et seq.) and regulations implementing that act, as set forth in Part 416.905 of Title 20 of the Federal Code of Regulations.

(2) A person who meets the definition of disability as defined in paragraphs (1), (2), and (3) of subsection (d) of Section 423 of Title II of the federal Social Security Act (42 U.S.C. Sec. 401 et seq.) and regulations implementing that act, as set forth in Part 404.1505 of Title 20 of the Federal Code of Regulations.

(3) A minor who meets the definition of disability, as set forth in Part 416.906 of Title 20 of the Federal Code of Regulations.

(4) A person with a developmental disability, as defined in Section 4512 of the Welfare and Institutions Code.

3604. (a) (1) If a court makes an order under Section 3602 or 3611 that money of a minor or person with a disability be paid to a special needs trust, the terms of the trust shall be reviewed and approved by the court and shall satisfy the requirements of this section. The trust is subject to continuing jurisdiction of the court, and is subject to court supervision to the extent determined by the court. The court may transfer jurisdiction to the court in the proper county for commencement of a proceeding as determined under Section 17005.

(2) If the court referred to in subdivision (a) could have made an order under Section 3602 or 3611 to place that money into a special needs trust, but that order was not requested, a parent, guardian, conservator, or other interested person may petition a court that exercises jurisdiction pursuant to Section 800 for that order. In doing so, notice shall be provided pursuant to subdivisions (e) and (f) of Section 3602, or subdivision (c) of Section 3611, and that notice shall be given at least 15 days before the hearing.

(b) A special needs trust may be established and continued under this section only if the court determines all of the following:

(1) That the minor or person with a disability has a disability that substantially impairs the individual's ability to provide for the individual's own care or custody and constitutes a substantial handicap.

(2) That the minor or person with a disability is likely to have special needs that will not be met without the trust.

(3) That money to be paid to the trust does not exceed the amount that appears reasonably necessary to meet the special needs of the minor or person with a disability.

(c) If at any time it appears (1) that any of the requirements of subdivision (b) are not satisfied or the trustee refuses without good cause to make payments from the trust for the special needs of the beneficiary, and (2) that the State Department of Health Care Services, the State Department of State Hospitals, the State Department of Developmental Services, or a county or city and county in this state has a claim against trust property, that department, county, or city and county may petition the court for an order terminating the trust.

(d) A court order under Section 3602 or 3611 for payment of money to a special needs trust shall include a provision that all statutory liens in favor of the State Department of Health Care Services, the State Department of State Hospitals, the State Department of Developmental Services, and any county or city and county in this state shall first be satisfied.

3605. (a) This section applies only to a special needs trust established under Section 3604 on or after January 1, 1993.

(b) While the special needs trust is in existence, the statute of limitations otherwise applicable to claims of the State Department of Health Care Services, the State Department of State Hospitals, the State Department of Developmental Services, and any county or city and county in this state is tolled. Notwithstanding any provision in the trust instrument, at the death of the special needs trust beneficiary or on termination of the trust, the trust property is subject to claims of the State Department of Health Care Services, the State Department of State Hospitals, the State Department of Developmental Services, and any county or city and county in this state to the extent authorized by law as if the trust property is owned by the beneficiary or is part of the beneficiary's estate.

(c) At the death of the special needs trust beneficiary or on termination of the trust, the trustee shall give notice of the beneficiary's death or the trust termination, in the manner provided in Section 1215, to all of the following:

(1) The State Department of Health Care Services, the State Department of State Hospitals, and the State Department of Developmental Services, addressed to the director of that department at the Sacramento office of the director.

(2) Any county or city and county in this state that has made a written request to the trustee for notice, addressed to that county or city and county at the address specified in the request.

(d) Failure to give the notice required by subdivision (c) prevents the running of the statute of limitations against the claim of the department, county, or city and county not given the notice.

(e) The department, county, or city and county has four months after notice is given in which to make a claim with the trustee. If the trustee rejects the claim, the department, county, or city and county making the claim may petition the court for an order under Chapter 3 (commencing with Section 17200) of Part 5 of Division 9, directing the trustee to pay the claim. A claim made under this subdivision shall be paid as a preferred claim prior to any other distribution.

If trust property is insufficient to pay all claims under this subdivision, the trustee shall petition the court for instructions and the claims shall be paid from trust property as the court deems just.

(f) If trust property is distributed before expiration of four months after notice is given without payment of the claim the department, county, or city and county has a claim against the distributees to the full extent of the claim, or each distributee's share of trust property, whichever is less. The claim against distributees includes interest at a rate equal to that earned in the Pooled Money Investment Account, Article 4.5 (commencing with Section 16480) of Chapter 3 of Part 2 of Division 4 of Title 2 of the Government Code, from the date of distribution or the date of filing the claim, whichever is later, plus other accruing costs as in the case of enforcement of a money judgment.

Article 2. Disposition Of Money Or Other Property Where No Guardianship Or Conservatorship

3610. When money or other property is to be paid or delivered for the benefit of a minor or person with a disability under a compromise, covenant, order or judgment, and there is no guardianship of the estate of the minor or conservatorship of the estate of the person with a disability, the remaining balance of the money and other property (after payment of all expenses, costs, and fees as approved and allowed by the court under Section 3601) shall be paid, delivered, deposited, or invested as provided in this article.

3611. In any case described in Section 3610, the court making the order or giving the judgment referred to in Section 3600 shall, upon application of counsel for the minor or person with a disability, order any one or more of the following:

(a) That a guardian of the estate or conservator of the estate be appointed and that the remaining balance of the money and other property be paid or delivered to the person so appointed.

(b) That the remaining balance of any money paid or to be paid be deposited in an insured account in a financial institution in this state, or in a single-premium deferred annuity, subject to withdrawal only upon the authorization of the court, and that the remaining balance of any other property delivered or to be delivered be held on conditions the court determines to be in the best interest of the minor or person with a disability.

(c) After a hearing by the court, that the remaining balance of any money and other property be paid to a special needs trust established under Section 3604 for the benefit of the minor or person with a disability. Notice of the time and place of the hearing and a copy of the petition shall be mailed to the State Director of Health Care Services, the Director of State Hospitals, and the Director of Developmental Services at the office of each director in Sacramento at least 15 days before the hearing.

(d) If the remaining balance of the money to be paid or delivered does not exceed twenty thousand dollars ($20,000), that all or any part of the money be held on any other conditions the court in its discretion determines to be in the best interest of the minor or person with a disability.

(e) If the remaining balance of the money and other property to be paid or delivered does not exceed five thousand dollars ($5,000) in value and is to be paid or delivered for the benefit of a minor, that all or any part of the money and the other property be paid or delivered to a parent of the minor, without bond, upon the terms and under the conditions specified in Article 1 (commencing with Section 3400) of Chapter 2.

(f) If the remaining balance of the money and other property to be paid or delivered is to be paid or delivered for the benefit of the minor, that all or any part of the money and other property be transferred to a custodian for the benefit of the minor under the California Uniform Transfers to Minors Act, Part 9 (commencing with Section 3900).

(g) That the remaining balance of the money and other property be paid or delivered to the trustee of a trust which is created by, or approved of, in the order or judgment referred to in Section 3600. This trust shall be revocable by the minor upon attaining the age of 18 years, and shall contain other terms and conditions, including, but not limited to, terms and conditions concerning trustee's accounts and trustee's bond, as the court determines to be necessary to protect the minor's interests.

(h) That the remaining balance of any money paid or to be paid be deposited with the county treasurer, if all of the following conditions are met:

(1) The county treasurer has been authorized by the county board of supervisors to handle the deposits.

(2) The county treasurer shall receive and safely keep all money deposited with the county treasurer pursuant to this subdivision, shall pay the money out only upon the order of the court, and shall credit each estate with the interest earned by the funds deposited less the county treasurer's actual cost authorized to be recovered under Section 27013 of the Government Code.

(3) The county treasurer and sureties on the official bond of the county treasurer are responsible for the safekeeping and payment of the money.

(4) The county treasurer shall ensure that the money deposited is to earn interest or dividends, or both, at the highest rate which the county can reasonably obtain as a prudent investor.

(5) Funds so deposited with the county treasurer shall only be invested or deposited in compliance with the provisions governing the investment or deposit of state funds set forth in Chapter 5 (commencing with Section 16640) of Part 2 of Division 4 of Title 2 of the Government Code, the investment or deposit of county funds set forth in Chapter 4 (commencing with Section 53600) of Part 1 of Division 2 of Title 5 of the Government Code, or as authorized under Chapter 6 (commencing with Section 2400) of Part 4.

(i) That the remaining balance of the money and other property be paid or delivered to the person with a disability.

3612. (a) Notwithstanding any other provision of law and except to the extent the court orders otherwise, the court making the order under Section 3611 shall have continuing jurisdiction of the money and other property paid, delivered, deposited, or invested under this article until the minor reaches 18 years of age.

(b) Notwithstanding subdivision (a), the trust of an individual who meets the definition of a person with a disability under paragraph (3) of subdivision (b) of Section 3603 and who reaches 18 years of age, shall continue and be under continuing court jurisdiction until terminated by the court.

3613. Notwithstanding any other provision of this chapter, a court may not make an order or give a judgment pursuant to Section 3600, 3601, 3602, 3610, or 3611 with respect to an adult who has the capacity within the meaning of Section 812 to consent to the order and who has no conservator of the estate with authority to make that decision , without the express consent of that person.

Chapter 5. Property Of Absent Federal Personnel

Article 1. Definitions

3700. As used in this chapter:

(a) "Absentee" is defined in Section 1403.

(b) "Certificate of missing status" means the official written report complying with Section 1283 of the Evidence Code and showing the determination of the secretary of the military department or the head of the department or agency concerned or the delegate of the secretary or head that the absentee is in missing status.

(c) "Eligible spouse" means the spouse of an absentee who has not commenced an action or proceeding for judicial or legal separation, annulment, adjudication of nullity, or dissolution of the marriage of the spouse and the absentee.

(d) "Family of an absentee" means an eligible spouse, if any, or if no eligible spouse, the child or children of an absentee, equally, or if no child or children, the parent or parents of an absentee, equally, provided these persons are dependents of the absentee as defined in Section 401 of Title 37 of the United States Code, and the guardian of the estate or conservator of the estate of any person bearing such relationship to the absentee.

(e) "Secretary concerned" is defined in Section 1440.

Article 2. Court Proceeding To Set Aside Personal Property Of Absentee

3701. Upon petition as provided in this chapter, the court may set aside to the family of an absentee personal property of the absentee situated in this state for the purpose of managing, controlling, encumbering, selling, or conveying, or otherwise engaging in any transaction with respect to the property, if the court determines that to do so will be in the best interest of the absentee, including the interest of the absentee in providing for shelter, food, health care, education, transportation, or the maintenance of a reasonable and adequate standard of living for the family of the absentee. The absentee's interest in the property set aside shall not exceed twenty thousand dollars ($20,000).

3702. A petition that personal property of an absentee be set aside as provided in this chapter may be filed by any of the following persons:

(a) A person in whose favor the personal property of the absentee may be set aside.

(b) A person to whom the absentee has issued a general power of attorney while serving in the armed forces of the United States or while an employee of any agency or department of the United States, provided the power of attorney was valid and effective at the time issued, regardless whether it has expired or terminated.

3703. (a) The petition shall contain all of the following:

(1) A statement that the petition is filed under this chapter.

(2) In its caption, the last known military rank or grade and the social security account number of the absentee.

(3) A specific description and estimate of the value of all of the absentee's property, wherever situated (including all sums due the absentee from the United States).

(4) A designation of the property to be set aside, and the facts establishing that setting aside the property is necessary and in the best interest of the absentee.

(5) If the property is to be set aside for the benefit of the spouse of the absentee, an allegation that the spouse is an eligible spouse.

(6) So far as known to the petitioner, the names and addresses of all persons comprising the family of the absentee, and an allegation whether a guardian of the estate or a conservator of the estate of any member of the family of the absentee has been appointed.

(b) There shall be attached to the petition a certificate of missing status. The certificate of missing status shall be received as evidence of that fact and the court shall not determine the status of the absentee inconsistent with the status shown in the certificate.

3704. (a) Notice of the nature of the proceedings and the time and place of the hearing shall be given by the petitioner at least 15 days before the hearing date by all of the following means:

(1) By mail, together with a copy of the petition, to all persons comprising the family of the absentee.

(2) By delivery by a method that would be sufficient for service of summons in a civil action, together with a copy of the petition, to the secretary concerned or to the head of the United States department or agency concerned.

(3) By publication pursuant to Section 6061 of the Government Code in a newspaper of general circulation in the county in which the proceedings will be held.

(b) Whenever notice to an officer or agency of this state or of the United States would be required under Section 1461 or Section 1822 upon petition for appointment of a conservator, like notice shall be given of the petition under this chapter.

3705. (a) Upon the hearing of the petition, any officer or agency of this state or the United States or the authorized delegate of the officer or agency, or any relative or friend of the absentee, may appear and support or oppose the petition.

(b) If the court determines that the allegations of the petition are true and correct, the court may order set aside to the family of the absentee personal property of the absentee situated in this state (excluding any sums due the absentee from the United States) in which the absentee's interest does not exceed twenty thousand dollars ($20,000). The property set aside shall be specified in the order.

(c) No bond shall be required of any person to whom property of the absentee has been set aside by order of the court pursuant to this chapter.

3706. A determination by the court that the value of all of the absentee's property, wherever situated, exceeds twenty thousand dollars ($20,000) or that the absentee owns or has an interest in real property, wherever situated, does not deprive the court of jurisdiction to set aside to the family of the absentee personal property of the absentee situated in this state in which the absentee's interest does not exceed twenty thousand dollars ($20,000), and the court shall order set aside such personal property to the family of the absentee if the court finds that all of the other provisions of this chapter have been complied with. The property set aside shall be specified in the order.

3707. For the purposes of this chapter, any property or interest therein or lien thereon that the absentee holds as joint tenant shall be included in determining the property of the absentee and its value. The joint tenancy interest may be set aside to the family of the absentee as provided in this chapter but may only be set aside to a member of the absentee's family who was a joint tenant with the absentee in the property.

3708. (a) Within six months after the absentee has returned to the controllable jurisdiction of the military department or civilian agency or department concerned, or within six months after the determination of death of the absentee by the secretary concerned or the head of the department or agency concerned or the delegate of the secretary or head, the former absentee or the personal representative of the deceased absentee may, by motion in the same proceeding, require the person or persons to whom the property of the absentee was set aside to account for the property and the proceeds, if any. The time of return to the controllable jurisdiction of the military department or civilian department or agency concerned or the determination of the time of death of the absentee shall be determined by the court under 37 United States Code, Section 556, or 5 United States Code, Section 5566. An official written report or record of the military department or civilian department or agency that the absentee has returned to its controllable jurisdiction or is deceased shall be received as evidence of that fact.

(b) This section does not in any manner derogate the finality and conclusiveness of any order, judgment, or decree previously entered in the proceeding.

Article 3. Management And Disposition Of Personal Property Of Absentee Without Court Proceeding

3710. The family of an absentee may collect, receive, dispose of, or engage in any transaction relating to the absentee's personal property situated in this state without any judicial proceeding if all the following conditions are satisfied:

(a) The absentee owns no real property situated in this state.

(b) The aggregate value of all of the absentee's personal property situated in this state is five thousand dollars ($5,000) or less, excluding any money owed the absentee by the United States.

(c) The family of the absentee needs to dispose of such personal property to provide for shelter, food, health care, education, transportation, or the maintenance of a reasonable and adequate standard of living for the family of the absentee.

3711. (a) If the conditions set forth in Section 3710 are satisfied, the family of the absentee may have any evidence of interest, indebtedness, or right attributable to the absentee's personal property transferred to the family of the absentee, or transferred to

the person to whom the property is to be sold or transferred by the family of the absentee, upon furnishing the person (including any governmental body) having custody of the property both of the following:

(1) A certificate of missing status.

(2) An affidavit stating under oath that the provisions of this article are applicable and that the aggregate value of all property received pursuant to this affidavit, together with all other property previously received under this article, does not exceed five thousand dollars ($5,000).

(b) The receipt of a certificate of missing status and affidavit under subdivision (a) constitutes sufficient acquittance for any payment of money or delivery of property made pursuant to this article and fully discharges the recipient from any further liability concerning the money or property without the necessity of inquiring into the truth of any of the facts stated in the affidavit.

3712. The time within which an absentee may commence an action against any person who executes an affidavit and receives property pursuant to this article commences to run on the earlier of the following dates:

(a) Ninety days after the absentee returns to the United States after the termination of the condition that caused the classification of an absentee.

(b) Two years after the termination of the condition that caused the classification of an absentee.

Article 4. Absentee's Power Of Attorney

3720. If an absentee executed a power of attorney that expires during the period that occasions absentee status, the power of attorney continues in full force and effect until 30 days after the absentee status is terminated. Any person who acts in reliance upon the power of attorney when accompanied by a copy of a certificate of missing status is not liable for relying and acting upon the power of attorney.

3721. For the purposes of Chapter 5 (commencing with Section 4300) of Part 2 of Division 4.5, in the case of a principal who is an absentee, an attorney-in-fact or third person shall be deemed to be without actual knowledge of the following:

(a) The principal's death or incapacity while the absentee continues in missing status and until the attorney-in-fact or third person receives notice of the determination of the absentee's death by the secretary concerned or the head of the department or agency concerned or the delegate of the secretary or head.

(b) Revocation by the principal during the period described in subdivision (a).

3722. If after the absentee executes a power of attorney, the principal's spouse who is the attorney-in-fact commences a proceeding for dissolution, annulment, or legal separation, or a legal separation is ordered, the attorney-in-fact's authority is revoked. This section is in addition to the provisions of Sections 4154 and 4697.

Chapter 6. Removal Of Property Of Nonresident

3800. (a) If a nonresident has a duly appointed, qualified, and acting guardian, conservator, committee, or comparable fiduciary in the place of residence and if no proceeding for guardianship or conservatorship of the nonresident is pending or contemplated in this state, the nonresident fiduciary may petition to have property owned by the nonresident removed to the place of residence.

(b) The petition for removal of property of the nonresident shall be filed in the superior court of the county in which the nonresident is or has been temporarily present or in which the property of the nonresident, or the principal part thereof, is located.

3801. (a) The petition shall be made upon 15 days' notice, by mail or personal delivery, to all of the following persons:

(1) The personal representative or other person in whose possession the property may be.

(2) Persons in this state, known to the petitioner, who are obligated to pay a debt, perform an obligation, or issue a security to the nonresident or the estate of the nonresident.

(b) The petition shall be made upon such additional notice, if any, as the court may order.

3802. (a) The nonresident fiduciary shall produce and file one of the following certificates:

(1) A certificate that the fiduciary is entitled, by the laws of the place of appointment of the fiduciary, to the possession of the estate of the nonresident. The certificate shall be under the hand of the clerk and seal of the court from which the appointment of the fiduciary was derived and shall show a transcript of the record of appointment and that the fiduciary has entered upon the discharge of the duties of the fiduciary.

(2) A certificate that the fiduciary is entitled, by the laws of the place of residence, to custody of the estate of the nonresident, without the appointment of any court. The certificate shall be under the hand of the clerk and seal of either (i) the court in the place of residence having jurisdiction of estates of persons that have a guardian, conservator, committee, or comparable fiduciary or (ii) the highest court in the place of residence.

(b) In the case of a foreign country, the certificate shall be accompanied by a final statement certifying the genuineness of the signature and official position of (1) the court clerk making the original certificate or (2) any foreign official who has certified either the genuineness of the signature and

official position of the court clerk making the original certificate or the genuineness of the signature and official position of another foreign official who has executed a similar certificate in a chain of such certificates beginning with a certificate of the genuineness of the signature and official position of the clerk making the original certificate. The final statement may be made only by a secretary of an embassy or legation, consul general, consul, vice consul, or consular agent of the United States, or a diplomatic or consular official of the foreign country assigned or accredited to the United States.

3803. (a) Upon the petition, if the court determines that removal of the property will not conflict with any restriction or limitation on the property or impair the right of the nonresident to the property or the rights of creditors or claimants in this state, the court shall make an order granting to the nonresident fiduciary leave to remove the property of the nonresident to the place of residence unless good cause to the contrary is shown.

(b) The order is authority to the fiduciary to sue for and receive the property in his or her own name for the use and benefit of the nonresident.

(c) The order is a discharge of the personal representative or other person in whose possession the property may be at the time the order is made and of the person obligated to pay a debt, perform an obligation, or issue a security to the nonresident or the estate of the nonresident, upon filing with the clerk of the court the receipt of the nonresident fiduciary for the property and transmitting a duplicate receipt, or a certified copy of the receipt, to the court, if any, from which the nonresident fiduciary received his or her appointment.

Part 9. California Uniform Transfers To Minors Act

3900. This part may be cited as the "California Uniform Transfers to Minors Act."

3901. In this part:

(a) "Adult" means an individual who has attained the age of 18 years.

(b) "Benefit plan" means an employer's plan for the benefit of an employee or partner.

(c) "Broker" means a person lawfully engaged in the business of effecting transactions in securities or commodities for the person's own account or for the account of others.

(d) "Conservator" means a person appointed or qualified by a court to act as general, limited, or temporary guardian of a minor's property or a person legally authorized to perform substantially the same functions.

(e) "Court" means the superior court.

(f) "Custodial property" means (1) any interest in property transferred to a custodian under this part and (2) the income from and proceeds of that interest in property.

(g) "Custodian" means a person so designated under Section 3909 or a successor or substitute custodian designated under Section 3918.

(h) "Financial institution" means a bank, trust company, savings institution, or credit union, chartered and supervised under state or federal law or an industrial loan company licensed and supervised under the laws of this state.

(i) "Legal representative" means an individual's personal representative or conservator.

(j) "Member of the minor's family" means the minor's parent, stepparent, spouse, grandparent, brother, sister, uncle, or aunt, whether of the whole or half blood or by adoption.

(k) "Minor" means:

(1) Except as provided in paragraph (2), an individual who has not attained the age of 18 years.

(2) When used with reference to the beneficiary for whose benefit custodial property is held or is to be held, an individual who has not attained the age at which the custodian is required under Sections 3920 and 3920.5 to transfer the custodial property to the beneficiary.

(l) "Person" means an individual, corporation, organization, or other legal entity.

(m) "Personal representative" means an executor, administrator, successor personal representative, or special administrator of a decedent's estate or a person legally authorized to perform substantially the same functions.

(n) "State" includes any state of the United States, the District of Columbia, the Commonwealth of Puerto Rico, and any territory or possession subject to the legislative authority of the United States.

(o) "Transfer" means a transaction that creates custodial property under Section 3909.

(p) "Transferor" means a person who makes a transfer under this part.

(q) "Trust company" means a financial institution, corporation, or other legal entity, authorized to exercise general trust powers.

3902. (a) This part applies to a transfer that refers to this part in the designation under subdivision (a) of Section 3909 by which the transfer is made if at the time of the transfer, the transferor, the minor, or the custodian is a resident of this state or the custodial property is located in this state. The custodianship so created remains subject to this part despite a subsequent change in residence of a transferor, the minor, or the custodian, or the removal of custodial property from this state.

(b) A person designated as custodian under this part is subject to personal jurisdiction in this state with respect to any matter relating to the custodianship.

(c) A transfer that purports to be made and which is valid under the Uniform Transfers to Minors Act, the Uniform Gifts to Minors Act, or a substantially similar act, of another state is governed by the law of the designated state and may be executed and is enforceable in this state if at the time of the transfer, the transferor, the minor, or the custodian is a resident of the designated state or the custodial property is located in the designated state.

3903. (a) A person having the right to designate the recipient of property transferable upon the occurrence of a future event may revocably nominate a custodian to receive the property for a minor beneficiary upon the occurrence of the event by naming the custodian followed in substance by the words:
"as custodian for _____
(Name of Minor)
under the California Uniform Transfers to Minors Act."

The nomination may name one or more persons as substitute custodians to whom the property must be transferred, in the order named, if the first nominated custodian dies before the transfer or is unable, declines, or is ineligible to serve. The nomination may be made in a will, a trust, a deed, an instrument exercising a power of appointment, or in a writing designating a beneficiary of contractual rights which is registered with or delivered to the payor, issuer, or other obligor of the contractual rights.

(b) A custodian nominated under this section must be a person to whom a transfer of property of that kind may be made under subdivision (a) of Section 3909.

(c) The nomination of a custodian under this section does not create custodial property until the nominating instrument becomes irrevocable or a transfer to the nominated custodian is completed under Section 3909. Unless the nomination of a custodian has been revoked, upon the occurrence of the future event, the custodianship becomes effective, and the custodian shall enforce a transfer of the custodial property pursuant to Section 3909.

3904. A person may make a transfer by irrevocable gift to, or the irrevocable exercise of a power of appointment in favor of, a custodian for the benefit of a minor pursuant to Section 3909.

3905. (a) A personal representative or trustee may make an irrevocable transfer pursuant to Section 3909 to a custodian for the benefit of a minor as authorized in the governing will or trust.

(b) If the testator or settlor has nominated a custodian under Section 3903 to receive the custodial property, the transfer shall be made to that person.

(c) If the testator or settlor has not nominated a custodian under Section 3903, or all persons so nominated as custodian die before the transfer or are unable, decline, or are ineligible to serve, the personal representative or the trustee, as the case may be, shall designate the custodian from among those eligible to serve as custodian for property of that kind under subdivision (a) of Section 3909.

3906. (a) Subject to subdivision (c), a personal representative or trustee may make an irrevocable transfer to another adult or trust company as custodian for the benefit of a minor pursuant to Section 3909, in the absence of a will or under a will or trust that does not contain an authorization to do so.

(b) Subject to subdivision (c), a conservator may make an irrevocable transfer to another adult or trust company as custodian for the benefit of the minor pursuant to Section 3909.

(c) A transfer under subdivision (a) or (b) may be made only if all of the following requirements are satisfied:

(1) The personal representative, trustee, or conservator considers the transfer to be in the best interest of the minor.

(2) The transfer is not prohibited by or inconsistent with provisions of the applicable will, trust agreement, or other governing instrument. For the purposes of this subdivision, a spendthrift provision (such as that described in Section 15300) shall not prohibit or be inconsistent with the transfer.

(3) The transfer is authorized by the court if it exceeds ten thousand dollars ($10,000) in value; provided, however, that such court authorization shall not be required when the transfer is to a custodian who is either (A) a trust company or (B) an individual designated as a trustee by the terms of a trust instrument which does not require a bond.

3907. (a) Subject to subdivisions (b) and (c), a person not subject to Section 3905 or 3906 who holds property of, or owes a liquidated debt to, a minor not having a conservator may make an irrevocable transfer to a custodian for the benefit of the minor pursuant to Section 3909.

(b) If a person having the right to do so under Section 3903 has nominated a custodian under that section to receive the custodial property, the transfer shall be made to that person.

(c) If no custodian has been nominated under Section 3903, or all persons so nominated as custodian die before the transfer or are unable, decline, or are ineligible to serve, a transfer under this section may be made to an adult member of the minor's family or to a trust company unless the property exceeds ten thousand dollars ($10,000) in value.

3908. A written acknowledgment of delivery by a custodian constitutes a sufficient receipt and discharge for custodial property transferred to the custodian pursuant to this part.

3909. (a) Custodial property is created

and a transfer is made whenever any of the following occurs:

(1) An uncertificated security or a certificated security in registered form is either:

(A) Registered in the name of the transferor, an adult other than the transferor, or a trust company, followed in substance by the words:
"as custodian for _____
                    (Name of Minor)
under the California Uniform Transfers to Minors Act."

(B) Delivered if in certificated form, or any document necessary for the transfer of an uncertificated security is delivered, together with any necessary endorsement to an adult other than the transferor or to a trust company as custodian, accompanied by an instrument in substantially the form set forth in subdivision (b).

(2) Money is paid or delivered, or a security held in the name of a broker, financial institution, or its nominee is transferred, to a broker or financial institution for credit to an account in the name of the transferor, an adult other than the transferor, or a trust company, followed in substance by the words:
"as custodian for _____
                    (Name of Minor)
under the California Uniform Transfers to Minors Act."

(3) The ownership of a life or endowment insurance policy or annuity contract is either:

(A) Registered with the issuer in the name of the transferor, an adult other than the transferor, or a trust company, followed in substance by the words:
"as custodian for _____
                    (Name of Minor)
under the California Uniform Transfers to Minors Act."

(B) Assigned in a writing delivered to an adult other than the transferor or to a trust company whose name in the assignment is followed in substance by the words:
"as custodian for _____
                    (Name of Minor)
under the California Uniform Transfers to Minors Act."

(4) An irrevocable exercise of a power of appointment or an irrevocable present right to future payment under a contract is the subject of a written notification delivered to the payor, issuer, or other obligor that the right is transferred to the transferor, an adult other than the transferor, or a trust company, whose name in the notification is followed in substance by the words:
"as custodian for _____
                    (Name of Minor)
under the California Uniform Transfers to Minors Act."

(5) An interest in real property is recorded in the name of the transferor, an adult other than the transferor, or a trust company, followed in substance by the words:
"as custodian for _____

(Name of Minor)
under the California Uniform Transfers to Minors Act."

(6) A certificate of title issued by a department or agency of a state or of the United States which evidences title to tangible personal property is either:

(A) Issued in the name of the transferor, an adult other than the transferor, or a trust company, followed in substance by the words:
"as custodian for _____
(Name of Minor)
under the California Uniform Transfers to Minors Act."

(B) Delivered to an adult other than the transferor or to a trust company, endorsed to that person followed in substance by the words:
"as custodian for _____
(Name of Minor)
under the California Uniform Transfers to Minors Act."

(7) An interest in any property not described in paragraphs (1) through (6) is transferred to an adult other than the transferor or to a trust company by a written instrument in substantially the form set forth in subdivision (b).

(b) An instrument in the following form satisfies the requirements of subparagraph (B) of paragraph (1) and paragraph (7) of subdivision (a):

PLEASE SEE THE APPENDIX

(c) A transferor shall place the custodian in control of the custodial property as soon as practicable.

3910. A transfer may be made only for one minor, and only one person may be the custodian. All custodial property held under this part by the same custodian for the benefit of the same minor constitutes a single custodianship.

3911. (a) The validity of a transfer made in a manner prescribed in this part is not affected by any of the following:

(1) Failure of the transferor to comply with subdivision (c) of Section 3909.

(2) Designation of an ineligible custodian, except designation of the transferor in the case of property for which the transferor is ineligible to serve as custodian under subdivision (a) of Section 3909.

(3) Death or incapacity of a person nominated under Section 3903 or designated under Section 3909 as custodian, or the disclaimer of the office by that person.

(b) A transfer made pursuant to Section 3909 is irrevocable, and the custodial property is indefeasibly vested in the minor, but the custodian has all the rights, powers, duties, and authority provided in this part, and neither the minor nor the minor's legal representative has any right, power, duty, or authority with respect to the custodial property except as provided in this part.

(c) By making a transfer, the transferor incorporates in the disposition all the provisions of this part and grants to the custodian, and to any third person dealing with a person designated as custodian, the respective powers, rights, and immunities provided in this part.

(d) A person is not precluded from being a custodian for a minor under this part with respect to some property because the person is a conservator of the minor with respect to other property.

(e) A person who is the conservator of the minor is not precluded from being a custodian for a minor under this part because the custodial property has or will be transferred to the custodian from the guardianship estate of the minor. In such case, for the purposes of Section 3909, the custodian shall be deemed to be "an adult other than the transferor."

(f) In the cases described in subdivisions (d) and (e), with respect to the property transferred to the custodian, this part applies to the extent it would apply if the person to whom the custodial property is transferred were not and had not been a conservator of the minor.

3912. (a) A custodian shall do all of the following:

(1) Take control of custodial property.

(2) Register or record title to custodial property if appropriate.

(3) Collect, hold, manage, invest, and reinvest custodial property.

(b) In dealing with custodial property, a custodian shall observe the standard of care that would be observed by a prudent person dealing with property of another and is not limited by any other statute restricting investments by fiduciaries except that:

(1) If a custodian is not compensated for his or her services, the custodian is not liable for losses to custodial property unless they result from the custodian's bad faith, intentional wrongdoing, or gross negligence, or from the custodian's failure to maintain the standard of prudence in investing the custodial property provided in this section.

(2) A custodian, in the custodian's discretion and without liability to the minor or the minor's estate, may retain any custodial property received from a transferor.

(c) A custodian may invest in or pay premiums on life insurance or endowment policies on (1) the life of the minor only if the minor or the minor's estate is the sole beneficiary or (2) the life of another person in whom the minor has an insurable interest only to the extent that the minor, the minor's estate, or the custodian in the capacity of custodian, is the irrevocable beneficiary.

(d) A custodian at all times shall keep custodial property separate and distinct from all other property in a manner sufficient to identify it clearly as custodial property of the minor. Custodial property consisting of an undivided interest is so identified if the minor's interest is held as a tenant in common and is fixed. Custodial property subject to recordation is so identified if it is recorded, and custodial property subject to registration is so identified if it is either registered, or held in an account designated, in the name of the custodian, followed in substance by the words:

"as custodian for _____
(Name of Minor)
under the California Uniform Transfers to Minors Act."

(e) A custodian shall keep records of all transactions with respect to custodial property, including information necessary for the preparation of the minor's tax returns, and shall make them available for inspection at reasonable intervals by a parent or legal representative of the minor or by the minor if the minor has attained the age of 14 years.

3913. (a) A custodian, acting in a custodial capacity, has all the rights, powers, and authority over custodial property that unmarried adult owners have over their own property, but a custodian may exercise those rights, powers, and authority in that capacity only.

(b) This section does not relieve a custodian from liability for breach of Section 3912.

3914. (a) A custodian may deliver or pay to the minor or expend for the minor's benefit as much of the custodial property as the custodian considers advisable for the use and benefit of the minor, without court order and without regard to (1) the duty or ability of the custodian personally, or of any other person, to support the minor or (2) any other income or property of the minor which may be applicable or available for that purpose.

(b) On petition of an interested person or the minor if the minor has attained the age of 14 years, the court may order the custodian to deliver or pay to the minor or expend for the minor's benefit so much of the custodial property as the court considers advisable for the use and benefit of the minor.

(c) A delivery, payment, or expenditure under this section is in addition to, not in substitution for, and does not affect, any obligation of a person to support the minor.

(d) In lieu of the powers and duties described in subdivision (a), a transferor who is also the custodian may elect to govern his or her custodial powers and duties under this subdivision. If such election is made, the custodian shall not pay over to the minor for expenditure by the minor, and shall not expend for the minor's use or benefit, any part of the custodial property for any purpose prior to the time specified in Section 3920, except by order of the court upon a showing that the expenditure is necessary for the support, maintenance, or education of the minor. When the powers and duties of the custodian are governed by this subdivision, the transferor-custodian shall file with the

clerk of the court a declaration in substantially the following form:

| PLEASE SEE THE APPENDIX |

3915. (a) A custodian is entitled to reimbursement from custodial property for reasonable expenses incurred in the performance of the custodian's duties.

(b) Except for one who is a transferor under Section 3904, a custodian has a noncumulative election during each calendar year to charge reasonable compensation for services performed during that year.

(c) Except as provided in subdivision (f) of Section 3918, a custodian need not give a bond.

3916. A third person in good faith and without court order may act on the instructions of, or otherwise deal with, any person purporting to make a transfer or purporting to act in the capacity of a custodian and, in the absence of knowledge, is not responsible for determining any of the following:

(a) The validity of the purported custodian's designation.

(b) The propriety of, or the authority under this part for, any act of the purported custodian.

(c) The validity or propriety under this part of any instrument or instructions executed or given either by the person purporting to make a transfer or by the purported custodian.

(d) The propriety of the application of any property of the minor delivered to the purported custodian.

3917. (a) A claim based on (1) a contract entered into by a custodian acting in a custodial capacity, (2) an obligation arising from the ownership or control of custodial property, or (3) a tort committed during the custodianship, may be asserted against the custodial property by proceeding against the custodian in the custodial capacity, whether or not the custodian or the minor is personally liable therefor.

(b) A custodian is not personally liable for either of the following:

(1) On a contract properly entered into in the custodial capacity unless the custodian fails to reveal that capacity and to identify the custodianship in the contract.

(2) For an obligation arising from control of custodial property or for a tort committed during the custodianship unless the custodian is personally at fault.

(c) A minor is not personally liable for an obligation arising from ownership of custodial property or for a tort committed during the custodianship unless the minor is personally at fault.

3918. (a) A person nominated under Section 3903 or designated under Section 3909 as custodian may decline to serve by delivering a valid disclaimer under Part 8 (commencing with Section 260) of Division

2 to the person who made the nomination or to the transferor or the transferor's legal representative. If the event giving rise to a transfer has not occurred and no substitute custodian able, willing, and eligible to serve was nominated under Section 3903, the person who made the nomination may nominate a substitute custodian under Section 3903; otherwise the transferor or the transferor's legal representative shall designate a substitute custodian at the time of the transfer, in either case from among the persons eligible to serve as custodian for that kind of property under subdivision (a) of Section 3909. The custodian so designated has the rights of a successor custodian.

(b) A custodian at any time may designate a trust company or an adult other than a transferor under Section 3904 as successor custodian by executing and dating an instrument of designation before a subscribing witness other than the successor. If the instrument of designation does not contain or is not accompanied by the resignation of the custodian, the designation of the successor does not take effect until the custodian resigns, dies, becomes incapacitated, or is removed. The transferor may designate one or more persons as successor custodians to serve, in the designated order of priority, in case the custodian originally designated or a prior successor custodian is unable, declines, or is ineligible to serve or resigns, dies, becomes incapacitated, or is removed. The designation either (1) shall be made in the same transaction and by the same document by which the transfer is made or (2) shall be made by executing and dating a separate instrument of designation before a subscribing witness other than a successor as a part of the same transaction and contemporaneously with the execution of the document by which the transfer is made. The designation is made by setting forth the successor custodian's name, followed in substance by the words: "is designated [first, second, etc., where applicable] successor custodian." A successor custodian designated by the transferor may be a trust company or an adult other than a transferor under Section 3904. A successor custodian effectively designated by the transferor has priority over a successor custodian designated by a custodian.

(c) A custodian may resign at any time by delivering written notice to the minor if the minor has attained the age of 14 years and to the successor custodian and by delivering the custodial property to the successor custodian.

(d) If the transferor has not effectively designated a successor custodian, and a custodian is ineligible, dies, or becomes incapacitated without having effectively designated a successor and the minor has attained the age of 14 years, the minor may designate as successor custodian, in the manner prescribed in subdivision (b), an adult member of the minor's family, a conservator of the minor, or a trust company. If the minor has not attained the age of 14 years or fails to act within 60 days after the ineligibility, death, or incapacity, the conservator of the minor becomes successor custodian. If the minor has no conservator or the conservator declines to act, the transferor, the legal representative of the transferor or of the custodian, an adult member of the minor's family, or any other interested person may petition the court to designate a successor custodian.

(e) A custodian who declines to serve under subdivision (a) or resigns under subdivision (c), or the legal representative of a deceased or incapacitated custodian, as soon as practicable, shall put the custodial property and records in the possession and control of the successor custodian. The successor custodian by action may enforce the obligation to deliver custodial property and records and becomes responsible for each item as received.

(f) A transferor, the legal representative of a transferor, an adult member of the minor's family, a guardian of the person of the minor, the conservator of the minor, or the minor if the minor has attained the age of 14 years, may petition the court to remove the custodian for cause and to designate a successor custodian other than a transferor under Section 3904 or to require the custodian to give appropriate bond.

(g) At least 15 days before the hearing on a petition under subdivision (d) or (f), the petitioner shall serve notice by mail or personal delivery on each of the following persons:

(1) The minor.
(2) The parent or parents of the minor.
(3) The transferor.

(h) Upon consideration of the petition under subdivision (d) or (f), the court may grant the relief that the court finds to be in the best interests of the minor.

3919. (a) A minor who has attained the age of 14 years, the minor's guardian of the person or legal representative, an adult member of the minor's family, a transferor, or a transferor's legal representative may petition the court for any of the following:

(1) An accounting by the custodian or the custodian's legal representative.

(2) A determination of responsibility, as between the custodial property and the custodian personally, for claims against the custodial property unless the responsibility has been adjudicated in an action under Section 3917 to which the minor or the minor's legal representative was a party.

(b) A successor custodian may petition the court for an accounting by the predecessor custodian.

(c) The court, in a proceeding under this part or in any other proceeding, may require or permit the custodian or the custodian's legal representative to account.

(d) If a custodian is removed under sub-

152

division (f) of Section 3918, the court shall require an accounting and order delivery of the custodial property and records to the successor custodian and the execution of all instruments required for transfer of the custodial property.

(e) The right to petition for an accounting shall continue for one year after the filing of a final accounting by the custodian or the custodian's legal representative and delivery of the custodial property to the minor or the minor's estate.

3920. The custodian shall transfer in an appropriate manner the custodial property to the minor or to the minor's estate upon the earlier of the following:

(a) The minor's attainment of 18 years of age unless the time of transfer of the custodial property to the minor is delayed under Section 3920.5 to a time after the time the minor attains the age of 18 years.

(b) The time specified in the transfer pursuant to Section 3909 if the time of transfer of the custodial property to the minor is delayed under Section 3920.5 to a time after the time the minor attains the age of 18 years.

(c) The minor's death.

3920.5. (a) Subject to the requirements and limitations of this section, the time for transfer to the minor of custodial property transferred under or pursuant to Section 3903, 3904, 3905, or 3906, may be delayed until a specified time after the time the minor attains the age of 18 years, which time shall be specified in the transfer pursuant to Section 3909.

(b) To specify a delayed time for transfer to the minor of the custodial property, the words
"as custodian for _____
(Name of Minor) until age
_____
(Age for Delivery of Property to Minor)
under the California Uniform Transfers to Minors Act"
shall be substituted in substance for the words
"as custodian for _____
(Name of Minor)
under the California Uniform Transfers to Minors Act"
in making the transfer pursuant to Section 3909.

(c) The time for transfer to the minor of custodial property transferred under or pursuant to Section 3903 or 3905 may be delayed under this section only if the governing will or trust or nomination provides in substance that the custodianship is to continue until the time the minor attains a specified age, which time may not be later than the time the minor attains 25 years of age, and in that case the governing will or trust or nomination shall determine the time to be specified in the transfer pursuant to Section 3909.

(d) The time for transfer to the minor of custodial property transferred by the irrevocable exercise of a power of appointment under Section 3904 may be delayed under this section only if the transfer pursuant to Section 3909 provides in substance that the custodianship is to continue until the time the minor attains a specified age, which time may not be later than the time the minor attains 25 years of age.

(e) The time for transfer to the minor of custodial property transferred by irrevocable gift under Section 3904 may be delayed under this section only if the transfer pursuant to Section 3909 provides in substance that the custodianship is to continue until the time the minor attains a specified age, which time may not be later than the time the minor attains 21 years of age.

(f) The time for transfer to the minor of custodial property transferred by a trustee under Section 3906 may be delayed under this section only if the transfer pursuant to Section 3909 provides that the custodianship is to continue until a specified time not later than the time the minor attains 25 years of age or the time of termination of all present beneficial interests of the minor in the trust from which the custodial property was transferred, whichever is to occur first.

(g) If the transfer pursuant to Section 3909 does not specify any age, the time for the transfer of the custodial property to the minor under Section 3920 is the time when the minor attains 18 years of age.

(h) If the transfer pursuant to Section 3909 provides in substance that the duration of the custodianship is for a time longer than the maximum time permitted by this section for the duration of a custodianship created by that type of transfer, the custodianship shall be deemed to continue only until the time the minor attains the maximum age permitted by this section for the duration of a custodianship created by that type of transfer.

3921. Subject to the power of the court to transfer actions and proceedings as provided in the Code of Civil Procedure, a petition filed under this part shall be heard and proceedings thereon held in the superior court in the proper county, which shall be determined as follows:

(a) If the minor resides in this state, in either of the following counties:

(1) Where the minor resides.

(2) Where the custodian resides.

(b) If the minor does not reside within this state, in any of the following counties:

(1) Where the transferor resides.

(2) Where the custodian resides.

(3) Where the estate of a deceased or legally incapacitated custodian is being administered.

(4) Where a parent of the minor resides.

(c) If neither the minor, nor the transferor, nor any parent resides within this state, and no estate of a deceased or legally incapacitated custodian is being administered within this state, in any county.

3922. This part applies to a transfer within the scope of Section 3902 made on or after January 1, 1985, if either of the following requirements is satisfied:

(a) The transfer purports to have been made under the California Uniform Gifts to Minors Act.

(b) The instrument by which the transfer purports to have been made uses in substance the designation "as custodian under the Uniform Gifts to Minors Act" or "as custodian under the Uniform Transfers to Minors Act" of any other state, and the application of this part is necessary to validate the transfer.

3923. (a) As used in this section, "California Uniform Gifts to Minors Act" means former Article 4 (commencing with Section 1154) of Chapter 3 of Title 4 of Part 4 of Division 2 of the Civil Code.

(b) Any transfer of custodial property, as now defined in this part, made before January 1, 1985, is validated, notwithstanding that there was no specific authority in the California Uniform Gifts to Minors Act for the coverage of custodial property of that kind or for a transfer from that source at the time the transfer was made.

(c) This part applies to all transfers made before January 1, 1985, in a manner and form prescribed in the California Uniform Gifts to Minors Act, except insofar as the application impairs constitutionally vested rights.

(d) To the extent that this part, by virtue of subdivision (c), does not apply to transfers made in a manner prescribed in the California Uniform Gifts to Minors Act or to the powers, duties, and immunities conferred by transfers in that manner upon custodians and persons dealing with custodians, the repeal of the California Uniform Gifts to Minors Act does not affect those transfers or those powers, duties, and immunities.

3925. This part shall not be construed as providing an exclusive method for making gifts or other transfers to minors.

Division 4.5. Powers Of Attorney

Part 1. Definitions And General Provisions

Chapter 1. Short Title And Definitions

4000. This division may be cited as the Power of Attorney Law.

4001. Sections 4124, 4125, 4126, 4127, 4206, 4304, and 4305 may be cited as the Uniform Durable Power of Attorney Act.

4010. Unless the provision or context otherwise requires, the definitions in this chapter govern the construction of this division.

4014. (a) "Attorney-in-fact" means a person granted authority to act for the principal in a power of attorney, regardless of whether the person is known as an attorney-in-fact or agent, or by some other term.

(b) "Attorney-in-fact" includes a successor or alternate attorney-in-fact and a person delegated authority by an attorney-in-fact.

4018. "Durable power of attorney" means a power of attorney that satisfies the requirements for durability provided in Section 4124.

4022. "Power of attorney" means a written instrument, however denominated, that is executed by a natural person having the capacity to contract and that grants authority to an attorney-in-fact. A power of attorney may be durable or nondurable.

4026. "Principal" means a natural person who executes a power of attorney.

4030. "Springing power of attorney" means a power of attorney that by its terms becomes effective at a specified future time or on the occurrence of a specified future event or contingency, including, but not limited to, the subsequent incapacity of the principal. A springing power of attorney may be a durable power of attorney or a nondurable power of attorney.

4034. "Third person" means any person other than the principal or attorney-in-fact.

Chapter 2. General Provisions

4050. (a) This division applies to the following:

(1) Durable powers of attorney, other than powers of attorney for health care governed by Division 4.7 (commencing with Section 4600).

(2) Statutory form powers of attorney under Part 3 (commencing with Section 4400).

(3) Any other power of attorney that incorporates or refers to this division or the provisions of this division.

(b) This division does not apply to the following:

(1) A power of attorney to the extent that the authority of the attorney-in-fact is coupled with an interest in the subject of the power of attorney.

(2) Reciprocal or interinsurance exchanges and their contracts, subscribers, attorneys-in-fact, agents, and representatives.

(3) A proxy given by an attorney-in-fact to another person to exercise voting rights.

(c) This division is not intended to affect the validity of any instrument or arrangement that is not described in subdivision (a).

4051. Except where this division provides a specific rule, the general law of agency, including Article 2 (commencing with Section 2019) of Chapter 2 of Title 6 of, and Title 9 (commencing with Section 2295) of, Part 4 of Division 3 of the Civil Code, applies to powers of attorney.

4052. (a) If a power of attorney provides that the Power of Attorney Law of this state governs the power of attorney or otherwise indicates the principal's intention that the Power of Attorney Law of this state governs the power of attorney, this division governs the power of attorney and applies to acts and transactions of the attorney-in-fact in this state or outside this state where any of the following conditions is satisfied:

(1) The principal or attorney-in-fact was domiciled in this state when the principal executed the power of attorney.

(2) The authority conferred on the attorney-in-fact relates to property, acts, or transactions in this state.

(3) The acts or transactions of the attorney-in-fact occurred or were intended to occur in this state.

(4) The principal executed the power of attorney in this state.

(5) There is otherwise a reasonable relationship between this state and the subject matter of the power of attorney.

(b) If subdivision (a) does not apply to the power of attorney, this division governs the power of attorney and applies to the acts and transactions of the attorney-in-fact in this state where either of the following conditions is satisfied:

(1) The principal was domiciled in this state when the principal executed the power of attorney.

(2) The principal executed the power of attorney in this state.

(c) A power of attorney described in this section remains subject to this division despite a change in domicile of the principal or the attorney-in-fact, or the removal from this state of property that was the subject of the power of attorney.

4053. A durable power of attorney executed in another state or jurisdiction in compliance with the law of that state or jurisdiction or the law of this state is valid and enforceable in this state to the same extent as a durable power of attorney executed in this state, regardless of whether the principal is a domiciliary of this state.

4054. Except as otherwise provided by statute:

(a) On and after January 1, 1995, this division applies to all powers of attorney regardless of whether they were executed before, on, or after January 1, 1995.

(b) This division applies to all proceedings concerning powers of attorney commenced on or after January 1, 1995.

(c) This division applies to all proceedings concerning powers of attorney commenced before January 1, 1995, unless the court determines that application of a particular provision of this division would substantially interfere with the effective conduct of the proceedings or the rights of the parties and other interested persons, in which case the particular provision of this division does not apply and prior law applies.

(d) Nothing in this division affects the validity of a power of attorney executed before January 1, 1995, that was valid under prior law.

Part 2. Powers Of Attorney Generally

Chapter 1. General Provisions

4100. This part applies to all powers of attorney under this division, subject to any special rules applicable to statutory form powers of attorney under Part 3 (commencing with Section 4400).

4101. (a) Except as provided in subdivision (b), the principal may limit the application of any provision of this division by an express statement in the power of attorney or by providing an inconsistent rule in the power of attorney.

(b) A power of attorney may not limit either the application of a statute specifically providing that it is not subject to limitation in the power of attorney or a statute concerning any of the following:

(1) Warnings or notices required to be included in a power of attorney.

(2) Operative dates of statutory enactments or amendments.

(3) Execution formalities.

(4) Qualifications of witnesses.

(5) Qualifications of attorneys-in-fact.

(6) Protection of third persons from liability.

4102. Notwithstanding Section 4128:

(a) Except as provided in subdivision (b), on and after January 1, 1995, a printed form of a durable power of attorney may be sold or otherwise distributed if it satisfies the requirements of former Section 2510.5 of the Civil Code.

(b) A printed form of a durable power of attorney printed on or after January 1, 1986, that is sold or otherwise distributed in this state for use by a person who does not have the advice of legal counsel shall comply with former Section 2510 of the Civil Code or with Section 4128 of this code.

(c) A durable power of attorney executed on or after January 1, 1995, using a printed form that complies with subdivision (b) of former Section 2400 of the Civil Code, as enacted by Chapter 511 of the Statutes of 1981, or with former Section 2510 of the Civil Code, is as valid as if it had been executed using a printed form that complies with Section 4128 of this code.

Chapter 2. Creation And Effect Of Powers Of Attorney

4120. A natural person having the capacity to contract may execute a power of attorney.

4121. A power of attorney is legally sufficient if all of the following requirements are satisfied:

(a) The power of attorney contains the date of its execution.

(b) The power of attorney is signed either (1) by the principal or (2) in the principal's name by another adult in the principal's presence and at the principal's direction.

(c) The power of attorney is either (1) acknowledged before a notary public or (2) signed by at least two witnesses who satisfy the requirements of Section 4122.

4122. If the power of attorney is signed by witnesses, as provided in Section 4121, the following requirements shall be satisfied:

(a) The witnesses shall be adults.

(b) The attorney-in-fact may not act as a witness.

(c) Each witness signing the power of attorney shall witness either the signing of the instrument by the principal or the principal's acknowledgment of the signature or the power of attorney.

4123. (a) In a power of attorney under this division, a principal may grant authority to an attorney-in-fact to act on the principal's behalf with respect to all lawful subjects and purposes or with respect to one or more express subjects or purposes. The attorney-in-fact may be granted authority with regard to the principal's property, personal care, or any other matter.

(b) With regard to property matters, a power of attorney may grant authority to make decisions concerning all or part of the principal' s real and personal property, whether owned by the principal at the time of the execution of the power of attorney or thereafter acquired or whether located in this state or elsewhere, without the need for a description of each item or parcel of property.

(c) With regard to personal care, a power of attorney may grant authority to make decisions relating to the personal care of the principal, including, but not limited to, determining where the principal will live, providing meals, hiring household employees, providing transportation, handling mail, and arranging recreation and entertainment.

4124. A durable power of attorney is a power of attorney by which a principal designates another person as attorney-in-fact in writing and the power of attorney contains any of the following statements:

(a) "This power of attorney shall not be affected by subsequent incapacity of the principal."

(b) "This power of attorney shall become effective upon the incapacity of the principal."

(c) Similar words showing the intent of the principal that the authority conferred shall be exercisable notwithstanding the principal's subsequent incapacity.

4125. All acts done by an attorney-in-fact pursuant to a durable power of attorney during any period of incapacity of the principal have the same effect and inure to the benefit of and bind the principal and the principal's successors in interest as if the principal had capacity.

4126. (a) A principal may nominate, by a durable power of attorney, a conservator of the person or estate or both, or a guardian of the person or estate or both, for consideration by the court if protective proceedings for the principal's person or estate are thereafter commenced.

(b) If the protective proceedings are conservatorship proceedings in this state, the nomination has the effect provided in Section 1810 and the court shall give effect to the most recent writing executed in accordance with Section 1810, whether or not the writing is a durable power of attorney.

4127. Unless a power of attorney states a time of termination, the authority of the attorney-in-fact is exercisable notwithstanding any lapse of time since execution of the power of attorney.

4128. (a) Subject to subdivision (b), a printed form of a durable power of attorney that is sold or otherwise distributed in this state for use by a person who does not have the advice of legal counsel shall contain, in not less than 10-point boldface type or a reasonable equivalent thereof, the following warning statements:

PLEASE SEE THE APPENDIX

(b) Nothing in subdivision (a) invalidates any transaction in which a third person relied in good faith on the authority created by the durable power of attorney.

(c) This section does not apply to a statutory form power of attorney under Part 3 (commencing with Section 4400).

4129. (a) In a springing power of attorney, the principal may designate one or more persons who, by a written declaration under penalty of perjury, have the power to determine conclusively that the specified event or contingency has occurred. The principal may designate the attorney-in-fact or another person to perform this function, either alone or jointly with other persons.

(b) A springing power of attorney containing the designation described in subdivision (a) becomes effective when the person or persons designated in the power of attorney execute a written declaration under penalty of perjury that the specified event or contingency has occurred, and any person may act in reliance on the written declaration without liability to the principal or to any other person, regardless of whether the specified event or contingency has actually occurred.

(c) This section applies to a power of attorney whether executed before, on, or after January 1, 1991, if the power of attorney contains the designation described in subdivision (a).

(d) This section does not provide the exclusive method by which a power of attorney may be limited to take effect on the occurrence of a specified event or contingency.

4130. (a) If a principal grants inconsistent authority to one or more attorneys-in-fact in two or more powers of attorney, the authority granted last controls to the extent of the inconsistency.

(b) This section is not subject to limitation in the power of attorney.

Chapter 3. Modification And Revocation Of Powers Of Attorney

4150. (a) A principal may modify a power of attorney as follows:

(1) In accordance with the terms of the power of attorney.

(2) By an instrument executed in the same manner as a power of attorney may be executed.

(b) An attorney-in-fact or third person who does not have notice of the modification is protected from liability as provided in Chapter 5 (commencing with Section 4300).

4151. (a) A principal may revoke a power of attorney as follows:

(1) In accordance with the terms of the power of attorney.

(2) By a writing. This paragraph is not subject to limitation in the power of attorney.

(b) An attorney-in-fact or third person who does not have notice of the revocation is protected from liability as provided in Chapter 5 (commencing with Section 4300).

4152. (a) Subject to subdivision (b), the authority of an attorney-in-fact under a power of attorney is terminated by any of the following events:

(1) In accordance with the terms of the power of attorney.

(2) Extinction of the subject or fulfillment of the purpose of the power of attorney.

(3) Revocation of the attorney-in-fact's authority, as provided in Section 4153.

(4) Death of the principal, except as to specific authority permitted by statute to be exercised after the principal's death.

(5) Removal of the attorney-in-fact.

(6) Resignation of the attorney-in-fact.

(7) Incapacity of the attorney-in-fact, except that a temporary incapacity suspends the attorney-in-fact's authority only during the period of the incapacity.

(8) Dissolution or annulment of the marriage of the attorney-in-fact and principal, as provided in Section 4154.

(9) Death of the attorney-in-fact.

(b) An attorney-in-fact or third person who does not have notice of an event that terminates the power of attorney or the authority of an attorney-in-fact is protected from liability as provided in Chapter 5 (commencing with Section 4300).

4153. (a) The authority of an attorney-in-fact under a power of attorney may be revoked as follows:

(1) In accordance with the terms of the power of attorney.

(2) Where the principal informs the attorney-in-fact orally or in writing that the attorney-in-fact's authority is revoked or when and under what circumstances it is revoked. This paragraph is not subject to limitation in the power of attorney.

(3) Where the principal's legal representative, with approval of the court as provided in Section 4206, informs the attorney-in-fact in writing that the attorney-in-fact's authority is revoked or when and under what circumstances it is revoked. This paragraph is not subject to limitation in the power of attorney.

(b) An attorney-in-fact or third person who does not have notice of the revocation is protected from liability as provided in Chapter 5 (commencing with Section 4300).

4154. (a) If after executing a power of attorney the principal's marriage to the attorney-in-fact is dissolved or annulled, the principal's designation of the former spouse as an attorney-in-fact is revoked.

(b) If the attorney-in-fact's authority is revoked solely by subdivision (a), it is revived by the principal's remarriage to the attorney-in-fact.

4155. (a) Subject to subdivision (b), the authority of an attorney-in-fact under a nondurable power of attorney is terminated by the incapacity of the principal to contract.

(b) An attorney-in-fact or third person who does not have notice of the incapacity of the principal is protected from liability as provided in Chapter 5 (commencing with Section 4300).

(c) This section is not subject to limitation in the power of attorney.

Chapter 4. Attorneys-In-Fact

Article 1. Qualifications And Authority Of Attorneys-In-Fact

4200. Only a person having the capacity to contract is qualified to act as an attorney-in-fact.

4201. Designating an unqualified person as an attorney-in-fact does not affect the immunities of third persons nor relieve the unqualified person of any applicable duties to the principal or the principal's successors.

4202. (a) A principal may designate more than one attorney-in-fact in one or more powers of attorney.

(b) Authority granted to two or more attorneys-in-fact is exercisable only by their unanimous action.

(c) If a vacancy occurs, the remaining attorneys-in-fact may exercise the authority conferred as if they are the only attorneys-in-fact.

(d) If an attorney-in-fact is unavailable because of absence, illness, or other temporary incapacity, the other attorneys-in-fact may exercise the authority under the power of attorney as if they are the only attorneys-in-fact, where necessary to accomplish the purposes of the power of attorney or to avoid irreparable injury to the principal's interests.

(e) An attorney-in-fact is not liable for the actions of other attorneys-in-fact, unless the attorney-in-fact participates in, knowingly acquiesces in, or conceals a breach of fiduciary duty committed by another attorney-in-fact.

4203. (a) A principal may designate one or more successor attorneys-in-fact to act if the authority of a predecessor attorney-in-fact terminates.

(b) The principal may grant authority to another person, designated by name, by office, or by function, including the initial and any successor attorneys-in-fact, to designate at any time one or more successor attorneys-in-fact.

(c) A successor attorney-in-fact is not liable for the actions of the predecessor attorney-in-fact.

4204. An attorney-in-fact is entitled to reasonable compensation for services rendered to the principal as attorney-in-fact and to reimbursement for reasonable expenses incurred as a result of acting as attorney-in-fact.

4205. (a) An attorney-in-fact may revocably delegate authority to perform mechanical acts to one or more persons qualified to exercise the authority delegated.

(b) The attorney-in-fact making a delegation remains responsible to the principal for the exercise or nonexercise of the delegated authority.

4206. (a) If, following execution of a durable power of attorney, a court of the principal's domicile appoints a conservator of the estate, guardian of the estate, or other fiduciary charged with the management of all of the principal's property or all of the principal's property except specified exclusions, the attorney-in-fact is accountable to the fiduciary as well as to the principal. Except as provided in subdivision (b), the fiduciary has the same power to revoke or amend the durable power of attorney that the principal would have had if not incapacitated, subject to any required court approval.

(b) If a conservator of the estate is appointed by a court of this state, the conservator can revoke or amend the durable power of attorney only if the court in which the conservatorship proceeding is pending has first made an order authorizing or requiring the fiduciary to modify or revoke the durable power of attorney and the modification or revocation is in accord with the order.

(c) This section is not subject to limitation in the power of attorney.

4207. (a) An attorney-in-fact may resign by any of the following means:

(1) If the principal is competent, by giving notice to the principal.

(2) If a conservator has been appointed, by giving notice to the conservator.

(3) On written agreement of a successor who is designated in the power of attorney or pursuant to the terms of the power of attorney to serve as attorney-in-fact.

(4) Pursuant to a court order.

(b) This section is not subject to limitation in the power of attorney.

Article 2. Duties Of Attorneys-In-Fact

4230. (a) Except as provided in subdivisions (b) and (c), a person who is designated as an attorney-in-fact has no duty to exercise the authority granted in the power of attorney and is not subject to the other duties of an attorney-in-fact, regardless of whether the principal has become incapacitated, is missing, or is otherwise unable to act.

(b) Acting for the principal in one or more transactions does not obligate an attorney-in-fact to act for the principal in a subsequent transaction, but the attorney-in-fact has a duty to complete a transaction that the attorney-in-fact has commenced.

(c) If an attorney-in-fact has expressly agreed in writing to act for the principal, the attorney-in-fact has a duty to act pursuant to the terms of the agreement. The agreement to act on behalf of the principal is enforceable against the attorney-in-fact as a fiduciary regardless of whether there is any consideration to support a contractual obligation.

4231. (a) Except as provided in subdivision (b), in dealing with property of the principal, an attorney-in-fact shall observe the standard of care that would be observed by a prudent person dealing with property of another and is not limited by any other statute restricting investments by fiduciaries.

(b) An attorney-in-fact who has special skills or expertise or was designated as an attorney-in-fact on the basis of representations of special skills or expertise shall observe the standard of care that would be observed by others with similar skills or expertise.

4231.5. (a) If the attorney-in-fact breaches a duty pursuant to this division, the attorney-in-fact is chargeable with any of the following, as appropriate under the circumstances:

(1) Any loss or depreciation in value of the principal's property resulting from the breach of duty, with interest.

(2) Any profit made by the attorney-in-fact through the breach of duty, with interest.

(3) Any profit that would have accrued to the principal if the loss of profit is the result of the breach of duty.

(b) If the attorney-in-fact has acted reasonably and in good faith under the circumstances as known to the attorney-in-fact, the court, in its discretion, may excuse the attorney-in-fact in whole or in part from liability under subdivision (a) if it would be equitable to do so.

(c) If a court finds that a person has in bad faith wrongfully taken, concealed, or disposed of property that belongs to a principal under a power of attorney, or has taken, concealed, or disposed of property that belongs to a principal under a power of attorney by the use of undue influence in bad faith or through the commission of elder or dependent adult financial abuse, as defined in Section 15610.30 of the Welfare and Institutions Code, the person shall be liable for twice the value of the property recovered by an action to recover the property or for surcharge. In addition, except as otherwise required by law, including Section 15657.5 of the Welfare and Institutions Code, the person may, in the court's discretion, be liable for reasonable attorney's fees and costs to the prevailing party. The remedies provided in this section shall be in addition to any other remedies available in law to the principal or any successor in interest of the principal.

4232. (a) An attorney-in-fact has a duty to act solely in the interest of the principal and to avoid conflicts of interest.

(b) An attorney-in-fact is not in violation of the duty provided in subdivision (a) solely because the attorney-in-fact also benefits from acting for the principal, has conflicting interests in relation to the property, care, or affairs of the principal, or acts in an inconsistent manner regarding the respective interests of the principal and the attorney-in-fact.

4233. (a) The attorney-in-fact shall keep the principal's property separate and distinct from other property in a manner adequate to identify the property clearly as belonging to the principal.

(b) An attorney-in-fact holding property for a principal complies with subdivision (a) if the property is held in the name of the principal or in the name of the attorney-in-fact as attorney-in-fact for the principal.

4234. (a) To the extent reasonably practicable under the circumstances, an attorney-in-fact has a duty to keep in regular contact with the principal, to communicate with the principal, and to follow the instructions of the principal.

(b) With court approval, the attorney-in-fact may disobey instructions of the principal.

4235. If the principal becomes wholly or partially incapacitated, or if there is a question concerning the capacity of the principal to give instructions to and supervise the attorney-in-fact, the attorney-in-fact may consult with a person previously designated by the principal for this purpose, and may also consult with and obtain information needed to carry out the attorney-in-fact's duties from the principal's spouse, physician, attorney, accountant, a member of the principal's family, or other person, business entity, or government agency with respect to matters to be undertaken on the principal's behalf and affecting the principal's personal affairs, welfare, family, property, and business interests. A person from whom information is requested shall disclose relevant information to the attorney-in-fact. Disclosure under this section is not a waiver of any privilege that may apply to the information disclosed.

4236. (a) The attorney-in-fact shall keep records of all transactions entered into by the attorney-in-fact on behalf of the principal.

(b) The attorney-in-fact does not have a duty to make an account of transactions entered into on behalf of the principal, except in the following circumstances:

(1) At any time requested by the principal.

(2) Where the power of attorney requires the attorney-in-fact to account and specifies to whom the account is to be made.

(3) On request by the conservator of the estate of the principal while the principal is living.

(4) On request by the principal's personal representative or successor in interest after the death of the principal.

(5) Pursuant to court order.

(c) The following persons are entitled to examine and copy the records kept by the attorney-in-fact:

(1) The principal.

(2) The conservator of the estate of the principal while the principal is living.

(3) The principal's personal representative or successor in interest after the death of the principal.

(4) Any other person, pursuant to court

order.

(d) This section is not subject to limitation in the power of attorney.

4237. An attorney-in-fact with special skills has a duty to apply the full extent of those skills.

4238. (a) On termination of an attorney-in-fact's authority, the attorney-in-fact shall promptly deliver possession or control of the principal's property as follows:

(1) If the principal is not incapacitated, to the principal or as directed by the principal.

(2) If the principal is incapacitated, to the following persons with the following priority:

(A) To a qualified successor attorney-in-fact.

(B) As to any community property, to the principal's spouse.

(C) To the principal's conservator of the estate or guardian of the estate.

(3) In the case of the death of the principal, to the principal's personal representative, if any, or the principal's successors.

(b) On termination of an attorney-in-fact's authority, the attorney-in-fact shall deliver copies of any records relating to transactions undertaken on the principal's behalf that are requested by the person to whom possession or control of the property is delivered.

(c) Termination of an attorney-in-fact's authority does not relieve the attorney-in-fact of any duty to render an account of actions taken as attorney-in-fact.

(d) The attorney-in-fact has the powers reasonably necessary under the circumstances to perform the duties provided by this section.

Article 3. Authority Of Attorneys-In-Fact

4260. (a) Except as specified in subdivision (b), this article applies to all powers of attorney under this division.

(b) Sections 4261 and 4263 do not apply to the provisions of Part 3 (commencing with Section 4400).

4261. If a power of attorney grants general authority to an attorney-in-fact and is not limited to one or more express actions, subjects, or purposes for which general authority is conferred, the attorney-in-fact has all the authority to act that a person having the capacity to contract may carry out through an attorney-in-fact specifically authorized to take the action.

4262. Subject to this article, if a power of attorney grants limited authority to an attorney-in-fact, the attorney-in-fact has the following authority:

(a) The authority granted in the power of attorney, as limited with respect to permissible actions, subjects, or purposes.

(b) The authority incidental, necessary, or proper to carry out the granted authority.

4263. (a) A power of attorney may grant authority to the attorney-in-fact by incorporating powers by reference to another statute, including, but not limited to, the following:

(1) Powers of attorneys-in-fact provided by the Uniform Statutory Form Power of Attorney Act (Part 3 (commencing with Section 4400)).

(2) Powers of guardians and conservators provided by Chapter 5 (commencing with Section 2350) and Chapter 6 (commencing with Section 2400) of Part 4 of Division 4.

(3) Powers of trustees provided by Chapter 2 (commencing with Section 16200) of Part 4 of Division 9.

(b) Incorporation by reference to another statute includes any amendments made to the incorporated provisions after the date of execution of the power of attorney.

4264. An attorney-in-fact under a power of attorney may perform any of the following acts on behalf of the principal or with the property of the principal only if the power of attorney expressly grants that authority to the attorney-in-fact:

(a) Create, modify, revoke, or terminate a trust, in whole or in part. If a power of attorney under this division empowers the attorney-in-fact to modify or revoke a trust created by the principal, the trust may be modified or revoked by the attorney-in-fact only as provided in the trust instrument.

(b) Fund with the principal's property a trust not created by the principal or a person authorized to create a trust on behalf of the principal.

(c) Make or revoke a gift of the principal's property in trust or otherwise.

(d) Exercise the right to reject, disclaim, release, or consent to a reduction in, or modification of, a share in, or payment from, an estate, trust, or other fund on behalf of the principal. This subdivision does not limit the attorney-in-fact's authority to disclaim a detrimental transfer to the principal with the approval of the court.

(e) Create or change survivorship interests in the principal's property or in property in which the principal may have an interest.

(f) Designate or change the designation of beneficiaries to receive any property, benefit, or contract right on the principal's death.

(g) Make a loan to the attorney-in-fact.

4265. A power of attorney may not authorize an attorney-in-fact to make, publish, declare, amend, or revoke the principal's will.

4266. The grant of authority to an attorney-in-fact, whether by the power of attorney, by statute, or by the court, does not in itself require or permit the exercise of the power. The exercise of authority by an attorney-in-fact is subject to the attorney-in-fact's fiduciary duties.

Chapter 5. Relations With Third Persons

4300. A third person shall accord an attorney-in-fact acting pursuant to the provisions of a power of attorney the same rights and privileges that would be accorded the principal if the principal were personally present and seeking to act. However, a third person is not required to honor the attorney-in-fact's authority or conduct business with the attorney-in-fact if the principal cannot require the third person to act or conduct business in the same circumstances.

4301. A third person may rely on, contract with, and deal with an attorney-in-fact with respect to the subjects and purposes encompassed or expressed in the power of attorney without regard to whether the power of attorney expressly authorizes the specific act, transaction, or decision by the attorney-in-fact.

4302. When requested to engage in transactions with an attorney-in-fact, a third person, before incurring any duty to comply with the power of attorney, may require the attorney-in-fact to provide identification, specimens of the signatures of the principal and the attorney-in-fact, and any other information reasonably necessary or appropriate to identify the principal and the attorney-in-fact and to facilitate the actions of the third person in transacting business with the attorney-in-fact. A third person may require an attorney-in-fact to provide the current and permanent residence addresses of the principal before agreeing to engage in a transaction with the attorney-in-fact.

4303. (a) A third person who acts in good faith reliance on a power of attorney is not liable to the principal or to any other person for so acting if all of the following requirements are satisfied:

(1) The power of attorney is presented to the third person by the attorney-in-fact designated in the power of attorney.

(2) The power of attorney appears on its face to be valid.

(3) The power of attorney includes a notary public's certificate of acknowledgment or is signed by two witnesses.

(b) Nothing in this section is intended to create an implication that a third person is liable for acting in reliance on a power of attorney under circumstances where the requirements of subdivision (a) are not satisfied. Nothing in this section affects any immunity that may otherwise exist apart from this section.

4304. (a) The death of a principal who has executed a power of attorney, whether durable or nondurable, does not revoke or terminate the agency as to the attorney-in-fact or a third person who, without actual knowledge of the principal's death, acts in good faith under the power of attorney. Any action so taken, unless otherwise invalid or unenforceable, binds the principal's successors in interest.

(b) The incapacity of a principal who has previously executed a nondurable power of attorney does not revoke or terminate the agency as to the attorney-in-fact or a third person who, without actual knowledge of the incapacity of the principal, acts in good faith under the power of attorney. Any action so taken, unless otherwise invalid or unenforceable, binds the principal and the principal's successors in interest.

4305. (a) As to acts undertaken in good faith reliance thereon, an affidavit executed by the attorney-in-fact under a power of attorney, whether durable or nondurable, stating that, at the time of the exercise of the power, the attorney-in-fact did not have actual knowledge of the termination of the power of attorney or the attorney-in-fact's authority by revocation or of the principal's death or incapacity is conclusive proof of the nonrevocation or nontermination of the power at that time. If the exercise of the power of attorney requires execution and delivery of any instrument that is recordable, the affidavit when authenticated for record is likewise recordable.

(b) This section does not affect any provision in a power of attorney for its termination by expiration of time or occurrence of an event other than express revocation or a change in the principal's capacity.

4306. (a) If an attorney-in-fact furnishes an affidavit pursuant to Section 4305, whether voluntarily or on demand, a third person dealing with the attorney-in-fact who refuses to accept the exercise of the attorney-in-fact's authority referred to in the affidavit is liable for attorney's fees incurred in an action or proceeding necessary to confirm the attorney-in-fact's qualifications or authority, unless the court determines that the third person believed in good faith that the attorney-in-fact was not qualified or was attempting to exceed or improperly exercise the attorney-in-fact's authority.

(b) The failure of a third person to demand an affidavit pursuant to Section 4305 does not affect the protection provided the third person by this chapter, and no inference as to whether a third person has acted in good faith may be drawn from the failure to demand an affidavit from the attorney-in-fact.

4307. (a) A copy of a power of attorney certified under this section has the same force and effect as the original power of attorney.

(b) A copy of a power of attorney may be certified by any of the following:

(1) An attorney authorized to practice law in this state.

(2) A notary public in this state.

(3) An official of a state or of a political subdivision who is authorized to make certifications.

(c) The certification shall state that the certifying person has examined the original power of attorney and the copy and that the copy is a true and correct copy of the original power of attorney.

(d) Nothing in this section is intended to create an implication that a third person may be liable for acting in good faith reliance on a copy of a power of attorney that has not been certified under this section.

4308. (a) A third person who conducts activities through employees is not charged under this chapter with actual knowledge of any fact relating to a power of attorney, nor of a change in the authority of an attorney-in-fact, unless both of the following requirements are satisfied:

(1) The information is received at a home office or a place where there is an employee with responsibility to act on the information.

(2) The employee has a reasonable time in which to act on the information using the procedure and facilities that are available to the third person in the regular course of its operations.

(b) Knowledge of an employee in one branch or office of an entity that conducts business through branches or multiple offices is not attributable to an employee in another branch or office.

4309. Nothing in this chapter requires a third person to engage in any transaction with an attorney-in-fact if the attorney-in-fact has previously breached any agreement with the third person.

4310. Without limiting the generality of Section 4300, nothing in this chapter requires a financial institution to open a deposit account for a principal at the request of an attorney-in-fact if the principal is not currently a depositor of the financial institution or to make a loan to the attorney-in-fact on the principal's behalf if the principal is not currently a borrower of the financial institution.

Part 3. Uniform Statutory Form Power Of Attorney

Chapter 1. General Provisions

4400. This part may be cited as the Uniform Statutory Form Power of Attorney Act.

4401. The following statutory form power of attorney is legally sufficient when the requirements of Section 4402 are satisfied:

PLEASE SEE THE APPENDIX

4402. A statutory form power of attorney under this part is legally sufficient if all of the following requirements are satisfied:

(a) The wording of the form complies substantially with Section 4401. A form does not fail to comply substantially with Section 4401 merely because the form does not include the provisions of Section 4401 relating to designation of co-agents. A form does not fail to comply substantially with Section 4401 merely because the form uses the sentence "Revocation of the power of attorney is not effective as to a third party until the third party learns of the revocation" in place of the sentence "Revocation of the power of attorney is not effective as to a third party until the third party has actual knowledge of the revocation," in which case the form shall be interpreted as if it contained the sentence "Revocation of the power of attorney is not effective as to a third party until the third party has actual knowledge of the revocation."

(b) The form is properly completed.

(c) The signature of the principal is acknowledged.

4403. If the line in front of (N) of the statutory form under Section 4401 is initialed, an initial on the line in front of any other power does not limit the powers granted by line (N).

4404. A statutory form power of attorney legally sufficient under this part is durable to the extent that the power of attorney contains language, such as "This power of attorney will continue to be effective even though I become incapacitated," showing the intent of the principal that the power granted may be exercised notwithstanding later incapacity.

4405. (a) A statutory form power of attorney under this part that limits the power to take effect upon the occurrence of a specified event or contingency, including, but not limited to, the incapacity of the principal, may contain a provision designating one or more persons who, by a written declaration under penalty of perjury, have the power to determine conclusively that the specified event or contingency has occurred.

(b) A statutory form power of attorney that contains the provision described in subdivision (a) becomes effective when the person or persons designated in the power of attorney execute a written declaration under penalty of perjury that the specified event or contingency has occurred, and any person may act in reliance on the written declaration without liability to the principal or to any other person, regardless whether the specified event or contingency has actually occurred.

(c) The provision described in subdivision (a) may be included in the "Special Instructions" portion of the form set forth in Section 4401.

(d) Subdivisions (a) and (b) do not provide the exclusive method by which a statutory form power of attorney under this part may be limited to take effect upon the occurrence of a specified event or contingency.

4406. (a) If a third person to whom a properly executed statutory form power of attorney under this part is presented refuses to honor the agent's authority under the power of attorney within a reasonable time, the third person may be compelled to honor the agent's authority under the power of attorney in an action brought against the third person for this purpose, except that the third person may not be compelled to honor the agent's authority if the principal could not compel the third person to act in the same circumstances.

(b) If an action is brought under this section, the court shall award attorney's fees to the agent if the court finds that the third person acted unreasonably in refusing to accept the agent's authority under the statutory form power of attorney.

(c) For the purpose of subdivision (b), and without limiting any other grounds that may constitute a reasonable refusal to accept an agent's authority under a statutory form power of attorney, a third person shall not be deemed to have acted unreasonably in refusing to accept an agent's authority if the refusal is authorized or required by state or federal statute or regulation.

(d) Notwithstanding subdivision (c), a third person's refusal to accept an agent's authority under a statutory form power of attorney under this part shall be deemed unreasonable if the only reason for the refusal is that the power of attorney is not on a form prescribed by the third person to whom the power of attorney is presented.

(e) The remedy provided in this section is cumulative and nonexclusive.

4407. The provisions of this division apply to a statutory form power of attorney except when there is a conflicting provision in this part, in which case the provision of this part governs, or when a provision of this division is expressly made inapplicable to a statutory form power of attorney.

4408. Nothing in this part affects or limits the use of any other form for a power of attorney. A form that complies with the requirements of any law other than the provisions of this part may be used instead of the form set forth in Section 4401, and none of the provisions of this part apply if the other form is used.

4409. (a) A statutory short form power of attorney executed before, on, or after the repeal of Chapter 3 (commencing with Section 2450) of Title 9 of Part 4 of Division 3 of the Civil Code by Chapter 986 of the Statutes of 1990, using a form that complied with former Section 2450 of the Civil Code, as originally enacted by Chapter 602 of the Statutes of 1984, or as amended by Chapter 403 of the Statutes of 1985, is as valid as if Chapter 3 (commencing with Section 2450) of Title 9 of Part 4 of Division 3 of the Civil Code had not been repealed by, and former Section 2511 of the Civil Code amended by, Chapter 986 of the Statutes of 1990.

(b) A statutory form power of attorney executed before, on, or after the repeal of Chapter 3.5 (commencing with Section 2475)

of Title 9 of Part 4 of Division 3 of the Civil Code by the act that enacted this section, using a form that complied with the repealed chapter of the Civil Code is as valid as if that chapter had not been repealed.

Chapter 2. Construction Of Powers

4450. By executing a statutory form power of attorney with respect to a subject listed in Section 4401, the principal, except as limited or extended by the principal in the power of attorney, empowers the agent, for that subject, to do all of the following:

(a) Demand, receive, and obtain by litigation or otherwise, money or other thing of value to which the principal is, may become, or claims to be entitled, and conserve, invest, disburse, or use anything so received for the purposes intended.

(b) Contract in any manner with any person, on terms agreeable to the agent, to accomplish a purpose of a transaction, and perform, rescind, reform, release, or modify the contract or another contract made by or on behalf of the principal.

(c) Execute, acknowledge, seal, and deliver a deed, revocation, mortgage, lease, notice, check, release, or other instrument the agent considers desirable to accomplish a purpose of a transaction.

(d) Prosecute, defend, submit to arbitration, settle, and propose or accept a compromise with respect to, a claim existing in favor of or against the principal or intervene in litigation relating to the claim.

(e) Seek on the principal's behalf the assistance of a court to carry out an act authorized by the power of attorney.

(f) Engage, compensate, and discharge an attorney, accountant, expert witness, or other assistant.

(g) Keep appropriate records of each transaction, including an accounting of receipts and disbursements.

(h) Prepare, execute, and file a record, report, or other document the agent considers desirable to safeguard or promote the principal's interest under a statute or governmental regulation.

(i) Reimburse the agent for expenditures properly made by the agent in exercising the powers granted by the power of attorney.

(j) In general, do any other lawful act with respect to the subject.

4451. In a statutory form power of attorney, the language granting power with respect to real property transactions empowers the agent to do all of the following:

(a) Accept as a gift or as security for a loan, reject, demand, buy, lease, receive, or otherwise acquire, an interest in real property or a right incident to real property.

(b) Sell, exchange, convey with or without covenants, quitclaim, release, surrender, mortgage, encumber, partition, consent to partitioning, subdivide, apply for zoning, rezoning, or other governmental permits, plat or consent to platting, develop, grant options concerning, lease, sublease, or otherwise dispose of, an interest in real property or a right incident to real property.

(c) Release, assign, satisfy, and enforce by litigation or otherwise, a mortgage, deed of trust, encumbrance, lien, or other claim to real property which exists or is asserted.

(d) Do any act of management or of conservation with respect to an interest in real property, or a right incident to real property, owned, or claimed to be owned, by the principal, including all of the following:

(1) Insuring against a casualty, liability, or loss.

(2) Obtaining or regaining possession, or protecting the interest or right, by litigation or otherwise.

(3) Paying, compromising, or contesting taxes or assessments, or applying for and receiving refunds in connection with them.

(4) Purchasing supplies, hiring assistance or labor, and making repairs or alterations in the real property.

(e) Use, develop, alter, replace, remove, erect, or install structures or other improvements upon real property in or incident to which the principal has, or claims to have, an interest or right.

(f) Participate in a reorganization with respect to real property or a legal entity that owns an interest in or right incident to real property and receive and hold shares of stock or obligations received in a plan of reorganization, and act with respect to them, including all of the following:

(1) Selling or otherwise disposing of them.

(2) Exercising or selling an option, conversion, or similar right with respect to them.

(3) Voting them in person or by proxy.

(g) Change the form of title of an interest in or right incident to real property.

(h) Dedicate to public use, with or without consideration, easements or other real property in which the principal has, or claims to have, an interest or right.

4452. In a statutory form power of attorney, the language granting power with respect to tangible personal property transactions empowers the agent to do all of the following:

(a) Accept as a gift or as security for a loan, reject, demand, buy, receive, or otherwise acquire ownership or possession of tangible personal property or an interest in tangible personal property.

(b) Sell, exchange, convey with or without covenants, release, surrender, mortgage, encumber, pledge, hypothecate, create a security interest in, pawn, grant options concerning, lease, sublease to others, or otherwise dispose of tangible personal property or an interest in tangible personal property.

(c) Release, assign, satisfy, or enforce by litigation or otherwise, a mortgage, security interest, encumbrance, lien, or other claim on behalf of the principal, with respect to tangible personal property or an interest in tangible personal property.

(d) Do an act of management or conservation with respect to tangible personal property or an interest in tangible personal property on behalf of the principal, including all of the following:

(1) Insuring against casualty, liability, or loss.

(2) Obtaining or regaining possession, or protecting the property or interest, by litigation or otherwise.

(3) Paying, compromising, or contesting taxes or assessments or applying for and receiving refunds in connection with taxes or assessments.

(4) Moving from place to place.

(5) Storing for hire or on a gratuitous bailment.

(6) Using, altering, and making repairs or alterations.

4453. In a statutory form power of attorney, the language granting power with respect to stock and bond transactions empowers the agent to do all of the following:

(a) Buy, sell, and exchange stocks, bonds, mutual funds, and all other types of securities and financial instruments except commodity futures contracts and call and put options on stocks and stock indexes.

(b) Receive certificates and other evidences of ownership with respect to securities.

(c) Exercise voting rights with respect to securities in person or by proxy, enter into voting trusts, and consent to limitations on the right to vote.

4454. In a statutory form power of attorney, the language granting power with respect to commodity and option transactions empowers the agent to do all of the following:

(a) Buy, sell, exchange, assign, settle, and exercise commodity futures contracts and call and put options on stocks and stock indexes traded on a regulated option exchange.

(b) Establish, continue, modify, and terminate option accounts with a broker.

4455. In a statutory form power of attorney, the language granting power with respect to banking and other financial institution transactions empowers the agent to do all of the following:

(a) Continue, modify, and terminate an account or other banking arrangement made by or on behalf of the principal.

(b) Establish, modify, and terminate an account or other banking arrangement with a bank, trust company, savings and loan association, credit union, thrift company, industrial loan company, brokerage firm, or other financial institution selected by the agent.

(c) Hire or close a safe deposit box or space in a vault.

(d) Contract to procure other services available from a financial institution as the agent considers desirable.

(e) Withdraw by check, order, or otherwise money or property of the principal deposited with or left in the custody of a financial institution.

(f) Receive bank statements, vouchers, notices, and similar documents from a financial institution and act with respect to them.

(g) Enter a safe deposit box or vault and withdraw or add to the contents.

(h) Borrow money at an interest rate agreeable to the agent and pledge as security personal property of the principal necessary in order to borrow, pay, renew, or extend the time of payment of a debt of the principal.

(i) Make, assign, draw, endorse, discount, guarantee, and negotiate promissory notes, checks, drafts, and other negotiable or non-negotiable paper of the principal, or payable to the principal or the principal's order, receive the cash or other proceeds of those transactions, and accept a draft drawn by a person upon the principal and pay it when due.

(j) Receive for the principal and act upon a sight draft, warehouse receipt, or other negotiable or nonnegotiable instrument.

(k) Apply for and receive letters of credit, credit cards, and traveler's checks from a financial institution, and give an indemnity or other agreement in connection with letters of credit.

(l) Consent to an extension of the time of payment with respect to commercial paper or a financial transaction with a financial institution.

4456. In a statutory form power of attorney, the language granting power with respect to business operating transactions empowers the agent to do all of the following:

(a) Operate, buy, sell, enlarge, reduce, and terminate a business interest.

(b) To the extent that an agent is permitted by law to act for a principal and subject to the terms of the partnership agreement:

(1) Perform a duty or discharge a liability and exercise a right, power, privilege, or option that the principal has, may have, or claims to have, under a partnership agreement, whether or not the principal is a partner.

(2) Enforce the terms of a partnership agreement by litigation or otherwise.

(3) Defend, submit to arbitration, settle, or compromise litigation to which the principal is a party because of membership in the partnership.

(c) Exercise in person or by proxy, or enforce by litigation or otherwise, a right, power, privilege, or option the principal has or claims to have as the holder of a bond, share, or other instrument of similar character, and defend, submit to arbitration, settle, or compromise litigation to which the principal is a party because of a bond, share, or similar instrument.

(d) With respect to a business owned solely by the principal:

(1) Continue, modify, renegotiate, extend, and terminate a contract made with an individual or a legal entity, firm, association, or corporation by or on behalf of the principal with respect to the business before execution of the power of attorney.

(2) Determine the policy of the business as to (A) the location of its operation, (B) the nature and extent of its business, (C) the methods of manufacturing, selling, merchandising, financing, accounting, and advertising employed in its operation, (D) the amount and types of insurance carried, and (E) the mode of engaging, compensating, and dealing with its accountants, attorneys, and other agents and employees.

(3) Change the name or form of organization under which the business is operated and enter into a partnership agreement with other persons or organize a corporation to take over all or part of the operation of the business.

(4) Demand and receive money due or claimed by the principal or on the principal's behalf in the operation of the business, and control and disburse the money in the operation of the business.

(e) Put additional capital into a business in which the principal has an interest.

(f) Join in a plan of reorganization, consolidation, or merger of the business.

(g) Sell or liquidate a business or part of it at the time and upon the terms the agent considers desirable.

(h) Represent the principal in establishing the value of a business under a buy-out agreement to which the principal is a party.

(i) Prepare, sign, file, and deliver reports, compilations of information, returns, or other papers with respect to a business which are required by a governmental agency or instrumentality or which the agent considers desirable, and make related payments.

(j) Pay, compromise, or contest taxes or assessments and do any other act which the agent considers desirable to protect the principal from illegal or unnecessary taxation, fines, penalties, or assessments with respect to a business, including attempts to recover, in any manner permitted by law, money paid before or after the execution of the power of attorney.

4457. In a statutory form power of attorney, the language granting power with respect to insurance and annuity transactions empowers the agent to do all of the following:

(a) Continue, pay the premium or assessment on, modify, rescind, release, or terminate a contract procured by or on behalf of the principal that insures or provides an annuity to either the principal or another person, whether or not the principal is a beneficiary under the contract.

(b) Procure new, different, and additional contracts of insurance and annuities for the principal and the principal's spouse, children, and other dependents, and select the amount, type of insurance or annuity, and mode of payment.

(c) Pay the premium or assessment on, modify, rescind, release, or terminate a contract of insurance or annuity procured by the agent.

(d) Apply for and receive a loan on the security of the contract of insurance or annuity.

(e) Surrender and receive the cash surrender value.

(f) Exercise an election.

(g) Change the manner of paying premiums.

(h) Change or convert the type of insurance contract or annuity as to any insurance contract or annuity with respect to which the principal has or claims to have a power described in this section.

(i) Apply for and procure government aid to guarantee or pay premiums of a contract of insurance on the life of the principal.

(j) Collect, sell, assign, hypothecate, borrow upon, or pledge the interest of the principal in a contract of insurance or annuity.

(k) Pay from proceeds or otherwise, compromise or contest, and apply for refunds in connection with, a tax or assessment levied by a taxing authority with respect to a contract of insurance or annuity or its proceeds or liability accruing by reason of the tax or assessment.

4458. In a statutory form power of attorney, the language granting power with respect to estate, trust, and other beneficiary transactions, empowers the agent to act for the principal in all matters that affect a trust, probate estate, guardianship, conservatorship, escrow, custodianship, or other fund from which the principal is, may become, or claims to be entitled, as a beneficiary, to a share or payment, including the power to do all of the following:

(a) Accept, receive, receipt for, sell, assign, pledge, or exchange, a share in, or payment from, the fund.

(b) Demand or obtain by litigation or otherwise money or other thing of value to which the principal is, may become, or claims to be entitled by reason of the fund.

(c) Initiate, participate in, and oppose litigation to ascertain the meaning, validity, or effect of a deed, will, declaration of trust, or other instrument or transaction affecting the interest of the principal.

(d) Initiate, participate in, and oppose litigation to remove, substitute, or surcharge a fiduciary.

(e) Conserve, invest, disburse, and use anything received for an authorized purpose.

(f) Transfer an interest of the principal in real property, stocks, bonds, accounts with financial institutions, insurance, and other property, to the trustee of a revocable trust created by the principal as settlor.

(g) Disclaim a detrimental transfer to the principal with the approval of the court.

4459. In a statutory form power of attorney, the language with respect to claims and litigation empowers the agent to do all of the following:

(a) Assert and prosecute before a court or administrative agency a claim, claim for relief, cause of action, counterclaim, cross-complaint, or offset, and defend against an individual, a legal entity, or government, including suits to recover property or other thing of value, to recover damages sustained by the principal, to eliminate or modify tax liability, or to seek an injunction, specific performance, or other relief.

(b) Bring an action to determine adverse claims, intervene in litigation, and act as amicus curiae.

(c) In connection with litigation:

(1) Procure an attachment, garnishment, libel, order of arrest, or other preliminary, provisional, or intermediate relief and use any available procedure to effect, enforce, or satisfy a judgment, order, or decree.

(2) Perform any lawful act, including acceptance of tender, offer of judgment, admission of facts, submission of a controversy on an agreed statement of facts, consent to examination before trial, and binding the principal in litigation.

(d) Submit to arbitration, settle, and propose or accept a compromise with respect to a claim or litigation.

(e) Waive the issuance and service of process upon the principal, accept service of process, appear for the principal, designate persons upon whom process directed to the principal may be served, execute and file or deliver stipulations on the principal's behalf, verify pleadings, seek appellate review, procure and give surety and indemnity bonds, contract and pay for the preparation and printing of records and briefs, receive and execute and file or deliver a consent, waiver, release, confession of judgment, satisfaction of judgment, notice, agreement, or other instrument in connection with the prosecution, settlement, or defense of a claim or litigation.

(f) Act for the principal with respect to bankruptcy or insolvency proceedings, whether voluntary or involuntary, concerning the principal or some other person, or with respect to a reorganization proceeding, or with respect to an assignment for the benefit of creditors, receivership, or application for the appointment of a receiver or trustee which affects an interest of the principal in property or other thing of value.

(g) Pay a judgment against the principal or a settlement made in connection with litigation and receive and conserve money or other thing of value paid in settlement of or as proceeds of a claim or litigation.

4460. (a) In a statutory form power of attorney, the language granting power with respect to personal and family maintenance empowers the agent to do all of the following:

(1) Do the acts necessary to maintain the customary standard of living of the principal, the principal's spouse, children, and other individuals customarily or legally entitled to be supported by the principal, including providing living quarters by purchase, lease, or other contract, or paying the operating costs, including interest, amortization payments, repairs, and taxes on premises owned by the principal and occupied by those individuals.

(2) Provide for the individuals described in paragraph (1) all of the following:

(A) Normal domestic help.

(B) Usual vacations and travel expenses.

(C) Funds for shelter, clothing, food, appropriate education, and other current living costs.

(3) Pay for the individuals described in paragraph (1) necessary medical, dental, and surgical care, hospitalization, and custodial care.

(4) Continue any provision made by the principal, for the individuals described in paragraph (1), for automobiles or other means of transportation, including registering, licensing, insuring, and replacing them.

(5) Maintain or open charge accounts for the convenience of the individuals described in paragraph (1) and open new accounts the agent considers desirable to accomplish a lawful purpose.

(6) Continue payments incidental to the membership or affiliation of the principal in a church, club, society, order, or other organization and continue contributions to those organizations.

(b) The authority of an agent with respect to personal and family maintenance under this section is not dependent on any other grant of authority to the agent to make gifts on the principal's behalf and is not limited by any limitation that otherwise applies to the authority of the agent to make gifts on the principal's behalf.

4461. In a statutory form power of attorney, the language granting power with respect to benefits from social security, Medicare, Medicaid, or other governmental programs, or civil or military service, empowers the agent to do all of the following:

(a) Execute vouchers in the name of the principal for allowances and reimbursements payable by the United States or a foreign government or by a state or subdivision of a state to the principal, including allowances and reimbursements for transportation of the individuals described in paragraph (1) of subdivision (a) of Section 4460, and for shipment of their household effects.

(b) Take possession and order the removal and shipment of property of the principal from a post, warehouse, depot, dock, or other place of storage or safekeeping, either governmental or private, and execute and deliver a release, voucher, receipt, bill of lading, shipping ticket, certificate, or other instrument for that purpose.

(c) Prepare, file, and prosecute a claim of the principal to a benefit or assistance, financial or otherwise, to which the principal claims to be entitled, under a statute or governmental regulation.

(d) Prosecute, defend, submit to arbitration, settle, and propose or accept a compromise with respect to any benefits the principal may be entitled to receive.

(e) Receive the financial proceeds of a claim of the type described in this section, conserve, invest, disburse, or use anything received for a lawful purpose.

4462. In a statutory form power of attorney, the language granting power with respect to retirement plan transactions empowers the agent to do all of the following:

(a) Select payment options under any retirement plan in which the principal participates, including plans for self-employed individuals.

(b) Make voluntary contributions to those plans.

(c) Exercise the investment powers available under any self-directed retirement plan.

(d) Make rollovers of plan benefits into other retirement plans.

(e) If authorized by the plan, borrow from, sell assets to, and purchase assets from the plan.

(f) Waive the right of the principal to be a beneficiary of a joint or survivor annuity if the principal is a spouse who is not employed.

4463. In a statutory form power of attorney, the language granting power with respect to tax matters empowers the agent to do all of the following:

(a) Prepare, sign, and file federal, state, local, and foreign income, gift, payroll, Federal Insurance Contributions Act returns, and other tax returns, claims for refunds, requests for extension of time, petitions regarding tax matters, and any other tax-related documents, including receipts, offers, waivers, consents (including consents and agreements under Internal Revenue Code Section 2032A or any successor section), closing agreements, and any power of attorney required by the Internal Revenue Service or other taxing authority with respect to a tax year upon which the statute of limitations has not run and to the tax year in which the power of attorney was executed and any subsequent tax year.

(b) Pay taxes due, collect refunds, post bonds, receive confidential information, and contest deficiencies determined by the Internal Revenue Service or other taxing authority.

(c) Exercise any election available to the principal under federal, state, local, or foreign tax law.

(d) Act for the principal in all tax matters for all periods before the Internal Revenue Service and any other taxing authority.

4464. The powers described in this chapter are exercisable equally with respect to an interest the principal has when the statutory form power of attorney is executed or acquires later, whether or not the property is located in this state, and whether or not the powers are exercised or the power of attorney is executed in this state.

4465. A statutory form power of attorney under this part does not empower the agent to take any of the actions specified in Section 4264 unless the statutory form power of attorney expressly grants that authority to the attorney-in-fact.

Part 4. Judicial Proceedings Concerning Powers Of Attorney

Chapter 1. General Provisions

4500. A power of attorney is exercisable free of judicial intervention, subject to this part.

4501. The remedies provided in this part are cumulative and not exclusive of any other remedies provided by law.

4502. Except as provided in Section 4503, this part is not subject to limitation in the power of attorney.

4503. (a) Subject to subdivision (b), a power of attorney may expressly eliminate the authority of a person listed in Section 4540 to petition the court for any one or more of the purposes enumerated in Section 4541 if both of the following requirements are satisfied:

(1) The power of attorney is executed by the principal at a time when the principal has the advice of a lawyer authorized to practice law in the state where the power of attorney is executed.

(2) The principal's lawyer signs a certificate stating in substance:

"I am a lawyer authorized to practice law in the state where this power of attorney was executed, and the principal was my client at the time this power of attorney was executed. I have advised my client concerning his or her rights in connection with this power of attorney and the applicable law and the consequences of signing or not signing this power of attorney, and my client, after being so advised, has executed this power of attorney."

(b) A power of attorney may not limit the authority of the attorney-in-fact, the principal, the conservator of the person or estate of the principal, or the public guardian to petition under this part.

4504. There is no right to a jury trial in proceedings under this division.

4505. Except as otherwise provided in this division, the general provisions in Division 3 (commencing with Section 1000) apply to proceedings under this division.

Chapter 2. Jurisdiction And Venue

4520. (a) The superior court has jurisdiction in proceedings under this division.

(b) The court in proceedings under this division is a court of general jurisdiction and the court, or a judge of the court, has the same power and authority with respect to the proceedings as otherwise provided by law for a superior court, or a judge of the superior court, including, but not limited to, the matters authorized by Section 128 of the Code of Civil Procedure.

4521. The court may exercise jurisdiction in proceedings under this division on any basis permitted by Section 410.10 of the Code of Civil Procedure.

4522. Without limiting Section 4521, a person who acts as an attorney-in-fact under a power of attorney governed by this division is subject to personal jurisdiction in this state with respect to matters relating to acts and transactions of the attorney-in-fact performed in this state or affecting property or a principal in this state.

4523. The proper county for commencement of a proceeding under this division shall be determined in the following order of priority:

(a) The county in which the principal resides.

(b) The county in which the attorney-in-fact resides.

(c) A county in which property subject to the power of attorney is located.

(d) Any other county that is in the principal's best interest.

Chapter 3. Petitions, Orders, Appeals

4540. Subject to Section 4503, a petition may be filed under this part by any of the following persons:

(a) The attorney-in-fact.

(b) The principal.

(c) The spouse of the principal.

(d) A relative of the principal.

(e) The conservator of the person or estate of the principal.

(f) The court investigator, described in Section 1454, of the county where the power of attorney was executed or where the principal resides.

(g) The public guardian of the county where the power of attorney was executed or where the principal resides.

(h) The personal representative or trustee of the principal's estate.

(i) The principal's successor in interest.

(j) A person who is requested in writing by an attorney-in-fact to take action.

(k) Any other interested person or friend of the principal.

4541. A petition may be filed under this part for any one or more of the following purposes:

(a) Determining whether the power of attorney is in effect or has terminated.

(b) Passing on the acts or proposed acts of the attorney-in-fact, including approval of authority to disobey the principal's instructions pursuant to subdivision (b) of Section 4234.

(c) Compelling the attorney-in-fact to submit the attorney-in-fact' s accounts or report the attorney-in-fact's acts as attorney-in-fact to the principal, the spouse of the principal, the conservator of the person or the estate of the principal, or to any other person required by the court in its discretion, if the attorney-in-fact has failed to submit an accounting or report within 60 days after written request from the person filing the petition.

(d) Declaring that the authority of the attorney-in-fact is revoked on a determination by the court of all of the following:

(1) The attorney-in-fact has violated or is unfit to perform the fiduciary duties under the power of attorney.

(2) At the time of the determination by the court, the principal lacks the capacity to give or to revoke a power of attorney.

(3) The revocation of the attorney-in-fact's authority is in the best interest of the principal or the principal's estate.

(e) Approving the resignation of the attorney-in-fact:

(1) If the attorney-in-fact is subject to a duty to act under Section 4230, the court may approve the resignation, subject to any orders the court determines are necessary to protect the principal's interests.

(2) If the attorney-in-fact is not subject to a duty to act under Section 4230, the court shall approve the resignation, subject to the court's discretion to require the attorney-in-fact to give notice to other interested persons.

(f) Compelling a third person to honor the authority of an attorney-in-fact.

4542. A proceeding under this part is commenced by filing a petition stating facts showing that the petition is authorized under this part, the grounds of the petition, and, if known to the petitioner, the terms of the power of attorney.

4543. The court may dismiss a petition if it appears that the proceeding is not reasonably necessary for the protection of the interests of the principal or the principal's estate and shall stay or dismiss the proceeding in whole or in part when required by Section 410.30 of the Code of Civil Procedure.

4544. (a) Subject to subdivision (b), at least 15 days before the time set for hearing, the petitioner shall serve notice of the time and place of the hearing, together with a copy of the petition, on the following:

(1) The attorney-in-fact if not the petitioner.

(2) The principal if not the petitioner.

(b) In the case of a petition to compel a third person to honor the authority of an attorney-in-fact, notice of the time and place of the hearing, together with a copy of the petition, shall be served on the third person in the manner provided in Chapter 4 (commencing with Section 413.10) of Title 5 of Part 2 of the Code of Civil Procedure.

4545. In a proceeding under this part commenced by the filing of a petition by a person other than the attorney-in-fact, the court may in its discretion award reasonable attorney's fees to one of the following:

(a) The attorney-in-fact, if the court determines that the proceeding was commenced without any reasonable cause.

(b) The person commencing the proceeding, if the court determines that the attorney-in-fact has clearly violated the fiduciary duties under the power of attorney or has failed without any reasonable cause or justification to submit accounts or report acts to the principal or conservator of the estate or of the person, as the case may be, after written request from the principal or conservator.

Division 4.7. Health Care Decisions

Part 1. Definitions And General

Chapter 1. Short Title And Definitions

4600. This division may be cited as the Health Care Decisions Law.

4603. Unless the provision or context otherwise requires, the definitions in this chapter govern the construction of this division.

4605. "Advance health care directive" or "advance directive" means either an individual health care instruction or a power of attorney for health care.

4607. (a) "Agent" means an individual designated in a power of attorney for health care to make a health care decision for the principal, regardless of whether the person is known as an agent or attorney-in-fact, or by some other term.

(b) "Agent" includes a successor or alternate agent.

4609. "Capacity" means a person's ability to understand the nature and consequences of a decision and to make and communicate a decision, and includes in the case of proposed health care, the ability to understand its significant benefits, risks, and alternatives.

4611. "Community care facility" means a "community care facility" as defined in Section 1502 of the Health and Safety Code.

4613. "Conservator" means a court-appointed conservator having authority to make a health care decision for a patient.

4615. "Health care" means any care, treatment, service, or procedure to maintain, diagnose, or otherwise affect a patient's physical or mental condition.

4617. "Health care decision" means a decision made by a patient or the patient's agent, conservator, or surrogate, regarding the patient' s health care, including the following:

(a) Selection and discharge of health care providers and institutions.

(b) Approval or disapproval of diagnostic tests, surgical procedures, and programs of medication.

(c) Directions to provide, withhold, or withdraw artificial nutrition and hydration and all other forms of health care, including cardiopulmonary resuscitation.

4619. "Health care institution" means an institution, facility, or agency licensed, certified, or otherwise authorized or permitted by law to provide health care in the ordinary course of business.

4621. "Health care provider" means an individual licensed, certified, or otherwise authorized or permitted by the law of this state to provide health care in the ordinary course of business or practice of a profession.

4623. "Individual health care instruction" or "individual instruction" means a patient's written or oral direction concerning a health care decision for the patient.

4625. "Patient" means an adult whose health care is under consideration, and includes a principal under a power of attorney for health care and an adult who has given an individual health care instruction or designated a surrogate.

4627. "Physician" means a physician and surgeon licensed by the Medical Board of California or the Osteopathic Medical Board of California.

4629. "Power of attorney for health care" means a written instrument designating an agent to make health care decisions for the principal.

4631. "Primary physician" means a physician designated by a patient or the patient's agent, conservator, or surrogate, to have primary responsibility for the patient's health care or, in the absence of a designation or if the designated physician is not reasonably available or declines to act as primary physician, a physician who undertakes the responsibility.

4633. "Principal" means an adult who executes a power of attorney for health care.

4635. "Reasonably available" means readily able to be contacted without undue effort and willing and able to act in a timely manner considering the urgency of the patient's health care needs.

4637. "Residential care facility for the elderly" means a "residential care facility for the elderly" as defined in Section 1569.2 of the Health and Safety Code.

4639. "Skilled nursing facility" means a "skilled nursing facility" as defined in Section 1250 of the Health and Safety Code.

4641. "Supervising health care provider" means the primary physician or, if there is no primary physician or the primary physician is not reasonably available, the health care provider who has undertaken primary responsibility for a patient's health care.

4643. "Surrogate" means an adult, other than a patient's agent or conservator, authorized under this division to make a health care decision for the patient.

Chapter 2. General Provisions

4650. The Legislature finds the following:

(a) In recognition of the dignity and privacy a person has a right to expect, the law recognizes that an adult has the fundamental right to control the decisions relating to his or her own health care, including the decision to have life-sustaining treatment withheld or withdrawn.

(b) Modern medical technology has made possible the artificial prolongation of human life beyond natural limits. In the interest of protecting individual autonomy, this prolongation of the process of dying for a person for whom continued health care does not improve the prognosis for recovery may violate patient dignity and cause unnecessary pain and suffering, while providing nothing medically necessary or beneficial to the person.

(c) In the absence of controversy, a court is normally not the proper forum in which to make health care decisions, including decisions regarding life-sustaining treatment.

4651. (a) Except as otherwise provided, this division applies to health care decisions for adults who lack capacity to make health care decisions for themselves.

(b) This division does not affect any of the following:

(1) The right of an individual to make health care decisions while having the capacity to do so.

(2) The law governing health care in an emergency.

(3) The law governing health care for unemancipated minors.

4652. This division does not authorize consent to any of the following on behalf of a patient:

(a) Commitment to or placement in a mental health treatment facility.

(b) Convulsive treatment (as defined in Section 5325 of the Welfare and Institutions Code).

(c) Psychosurgery (as defined in Section 5325 of the Welfare and Institutions Code).

(d) Sterilization.

(e) Abortion.

4653. Nothing in this division shall be construed to condone, authorize, or approve mercy killing, assisted suicide, or euthanasia. This division is not intended to permit any affirmative or deliberate act or omission to end life other than withholding or withdrawing health care pursuant to an advance health care directive, by a surrogate, or as otherwise provided, so as to permit the natural process of dying.

4654. This division does not authorize or require a health care provider or health care institution to provide health care contrary to generally accepted health care standards applicable to the health care provider or health care institution.

4655. (a) This division does not create a presumption concerning the intention of a patient who has not made or who has revoked an advance health care directive.

(b) In making health care decisions under this division, a patient's attempted suicide shall not be construed to indicate a desire of the patient that health care be restricted or inhibited.

4656. Death resulting from withholding or withdrawing health care in accordance with this division does not for any purpose constitute a suicide or homicide or legally impair or invalidate a policy of insurance or an annuity providing a death benefit, notwithstanding any term of the policy or annuity to the contrary.

4657. A patient is presumed to have the capacity to make a health care decision, to give or revoke an advance health care directive, and to designate or disqualify a surrogate. This presumption is a presumption affecting the burden of proof.

4658. Unless otherwise specified in a written advance health care directive, for the purposes of this division, a determination that a patient lacks or has recovered capacity, or that another condition exists that affects an individual health care instruction or the authority of an agent or surrogate, shall be made by the primary physician.

4659. (a) Except as provided in subdivision (b), none of the following persons may make health care decisions as an agent under a power of attorney for health care or a surrogate under this division:

(1) The supervising health care provider or an employee of the health care institution where the patient is receiving care.

(2) An operator or employee of a community care facility or residential care facility where the patient is receiving care.

(b) The prohibition in subdivision (a) does not apply to the following persons:

(1) An employee, other than the supervising health care provider, who is related to the patient by blood, marriage, or adoption, or is a registered domestic partner of the patient.

(2) An employee, other than the supervising health care provider, who is employed by the same health care institution, community care facility, or residential care facility for the elderly as the patient.

(c) A conservator under the Lanterman-Petris-Short Act (Part 1 (commencing with Section 5000) of Division 5 of the Welfare and Institutions Code) may not be designated as an agent or surrogate to make health care decisions by the conservatee, unless all of the following are satisfied:

(1) The advance health care directive is otherwise valid.

(2) The conservatee is represented by legal counsel.

(3) The lawyer representing the conservatee signs a certificate stating in substance:

"I am a lawyer authorized to practice law in the state where this advance health care directive was executed, and the principal or patient was my client at the time this advance directive was executed. I have advised my client concerning his or her rights in connection with this advance directive and the applicable law and the consequences of signing or not signing this advance directive, and my client, after being so advised, has executed this advance directive."

4660. A copy of a written advance health care directive, revocation of an advance directive, or designation or disqualification of a surrogate has the same effect as the original.

Chapter 3. Transitional Provisions

4665. Except as otherwise provided by statute:

(a) On and after July 1, 2000, this division applies to all advance health care directives, including, but not limited to, durable powers of attorney for health care and declarations under the Natural Death Act (former Chapter 3.9 (commencing with Section 7185) of Part 1 of Division 7 of the Health and Safety Code), regardless of whether they were given or executed before, on, or after July 1, 2000.

(b) This division applies to all proceedings concerning advance health care directives commenced on or after July 1, 2000.

(c) This division applies to all proceedings concerning written advance health care directives commenced before July 1, 2000, unless the court determines that application of a particular provision of this division would substantially interfere with the effective conduct of the proceedings or the rights of the parties and other interested persons, in which case the particular provision of this division does not apply and prior law applies.

(d) Nothing in this division affects the validity of an advance health care directive executed before July 1, 2000, that was valid under prior law.

(e) Nothing in this division affects the validity of a durable power of attorney for health care executed on a printed form that was valid under prior law, regardless of whether execution occurred before, on, or after July 1, 2000.

Part 2. Uniform Health Care Decisions Act

Chapter 1. Advance Health Care Directives

Article 1. General Provisions

4670. An adult having capacity may give an individual health care instruction. The individual instruction may be oral or written. The individual instruction may be limited to take effect only if a specified condition arises.

4671. (a) An adult having capacity may execute a power of attorney for health care, as provided in Article 2 (commencing with Section 4680). The power of attorney for health care may authorize the agent to make health care decisions and may also include individual health care instructions.

(b) The principal in a power of attorney for health care may grant authority to make decisions relating to the personal care of the principal, including, but not limited to, de-

termining where the principal will live, providing meals, hiring household employees, providing transportation, handling mail, and arranging recreation and entertainment.

4672. (a) A written advance health care directive may include the individual's nomination of a conservator of the person or estate or both, or a guardian of the person or estate or both, for consideration by the court if protective proceedings for the individual's person or estate are thereafter commenced.

(b) If the protective proceedings are conservatorship proceedings in this state, the nomination has the effect provided in Section 1810 and the court shall give effect to the most recent writing executed in accordance with Section 1810, whether or not the writing is a written advance health care directive.

4673. (a) A written advance health care directive is legally sufficient if all of the following requirements are satisfied:

(1) The advance directive contains the date of its execution.

(2) The advance directive is signed either by the patient or in the patient's name by another adult in the patient's presence and at the patient's direction.

(3) The advance directive is either acknowledged before a notary public or signed by at least two witnesses who satisfy the requirements of Sections 4674 and 4675.

(b) An electronic advance health care directive or power of attorney for health care is legally sufficient if the requirements in subdivision (a) are satisfied, except that for the purposes of paragraph (3) of subdivision (a), an acknowledgment before a notary public shall be required, and if a digital signature is used, it meets all of the following requirements:

(1) The digital signature either meets the requirements of Section 16.5 of the Government Code and Chapter 10 (commencing with Section 22000) of Division 7 of Title 2 of the California Code of Regulations or the digital signature uses an algorithm approved by the National Institute of Standards and Technology.

(2) The digital signature is unique to the person using it.

(3) The digital signature is capable of verification.

(4) The digital signature is under the sole control of the person using it.

(5) The digital signature is linked to data in such a manner that if the data are changed, the digital signature is invalidated.

(6) The digital signature persists with the document and not by association in separate files.

(7) The digital signature is bound to a digital certificate.

4674. If the written advance health care directive is signed by witnesses, as provided in Section 4673, the following requirements shall be satisfied:

(a) The witnesses shall be adults.

(b) Each witness signing the advance directive shall witness either the signing of the advance directive by the patient or the patient's acknowledgment of the signature or the advance directive.

(c) None of the following persons may act as a witness:

(1) The patient's health care provider or an employee of the patient's health care provider.

(2) The operator or an employee of a community care facility.

(3) The operator or an employee of a residential care facility for the elderly.

(4) The agent, where the advance directive is a power of attorney for health care.

(d) Each witness shall make the following declaration in substance:

"I declare under penalty of perjury under the laws of California (1) that the individual who signed or acknowledged this advance health care directive is personally known to me, or that the individual's identity was proven to me by convincing evidence, (2) that the individual signed or acknowledged this advance directive in my presence, (3) that the individual appears to be of sound mind and under no duress, fraud, or undue influence, (4) that I am not a person appointed as agent by this advance directive, and (5) that I am not the individual's health care provider, an employee of the individual's health care provider, the operator of a community care facility, an employee of an operator of a community care facility, the operator of a residential care facility for the elderly, nor an employee of an operator of a residential care facility for the elderly."

(e) At least one of the witnesses shall be an individual who is neither related to the patient by blood, marriage, or adoption, nor entitled to any portion of the patient's estate upon the patient's death under a will existing when the advance directive is executed or by operation of law then existing.

(f) The witness satisfying the requirement of subdivision (e) shall also sign the following declaration in substance:

"I further declare under penalty of perjury under the laws of California that I am not related to the individual executing this advance health care directive by blood, marriage, or adoption, and, to the best of my knowledge, I am not entitled to any part of the individual's estate upon his or her death under a will now existing or by operation of law."

(g) The provisions of this section applicable to witnesses do not apply to a notary public before whom an advance health care directive is acknowledged.

4675. (a) If an individual is a patient in a skilled nursing facility when a written advance health care directive is executed, the advance directive is not effective unless a patient advocate or ombudsman, as may be designated by the Department of Aging for this purpose pursuant to any other applicable provision of law, signs the advance directive as a witness, either as one of two witnesses or in addition to notarization. The patient advocate or ombudsman shall declare that he or she is serving as a witness as required by this subdivision. It is the intent of this subdivision to recognize that some patients in skilled nursing facilities are insulated from a voluntary decisionmaking role, by virtue of the custodial nature of their care, so as to require special assurance that they are capable of willfully and voluntarily executing an advance directive.

(b) A witness who is a patient advocate or ombudsman may rely on the representations of the administrators or staff of the skilled nursing facility, or of family members, as convincing evidence of the identity of the patient if the patient advocate or ombudsman believes that the representations provide a reasonable basis for determining the identity of the patient.

4676. (a) A written advance health care directive or similar instrument executed in another state or jurisdiction in compliance with the laws of that state or jurisdiction or of this state, is valid and enforceable in this state to the same extent as a written advance directive validly executed in this state.

(b) In the absence of knowledge to the contrary, a physician or other health care provider may presume that a written advance health care directive or similar instrument, whether executed in another state or jurisdiction or in this state, is valid.

4677. A health care provider, health care service plan, health care institution, disability insurer, self-insured employee welfare plan, or nonprofit hospital plan or a similar insurance plan may not require or prohibit the execution or revocation of an advance health care directive as a condition for providing health care, admission to a facility, or furnishing insurance.

4678. Unless otherwise specified in an advance health care directive, a person then authorized to make health care decisions for a patient has the same rights as the patient to request, receive, examine, copy, and consent to the disclosure of medical or any other health care information.

Article 2. Powers Of Attorney For Health Care

4680. A power of attorney for health care is legally sufficient if it satisfies the requirements of Section 4673.

4681. (a) Except as provided in subdivision (b), the principal may limit the application of any provision of this division by an express statement in the power of attorney for health care or by providing an inconsistent rule in the power of attorney.

(b) A power of attorney for health care may not limit either the application of a statute specifically providing that it is not subject to limitation in the power of attorney or a statute concerning any of the following:

(1) Statements required to be included in a power of attorney.

(2) Operative dates of statutory enactments or amendments.

(3) Formalities for execution of a power of attorney for health care.

(4) Qualifications of witnesses.

(5) Qualifications of agents.

(6) Protection of third persons from liability.

4682. Unless otherwise provided in a power of attorney for health care, the authority of an agent becomes effective only on a determination that the principal lacks capacity, and ceases to be effective on a determination that the principal has recovered capacity.

4683. Subject to any limitations in the power of attorney for health care:

(a) An agent designated in the power of attorney may make health care decisions for the principal to the same extent the principal could make health care decisions if the principal had the capacity to do so.

(b) The agent may also make decisions that may be effective after the principal's death, including the following:

(1) Making a disposition under the Uniform Anatomical Gift Act (Chapter 3.5 (commencing with Section 7150) of Part 1 of Division 7 of the Health and Safety Code).

(2) Authorizing an autopsy under Section 7113 of the Health and Safety Code.

(3) Directing the disposition of remains under Section 7100 of the Health and Safety Code.

(4) Authorizing the release of the records of the principal to the extent necessary for the agent to fulfill his or her duties as set forth in this division.

4684. An agent shall make a health care decision in accordance with the principal's individual health care instructions, if any, and other wishes to the extent known to the agent. Otherwise, the agent shall make the decision in accordance with the agent's determination of the principal's best interest. In determining the principal's best interest, the agent shall consider the principal's personal values to the extent known to the agent.

4685. Unless the power of attorney for health care provides otherwise, the agent designated in the power of attorney who is known to the health care provider to be reasonably available and willing to make health care decisions has priority over any other person in making health care decisions for the principal.

4686. Unless the power of attorney for health care provides a time of termination, the authority of the agent is exercisable notwithstanding any lapse of time since execu-

tion of the power of attorney.

4687. Nothing in this division affects any right the person designated as an agent under a power of attorney for health care may have, apart from the power of attorney, to make or participate in making health care decisions for the principal.

4688. Where this division does not provide a rule governing agents under powers of attorney, the law of agency applies.

4689. Nothing in this division authorizes an agent under a power of attorney for health care to make a health care decision if the principal objects to the decision. If the principal objects to the health care decision of the agent under a power of attorney, the matter shall be governed by the law that would apply if there were no power of attorney for health care.

4690. (a) If the principal becomes wholly or partially incapacitated, or if there is a question concerning the capacity of the principal, the agent may consult with a person previously designated by the principal for this purpose, and may also consult with and obtain information needed to carry out the agent's duties from the principal's spouse, physician, supervising health care provider, attorney, a member of the principal's family, or other person, including a business entity or government agency, with respect to matters covered by the power of attorney for health care.

(b) A person described in subdivision (a) from whom information is requested shall disclose information that the agent requires to carry out his or her duties. Disclosure under this section is not a waiver of any privilege that may apply to the information disclosed.

Article 3. Revocation Of Advance Directives

4695. (a) A patient having capacity may revoke the designation of an agent only by a signed writing or by personally informing the supervising health care provider.

(b) A patient having capacity may revoke all or part of an advance health care directive, other than the designation of an agent, at any time and in any manner that communicates an intent to revoke.

4696. A health care provider, agent, conservator, or surrogate who is informed of a revocation of an advance health care directive shall promptly communicate the fact of the revocation to the supervising health care provider and to any health care institution where the patient is receiving care.

4697. (a) If after executing a power of attorney for health care the principal's marriage to the agent is dissolved or annulled, the principal's designation of the former spouse as an agent to make health care decisions for the principal is revoked.

(b) If the agent's authority is revoked solely by subdivision (a), it is revived by the principal's remarriage to the agent.

4698. An advance health care directive that conflicts with an earlier advance directive revokes the earlier advance directive to the extent of the conflict.

Chapter 2. Advance Health Care Directive Forms

4700. The form provided in Section 4701 may, but need not, be used to create an advance health care directive. The other sections of this division govern the effect of the form or any other writing used to create an advance health care directive. An individual may complete or modify all or any part of the form in Section 4701.

4701. The statutory advance health care directive form is as follows:

PLEASE SEE THE APPENDIX

Chapter 3. Health Care Surrogates

4711. (a) A patient may designate an adult as a surrogate to make health care decisions by personally informing the supervising health care provider. The designation of a surrogate shall be promptly recorded in the patient's health care record.

(b) Unless the patient specifies a shorter period, a surrogate designation under subdivision (a) is effective only during the course of treatment or illness or during the stay in the health care institution when the surrogate designation is made, or for 60 days, whichever period is shorter.

(c) The expiration of a surrogate designation under subdivision (b) does not affect any role the person designated under subdivision (a) may have in making health care decisions for the patient under any other law or standards of practice.

(d) If the patient has designated an agent under a power of attorney for health care, the surrogate designated under subdivision (a) has priority over the agent for the period provided in subdivision (b), but the designation of a surrogate does not revoke the designation of an agent unless the patient communicates the intention to revoke in compliance with subdivision (a) of Section 4695.

4714. A surrogate, including a person acting as a surrogate, shall make a health care decision in accordance with the patient's individual health care instructions, if any, and other wishes to the extent known to the surrogate. Otherwise, the surrogate shall make the decision in accordance with the surrogate's determination of the patient's best interest. In determining the patient's best interest, the surrogate shall consider the patient's personal values to the extent known to the surrogate.

4715. A patient having capacity at any time may disqualify another person, including a member of the patient's family, from acting as the patient's surrogate by a signed writing or by personally informing the supervising health care provider of the disqualification.

4716. (a) If a patient lacks the capacity to make a health care decision, the patient's domestic partner shall have the same authority as a spouse has to make a health care decision for his or her incapacitated spouse. This section may not be construed to expand or restrict the ability of a spouse to make a health care decision for an incapacitated spouse.

(b) For the purposes of this section, the following definitions shall apply:

(1) "Capacity" has the same meaning as defined in Section 4609.

(2) "Health care" has the same meaning as defined in Section 4615.

(3) "Health care decision" has the same meaning as defined in Section 4617.

(4) "Domestic partner" has the same meaning as that term is used in Section 297 of the Family Code.

4717. (a) Notwithstanding any other provision of law, within 24 hours of the arrival in the emergency department of a general acute care hospital of a patient who is unconscious or otherwise incapable of communication, the hospital shall make reasonable efforts to contact the patient's agent, surrogate, or a family member or other person the hospital reasonably believes has the authority to make health care decisions on behalf of the patient. A hospital shall be deemed to have made reasonable efforts, and to have discharged its duty under this section, if it does all of the following:

(1) Examines the personal effects, if any, accompanying the patient and any medical records regarding the patient in its possession, and reviews any verbal or written report made by emergency medical technicians or the police, to identify the name of any agent, surrogate, or a family member or other person the hospital reasonably believes has the authority to make health care decisions on behalf of the patient.

(2) Contacts or attempts to contact any agent, surrogate, or a family member or other person the hospital reasonably believes has the authority to make health care decisions on behalf of the patient, as identified in paragraph (1).

(3) Contacts the Secretary of State directly or indirectly, including by voice mail or facsimile, to inquire whether the patient has registered an advance health care directive with the Advance Health Care Directive Registry, if the hospital finds evidence of the patient's Advance Health Care Directive Registry identification card either from the patient or from the patient's family or authorized agent.

(b) The hospital shall document in the patient's medical record all efforts made to contact any agent, surrogate, or a family member or other person the hospital reasonably believes has the authority to make health care decisions on behalf of the patient.

(c) Application of this section shall be suspended during any period in which the hospital implements its disaster and mass casualty program, or its fire and internal disaster program.

Chapter 4. Duties Of Health Care Providers

4730. Before implementing a health care decision made for a patient, a supervising health care provider, if possible, shall promptly communicate to the patient the decision made and the identity of the person making the decision.

4731. (a) A supervising health care provider who knows of the existence of an advance health care directive, a revocation of an advance health care directive, or a designation or disqualification of a surrogate, shall promptly record its existence in the patient's health care record and, if it is in writing, shall request a copy. If a copy is furnished, the supervising health care provider shall arrange for its maintenance in the patient's health care record.

(b) A supervising health care provider who knows of a revocation of a power of attorney for health care or a disqualification of a surrogate shall make a reasonable effort to notify the agent or surrogate of the revocation or disqualification.

4732. A primary physician who makes or is informed of a determination that a patient lacks or has recovered capacity, or that another condition exists affecting an individual health care instruction or the authority of an agent, conservator of the person, or surrogate, shall promptly record the determination in the patient' s health care record and communicate the determination to the patient, if possible, and to a person then authorized to make health care decisions for the patient.

4733. Except as provided in Sections 4734 and 4735, a health care provider or health care institution providing care to a patient shall do the following:

(a) Comply with an individual health care instruction of the patient and with a reasonable interpretation of that instruction made by a person then authorized to make health care decisions for the patient.

(b) Comply with a health care decision for the patient made by a person then authorized to make health care decisions for the patient to the same extent as if the decision had been made by the patient while having capacity.

4734. (a) A health care provider may decline to comply with an individual health care instruction or health care decision for reasons of conscience.

(b) A health care institution may decline to comply with an individual health care instruction or health care decision if the instruction or decision is contrary to a policy of the institution that is expressly based on reasons of conscience and if the policy was timely communicated to the patient or to a person then authorized to make health care decisions for the patient.

4735. A health care provider or health care institution may decline to comply with an individual health care instruction or health care decision that requires medically ineffective health care or health care contrary to generally accepted health care standards applicable to the health care provider or institution.

4736. A health care provider or health care institution that declines to comply with an individual health care instruction or health care decision shall do all of the following:

(a) Promptly so inform the patient, if possible, and any person then authorized to make health care decisions for the patient.

(b) Unless the patient or person then authorized to make health care decisions for the patient refuses assistance, immediately make all reasonable efforts to assist in the transfer of the patient to another health care provider or institution that is willing to comply with the instruction or decision.

(c) Provide continuing care to the patient until a transfer can be accomplished or until it appears that a transfer cannot be accomplished. In all cases, appropriate pain relief and other palliative care shall be continued.

Chapter 5. Immunities And Liabilities

4740. A health care provider or health care institution acting in good faith and in accordance with generally accepted health care standards applicable to the health care provider or institution is not subject to civil or criminal liability or to discipline for unprofessional conduct for any actions in compliance with this division, including, but not limited to, any of the following conduct:

(a) Complying with a health care decision of a person that the health care provider or health care institution believes in good faith has the authority to make a health care decision for a patient, including a decision to withhold or withdraw health care.

(b) Declining to comply with a health care decision of a person based on a belief that the person then lacked authority.

(c) Complying with an advance health care directive and assuming that the directive was valid when made and has not been revoked or terminated.

(d) Declining to comply with an individual health care instruction or health care decision, in accordance with Sections 4734 to 4736, inclusive.

4741. A person acting as agent or surrogate under this part is not subject to civil or criminal liability or to discipline for unprofessional conduct for health care decisions made in good faith.

4742. (a) A health care provider or health care institution that intentionally violates this part is subject to liability to the aggrieved individual for damages of two thousand five hundred dollars ($2,500) or actual damages resulting from the violation, whichever is greater, plus reasonable attorney's fees.

(b) A person who intentionally falsifies, forges, conceals, defaces, or obliterates an individual's advance health care directive or a revocation of an advance health care directive without the individual's consent, or who coerces or fraudulently induces an individual to give, revoke, or not to give an advance health care directive, is subject to liability to that individual for damages of ten thousand dollars ($10,000) or actual damages resulting from the action, whichever is greater, plus reasonable attorney's fees.

(c) The damages provided in this section are cumulative and not exclusive of any other remedies provided by law.

4743. Any person who alters or forges a written advance health care directive of another, or willfully conceals or withholds personal knowledge of a revocation of an advance directive, with the intent to cause a withholding or withdrawal of health care necessary to keep the patient alive contrary to the desires of the patient, and thereby directly causes health care necessary to keep the patient alive to be withheld or withdrawn and the death of the patient thereby to be hastened, is subject to prosecution for unlawful homicide as provided in Chapter 1 (commencing with Section 187) of Title 8 of Part 1 of the Penal Code.

Part 3. Judicial Proceedings

Chapter 1. General Provisions

4750. Subject to this division:

(a) An advance health care directive is effective and exercisable free of judicial intervention.

(b) A health care decision made by an agent for a principal is effective without judicial approval.

(c) A health care decision made by a surrogate for a patient is effective without judicial approval.

4751. The remedies provided in this part are cumulative and not exclusive of any other remedies provided by law.

4752. Except as provided in Section 4753, this part is not subject to limitation in an advance health care directive.

4753. (a) Subject to subdivision (b), an advance health care directive may expressly eliminate the authority of a person listed in Section 4765 to petition the court for any one or more of the purposes enumerated in Section 4766, if both of the following requirements are satisfied:

(1) The advance directive is executed by an individual having the advice of a lawyer authorized to practice law in the state where the advance directive is executed.

(2) The individual's lawyer signs a certificate stating in substance:

"I am a lawyer authorized to practice law in the state where this advance health care directive was executed, and _____ [insert name] was my client at the time this advance directive was executed. I have advised my client concerning his or her rights in connection with this advance directive and the applicable law and the consequences of signing or not signing this advance directive, and my client, after being so advised, has executed this advance directive."

(b) An advance health care directive may not limit the authority of the following persons to petition under this part:

(1) The conservator of the person, with respect to a petition relating to an advance directive, for a purpose specified in subdivision (b) or (d) of Section 4766.

(2) The agent, with respect to a petition relating to a power of attorney for health care, for a purpose specified in subdivision (b) or (c) of Section 4766.

4754. There is no right to a jury trial in proceedings under this division.

4755. Except as otherwise provided in this division, the general provisions in Division 3 (commencing with Section 1000) apply to proceedings under this division.

Chapter 2. Jurisdiction And Venue

4760. (a) The superior court has jurisdiction in proceedings under this division.

(b) The court in proceedings under this division is a court of general jurisdiction and the court, or a judge of the court, has the same power and authority with respect to the proceedings as otherwise provided by law for a superior court, or a judge of the superior court, including, but not limited to, the matters authorized by Section 128 of the Code of Civil Procedure.

4761. The court may exercise jurisdiction in proceedings under this division on any basis permitted by Section 410.10 of the Code of Civil Procedure.

4762. Without limiting Section 4761, a person who acts as an agent under a power of attorney for health care or as a surrogate under this division is subject to personal jurisdiction in this state with respect to matters relating to acts and transactions of the agent or surrogate performed in this state or affecting a patient in this state.

4763. The proper county for commencement of a proceeding under this division shall be determined in the following order of priority:

(a) The county in which the patient resides.

(b) The county in which the agent or surrogate resides.

(c) Any other county that is in the patient's best interest.

Chapter 3. Petitions And Orders

4765. Subject to Section 4753, a petition may be filed under this part by any of the following persons:

(a) The patient.

(b) The patient's spouse, unless legally separated.

(c) A relative of the patient.

(d) The patient's agent or surrogate.

(e) The conservator of the person of the patient.

(f) The court investigator, described in Section 1454, of the county where the patient resides.

(g) The public guardian of the county where the patient resides.

(h) The supervising health care provider or health care institution involved with the patient's care.

(i) Any other interested person or friend of the patient.

4766. A petition may be filed under this part for any one or more of the following purposes:

(a) Determining whether or not the patient has capacity to make health care decisions.

(b) Determining whether an advance health care directive is in effect or has terminated.

(c) Determining whether the acts or proposed acts of an agent or surrogate are consistent with the patient's desires as expressed in an advance health care directive or otherwise made known to the court or, where the patient's desires are unknown or unclear, whether the acts or proposed acts of the agent or surrogate are in the patient's best interest.

(d) Declaring that the authority of an agent or surrogate is terminated, upon a determination by the court that the agent or surrogate has made a health care decision for the patient that authorized anything illegal or upon a determination by the court of both of the following:

(1) The agent or surrogate has violated, has failed to perform, or is unfit to perform, the duty under an advance health care directive to act consistent with the patient's desires or, where the patient's desires are unknown or unclear, is acting (by action or

inaction) in a manner that is clearly contrary to the patient's best interest.

(2) At the time of the determination by the court, the patient lacks the capacity to execute or to revoke an advance health care directive or disqualify a surrogate.

(e) Compelling a third person to honor individual health care instructions or the authority of an agent or surrogate.

4767. A proceeding under this part is commenced by filing a petition stating facts showing that the petition is authorized under this part, the grounds of the petition, and, if known to the petitioner, the terms of any advance health care directive in question.

4768. The court may dismiss a petition if it appears that the proceeding is not reasonably necessary for the protection of the interests of the patient and shall stay or dismiss the proceeding in whole or in part when required by Section 410.30 of the Code of Civil Procedure.

4769. (a) Subject to subdivision (b), at least 15 days before the time set for hearing, the petitioner shall serve notice of the time and place of the hearing, together with a copy of the petition, on the following:

(1) The agent or surrogate, if not the petitioner.

(2) The patient, if not the petitioner.

(b) In the case of a petition to compel a third person to honor individual health care instructions or the authority of an agent or surrogate, notice of the time and place of the hearing, together with a copy of the petition, shall be served on the third person in the manner provided in Chapter 4 (commencing with Section 413.10) of Title 5 of Part 2 of the Code of Civil Procedure.

4770. The court in its discretion, on a showing of good cause, may issue a temporary order prescribing the health care of the patient until the disposition of the petition filed under Section 4766. If a power of attorney for health care is in effect and a conservator (including a temporary conservator) of the person is appointed for the principal, the court that appoints the conservator in its discretion, on a showing of good cause, may issue a temporary order prescribing the health care of the principal, the order to continue in effect for the period ordered by the court but in no case longer than the period necessary to permit the filing and determination of a petition filed under Section 4766.

4771. In a proceeding under this part commenced by the filing of a petition by a person other than the agent or surrogate, the court may in its discretion award reasonable attorney's fees to one of the following:

(a) The agent or surrogate, if the court determines that the proceeding was commenced without any reasonable cause.

(b) The person commencing the proceeding, if the court determines that the agent or surrogate has clearly violated the duties under the advance health care directive.

Part 4. Request Regarding Resuscitative Measures

4780. (a) As used in this part:

(1) "Request regarding resuscitative measures" means a written document, signed by (A) an individual with capacity, or a legally recognized health care decisionmaker, and (B) the individual's physician, that directs a health care provider regarding resuscitative measures. A request regarding resuscitative measures is not an advance health care directive.

(2) "Request regarding resuscitative measures" includes one, or both of, the following:

(A) A prehospital "do not resuscitate" form as developed by the Emergency Medical Services Authority or other substantially similar form.

(B) A Physician Orders for Life Sustaining Treatment form, as approved by the Emergency Medical Services Authority.

(3) "Physician Orders for Life Sustaining Treatment form" means a request regarding resuscitative measures that directs a health care provider regarding resuscitative and life-sustaining measures.

(b) A legally recognized health care decisionmaker may execute the Physician Orders for Life Sustaining Treatment form only if the individual lacks capacity, or the individual has designated that the decisionmaker's authority is effective pursuant to Section 4682.

(c) The Physician Orders for Life Sustaining Treatment form and medical intervention and procedures offered by the form shall be explained by a health care provider, as defined in Section 4621. The form shall be completed by a health care provider based on patient preferences and medical indications, and signed by a physician and the patient or his or her legally recognized health care decisionmaker. The health care provider, during the process of completing the Physician Orders for Life Sustaining Treatment form, should inform the patient about the difference between an advance health care directive and the Physician Orders for Life Sustaining Treatment form.

(d) An individual having capacity may revoke a Physician Orders for Life Sustaining Treatment form at any time and in any manner that communicates an intent to revoke, consistent with Section 4695.

(e) A request regarding resuscitative measures may also be evidenced by a medallion engraved with the words "do not resuscitate" or the letters "DNR," a patient identification number, and a 24-hour toll-free telephone number, issued by a person pursuant to an agreement with the Emergency Medical Services Authority.

4781. As used in this part, "health care provider" includes, but is not limited to, the following:

(a) Persons described in Section 4621.

(b) Emergency response employees, including, but not limited to, firefighters, law enforcement officers, emergency medical technicians I and II, paramedics, and employees and volunteer members of legally organized and recognized volunteer organizations, who are trained in accordance with standards adopted as regulations by the Emergency Medical Services Authority pursuant to Sections 1797.170, 1797.171, 1797.172, 1797.182, and 1797.183 of the Health and Safety Code to respond to medical emergencies in the course of performing their volunteer or employee duties with the organization.

4781.2. (a) A health care provider shall treat an individual in accordance with a Physician Orders for Life Sustaining Treatment form.

(b) Subdivision (a) does not apply if the Physician Orders for Life Sustaining Treatment form requires medically ineffective health care or health care contrary to generally accepted health care standards applicable to the health care provider or institution.

(c) A physician may conduct an evaluation of the individual and, if possible, in consultation with the individual, or the individual's legally recognized health care decisionmaker, issue a new order consistent with the most current information available about the individual's health status and goals of care.

(d) The legally recognized health care decisionmaker of an individual without capacity shall consult with the physician who is, at that time, the individual's treating physician prior to making a request to modify that individual's Physician Orders for Life Sustaining Treatment form.

(e) An individual with capacity may, at any time, request alternative treatment to that treatment that was ordered on the form.

4781.4. If the orders in an individual's request regarding resuscitative measures directly conflict with his or her individual health care instruction, as defined in Section 4623, then, to the extent of the conflict, the most recent order or instruction is effective.

4781.5. The legally recognized health care decisionmaker shall make health care decisions pursuant to this part in accordance with Sections 4684 and 4714.

4782. A health care provider who honors a request regarding resuscitative measures is not subject to criminal prosecution, civil liability, discipline for unprofessional conduct, administrative sanction, or any other sanction, as a result of his or her reliance on the request, if the health care provider (a) believes in good faith that the action or decision is consistent with this part, and (b) has no knowledge that the action or decision would be inconsistent with a health care decision that the individual signing the request would have made on his or her own behalf under like circumstances.

4783. (a) Forms for requests regarding resuscitative measures printed after January 1, 1995, shall contain the following:

"By signing this form, the legally recognized health care decisionmaker acknowledges that this request regarding resuscitative measures is consistent with the known desires of, and with the best interest of, the individual who is the subject of the form."

(b) A printed form substantially similar to that described in subparagraph (A) of paragraph (2) of subdivision (a) of Section 4780 is valid and enforceable if all of the following conditions are met:

(1) The form is signed by the individual, or the individual's legally recognized health care decisionmaker, and a physician.

(2) The form directs health care providers regarding resuscitative measures.

(3) The form contains all other information required by this section.

4784. In the absence of knowledge to the contrary, a health care provider may presume that a request regarding resuscitative measures is valid and unrevoked.

4785. This part applies regardless of whether the individual executing a request regarding resuscitative measures is within or outside a hospital or other health care institution.

4786. This part does not repeal or narrow laws relating to health care decisionmaking.

Part 5. Advance Health Care Directive Registry

4800. (a) The Secretary of State shall establish a registry system through which a person who has executed a written advance health care directive may register in a central information center, information regarding the advance directive, making that information available upon request to any health care provider, the public guardian, or the legal representative of the registrant. A request for information pursuant to this section shall state the need for the information.

(b) The Secretary of State shall respond by the close of business on the next business day to a request for information made pursuant to Section 4717 by the emergency department of a general acute care hospital.

(c) Information that may be received is limited to the registrant's name, social security number, driver's license number, or other individual identifying number established by law, if any, address, date and place of birth, the registrant's advance health care directive, an intended place of deposit or safekeeping of a written advance health care directive, and the name and telephone number of the agent and any alternative agent. Information that may be released upon request may not include the registrant's social security number except when necessary to verify the identity of the registrant.

(d) When the Secretary of State receives information from a registrant, the secretary shall issue the registrant an Advance Health Care Directive Registry identification card indicating that an advance health care directive, or information regarding an advance health care directive, has been deposited with the registry. Costs associated with issuance of the card shall be offset by the fee charged by the Secretary of State to receive and register information at the registry.

(e) The Secretary of State, at the request of the registrant or his or her legal representative, shall transmit the information received regarding the written advance health care directive to the registry system of another jurisdiction as identified by the registrant, or his or her legal representative.

(f) The Secretary of State shall charge a fee to each registrant in an amount such that, when all fees charged to registrants are aggregated, the aggregated fees do not exceed the actual cost of establishing and maintaining the registry.

4801. The Secretary of State shall establish procedures to verify the identities of health care providers, the public guardian, and other authorized persons requesting information pursuant to Section 4800. No fee shall be charged to any health care provider, the public guardian, or other authorized person requesting information pursuant to Section 4800.

4802. The Secretary of State shall establish procedures to advise each registrant of the following:

(a) A health care provider may not honor a written advance health care directive until it receives a copy from the registrant.

(b) Each registrant must notify the registry upon revocation of the advance directive.

(c) Each registrant must reregister upon execution of a subsequent advance directive.

4803. Failure to register with the Secretary of State does not affect the validity of any advance health care directive.

4804. Registration with the Secretary of State does not affect the ability of the registrant to revoke the registrant's advance health care directive or a later executed advance directive, nor does registration raise any presumption of validity or superiority among any competing advance directives or revocations.

4805. Nothing in this part shall be construed to affect the duty of a health care provider to provide information to a patient regarding advance health care directives pursuant to any provision of federal law.

4806. (a) The Secretary of State shall work with the State Department of Health Services and the office of the Attorney

General to develop information about end of life care, advance health care directives, and registration of the advance health care directives at the registry established pursuant to subdivision (a) of Section 4800. This information shall be developed utilizing existing information developed by the office of the Attorney General.

(b) Links to the information specified in subdivision (a) and to the registry shall be available on the Web sites of the Secretary of State, the State Department of Health Services, the office of the Attorney General, the Department of Managed Health Care, the Department of Insurance, the Board of Registered Nursing, and the Medical Board of California.

Division 5. Nonprobate Transfers

Part 1. Provisions Relating To Effect Of Death

Chapter 1. General Provisions

5000. (a) A provision for a nonprobate transfer on death in an insurance policy, contract of employment, bond, mortgage, promissory note, certificated or uncertificated security, account agreement, custodial agreement, deposit agreement, compensation plan, pension plan, individual retirement plan, employee benefit plan, trust, conveyance, deed of gift, marital property agreement, or other written instrument of a similar nature is not invalid because the instrument does not comply with the requirements for execution of a will, and this code does not invalidate the instrument.

(b) Included within subdivision (a) are the following:

(1) A written provision that money or other benefits due to, controlled by, or owned by a decedent before death shall be paid after the decedent's death to a person whom the decedent designates either in the instrument or in a separate writing, including a will, executed either before or at the same time as the instrument, or later.

(2) A written provision that money due or to become due under the instrument shall cease to be payable in event of the death of the promisee or the promisor before payment or demand.

(3) A written provision that any property controlled by or owned by the decedent before death that is the subject of the instrument shall pass to a person whom the decedent designates either in the instrument or in a separate writing, including a will, executed either before or at the same time as the instrument, or later.

(c) Nothing in this section limits the rights of creditors under any other law.

5002. Notwithstanding any other provision of this part, a holder of property under an instrument of a type described in Section 5000 is not required to receive, hold, or transfer the property in compliance with a provision for a nonprobate transfer on death executed by a person who has an interest in the property if either (1) the person is not authorized by the terms of the instrument to execute a provision for transfer of the property, or (2) the provision for transfer of the property does not otherwise satisfy the terms of the instrument.

5003. (a) A holder of property under an instrument of a type described in Section 5000 may transfer the property in compliance with a provision for a nonprobate transfer on death that satisfies the terms of the instrument, whether or not the transfer is consistent with the beneficial ownership of the property as between the person who executed the provision for transfer of the property and other persons having an interest in the property or their successors, and whether or not the transfer is consistent with the rights of the person named as beneficiary.

(b) Except as provided in this subdivision, no notice or other information shown to have been available to the holder of the property affects the right of the holder to the protection provided by subdivision (a). The protection provided by subdivision (a) does not extend to a transfer made after either of the following events:

(1) The holder of the property has been served with a contrary court order.

(2) The holder of the property has been served with a written notice of a person claiming an adverse interest in the property. However, this paragraph does not apply to a pension plan to the extent the transfer is a periodic payment pursuant to the plan.

(c) The protection provided by this section does not affect the rights of the person who executed the provision for transfer of the property and other persons having an interest in the property or their successors in disputes among themselves concerning the beneficial ownership of the property.

(d) The protection provided by this section is not exclusive of any protection provided the holder of the property by any other provision of law.

(e) A person shall not serve notice under paragraph (2) of subdivision (b) in bad faith. If the court in an action or proceeding relating to the rights of the parties determines that a person has served notice under paragraph (2) of subdivision (b) in bad faith, the court shall award against the person the cost of the action or proceeding, including a reasonable attorney's fee, and the damages caused by the service.

Chapter 2. Nonprobate Transfers Of Community Property

Article 1. General Provisions

5010. As used in this chapter, "written consent" to a provision for a nonprobate transfer of community property on death includes a written joinder in such a provision.

5011. Notwithstanding any other provision of this part, the rights of the parties in a nonprobate transfer of community property on death are subject to all of the following:

(a) The terms of the instrument under which the nonprobate transfer is made.

(b) A contrary state statute specifically applicable to the instrument under which the nonprobate transfer is made.

(c) A written expression of intent of a party in the provision for transfer of the property or in a written consent to the provision.

5012. A provision of this chapter concerning rights between a married person and the person's spouse in community property is relevant only to controversies between the person and spouse and their successors and does not affect the obligation of a holder of community property under an instrument of a type described in Section 5000 to hold, receive, or transfer the property in compliance with a provision for a nonprobate transfer on death, or the protection provided the holder by Section 5003.

5013. Nothing in this chapter limits the effect of a surviving spouse's waiver of rights in community property under Chapter 1 (commencing with Section 140) of Part 3 of Division 2 or other instrument or agreement that affects a married person's interest in community property.

5014. (a) Except as provided in subdivision (b), this chapter applies to a provision for a nonprobate transfer of community property on the death of a married person, regardless of whether the provision for transfer of the property was executed by the person, or written consent to the provision for transfer of the property was given by the person's spouse, before, on, or after January 1, 1993.

(b) Subdivision (c) of Section 5030 does not apply, and the applicable law in effect on the date of death does apply, to revocation of a written consent given by a spouse who died before January 1, 1993.

5015. Nothing in this chapter limits the application of principles of fraud, undue influence, duress, mistake, or other invalidating cause to a written consent to a provision for a nonprobate transfer of community property on death.

Article 2. Consent To Nonprobate Transfer

5020. A provision for a nonprobate transfer of community property on death executed by a married person without the written consent of the person's spouse (1) is not effective as to the nonconsenting spouse's interest in the property and (2) does not affect the nonconsenting spouse's disposition on death of the nonconsenting spouse's interest in the community property by will, intestate succession, or nonprobate transfer.

5021. (a) In a proceeding to set aside a nonprobate transfer of community property on death made pursuant to a provision for transfer of the property executed by a married person without the written consent of the person's spouse, the court shall set aside the transfer as to the nonconsenting spouse's interest in the property, subject to terms and conditions or other remedies that appear equitable under the circumstances of the case, taking into account the rights of all interested persons.

(b) Nothing in subdivision (a) affects any additional remedy the nonconsenting spouse may have against the person's estate for a nonprobate transfer of community property on death without the spouse's written consent.

5022. (a) Except as provided in subdivision (b), a spouse's written consent to a provision for a nonprobate transfer of community property on death is not a transmutation of the consenting spouse's interest in the property.

(b) This chapter does not apply to a spouse's written consent to a provision for a nonprobate transfer of community property on death that satisfies Section 852 of the Family Code. Such a consent is a transmutation and is governed by the law applicable to transmutations.

5023. (a) As used in this section "modification" means revocation of a provision for a nonprobate transfer on death in whole or part, designation of a different beneficiary, or election of a different benefit or payment option. As used in this section, "modification" does not mean, and this section does not apply to, the exercise of a power of appointment under a trust.

(b) If a married person executes a provision for a nonprobate transfer of community property on death with the written consent of the person's spouse and thereafter executes a modification of the provision for transfer of the property without written consent of the spouse, the modification is effective as to the person's interest in the community property and has the following effect on the spouse's interest in the community property:

(1) If the person executes the modification during the spouse's lifetime, the modification revokes the spouse's previous written consent to the provision for transfer of the property.

(2) If the person executes the modification after the spouse's death, the modification does not affect the spouse's previous written consent to the provision for transfer of the property, and the spouse's interest in the community property is subject to the nonprobate transfer on death as consented to by the spouse.

(3) If a written expression of intent of a party in the provision for transfer of the property or in the written consent to the provision for transfer of the property authorizes the person to execute a modification after the spouse's death, the spouse's interest in the community property is deemed transferred to the married person on the spouse's death, and the modification is effective as to both the person's and the spouse's interests in the community property.

Article 3. Revocation Of Consent

5030. (a) A spouse's written consent to a provision for a nonprobate transfer of community property on death is revocable during the marriage.

(b) On termination of the marriage by dissolution or on legal separation, the written consent is revocable and the community property is subject to division under Division 7 (commencing with Section 2500) of the Family Code or other disposition on order within the jurisdiction of the court.

(c) On the death of either spouse, the written consent is irrevocable.

5031. (a) If a married person executes a provision for a nonprobate transfer of community property on death with the written consent of the person's spouse, the consenting spouse may revoke the consent by a writing, including a will, that identifies the provision for transfer of the property being revoked, and that is served on the married person before the married person's death.

(b) Revocation of a spouse's written consent to a provision for a nonprobate transfer of community property on death does not affect the authority of the holder of the property to transfer the property in compliance with the provision for transfer of the property to the extent provided in Section 5003.

5032. On revocation of a spouse's written consent to a nonprobate transfer of community property on death, the property passes in the same manner as if the consent had not been given.

Part 2. Multiple-Party Accounts

Chapter 1. Short Title And Definitions

Article 1. Short Title

5100. This part may be cited as the California Multiple-Party Accounts Law.

Article 2. Definitions

5120. Unless the provision or context otherwise requires, the definitions in this article govern the construction of this part.

5122. (a) "Account" means a contract of deposit of funds between a depositor and a financial institution, and includes a checking account, savings account, certificate of deposit, share account, and other like arrangement.

(b) "Account" does not include:

(1) An account established for deposit of funds of a partnership, joint venture, or other association for business purposes.

(2) An account controlled by one or more persons as the duly authorized agent or trustee for a corporation, unincorporated association, or charitable or civic organization.

(3) A regular fiduciary or trust account where the relationship is established other than by deposit agreement.

(4) An account established for the deposit of funds of the estate of a ward, conservatee, or decedent.

5124. "Agent" means a person who has a present right, subject to request, to payment from an account as an attorney in fact under a power of attorney.

5126. "Beneficiary" means a person named in a Totten trust account as one for whom a party to the account is named as trustee.

5128. "Financial institution" includes:

(a) A financial institution as defined in Section 40.

(b) An industrial loan company as defined in Section 18003 of the Financial Code.

5130. "Joint account" means an account payable on request to one or more of two or more parties whether or not mention is made of any right of survivorship.

5132. A "multiple-party account" is any of the following types of account:

(a) A joint account.

(b) A P.O.D. account.

(c) A Totten trust account.

5134. (a) "Net contribution" of a party to an account as of any given time is the sum of all of the following:

(1) All deposits thereto made by or for the party, less all withdrawals made by or for the party that have not been paid to or applied to the use of any other party.

(2) A pro rata share of any interest or dividends earned, whether or not included in the current balance.

(3) Any proceeds of deposit life insurance added to the account by reason of the death of the party whose net contribution is in question.

(b) In the absence of proof otherwise:

(1) Only parties who have a present right of withdrawal shall be considered as having a net contribution.

(2) The net contribution of each of the parties having a present right of withdrawal is deemed to be an equal amount.

(c) It is the intent of the Legislature in enacting this section to provide a definition for the purpose of determining ownership interests in an account as between the parties to the account, and not as between the parties and the financial institution.

5136. (a) "Party" means a person who, by the terms of the account, has a present right, subject to request, to payment from a multiple-party account other than as an agent.

(b) A P.O.D. payee is a party, by reason of being a P.O.D. payee, only after the account becomes payable to the payee by reason of surviving all persons named as original payees.

(c) A beneficiary of a Totten trust account is a party, by reason of being a beneficiary, only after the account becomes payable to the beneficiary by reason of surviving all persons named as trustees.

5138. "Payment" of sums on deposit includes all of the following:

(a) A withdrawal, including payment on check or other directive of a party.

(b) A pledge of sums of deposit.

(c) A setoff, reduction, or other disposition of all or part of an account pursuant to a pledge.

5139. "P.O.D." means pay on death.

5140. "P.O.D. account" means any of the following:

(a) An account payable on request to one person during the person' s lifetime and on the person's death to one or more P.O.D. payees.

(b) An account payable on request to one or more persons during their lifetimes and on the death of all of them to one or more P.O.D. payees.

5142. "P.O.D. payee" means a person designated on a P.O.D. account as one to whom the account is payable on request after the death of one or more persons.

5144. "Proof of death" includes any of the following:

(a) An original or attested or certified copy of a death certificate.

(b) A record or report that is prima facie evidence of death under Section 103550 of the Health and Safety Code, Sections 1530 to 1532, inclusive, of the Evidence Code, or another statute of this state.

5146. Except to the extent the terms of the account or deposit agreement expressly provide otherwise, a financial institution "receives" an order or notice under this part when it is received by the particular office or branch office of the financial instutition where the account is carried.

5148. "Request" means a proper request for withdrawal, including a check or order for payment, that complies with all conditions of the account (including special requirements concerning necessary signatures) and regulations of the financial institution; but, if the financial institution conditions withdrawal or payment on advance notice, for purposes of this part the request for withdrawal or payment is treated as immediately effective and a notice of intent to withdraw is treated as a request for withdrawal.

5150. "Sums on deposit" means both of the following:

(a) The balance payable on an account, including interest and dividends earned, whether or not included in the current balance.

(b) Any life insurance proceeds added to the account by reason of the death of a party.

5152. "Withdrawal" includes payment to a third person pursuant to a check or other directive of a party or an agent.

Chapter 2. General Provisions

5201. (a) The provisions of Chapter 3 (commencing with Section 5301) concerning beneficial ownership as between parties, or as between parties and P.O.D. payees or beneficiaries of multiple-party accounts, are relevant only to controversies between these persons and their creditors and other successors, and have no bearing on the power of withdrawal of these persons as determined by the terms of account contracts.

(b) The provisions of Chapter 4 (commencing with Section 5401) govern the liability of financial institutions who make payments pursuant to that chapter.

5202. Nothing in this part affects the law relating to transfers in fraud of creditors.

5203. (a) Words in substantially the following form in a signature card, passbook, contract, or instrument evidencing an account, or words to the same effect, executed before, on, or after July 1, 1990, create the following accounts:

(1) Joint account: "This account or certificate is owned by the named parties. Upon the death of any of them, ownership passes to the survivor(s)."

(2) P.O.D. account with single party: "This account or certificate is owned by the named party. Upon the death of that party, ownership passes to the named pay-on-death payee(s)."

(3) P.O.D. account with multiple parties: "This account or certificate is owned by the named parties. Upon the death of any of them, ownership passes to the survivor(s). Upon the death of all of them, ownership passes to the named pay-on-death payee(s)."

(4) Joint account of husband and wife with right of survivorship: "This account or certificate is owned by the named parties, who are husband and wife, and is presumed to be their community property. Upon the death of either of them, ownership passes to the survivor."

(5) Community property account of husband and wife: "This account or certificate is the community property of the named parties who are husband and wife. The ownership during lifetime and after the death of a spouse is determined by the law applicable to community property generally and may be affected by a will."

(6) Tenancy in common account: "This account or certificate is owned by the named parties as tenants in common. Upon the death of any party, the ownership interest of that party passes to the named pay-on-death payee(s) of that party or, if none, to the estate of that party."

(b) Use of the form language provided in this section is not necessary to create an account that is governed by this part. If the contract of deposit creates substantially the same relationsip between the parties as an account created using the form language provided in this section, this part applies to the same extent as if the form language had been used.

5204. (a) In addition to a power of attorney otherwise authorized by law, a special power of attorney is authorized under this section to apply to one or more accounts at a financial institution or to one or more contracts with a financial institution concerning safe deposit services. For the purposes of this section, "account" includes checking accounts, savings accounts, certificates of deposit, savings certificates, and any other depository relationship with the financial institution.

(b) The special power of attorney under this section shall:

(1) Be in writing.

(2) Be signed by the person or persons giving the power of attorney.

(3) Explicitly identify the attorney-in-fact or attorneys-in-fact, the financial institution, and the accounts or contracts subject to the power.

(c) The special power of attorney shall contain language in substantially the following form:

"WARNING TO PERSON EXECUTING THIS DOCUMENT: This is an important legal document. It creates a power of attorney that provides the person you designate as your attorney-in-fact with the broad powers it sets forth. You have the right to terminate this power of attorney. If there is anything about this form that you do not understand, you should ask a lawyer to explain it to you."

(d) In addition to the language required by subdivision (c), special powers of attorney that are or may be durable shall also contain substantially the following language:

"These powers of attorney shall continue even if you later become disabled or incapacitated."

(e) The power of attorney granted under this section shall endure as between the grantor and grantee of the power until the earliest of the following occurs:

(1) Revocation by the grantor of the power.

(2) Termination of the account.

(3) Death of the grantor of the power.

(4) In the case of a nondurable power of attorney, appointment of a guardian or conservator of the estate of the grantor of the power.

(f) A financial institution may rely in good faith upon the validity of the power of attorney granted under this section and is not liable to the principal or any other person for doing so if (1) the power of attorney is on file with the financial institution and the transaction is made by the attorney-in-fact named in the power of attorney, (2) the power of attorney appears on its face to be valid, and (3) the financial institution has convincing evidence of the identity of the person signing the power of attorney as principal.

(g) For the purposes of subdivision (f), "convincing evidence" requires both of the following:

(1) Reasonable reliance on a document that satisfies the requirement of Section 4751.

(2) The absence of any information, evi-

dence, or other circumstances that would lead a reasonable person to believe that the person signing the power of attorney as principal is not the individual he or she claims to be.

(h) The protection provided by subdivision (f) does not extend to payments made after written notice is received by the financial institution as to any of the events of termination of the power under subdivision (e) if the financial institution has had a reasonable time to act on the notice. No other notice or any other information shown to have been available to the financial institution shall affect its right to the protection provided by this subdivision.

(i) The attorney-in-fact acting under the power of attorney granted under this section shall maintain books or records to permit an accounting of the acts of the attorney-in-fact if an accounting is requested by a legal representative of the grantor of the power.

(j) The attorney-in-fact acting under a power of attorney granted under this section is liable for any disbursement other than a disbursement to or for the benefit of the grantor of the power, unless the grantor has authorized the disbursement in writing.

(k) Nothing in this section limits the use or effect of any other form of power of attorney for transactions with a financial institution. Nothing in this section creates an implication that a financial institution is liable for acting in reliance upon a power of attorney under circumstances where the requirements of subdivision (f) are not satisfied. Nothing in this section affects any immunity that may otherwise exist apart from this section.

(l) Nothing in this section prevents the attorney-in-fact from also being designated as a P.O.D. payee.

(m) Except as otherwise provided in this section, the Power of Attorney Law, Division 4.5 (commencing with Section 4000) shall not apply to a special power of attorney under this section. Section 4130 and Part 5 (commencing with Section 4900) of Division 4.5 shall apply to a special power of attorney under this section.

5205. This part applies to accounts in existence on July 1, 1990, and accounts thereafter established.

Chapter 3. Ownership Between Parties And Their Creditors And Successors

5301. (a) An account belongs, during the lifetime of all parties, to the parties in proportion to the net contributions by each, unless there is clear and convincing evidence of a different intent.

(b) If a party makes an excess withdrawal from an account, the other parties to the account shall have an ownership interest in the excess withdrawal in proportion to the net contributions of each to the amount on deposit in the account immediately following the excess withdrawal, unless there is clear and convincing evidence of a contrary agreement between the parties.

(c) Only a living party, or a conservator, guardian, or agent acting on behalf of a living party, shall be permitted to make a claim to recover the living party's ownership interest in an excess withdrawal, pursuant to subdivision (b). A court may, at its discretion, and in the interest of justice, reduce any recovery under this section to reflect funds withdrawn and applied for the benefit of the claiming party.

(d) In the case of a P.O.D. account, the P.O.D. payee has no rights to the sums on deposit during the lifetime of any party, unless there is clear and convincing evidence of a different intent.

(e) In the case of a Totten trust account, the beneficiary has no rights to the sums on deposit during the lifetime of any party, unless there is clear and convincing evidence of a different intent. If there is an irrevocable trust, the account belongs beneficially to the beneficiary.

(f) For purposes of this section, "excess withdrawal" means the amount of a party's withdrawal that exceeds that party's net contribution on deposit in the account immediately preceding the withdrawal.

5302. Subject to Section 5600:

(a) Sums remaining on deposit at the death of a party to a joint

account belong to the surviving party or parties as against the estate of the decedent unless there is clear and convincing evidence of a different intent. If there are two or more surviving parties, their respective ownerships during lifetime are in proportion to their previous ownership interests under Section 5301 augmented by an equal share for each survivor of any interest the decedent may have owned in the account immediately before the decedent's death; and the right of survivorship continues between the surviving parties.

(b) If the account is a P.O.D. account:

(1) On death of one of two or more parties, the rights to any sums remaining on deposit are governed by subdivision (a).

(2) On death of the sole party or of the survivor of two or more parties, (A) any sums remaining on deposit belong to the P.O.D. payee or payees if surviving, or to the survivor of them if one or more die before the party, (B) if two or more P.O.D. payees survive, any sums remaining on deposit belong to them in equal and undivided shares unless the terms of the account or deposit agreement expressly provide for different shares, and (C) if two or more P.O.D. payees survive, there is no right of survivorship in the event of death of a P.O.D. payee thereafter unless the terms of the account or deposit agreement expressly provide for survivorship between them.

(c) If the account is a Totten trust account:

(1) On death of one of two or more trustees, the rights to any sums remaining on deposit are governed by subdivision (a).

(2) On death of the sole trustee or the survivor of two or more trustees, (A) any sums remaining on deposit belong to the person or persons named as beneficiaries, if surviving, or to the survivor of them if one or more die before the trustee, unless there is clear and convincing evidence of a different intent, (B) if two or more beneficiaries survive, any sums remaining on deposit belong to them in equal and undivided shares unless the terms of the account or deposit agreement expressly provide for different shares, and (C) if two or more beneficiaries survive, there is no right of survivorship in event of death of any beneficiary thereafter unless the terms of the account or deposit agreement expressly provide for survivorship between them.

(d) In other cases, the death of any party to a multiple-party account has no effect on beneficial ownership of the account other than to transfer the rights of the decedent as part of the decedent's estate.

(e) A right of survivorship arising from the express terms of the account or under this section, a beneficiary designation in a Totten trust account, or a P.O.D. payee designation, cannot be changed by will.

5303. (a) The provisions of Section 5302 as to rights of survivorship are determined by the form of the account at the death of a party.

(b) Once established, the terms of a multiple-party account can be changed only by any of the following methods:

(1) Closing the account and reopening it under different terms.

(2) Presenting to the financial institution a modification agreement that is signed by all parties with a present right of withdrawal. If the financial institution has a form for this purpose, it may require use of the form.

(3) If the provisions of the terms of the account or deposit agreement provide a method of modification of the terms of the account, complying with those provisions.

(4) As provided in subdivision (c) of Section 5405.

(c) During the lifetime of a party, the terms of the account may be changed as provided in subdivision (b) to eliminate or to add rights of survivorship. Withdrawal of funds from the account by a party also eliminates rights of survivorship with respect to the funds withdrawn to the extent of the withdrawing party's net contribution to the account.

5304. Any transfers resulting from the application of Section 5302 are effective by reason of the account contracts involved and this part and are not to be considered as testamentary. The right under this part of a surviving party to a joint account, or of a beneficiary, or of a P.O.D. payee, to the sums on deposit on the death of a party to a multiple-party account shall not be denied, abridged, or affected because such right has not been created by a writing executed in accordance with the laws of this state prescribing the requirements to effect a valid testamentary disposition of property.

5305. (a) Notwithstanding Sections 5301 to 5303, inclusive, if parties to an account are married to each other, whether or not they are so described in the deposit agreement, their net contribution to the account is presumed to be and remain their community property.

(b) Notwithstanding Sections 2581 and 2640 of the Family Code, the presumption established by this section is a presumption affecting the burden of proof and may be rebutted by proof of either of the following:

(1) The sums on deposit that are claimed to be separate property can be traced from separate property unless it is proved that the married persons made a written agreement that expressed their clear intent that the sums be their community property.

(2) The married persons made a written agreement, separate from the deposit agreement, that expressly provided that the sums on deposit, claimed not to be community property, were not to be community property.

(c) Except as provided in Section 5307, a right of survivorship arising from the express terms of the account or under Section 5302, a beneficiary designation in a Totten trust account, or a P.O.D. payee designation, may not be changed by will.

(d) Except as provided in subdivisions (b) and (c), a multiple-party account created with community property funds does not in any way alter community property rights.

5306. For the purposes of this chapter, if an account is expressly described in the deposit agreement as a "tenancy in common" account, no right of survivorship arises from the terms of the account or under Section 5302 unless the terms of the account or deposit agreement expressly provide for survivorship.

5307. For the purposes of this chapter, except to the extent the terms of the account or deposit agreement expressly provide otherwise, if the parties to an account are married to each other and the account is expressly described in the account agreement as a "community property" account, the ownership of the account during lifetime and after the death of a spouse is governed by the law governing community property generally.

Chapter 4. Protection Of Financial Institution

5401. (a) Financial institutions may enter into multiple-party accounts to the same extent that they may enter into single-party accounts. Any multiple-party account may be paid, on request and according to its terms, to any one or more of the parties or agents.

(b) The terms of the account or deposit agreement may require the signatures of more than one of the parties to a multiple-party account during their lifetimes or of more than one of the survivors after the death of any one of them on any check, check endorsement, receipt, notice of withdrawal, request for withdrawal, or withdrawal order. In such case, the financial institution shall pay the sums on deposit only in accordance with such terms, but those terms do not limit the right of the sole survivor or of all of the survivors to receive the sums on deposit.

(c) A financial institution is not required to do any of the following pursuant to Section 5301, 5303, or any other provision of this part:

(1) Inquire as to the source of funds received for deposit to a multiple-party account, or inquire as to the proposed application of any sum withdrawn from an account, for purposes of establishing net contributions.

(2) Determine any party's net contribution.

(3) Limit withdrawals or any other use of an account based on the net contribution of any party, whether or not the financial institution has actual knowledge of each party's contribution.

(d) All funds in an account, unless otherwise agreed in writing by the financial institution and the parties to the account, remain subject to liens, security interests, rights of setoff, and charges, notwithstanding the determination or allocation of net contributions with respect to the parties.

5402. Any sums in a joint account may be paid, on request and according to its terms, to any party without regard to whether any other party is incapacitated or deceased at the time the payment is demanded; but payment may not be made to the personal representative or heirs of a deceased party unless proof of death is presented to the financial institution showing that the decedent was the last surviving party or unless there is no right of survivorship under Section 5302.

5403. Any P.O.D. account may be paid, on request and according to its terms, to any original party to the account. Payment may be made, on request, to the P. O.D. payee or to the personal representative or heirs of a deceased P.O.D. payee upon presentation to the financial institution of proof of death showing that the P.O.D. payee survived all persons named as original payees. Payment may be made to the personal representative or heirs of a deceased original payee if proof of death is presented to the financial institution showing that the deceased original payee was the survivor of all other persons named on the account either as an original payee or as P.O.D. payee.

5404. Any Totten trust account may be paid, on request and according to its terms, to any trustee. Unless the financial institution has received written notice that the beneficiary has a vested interest not dependent upon surviving the trustee, payment may be made to the personal representative or heirs of a deceased trustee if proof of death is presented to the financial institution showing that the deceased trustee was the survivor of all other persons named on the account either as trustee or beneficiary. A Totten trust account may be paid to a beneficiary or beneficiaries or the personal representative or heirs of a beneficiary or beneficiaries if proof of death is presented to the financial institution showing that the beneficiary or beneficiaries survived all persons named as trustees.

5405. (a) Payment made pursuant to Section 5401, 5402, 5403, or 5404 discharges the financial institution from all claims for amounts so paid whether or not the payment is consistent with the beneficial ownership of the account as between parties, P.O.D. payees, or beneficiaries, or their successors.

(b) The protection provided by subdivision (a) does not extend to payments made after the financial institution has been served with a court order restraining payment. No other notice or any other information shown to have been available to a financial institution shall affect its right to the protection provided by subdivision (a).

(c) Unless the notice is withdrawn by a subsequent writing, after receipt of a written notice from any party that withdrawals in accordance with the terms of the account, other than a checking account, share draft account, or other similar third-party payment instrument, should not be permitted, except with the signatures of more than one of the parties during their lifetimes or of more than one of the survivors after the death of any one of the parties, the financial institution may only pay the sums on deposit in accordance with the written instructions pending determination of the rights of the parties or their successors. No liability shall attach to the financial institution for complying with the terms of any written notice provided pursuant to this subdivision.

(d) The protection provided by this section has no bearing on the rights of parties in disputes between themselves or their successors concerning the beneficial ownership of funds in, or withdrawn from, multiple-party accounts and is in addition to, and not exclusive of, any protection provided the financial institution by any other provision of law.

5406. The provisions of this chapter that apply to the payment of a Totten trust account apply to an account in the name of one or more parties as trustee for one or more other persons if the financial institution has no other or further notice in writing that the account is not a Totten trust account as defined in Section 80.

5407. If a financial institution is required or permitted to make payment pursuant to this chapter to a person who is a minor:

(a) If the minor is a party to a multiple-party account, payment may be made to the minor or to the minor's order, and payment so made is a valid release and discharge of the financial institution, but this subdivision does not apply if the account is to be paid to the minor because the minor was designated as a P.O. D. payee or as a beneficiary of a Totten trust account.

(b) In cases where subdivision (a) does not apply, payment shall be made pursuant to the California Uniform Transfers to Minors Act (Part 9 (commencing with Section 3900) of Division 4), or as provided in Chapter 2 (commencing with Section 3400) of Part 8 of Division 4.

Part 3. Uniform TOD Security Registration Act

5500. (a) This part shall be known as and may be cited as the Uniform TOD Security Registration Act.

(b) This part shall be liberally construed and applied to promote its underlying purposes and policy.

(c) The underlying purposes and policy of this act are to (1) encourage development of a title form for use by individuals that is effective, without probate and estate administration, for transferring property at death in accordance with directions of a deceased owner of a security as included in the title form in which the security is held and (2) protect issuers offering and implementing the new title form.

(d) Unless displaced by the particular provisions of this part, the principles of law and equity supplement its provisions.

5501. For purposes of this part:

(a) "Beneficiary form" means a registration of a security that indicates the present owner of the security and the intention of the owner regarding the person who will become the owner of the security upon the death of the owner.

(b) "Register," including its derivatives, means to issue a certificate showing the ownership of a certificated security or, in the case of an uncertificated security, to initiate or transfer an account showing ownership of securities.

(c) "Registering entity" means a person who originates or transfers a security title by registration, and includes a broker maintaining security accounts for customers and a transfer agent or other person acting for or as an issuer of securities.

(d) "Security" means a share, participation, or other interest in property, in a business, or in an obligation of an enterprise or other issuer, and includes a certificated security, an uncertificated security, and a security account.

(e) (1) "Security account" means any of the following:

(A) A reinvestment account associated with a security, a securities account with a broker, a cash balance in a brokerage account, cash, cash equivalents, interest, earnings, or dividends earned or declared on a security in an account, a reinvestment account, or a brokerage account, whether or not credited to the account before the owner's death.

(B) An investment management or custody account with a trust company or a trust department of a bank with trust powers, including the securities in the account, the cash balance in the account, and cash equivalents, and interest, earnings, or dividends earned or declared on a security in the account, whether or not credited to the account before the owner's death.

(C) A cash balance or other property held for or due to the owner of a security as a replacement for or product of an account security, whether or not credited to the account before the owner's death.

(2) For the purposes of this subdivision, "cash equivalent" means an investment that is easily converted into cash, including, treasury bills, treasury notes, money market funds, savings bonds, short-term instruments, and short-term obligations.

(f) This section may not be construed to govern cash equivalents in multiple-party accounts that are governed by the California Multiple-Party Accounts Law, Part 2 (commencing with Section 5100).

5502. Only individuals whose registration of a security shows sole ownership by one individual or multiple ownership by two or more individuals with right of survivorship, rather than as tenants in common, may obtain registration in beneficiary form. Multiple owners of a security registered in beneficiary form hold as joint tenants with right of survivorship, as tenants by the entireties, or as owners of community property held in survivorship form, and not as tenants in common.

5503. A security may be registered in beneficiary form if the form is authorized by this or a similar statute of the state of organization of the issuer or registering entity, the location of the registering entity's principal office, the office of its transfer agent or its office making the registration, or by this or a similar statute of the law of the state listed as the owner's address at the time of registration. A registration governed by the law of a jurisdiction in which this or similar legislation is not in force or was not in force when a registration in beneficiary form was made is nevertheless presumed to be valid and authorized as a matter of contract law.

5504. A security, whether evidenced by certificate or account, is registered in beneficiary form when the registration includes a designation of a beneficiary to take the ownership at the death of the owner or the deaths of all multiple owners.

5505. Registration in beneficiary form may be shown by the words "transfer on death" or the abbreviation "TOD," or by the words "pay on death" or the abbreviation "POD," after the name of the registered owner and before the name of a beneficiary.

5506. The designation of a TOD beneficiary on a registration in beneficiary form has no effect on ownership until the owner's death. A registration of a security in beneficiary form may be canceled or changed at any time by the sole owner or all then surviving owners without the consent of the beneficiary.

5507. On death of a sole owner or the last to die of all multiple owners, ownership of securities registered in beneficiary form passes to the beneficiary or beneficiaries who survive all owners. On proof of death of all owners and compliance with any applicable requirements of the registering entity, a security registered in beneficiary form may be reregistered in the name of the beneficiary or beneficiaries who survive the death of all owners. Until division of the security after the death of all owners, multiple beneficiaries surviving the death of all owners hold their interests as tenants in common. If no beneficiary survives the death of all owners, the security belongs to the estate of the deceased sole owner or the estate of the last to die of all multiple owners.

5508. (a) A registering entity is not required to offer or to accept requests for security registration in beneficiary form. If a registration in beneficiary form is offered by a registering entity, the owner requesting registration in beneficiary form assents to the protections given to the registering entity by this part.

(b) By accepting a request for registration of a security in beneficiary form, the registering entity agrees that the registration will be implemented as provided in this part.

(c) A registering entity is discharged from all claims to a security by the estate, creditors, heirs, or devisees of a deceased owner if it registers a transfer of the security in accordance with Section 5507 and does so in good faith reliance (1) on the registration, (2) on this part, and (3) on information provided to it by affidavit of the personal representative of the deceased owner, or by the surviving beneficiary or the surviving beneficiary's representatives, or other information available to the registering entity. The protections of this part do not extend to a reregistration or payment made after a registering entity has received written notice from any claimant to any interest in the security objecting to implementation of a registration in beneficiary form. No other notice or other information available to the registering entity shall affect its right to protection under this part.

(d) The protection provided by this part to the registering entity of a security does not affect the rights of beneficiaries in disputes between themselves and other claimants to ownership of the security transferred or its value or proceeds.

5509. (a) Any transfer on death resulting from a registration in beneficiary form is effective by reason of the contract regarding the registration between the owner and the registering entity and this part and is not testamentary.

(b) This part does not limit the rights of a surviving spouse or creditors of security owners against beneficiaries and other transferees under other laws of this state.

5510. (a) A registering entity offering to accept registrations in beneficiary form may establish the terms and conditions under which it will receive requests for (1) registrations in beneficiary form, and (2) implementation of registrations in beneficiary form, including requests for cancellation of previously registered TOD beneficiary designations and requests for reregistration to effect a change of beneficiary.

(b) The terms and conditions established pursuant to subdivision (a) may provide for (1) proving death, (2) avoiding or resolving any problems concerning fractional shares, (3) designating primary and contingent beneficiaries, and (4) substituting a named beneficiary's descendants to take in the place of the named beneficiary in the event of the beneficiary's death. Substitution may be indicated by appending to the name of the primary beneficiary the letters LDPS, standing for "lineal descendants per stirpes." This designation substitutes a deceased beneficiary's descendants who survive the owner for a beneficiary who fails to so survive, the descendants to be identified and to share in accordance with the law of the beneficiary's domicile at the owner's death governing inheritance by descendants of an intestate. Other forms of identifying beneficiaries who are to take on one or more contingencies, and rules for providing proofs and assurances needed to satisfy reasonable concerns by registering entities regarding conditions and identities relevant to accurate implementation of registrations in beneficiary form, may be contained in a registering entity's terms and conditions.

(c) The following are illustrations of registrations in beneficiary form that a registering entity may authorize:

(1) Sole owner-sole beneficiary: John S. Brown TOD (or POD) John S. Brown, Jr.

(2) Multiple owners-sole beneficiary: John S. Brown Mary B. Brown, JT TEN TOD John S. Brown, Jr.

(3) Multiple owners-primary and secondary (substituted) beneficiaries: John S. Brown Mary B. Brown, JT TEN TOD John S. Brown, Jr. SUB BENE Peter Q. Brown ,

or John S. Brown Mary B. Brown JT TEN TOD John S. Brown Jr. LDPS.

5511. Nothing in this part alters the community character of community property or community rights in community property. This part is subject to Chapter 2 (commencing with Section 5010) of Part 1 of Division 5.

5512. This part applies to registrations of securities in beneficiary form made before, on, or after January 1, 1999, by decedents dying on or after January 1, 1999.

Part 4. Nonprobate Transfer To Former Spouse

5600. (a) Except as provided in subdivision (b), a nonprobate transfer to the transferor's former spouse, in an instrument executed by the transferor before or during the marriage, fails if, at the time of the transferor's death, the former spouse is not the transferor's surviving spouse as defined in Section 78, as a result of the dissolution or annulment of the marriage. A judgment of legal separation that does not terminate the status of husband and wife is not a dissolution for purposes of this section.

(b) Subdivision (a) does not cause a nonprobate transfer to fail in any of the following cases:

(1) The nonprobate transfer is not subject to revocation by the transferor at the time of the transferor's death.

(2) There is clear and convincing evidence that the transferor intended to preserve the nonprobate transfer to the former spouse.

(3) A court order that the nonprobate transfer be maintained on behalf of the former spouse is in effect at the time of the transferor's death.

(c) Where a nonprobate transfer fails by operation of this section, the instrument making the nonprobate transfer shall be treated as it would if the former spouse failed to survive the transferor.

(d) Nothing in this section affects the rights of a subsequent purchaser or encumbrancer for value in good faith who relies on the apparent failure of a nonprobate transfer under this section or who lacks knowledge of the failure of a nonprobate transfer under this section.

(e) As used in this section, "nonprobate transfer" means a provision, other than a provision of a life insurance policy, of either of the following types:

(1) A provision of a type described in Section 5000.

(2) A provision in an instrument that operates on death, other than a will, conferring a power of appointment or naming a trustee.

5601. (a) Except as provided in subdivision (b), a joint tenancy between the decedent and the decedent's former spouse, created before or during the marriage, is severed as to the decedent's interest if, at the time of the decedent's death, the former spouse is not the decedent's surviving spouse as defined in Section 78, as a result of the dissolution or annulment of the marriage. A judgment of legal separation that does not terminate the status of husband and wife is not a dissolution for purposes of this section.

(b) Subdivision (a) does not sever a joint tenancy in either of the following cases:

(1) The joint tenancy is not subject to severance by the decedent at the time of the decedent's death.

(2) There is clear and convincing evidence that the decedent intended to preserve the joint tenancy in favor of the former spouse.

(c) Nothing in this section affects the rights of a subsequent purchaser or encumbrancer for value in good faith who relies on an apparent severance under this section or who lacks knowledge of a severance under this section.

(d) For purposes of this section, property held in "joint tenancy" includes property held as community property with right of survivorship, as described in Section 682.1 of the Civil Code.

5602. (a) Nothing in this part affects the rights of a purchaser or encumbrancer of real property for value who in good faith relies on an affidavit or a declaration under penalty of perjury under the laws of this state that states all of the following:

(1) The name of the decedent.

(2) The date and place of the decedent's death.

(3) A description of the real property transferred to the affiant or declarant by an instrument making a nonprobate transfer or by operation of joint tenancy survivorship.

(4) Either of the following, as appropriate:

(A) The affiant or declarant is the surviving spouse of the decedent.

(B) The affiant or declarant is not the surviving spouse of the decedent, but the rights of the affiant or declarant to the described property are not affected by Section 5600 or 5601.

(b) A person relying on an affidavit or declaration made pursuant to subdivision (a) has no duty to inquire into the truth of the matters stated in the affidavit or declaration.

(c) An affidavit or declaration made pursuant to subdivision (a) may be recorded.

5603. Nothing in this part is intended to limit the court's authority to order a party to a dissolution or annulment of marriage to maintain the former spouse as a beneficiary on any nonprobate transfer described in this part, or to preserve a joint tenancy in favor of the former spouse.

5604. (a) This part is operative on January 1, 2002.

(b) Except as provided in subdivision (c), this part applies to an instrument making a nonprobate transfer or creating a joint tenancy whether executed before, on, or after the operative date of this part.

(c) Sections 5600 and 5601 do not apply, and the applicable law in effect before the operative date of this part applies, to an instrument making a nonprobate transfer or creating a joint tenancy in either of the following circumstances:

(1) The person making the nonprobate transfer or creating the joint tenancy dies before the operative date of this part.

(2) The dissolution of marriage or other event that terminates the status of the nonprobate transfer beneficiary or joint tenant as a surviving spouse occurs before the operative date of this part.

Part 5. Gifts In View Of Impending Death

5700. As used in this part, "gift" means a transfer of personal property made voluntarily and without consideration.

5701. Except as provided in this part, a gift in view of impending death is subject to the general law relating to gifts of personal property.

5702. (a) A gift in view of impending death is one which is made in contemplation, fear, or peril of impending death, whether from illness or other cause, and with intent that it shall be revoked if the giver recovers from the illness or escapes from the peril.

(b) A reference in a statute to a gift in view of death means a gift in view of impending death.

5703. A gift made during the last illness of the giver, or under circumstances which would naturally impress the giver with an expectation of speedy death, is presumed to be a gift in view of impending death.

5704. (a) A gift in view of impending death is revoked by:

(1) The giver's recovery from the illness, or escape from the peril, under the presence of which it was made.

(2) The death of the donee before the death of the giver.

(b) A gift in view of impending death may be revoked by:

(1) The giver at any time.

(2) The giver's will if the will expresses an intention to revoke the gift.

(c) A gift in view of impending death is not affected by a previous will of the giver.

(d) Notwithstanding subdivisions (a) and (b), when the gift has been delivered to the donee, the rights of a purchaser or encumbrancer, acting before the revocation in good faith, for a valuable consideration, and without knowledge of the conditional nature of the gift, are not affected by the revocation.

5705. A gift in view of impending death is subject to Section 9653.

Division 6. Wills And Intestate Succession

Part 1. Wills

Chapter 1. General Provisions

6100. (a) An individual 18 or more years of age who is of sound mind may make a will.

(b) A conservator may make a will for the conservatee if the conservator has been so authorized by a court order pursuant to Section 2580. Nothing in this section shall impair the right of a conservatee who is mentally competent to make a will from revoking or amending a will made by the conservator or making a new and inconsistent will.

6100.5. (a) An individual is not mentally competent to make a will if at the time of making the will either of the following is true:

(1) The individual does not have sufficient mental capacity to be able to (A) understand the nature of the testamentary act, (B) understand and recollect the nature and situation of the individual's property, or (C) remember and understand the individual's relations to living descendants, spouse, and parents, and those whose interests are affected by the will.

(2) The individual suffers from a mental disorder with symptoms including delusions or hallucinations, which delusions or hallucinations result in the individual's devising property in a way which, except for the existence of the delusions or hallucinations, the individual would not have done.

(b) Nothing in this section supersedes existing law relating to the admissibility of evidence to prove the existence of mental incompetence or mental disorders.

(c) Notwithstanding subdivision (a), a conservator may make a will on behalf of a conservatee if the conservator has been so authorized by a court order pursuant to Section 2580.

6101. A will may dispose of the following property:

(a) The testator's separate property.

(b) The one-half of the community property that belongs to the testator under Section 100.

(c) The one-half of the testator's quasi-community property that belongs to the testator under Section 101.

6102. A will may make a disposition of property to any person, including but not limited to any of the following:

(a) An individual.

(b) A corporation.

(c) An unincorporated association, society, lodge, or any branch thereof.

(d) A county, city, city and county, or any municipal corporation.

(e) Any state, including this state.

(f) The United States or any instrumentality thereof.

(g) A foreign country or a governmental entity therein.

6103. Except as otherwise specifically provided, Chapter 1 (commencing with Section 6100), Chapter 2 (commencing with Section 6110), Chapter 3 (commencing with Section 6120), Chapter 4 (commencing with Section 6130), Chapter 6 (commencing with Section 6200), and Chapter 7 (commencing with Section 6300) of this division, and Part 1 (commencing with Section 21101) of Division 11, do not apply where the testator died before January 1, 1985, and the law applicable prior to January 1, 1985, continues to apply where the testator died before January 1, 1985.

6104. The execution or revocation of a will or a part of a will is ineffective to the extent the execution or revocation was procured by duress, menace, fraud, or undue influence.

6105. A will, the validity of which is made conditional by its own terms, shall be admitted to probate or rejected, or denied effect after admission to probate, in conformity with the condition.

Chapter 2. Execution Of Wills

6110. (a) Except as provided in this part, a will shall be in writing and satisfy the requirements of this section.

(b) The will shall be signed by one of the following:

(1) By the testator.

(2) In the testator's name by some other person in the testator's presence and by the testator's direction.

(3) By a conservator pursuant to a court order to make a will under Section 2580.

(c) (1) Except as provided in paragraph (2), the will shall be witnessed by being signed, during the testator's lifetime, by at least two persons each of whom (A) being present at the same time, witnessed either the signing of the will or the testator's acknowledgment of the signature or of the will and (B) understand that the instrument they sign is the testator's will.

(2) If a will was not executed in compliance with paragraph (1), the will shall be treated as if it was executed in compliance with that paragraph if the proponent of the will establishes by clear and convincing evidence that, at the time the testator signed the will, the testator intended the will to constitute the testator's will.

6111. (a) A will that does not comply with Section 6110 is valid as a holographic will, whether or not witnessed, if the signature and the material provisions are in the handwriting of the testator.

(b) If a holographic will does not contain a statement as to the date of its execution and:

(1) If the omission results in doubt as to whether its provisions or the inconsistent provisions of another will are controlling, the holographic will is invalid to the extent of the inconsistency unless the time of its execution is established to be after the date of execution of the other will.

(2) If it is established that the testator lacked testamentary capacity at any time during which the will might have been executed, the will is invalid unless it is established that it was executed at a time when the testator had testamentary capacity.

(c) Any statement of testamentary intent contained in a holographic will may be set forth either in the testator's own handwriting or as part of a commercially printed form will.

6111.5. Extrinsic evidence is admissible to determine whether a document constitutes a will pursuant to Section 6110 or 6111, or to determine the meaning of a will or a portion of a will if the meaning is unclear.

6112. (a) Any person generally competent to be a witness may act as a witness to a will.

(b) A will or any provision thereof is not invalid because the will is signed by an interested witness.

(c) Unless there are at least two other subscribing witnesses to the will who are disinterested witnesses, the fact that the will makes a devise to a subscribing witness creates a presumption that the witness procured the devise by duress, menace, fraud, or undue influence. This presumption is a presumption affecting the burden of proof. This presumption does not apply where the witness is a person to whom the devise is made solely in a fiduciary capacity.

(d) If a devise made by the will to an interested witness fails because the presumption established by subdivision (c) applies to the devise and the witness fails to rebut the presumption, the interested witness shall take such proportion of the devise made to the witness in the will as does not exceed the share of the estate which would be distributed to the witness if the will were not established. Nothing in this subdivision affects the law that applies where it is established that the witness procured a devise by duress, menace, fraud, or undue influence.

6113. A written will is validly executed if its execution complies with any of the following:

(a) The will is executed in compliance with Section 6110 or 6111 or Chapter 6 (commencing with Section 6200) (California statutory will) or Chapter 11 (commencing with Section 6380) (Uniform International Wills Act).

(b) The execution of the will complies with the law at the time of execution of the place where the will is executed.

(c) The execution of the will complies with the law of the place where at the time of execution or at the time of death the testator is domiciled, has a place of abode, or is a national.

Chapter 3. Revocation And Revival

6120. A will or any part thereof is revoked by any of the following:

(a) A subsequent will which revokes the prior will or part expressly or by inconsistency.

(b) Being burned, torn, canceled, obliterated, or destroyed, with the intent and for the purpose of revoking it, by either (1) the testator or (2) another person in the testator's presence and by the testator's direction.

6121. A will executed in duplicate or any part thereof is revoked if one of the duplicates is burned, torn, canceled, obliterated, or destroyed, with the intent and for the purpose of revoking it, by either (1) the testator or (2) another person in the testator's presence and by the testator's direction.

6122. (a) Unless the will expressly provides otherwise, if after executing a will the testator's marriage is dissolved or annulled, the dissolution or annulment revokes all of the following:

(1) Any disposition or appointment of property made by the will to the former spouse.

(2) Any provision of the will conferring a general or special power of appointment on the former spouse.

(3) Any provision of the will nominating the former spouse as executor, trustee, conservator, or guardian.

(b) If any disposition or other provision of a will is revoked solely by this section, it is revived by the testator's remarriage to the former spouse.

(c) In case of revocation by dissolution or annulment:

(1) Property prevented from passing to a former spouse because of the revocation passes as if the former spouse failed to survive the testator.

(2) Other provisions of the will conferring some power or office on the former spouse shall be interpreted as if the former spouse failed to survive the testator.

(d) For purposes of this section, dissolution or annulment means any dissolution or annulment which would exclude the spouse as a surviving spouse within the meaning of Section 78. A decree of legal separation which does not terminate the status of husband and wife is not a dissolution for purposes of this section.

(e) Except as provided in Section 6122.1, no change of circumstances other than as described in this section revokes a will.

(f) Subdivisions (a) to (d), inclusive, do not apply to any case where the final judgment of dissolution or annulment of marriage occurs before January 1, 1985. That case is governed by the law in effect prior to January 1, 1985.

6122.1. (a) Unless the will expressly provides otherwise, if after executing a will the testator's domestic partnership is terminated, the termination revokes all of the following:

(1) Any disposition or appointment of property made by the will to the former domestic partner.

(2) Any provision of the will conferring a general or special power of appointment on the former domestic partner.

(3) Any provision of the will nominating the former domestic partner as executor, trustee, conservator, or guardian.

(b) If any disposition or other provision of a will is revoked solely by this section, it is revived by the testator establishing another domestic partnership with the former domestic partner.

(c) In case of revocation by termination of a domestic partnership:

(1) Property prevented from passing to a former domestic partner because of the revocation passes as if the former domestic partner failed to survive the testator.

(2) Other provisions of the will conferring some power or office on the former domestic partner shall be interpreted as if the former domestic partner failed to survive the testator.

(d) This section shall apply only to wills executed on or after January 1, 2002.

6123. (a) If a second will which, had it remained effective at death, would have revoked the first will in whole or in part, is thereafter revoked by acts under Section 6120 or 6121, the first will is revoked in whole or in part unless it is evident from the circumstances of the revocation of the second will or from the testator's contemporary or subsequent declarations that the testator intended the first will to take effect as executed.

(b) If a second will which, had it remained effective at death, would have revoked the first will in whole or in part, is thereafter revoked by a third will, the first will is revoked in whole or in part, except to the extent it appears from the terms of the third will that the testator intended the first will to take effect.

6124. If the testator's will was last in the testator's possession, the testator was competent until death, and neither the will nor a duplicate original of the will can be found after the testator's death, it is presumed that the testator destroyed the will with intent to revoke it. This presumption is a presumption affecting the burden of producing evidence.

Chapter 4. Reference To Matters Outside The Will

6130. A writing in existence when a will is executed may be incorporated by reference if the language of the will manifests this intent and describes the writing sufficiently to permit its identification.

6131. A will may dispose of property by reference to acts and events that have significance apart from their effect upon the dispositions made by the will, whether the acts and events occur before or after the execution of the will or before or after the testator's death. The execution or revocation of a will of another person is such an event.

6132. (a) Notwithstanding any other provision, a will may refer to a writing that directs disposition of tangible personal property not otherwise specifically disposed of by the will, except for money that is common coin or currency and property used primarily in a trade or business. A writing directing disposition of a testator's tangible personal property is effective if all of the following conditions are satisfied:

(1) An unrevoked will refers to the writing.

(2) The writing is dated and is either in the handwriting of, or signed by, the testator.

(3) The writing describes the items and the recipients of the property with reasonable certainty.

(b) The failure of a writing to conform to the conditions described in paragraph (2) of subdivision (a) does not preclude the introduction of evidence of the existence of the testator's intent regarding the disposition of tangible personal property as authorized by this section.

(c) The writing may be written or signed before or after the execution of the will and need not have significance apart from its effect upon the dispositions of property made by the will. A writing that meets the requirements of this section shall be given effect as if it were actually contained in the will itself, except that if any person designated to receive property in the writing dies before the testator, the property shall pass as further directed in the writing and, in the absence of any further directions, the disposition shall lapse.

(d) The testator may make subsequent handwritten or signed changes to any writing. If there is an inconsistent disposition of tangible personal property as between writings, the most recent writing controls.

(e) (1) If the writing directing disposition of tangible personal property omits a statement as to the date of its execution, and if the omission results in doubt whether its provisions or the provisions of another writing inconsistent with it are controlling, then the writing omitting the statement is invalid to the extent of its inconsistency unless the time of its execution is established to be after the date of execution of the other writing.

(2) If the writing directing disposition of tangible personal property omits a statement as to the date of its execution, and it is established that the testator lacked testamentary capacity at any time during which the writing may have been executed, the writing is invalid unless it is established that it was executed at a time when the testator had testamentary capacity.

(f) (1) Concurrent with the filing of the inventory and appraisal required by Section 8800, the personal representative shall also file the writing that directs disposition of the testator's tangible personal property.

(2) Notwithstanding paragraph (1), if the writing has not been found or is not available at the time of the filing of the inventory and appraisal, the personal representative shall file the writing no later than 60 days prior to filing the petition for final distribution pursuant to Section 11640.

(g) The total value of tangible personal property identified and disposed of in the writing shall not exceed twenty-five thousand dollars ($25,000). If the value of an item of tangible personal property described in the writing exceeds five thousand dollars ($5,000), that item shall not be subject to this section and that item shall be disposed of pursuant to the remainder clause of the will. The value of an item of tangible personal property that is disposed of pursuant to the remainder clause of the will shall not be counted towards the twenty-five thousand dollar ($25,000) limit described in this subdivision.

(h) As used in this section, the following definitions shall apply:

(1) "Tangible personal property" means articles of personal or household use or ornament, including, but not limited to, furniture, furnishings, automobiles, boats, and jewelry, as well as precious metals in any tangible form, such as bullion or coins and articles held for investment purposes The term "tangible personal property" does not mean real property, a mobilehome as defined in Section 798.3 of the Civil Code, intangible property, such as evidences of indebtedness, bank accounts and other monetary deposits, documents of title, or securities.

(2) "Common coin or currency" means the coins and currency of the United States that are legal tender for the payment of public and private debts, but does not include coins or currency kept or acquired for their historical, artistic, collectable, or investment value apart from their normal use as legal tender for payment.

Chapter 6. California Statutory Will

Article 1. Definitions And Rules Of Construction

6200. Unless the provision or context clearly requires otherwise, these definitions and rules of construction govern the construction of this chapter.

6201. "Testator" means a person choosing to adopt a California statutory will.

6203. "Executor" means both the person so designated in a California statutory will and any other person acting at any time as the executor or administrator under a

California statutory will.

6204. "Trustee" means both the person so designated in a California statutory will and any other person acting at any time as the trustee under a California statutory will.

6205. "Descendants" mean children, grandchildren, and their lineal descendants of all generations, with the relationship of parent and child at each generation being determined as provided in Section 21115. A reference to "descendants" in the plural includes a single descendant where the context so requires.

6206. A reference in a California statutory will to the "Uniform Gifts to Minors Act of any state" or the "Uniform Transfers to Minors Act of any state" includes both the Uniform Gifts to Minors Act of any state and the Uniform Transfers to Minors Act of any state. A reference to a "custodian" means the person so designated in a California statutory will or any other person acting at any time as a custodian under a Uniform Gifts to Minors Act or Uniform Transfers to Minors Act.

6207. Masculine pronouns include the feminine, and plural and singular words include each other, where appropriate.

6208. (a) If a California statutory will states that a person shall perform an act, the person is required to perform that act.

(b) If a California statutory will states that a person may do an act, the person's decision to do or not to do the act shall be made in the exercise of the person's fiduciary powers.

6209. Whenever a distribution under a California statutory will is to be made to a person's descendants, the property shall be divided into as many equal shares as there are then living descendants of the nearest degree of living descendants and deceased descendants of that same degree who leave descendants then living; and each living descendant of the nearest degree shall receive one share and the share of each deceased descendant of that same degree shall be divided among his or her descendants in the same manner.

6210. "Person" includes individuals and institutions.

6211. Reference to a person "if living" or who "survives me" means a person who survives the decedent by 120 hours. A person who fails to survive the decedent by 120 hours is deemed to have predeceased the decedent for the purpose of a California statutory will, and the beneficiaries are determined accordingly. If it cannot be established by clear and convincing evidence that a person who would otherwise be a beneficiary has survived the decedent by 120 hours, it is deemed that the person failed to survive for the required period. The requirement of this section that a person who survives the decedent must survive the decedent by 120 hours does not apply if the application of the 120-hour survival requirement would result in the escheat of property to the state.

Article 2. General Provisions

6220. Any individual of sound mind and over the age of 18 may execute a California statutory will under the provisions of this chapter.

6221. A California statutory will shall be executed only as follows:

(a) The testator shall complete the appropriate blanks and shall sign the will.

(b) Each witness shall observe the testator's signing and each witness shall sign his or her name in the presence of the testator.

6222. The execution of the attestation clause provided in the California statutory will by two or more witnesses satisfies Section 8220.

6223. (a) There is only one California statutory will.

(b) The California statutory will includes all of the following:

(1) The contents of the California statutory will form set out in Section 6240, excluding the questions and answers at the beginning of the California statutory will.

(2) By reference, the full texts of each of the following:

(A) The definitions and rules of construction set forth in Article 1 (commencing with Section 6200).

(B) The property disposition clauses adopted by the testator. If no property disposition clause is adopted, Section 6224 shall apply.

(C) The mandatory clauses set forth in Section 6241.

(c) Notwithstanding this section, any California statutory will or California statutory will with trust executed on a form allowed under prior law shall be governed by the law that applied prior to January 1, 1992.

6224. If more than one property disposition clause appearing in paragraphs 2 or 3 of a California statutory will is selected, no gift is made. If more than one property disposition clause in paragraph 5 of a California statutory will form is selected, or if none is selected, the residuary estate of a testator who signs a California statutory will shall be distributed to the testator's heirs as if the testator did not make a will.

6225. Only the texts of property disposition clauses and the mandatory clauses shall be considered in determining their meaning. Their titles shall be disregarded.

6226. (a) A California statutory will may be revoked and may be amended by codicil in the same manner as other wills.

(b) Any additions to or deletions from the California statutory will on the face of the California statutory will form, other than in accordance with the instructions, shall be given effect only where clear and convincing evidence shows that they would effectuate the clear intent of the testator. In the absence of such a showing, the court either may determine that the addition or deletion is ineffective and shall be disregarded, or may determine that all or a portion of the California statutory will is invalid, whichever is more likely to be consistent with the intent of the testator.

(c) Notwithstanding Section 6110, a document executed on a California statutory will form is valid as a will if all of the following requirements are shown to be satisfied by clear and convincing evidence:

(1) The form is signed by the testator.

(2) The court is satisfied that the testator knew and approved of the contents of the will and intended it to have testamentary effect.

(3) The testamentary intent of the maker as reflected in the document is clear.

6227. (a) If after executing a California statutory will the testator's marriage is dissolved or annulled, the dissolution or annulment revokes any disposition of property made by the will to the former spouse and any nomination of the former spouse as executor, trustee, guardian, or custodian made by the will. If any disposition or nomination is revoked solely by this section, it is revived by the testator's remarriage to the former spouse.

(b) In case of revocation by dissolution or annulment:

(1) Property prevented from passing to a former spouse because of the revocation passes as if the former spouse failed to survive the testator.

(2) Provisions nominating the former spouse as executor, trustee, guardian, or custodian shall be interpreted as if the former spouse failed to survive the testator.

(c) For purposes of this section, dissolution or annulment means any dissolution or annulment that would exclude the spouse as a surviving spouse within the meaning of Section 78. A decree of legal separation which does not terminate the status of husband and wife is not a dissolution or annulment for purposes of this section.

(d) This section applies to any California statutory will, without regard to the time when the will was executed, but this section does not apply to any case where the final judgment of dissolution or annulment of marriage occurs before January 1, 1985; and, if the final judgment of dissolution or annulment of marriage occurs before January 1, 1985, the case is governed by the law that applied prior to January 1, 1985.

Article 3. Form And Full Text Of Clauses

6240. The following is the California Statutory Will form:

```
PLEASE SEE THE APPENDIX
```

6241. The mandatory clauses of the California statutory will form are as follows:

(a) Intestate Disposition. If the testator has not made an effective disposition of the residuary estate, the executor shall distribute it to the testator's heirs at law, their identities and respective shares to be determined according to the laws of the State of California in effect on the date of the testator's death relating to intestate succession of property not acquired from a predeceased spouse.

(b) Powers of Executor.

(1) In addition to any powers now or hereafter conferred upon executors by law, including all powers granted under the Independent Administration of Estates Act, the executor shall have the power to:

(A) Sell estate assets at public or private sale, for cash or on credit terms.

(B) Lease estate assets without restriction as to duration.

(C) Invest any surplus moneys of the estate in real or personal property, as the executor deems advisable.

(2) The executor may distribute estate assets otherwise distributable to a minor beneficiary to one of the following:

(A) The guardian of the minor's person or estate.

(B) Any adult person with whom the minor resides and who has the care, custody, or control of the minor.

(C) A custodian of the minor under the Uniform Transfers to Minors Act as designated in the California statutory will form.

The executor is free of liability and is discharged from any further accountability for distributing assets in compliance with the provisions of this paragraph.

(3) On any distribution of assets from the estate, the executor shall have the discretion to partition, allot, and distribute the assets in the following manner:

(A) In kind, including undivided interest in an asset or in any part of it.

(B) Partly in cash and partly in kind.

(C) Entirely in cash.

If a distribution is being made to more than one beneficiary, the executor shall have the discretion to distribute assets among them on a pro rata or non pro rata basis, with the assets valued as of the date of distribution.

(c) Powers of Guardian. A guardian of the person nominated in the California statutory will shall have the same authority with respect to the person of the ward as a parent having legal custody of a child would have. All powers granted to guardians in this paragraph may be exercised without court authorization.

6242. (a) Except as specifically provided in this chapter, a California statutory will shall include only the texts of the property disposition clauses and the mandatory clauses as they exist on the day the California statutory will is executed.

(b) Sections 6205, 6206, and 6227 apply to every California statutory will, including those executed before January 1, 1985. Section 6211 applies only to California statutory wills executed after July 1, 1991.

(c) Notwithstanding Section 6222, and except as provided in subdivision (b), a California statutory will is governed by the law that applied prior to January 1, 1992, if the California statutory will is executed on a form that (1) was prepared for use under former Sections 56 to 56.14, inclusive, or former Sections 6200 to 6248, inclusive, of the Probate Code, and (2) satisfied the requirements of law that applied prior to January 1, 1992.

(d) A California statutory will does not fail to satisfy the requirements of subdivision (a) merely because the will is executed on a form that incorporates the mandatory clauses of Section 6241 that refer to former Section 1120.2. If the will incorporates the mandatory clauses with a reference to former Section 1120.2, the trustee has the powers listed in Article 2 (commencing with Section 16220) of Chapter 2 of Part 4 of Division 9.

6243. Except as specifically provided in this chapter, the general law of California applies to a California statutory will.

Chapter 7. Uniform Testamentary Additions To Trusts Act

6300. A devise, the validity of which is determinable by the law of this state, may be made by a will to the trustee of a trust established or to be established by the testator or by the testator and some other person or by some other person (including a funded or unfunded life insurance trust, although the settlor has reserved any or all rights of ownership of the insurance contracts) if the trust is identified in the testator's will and its terms are set forth in a written instrument (other than a will) executed before or concurrently with the execution of the testator's will or in the valid last will of a person who has predeceased the testator (regardless of the existence, size, or character of the trust property). The devise is not invalid because the trust is amendable or revocable, or both, or because the trust was amended after the execution of the will or after the death of the testator. Unless the testator's will provides otherwise, the property so devised (1) is not deemed to be held under a testamentary trust of the testator but becomes a part of the trust to which it is given and (2) shall be administered and disposed of in accordance with the provisions of the instrument or will setting forth the terms of the trust, including any amendments thereto made before or after the death of the testator (regardless of whether made before or after the execution of the testator's will). Unless otherwise pro-

vided in the will, a revocation or termination of the trust before the death of the testator causes the devise to lapse.

6301. This chapter does not invalidate any devise made by a will executed prior to September 17, 1965.

6303. This chapter may be cited as the Uniform Testamentary Additions to Trusts Act.

Chapter 8. Nonprobate Transfer To Trustee Named In Decedent's Will

6320. As used in this chapter, unless the context otherwise requires:

(a) "Designation" means a designation made pursuant to Section 6321.

(b) "Instrument" includes all of the following:

(1) An insurance, annuity, or endowment contract (including any agreement issued or entered into by the insurer in connection therewith, supplemental thereto, or in settlement thereof).

(2) A pension, retirement benefit, death benefit, stock bonus, profit-sharing or employees' saving plan, employee benefit plan, or contract created or entered into by an employer for the benefit of some or all of his or her employees.

(3) A self-employed retirement plan, or an individual retirement annuity or account, established or held pursuant to the Internal Revenue Code.

(4) A multiple-party account, as defined in Section 5132.

(5) Any other written instrument of a type described in Section 5000.

6321. An instrument may designate as a primary or contingent beneficiary, payee, or owner a trustee named or to be named in the will of the person entitled to designate the beneficiary, payee, or owner. The designation shall be made in accordance with the provisions of the contract or plan or, in the absence of such provisions, in a manner approved by the insurer if an insurance, annuity, or endowment contract is involved, and by the trustee, custodian, or person or entity administering the contract or plan, if any. The designation may be made before or after the execution of the designator's will and is not required to comply with the formalities for execution of a will.

6322. The designation is ineffective unless the designator's will contains provisions creating the trust or makes a disposition valid under Section 6300.

6323. Subject to the provisions of Section 6325, the benefits or rights resulting from the designation are payable or transferable directly to the trustee, without becoming subject to administration, upon or at any time after admission of the designator's will to probate. A designation pursuant to this chapter does not have the effect of naming a trustee of a separate inter vivos trust but the rights and benefits or the proceeds thereof when paid to the trustee are, or become a part of, the testamentary trust or trusts established pursuant to the designator's will or shall be added to an inter vivos trust or trusts if the disposition is governed by Section 6300.

6324. Except as otherwise provided in the designator's will, the rights and benefits and their proceeds paid or transferred to the trustee are not subject to the debts of the designator to any greater extent than if they were paid or transferred to a named beneficiary, payee, or owner other than the estate of the designator.

6325. (a) The court in which the proceedings are pending for administration of the estate of the decedent has jurisdiction, before or after payment or transfer of benefits and rights or their proceeds to the trustee, to:

(1) Determine the validity of the trust.

(2) Determine the terms of the trust.

(3) Fill vacancies in the office of trustee.

(4) Require a bond of a trustee in its discretion and in such amount as the court may determine for the faithful performance of duties as trustee, subject to the provisions of Article 3 (commencing with Section 1540) of Chapter 12 of Division 1 of the Financial Code and Section 15602 of this code.

(5) Grant additional powers to the trustee, as provided in Section 16201.

(6) Instruct the trustee.

(7) Fix or allow payment of compensation of a trustee as provided in Sections 15680 to 15683, inclusive.

(8) Hear and determine adverse claims to the trust property by the personal representative, surviving spouse, or other third person.

(9) Determine the identity of the trustee and the trustee's acceptance or rejection of the office and, upon request, furnish evidence of trusteeship to a trustee.

(10) Order postponement of the payment or transfer of the benefits and rights or their proceeds.

(11) Authorize or direct removal of the trust or trust property to another jurisdiction pursuant to the procedure provided in Chapter 5 (commencing with Section 17400) of Part 5 of Division 9.

(12) Make any order incident to the foregoing or to the accomplishment of the purposes of this chapter.

(b) The personal representative of the designator's estate, any trustee named in the will or designation or successor to such trustee, or any person interested in the estate or trust may petition the court for an order under this section. Notice of hearing of the petition shall be given in the manner provided in Section 17203, except as the court may otherwise order.

6326. As to matters not specifically provided in Section 6325, the provisions of Division 9 (commencing with Section 15000) apply to the trust.

6327. An appeal may be taken from any of the following:

(a) Any order described in Part 3 (commencing with Section 1300) of Division 3 made pursuant to this chapter.

(b) An order making or refusing to make a determination specified in paragraph (1), (2), or (8) of subdivision (a) of Section 6325.

(c) As provided in Section 1304 for an order made pursuant to Section 6326.

6328. If no qualified trustee makes claim to the benefits or rights or proceeds within one year after the death of the designator, or if satisfactory evidence is furnished within such one-year period showing that no trustee can qualify to receive them, payment or transfer may be made, unless the designator has otherwise provided, by the obligor to the personal representative of the designator or to those thereafter entitled, and the obligor is discharged from liability.

6329. Enactment of this chapter does not invalidate trusts, otherwise valid, not made pursuant to the provisions of this chapter.

6330. This chapter, insofar as it is substantially the same as former Chapter 10 (commencing with Section 175) of former Division 1, repealed by Section 18 of Chapter 842 of the Statutes of 1983, shall be construed as a restatement and continuation thereof and not as a new enactment. After December 31, 1984, a reference in a written instrument to the previously existing provisions relating to the subject matter of this chapter shall be deemed to be a reference to the corresponding provisions of this chapter.

Chapter 9. Devise Subject To California Uniform Transfers To Minors Act

6341. If a testator's will provides that devised property shall be paid or delivered or transferred to a custodian subject to the California Uniform Gifts to Minors Act or the California Uniform Transfers to Minors Act:

(a) All of the provisions of the California Uniform Transfers to Minors Act, Part 9 (commencing with Section 3900) of Division 4, including, but not limited to, the definitions and the provisions concerning powers, rights, and immunities contained in that act, are applicable to the devise during the period prior to distribution of the property.

(b) Unless the will clearly requires otherwise, if the person named as the beneficiary for whose benefit the custodial property is to be held attains the age at which the custodianship was to terminate prior to the order of distribution, the devise shall be deemed to be a direct devise to the person named as the beneficiary for whose benefit the custodial property was to be held.

(c) The personal representative of the testator's estate, upon entry of an order for distribution, shall make distribution pursuant to the order for distribution by transferring the devised property in the form and manner provided by the California Uniform Transfers to Minors Act.

(d) If a vacancy in the custodianship exists prior to full distribution of the devised property by the personal representative, a successor custodian shall be appointed for any undistributed property in the manner provided by the California Uniform Transfers to Minors Act.

6345. The will may provide for successor or substitute custodians and may specify the standard of compensation of the custodian.

6347. (a) Except as otherwise provided in the will or ordered by a court, each custodian designated in the will and the person for whom the property is to be held shall be deemed a devisee for the purpose of receiving notices which may be required or permitted to be sent to a devisee in the estate of the testator.

(b) Unless required by the will or ordered by the court, a custodian does not have a duty to participate in the proceedings in the estate on behalf of the minor, and in no event does the custodian have a duty to so participate until the custodian has filed a written notice of acceptance of the office of custodian with the clerk of the court in which administration of the estate of the testator is pending.

6348. Until distribution of the property pursuant to an order for distribution is completed, the court in which administration of the estate of the testator is pending has exclusive jurisdiction over all proceedings and matters concerning undistributed property, including, but not limited to, the appointment, declination, resignation, removal, bonding, and compensation of, and the delivery or transfer of the undistributed property to, a custodian. After distribution of any property is completed, the court has no further jurisdiction over the distributed property and the property shall be held subject to the California Uniform Transfers to Minors Act.

6349. (a) This chapter shall not be construed as providing an exclusive method for making devises to or for the benefit of minors.

(b) Nothing in this chapter limits any provision of the California Uniform Transfers to Minors Act, Part 9 (commencing with Section 3900) of Division 4.

Chapter 11. Uniform International Wills Act

6380. In this chapter:

(a) "International will" means a will executed in conformity with Sections 6381 to 6384, inclusive.

(b) "Authorized person" and "person authorized to act in connection with international wills" means a person who by Section 6388, or by the laws of the United States including members of the diplomatic and consular service of the United States designated by Foreign Service Regulations, is empowered to supervise the execution of international wills.

6381. (a) A will is valid as regards form, irrespective particularly of the place where it is made, of the location of the assets and of the nationality, domicile, or residence of the testator, if it is made in the form of an international will complying with the requirements of this chapter.

(b) The invalidity of the will as an international will does not affect its formal validity as a will of another kind.

(c) This chapter does not apply to the form of testamentary dispositions made by two or more persons in one instrument.

6382. (a) The will shall be made in writing. It need not be written by the testator himself or herself. It may be written in any language, by hand or by any other means.

(b) The testator shall declare in the presence of two witnesses and of a person authorized to act in connection with international wills that the document is the testator's will and that the testator knows the contents thereof. The testator need not inform the witnesses, or the authorized person, of the contents of the will.

(c) In the presence of the witnesses, and of the authorized person, the testator shall sign the will or, if the testator has previously signed it, shall acknowledge his or her signature.

(d) If the testator is unable to sign, the absence of the testator' s signature does not affect the validity of the international will if the testator indicates the reason for his or her inability to sign and the authorized person makes note thereof on the will. In that case, it is permissible for any other person present, including the authorized person or one of the witnesses, at the direction of the testator, to sign the testator's name for the testator if the authorized person makes note of this also on the will, but it is not required that any person sign the testator's name for the testator.

(e) The witnesses and the authorized person shall there and then attest the will by signing in the presence of the testator.

6383. (a) The signatures shall be placed at the end of the will. If the will consists of several sheets, each sheet shall be signed by the testator or, if the testator is unable to sign, by the person signing on his or her behalf or, if there is no such person, by the authorized person. In addition, each sheet shall be numbered.

(b) The date of the will shall be the date of its signature by the authorized person. That date shall be noted at the end of the will by the authorized person.

(c) The authorized person shall ask the testator whether the testator wishes to make a declaration concerning the safe-keeping of the will. If so and at the express request of the testator, the place where the testator intends to have the will kept shall be mentioned in the certificate provided for in Section 6384.

(d) A will executed in compliance with Section 6382 is not invalid merely because it does not comply with this section.

6384. The authorized person shall attach to the will a certificate to be signed by the authorized person establishing that the requirements of this chapter for valid execution of an international will have been fulfilled. The authorized person shall keep a copy of the certificate and deliver another to the testator. The certificate shall be substantially in the following form:

> PLEASE SEE THE APPENDIX

6385. In the absence of evidence to the contrary, the certificate of the authorized person is conclusive of the formal validity of the instrument as a will under this chapter. The absence or irregularity of a certificate does not affect the formal validity of a will under this chapter.

6386. The international will is subject to the ordinary rules of revocation of wills.

6387. Sections 6380 to 6386, inclusive, derive from Annex to Convention of October 26, 1973, Providing a Uniform Law on the Form of an International Will. In interpreting and applying this chapter, regard shall be had to its international origin and to the need for uniformity in its interpretation.

6388. Individuals who have been admitted to practice law before the courts of this state and who are in good standing as active law practitioners of this state are authorized persons in relation to international wills.

6389. The Secretary of State shall establish a registry system by which authorized persons may register in a central information center information regarding the execution of international wills, keeping that information in strictest confidence until the death of the maker and then making it available to any person desiring information about any will who presents a death certificate or other satisfactory evidence of the testator's death to the center. Information that may be received, preserved in confidence until death, and reported as indicated is limited to the name, social security or other individual identifying number established by law, if any, address, date and place of birth of the testator, and the intended place of deposit or safekeeping of the instrument pending the death of the maker. The Secretary of State, at the request of the authorized person, may cause the information it receives about execution of any interna-

tional will to be transmitted to the registry system of another jurisdiction as identified by the testator, if that other system adheres to rules protecting the confidentiality of the information similar to those established in this state.

6390. After December 31, 1984, a reference in a written instrument, including a will, to the former law (repealed by Chapter 892 of the Statutes of 1984) shall be deemed to be a reference to the corresponding provision of this chapter.

Part 2. Intestate Succession

Chapter 1. Intestate Succession Generally

6400. Any part of the estate of a decedent not effectively disposed of by will passes to the decedent's heirs as prescribed in this part.

6401. (a) As to community property, the intestate share of the surviving spouse is the one-half of the community property that belongs to the decedent under Section 100.

(b) As to quasi-community property, the intestate share of the surviving spouse is the one-half of the quasi-community property that belongs to the decedent under Section 101.

(c) As to separate property, the intestate share of the surviving spouse or surviving domestic partner, as defined in subdivision (b) of Section 37, is as follows:

(1) The entire intestate estate if the decedent did not leave any surviving issue parent, brother, sister, or issue of a deceased brother or sister.

(2) One-half of the intestate estate in the following cases:

(A) Where the decedent leaves only one child or the issue of one deceased child.

(B) Where the decedent leaves no issue but leaves a parent or parents or their issue or the issue of either of them.

(3) One-third of the intestate estate in the following cases:

(A) Where the decedent leaves more than one child.

(B) Where the decedent leaves one child and the issue of one or more deceased children.

(C) Where the decedent leaves issue of two or more deceased children.

6402. Except as provided in Section 6402.5, the part of the intestate estate not passing to the surviving spouse or surviving domestic partner, as defined in subdivision (b) of Section 37, under Section 6401, or the entire intestate estate if there is no surviving spouse or domestic partner, passes as follows:

(a) To the issue of the decedent, the issue taking equally if they are all of the same degree of kinship to the decedent, but if of unequal degree those of more remote degree take in the manner provided in Section 240.

(b) If there is no surviving issue, to the decedent's parent or parents equally.

(c) If there is no surviving issue or parent, to the issue of the parents or either of them, the issue taking equally if they are all of the same degree of kinship to the decedent, but if of unequal degree those of more remote degree take in the manner provided in Section 240.

(d) If there is no surviving issue, parent or issue of a parent, but the decedent is survived by one or more grandparents or issue of grandparents, to the grandparent or grandparents equally, or to the issue of those grandparents if there is no surviving grandparent, the issue taking equally if they are all of the same degree of kinship to the decedent, but if of unequal degree those of more remote degree take in the manner provided in Section 240.

(e) If there is no surviving issue, parent or issue of a parent, grandparent or issue of a grandparent, but the decedent is survived by the issue of a predeceased spouse, to that issue, the issue taking equally if they are all of the same degree of kinship to the predeceased spouse, but if of unequal degree those of more remote degree take in the manner provided in Section 240.

(f) If there is no surviving issue, parent or issue of a parent, grandparent or issue of a grandparent, or issue of a predeceased spouse, but the decedent is survived by next of kin, to the next of kin in equal degree, but where there are two or more collateral kindred in equal degree who claim through different ancestors, those who claim through the nearest ancestor are preferred to those claiming through an ancestor more remote.

(g) If there is no surviving next of kin of the decedent and no surviving issue of a predeceased spouse of the decedent, but the decedent is survived by the parents of a predeceased spouse or the issue of those parents, to the parent or parents equally, or to the issue of those parents if both are deceased, the issue taking equally if they are all of the same degree of kinship to the predeceased spouse, but if of unequal degree those of more remote degree take in the manner provided in Section 240.

6402.5. (a) For purposes of distributing real property under this section if the decedent had a predeceased spouse who died not more than 15 years before the decedent and there is no surviving spouse or issue of the decedent, the portion of the decedent's estate attributable to the decedent's predeceased spouse passes as follows:

(1) If the decedent is survived by issue of the predeceased spouse, to the surviving issue of the predeceased spouse; if they are all of the same degree of kinship to the predeceased spouse they take equally, but if of unequal degree those of more remote degree

take in the manner provided in Section 240.

(2) If there is no surviving issue of the predeceased spouse but the decedent is survived by a parent or parents of the predeceased spouse, to the predeceased spouse's surviving parent or parents equally.

(3) If there is no surviving issue or parent of the predeceased spouse but the decedent is survived by issue of a parent of the predeceased spouse, to the surviving issue of the parents of the predeceased spouse or either of them, the issue taking equally if they are all of the same degree of kinship to the predeceased spouse, but if of unequal degree those of more remote degree take in the manner provided in Section 240.

(4) If the decedent is not survived by issue, parent, or issue of a parent of the predeceased spouse, to the next of kin of the decedent in the manner provided in Section 6402.

(5) If the portion of the decedent's estate attributable to the decedent's predeceased spouse would otherwise escheat to the state because there is no kin of the decedent to take under Section 6402, the portion of the decedent's estate attributable to the predeceased spouse passes to the next of kin of the predeceased spouse who shall take in the same manner as the next of kin of the decedent take under Section 6402.

(b) For purposes of distributing personal property under this section if the decedent had a predeceased spouse who died not more than five years before the decedent, and there is no surviving spouse or issue of the decedent, the portion of the decedent's estate attributable to the decedent's predeceased spouse passes as follows:

(1) If the decedent is survived by issue of the predeceased spouse, to the surviving issue of the predeceased spouse; if they are all of the same degree of kinship to the predeceased spouse they take equally, but if of unequal degree those of more remote degree take in the manner provided in Section 240.

(2) If there is no surviving issue of the predeceased spouse but the decedent is survived by a parent or parents of the predeceased spouse, to the predeceased spouse's surviving parent or parents equally.

(3) If there is no surviving issue or parent of the predeceased spouse but the decedent is survived by issue of a parent of the predeceased spouse, to the surviving issue of the parents of the predeceased spouse or either of them, the issue taking equally if they are all of the same degree of kinship to the predeceased spouse, but if of unequal degree those of more remote degree take in the manner provided in Section 240.

(4) If the decedent is not survived by issue, parent, or issue of a parent of the predeceased spouse, to the next of kin of the decedent in the manner provided in Section 6402.

(5) If the portion of the decedent's estate attributable to the decedent's predeceased

spouse would otherwise escheat to the state because there is no kin of the decedent to take under Section 6402, the portion of the decedent's estate attributable to the predeceased spouse passes to the next of kin of the predeceased spouse who shall take in the same manner as the next of kin of the decedent take under Section 6402.

(c) For purposes of disposing of personal property under subdivision (b), the claimant heir bears the burden of proof to show the exact personal property to be disposed of to the heir.

(d) For purposes of providing notice under any provision of this code with respect to an estate that may include personal property subject to distribution under subdivision (b), if the aggregate fair market value of tangible and intangible personal property with a written record of title or ownership in the estate is believed in good faith by the petitioning party to be less than ten thousand dollars ($10,000), the petitioning party need not give notice to the issue or next of kin of the predeceased spouse. If the personal property is subsequently determined to have an aggregate fair market value in excess of ten thousand dollars ($10,000), notice shall be given to the issue or next of kin of the predeceased spouse as provided by law.

(e) For the purposes of disposing of property pursuant to subdivision (b), "personal property" means that personal property in which there is a written record of title or ownership and the value of which in the aggregate is ten thousand dollars ($10,000) or more.

(f) For the purposes of this section, the "portion of the decedent' s estate attributable to the decedent's predeceased spouse" means all of the following property in the decedent's estate:

(1) One-half of the community property in existence at the time of the death of the predeceased spouse.

(2) One-half of any community property, in existence at the time of death of the predeceased spouse, which was given to the decedent by the predeceased spouse by way of gift, descent, or devise.

(3) That portion of any community property in which the predeceased spouse had any incident of ownership and which vested in the decedent upon the death of the predeceased spouse by right of survivorship.

(4) Any separate property of the predeceased spouse which came to the decedent by gift, descent, or devise of the predeceased spouse or which vested in the decedent upon the death of the predeceased spouse by right of survivorship.

(g) For the purposes of this section, quasi-community property shall be treated the same as community property.

(h) For the purposes of this section:

(1) Relatives of the predeceased spouse conceived before the decedent's death but born thereafter inherit as if they had been born in the lifetime of the decedent.

(2) A person who is related to the predeceased spouse through two lines of relationship is entitled to only a single share based on the relationship which would entitle the person to the larger share.

6403. (a) A person who fails to survive the decedent by 120 hours is deemed to have predeceased the decedent for the purpose of intestate succession, and the heirs are determined accordingly. If it cannot be established by clear and convincing evidence that a person who would otherwise be an heir has survived the decedent by 120 hours, it is deemed that the person failed to survive for the required period. The requirement of this section that a person who survives the decedent must survive the decedent by 120 hours does not apply if the application of the 120-hour survival requirement would result in the escheat of property to the state.

(b) This section does not apply to the case where any of the persons upon whose time of death the disposition of property depends died before January 1, 1990, and such case continues to be governed by the law applicable before January 1, 1990.

6404. Part 4 (commencing with Section 6800) (escheat) applies if there is no taker of the intestate estate under the provisions of this part.

6406. Except as provided in Section 6451, relatives of the halfblood inherit the same share they would inherit if they were of the whole blood.

6407. Relatives of the decedent conceived before the decedent's death but born thereafter inherit as if they had been born in the lifetime of the decedent.

6409. (a) If a person dies intestate as to all or part of his or her estate, property the decedent gave during lifetime to an heir is treated as an advancement against that heir's share of the intestate estate only if one of the following conditions is satisfied:

(1) The decedent declares in a contemporaneous writing that the gift is an advancement against the heir's share of the estate or that its value is to be deducted from the value of the heir's share of the estate.

(2) The heir acknowledges in writing that the gift is to be so deducted or is an advancement or that its value is to be deducted from the value of the heir's share of the estate.

(b) Subject to subdivision (c), the property advanced is to be valued as of the time the heir came into possession or enjoyment of the property or as of the time of death of the decedent, whichever occurs first.

(c) If the value of the property advanced is expressed in the contemporaneous writing of the decedent, or in an acknowledgment of the heir made contemporaneously with the advancement, that value is conclusive in the division and distribution of the intestate estate.

(d) If the recipient of the property advanced fails to survive the decedent, the property is not taken into account in computing the intestate share to be received by the recipient's issue unless the declaration or acknowledgment provides otherwise.

6410. (a) A debt owed to the decedent is not charged against the intestate share of any person except the debtor.

(b) If the debtor fails to survive the decedent, the debt is not taken into account in computing the intestate share of the debtor's issue.

6411. No person is disqualified to take as an heir because that person or a person through whom he or she claims is or has been an alien.

6412. Except to the extent provided in Section 120, the estates of dower and curtesy are not recognized.

6413. A person who is related to the decedent through two lines of relationship is entitled to only a single share based on the relationship which would entitle the person to the larger share.

6414. (a) Except as provided in subdivision (b), this part does not apply where the decedent died before January 1, 1985, and the law applicable prior to January 1, 1985, continues to apply where the decedent died before January 1, 1985.

(b) Section 6412 applies whether the decedent died before, on, or after January 1, 1985.

(c) Where any of the following provisions is applied in a case where the decedent died before January 1, 1985, any reference in that provision to this part shall be deemed to be a reference to former Division 2 (commencing with Section 200) which was repealed by Section 19 of Chapter 842 of the Statutes of 1983:

(1) Section 377 of the Code of Civil Procedure.

(2) Section 3524 of the Penal Code.

Chapter 2. Parent And Child Relationship

6450. Subject to the provisions of this chapter, a relationship of parent and child exists for the purpose of determining intestate succession by, through, or from a person in the following circumstances:

(a) The relationship of parent and child exists between a person and the person's natural parents, regardless of the marital status of the natural parents.

(b) The relationship of parent and child exists between an adopted person and the person's adopting parent or parents.

6451. (a) An adoption severs the relationship of parent and child between an adopted person and a natural parent of the adopted person unless both of the following requirements are satisfied:

(1) The natural parent and the adopted person lived together at any time as parent and child, or the natural parent was married to or cohabiting with the other natural parent at the time the person was conceived and died before the person's birth.

(2) The adoption was by the spouse of either of the natural parents or after the death of either of the natural parents.

(b) Neither a natural parent nor a relative of a natural parent, except for a wholeblood brother or sister of the adopted person or the issue of that brother or sister, inherits from or through the adopted person on the basis of a parent and child relationship between the adopted person and the natural parent that satisfies the requirements of paragraphs (1) and (2) of subdivision (a), unless the adoption is by the spouse or surviving spouse of that parent.

(c) For the purpose of this section, a prior adoptive parent and child relationship is treated as a natural parent and child relationship.

6452. (a) A parent does not inherit from or through a child on the basis of the parent and child relationship if any of the following apply:

(1) The parent's parental rights were terminated and the parent-child relationship was not judicially reestablished.

(2) The parent did not acknowledge the child.

(3) The parent left the child during the child's minority without an effort to provide for the child's support or without communication from the parent, for at least seven consecutive years that continued until the end of the child's minority, with the intent on the part of the parent to abandon the child. The failure to provide support or to communicate for the prescribed period is presumptive evidence of an intent to abandon.

(b) A parent who does not inherit from or through the child as provided in subdivision (a) shall be deemed to have predeceased the child, and the intestate estate shall pass as otherwise required under Section 6402.

6453. For the purpose of determining whether a person is a "natural parent" as that term is used in this chapter:

(a) A natural parent and child relationship is established where that relationship is presumed and not rebutted pursuant to the Uniform Parentage Act (Part 3 (commencing with Section 7600) of Division 12 of the Family Code).

(b) A natural parent and child relationship may be established pursuant to any other provisions of the Uniform Parentage Act, except that the relationship may not be established by an action under subdivision (c) of Section 7630 of the Family Code unless any of the following conditions exist:

(1) A court order was entered during the father's lifetime declaring paternity.

(2) Paternity is established by clear and convincing evidence that the father has openly held out the child as his own.

(3) It was impossible for the father to hold out the child as his own and paternity is established by clear and convincing evidence.

(c) A natural parent and child relationship may be established pursuant to Section 249.5.

6454. For the purpose of determining intestate succession by a person or the person's issue from or through a foster parent or stepparent, the relationship of parent and child exists between that person and the person's foster parent or stepparent if both of the following requirements are satisfied:

(a) The relationship began during the person's minority and continued throughout the joint lifetimes of the person and the person's foster parent or stepparent.

(b) It is established by clear and convincing evidence that the foster parent or stepparent would have adopted the person but for a legal barrier.

6455. Nothing in this chapter affects or limits application of the judicial doctrine of equitable adoption for the benefit of the child or the child's issue.

Part 3. Family Protection

Chapter 1. Temporary Possession Of Family Dwelling And Exempt Property

6500. Until the inventory is filed and for a period of 60 days thereafter, or for such other period as may be ordered by the court for good cause on petition therefor, the decedent's surviving spouse and minor children are entitled to remain in possession of the family dwelling, the wearing apparel of the family, the household furniture, and the other property of the decedent exempt from enforcement of a money judgment.

6501. A petition for an order under Section 6500 may be filed by any interested person. Notice of the hearing on the petition shall be given as provided in Section 1220.

Chapter 2. Setting Aside Exempt Property Other Than Family Dwelling

6510. Upon the filing of the inventory or at any subsequent time during the administration of the estate, the court in its discretion may on petition therefor set apart all or any part of the property of the decedent exempt from enforcement of a money judgment, other than the family dwelling, to any one or more of the following:

(a) The surviving spouse.

(b) The minor children of the decedent.

6511. A petition for an order under Section 6510 may be filed by any interested person. Notice of the hearing on the petition shall be given as provided in Section 1220.

Chapter 3. Setting Aside Probate Homestead

6520. Upon the filing of the inventory or at any subsequent time during the administration of the estate, the court in its discretion may on petition therefor select and set apart one probate homestead in the manner provided in this chapter.

6521. The probate homestead shall be set apart for the use of one or more of the following persons:

(a) The surviving spouse.

(b) The minor children of the decedent.

6522. (a) The probate homestead shall be selected out of the following property, giving first preference to the community and quasi-community property of, or property owned in common by, the decedent and the person entitled to have the homestead set apart:

(1) If the homestead is set apart for the use of the surviving spouse or for the use of the surviving spouse and minor children, out of community property or quasi-community property.

(2) If the homestead is set apart for the use of the surviving spouse or for the use of the minor children or for the use of the surviving spouse and minor children, out of property owned in common by the decedent and the persons entitled to have the homestead set apart, or out of the separate property of the decedent or, if the decedent was not married at the time of death, out of property owned by the decedent.

(b) The probate homestead shall not be selected out of property the right to possession of which is vested in a third person unless the third person consents thereto. As used in this subdivision, "third person" means a person whose right to possession of the property (1) existed at the time of the death of the decedent or came into existence upon the death of the decedent and (2) was not created by testate or intestate succession from the decedent.

6523. (a) In selecting and setting apart the probate homestead, the court shall consider the needs of the surviving spouse and minor children, the liens and encumbrances on the property, the claims of creditors, the needs of the heirs or devisees of the decedent, and the intent of the decedent with respect to the property in the estate and the estate plan of the decedent as expressed in inter vivos and testamentary transfers or by other means.

(b) The court, in light of subdivision (a) and other relevant considerations as determined by the court in its discretion, shall:

(1) Select as a probate homestead the most appropriate property available that is suitable for that use, including in addition to the dwelling itself such adjoining property as appears reasonable.

(2) Set the probate homestead so selected apart for such a term and upon such condi-

tions (including, but not limited to, assignment by the homestead recipient of other property to the heirs or devisees of the property set apart as a homestead) as appear proper.

6524. The property set apart as a probate homestead shall be set apart only for a limited period, to be designated in the order, and in no case beyond the lifetime of the surviving spouse, or, as to a child, beyond its minority. Subject to the probate homestead right, the property of the decedent remains subject to administration including testate and intestate succession. The rights of the parties during the period for which the probate homestead is set apart are governed, to the extent applicable, by the Legal Estates Principal and Income Law, Chapter 2.6 (commencing with Section 731) of Title 2 of Part 1 of Division 2 of the Civil Code.

6525. (a) A petition to select and set apart a probate homestead may be filed by any interested person.

(b) Notice of the hearing on the petition shall be given as provided in Section 1220 to all of the following persons:

(1) Each person listed in Section 1220.

(2) Each known heir whose interest in the estate would be affected by the petition.

(3) Each known devisee whose interest in the estate would be affected by the petition.

6526. (a) Property of the decedent set apart as a probate homestead is liable for claims against the estate of the decedent, subject to the probate homestead right. The probate homestead right in property of the decedent is liable for claims that are secured by liens and encumbrances on the property at the time of the decedent's death but is exempt to the extent of the homestead exemption as to any claim that would have been subject to a homestead exemption at the time of the decedent's death under Article 4 (commencing with Section 704.710) of Chapter 4 of Division 2 of Title 9 of Part 2 of the Code of Civil Procedure.

(b) The probate homestead right in the property of the decedent is not liable for claims against the person for whose use the probate homestead is set apart.

(c) Property of the decedent set apart as a probate homestead is liable for claims against the testate or intestate successors of the decedent or other successors to the property after administration, subject to the probate homestead right.

6527. (a) The court may by order modify the term or conditions of the probate homestead right or terminate the probate homestead right at any time prior to entry of an order for final distribution of the decedent's estate if in the court's discretion to do so appears appropriate under the circumstances of the case.

(b) A petition for an order under this section may be filed by any of the following:

(1) The person for whose use the probate

homestead is set apart.

(2) The testate or intestate successors of the decedent or other successors to the property set apart as a probate homestead.

(3) Persons having claims secured by liens or encumbrances on the property set apart as a probate homestead.

(c) Notice of the hearing on the petition shall be given to all the persons listed in subdivision (b) as provided in Section 1220.

6528. Nothing in this chapter terminates or otherwise affects a declaration of homestead by, or for the benefit of, a surviving spouse or minor child of the decedent with respect to the community, quasi-community, or common interest of the surviving spouse or minor child in property in the decedent's estate. This section is declaratory of, and does not constitute a change in, existing law.

Chapter 4. Family Allowance

6540. (a) The following are entitled to such reasonable family allowance out of the estate as is necessary for their maintenance according to their circumstances during administration of the estate:

(1) The surviving spouse of the decedent.

(2) Minor children of the decedent.

(3) Adult children of the decedent who are physically or mentally incapacitated from earning a living and were actually dependent in whole or in part upon the decedent for support.

(b) The following may be given such reasonable family allowance out of the estate as the court in its discretion determines is necessary for their maintenance according to their circumstances during administration of the estate:

(1) Other adult children of the decedent who were actually dependent in whole or in part upon the decedent for support.

(2) A parent of the decedent who was actually dependent in whole or in part upon the decedent for support.

(c) If a person otherwise eligible for family allowance has a reasonable maintenance from other sources and there are one or more other persons entitled to a family allowance, the family allowance shall be granted only to those who do not have a reasonable maintenance from other sources.

6541. (a) The court may grant or modify a family allowance on petition of any interested person.

(b) With respect to an order for the family allowance provided for in subdivision (a) of Section 6540:

(1) Before the inventory is filed, the order may be made or modified either (A) ex parte or (B) after notice of the hearing on the petition has been given as provided in Section 1220.

(2) After the inventory is filed, the order may be made or modified only after notice of the hearing on the petition has been given as provided in Section 1220.

(c) An order for the family allowance provided in subdivision (b) of Section 6540 may be made only after notice of the hearing on the petition has been given as provided in Section 1220 to all of the following persons:

(1) Each person listed in Section 1220.

(2) Each known heir whose interest in the estate would be affected by the petition.

(3) Each known devisee whose interest in the estate would be affected by the petition.

6542. A family allowance commences on the date of the court's order or such other time as may be provided in the court's order, whether before or after the date of the order, as the court in its discretion determines, but the allowance may not be made retroactive to a date earlier than the date of the decedent's death.

6543. (a) A family allowance shall terminate no later than the entry of the order for final distribution of the estate or, if the estate is insolvent, no later than one year after the granting of letters.

(b) Subject to subdivision (a), a family allowance shall continue until modified or terminated by the court or until such time as the court may provide in its order.

6544. The costs of proceedings under this chapter shall be paid by the estate as expenses of administration.

6545. Notwithstanding Chapter 2 (commencing with Section 916) of Title 13 of Part 2 of the Code of Civil Procedure, the perfecting of an appeal from an order made under this chapter does not stay proceedings under this chapter or the enforcement of the order appealed from if the person in whose favor the order is made gives an undertaking in double the amount of the payment or payments to be made to that person. The undertaking shall be conditioned that if the order appealed from is modified or reversed so that the payment or any part thereof to the person proves to have been unwarranted, the payment or part thereof shall, unless deducted from any preliminary or final distribution ordered in favor of the person, be repaid and refunded into the estate within 30 days after the court so orders following the modification or reversal, together with interest and costs.

Chapter 6. Small Estate Set-Aside

6600. (a) Subject to subdivision (b), for the purposes of this chapter, "decedent's estate" means all the decedent's personal property, wherever located, and all the decedent's real property located in this state.

(b) For the purposes of this chapter:

(1) Any property or interest or lien thereon which, at the time of the decedent's death, was held by the decedent as a joint tenant, or in which the decedent had a life or other interest terminable upon the decedent's death, shall be excluded in determining the estate

of the decedent or its value.

(2) A multiple-party account to which the decedent was a party at the time of the decedent's death shall be excluded in determining the estate of the decedent or its value, whether or not all or a portion of the sums on deposit are community property, to the extent that the sums on deposit belong after the death of the decedent to a surviving party, P.O.D. payee, or beneficiary. As used in this paragraph, the terms "multiple-party account," "party," "P.O.D. payee," and "beneficiary" have the meanings given those terms in Article 2 (commencing with Section 5120) of Chapter 1 of Part 2 of Division 5.

6601. As used in this chapter, "minor child" means a child of the decedent who was under the age of 18 at the time of the decedent's death and who survived the decedent.

6602. A petition may be filed under this chapter requesting an order setting aside the decedent's estate to the decedent's surviving spouse and minor children, or one or more of them, as provided in this chapter, if the net value of the decedent's estate, over and above all liens and encumbrances at the date of death and over and above the value of any probate homestead interest set apart out of the decedent's estate under Section 6520, does not exceed twenty thousand dollars ($20,000).

6603. The petition shall be filed in the superior court of a county in which the estate of the decedent may be administered.

6604. (a) The petition shall allege that this chapter applies and request that an order be made setting aside the estate of the decedent as provided in this chapter.

(b) The petition shall include the following:

(1) If proceedings for administration of the estate are not pending, the facts necessary to determine the county in which the estate of the decedent may be administered.

(2) The name, age, address, and relation to the decedent of each heir and devisee of the decedent, so far as known to the petitioner.

(3) A specific description and estimate of the value of the decedent's estate and a list of all liens and encumbrances at the date of death.

(4) A specific description and estimate of the value of any of the decedent's real property located outside this state that passed to the surviving spouse and minor children of the decedent, or any one or more of them, under the will of the decedent or by intestate succession.

(5) A specific description and estimate of the value of any of the decedent's property described in subdivision (b) of Section 6600 that passed to the surviving spouse and minor children of the decedent, or any one or more of them, upon the death of the decedent.

(6) A designation of any property as to

which a probate homestead is set apart out of the decedent's estate under Section 6520.

(7) A statement of any unpaid liabilities for expenses of the last illness, funeral charges, and expenses of administration.

(8) The requested disposition of the estate of the decedent under this chapter and the considerations that justify the requested disposition.

6605. (a) If proceedings for the administration of the estate of the decedent are pending, a petition under this chapter shall be filed in those proceedings without the payment of an additional fee.

(b) If proceedings for the administration of the estate of the decedent have not yet been commenced, a petition under this chapter may be filed concurrently with a petition for the probate of the decedent's will or for administration of the estate of the decedent, or, if no petition for probate or for administration is being filed, a petition under this chapter may be filed independently.

(c) A petition may be filed under this chapter at any time prior to the entry of the order for final distribution of the estate.

6606. (a) A petition may be filed under this chapter by any of the following:

(1) The person named in the will of the decedent as executor.

(2) The surviving spouse of the decedent.

(3) The guardian of a minor child of the decedent.

(4) A child of the decedent who was a minor at the time the decedent died.

(5) The personal representative if a personal representative has been appointed for the decedent's estate.

(b) The guardian of a minor child of the decedent may file the petition without authorization or approval of the court in which the guardianship proceeding is pending.

6607. (a) Where proceedings for the administration of the estate of the decedent are not pending when the petition is filed under this chapter and the petition under this chapter is not joined with a petition for the probate of the decedent's will or for administration of the estate of the decedent, the petitioner shall give notice of the hearing on the petition as provided in Section 1220 to (1) each person named as executor in the decedent's will and to (2) each heir or devisee of the decedent, if known to the petitioner. A copy of the petition shall be sent with the notice of hearing to the surviving spouse, each child, and each devisee who is not petitioning.

(b) If the petition under this chapter is filed with a petition for the probate of the decedent's will or with a petition for administration of the estate of the deceased spouse, notice of the hearing on the petition shall be given to the persons and in the manner prescribed by Section 8003 and shall be included in the notice required by that section.

(c) If proceedings for the administration of the estate of the decedent are pending when the petition is filed under this chapter and the hearing of the petition for probate of the will or administration of the estate of the decedent is set for a day more than 15 days after the filing of the petition filed under this chapter, the petition under this chapter shall be set for hearing at the same time as the petition for probate of the will or for administration of the estate, and notice of hearing on the petition filed under this chapter shall be given by the petitioner as provided in Section 1220. If the hearing of the petition for probate of the will or for administration of the estate is not set for hearing for a day more than 15 days after the filing of the petition under this chapter, (1) the petition filed under this chapter shall be set for hearing at least 15 days after the date on which it is filed, (2) notice of the hearing on the petition filed under this chapter shall be given by the petitioner as provided in Section 1220, and (3) if the petition for probate of the will or for administration of the estate has not already been heard, that petition shall be continued until that date and heard at the same time unless the court otherwise orders.

6608. If a petition is filed under this chapter, the personal representative, or the petitioner if no personal representative has been appointed, shall file with the clerk of the court, prior to the hearing of the petition, an inventory and appraisal made as provided in Part 3 (commencing with Section 8800) of Division 7. The personal representative or the petitioner, as the case may be, may appraise the assets which a personal representative could appraise under Section 8901.

6609. (a) If the court determines that the net value of the decedent's estate, over and above all liens and encumbrances at the date of death of the decedent and over and above the value of any probate homestead interest set apart out of the decedent's estate under Section 6520, does not exceed twenty thousand dollars ($20,000) as of the date of the decedent's death, the court shall make an order under this section unless the court determines that making an order under this section would be inequitable under the circumstances of the particular case.

(b) In determining whether to make an order under this section, the court shall consider the needs of the surviving spouse and minor children, the liens and encumbrances on the property of the decedent's estate, the claims of creditors, the needs of the heirs or devisees of the decedent, the intent of the decedent with respect to the property in the estate and the estate plan of the decedent as expressed in inter vivos and testamentary transfers or by other means, and any other relevant considerations. If the surviving spouse has remarried at the time the petition is heard, it shall be presumed that the needs of the surviving spouse do not justify the setting aside of the small estate, or any portion thereof, to the surviving spouse. This presumption is a presumption affecting the burden of proof.

(c) Subject to subdivision (d), if the court makes an order under this section, the court shall assign the whole of the decedent's estate, subject to all liens and encumbrances on property in the estate at the date of the decedent's death, to the surviving spouse and the minor children of the decedent, or any one or more of them.

(d) If there are any liabilities for expenses of the last illness, funeral charges, or expenses of administration that are unpaid at the time the court makes an order under this section, the court shall make such orders as are necessary so that those unpaid liabilities are paid.

(e) Title to property in the decedent's estate vests absolutely in the surviving spouse, minor children, or any or all of them, as provided in the order, subject to all liens and encumbrances on property in the estate at the date of the decedent's death, and there shall be no further proceedings in the administration of the decedent's estate unless additional property in the decedent's estate is discovered.

6610. Upon becoming final, an order under Section 6609 shall be conclusive on all persons, whether or not they are then in being.

6611. (a) Subject to the limitations and conditions specified in this section, the person or persons in whom title vested pursuant to Section 6609 are personally liable for the unsecured debts of the decedent.

(b) The personal liability of a person under this section does not exceed the fair market value at the date of the decedent's death of the property title to which vested in that person pursuant to Section 6609, less the total of all of the following:

(1) The amount of any liens and encumbrances on that property.

(2) The value of any probate homestead interest set apart under Section 6520 out of that property.

(3) The value of any other property set aside under Section 6510 out of that property.

(c) In any action or proceeding based upon an unsecured debt of the decedent, the surviving spouse of the decedent, the child or children of the decedent, or the guardian of the minor child or children of the decedent, may assert any defense, cross-complaint, or setoff which would have been available to the decedent if the decedent had not died.

(d) If proceedings are commenced in this state for the administration of the estate of the decedent and the time for filing claims has commenced, any action upon the personal liability of a person under this section is barred to the same extent as provided for claims under Part 4 (commencing with Section 9000) of Division 7, except as to the following:

(1) Creditors who commence judicial proceedings for the enforcement of the debt and serve the person liable under this section with the complaint therein prior to the expiration of the time for filing claims.

(2) Creditors who have or who secure an acknowledgment in writing of the person liable under this section that that person is liable for the debts.

(3) Creditors who file a timely claim in the proceedings for the administration of the estate of the decedent.

(e) Section 366.2 of the Code of Civil Procedure applies in an action under this section.

6612. If a petition filed under this chapter is filed with a petition for the probate of the decedent's will or for administration of the estate of the decedent and the court determines not to make an order under Section 6609, the court shall act on the petition for probate of the decedent's will or for administration of the estate of the decedent in the same manner as if no petition had been filed under this chapter, and the estate shall then be administered in the same manner as if no petition had been filed under this chapter.

6613. The attorney's fees for services performed in connection with the filing of a petition and the obtaining of a court order under this chapter shall be determined by private agreement between the attorney and the client and are not subject to approval by the court. If there is no agreement between the attorney and the client concerning the attorney's fees for services performed in connection with the filing of a petition and obtaining of a court order under this chapter and there is a dispute concerning the reasonableness of the attorney's fees for those services, a petition may be filed with the court in the same proceeding requesting that the court determine the reasonableness of the attorney's fees for those services. If there is an agreement between the attorney and the client concerning the attorney's fees for services performed in connection with the filing of a petition and obtaining a court order under this chapter and there is a dispute concerning the meaning of the agreement, a petition may be filed with the court in the same proceeding requesting that the court determine the dispute.

6614. Sections 6600 to 6613, inclusive, do not apply if the decedent died before July 1, 1987. If the decedent died before July 1, 1987, the case continues to be governed by the law applicable to the case prior to July 1, 1987.

6615. A reference in any statute of this state or in a written instrument, including a will or trust, to a provision of former Sections 640 to 647.5, inclusive, repealed by Chapter 783 of the Statutes of 1986, shall be deemed to be a reference to the comparable provisions of this chapter.

Part 4. Escheat Of Decedent's Property

6800. (a) If a decedent, whether or not the decedent was domiciled in this state, leaves no one to take the decedent's estate or any portion thereof by testate succession, and no one other than a government or governmental subdivision or agency to take the estate or a portion thereof by intestate succession, under the laws of this state or of any other jurisdiction, the same escheats at the time of the decedent's death in accordance with this part.

(b) Property that escheats to the state under this part, whether held by the state or its officers, is subject to the same charges and trusts to which it would have been subject if it had passed by succession and is also subject to the provisions of Title 10 (commencing with Section 1300) of Part 3 of the Code of Civil Procedure relating to escheated estates.

6801. Real property in this state escheats to this state in accordance with Section 6800.

6802. All tangible personal property owned by the decedent, wherever located at the decedent's death, that was customarily kept in this state prior to the decedent's death, escheats to this state in accordance with Section 6800.

6803. (a) Subject to subdivision (b), all tangible personal property owned by the decedent that is subject to the control of a superior court of this state for purposes of administration under this code escheats to this state in accordance with Section 6800.

(b) The property described in subdivision (a) does not escheat to this state but goes to another jurisdiction if the other jurisdiction claims the property and establishes all of the following:

(1) The other jurisdiction is entitled to the property under its law.

(2) The decedent customarily kept the property in that jurisdiction prior to the decedent's death.

(3) This state has the right to escheat and take tangible personal property being administered as part of a decedent's estate in that jurisdiction if the decedent customarily kept the property in this state prior to the decedent's death.

6804. All intangible property owned by the decedent escheats to this state in accordance with Section 6800 if the decedent was domiciled in this state at the time of the decedent's death.

6805. (a) Subject to subdivision (b), all intangible property owned by the decedent that is subject to the control of a superior court of this state for purposes of administration under this code escheats to this state in accordance with Section 6800 whether or not the decedent was domiciled in this state at the time of the decedent's death.

(b) The property described in subdivision (a) does not escheat to this state but goes to another jurisdiction if the other jurisdiction claims the property and establishes all of the following:

(1) The other jurisdiction is entitled to the property under its laws.

(2) The decedent was domiciled in that jurisdiction at the time of the decedent's death.

(3) This state has the right to escheat and take intangible property being administered as part of a decedent's estate in that jurisdiction if the decedent was domiciled in this state at the time of the decedent's death.

6806. Notwithstanding any other provision of law, a benefit consisting of money or other property distributable from a trust established under a plan providing health and welfare, pension, vacation, severance, retirement benefit, death benefit, unemployment insurance or similar benefits does not pass to or escheat to the state under this part but goes to the trust or fund from which it is distributable, subject to the provisions of Section 1521 of the Code of Civil Procedure. However, if such plan has terminated and the trust or fund has been distributed to the beneficiaries thereof prior to distribution of such benefit from the estate, such benefit passes to the state and escheats to the state under this part.

Division 7. Administration Of Estates Of Decedents

Part 1. General Provisions

Chapter 1. Passage Of Decedent's Property

7000. Subject to Section 7001, title to a decedent's property passes on the decedent's death to the person to whom it is devised in the decedent's last will or, in the absence of such a devise, to the decedent's heirs as prescribed in the laws governing intestate succession.

7001. The decedent's property is subject to administration under this code, except as otherwise provided by law, and is subject to the rights of beneficiaries, creditors, and other persons as provided by law.

Chapter 2. Jurisdiction And Courts

Article 1. Jurisdiction And Venue

7050. The superior court has jurisdiction of proceedings under this code concerning the administration of the decedent's estate.

7051. If the decedent was domiciled in this state at the time of death, the proper county for proceedings concerning administration of the decedent's estate is the county in which the decedent was domiciled, regardless of where the decedent died.

7052. If the decedent was not domiciled in this state at the time of death, the proper county for proceedings under this code concerning the administration of the decedent's estate is one of the following:

(a) If property of the nondomiciliary decedent is located in the county in which the nondomiciliary decedent died, the county in which the nondomiciliary decedent died.

(b) If no property of the nondomiciliary decedent is located in the county in which the nondomiciliary decedent died or if the nondomiciliary decedent did not die in this state, any county in which property of the nondomiciliary decedent is located, regardless of where the nondomiciliary decedent died. If property of the nondomiciliary decedent is located in more than one county, the proper county is the county in which a petition for ancillary administration is first filed, and the court in that county has jurisdiction of the administration of the estate.

Article 2. Disqualification Of Judge

7060. (a) In addition to any other ground provided by law for disqualification of a judge, a judge is disqualified from acting in proceedings under this code concerning the administration of the decedent's estate, except to order the transfer of a proceeding as provided in Article 3 (commencing with Section 7070), if any of the following circumstances exist:

(1) The judge is interested as a beneficiary or creditor.

(2) The judge is named as executor or trustee in the will.

(3) The judge is otherwise interested.

(b) A judge who participates in any manner in the drafting or execution of a will, including acting as a witness to the will, is disqualified from acting in any proceeding prior to and including the admission of the will to probate or in any proceeding involving its validity or interpretation.

(c) The amendments made to former Section 303 by Section 27 of Chapter 923 of the Statutes of 1987 do not apply in any proceeding commenced prior to July 1, 1988.

Article 3. Transfer Of Proceedings

7070. The court or judge shall order a proceeding under this code concerning the administration of the decedent's estate transferred to another county if there is no judge of the court in which the proceeding is pending who is qualified to act. This section does not apply if a judge qualified to act is assigned by the chairman of the Judicial Council to sit in the county and hear the proceeding.

7071. Transfer of a proceeding under this article shall be to another county in which property of the decedent is located or, if there is no other county in which property of the decedent is located, to an adjoining county.

7072. Upon petition of the personal representative or other interested person before entry of the order for final distribution of the estate, a proceeding transferred under this article may be retransferred to the court in which the proceeding was originally commenced if the court determines that both of the following conditions are satisfied:

(a) Another person has become judge of the court where the proceeding was originally commenced who is not disqualified to act in the administration of the estate.

(b) The convenience of the parties interested would be promoted by the retransfer.

Chapter 3. Rules Of Procedure

Article 1. Trial By Jury

Article 2. New Trials

7220. In proceedings under this code concerning the administration of the decedent's estate, a motion for a new trial may be made only in the following cases:

(a) Contest of a will or revocation of probate of a will.

(b) Cases in which a right to jury trial is

expressly granted, whether or not the case was tried by a jury.

Article 3.5. Judgments And Orders

7250. (a) When a judgment or order made pursuant to the provisions of this code concerning the administration of the decedent's estate becomes final, it releases the personal representative and the sureties from all claims of the heirs or devisees and of any persons affected thereby based upon any act or omission directly authorized, approved, or confirmed in the judgment or order. For the purposes of this section, "order" includes an order settling an account of the personal representative, whether an interim or final account.

(b) Nothing in this section affects any order, judgment, or decree made, or any action taken, before July 1, 1988. The validity of any action taken before July 1, 1988, is determined by the applicable law in effect before July 1, 1988, and not by this section.

(c) This section shall not apply where the judgment or order is obtained by fraud or conspiracy or by misrepresentation contained in the petition or account or in the judgment as to any material fact. For purposes of this subdivision, misrepresentation includes, but shall not be limited to, the omission of a material fact.

Article 4. Orders And Transactions Affecting Property

7260. As used in this article, "transaction" means a transaction affecting title to property in the estate, including, but not limited to, the following:

(a) In the case of real property, a conveyance (including a sale, option, or order confirming a sale or option), a lease, the creation of a mortgage, deed of trust, or other lien or encumbrance, the setting apart of a probate homestead, or the distribution of property.

(b) In the case of personal property, a transfer of the property or the creation of a security interest or other lien on the property.

7261. If a transaction affecting real property in the estate is executed by the personal representative in accordance with the terms of a court order, the instrument shall include a statement that the transaction is made by authority of the order authorizing or directing the transaction and shall give the date of the order.

7262. A transaction executed by the personal representative in accordance with an order authorizing or directing the transaction has the same effect as if the decedent were living at the time of the transaction and had carried it out in person while having legal capacity to do so.

7263. If an order is made setting apart a probate homestead, confirming a sale or making a distribution of real property, or

determining any other matter affecting title to real property in the estate, the personal representative shall record a certified copy of the order in the office of the county recorder in each county in which any portion of the real property is located.

Article 5. United States As Interested Person

7280. Where compensation, pension, insurance, or other allowance is made or awarded by a department or bureau of the United States government to a decedent's estate, the department or bureau has the same right as an interested person to do any of the following:

(a) Request special notice.

(b) Commence and prosecute an action on the bond of a personal representative.

(c) Contest an account of a personal representative.

Chapter 4. Public Administrators

Article 1. Taking Temporary Possession Or Control Of Property

7600. If a public officer or employee knows of property of a decedent that is subject to loss, injury, waste, or misappropriation and that ought to be in the possession or control of the public administrator, the officer or employee shall inform the public administrator.

7600.5. If a person dies in a hospital, convalescent hospital, or board and care facility without known next of kin, the person in charge of the hospital or facility shall give immediate notice of that fact to the public administrator of the county in which the hospital or facility is located. If the notice required by this section is not given, the hospital or facility is liable for (1) any cost of interment incurred by the estate or the county as a result of the failure and (2) any loss to the estate or beneficiaries caused by loss, injury, waste, or misappropriation of property of the decedent as a result of the failure.

7600.6. A funeral director in control of the decedent's remains pursuant to subdivision (c) of Section 7100 of the Health and Safety Code shall notify the public administrator if none of the persons described in paragraphs (2) to (6), inclusive, of subdivision (a) of Section 7100 of the Health and Safety Code exist, can be found after reasonable inquiry, or can be contacted by reasonable means.

7601. (a) If no personal representative has been appointed, the public administrator of a county shall take prompt possession or control of property of a decedent in the county that is deemed by the public administrator to be subject to loss, injury, waste, or misappropriation, or that the court orders into the possession or control of the public administrator after notice to the public administrator as provided in Section 1220.

(b) If property described in subdivision (a) is beyond the ability of the public administrator to take possession or control, the public administrator is not liable for failing to take possession or control of the property.

7602. (a) A public administrator who is authorized to take possession or control of property of a decedent under this article shall make a prompt search for other property, a will, and instructions for disposition of the decedent's remains.

(b) If a will is found, the public administrator or custodian of the will shall deliver the will as provided in Section 8200.

(c) If instructions for disposition of the decedent's remains are found, the public administrator shall promptly deliver the instructions to the person upon whom the right to control disposition of the decedent's remains devolves as provided in Section 7100 of the Health and Safety Code.

(d) If other property is located, the public administrator shall take possession or control of any property that, in the sole discretion of the public administrator, is deemed to be subject to loss, injury, waste, or misappropriation and that is located anywhere in this state or that is subject to the laws of this state. The public administrator does not have any liability for loss, injury, waste, or misappropriation of property of which he or she is unable to take possession or control.

7603. (a) A public administrator who is authorized to take possession or control of property of a decedent pursuant to this article may issue a written certification of that fact. The written certification is effective for 30 days after the date of issuance.

(b) The public administrator may record a copy of the written certification in any county in which is located real property of which the public administrator is authorized to take possession or control under this article.

(c) A financial institution, government or private agency, retirement fund administrator, insurance company, licensed securities dealer, or other person shall, without the necessity of inquiring into the truth of the written certification, without requiring a death certificate, without charge, and without court order or letters being issued:

(1) Provide the public administrator complete information concerning property held in the sole name of the decedent, including the names and addresses of any beneficiaries.

(2) Grant the public administrator access to a safe-deposit box rented in the sole name of the decedent for the purpose of inspection and removal of any will or instructions for disposition of the decedent's remains. Costs and expenses incurred in drilling or forcing a safe-deposit box shall be borne by the estate of the decedent.

(3) Surrender to the public administra-

tor any property of the decedent that, in the sole discretion of the public administrator, is deemed to be subject to loss, injury, waste, or misappropriation.

(d) Receipt of the written certification provided by this section:

(1) Constitutes sufficient acquittance for providing information or granting access to the safe-deposit box, for removal of the decedent's will and instructions for disposition of the decedent's remains, and for surrendering property of the decedent.

(2) Fully discharges the financial institution, government or private agency, retirement fund administrator, insurance company, licensed securities dealer, or other person from any liability for any act or omission of the public administrator with respect to the property or the safe-deposit box.

7604. If the public administrator takes possession or control of property of a decedent under this article, but another person is subsequently appointed personal representative or subsequently takes control or possession, the public administrator is entitled to reasonable costs incurred for the preservation of the estate, together with reasonable compensation for services. The costs and compensation are a proper expense of administration.

7605. On or before January 1, 2010, the public administrator shall comply with the continuing education requirements that are established by the California State Association of Public Administrators, Public Guardians, and Public Conservators.

Article 2. Appointment As Personal Representative

7620. The public administrator of the county in which the estate of a decedent may be administered shall promptly:

(a) Petition for appointment as personal representative of the estate if no person having higher priority has petitioned for appointment and the total value of the property in the decedent's estate exceeds one hundred fifty thousand dollars ($150,000).

(b) Petition for appointment as personal representative of any other estate the public administrator determines is proper.

(c) Accept appointment as personal representative of an estate when so ordered by the court, whether or not on petition of the public administrator, after notice to the public administrator as provided in Section 7321.

(d) Proceed with summary disposition of the estate as authorized by Article 4 (commencing with Section 7660), if the total value of the property in the decedent's estate does not exceed the amount prescribed in Section 13100 and a person having higher priority has not assumed responsibility for administration of the estate.

7621. (a) Except as otherwise provided in this section, appointment of the public administrator as personal representative shall be made, and letters issued, in the same manner and pursuant to the same procedure as for appointment of and issuance of letters to personal representatives generally.

(b) Appointment of the public administrator may be made on the court's own motion, after notice to the public administrator as provided in Section 1220.

(c) Letters may be issued to "the public administrator" of the county without naming the public administrator.

(d) The public administrator's oath and official bond are in lieu of the personal representative's oath and bond. Every estate administered under this chapter shall be charged an annual bond fee in the amount of twenty-five dollars ($25) plus one-fourth of one percent of the amount of an estate greater than ten thousand dollars ($10,000). The amount charged is an expense of administration and that amount shall be deposited in the county treasury. If a successor personal representative is appointed, the amount of the bond fee shall be prorated over the period of months during which the public administrator acted as personal representative. Upon final distribution by the public administrator, any amount of bond charges in excess of one year shall be a prorated charge to the estate.

7622. Except as otherwise provided in this chapter:

(a) The public administrator shall administer the estate in the same manner as a personal representative generally, and the provisions of this code concerning the administration of the decedent' s estate apply to administration by the public administrator.

(b) The public administrator is entitled to receive the same compensation as is granted by this division to a personal representative generally. The attorney for the public administrator is entitled to receive the same compensation as is granted by this division to an attorney for a personal representative generally. However, the compensation of the public administrator and the public administrator's attorney may not be less than the compensation in effect at the time of appointment of the public administrator or the minimum amount provided in subdivision (b) of Section 7666, whichever is greater.

7623. (a) As used in this section, "additional compensation" means the difference between the reasonable compensation of the public administrator in administering the estate and the compensation awarded the public administrator under Chapter 1 (commencing with Section 10800) of Part 7.

(b) The public administrator may be awarded additional compensation if any of the following conditions are satisfied:

(1) A person having priority for appointment as personal representative has been given notice under Section 8110 of the public administrator's petition for appointment,

and the person has not petitioned for appointment in preference to the public administrator.

(2) The public administrator has been appointed after the resignation or removal of a personal representative.

7624. (a) If after final distribution of an estate any money remains in the possession of the public administrator that should be paid over to the county treasurer pursuant to Chapter 5 (commencing with Section 11850) of Part 10, the court shall order payment to be made within 60 days.

(b) Upon failure of the public administrator to comply with an order made pursuant to subdivision (a), the district attorney of the county shall promptly institute proceedings against the public administrator and the sureties on the official bond for the amount ordered to be paid, plus costs.

Article 3. Deposit Of Money Of Estate

7640. (a) The public administrator shall, upon receipt, deposit all money of the estate in an insured account in a financial institution or with the county treasurer of the county in which the proceedings are pending.

(b) Upon deposit under this section the public administrator is discharged from further responsibility for the money deposited until the public administrator withdraws the money.

7641. Money deposited in a financial institution or with the county treasurer under this article may be withdrawn upon the order of the public administrator when required for the purposes of administration.

7642. (a) The public administrator shall credit each estate with the highest rate of interest or dividends that the estate would have received if the funds available for deposit had been individually and separately deposited.

(b) Interest or dividends credited to the account of the public administrator in excess of the amount credited to the estates pursuant to subdivision (a) shall be deposited in the county general fund.

7643. (a) The county treasurer shall receive and safely keep all money deposited with the county treasurer under this chapter and pay the money out on the order of the public administrator when required for the purposes of administration. The county treasurer and sureties on the official bond of the county treasurer are responsible for the safekeeping and payment of the money.

(b) The county treasurer shall deliver to the State Treasurer or the Controller all money in the possession of the county treasurer belonging to the estate, if there are no beneficiaries or other persons entitled to the money, or the beneficiaries or other persons entitled to the money do not appear and claim it. Delivery shall be made under the provisions of Article 1 (commencing with

Section 1440) of Chapter 6 of Title 10 of Part 3 of the Code of Civil Procedure.

7644. (a) If a deposit in a financial institution is made under this article, money remaining unclaimed at the expiration of five years after the date of the deposit, together with the increase and proceeds of the deposit, shall be presumed abandoned in any of the following circumstances:

(1) The deposit belongs to the estate of a known decedent for which a personal representative has never been appointed.

(2) The deposit belongs to the estate of a known decedent for which a personal representative has been appointed but no order of distribution has been made due to the absence of interested persons or the failure of interested persons diligently to protect their interests by taking reasonable steps for the purpose of securing a distribution of the estate.

(b) The Controller may, at any time after the expiration of the five-year period, file a petition with the court setting forth the fact that the money has remained on deposit in a financial institution under the circumstances described in subdivision (a) for the five-year period, and requesting an order declaring that the money is presumptively abandoned and directing the holder of the money to pay the money to the State Treasurer.

(c) Upon presentation of a certified copy of a court order made under subdivision (b), the financial institution shall forthwith transmit the money to the State Treasurer for deposit in the State Treasury. The deposit shall be made as provided in Section 1310 of the Code of Civil Procedure. All money deposited in the State Treasury under the provisions of this section shall be deemed to be deposited in the State Treasury under the provisions of Article 1 (commencing with Section 1440) of Chapter 6 of Title 10 of Part 3 of the Code of Civil Procedure. The deposit shall be transmitted, received, accounted for, and disposed of as provided by Title 10 (commencing with Section 1300) of Part 3 of the Code of Civil Procedure.

Article 4. Summary Disposition Of Small Estates

7660. (a) If a public administrator takes possession or control of an estate pursuant to this chapter, the public administrator may, acting as personal representative of the estate, summarily dispose of the estate in the manner provided in this article in either of the following circumstances:

(1) The total value of the property in the decedent's estate does not exceed the amount prescribed in Section 13100. The authority provided by this paragraph may be exercised only upon order of the court. The order may be made upon ex parte application. The fee to be allowed to the clerk for the filing of the application is two hundred five dollars

($205). The authority for this summary administration of the estate shall be evidenced by a court order for summary disposition.

(2) The total value of the property in the decedent's estate does not exceed fifty thousand dollars ($50,000). The authority provided by this paragraph may be exercised without court authorization.

(A) A public administrator who is authorized to summarily dispose of property of a decedent pursuant to this paragraph may issue a written certification of Authority for Summary Administration. The written certification is effective for 30 days after the date of issuance.

(B) A financial institution, government or private agency, retirement fund administrator, insurance company, licensed securities dealer, or other person shall, without the necessity of inquiring into the truth of the written certification of Authority for Summary Administration and without court order or letters being issued, do all of the following:

(i) Provide the public administrator complete information concerning any property held in the name of the decedent, including the names and addresses of any beneficiaries or joint owners.

(ii) Grant the public administrator access to a safe-deposit box or storage facility rented in the name of the decedent for the purpose of inspection and removal of property of the decedent. Costs and expenses incurred in accessing a safe-deposit box or storage facility shall be borne by the estate of the decedent.

(iii) Surrender to the public administrator any property of the decedent that is held or controlled by the financial institution, agency, retirement fund administrator, insurance company, licensed securities dealer, or other person.

(C) Receipt by a financial institution, government or private agency, retirement fund administrator, insurance company, licensed securities dealer, or other person of the written certification provided by this article shall do both of the following:

(i) Constitute sufficient acquittance for providing information or granting access to a safe-deposit box or a storage facility and for surrendering any property of the decedent.

(ii) Fully discharge the financial institution, government or private agency, retirement fund administrator, insurance company, licensed securities dealer, or other person from liability for any act or omission of the public administrator with respect to the property, a safe-deposit box, or a storage facility.

(b) Summary disposition may be made notwithstanding the existence of the decedent's will, if the will does not name an executor or if the named executor refuses to act.

(c) Nothing in this article precludes the public administrator from filing a petition with the court under any other provision of this code concerning the administration of the decedent's estate.

(d) Petitions filed pursuant to this article shall contain the information required by Section 8002.

(e) If a public administrator takes possession or control of an estate pursuant to this chapter, this article conveys the authority of a personal representative as described in Section 9650 to the public administrator to summarily dispose of the estates pursuant to the procedures described in paragraphs (1) and (2) of subdivision (a).

(f) The fee charged under paragraph (1) of subdivision (a) shall be distributed as provided in Section 68085.4 of the Government Code. When an application is filed under that paragraph, no other fees shall be charged in addition to the uniform filing fee provided for in Section 68085.4 of the Government Code.

7661. A public administrator acting under authority of this article may:

(a) Withdraw money or take possession of any other property of the decedent that is in the possession or control of a financial institution, government or private agency, retirement fund administrator, insurance company, licensed securities dealer, or other person.

(b) Collect any debts owed to the decedent, including, but not limited to, any rents, issues, or profits from the real and personal property in the estate until the estate is distributed.

(c) Sell any personal property of the decedent, including, but not limited to, stocks, bonds, mutual funds and other types of securities. Sales may be made with or without notice, as the public administrator elects. Title to the property sold passes without the need for confirmation by the court.

(d) Sell any real property of the decedent. The sale shall be accomplished through one of the following procedures:

(1) The sale may be conducted subject to Article 6 (commencing with Section 10300) of Chapter 18 of Part 5.

(2) With approval specified in the original court order for summary disposition of the estate, the sale of real property may be accomplished using a Notice of Proposed Action according to the following requirements:

(A) The publication of the sale shall be accomplished according to Sections 10300 to 10307, inclusive.

(B) The appraisal of the property and determination of the minimum sale price of 90 percent of the appraised value shall be accomplished according to Section 10309.

(C) If an offer meets the approval of the public administrator and the offered price is at least 90 percent of the appraised value, a notice of proposed action shall be made according to Sections 10581 to 10588, inclusive. If objection is not made to the notice of

proposed action, the sale may be completed without a court confirmation of the sale. The sale may be consummated by recording a public administrator's deed and a copy of the court order for summary disposition that authorized the use of the notice of proposed action.

(D) If an objection to the notice of proposed action is made pursuant to Section 10587, the sale shall be confirmed in court according to Sections 10308 to 10316, inclusive. The sale may be consummated by recording an administrator's deed and a copy of the court order confirming the sale.

(E) If objection to the notice of proposed action is not made under Section 10587, the public administrator may still elect to have the sale confirmed in court according to Sections 10308 to 10316, inclusive, if the public administrator deems that is in the best interest of the estate. Title to the property sold passes with the public administrator's deed.

7662. The public administrator acting under authority of this article shall pay out the money of the estate in the order prescribed in Section 11420, for expenses of administration, charges against the estate, and claims presented to the public administrator before distribution of the decedent's property pursuant to Section 7663. A creditor whose claim is paid under this section is not liable for contribution to a creditor whose claim is presented after the payment.

7663. (a) After payment of debts pursuant to Section 7662, but in no case before four months after court authorization of the public administrator to act under this article or after the public administrator takes possession or control of the estate, the public administrator shall distribute to the decedent's beneficiaries any money or other property of the decedent remaining in the possession of the public administrator.

(b) If there are no beneficiaries, the public administrator shall deposit the balance with the county treasurer for use in the general fund of the county, subject to Article 3 (commencing with Section 50050) of Chapter 1 of Part 1 of Division 1 of Title 5 of the Government Code. If the amount deposited exceeds five thousand dollars ($5,000), the public administrator shall at the time of the deposit give the Controller written notice of the information specified in Section 1311 of the Code of Civil Procedure.

7664. A person to whom property is distributed under this article is personally liable for the unsecured debts of the decedent. Such a debt may be enforced against the person in the same manner as it could have been enforced against the decedent if the decedent had not died. In an action based on the debt, the person may assert any defenses available to the decedent if the decedent had not died. The aggregate personal liability of a person under this section shall not exceed the fair market value of the property distributed to the person, valued as of the date of the distribution, less the amount of any liens and encumbrances on the property on that date. Section 366.2 of the Code of Civil Procedure applies in an action under this section.

7665. (a) The public administrator shall file with the clerk a statement showing the property of the decedent that came into possession of the public administrator and the disposition made of the property, together with receipts for all distributions. This subdivision does not apply to proceedings under paragraph (2) of subdivision (a) of Section 7660.

(b) The public administrator shall maintain a file of all receipts and records of expenditures for a period of three years after disposition of the property pursuant to Section 7663.

7666. (a) Except as provided in Section 7623 and in subdivision (b), the compensation payable to the public administrator and the attorney, if any, for the public administrator for the filing of an application pursuant to this chapter and for performance of any duty or service connected therewith is that set out in Part 7 (commencing with Section 10800).

(b) The public administrator is entitled to a minimum compensation of one thousand dollars ($1,000).

Part 2. Opening Estate Administration

Chapter 1. Commencement Of Proceedings

8000. (a) At any time after a decedent's death, any interested person may commence proceedings for administration of the estate of the decedent by a petition to the court for an order determining the date and place of the decedent's death and for either or both of the following:

(1) Appointment of a personal representative.

(2) Probate of the decedent's will.

(b) A petition for probate of the decedent's will may be made regardless of whether the will is in the petitioner's possession or is lost, destroyed, or beyond the jurisdiction of the state.

8001. Unless good cause for delay is shown, if a person named in a will as executor fails to petition the court for administration of the estate within 30 days after the person has knowledge of the death of the decedent and that the person is named as executor, the person may be held to have waived the right to appointment as personal representative.

8002. (a) The petition shall contain all of the following information:

(1) The date and place of the decedent's death.

(2) The street number, street, and city, or other address, and the county, of the decedent's residence at the time of death.

(3) The name, age, address, and relation to the decedent of each heir and devisee of the decedent, so far as known to or reasonably ascertainable by the petitioner.

(4) The character and estimated value of the property in the estate.

(5) The name of the person for whom appointment as personal representative is petitioned.

(b) If the decedent left a will:

(1) The petitioner shall attach to the petition a photographic copy of the will. In the case of a holographic will or other will of which material provisions are handwritten, the petitioner shall also attach a typed copy of the will.

(2) If the will is in a foreign language, the petitioner shall attach an English language translation. On admission of the will to probate, the court shall certify to a correct translation into English, and the certified translation shall be filed with the will.

(3) The petition shall state whether the person named as executor in the will consents to act or waives the right to appointment.

8003. (a) The hearing on the petition shall be set for a day not less than 15 nor more than 30 days after the petition is filed. At the request of the petitioner made at the time the petition is filed, the hearing on the petition shall be set for a day not less than 30 nor more than 45 days after the petition is filed. The court may not shorten the time for giving the notice of hearing under this section.

(b) The petitioner shall serve and publish notice of the hearing in the manner prescribed in Chapter 2 (commencing with Section 8100).

8004. (a) If appointment of the personal representative is contested, the grounds of opposition may include a challenge to the competency of the personal representative or the right to appointment. If the contest asserts the right of another person to appointment as personal representative, the contestant shall also file a petition and serve notice in the manner provided in Article 2 (commencing with Section 8110) of Chapter 2, and the court shall hear the two petitions together.

(b) If a will is contested, the applicable procedure is that provided in Article 3 (commencing with Section 8250) of Chapter 3.

8005. (a) At the hearing on the petition, the court may examine and compel any person to attend as a witness concerning any of the following matters:

(1) The time, place, and manner of the decedent's death.

(2) The place of the decedent's domicile and residence at the time of death.

(3) The character and value of the decedent's property.

(4) Whether or not the decedent left a will.

(b) The following matters shall be established:

(1) The jurisdictional facts, including:

(A) The date and place of the decedent's death.

(B) That the decedent was domiciled in this state or left property in this state at the time of death.

(C) The publication of notice under Article 3 (commencing with Section 8120) of Chapter 2.

(2) The existence or nonexistence of the decedent's will.

(3) That notice of the hearing was served as provided in Article 2 (commencing with Section 8110) of Chapter 2.

8006. (a) If the court finds that the matters referred to in paragraph (1) of subdivision (b) of Section 8005 are established, the court shall make an order determining the time and place of the decedent's death and the jurisdiction of the court. Where appropriate and on satisfactory proof, the order shall admit the decedent's will to probate and appoint a personal representative. The date the will is admitted to probate shall be included in the order.

(b) If through defect of form or error the matters referred to in paragraph (1) of subdivision (b) of Section 8005 are incorrectly stated in the petition but actually are established, the court has and retains jurisdiction to correct the defect or error at any time. No such defect or error makes void an order admitting the will to probate or appointing a personal representative or an order made in any subsequent proceeding.

8007. (a) Except as provided in subdivision (b), an order admitting a will to probate or appointing a personal representative, when it becomes final, is a conclusive determination of the jurisdiction of the court and cannot be collaterally attacked.

(b) Subdivision (a) does not apply in either of the following cases:

(1) The presence of extrinsic fraud in the procurement of the court order.

(2) The court order is based on the erroneous determination of the decedent's death.

Chapter 2. Notice Of Hearing

Article 1. Contents

8100. The notice of hearing of a petition for administration of a decedent's estate, whether served under Article 2 (commencing with Section 8110) or published under Article 3 (commencing with Section 8120), shall state substantially as follows:

> PLEASE SEE THE APPENDIX

Article 2. Service Of Notice Of Hearing

8110. At least 15 days before the hearing of a petition for administration of a decedent's estate, the petitioner shall serve notice of the hearing by mail or personal delivery on all of the following persons:

(a) Each heir of the decedent, so far as known to or reasonably ascertainable by the petitioner.

(b) Each devisee, executor, and alternative executor named in any will being offered for probate, regardless of whether the devise or appointment is purportedly revoked in a subsequent instrument.

8111. If the decedent's will involves or may involve a testamentary trust of property for charitable purposes other than a charitable trust with a designated trustee resident in this state, or involves or may involve a devise for charitable purposes without an identified devisee, notice of hearing accompanied by a copy of the petition and of the will shall be served on the Attorney General as provided in Section 1209.

8112. A general personal representative shall give notice of administration of the estate of the decedent to creditors under Chapter 2 (commencing with Section 9050), and to public entities under Chapter 5 (commencing with Section 9200), of Part 4.

8113. If a citizen of a foreign country dies without leaving a will or leaves a will without naming an executor, or if it appears that property will pass to a citizen of a foreign country, notice shall be given to a recognized diplomatic or consular official of the foreign country maintaining an office in the United States.

Article 3. Publication

8120. In addition to service of the notice of hearing as provided in Article 2 (commencing with Section 8110), notice of hearing of a petition for administration of a decedent's estate shall also be published before the hearing in the manner provided in this article.

8121. (a) The first publication date of the notice shall be at least 15 days before the hearing. Three publications in a newspaper published once a week or more often, with at least five days intervening between the first and last publication dates, not counting the publication dates, are sufficient.

(b) Notice shall be published in a newspaper of general circulation in the city where the decedent resided at the time of death, or where the decedent's property is located if the court has jurisdiction under Section 7052. If there is no such newspaper, or if the decedent did not reside in a city, or if the property is not located in a city, then notice shall be published in a newspaper of general circulation in the county which is circulated within the area of the county in which the decedent resided or the property is located. If there is no such newspaper, notice shall be published in a newspaper of general circulation published in this state nearest to the county seat of the county in which the decedent resided or the property is located, and which is circulated within the area of the county in which the decedent resided or the property is located.

(c) For purposes of this section, "city" means a charter city as defined in Section 34101 of the Government Code or a general law city as defined in Section 34102 of the Government Code.

8122. The Legislature finds and declares that, to be most effective, notice of hearing should be published in compliance with Section 8121. However, the Legislature recognizes the possibility that in unusual cases due to confusion over jurisdictional boundaries or oversight such notice may inadvertently be published in a newspaper that does not satisfy Section 8121. Therefore, to prevent a minor error in publication from invalidating what would otherwise be a proper proceeding, the Legislature further finds and declares that notice published in a good faith attempt to comply with Section 8121 is sufficient to provide notice of hearing and to establish jurisdiction if the court expressly finds that the notice was published in a newspaper of general circulation published within the county and widely circulated within a true cross-section of the area of the county in which the decedent resided or the property was located in substantial compliance with Section 8121.

8123. The caption of a notice under this article shall be in 8-point type or larger and the text shall be in 7-point type or larger.

8124. A petition for administration of a decedent's estate shall not be heard by the court unless an affidavit showing due publication of the notice of hearing has been filed with the court. The affidavit shall contain a copy of the notice and state the date of its publication.

8125. Notwithstanding Section 8100, after the notice of hearing is published and an affidavit filed, any subsequent publication of the notice ordered by the court may omit the information for creditors and contingent creditors.

Chapter 3. Probate Of Will

Article 1. Production Of Will

8200. (a) Unless a petition for probate of the will is earlier filed, the custodian of a will shall, within 30 days after having knowledge of the death of the testator, do both of the following:

(1) Deliver the will to the clerk of the superior court of the county in which the estate of the decedent may be administered.

(2) Mail a copy of the will to the person named in the will as executor, if the person's whereabouts is known to the custodian, or if not, to a person named in the will as a beneficiary, if the person's whereabouts is known to the custodian.

(b) A custodian of a will who fails to comply with the requirements of this section shall be liable for all damages sustained by any person injured by the failure.

(c) The clerk shall release a copy of a will delivered under this section for attachment to a petition for probate of the will or otherwise on receipt of payment of the required fee and either a court order for production of the will or a certified copy of a death certificate of the decedent.

(d) The fee for delivering a will to the clerk of the superior court pursuant to paragraph (1) of subdivision (a) shall be as provided in Section 70626 of the Government Code. If an estate is commenced for the decedent named in the will, the fee for any will delivered pursuant to paragraph (1) of subdivision (a) shall be reimbursable from the estate as an expense of administration.

8201. If, on petition to the superior court of the county in which the estate of the decedent is being or may be administered alleging that a person has possession of a decedent's will, the court is satisfied that the allegation is true, the court shall order the person to produce the will.

8202. If the will of a person who was domiciled in this state at the time of death is detained in a court of any other state or country and cannot be produced for probate in this state, a certified photographic copy of the will may be admitted to probate in this state with the same force and effect as the original will. The same proof shall be required as if the original will were produced.

8203. If a will has been delivered to the clerk of the superior court in a county in which no proceeding is pending to administer the testator's estate, that court may order the will transferred to the clerk of the superior court in a county in which such a proceeding is pending. A petition for the transfer may be presented and heard without notice, but shall not be granted without proof that a copy of the petition has been mailed to the petitioner and any persons who have requested special notice in the proceeding in the court to which the will is to be transferred. The petition and order shall include the case number of the proceeding in the court to which transfer is prayed. Certified copies of the petition, any supporting documents, and the order shall be transmitted by the clerk along with the original will, and these copies shall be filed in the proceeding by the clerk of the recipient court.

Article 2. Proof Of Will

8220. Unless there is a contest of a will:

(a) The will may be proved on the evidence of one of the subscribing witnesses only, if the evidence shows that the will was executed in all particulars as prescribed by law.

(b) Evidence of execution of a will may be received by an affidavit of a subscribing witness to which there is attached a photographic copy of the will, or by an affidavit in the original will that includes or incorporates the attestation clause.

(c) If no subscribing witness resides in the county, but the deposition of a witness can be taken elsewhere, the court may direct the deposition to be taken. On the examination, the court may authorize a photographic copy of the will to be made and presented to the witness, and the witness may be asked the same questions with respect to the photographic copy as if the original will were present.

8221. If no subscribing witness is available as a witness within the meaning of Section 240 of the Evidence Code, the court may, if the will on its face conforms to all requirements of law, permit proof of the will by proof of the handwriting of the testator and one of the following:

(a) Proof of the handwriting of any one subscribing witness.

(b) Receipt in evidence of one of the following documents reciting facts showing due execution of the will:

(1) A writing in the will bearing the signatures of all subscribing witnesses.

(2) An affidavit of a person with personal knowledge of the circumstances of the execution.

8222. A holographic will may be proved in the same manner as other writings.

8223. The petition for probate of a lost or destroyed will shall include a written statement of the testamentary words or their substance. If the will is proved, the provisions of the will shall be set forth in the order admitting the will to probate.

8224. The testimony of each witness in a proceeding concerning the execution or provisions of a will, the testamentary capacity of the decedent, and other issues of fact, may be reduced to writing, signed by the witness, and filed, whether or not the will is contested. The testimony so preserved, or an official reporter's transcript of the testimony, is admissible in evidence in any subsequent proceeding concerning the will if the witness has become unavailable as a witness within the meaning of Section 240 of the Evidence Code.

8225. When the court admits a will to probate, that fact shall be recorded in the minutes by the clerk and the will shall be filed.

8226. (a) If no person contests the validity of a will or petitions for revocation of probate of the will within the time provided in this chapter, admission of the will to probate is conclusive, subject to Section 8007.

(b) Subject to subdivision (c), a will may be admitted to probate notwithstanding prior admission to probate of another will or prior distribution of property in the proceeding. The will may not affect property previously distributed, but the court may determine how any provision of the will affects property not yet distributed and how any provision of the will affects provisions of another will.

(c) If the proponent of a will has received notice of a petition for probate or a petition for letters of administration for a general personal representative, the proponent of the will may petition for probate of the will only within the later of either of the following time periods:

(1) One hundred twenty days after issuance of the order admitting the first will to probate or determining the decedent to be intestate.

(2) Sixty days after the proponent of the will first obtains knowledge of the will.

Article 3. Contest Of Will

8250. (a) When a will is contested under Section 8004, the contestant shall file with the court an objection to probate of the will. Thereafter, a summons shall be issued and served, with a copy of the objection, on the persons required by Section 8110 to be served with notice of hearing of a petition for administration of the decedent's estate. The summons shall be issued and served as provided in Chapter 3 (commencing with Section 412.10) and Chapter 4 (commencing with Section 413.10) of Title 5 of Part 2 of the Code of Civil Procedure. The summons shall contain a direction that the persons summoned file with the court a written pleading in response to the contest within 30 days after service of the summons.

(b) A person named as executor in the will is under no duty to defend a contest until the person is appointed personal representative.

8251. (a) The petitioner and any other interested person may jointly or separately answer the objection or demur to the objection within the time prescribed in the summons.

(b) Demurrer may be made on any of the grounds of demurrer available in a civil action. If the demurrer is sustained, the court may allow the contestant a reasonable time, not exceeding 15 days, within which to amend the objection. If the demurrer is overruled, the petitioner and other interested persons may, within 15 days thereafter, answer the objection.

(c) If a person fails timely to respond to the summons:

(1) The case is at issue notwithstanding the failure and the case may proceed on the petition and other documents filed by the time of the hearing, and no further pleadings by other persons are necessary.

(2) The person may not participate further in the contest, but the person's inter-

est in the estate is not otherwise affected. Nothing in this paragraph precludes further participation by the petitioner.

(3) The person is bound by the decision in the proceeding.

8252. (a) At the trial, the proponents of the will have the burden of proof of due execution. The contestants of the will have the burden of proof of lack of testamentary intent or capacity, undue influence, fraud, duress, mistake, or revocation. If the will is opposed by the petition for probate of a later will revoking the former, it shall be determined first whether the later will is entitled to probate.

(b) The court shall try and determine any contested issue of fact that affects the validity of the will.

8253. At the trial, each subscribing witness shall be produced and examined. If no subscribing witness is available as a witness within the meaning of Section 240 of the Evidence Code, the court may admit the evidence of other witnesses to prove the due execution of the will.

8254. The court may make appropriate orders, including orders sustaining or denying objections, and shall render judgment either admitting the will to probate or rejecting it, in whole or in part, and appointing a personal representative.

Article 4. Revocation Of Probate

8270. (a) Within 120 days after a will is admitted to probate, any interested person, other than a party to a will contest and other than a person who had actual notice of a will contest in time to have joined in the contest, may petition the court to revoke the probate of the will. The petition shall include objections setting forth written grounds of opposition.

(b) Notwithstanding subdivision (a), a person who was a minor or who was incompetent and had no guardian or conservator at the time a will was admitted to probate may petition the court to revoke the probate of the will at any time before entry of an order for final distribution.

8271. (a) On the filing of the petition, a summons shall be directed to the personal representative and to the heirs and devisees of the decedent, so far as known to the petitioner. The summons shall contain a direction that the persons summoned file with the court a written pleading in response to the petition within 30 days after service of the summons. Failure of a person timely to respond to the summons precludes the person from further participation in the revocation proceeding, but does not otherwise affect the person's interest in the estate.

(b) The summons shall be issued and served with a copy of the petition and proceedings had as in the case of a contest of the will.

(c) If a person fails timely to respond to the summons:

(1) The case is at issue notwithstanding the failure and the case may proceed on the petition and other documents filed by the time of the hearing, and no further pleadings by other persons are necessary.

(2) The person may not participate further in the contest, but the person's interest in the estate is not otherwise affected.

(3) The person is bound by the decision in the proceeding.

8272. (a) If it appears on satisfactory proof that the will should be denied probate, the court shall revoke the probate of the will.

(b) Revocation of probate of a will terminates the powers of the personal representative. The personal representative is not liable for any otherwise proper act done in good faith before the revocation, nor is any transaction void by reason of the revocation if entered into with a third person dealing in good faith and for value.

Chapter 4. Appointment Of Personal Representative

Article 1. General Provisions

8400. (a) A person has no power to administer the estate until the person is appointed personal representative and the appointment becomes effective. Appointment of a personal representative becomes effective when the person appointed is issued letters.

(b) Subdivision (a) applies whether or not the person is named executor in the decedent's will, except that a person named executor in the decedent's will may, before the appointment is made or becomes effective, pay funeral expenses and take necessary measures for the maintenance and preservation of the estate.

(c) The order appointing a personal representative shall state in capital letters on the first page of the order, in at least 12-point type, the following:
"WARNING: THIS APPOINTMENT IS NOT EFFECTIVE UNTIL LETTERS HAVE ISSUED."

8401. (a) Notwithstanding Section 8400, a petitioner for appointment as personal representative may deliver property in the petitioner's possession to a trust company or financial institution for deposit, or allow a trust company or financial institution to retain on deposit property already in its possession, as provided in Chapter 3 (commencing with Section 9700) of Part 5.

(b) The petitioner shall obtain and file with the court a written receipt including the agreement of the trust company or financial institution that the property on deposit, including any earnings thereon, shall not be allowed to be withdrawn except on order of the court.

(c) In receiving and retaining property under this section, the trust company or financial institution is protected to the same extent as though it had received the property from a person who had been appointed personal representative.

8402. (a) Notwithstanding any other provision of this chapter, a person is not competent to act as personal representative in any of the following circumstances:

(1) The person is under the age of majority.

(2) The person is subject to a conservatorship of the estate or is otherwise incapable of executing, or is otherwise unfit to execute, the duties of the office.

(3) There are grounds for removal of the person from office under Section 8502.

(4) The person is not a resident of the United States.

(5) The person is a surviving partner of the decedent and an interested person objects to the appointment.

(b) Paragraphs (4) and (5) of subdivision (a) do not apply to a person named as executor or successor executor in the decedent's will.

8403. (a) Before letters are issued, the personal representative shall take and subscribe an oath to perform, according to law, the duties of the office. The oath may be taken and dated on or after the time the petition for appointment as personal representative is signed, and may be filed with the clerk at any time after the petition is granted.

(b) The oath constitutes an acceptance of the office and shall be attached to or endorsed on the letters.

8404. (a) Before letters are issued, the personal representative (other than a trust company or a public administrator) shall file an acknowledgment of receipt of a statement of duties and liabilities of the office of personal representative. The statement shall be in the form prescribed by the Judicial Council.

(b) The court may by local rule require the acknowledgment of receipt to include the personal representative's birth date and driver's license number, if any, provided that the court ensures their confidentiality.

(c) The statement of duties and liabilities prescribed by the Judicial Council does not supersede the law on which the statement is based.

8405. Letters shall be signed by the clerk under the seal of the court and shall include:

(a) The county from which the letters are issued.

(b) The name of the person appointed as personal representative and whether the personal representative is an executor, administrator, administrator with the will annexed, or special administrator.

(c) A notation whether the personal representative is authorized to act under the Independent Administration of Estates Act (Part 6 (commencing with Section 10400) of Division 7), and if so authorized whether the independent administration authority includes or excludes the power to do any of the following:

(1) Sell real property.

(2) Exchange real property.

(3) Grant an option to purchase real property.

(4) Borrow money with the loan secured by an encumbrance upon real property.

Article 2. Executors

8420. The person named as executor in the decedent's will has the right to appointment as personal representative.

8421. If a person is not named as executor in a will but it appears by the terms of the will that the testator intended to commit the execution of the will and the administration of the estate to the person, the person is entitled to appointment as personal representative in the same manner as if named as executor.

8422. (a) The testator may by will confer on a person the power to designate an executor or coexecutor, or successor executor or coexecutor. The will may provide that the persons so designated may serve without bond.

(b) A designation shall be in writing and filed with the court. Unless the will provides otherwise, if there are two or more holders of the power to designate, the designation shall be unanimous, unless one of the holders of the power is unable or unwilling to act, in which case the remaining holder or holders may exercise the power.

(c) Except as provided in this section, an executor does not have authority to name a coexecutor, or a successor executor or coexecutor.

8423. If the executor named in the will is a trust company that has sold its business and assets to, has consolidated or merged with, or is in any manner provided by law succeeded by, another trust company, the court may, and to the extent required by the Banking Law (Division 1 (commencing with Section 99) of the Financial Code) shall, appoint the successor trust company as executor.

8424. (a) If a person named as executor is under the age of majority and there is another person named as executor, the other person may be appointed and may administer the estate until the majority of the minor, who may then be appointed as coexecutor.

(b) If a person named as executor is under the age of majority and there is no other person named as executor, another person may be appointed as personal representative, but the court may revoke the appointment on the majority of the minor, who may then be appointed as executor.

8425. If the court does not appoint all the persons named in the will as executors, those appointed have the same authority to act in every respect as all would have if appointed.

Article 3. Administrators With The Will Annexed

8440. An administrator with the will annexed shall be appointed as personal representative if no executor is named in the will or if the sole executor or all the executors named in the will have waived the right to appointment or are for any reason unwilling or unable to act.

8441. (a) Except as provided in subdivision (b), persons and their nominees are entitled to appointment as administrator with the will annexed in the same order of priority as for appointment of an administrator.

(b) A person who takes under the will has priority over a person who does not, but the court in its discretion may give priority to a person who does not take under the will if the person is entitled to a statutory interest that is a substantially greater portion of the estate than the devise to the person who takes under the will and the priority appears appropriate under the circumstances. A person who takes more than 50 percent of the value of the estate under the will or the person's nominee, or the nominee of several persons who together take more than 50 percent of the value of the estate under the will, has priority over other persons who take under the will.

8442. (a) Subject to subdivision (b), an administrator with the will annexed has the same authority over the decedent's estate as an executor named in the will would have.

(b) If the will confers a discretionary power or authority on an executor that is not conferred by law and the will does not extend the power or authority to other personal representatives, the power or authority shall not be deemed to be conferred on an administrator with the will annexed, but the court in its discretion may authorize the exercise of the power or authority.

Article 4. Administrators

8460. (a) If the decedent dies intestate, the court shall appoint an administrator as personal representative.

(b) The court may appoint one or more persons as administrator.

8461. Subject to the provisions of this article, a person in the following relation to the decedent is entitled to appointment as administrator in the following order of priority:

(a) Surviving spouse or domestic partner as defined in Section 37.

(b) Children.

(c) Grandchildren.

(d) Other issue.

(e) Parents.

(f) Brothers and sisters.

(g) Issue of brothers and sisters.

(h) Grandparents.

(i) Issue of grandparents.

(j) Children of a predeceased spouse or domestic partner.

(k) Other issue of a predeceased spouse or domestic partner.

(l) Other next of kin.

(m) Parents of a predeceased spouse or domestic partner.

(n) Issue of parents of a predeceased spouse or domestic partner.

(o) Conservator or guardian of the estate acting in that capacity at the time of death who has filed a first account and is not acting as conservator or guardian for any other person.

(p) Public administrator.

(q) Creditors.

(r) Any other person.

8462. The surviving spouse or domestic partner of the decedent, a relative of the decedent, or a relative of a predeceased spouse or domestic partner of the decedent, has priority under Section 8461 only if one of the following conditions is satisfied:

(a) The surviving spouse, domestic partner, or relative is entitled to succeed to all or part of the estate.

(b) The surviving spouse, domestic partner, or relative either takes under the will of, or is entitled to succeed to all or part of the estate of, another deceased person who is entitled to succeed to all or part of the estate of the decedent.

8463. If the surviving spouse is a party to an action for separate maintenance, annulment, or dissolution of the marriage of the decedent and the surviving spouse, and was living apart from the decedent on the date of the decedent's death, the surviving spouse has priority next after brothers and sisters and not the priority prescribed in Section 8461.

8464. If a person otherwise entitled to appointment as administrator is a person under the age of majority or a person for whom a guardian or conservator of the estate has been appointed, the court in its discretion may appoint the guardian or conservator or another person entitled to appointment.

8465. (a) The court may appoint as administrator a person nominated by any of the following persons:

(1) A person otherwise entitled to appointment.

(2) A person who would otherwise be entitled for appointment but who is ineligible for appointment under paragraph (4) of subdivision (a) of Section 8402 because he or she is not a resident of the United States.

(3) The guardian or conservator of the estate of a person otherwise entitled to appointment. The nomination shall be made in writing and filed with the court.

(b) If a person making a nomination for appointment of an administrator is the surviving spouse or domestic partner, child, grandchild, other issue, parent, brother or sister, or grandparent of the decedent, the nominee has priority next after those in the class of the person making the nomination.

(c) If a person making a nomination for appointment of an administrator is other than a person described in subdivision (b), the court in its discretion may appoint either the nominee or a person of a class lower in priority to that of the person making the nomination, but other persons of the class of the person making the nomination have priority over the nominee.

(d) If a person making a nomination for appointment of an administrator is a person described in paragraph (2) of subdivision (a), the court shall not appoint a nominee who is not a California resident to act as administrator. For California residents nominated under paragraph (2) of subdivision (a), the court shall consider whether the nominee is capable of faithfully executing the duties of the office. The court may in its discretion deny the appointment and appoint another person. In determining whether to appoint the nominee, the factors the court may consider include, but are not limited to, the following:

(1) Whether the nominee has a conflict of interest with the heirs or any other interested party.

(2) Whether the nominee had a business or personal relationship with the decedent or decedent's family before the decedent's death.

(3) Whether the nominee is engaged in or acting on behalf of an individual, a business, or other entity that solicits heirs to obtain the person's nomination for appointment as administrator.

(4) Whether the nominee has been appointed as a personal representative in any other estate.

(e) If the court decides to appoint a nominee under the circumstances described in subdivision (d), the court shall require the nominee to obtain bond, unless the court orders otherwise for good cause. Any order for good cause must be supported by specific findings of fact, and shall consider the need for the protection of creditors, heirs, and any other interested parties. Before waiving a bond, the court shall consider all other alternatives, including, but not limited to, the deposit of property in the estate pursuant to Chapter 3 (commencing with Section 9700) of Part 5 on the condition that the property, including any earnings thereon, will not be withdrawn except on authorization of the court. The waiver of all of the heirs of the requirement of a bond shall not constitute good cause.

(f) If the appointed nominee ceases to be a California resident following his or her appointment, he or she shall be deemed to have resigned as administrator for the purposes of Article 7 (commencing with Section 8520). The court shall not lose jurisdiction of the proceeding by any resignation under this subdivision.

(g) By accepting appointment as personal representative, the nominee shall submit personally to the jurisdiction of the court.

(h) This section shall remain in effect only until January 1, 2016, and as of that date is repealed, unless a later enacted statute, that is enacted before January 1, 2016, deletes or extends that date.

8465. (a) The court may appoint as administrator a person nominated by a person otherwise entitled to appointment or by the guardian or conservator of the estate of a person otherwise entitled to appointment. The nomination shall be made in writing and filed with the court.

(b) If a person making a nomination for appointment of an administrator is the surviving spouse or domestic partner, child, grandchild, other issue, parent, brother or sister, or grandparent of the decedent, the nominee has priority next after those in the class of the person making the nomination.

(c) If a person making a nomination for appointment of an administrator is other than a person described in subdivision (b), the court in its discretion may appoint either the nominee or a person of a class lower in priority to that of the person making the nomination, but other persons of the class of the person making the nomination have priority over the nominee.

(d) This section shall become operative on January 1, 2016.

8466. If a person whose only priority is that of a creditor claims appointment as administrator, the court in its discretion may deny the appointment and appoint another person.

8467. If several persons have equal priority for appointment as administrator, the court may appoint one or more of them, or if such persons are unable to agree, the court may appoint the public administrator or a disinterested person in the same or the next lower class of priority as the persons who are unable to agree.

8468. If persons having priority fail to claim appointment as administrator, the court may appoint any person who claims appointment.

8469. (a) For good cause, the court may allow the priority given by Section 8461 to a conservator or guardian of the estate of the decedent serving in that capacity at the time of death that has not filed a first account, or that is acting as guardian or conservator for another person, or both.

(b) If the petition for appointment as administrator requests the court to allow the priority permitted by subdivision (a), the petitioner shall, in addition to the notice otherwise required by statute, serve notice of the hearing by mail or personal delivery on the public administrator.

Article 5. Bond

8480. (a) Except as otherwise provided by statute, every person appointed as personal representative shall, before letters are issued, give a bond approved by the court. If two or more persons are appointed, the court may require either a separate bond from each or a joint and several bond. If a joint bond is furnished, the liability on the bond is joint and several.

(b) The bond shall be for the benefit of interested persons and shall be conditioned on the personal representative's faithful execution of the duties of the office according to law.

(c) If the person appointed as personal representative fails to give the required bond, letters shall not be issued. If the person appointed as personal representative fails to give a new, additional, or supplemental bond, or to substitute a sufficient surety, under court order, the person may be removed from office.

8481. (a) A bond is not required in either of the following cases:

(1) The will waives the requirement of a bond.

(2) All beneficiaries waive in writing the requirement of a bond and the written waivers are attached to the petition for appointment of a personal representative. This paragraph does not apply if the will requires a bond.

(b) Notwithstanding the waiver of a bond by a will or by all the beneficiaries, on petition of any interested person or on its own motion, the court may for good cause require that a bond be given, either before or after issuance of letters.

8482. (a) The court in its discretion may fix the amount of the bond, but the amount of the bond shall be not more than the sum of:

(1) The estimated value of the personal property.

(2) The probable annual gross income of the estate.

(3) If independent administration is granted as to real property, the estimated value of the decedent's interest in the real property.

(b) Notwithstanding subdivision (a), if the bond is given by an admitted surety insurer, the court may establish a fixed minimum amount for the bond, based on the minimum premium required by the admitted surety insurer.

(c) If the bond is given by personal sureties, the amount of the bond shall be twice the amount fixed by the court under subdivision (a).

(d) Before confirming a sale of real property the court shall require such additional bond as may be proper, not exceeding the maximum requirements of this section, treating the expected proceeds of the sale as personal property.

8483. (a) This section applies where property in the estate has been deposited pursuant to Chapter 3 (commencing with Section 9700) of Part 5 on condition that the property, including any earnings thereon, will not

be withdrawn except on authorization of the court.

(b) In a proceeding to determine the amount of the bond of the personal representative (whether at the time of appointment or subsequently), on production of a receipt showing the deposit of property of the estate in the manner described in subdivision (a), the court may order that the property shall not be withdrawn except on authorization of the court and may, in its discretion, do either of the following:

(1) Exclude the property in determining the amount of the required bond or reduce the amount of the bond to an amount the court determines is reasonable.

(2) If a bond has already been given or the amount fixed, reduce the amount to an amount the court determines is reasonable.

8484. If a personal representative petitions to have the amount of the bond reduced, the petition shall include an affidavit setting forth the condition of the estate and notice of hearing shall be given as provided in Section 1220.

8485. A personal representative who petitions for substitution or release of a surety shall file with the petition an account in the form provided in Section 10900. The court shall not order a substitution or release unless the account is approved.

8486. The personal representative shall be allowed the reasonable cost of the bond for every year it remains in force.

8487. The provisions of the Bond and Undertaking Law (Chapter 2 (commencing with Section 995.010) of Title 14 of Part 2 of the Code of Civil Procedure) apply to a bond given under this division, except to the extent this division is inconsistent.

8488. (a) In case of a breach of a condition of the bond, an action may be brought against the sureties on the bond for the use and benefit of the decedent's estate or of any person interested in the estate.

(b) No action may be maintained against the sureties on the bond of the personal representative unless commenced within four years from the discharge or removal of the personal representative or within four years from the date the order surcharging the personal representative becomes final, whichever is later.

(c) In any case, and notwithstanding subdivision (c) of Section 7250, no action may be maintained against the sureties on the bond unless commenced within six years from the date the judgment under Section 7250 or the later of the orders under subdivision (b) of this section becomes final.

Article 6. Removal From Office

8500. (a) Any interested person may petition for removal of the personal representative from office. A petition for removal may be combined with a petition for appointment of a successor personal representative under

Article 7 (commencing with Section 8520). The petition shall state facts showing cause for removal.

(b) On a petition for removal, or if the court otherwise has reason to believe from the court's own knowledge or from other credible information, whether on the settlement of an account or otherwise, that there are grounds for removal, the court shall issue a citation to the personal representative to appear and show cause why the personal representative should not be removed. The court may suspend the powers of the personal representative and may make such orders as are necessary to deal with the property pending the hearing.

(c) Any interested person may appear at the hearing and file a written declaration showing that the personal representative should be removed or retained. The personal representative may demur to or answer the declaration. The court may compel the attendance of the personal representative and may compel the personal representative to answer questions, on oath, concerning the administration of the estate. Failure to attend or answer is cause for removal of the personal representative from office.

(d) The issues shall be heard and determined by the court. If the court is satisfied from the evidence that the citation has been duly served and cause for removal exists, the court shall remove the personal representative from office.

8501. On removal of a personal representative from office, the court shall revoke any letters issued to the personal representative, and the authority of the personal representative ceases.

8502. A personal representative may be removed from office for any of the following causes:

(a) The personal representative has wasted, embezzled, mismanaged, or committed a fraud on the estate, or is about to do so.

(b) The personal representative is incapable of properly executing the duties of the office or is otherwise not qualified for appointment as personal representative.

(c) The personal representative has wrongfully neglected the estate, or has long neglected to perform any act as personal representative.

(d) Removal is otherwise necessary for protection of the estate or interested persons.

(e) Any other cause provided by statute.

8503. (a) Subject to subdivision (b), an administrator may be removed from office on the petition of the surviving spouse or a relative of the decedent entitled to succeed to all or part of the estate, or the nominee of the surviving spouse or relative, if such person is higher in priority than the administrator.

(b) The court in its discretion may refuse to grant the petition:

(1) Where the petition is by a person or the nominee of a person who had actual notice of the proceeding in which the administrator was appointed and an opportunity to contest the appointment.

(2) Where to do so would be contrary to the sound administration of the estate.

8504. (a) After appointment of an administrator on the ground of intestacy, the personal representative shall be removed from office on the later admission to probate of a will.

(b) After appointment of an executor or administrator with the will annexed, the personal representative shall be removed from office on admission to probate of a later will.

8505. (a) A personal representative may be removed from office if the personal representative is found in contempt for disobeying an order of the court.

(b) Notwithstanding any other provision of this article, a personal representative may be removed from office under this section by a court order reciting the facts and without further showing or notice.

Article 7. Changes In Administration

8520. A vacancy occurs in the office of a personal representative who resigns, dies, or is removed from office under Article 6 (commencing with Section 8500), or whose authority is otherwise terminated.

8521. (a) Unless the will provides otherwise or the court in its discretion orders otherwise, if a vacancy occurs in the office of fewer than all personal representatives, the remaining personal representatives shall complete the administration of the estate.

(b) The court, on the filing of a petition alleging that a vacancy has occurred in the office of fewer than all personal representatives, may order the clerk to issue appropriate amended letters to the remaining personal representatives.

8522. (a) If a vacancy occurs in the office of a personal representative and there are no other personal representatives, the court shall appoint a successor personal representative.

(b) Appointment of a successor personal representative shall be made on petition and service of notice on interested persons in the manner provided in Article 2 (commencing with Section 8110) of Chapter 2, and shall be subject to the same priority as for an original appointment of a personal representative. The personal representative of a deceased personal representative is not, as such, entitled to appointment as successor personal representative.

8523. The court may make orders that are necessary to deal with the estate of the decedent between the time a vacancy occurs in the office of personal representative and appointment of a successor. Those orders may include appointment of a special administrator.

8524. (a) A successor personal representative is entitled to demand, sue for, recover and collect all the estate of the decedent remaining unadministered, and may prosecute to final judgment any suit commenced by the former personal representative before the vacancy.

(b) No notice, process, or claim given to or served on the former personal representative need be given to or served on the successor in order to preserve any position or right the person giving the notice or filing the claim may thereby have obtained or preserved with reference to the former personal representative.

(c) Except as provided in subdivision (b) of Section 8442 (authority of administrator with will annexed) or as otherwise ordered by the court, the successor personal representative has the powers and duties in respect to the continued administration that the former personal representative would have had.

8525. (a) The acts of the personal representative before a vacancy occurs are valid to the same extent as if no vacancy had later occurred.

(b) The liability of a personal representative whose office is vacant, or of the surety on the bond, is not discharged, released, or affected by the vacancy or by appointment of a successor, but continues until settlement of the accounts of the personal representative and delivery of all the estate of the decedent to the successor personal representative or other person appointed by the court to receive it. The personal representative shall render an account of the administration within the time that the court directs.

Article 8. Special Administrators

8540. (a) If the circumstances of the estate require the immediate appointment of a personal representative, the court may appoint a special administrator to exercise any powers that may be appropriate under the circumstances for the preservation of the estate.

(b) The appointment may be for a specified term, to perform particular acts, or on any other terms specified in the court order.

8541. (a) Appointment of a special administrator may be made at any time without notice or on such notice to interested persons as the court deems reasonable.

(b) In making the appointment, the court shall ordinarily give preference to the person entitled to appointment as personal representative. The court may appoint the public administrator.

(c) In the case of an appointment to perform a particular act, request for approval of the act may be included in the petition for appointment, and approval may be made on the same notice and at the same time as the appointment.

(d) The court may act, if necessary, to remedy any errors made in the appointment.

8542. (a) The clerk shall issue letters to the special administrator after both of the following conditions are satisfied:

(1) The special administrator gives any bond that may be required by the court under Section 8480.

(2) The special administrator takes the usual oath attached to or endorsed on the letters.

(b) Subdivision (a) does not apply to the public administrator.

(c) The letters of a special administrator appointed to perform a particular act shall include a notation of the particular act the special administrator was appointed to perform.

8543. Subject to subdivision (b) of Section 8481, the court shall direct that no bond be given in either of the following cases:

(a) The will waives the requirement of a bond and the person named as executor in the will is appointed special administrator.

(b) All beneficiaries waive in writing the requirement of a bond and the written waivers are attached to the petition for appointment of the special administrator. This paragraph does not apply if the will requires a bond.

8544. (a) Except to the extent the order appointing a special administrator prescribes terms, the special administrator has the power to do all of the following without further order of the court:

(1) Take possession of all of the real and personal property of the estate of the decedent and preserve it from damage, waste, and injury.

(2) Collect all claims, rents, and other income belonging to the estate.

(3) Commence and maintain or defend suits and other legal proceedings.

(4) Sell perishable property.

(b) Except to the extent the order prescribes terms, the special administrator has the power to do all of the following on order of the court:

(1) Borrow money, or lease, mortgage, or execute a deed of trust on real property, in the same manner as an administrator.

(2) Pay the interest due or all or any part of an obligation secured by a mortgage, lien, or deed of trust on property in the estate, where there is danger that the holder of the security may enforce or foreclose on the obligation and the property exceeds in value the amount of the obligation. This power may be ordered only on petition of the special administrator or any interested person, with any notice that the court deems proper, and shall remain in effect until appointment of a successor personal representative. The order may also direct that interest not yet accrued be paid as it becomes due, and the order

shall remain in effect and cover the future interest unless and until for good cause set aside or modified by the court in the same manner as for the original order.

(3) Exercise other powers that are conferred by order of the court.

(c) Except where the powers, duties, and obligations of a general personal representative are granted under Section 8545, the special administrator is not a proper party to an action on a claim against the decedent.

(d) A special administrator appointed to perform a particular act has no duty to take any other action to protect the estate.

8545. (a) Notwithstanding Section 8544, the court may grant a special administrator the same powers, duties, and obligations as a general personal representative where to do so appears proper. Notwithstanding Section 8541, if letters have not previously been issued to a general personal representative, the grant shall be on the same notice required under Section 8003 for appointment of a personal representative, unless the appointment is made at a hearing on a petition for appointment of a general personal representative and the notice of that petition required under Section 8003 has been given.

(b) Subject to Section 8543, the court may require as a condition of the grant that the special administrator give any additional bond that the court deems proper. From the time of approving and filing any required additional bond, the special administrator shall have the powers, duties, and obligations of a general personal representative.

(c) If a grant is made under this section, the letters shall recite that the special administrator has the powers, duties, and obligations of a general personal representative.

8546. (a) The powers of a special administrator cease on issuance of letters to a general personal representative or as otherwise directed by the court.

(b) The special administrator shall promptly deliver to the general personal representative:

(1) All property of the estate in the possession of the special administrator. The court may authorize the special administrator to complete a sale or other transaction affecting property in the possession of the special administrator.

(2) A list of all creditor claims of which the special administrator has knowledge. The list shall show the name and address of each creditor, the amount of the claim, and what action has been taken with respect to the claim. A copy of the list shall be filed in the court.

(c) The special administrator shall account in the same manner as a general personal representative is required to account. If the same person acts as both special administrator and general personal representative, the account of the special administrator may be combined with the first account of the general personal representative.

8547. (a) Subject to the limitations of this section, the court shall fix the compensation of the special administrator and the compensation of the attorney of the special administrator.

(b) The compensation of the special administrator shall not be allowed until the close of administration, unless the general personal representative joins in the petition for allowance of the special administrator's compensation or the court in its discretion so allows. Compensation for extraordinary services of a special administrator may be allowed on settlement of the final account of the special administrator. The total compensation paid to the special administrator and general personal representative shall not, together, exceed the sums provided in Part 7 (commencing with Section 10800) for compensation for the ordinary and extraordinary services of a personal representative. If the same person does not act as both special administrator and general personal representative, the compensation shall be divided in such proportions as the court determines to be just or as may be agreed to by the special administrator and general personal representative.

(c) The total compensation paid to the attorneys both of the special administrator and the general personal representative shall not, together, exceed the sums provided in Part 7 (commencing with Section 10800) as compensation for the ordinary and extraordinary services of attorneys for personal representatives. When the same attorney does not act for both the special administrator and general personal representative, the compensation shall be divided between the attorneys in such proportions as the court determines to be just or as agreed to by the attorneys.

(d) Compensation of an attorney for extraordinary services to a special administrator may be awarded in the same manner and subject to the same standards as for extraordinary services to a general personal representative, except that the award of compensation to the attorney may be made on settlement of the final account of the special administrator.

Article 9. Nonresident Personal Representative

8570. As used in this article, "nonresident personal representative" means a nonresident of this state appointed as personal representative, or a resident of this state appointed as personal representative who later removes from and resides without this state.

8571. Notwithstanding any other provision of this chapter and notwithstanding a waiver of a bond, the court in its discretion may require a nonresident personal representative to give a bond in an amount determined by the court.

8572. (a) Acceptance of appointment by a nonresident personal representative is equivalent to and constitutes an irrevocable and binding appointment by the nonresident personal representative of the Secretary of State to be the attorney of the personal representative for the purpose of this article. The appointment of the nonresident personal representative also applies to any personal representative of a deceased nonresident personal representative.

(b) All lawful processes, and notices of motion under Section 377.41 of the Code of Civil Procedure, in an action or proceeding against the nonresident personal representative with respect to the estate or founded on or arising out of the acts or omissions of the nonresident personal representative in that capacity may be served on the Secretary of State as the attorney for service of the nonresident personal representative.

8573. A nonresident personal representative shall sign and file with the court a statement of the permanent address of the nonresident personal representative. If the permanent address is changed, the nonresident personal representative shall promptly file in the same manner a statement of the change of address.

8574. (a) Service of process or notice of a motion under Section 377.41 of the Code of Civil Procedure in any action or proceeding against the nonresident personal representative shall be made by delivering to and leaving with the Secretary of State two copies of the summons and complaint or notice of motion and either of the following:

(1) A copy of the statement by the nonresident personal representative under Section 8573.

(2) If the nonresident personal representative has not filed a statement under Section 8573, a copy of the letters issued to the nonresident personal representative together with a written statement signed by the party or attorney of the party seeking service that sets forth an address for use by the Secretary of State.

(b) The Secretary of State shall promptly mail by registered mail one copy of the summons and complaint or notice of motion to the nonresident personal representative at the address shown on the statement delivered to the Secretary of State.

(c) Personal service of process, or notice of motion, on the nonresident personal representative wherever found shall be the equivalent of service as provided in this section.

8575. Proof of compliance with Section 8574 shall be made in the following manner:

(a) In the event of service by mail, by certificate of the Secretary of State, under official seal, showing the mailing. The certificate shall be filed with the court from which process issued.

(b) In the event of personal service outside this state, by the return of any duly constituted public officer qualified to serve like process, or notice of motion, of and in the jurisdiction where the nonresident personal representative is found, showing the service to have been made. The return shall be attached to the original summons, or notice of motion, and filed with the court from which process issued.

8576. (a) Except as provided in this section, service made under Section 8574 has the same legal force and validity as if made personally in this state.

(b) A nonresident personal representative served under Section 8574 may appear and answer the complaint within 30 days from the date of service.

(c) Notice of motion shall be served on a nonresident personal representative under Section 8574 not less than 30 days before the date of the hearing on the motion.

8577. (a) Failure of a nonresident personal representative to comply with Section 8573 is cause for removal from office.

(b) Nothing in this section limits the liability of, or the availability of any other remedy against, a nonresident personal representative who is removed from office under this section.

Part 3. Inventory And Appraisal

Chapter 1. General Provisions

8800. (a) The personal representative shall file with the court clerk an inventory of property to be administered in the decedent's estate together with an appraisal of property in the inventory. An inventory and appraisal shall be combined in a single document.

(b) The inventory and appraisal shall be filed within four months after letters are first issued to a general personal representative. The court may allow such further time for filing an inventory and appraisal as is reasonable under the circumstances of the particular case.

(c) The personal representative may file partial inventories and appraisals where appropriate under the circumstances of the particular case, but all inventories and appraisals shall be filed before expiration of the time allowed under subdivision (b)

(d) Concurrent with the filing of the inventory and appraisal pursuant to this section, the personal representative shall also file a certification that the requirements of Section 480 of the Revenue and Taxation Code either:

(1) Are not applicable because the decedent owned no real property in California at the time of death.

(2) Have been satisfied by the filing of a change in ownership statement with the

county recorder or assessor of each county in California in which the decedent owned property at the time of death.

8801. If the personal representative acquires knowledge of property to be administered in the decedent's estate that is not included in a prior inventory and appraisal, the personal representative shall file a supplemental inventory and appraisal of the property in the manner prescribed for an original inventory and appraisal. The supplemental inventory and appraisal shall be filed within four months after the personal representative acquires knowledge of the property. The court may allow such further time for filing a supplemental inventory and appraisal as is reasonable under the circumstances of the particular case.

8802. The inventory and appraisal shall separately list each item and shall state the fair market value of the item at the time of the decedent's death in monetary terms opposite the item.

8803. On the filing of an inventory and appraisal or a supplemental inventory and appraisal, the personal representative shall, pursuant to Section 1252, mail a copy to each person who has requested special notice.

8804. If the personal representative refuses or negligently fails to file an inventory and appraisal within the time allowed under this chapter, upon petition of an interested person:

(a) The court may compel the personal representative to file an inventory and appraisal pursuant to the procedure prescribed in Chapter 4 (commencing with Section 11050) of Part 8.

(b) The court may remove the personal representative from office.

(c) The court may impose on the personal representative personal liability for injury to the estate or to an interested person that directly results from the refusal or failure. The liability may include attorney's fees, in the court's discretion. Damages awarded pursuant to this subdivision are a liability on the bond of the personal representative, if any.

Chapter 2. Inventory

Article 1. General Provisions

8850. (a) The inventory, including partial and supplemental inventories, shall include all property to be administered in the decedent's estate.

(b) The inventory shall particularly specify the following property:

(1) Money owed to the decedent, including debts, bonds, and notes, with the name of each debtor, the date, the sum originally payable, and the endorsements, if any, with their dates. The inventory shall also specify security for the payment of money to the decedent, including mortgages and deeds of

trust. If security for the payment of money is real property, the inventory shall include the recording reference or, if not recorded, a legal description of the real property.

(2) A statement of the interest of the decedent in a partnership, appraised as a single item.

(3) All money and other cash items, as defined in Section 8901, of the decedent.

(c) The inventory shall show, to the extent ascertainable by the personal representative, the portions of the property that are community, quasi-community, and separate property of the decedent.

8851. The discharge or devise in a will of any debt or demand of the testator against the executor or any other person is not valid against creditors of the testator, but is a specific devise of the debt or demand. The debt or demand shall be included in the inventory. If necessary, the debt or demand shall be applied in the payment of the debts of the testator. If not necessary for that purpose, the debt or demand shall be distributed in the same manner and proportion as other specific devises.

8852. (a) The personal representative shall take and subscribe an oath that the inventory contains a true statement of the property to be administered in the decedent's estate of which the personal representative has knowledge, and particularly of money of the decedent and debts or demands of the decedent against the personal representative. The oath shall be endorsed upon or attached to the inventory.

(b) If there is more than one personal representative, each shall take and subscribe the oath. If the personal representatives are unable to agree as to property to be included in the inventory, any personal representative may petition for a court order determining whether the property is to be administered in the decedent's estate. The determination shall be made pursuant to the procedure provided in Part 19 (commencing with Section 850) of Division 2 or, if there is an issue of property belonging or passing to the surviving spouse, pursuant to Chapter 5 (commencing with Section 13650) of Part 2 of Division 8.

Article 2. Discovery Of Property Of Decedent

8870. (a) On petition by the personal representative or an interested person, the court may order that a citation be issued to a person to answer interrogatories, or to appear before the court and be examined under oath, or both, concerning any of the following allegations:

(1) The person has wrongfully taken, concealed, or disposed of property in the estate of the decedent.

(2) The person has knowledge or possession of any of the following:

(A) A deed, conveyance, bond, contract,

or other writing that contains evidence of or tends to disclose the right, title, interest, or claim of the decedent to property.

(B) A claim of the decedent.

(C) A lost will of the decedent.

(b) If the person does not reside in the county in which the estate is being administered, the superior court either of the county in which the person resides or of the county in which the estate is being administered may issue a citation under this section.

(c) Disobedience of a citation issued pursuant to this section may be punished as a contempt of the court issuing the citation.

(d) Notice to the personal representative of a proceeding under subdivision (a) shall be given for the period and in the manner provided in Section 1220. Other persons requesting notice of the hearing pursuant to Section 1250 shall be notified by the person filing the petition as set forth in Section 1252.

8871. Interrogatories may be put to a person cited to answer interrogatories pursuant to Section 8870. The interrogatories and answers shall be in writing. The answers shall be signed under penalty of perjury by the person cited. The interrogatories and answers shall be filed with the court.

8872. (a) At an examination witnesses may be produced and examined on either side.

(b) If upon the examination it appears that the allegations of the petition are true, the court may order the person to disclose the person's knowledge of the facts to the personal representative.

(c) If upon the examination it appears that the allegations of the petition are not true, the person's necessary expenses, including a reasonable attorney's fee, shall be charged against the petitioner or allowed out of the estate, in the discretion of the court.

8873. (a) On petition by the personal representative, the court may issue a citation to a person who has possession or control of property in the decedent's estate to appear before the court and make an account under oath of the property and the person's actions with respect to the property.

(b) Disobedience of a citation issued pursuant to this section may be punished as a contempt of the court issuing the citation.

Chapter 3. Appraisal

Article 1. Procedure

8900. The appraisal of property in the inventory shall be made by the personal representative, probate referee, or independent expert as provided in this chapter.

8901. The personal representative shall appraise the following property, excluding items whose fair market value is, in the opinion of the personal representative, an amount different from the face value of the property:

(a) Money and other cash items. As used in this subdivision, a "cash item" is a check, draft, money order, or similar instrument issued on or before the date of the decedent's death that can be immediately converted to cash.

(b) The following checks issued after the date of the decedent's death:

(1) Checks for wages earned before death.

(2) Refund checks, including tax and utility refunds, and Medicare, medical insurance, and other health care reimbursements and payments.

(c) Accounts (as defined in Section 21) in financial institutions.

(d) Cash deposits and money market mutual funds, as defined in subdivision (b) of Section 9730, whether in a financial institution or otherwise, including a brokerage cash account. All other mutual funds, stocks, bonds, and other securities shall be appraised pursuant to Sections 8902 to 8909, inclusive.

(e) Proceeds of life and accident insurance policies and retirement plans and annuities payable on death in lump sum amounts.

8902. Except as otherwise provided by statute:

(a) The personal representative shall deliver the inventory to the probate referee designated by the court, together with necessary supporting data to enable the probate referee to make an appraisal of the property in the inventory to be appraised by the probate referee.

(b) The probate referee shall appraise all property other than that appraised by the personal representative.

8903. (a) The court may, for good cause, waive appraisal by a probate referee in the manner provided in this section.

(b) The personal representative may apply for a waiver together with the petition for appointment of the personal representative or together with another petition, or may apply for a waiver in a separate petition filed in the administration proceedings, but the application may not be made later than the time the personal representative delivers the inventory to the probate referee, if a probate referee has been designated. A copy of the proposed inventory and appraisal and a statement that sets forth the good cause that justifies the waiver shall be attached to the petition.

(c) The hearing on the waiver shall be not sooner than 15 days after the petition is filed. Notice of the hearing on the petition, together with a copy of the petition and a copy of the proposed inventory and appraisal, shall be given as provided in Section 1220 to all of the following persons:

(1) Each person listed in Section 1220.

(2) Each known heir whose interest in the estate would be affected by the waiver.

(3) Each known devisee whose interest in the estate would be affected by the waiver.

(4) The Attorney General, at the office of the Attorney General in Sacramento, if any portion of the estate is to escheat to the state and its interest in the estate would be affected by the waiver.

(5) The probate referee, if a probate referee has been designated.

(d) A probate referee to whom notice is given under this section may oppose the waiver. If the opposition fails and the court determines the opposition was made without substantial justification, the court shall award litigation expenses, including reasonable attorney's fees, against the probate referee. If the opposition succeeds, the court may designate a different probate referee to appraise property in the estate.

(e) If the petition is granted, the inventory and appraisal attached to the petition shall be filed pursuant to Section 8800.

8904. (a) A unique, artistic, unusual, or special item of tangible personal property that would otherwise be appraised by the probate referee may, at the election of the personal representative, be appraised by an independent expert qualified to appraise the item.

(b) The personal representative shall make the election provided in subdivision (a) by a notation on the inventory delivered to the probate referee indicating the property to be appraised by an independent expert. The probate referee may, within five days after delivery of the inventory, petition for a court determination whether the property to be appraised by an independent expert is a unique, artistic, unusual, or special item of tangible personal property. If the petition fails and the court determines that the petition was made without substantial justification, the court shall award litigation expenses, including reasonable attorney's fees, against the probate referee.

8905. A person who appraises property, whether a personal representative, probate referee, or independent expert, shall sign the appraisal as to property appraised by that person, and shall take and subscribe an oath that the person has truly, honestly, and impartially appraised the property to the best of the person's ability.

8906. (a) At any time before the hearing on the petition for final distribution of the estate, the personal representative or an interested person may file with the court a written objection to the appraisal.

(b) The clerk shall fix a time, not less than 15 days after the filing, for a hearing on the objection.

(c) The person objecting shall give notice of the hearing, together with a copy of the objection, as provided in Section 1220. If the appraisal was made by a probate referee, the person objecting shall also mail notice of the hearing and a copy of the objection to the probate referee at least 15 days before the date set for the hearing.

(d) The person objecting to the appraisal has the burden of proof.

(e) Upon completion of the hearing, the court may make any orders that appear appropriate. If the court determines the objection was filed without reasonable cause or good faith, the court may order that the fees of the personal representative and attorney and any costs incurred for defending the appraisal be made a charge against the person filing the objection.

8907. Neither the personal representative nor the attorney for the personal representative is entitled to receive compensation for extraordinary services by reason of appraising any property in the estate.

8908. A probate referee who appraises property in the estate shall, upon demand by the personal representative or by a beneficiary:

(a) Provide any appraisal report or backup data in the possession of the probate referee used by the referee to appraise an item of property. The probate referee shall not disclose any information that is required by law to be confidential. The probate referee shall provide the appraisal report or backup data without charge. The cost of providing the appraisal report or backup data shall not be allowed as an expense of appraisal but is included in the commission for services of the probate referee.

(b) Justify the appraisal of an item of property if the appraisal is contested, whether by objection pursuant to Section 8906, by tax audit, or otherwise. The probate referee may be entitled to an additional fee for services provided to justify the appraisal, to be agreed upon by the personal representative or beneficiary and referee. If the personal representative or beneficiary and the probate referee are unable to agree, the court shall determine what fee, if any, is appropriate.

8909. A probate referee who appraises property in an estate shall retain possession of all appraisal reports and backup data used by the referee to appraise the property for a period of three years after the appraisal is filed. The probate referee shall, during the three-year period, offer the personal representative the reports and data used by the referee to appraise the property and deliver the reports and data to the personal representative on request. Any reports and data not requested by the personal representative may be destroyed at the end of the three-year period without further notice.

Article 2. Designation And Removal Of Probate Referee

8920. The probate referee, when designated by the court, shall be among the persons appointed by the Controller to act as a probate referee for the county. If there is no person available who is able to act or if, pursuant to authority of Section 8922 or otherwise, the court does not designate a person appointed for the county, the court may designate a probate referee from another county.

8921. The court may designate a person requested by the personal representative as probate referee, on a showing by the personal representative of good cause for the designation. The following circumstances are included within the meaning of good cause, as used in this section:

(a) The probate referee has recently appraised the same property that will be appraised in the administration proceeding.

(b) The probate referee will be making related appraisals in another proceeding.

(c) The probate referee has recently appraised similar property in another proceeding.

8922. The court has authority and discretion not to designate a particular person as probate referee even though appointed by the Controller to act as a probate referee for the county.

8923. The court may not designate as probate referee any of the following persons:

(a) The court clerk.

(b) A partner or employee of the judge or commissioner who orders the designation.

(c) The spouse of the judge or commissioner who orders the designation.

(d) A person, or the spouse of a person, who is related within the third degree either (1) to the judge or commissioner who orders the designation or (2) to the spouse of the judge or commissioner who orders the designation.

8924. (a) The court shall remove the designated probate referee in any of the following circumstances:

(1) The personal representative shows cause, including incompetence or undue delay in making the appraisal, that in the opinion of the court warrants removal of the probate referee. The showing shall be made at a hearing on petition of the personal representative. The personal representative shall mail notice of the hearing on the petition to the probate referee at least 15 days before the date set for the hearing.

(2) The personal representative has the right to remove the first probate referee who is designated by the court. No cause need be shown for removal under this paragraph. The personal representative may exercise the right at any time before the personal representative delivers the inventory to the probate referee. The personal representative shall exercise the right by filing an affidavit or declaration under penalty of perjury with the court and mailing a copy to the probate referee. Thereupon, the court shall remove the probate referee without any further act or proof.

(3) Any other cause provided by statute.

(b) Upon removal of the probate referee, the court shall designate another probate referee in the manner prescribed in Section 8920.

Article 3. Time For Probate Referee Appraisal

8940. (a) The probate referee shall promptly and with reasonable diligence appraise the property scheduled for appraisal by the probate referee in the inventory that the personal representative delivers to the referee.

(b) The probate referee shall, not later than 60 days after delivery of the inventory, do one of the following:

(1) Return the completed appraisal to the personal representative.

(2) Make a report of the status of the appraisal. The report shall show the reason why the property has not been appraised and an estimate of the time needed to complete the appraisal. The report shall be delivered to the personal representative and filed with the court.

8941. (a) The court shall, on petition of the personal representative or probate referee, or may, on the court's own motion, hear the report of the status of the appraisal. The court may issue a citation to compel the personal representative or the probate referee to attend the hearing.

(b) If the probate referee does not make the report of the status of the appraisal within the time required by this article or prescribed by the court, the court shall, on petition of the personal representative or may, on its own motion, cite the probate referee to appear before the court and show the reason why the property has not been appraised.

(c) Upon the hearing, the court may order any of the following:

(1) That the appraisal be completed within a time that appears reasonable.

(2) That the probate referee be removed. Upon removal of the probate referee the court shall designate another probate referee in the manner prescribed in Section 8920.

(3) That the commission of the probate referee be reduced by an amount the court deems appropriate, regardless of whether the commission otherwise allowable under the provisions of Sections 8960 to 8964 would be reasonable compensation for the services rendered.

(4) That the personal representative deliver to the probate referee all information necessary to allow the probate referee to complete the appraisal. Failure to comply with such an order is grounds for removal of the personal representative.

(5) Such other orders as may be appropriate.

Article 4. Commission And Expenses Of Probate Referee

8960. (a) The commission and expenses provided by this article as compensation for the services of the probate referee shall be paid from the estate.

(b) The probate referee may not withhold the appraisal until the commission and expenses are paid, but shall deliver the appraisal to the personal representative promptly upon completion.

(c) The commission and expenses of the probate referee are an expense of administration, entitled to the priority for payment provided by Section 11420, and shall be paid in the course of administration.

8961. As compensation for services the probate referee shall receive all of the following:

(a) A commission of one-tenth of one percent of the total value of the property for each estate appraised, subject to Section 8963. The commission shall be computed excluding property appraised by the personal representative pursuant to Section 8901 or by an independent expert pursuant to Section 8904.

(b) Actual and necessary expenses for each estate appraised. The referee shall file with, or list on, the inventory and appraisal a verified account of the referee's expenses.

8963. (a) Notwithstanding Section 8961 and subject to subdivision (b), the commission of the probate referee shall in no event be less than seventy-five dollars ($75) nor more than ten thousand dollars ($10,000) for any estate appraised.

(b) Upon application of the probate referee, the court may allow a commission in excess of ten thousand dollars ($10,000) if the court determines that the reasonable value of the referee's services exceeds that amount. Notice of the hearing under this subdivision shall be given as provided in Section 1220 to all of the following persons:

(1) Each person listed in Section 1220.

(2) Each known heir whose interest in the estate would be affected by the petition.

(3) Each known devisee whose interest in the estate would be affected by the petition.

(4) The Attorney General, at the office of the Attorney General in Sacramento, if any portion of the estate is to escheat to the state and its interest in the estate would be affected by the petition.

(5) Each person who has requested special notice of petitions filed in the proceeding.

8964. If more than one probate referee appraises or participates in the appraisal of property in the estate, each is entitled to the share of the commission agreed upon by the referees or, absent an agreement, that the court allows. In no case shall the total commission for all referees exceed the maximum commission that would be allowable for a single referee.

Article 5. Transitional Provision

8980. If an inventory is delivered to a probate referee for appraisal before July 1, 1989, all matters relating to the appraisal by the referee, including the property to be included in the appraisal, waiver of the appraisal, and compensation of the referee, are governed by the applicable law in effect before July 1, 1989, and are not governed by this chapter.

Part 4. Creditor Claims

Chapter 1. General Provisions

9000. As used in this division:

(a) "Claim" means a demand for payment for any of the following, whether due, not due, accrued or not accrued, or contingent, and whether liquidated or unliquidated:

(1) Liability of the decedent, whether arising in contract, tort, or otherwise.

(2) Liability for taxes incurred before the decedent's death, whether assessed before or after the decedent's death, other than property taxes and assessments secured by real property liens.

(3) Liability of the estate for funeral expenses of the decedent.

(b) "Claim" does not include a dispute regarding title of a decedent to specific property alleged to be included in the decedent's estate.

(c) "Creditor" means a person who may have a claim against estate property.

9001. (a) The publication of notice under Section 8120 and the giving of notice of administration of the estate of the decedent under Chapter 2 (commencing with Section 9050) constitute notice to creditors of the requirements of this part.

(b) Nothing in subdivision (a) affects a notice or request to a public entity required by Chapter 5 (commencing with Section 9200).

9002. Except as otherwise provided by statute:

(a) All claims shall be filed in the manner and within the time provided in this part.

(b) A claim that is not filed as provided in this part is barred.

9003. A claim that is established under this part shall be included among the debts to be paid in the course of administration.

9004. (a) This part does not apply in any proceeding for administration of a decedent's estate commenced before July 1, 1988.

(b) The applicable law in effect before July 1, 1988, governing the subject matter of this part continues to apply in any proceeding for administration of a decedent's estate commenced before July 1, 1988, notwithstanding its repeal by Chapter 923 of the Statutes of 1987.

Chapter 2. Notice To Creditors

9050. (a) Subject to Section 9054, the personal representative shall give notice of administration of the estate to the known or reasonably ascertainable creditors of the decedent. The notice shall be given as provided in Section 1215. For the purpose of this subdivision, a personal representative has knowledge of a creditor of the decedent if the personal representative is aware that the creditor has demanded payment from the decedent or the estate.

(b) The giving of notice under this chapter is in addition to the publication of the notice under Section 8120.

9051. The notice shall be given within the later of:

(a) Four months after the date letters are first issued.

(b) Thirty days after the personal representative first has knowledge of the creditor.

9052. The notice shall be in substantially the following form:

PLEASE SEE THE APPENDIX

9053. (a) If the personal representative believes that notice to a particular creditor is or may be required by this chapter and gives notice based on that belief, the personal representative is not liable to any person for giving the notice, whether or not required by this chapter.

(b) If the personal representative fails to give notice required by this chapter, the personal representative is not liable to any person for the failure, unless a creditor establishes all of the following:

(1) The failure was in bad faith.

(2) The creditor had no actual knowledge of the administration of the estate before expiration of the time for filing a claim, and payment would have been made on the creditor's claim in the course of administration if the claim had been properly filed.

(3) Within 16 months after letters were first issued to a general personal representative, the creditor did both of the following:

(A) Filed a petition requesting that the court in which the estate was administered make an order determining the liability of the personal representative under this subdivision.

(B) At least 30 days before the hearing on the petition, caused notice of the hearing and a copy of the petition to be served on the personal representative in the manner provided in Chapter 4 (commencing with Section 413.10) of Title 5 of Part 2 of the Code of Civil Procedure.

(c) Nothing in this section affects the liability of the estate, if any, for the claim of a creditor, and the personal representative is not liable for the claim to the extent it is paid out of the estate or could be paid out of the estate pursuant to Section 9103.

(d) A personal representative has a duty to make reasonably diligent efforts to identify reasonably ascertainable creditors of the decedent.

9054. Notwithstanding Section 9050, the personal representative need not give notice to a creditor even though the personal representative has knowledge of the creditor if any of the following conditions is satisfied:

(a) The creditor has filed a claim as provided in this part.

(b) The creditor has demanded payment and the personal representative elects to treat the demand as a claim under Section 9154.

Chapter 3. Time For Filing Claims

9100. (a) A creditor shall file a claim before expiration of the later of the following times:

(1) Four months after the date letters are first issued to a general personal representative.

(2) Sixty days after the date notice of administration is mailed or personally delivered to the creditor. Nothing in this paragraph extends the time provided in Section 366.2 of the Code of Civil Procedure.

(b) A reference in another statute to the time for filing a claim means the time provided in paragraph (1) of subdivision (a).

(c) Nothing in this section shall be interpreted to extend or toll any other statute of limitations or to revive a claim that is barred by any statute of limitations. The reference in this subdivision to a "statute of limitations" includes Section 366.2 of the Code of Civil Procedure.

9101. A vacancy in the office of the personal representative that occurs before expiration of the time for filing a claim does not extend the time.

9102. A claim that is filed before expiration of the time for filing the claim is timely even if acted on by the personal representative or by the court after expiration of the time for filing claims.

9103. (a) Upon petition by a creditor or the personal representative, the court may allow a claim to be filed after expiration of the time for filing a claim provided in Section 9100 if either of the following conditions is satisfied:

(1) The personal representative failed to send proper and timely notice of administration of the estate to the creditor, and that petition is filed within 60 days after the creditor has actual knowledge of the administration of the estate.

(2) The creditor had no knowledge of the facts reasonably giving rise to the existence of the claim more than 30 days prior to the time for filing a claim as provided in Section 9100, and the petition is filed within 60 days after the creditor has actual knowledge of both of the following:

(A) The existence of the facts reasonably giving rise to the existence of the claim.

(B) The administration of the estate.

(b) Notwithstanding subdivision (a), the court shall not allow a claim to be filed under this section after the court makes an order for final distribution of the estate.

(c) The court may condition the claim on terms that are just and equitable, and may require the appointment or reappointment of a personal representative if necessary. The court may deny the creditor's petition if a payment to general creditors has been made and it appears that the filing or establishment of the claim would cause or tend to cause unequal treatment among creditors.

(d) Regardless of whether the claim is later established in whole or in part, payments otherwise properly made before a claim is filed under this section are not subject to the claim. Except to the extent provided in Section 9392 and subject to Section 9053, the personal representative or payee is not liable on account of the prior payment. Nothing in this subdivision limits the liability of a person who receives a preliminary distribution of property to restore to the estate an amount sufficient for payment of the distributee's proper share of the claim, not exceeding the amount distributed.

(e) Notice of hearing on the petition shall be given as provided in Section 1220.

(f) Nothing in this section authorizes allowance or approval of a claim barred by, or extends the time provided in, Section 366.2 of the Code of Civil Procedure.

9104. (a) Subject to subdivision (b), if a claim is filed within the time provided in this chapter, the creditor may later amend or revise the claim. The amendment or revision shall be filed in the same manner as the claim.

(b) An amendment or revision may not be made to increase the amount of the claim after the time for filing a claim has expired. An amendment or revision to specify the amount of a claim that, at the time of filing, was not due, was contingent, or was not yet ascertainable, is not an increase in the amount of the claim within the meaning of this subdivision.

(c) An amendment or revision may not be made for any purpose after the earlier of the following times:

. (1) The time the court makes an order for final distribution of the estate.

(2) One year after letters are first issued to a general personal representative. This paragraph does not extend the time provided by Section 366.2 of the Code of Civil Procedure or authorize allowance or approval of a claim barred by that section.

Chapter 4. Filing Of Claims

9150. (a) A claim may be filed by the creditor or a person acting on behalf of the creditor.

(b) A claim shall be filed with the court and a copy shall be served on the personal representative, or on a person who is later appointed and qualified as personal representative.

(c) Service of the claim on the personal representative shall be made within the later of 30 days of the filing of the claim or four months after letters issue to a personal representative with general powers. Service shall not be required after the claim has been allowed or rejected.

(d) If the creditor does not file the claim with the court and serve the claim on the personal representative as provided in this section, the claim shall be invalid.

9151. (a) A claim shall be supported by the affidavit of the creditor or the person acting on behalf of the creditor stating:

(1) The claim is a just claim.

(2) If the claim is due, the facts supporting the claim, the amount of the claim, and that all payments on and offsets to the claim have been credited.

(3) If the claim is not due or contingent, or the amount is not yet ascertainable, the facts supporting the claim.

(4) If the affidavit is made by a person other than the creditor, the reason it is not made by the creditor.

(b) The personal representative may require satisfactory vouchers or proof to be produced to support the claim. An original voucher may be withdrawn after a copy is provided. If a copy is provided, the copy shall be attached to the claim.

9152. (a) If a claim is based on a written instrument, either the original or a copy of the original with all endorsements shall be attached to the claim. If a copy is attached, the original instrument shall be exhibited to the personal representative or court or judge on demand unless it is lost or destroyed, in which case the fact that it is lost or destroyed shall be stated in the claim.

(b) If the claim or a part of the claim is secured by a mortgage, deed of trust, or other lien that is recorded in the office of the recorder of the county in which the property subject to the lien is located, it is sufficient to describe the mortgage, deed of trust, or lien and the recording reference for the instrument that created the mortgage, deed of trust, or other lien.

9153. A claim form adopted by the Judicial Council shall inform the creditor that the claim must be filed with the court and a copy mailed or delivered to the personal representative. The claim form shall include a proof of mailing or delivery of a copy of the claim to the personal representative, which may be completed by the creditor.

9154. (a) Notwithstanding any other provision of this part, if a creditor makes a written demand for payment within four months after the date letters are first issued to a general personal representative, the personal representative may waive formal defects and elect to treat the demand as a claim that is filed and established under this part by paying the amount demanded before the expiration of 30 days after the four-month period if all of the following conditions are satisfied:

(1) The debt was justly due.

(2) The debt was paid in good faith.

(3) The amount paid was the true amount of the indebtedness over and above all payments and offsets.

(4) The estate is solvent.

(b) Nothing in this section limits application of (1) the doctrines of waiver, estoppel, laches, or detrimental reliance or (2) any other equitable principle.

Chapter 5. Claims By Public Entities

9200. (a) Except as provided in this chapter, a claim by a public entity shall be filed within the time otherwise provided in this part. A claim not so filed is barred, including any lien imposed for the claim.

(b) As used in this chapter, "public entity" has the meaning provided in Section 811.2 of the Government Code, and includes an officer authorized to act on behalf of the public entity.

9201. (a) Notwithstanding any other statute, if a claim of a public entity arises under a law, act, or code listed in subdivision (b):

(1) The public entity may provide a form to be used for the written notice or request to the public entity required by this chapter. Where appropriate, the form may require the decedent's social security number, if known.

(2) The claim is barred only after written notice or request to the public entity and expiration of the period provided in the applicable section. If no written notice or request is made, the claim is enforceable by the remedies, and is barred at the time, otherwise provided in the law, act, or code.

(b)

LAW, ACT, OR CODE	APPLICABLE SECTION
Sales and Use Tax Law (commencing with Section 6001 of the Revenue and Taxation Code)	Section 6487.1 of the Revenue and Taxation Code
Bradley-Burns Uniform Local Sales and Use Tax Law (commencing with Section 7200 of the Revenue and Taxation Code)	Section 6487.1 of the Revenue and Taxation Code

LAW, ACT, OR CODE	APPLICABLE SECTION
Transactions and Use Tax Law (commencing with Section 7251 of the Revenue and Taxation Code)	Section 6487.1 of the Revenue and Taxation Code
Motor Vehicle Fuel License Tax Law (commencing with Section 7301 of the Revenue and Taxation Code)	Section 7675.1 of the Revenue and Taxation Code
Use Fuel Tax Law (commencing with Section 8601 of the Revenue and Taxation Code)	Section 8782.1 of the Revenue and Taxation Code
Administration of Franchise and Income Tax Law (commencing with Section 18401 of the Revenue and Taxation Code)	Section 19517 of the Revenue and Taxation Code
Cigarette Tax Law (commencing with Section 30001 of the Revenue and Taxation Code)	Section 30207.1 of the Revenue and Taxation Code
Alcoholic Beverage Tax Law (commencing with Section 32001 of the Revenue and Taxation Code)	Section 32272.1 of the Revenue and Taxation Code
Unemployment Insurance Code	Section 1090 of the Unemployment Insurance Code
State Hospitals for the Mentally Disordered (commencing with Section 7200 of the Welfare and Institutions Code)	Section 7277.1 of the Welfare and Institutions Code
Medi-Cal Act (commencing with Section 14000 of the Welfare and Institutions Code)	Section 9202 of the Probate Code

LAW, ACT, OR CODE	APPLICABLE SECTION
Waxman-Duffy Prepaid Health Plan Act (commencing with Section 14200 of the Welfare and Institutions Code)	Section 9202 of the Probate Code

9202. (a) Not later than 90 days after the date letters are first issued to a general personal representative, the general personal representative or estate attorney shall give the Director of Health Care Services notice of the decedent's death in the manner provided in Section 215 if the general personal representative knows or has reason to believe that the decedent received health care under Chapter 7 (commencing with Section 14000) or Chapter 8 (commencing with Section 14200) of Part 3 of Division 9 of the Welfare and Institutions Code, or was the surviving spouse of a person who received that health care. The director has four months after notice is given in which to file a claim.

(b) Not later than 90 days after the date letters are first issued to a general personal representative, the general personal representative or estate attorney shall give the Director of the California Victim Compensation and Government Claims Board notice of the decedent's death in the manner provided in Section 216 if the general personal representative or estate attorney knows or has reason to believe that an heir is confined in a prison or facility under the jurisdiction of the Department of Corrections and Rehabilitation or confined in any county or city jail, road camp, industrial farm, or other local correctional facility. The director of the board shall have four months after that notice is received in which to pursue collection of any outstanding restitution fines or orders.

(c) (1) Not later than 90 days after the date letters are first issued to a general personal representative, the general personal representative or estate attorney shall give the Franchise Tax Board notice of the administration of the estate. The notice shall be given as provided in Section 1215.

(2) The provisions of this subdivision shall apply to estates for which letters are first issued on or after July 1, 2008.

9203. (a) Failure of a person to give the written notice or request required by this chapter does not affect the validity of any proceeding under this code concerning the administration of the decedent's estate.

(b) If property in the estate is distributed before expiration of the time allowed a public entity to file a claim, the public entity has a claim against the distributees to the full extent of the public entity's claim, or each distributee's share of the distributed property,

whichever is less. The public entity's claim against distributees includes interest at a rate equal to that specified in Section 19521 of the Revenue and Taxation Code, from the date of distribution or the date of filing the claim by the public entity, whichever is later, plus other accruing costs as in the case of enforcement of a money judgment.

9204. Nothing in this chapter shall be construed to affect the order of priority of claims provided for under other provisions of law.

9205. This chapter does not apply to liability for the restitution of amounts illegally acquired through the means of a fraudulent, false, or incorrect representation, or a forged or unauthorized endorsement.

Chapter 6. Allowance And Rejection Of Claims

9250. (a) When a claim is filed, the personal representative shall allow or reject the claim in whole or in part.

(b) The allowance or rejection shall be in writing. The personal representative shall file the allowance or rejection with the court clerk and give notice to the creditor as provided in Part 2 (commencing with Section 1200) of Division 3, together with a copy of the allowance or rejection.

(c) The allowance or rejection shall contain the following information:

(1) The name of the creditor.

(2) The total amount of the claim.

(3) The date of issuance of letters.

(4) The date of the decedent's death.

(5) The estimated value of the decedent's estate.

(6) The amount allowed or rejected by the personal representative.

(7) Whether the personal representative is authorized to act under the Independent Administration of Estates Act (Part 6 (commencing with Section 10400)).

(8) A statement that the creditor has 90 days in which to act on a rejected claim.

(d) The Judicial Council may prescribe an allowance or rejection form, which may be part of the claim form. Use of a form prescribed by the Judicial Council is deemed to satisfy the requirements of this section.

(e) This section does not apply to a demand the personal representative elects to treat as a claim under Section 9154.

9251. If the personal representative is not authorized to act under the Independent Administration of Estates Act (Part 6 (commencing with Section 10400)):

(a) Immediately on the filing of the allowance of a claim, the clerk shall present the claim and allowance to the court or judge for approval or rejection.

(b) On presentation of a claim and allowance, the court or judge may, in its discretion, examine the creditor and others on oath and receive any evidence relevant to the validity of the claim. The court or judge shall endorse on the claim whether the claim is approved or rejected and the date.

9252. (a) If the personal representative or the attorney for the personal representative is a creditor of the decedent, the clerk shall present the claim to the court or judge for approval or rejection. The court or judge may in its discretion require the creditor to file a petition and give notice of hearing.

(b) If the court or judge approves the claim, the claim is established and shall be included with other established claims to be paid in the course of administration.

(c) If the court or judge rejects the claim, the personal representative or attorney may bring an action against the estate. Summons shall be served on the judge, who shall appoint an attorney at the expense of the estate to defend the action.

9253. A claim barred by the statute of limitations may not be allowed by the personal representative or approved by the court or judge.

9254. (a) The validity of an allowed or approved claim may be contested by any interested person at any time before settlement of the report or account of the personal representative in which it is first reported as an allowed or approved claim. The burden of proof is on the contestant, except where the personal representative has acted under the Independent Administration of Estates Act (Part 6 (commencing Section 10400)), in which case the burden of proof is on the personal representative.

(b) Subdivision (a) does not apply to a claim established by a judgment.

9255. (a) The personal representative may allow a claim, or the court or judge may approve a claim, in part. The allowance or approval shall state the amount for which the claim is allowed or approved.

(b) A creditor who refuses to accept the amount allowed or approved in satisfaction of the claim may bring an action on the claim in the manner provided in Chapter 8 (commencing with Section 9350). The creditor may not recover costs in the action unless the creditor recovers an amount greater than that allowed or approved.

9256. If within 30 days after a claim is filed the personal representative or the court or judge has refused or neglected to act on the claim, the refusal or neglect may, at the option of the creditor, be deemed equivalent to giving a notice of rejection on the 30th day.

Chapter 7. Claims Established By Judgment

9300. (a) Except as provided in Section 9303, after the death of the decedent all money judgments against the decedent or against the personal representative on a claim against the decedent or estate are payable in the course of administration and are not enforceable against property in the estate of the decedent under the Enforcement of Judgments Law (Title 9 (commencing with Section 680.010) of Part 2 of the Code of Civil Procedure).

(b) Subject to Section 9301, a judgment referred to in subdivision (a) shall be filed in the same manner as other claims.

9301. When a money judgment against a personal representative in a representative capacity becomes final, it conclusively establishes the validity of the claim for the amount of the judgment. The judgment shall provide that it is payable out of property in the decedent's estate in the course of administration. An abstract of the judgment shall be filed in the administration proceedings.

9302. (a) Notwithstanding the death of the decedent, a judgment for possession of property or a judgment for sale of property may be enforced under the Enforcement of Judgments Law (Title 9 (commencing with Section 680.010) of Part 2 of the Code of Civil Procedure). Nothing in this subdivision authorizes enforcement under the Enforcement of Judgments Law against any property in the estate of the decedent other than the property described in the judgment for possession or sale.

(b) After the death of the decedent, a demand for money that is not satisfied from the property described in a judgment for sale of property shall be filed as a claim in the same manner as other claims and is payable in the course of administration.

9303. If property of the decedent is subject to an execution lien at the time of the decedent's death, enforcement against the property may proceed under the Enforcement of Judgments Law (Title 9 (commencing with Section 680.010) of Part 2 of the Code of Civil Procedure) to satisfy the judgment. The levying officer shall account to the personal representative for any surplus. If the judgment is not satisfied, the balance of the judgment remaining unsatisfied is payable in the course of administration.

9304. (a) An attachment lien may be converted into a judgment lien on property in the estate subject to the attachment lien, with the same priority as the attachment lien, in either of the following cases:

(1) Where the judgment debtor dies after entry of judgment in an action in which the property was attached.

(2) Where a judgment is entered after the death of the defendant in an action in which the property was attached.

(b) To convert the attachment lien into a judgment lien, the levying officer shall, after entry of judgment in the action in which the property was attached and before the expiration of the attachment lien, do one of the following:

(1) Serve an abstract of the judgment, and a notice that the attachment lien has become a judgment lien, on the person holding prop-

erty subject to the attachment lien.

(2) Record or file, in any office where the writ of attachment and notice of attachment are recorded or filed, an abstract of the judgment and a notice that the attachment lien has become a judgment lien. If the attached property is real property, the plaintiff or the plaintiff's attorney may record the required abstract and notice with the same effect as if recorded by the levying officer.

(c) After the death of the decedent, any members of the decedent's family who were supported in whole or in part by the decedent may claim an exemption provided in Section 487.020 of the Code of Civil Procedure for property levied on under the writ of attachment if the right to the exemption exists at the time the exemption is claimed. The personal representative may claim the exemption on behalf of members of the decedent's family. The claim of exemption may be made at any time before the time the abstract and notice are served, recorded, or filed under subdivision (b) with respect to the property claimed to be exempt. The claim of exemption shall be made in the same manner as an exemption is claimed under Section 482.100 of the Code of Civil Procedure.

Chapter 8. Claims In Litigation

Article 1. Claim Where No Pending Action Or Proceeding

9350. This article applies to any claim other than a claim on an action or proceeding pending against the decedent at the time of death.

9351. An action may not be commenced against a decedent's personal representative on a cause of action against the decedent unless a claim is first filed as provided in this part and the claim is rejected in whole or in part.

9352. (a) The filing of a claim or a petition under Section 9103 to file a claim tolls the statute of limitations otherwise applicable to the claim until allowance, approval, or rejection.

(b) The allowance or approval of a claim in whole or in part further tolls the statute of limitations during the administration of the estate as to the part allowed or approved.

9353. (a) Regardless of whether the statute of limitations otherwise applicable to a claim will expire before or after the following times, a claim rejected in whole or in part is barred as to the part rejected unless, within the following times, the creditor commences an action on the claim or the matter is referred to a referee or to arbitration:

(1) If the claim is due at the time the notice of rejection is given, 90 days after the notice is given.

(2) If the claim is not due at the time the notice of rejection is given, 90 days after the claim becomes due.

(b) The time during which there is a vacancy in the office of the personal representative shall be excluded from the period determined under subdivision (a).

9354. (a) In addition to any other county in which an action may be commenced, an action on the claim may be commenced in the county in which the proceeding for administration of the decedent's estate is pending.

(b) The plaintiff shall file a notice of the pendency of the action with the court clerk in the estate proceeding, together with proof of giving a copy of the notice to the personal representative as provided in Section 1215. Personal service of a copy of the summons and complaint on the personal representative is equivalent to the filing and giving of the notice. Any property distributed under court order, or any payment properly made, before the notice is filed and given is not subject to the claim. The personal representative, distributee, or payee is not liable on account of the prior distribution or payment.

(c) The prevailing party in the action shall be awarded court costs and, if the court determines that the prosecution or defense of the action against the prevailing party was unreasonable, the prevailing party shall be awarded reasonable litigation expenses, including attorney's fees.

Article 2. Claim Where Action Or Proceeding Pending

9370. (a) An action or proceeding pending against the decedent at the time of death may not be continued against the decedent's personal representative unless all of the following conditions are satisfied:

(1) A claim is first filed as provided in this part.

(2) The claim is rejected in whole or in part.

(3) Within three months after the notice of rejection is given, the plaintiff applies to the court in which the action or proceeding is pending for an order to substitute the personal representative in the action or proceeding. This paragraph applies only if the notice of rejection contains a statement that the plaintiff has three months within which to apply for an order for substitution.

(b) No recovery shall be allowed in the action against property in the decedent's estate unless proof is made of compliance with this section.

Article 3. Litigation Where No Claim Required

9390. (a) An action to establish the decedent's liability for which the decedent was protected by insurance may be commenced or continued under Section 550, and a judgment in the action may be enforced against the insurer, without first filing a claim as provided in this part.

(b) Unless a claim is first made as provided in this part, an action to establish the decedent's liability for damages outside the limits or coverage of the insurance may not be commenced or continued under Section 550.

(c) If the insurer seeks reimbursement under the insurance contract for any liability of the decedent, including, but not limited to, deductible amounts in the insurance coverage and costs and attorney's fees for which the decedent is liable under the contract, an insurer defending an action under Section 550 shall file a claim as provided in this part. Failure to file a claim is a waiver of reimbursement under the insurance contract for any liability of the decedent.

9391. Except as provided in Section 10361, the holder of a mortgage or other lien on property in the decedent's estate, including, but not limited to, a judgment lien, may commence an action to enforce the lien against the property that is subject to the lien, without first filing a claim as provided in this part, if in the complaint the holder of the lien expressly waives all recourse against other property in the estate. Section 366.2 of the Code of Civil Procedure does not apply to an action under this section. The personal representative shall have the authority to seek to enjoin any action of the lienholder to enforce a lien against property that is subject to the lien.

9392. (a) Subject to subdivision (b), a person to whom property is distributed is personally liable for the claim of a creditor, without a claim first having been filed, if all of the following conditions are satisfied:

(1) The identity of the creditor was known to, or reasonably ascertainable by, a general personal representative within four months after the date letters were first issued to the personal representative, and the claim of the creditor was not merely conjectural.

(2) Notice of administration of the estate was not given to the creditor under Chapter 2 (commencing with Section 9050) and neither the creditor nor the attorney representing the creditor in the matter had actual knowledge of the administration of the estate before the time the court made an order for final distribution of the property.

(3) The statute of limitations applicable to the claim under Section 353 of the Code of Civil Procedure has not expired at the time of commencement of an action under this section.

(b) Personal liability under this section is applicable only to the extent the claim of the creditor cannot be satisfied out of the decedent and is limited to the extent of the fair market value of the property on the date of the order for distribution, less the amount of any liens and encumbrances on the property at that time. Personal liability under this section is joint and several, based on the principles stated in Part 4 (commencing with Section 21400) of Division 11 (abatement).

(c) Nothing in this section affects the rights of a purchaser or encumbrancer of property in good faith and for value from a person who is personally liable under this section.

9392. (a) Subject to subdivision (b), a person to whom property is distributed is personally liable for the claim of a creditor, without a claim first having been filed, if all of the following conditions are satisfied:

(1) The identity of the creditor was known to, or reasonably ascertainable by, a general personal representative within four months after the date letters were first issued to the personal representative, and the claim of the creditor was not merely conjectural.

(2) Notice of administration of the estate was not given to the creditor under Chapter 2 (commencing with Section 9050) and neither the creditor nor the attorney representing the creditor in the matter has actual knowledge of the administration of the estate before the time the court made an order for final distribution of the property.

(3) The statute of limitations applicable to the claim under Section 366.2 of the Code of Civil Procedure has not expired at the time of commencement of an action under this section.

(b) Personal liability under this section is applicable only to the extent the claim of the creditor cannot be satisfied out of the estate of the decedent and is limited to a pro rata portion of the claim of the creditor, based on the proportion that the value of the property distributed to the person out of the estate bears to the total value of all property distributed to all persons out of the estate. Personal liability under this section for all claims of all creditors shall not exceed the value of the property distributed to the person out of the estate. As used in this section, the value of property is the fair market value of the property on the date of the order for distribution, less the amount of any liens and encumbrances on the property at that time.

(c) Nothing in this section affects the rights of a purchaser or encumbrancer of property in good faith and for value from a person who is personally liable under this section.

Article 4. Transitional Provision

9399. (a) This chapter does not apply to an action commenced before July 1, 1989.

(b) The applicable law in effect before July 1, 1989, continues to apply to an action commenced before July 1, 1989, notwithstanding its repeal by Chapter 1199 of the Statutes of 1988.

Part 5. Estate Management

Chapter 1. General Provisions

Article 1. Duties And Liabilities Of Personal Representative

9600. (a) The personal representative has the management and control of the estate and, in managing and controlling the estate, shall use ordinary care and diligence. What constitutes ordinary care and diligence is determined by all the circumstances of the particular estate.

(b) The personal representative:

(1) Shall exercise a power to the extent that ordinary care and diligence require that the power be exercised.

(2) Shall not exercise a power to the extent that ordinary care and diligence require that the power not be exercised.

9601. (a) If a personal representative breaches a fiduciary duty, the personal representative is chargeable with any of the following that is appropriate under the circumstances:

(1) Any loss or depreciation in value of the decedent's estate resulting from the breach of duty, with interest.

(2) Any profit made by the personal representative through the breach of duty, with interest.

(3) Any profit that would have accrued to the decedent's estate if the loss of profit is the result of the breach of duty.

(b) If the personal representative has acted reasonably and in good faith under the circumstances as known to the personal representative, the court, in its discretion, may excuse the personal representative in whole or in part from liability under subdivision (a) if it would be equitable to do so.

9602. (a) If the personal representative is liable for interest pursuant to Section 9601, the personal representative is liable for the greater of the following amounts:

(1) The amount of interest that accrues at the legal rate on judgments.

(2) The amount of interest actually received.

(b) If the personal representative has acted reasonably and in good faith under the circumstances as known to the personal representative, the court, in its discretion, may excuse the personal representative in whole or in part from liability under subdivision (a) if it would be equitable to do so.

9603. The provisions of Sections 9601 and 9602 for liability of a personal representative for breach of a fiduciary duty do not prevent resort to any other remedy available against the personal representative under the statutory or common law.

9604. No personal representative is chargeable upon a special promise to answer in damages for a liability of the decedent or to pay a debt of the decedent out of the personal representative's own estate unless the agreement for that purpose, or some memorandum or note thereof, is in writing and is signed by one of the following:

(a) The personal representative.

(b) Some other person specifically authorized by the personal representative in writing to sign the agreement or the memorandum or note.

9605. Appointment of a person as personal representative does not discharge any claim the decedent has against the person.

9606. Unless otherwise provided in the instrument or in this division, a personal representative is not personally liable on an instrument, including but not limited to a note, mortgage, deed of trust, or other contract, properly entered into in the personal representative's fiduciary capacity in the course of administration of the estate unless the personal representative fails to reveal the personal representative's representative capacity or identify the estate in the instrument.

Article 2. Court Supervision

9610. Unless this part specifically provides a proceeding to obtain court authorization or requires court authorization, the powers and duties set forth in this part may be exercised by the personal representative without court authorization, instruction, approval, or confirmation. Nothing in this section precludes the personal representative from seeking court authorization, instructions, approval, or confirmation.

9611. (a) In all cases where no other procedure is provided by statute, upon petition of the personal representative, the court may authorize and instruct the personal representative, or approve and confirm the acts of the personal representative, in the administration, management, investment, disposition, care, protection, operation, or preservation of the estate, or the incurring or payment of costs, fees, or expenses in connection therewith. Section 9613 does not preclude a petition for instructions under this section.

(b) Notice of the hearing on the petition shall be given as provided in Section 1220.

9613. (a) On petition of any interested person, and upon a showing that if the petition is not granted the estate will suffer great or irreparable injury, the court may direct the personal representative to act or not to act concerning the estate. The order may include terms and conditions the court determines are appropriate under the circumstances.

(b) Notice of the hearing on the petition shall be given as provided in Section 1220.

9614. (a) On petition of an interested person, the court may suspend the powers of the personal representative in whole or in part, for a time, as to specific property or circumstances or as to specific duties of the office, or may make any other order to secure proper performance of the duties of the personal representative, if it appears to the court that the personal representative otherwise may take some action that would jeopardize unreasonably the interest of the petitioner. Persons with whom the personal representative may transact business may be made parties.

(b) The matter shall be set for hearing within 10 days unless the parties agree otherwise. Notice as the court directs shall be given to the personal representative and attorney of record, if any, and to any other parties named in the petition.

(c) The court may, in its discretion, if it determines that the petition was brought unreasonably and for the purpose of hindering the personal representative in the performance of the duties of the office, assess attorney's fees against the petitioner and make the assessment a charge against the interest of the petitioner.

Article 3. Summary Determination Of Disputes

9620. If there is a dispute relating to the estate between the personal representative and a third person, the personal representative may do either of the following:

(a) Enter into an agreement in writing with the third person to refer the dispute to a temporary judge designated in the agreement. The agreement shall be filed with the clerk, who shall thereupon, with the approval of the court, enter an order referring the matter to the designated person. The temporary judge shall proceed promptly to hear and determine the matter in controversy by summary procedure, without pleadings or discovery. The decision of the designated person is subject to Section 632 of the Code of Civil Procedure. Judgment shall be entered on the decision and shall be as valid and effective as if rendered by a judge of the court in an action against the personal representative or the third person commenced by ordinary process.

(b) Enter into an agreement in writing with the third person that a judge, pursuant to the agreement and with the written consent of the judge, both filed with the clerk within the time specified in Section 9353 for bringing an independent suit on the matter in dispute, may hear and determine the dispute pursuant to the procedure provided in subdivision (a).

9621. If there is a dispute relating to the estate between the personal representative and a third person, the personal representative may enter into an agreement in writing with the third person to submit the dispute to arbitration under Title 9 (commencing with Section 1280) of Part 3 of the Code of Civil Procedure. The agreement is not effective unless it is first approved by the court

and a copy of the approved agreement is filed with the court. Notice of the hearing on the petition for approval of the agreement shall be given as provided in Section 1220. The order approving the agreement may be made ex parte.

Article 4. Joint Personal Representatives

9630. (a) Subject to subdivisions (b), (c), and (d):

(1) Where there are two personal representatives, both must concur to exercise a power.

(2) Where there are more than two personal representatives, a majority must concur to exercise a power.

(b) If one of the joint personal representatives dies or is removed or resigns, the powers and duties continue in the remaining joint personal representatives as if they were the only personal representatives until further appointment is made by the court.

(c) Where joint personal representatives have been appointed and one or more are (1) absent from the state and unable to act, or (2) otherwise unable to act, or (3) legally disqualified from serving, the court may, by order made with or without notice, authorize the remaining joint personal representatives to act as to all matters embraced within its order.

(d) Where there are two or more personal representatives, any of them may:

(1) Oppose a petition made by one or more of the other personal representatives or by any other person.

(2) Petition the court for an order requiring the personal representatives to take a specific action for the benefit of the estate or directing the personal representatives not to take a specific action. If a procedure is provided by statute for a petition to authorize the specific action by the personal representatives, the petitioner shall file the petition under the provision relating to that procedure. Otherwise, the petitioner shall file the petition under Section 9611.

9631. (a) Except as provided in subdivision (b), where there is more than one personal representative, one personal representative is not liable for a breach of fiduciary duty committed by another of the personal representatives.

(b) Where there is more than one personal representative, one personal representative is liable for a breach of fiduciary duty committed by another of the personal representatives under any of the following circumstances:

(1) Where the personal representative participates in a breach of fiduciary duty committed by the other personal representative.

(2) Where the personal representative improperly delegates the administration of the estate to the other personal representative.

(3) Where the personal representative approves, knowingly acquiesces in, or conceals a breach of fiduciary duty committed by the other personal representative.

(4) Where the personal representative's negligence enables the other personal representative to commit a breach of fiduciary duty.

(5) Where the personal representative knows or has information from which the personal representative reasonably should have known of the breach of fiduciary duty by the other personal representative and fails to take reasonable steps to compel the other personal representative to redress the breach.

(c) The liability of a personal representative for a breach of fiduciary duty committed by another of the personal representatives that occurred before July 1, 1988, is governed by prior law and not by this section.

Article 5. Independent Administration

9640. Nothing in this part limits or restricts any authority granted to a personal representative under the Independent Administration of Estates Act (Part 6 (commencing with Section 10400)) to administer the estate under that part.

Article 6. Transitional Provision

9645. (a) Subject to subdivisions (b) and (c), any petition or other matter filed or commenced before July 1, 1988, shall be continued under this part, so far as applicable, except where the court determines that application of a particular provision of this part would substantially interfere with the rights of the parties or other interested persons, in which case the particular provision of this part does not apply and the applicable law in effect before July 1, 1988, applies.

(b) Nothing in this part affects any order, judgment, or decree made, or any action taken, before July 1, 1988.

(c) Notwithstanding the enactment of this part:

(1) An order, judgment, or decree made before July 1, 1988, shall continue in full force and effect in accordance with its terms or until modified or terminated by the court.

(2) The validity of an order, judgment, or decree made before July 1, 1988, is determined by the applicable law in effect before July 1, 1988, and not by this part.

(3) The validity of any action taken before July 1, 1988, is determined by the applicable law in effect before July 1, 1988, and not by this part.

Chapter 2. Estate Management Generally

9650. (a) Except as provided by statute and subject to subdivision (c):

(1) The personal representative has the right to, and shall take possession or control of, all the property of the decedent to be administered in the decedent's estate and shall collect all debts due to the decedent or the estate. The personal representative is not accountable for any debts that remain uncollected without his or her fault.

(2) The personal representative is entitled to receive the rents, issues, and profits from the real and personal property in the estate until the estate is distributed.

(b) The personal representative shall pay taxes on, and take all steps reasonably necessary for the management, protection, and preservation of, the estate in his or her possession.

(c) Real property or tangible personal property may be left with or surrendered to the person presumptively entitled to it unless or until, in the judgment of the personal representative, possession of the property by the personal representative will be necessary for purposes of administration. The person holding the property shall surrender it to the personal representative on request by the personal representative.

9651. (a) A personal representative who in good faith takes into possession real or personal property, and reasonably believes that the property is part of the estate of the decedent, is not:

(1) Criminally liable for so doing.

(2) Civilly liable to any person for so doing.

(b) The personal representative shall make reasonable efforts to determine the true nature of, and title to, the property so taken into possession.

(c) During his or her possession, the personal representative is entitled to receive all rents, issues, and profits of the property. If the property is later determined not to be part of the estate of the decedent, the personal representative shall deliver the property, or cause it to be delivered, to the person legally entitled to it, together with all rents, issues, and profits of the property received by the personal representative, less any expenses incurred in protecting and maintaining the property and in collecting rents, issues, and profits. The personal representative may request court approval before delivering the property pursuant to this subdivision.

(d) The court may allow the personal representative reasonable compensation for services rendered in connection with the duties specified in this section as to property later determined not to be part of the estate of the decedent, if the court makes one of the following findings:

(1) The services were of benefit to the estate. If the court makes this finding, the compensation and the expenses and costs of litigation, including attorney's fees of the attorney hired by the personal representative to handle the matter, are a proper expense of administration.

(2) The services were essential to preserve, protect, and maintain the property. If the court makes this finding, the court shall award compensation and the expenses and costs of litigation, including attorney's fees of the attorney hired by the personal representative to handle the matter, as an expense deductible from the rents, issues, and profits received by the personal representative, or, if these are insufficient, as a lien against the property.

9652. (a) Except as provided in subdivisions (b) and (c), the personal representative shall keep all cash in his or her possession invested in interest-bearing accounts or other investments authorized by law.

(b) The requirement of subdivision (a) does not apply to the amount of cash that is reasonably necessary for orderly administration of the estate.

(c) The requirement of subdivision (a) does not apply to the extent that the testator's will otherwise provides.

9653. (a) On application of a creditor of the decedent or the estate, the personal representative shall commence and prosecute an action for the recovery of real or personal property of the decedent for the benefit of creditors if the personal representative has insufficient assets to pay creditors and the decedent during lifetime did any of the following with respect to the property:

(1) Made a conveyance of the property, or any right or interest in the property, that is fraudulent as to creditors under the Uniform Fraudulent Transfer Act (Chapter 1 (commencing with Section 3439) of Title 2 of Part 2 of Division 4 of the Civil Code).

(2) Made a gift of the property in view of impending death.

(3) Made a direction to transfer a vehicle, undocumented vessel, manufactured home, mobilehome, commercial coach, truck camper, or floating home to a designated beneficiary on the decedent's death pursuant to Section 18102.2 of the Health and Safety Code, or Section 5910.5 or 9916.5 of the Vehicle Code, and the property has been transferred as directed.

(b) A creditor making application under this section shall pay such part of the costs and expenses of the suit and attorney's fees, or give an undertaking to the personal representative for that purpose, as the personal representative and the creditor agree, or, absent an agreement, as the court or judge orders.

(c) The property recovered under this section shall be sold for the payment of debts in the same manner as if the decedent had died seized or possessed of the property. The proceeds of the sale shall be applied first to payment of the costs and expenses of suit, including attorney's fees, and then to payment of the debts of the decedent in the same manner as other property in possession of the personal representative. After all the debts of the decedent have been paid, the remainder of the proceeds shall be paid to the person from whom the property was recovered. The property may be sold in its entirety or in such portion as necessary to pay the debts.

9654. The heirs or devisees may themselves, or jointly with the personal representative, maintain an action for possession of property or to quiet title to property against any person except the personal representative.

9655. With respect to a share of stock of a domestic or foreign corporation held in the estate, a membership in a nonprofit corporation held in the estate, or other property held in the estate, a personal representative may do any one or more of the following:

(a) Vote in person, and give proxies to exercise, any voting rights with respect to the share, membership, or other property.

(b) Waive notice of a meeting or give consent to the holding of a meeting.

(c) Authorize, ratify, approve, or confirm any action which could be taken by shareholders, members, or property owners.

9656. The personal representative may insure the property of the estate against damage or loss and may insure himself or herself against liability to third persons.

9657. The personal representative shall not make profit by the increase, nor suffer loss by the decrease or destruction without his or her fault, of any part of the estate.

Chapter 3. Deposit Of Money And Personal Property With Financial Institutions

9700. The personal representative may deposit money of the estate in an insured account in a financial institution in this state. Unless otherwise provided by court order, the money may be withdrawn without order of the court.

9701. The personal representative may deposit personal property of the estate with a trust company for safekeeping. Unless otherwise provided by court order, the personal property may be withdrawn without order of the court.

9702. (a) A trust company serving as personal representative may deposit securities that constitute all or part of the estate in a securities depository as provided in Section 775 of the Financial Code.

(b) If securities have been deposited with a trust company by a personal representative pursuant to Section 9701, the trust company may deposit the securities in a securities depository as provided in Section 775 of the Financial Code.

(c) The securities depository may hold securities deposited with it in the manner authorized by Section 775 of the Financial Code.

9703. (a) Upon application of the personal representative, the court may, with or without notice, order that money or other personal property be deposited pursuant to Section 9700 or 9701 and be subject to withdrawal only upon authorization of the court.

(b) The personal representative shall deliver a copy of the court order to the financial institution or trust company at the time the deposit is made.

(c) No financial institution or trust company accepting a deposit pursuant to Section 9700 or 9701 shall be on notice of the existence of an order that the money or other property is subject to withdrawal only upon authorization of the court unless it has actual notice of the order.

9704. When an order for distribution of money or personal property deposited pursuant to this chapter is made, the financial institution, trust company, or securities depository may deliver the property directly to the distributees and shall file receipts therefor with the clerk.

9705. (a) Subject to subdivision (b), where a trust company is a personal representative and in the exercise of reasonable judgment deposits money of the estate in an account in any department of the corporation or association of which it is a part, it is chargeable with interest thereon at the rate of interest prevailing among banks of the locality on such deposits.

(b) Where it is to the advantage of the estate, the amount of cash that is reasonably necessary for orderly administration of the estate may be deposited in a checking account that does not earn interest which is maintained in a department of the corporation or association of which the trust company is a part.

Chapter 4. Investments And Purchase Of Property

9730. Pending distribution of the estate, the personal representative may invest money of the estate in possession of the personal representative in any one or more of the following:

(a) Direct obligations of the United States, or of the State of California, maturing not later than one year from the date of making the investment.

(b) An interest in a money market mutual fund registered under the Investment Company Act of 1940 (15 U.S.C. Sec. 80a-1, et seq.) or an investment vehicle authorized for the collective investment of trust funds pursuant to Section 9.18 of Part 9 of Title 12 of the Code of Federal Regulations, the portfolios of which are limited to United States government obligations maturing not later than five years from the date of investment and to repurchase agreements fully collateralized by United States government obligations.

(c) Units of a common trust fund described in Section 1564 of the Financial Code. The common trust fund shall have as its objective investment primarily in short term fixed income obligations and shall be permitted to value investments at cost pursuant to regulations of the appropriate regulatory authority.

9731. (a) Pending distribution of the estate, upon a showing that it is to the advantage of the estate, the court may order that money of the estate in possession of the personal representative be invested in securities of the United States or of this state.

(b) To obtain an order under this section, the personal representative or any interested person shall file a petition stating the types of securities that are proposed to be purchased and the advantage to the estate of the purchase.

(c) Notice of the hearing on the petition shall be given as provided in Section 1220.

9732. (a) The court may order that money of the estate in possession of the personal representative be invested in any manner provided by the will if all of the following conditions are satisfied:

(1) The time for filing claims has expired.

(2) All debts (as defined in Section 11401) have been paid or are sufficiently secured by mortgage or otherwise, or there is sufficient cash in the estate aside from the money to be invested to pay all the debts, or the court is otherwise satisfied that all the debts will be paid.

(3) The estate is not in a condition to be finally distributed.

(b) To obtain an order under this section, the personal representative or any interested person shall file a petition showing the general condition of the estate and the types of investments that are proposed to be made.

(c) Notice of the hearing on the petition shall be given as provided in Section 1220. In addition, the petitioner shall cause notice of the hearing and a copy of the petition to be mailed to all known devisees of property which is proposed to be invested. Where the property proposed to be invested is devised to a trust or trustee, notice of the hearing and a copy of the petition shall be mailed to the trustee or, if the trustee has not yet accepted the trust, to the person named in the will as trustee. Mailing pursuant to this subdivision shall be to the person's last known address as provided in Section 1220.

(d) If no objection has been filed by an interested person, the court may make an order authorizing or directing the personal representative to invest such portion of the money of the estate as the court deems advisable in the types of investments proposed in the petition and authorized by the will. If there is no objection by an interested person and no substantial reason why some or all of the investment powers given by the will should not be exercised, the court shall make the order. The order may be for a limited period or until the administration of the estate is completed. Upon petition of the personal representative or any interested person, the order may be renewed, modified, or terminated at any time.

9733. (a) Pending distribution of the estate or at the time the court makes an order for final distribution of the estate, on petition of the personal representative or any interested person, the court may, upon good cause shown, order that the personal representative purchase an annuity from an insurer admitted to do business in this state to satisfy a devise of an annuity or other direction in the will for periodic payments to a devisee.

(b) Notice of the hearing on the petition shall be given as provided in Section 1220.

9734. (a) If an asset of the estate consists of an option right, the personal representative may exercise the option after authorization by order of court upon a showing that the exercise would be to the advantage of the estate and would be in the best interest of the interested persons. The personal representative may use any funds or property in the estate to acquire the property covered by the option.

(b) A petition under this section may be filed by the personal representative or any interested person.

(c) Notice of the hearing on the petition shall be given as provided in Section 1220.

9735. (a) After authorization by order of court, the personal representative may purchase securities or commodities required to perform an incomplete contract of sale where the decedent died having sold but not delivered securities or commodities not owned by the decedent. The court's order shall fix the terms and conditions of purchase.

(b) A petition under this section may be filed by the personal representative or by any party to the contract. Notice of the hearing on the petition shall be given as provided in Section 1220.

(c) No notice of hearing need be given where the maximum purchase price is fixed or where the securities or commodities are to be purchased on an established stock, bond, or commodity exchange.

9736. The personal representative may hold a security in the name of a nominee or in any other form without disclosure of the estate so that title to the security may pass by delivery.

9737. (a) If an estate by reason of owning securities also owns or receives subscription rights for the purchase of additional securities, the personal representative may exercise the subscription rights after authorization by order of court upon a showing that it is to the advantage of the estate.

(b) To obtain an order under this section, the personal representative or any interested person shall file a petition stating the nature of the subscription rights and the advantage to the estate of exercising them.

(c) Notice of the hearing on the petition shall be given as provided in Section 1220.

Chapter 5. Operation Of Decedent's Business

9760. (a) As used in this section, "decedent's business" means an unincorporated business or venture in which the decedent was engaged or which was wholly or partly owned by the decedent at the time of the decedent's death, but does not include a business operated by a partnership in which the decedent was a partner.

(b) If it is to the advantage of the estate and in the best interest of the interested persons, the personal representative, with or without court authorization, may continue the operation of the decedent's business; but the personal representative may not continue the operation of the decedent's business for a period of more than six months from the date letters are first issued to a personal representative unless a court order has been obtained under this section authorizing the personal representative to continue the operation of the business.

(c) The personal representative or any interested person may file a petition requesting an order (1) authorizing the personal representative to continue the operation of the decedent's business or (2) directing the personal representative to discontinue the operation of the decedent's business. The petition shall show the advantage to the estate and the benefit to the interested persons of the order requested. Notice of the hearing on the petition shall be given as provided in Section 1220.

(d) If a petition is filed under this section, the court may make an order that either:

(1) Authorizes the personal representative to continue the operation of the decedent's business to such an extent and subject to such restrictions as the court determines to be to the advantage of the estate and in the best interest of the interested persons.

(2) Directs the personal representative to discontinue the operation of the decedent's business within the time specified in, and in accordance with the provisions of, the order.

9761. If a partnership existed between the decedent and another person at the time of the decedent's death, on application of the personal representative, the court may order any surviving partner to render an account pursuant to Section 15510, 15634, or 16807 of the Corporations Code. An order under this section may be enforced by the court's power to punish for contempt.

9762. (a) After authorization by order of court upon a showing that it would be to the advantage of the estate and in the best interest of the interested persons, the personal representative may continue as a general or a limited partner in any partnership in which the decedent was a general partner at the time of death. In its order, the court may specify any terms and conditions of the personal representative's participation as a partner that the court determines are to the advantage of the estate and in the best interest of the interested persons, but any terms and conditions that are inconsistent with the terms of any written partnership agreement are subject to the written consent of all of the surviving partners.

(b) If there is a written partnership agreement permitting the decedent's personal representative to participate as a partner, the personal representative has all the rights, powers, duties, and obligations provided in the written partnership agreement, except as otherwise ordered by the court pursuant to subdivision (a).

(c) If there is not a written partnership agreement, the personal representative has the rights, powers, duties, and obligations that the court specifies in its order pursuant to subdivision (a).

(d) To obtain an order under this section, the personal representative or any interested person shall file a petition showing that the order requested would be to the advantage of the estate and in the best interest of the interested persons. Notice of the hearing on the petition shall be given as provided in Section 1220. In addition, unless the court otherwise orders, the petitioner, not less than 15 days before the hearing, shall cause notice of hearing and a copy of the petition to be mailed to each of the surviving general partners at his or her last known address.

9763. (a) If the decedent was a general partner, the personal representative may commence and maintain any action against the surviving partner that the decedent could have commenced and maintained.

(b) The personal representative may exercise the decedent's rights as a limited partner as provided in Section 15675 of the Corporations Code.

9764. (a) The personal representative of the estate of a deceased attorney who was engaged in a practice of law at the time of his or her death or other person interested in the estate may bring a petition for appointment of an active member of the State Bar of California to take control of the files and assets of the practice of the deceased member.

(b) The petition may be filed and heard on such notice that the court determines is in the best interests of the estate of the deceased member. If the petition alleges that the immediate appointment of a practice administrator is required to safeguard the interests of the estate, the court may dispense with notice only if the personal representative is the petitioner or has joined in the petition or has otherwise waived notice of hearing on the petition.

(c) The petition shall indicate the powers sought for the practice administrator from the list of powers set forth in Section 6185 of the Business and Professions Code. These powers shall be specifically listed in the or-

der appointing the practice administrator.

(d) The petition shall allege the value of the assets that are to come under the control of the practice administrator, including, but not limited by the amount of funds in all accounts used by the deceased member. The court shall require the filing of a surety bond in the amount of the value of the personal property to be filed with the court by the practice administrator. No action may be taken by the practice administrator unless a bond has been fully filed with the court.

(e) The practice administrator shall not be the attorney representing the personal representative.

(f) The court shall appoint the attorney nominated by the deceased member in a writing, including, but not limited to, the deceased member's will, unless the court concludes that the appointment of the nominated person would be contrary to the best interests of the estate or would create a conflict of interest with any of the clients of the deceased member.

(g) The practice administrator shall be compensated only upon order of the court making the appointment for his or her reasonable and necessary services. The law practice shall be the source of the compensation for the practice administrator unless the assets are insufficient in which case, the compensation of the practice administrator shall be charged against the assets of the estate as a cost of administration. The practice administrator shall also be entitled to reimbursement of his or her costs.

(h) Upon conclusion of the services of the practice administrator, the practice administrator shall render an accounting and petition for its approval by the superior court making the appointment. Upon settlement of the accounting, the practice administrator shall be discharged and the surety on his or her bond exonerated.

(i) For the purposes of this section, the person appointed to take control of the practice of the deceased member shall be referred to as the "practice administrator" and the decedent shall be referred to as the "deceased member."

Chapter 6. Abandonment Of Tangible Personal Property

9780. Unless the property is specifically devised, subject to the requirements of this chapter, the personal representative may dispose of or abandon tangible personal property where the cost of collecting, maintaining, and safeguarding the property would exceed its fair market value.

9781. Unless otherwise provided in the will, subject to the requirements of this chapter, the personal representative may exercise the power provided in Section 9780 without court authorization or approval.

9782. (a) Except as provided in Section 9785, before disposing of or abandoning property under Section 9780, the personal representative shall give notice of the proposed disposition or abandonment as provided in subdivision (c) to all of the following:

(1) Each known devisee whose interest in the estate would be affected by the proposed action.

(2) Each known heir whose interest in the estate would be affected by the proposed action.

(3) Each person who has filed a request for special notice pursuant to Section 1250.

(4) The Attorney General, at the office of the Attorney General in Sacramento, if any portion of the estate is to escheat to the state and its interest in the estate would be affected by the proposed action.

(b) The notice of the proposed disposition or abandonment shall describe the property to be disposed of or abandoned, indicate the manner in which the property is to be disposed of or abandoned, and specify the date on or after which the property will be disposed of or abandoned.

(c) The notice shall be delivered personally to each person required to be given notice or shall be sent by mail to the person at the person's last known address. If the notice is delivered personally, it shall be delivered to the person not less than five days before the date specified in the notice as the date on or after which the property will be disposed of or abandoned. If the notice is sent by mail, it shall be deposited in the mail not less than 10 days before the date specified in the notice as the date on or after which the property will be disposed of or abandoned.

9783. A person described in Section 9782 may deliver or mail a written objection to the disposition or abandonment to the personal representative on or before the date specified in the notice as the date on or after which the property will be disposed of or abandoned. Subject to Section 9788, after receipt of the written objection, the personal representative shall not dispose of or abandon the property without authorization by order of the court obtained under Section 9611.

9784. (a) A person described in Section 9782 who objects to the disposition or abandonment of property by the personal representative under Section 9780 may apply to the court in which proceedings for administration of the estate are pending for an order restraining the personal representative from disposing of or abandoning the property without prior court authorization.

(b) The court shall grant the requested order without requiring notice to the personal representative and without cause being shown for the order if the court is satisfied that the estate will not suffer any loss or unreasonable expense if the order is granted. As a condition of granting the order, the court may require the person applying for the order (1) to pay the costs of storing and protecting the property or (2) to provide security by bond or cash deposit that the costs will be paid.

(c) The personal representative is deemed to have notice of the restraining order if it is served upon the personal representative in the manner provided in Section 415.10 or 415.30 of the Code of Civil Procedure, or in the manner authorized by the court, before the date specified in the notice as the date on or after which the property will be disposed of or abandoned.

9785. Notice of the proposed disposition or abandonment need not be given to any of the following:

(a) A person who consents in writing to the proposed disposition or abandonment.

(b) A person who, in writing, waives the right to notice of the proposed disposition or abandonment.

9786. A person who objects to the disposition or abandonment as provided in Section 9783, or who serves a restraining order issued under Section 9784 in the manner provided in that section, shall be given notice of any court hearing on a petition for court authorization of the disposition or abandonment of the property.

9787. (a) Except as provided in subdivision (b), a person described in Section 9782 who receives notice of the proposed disposition or abandonment as provided in Section 9782, waives the right to have the court later review the disposition or abandonment of the property unless the person does one of the following:

(1) Delivers or mails a written objection as provided in Section 9783.

(2) Serves a restraining order obtained under Section 9784 before whichever of the following is the later time:

(A) The date specified in the notice of proposed disposition or abandonment as the date on or after which the property will be disposed of or abandoned.

(B) The date the property has actually been disposed of or abandoned.

(b) Subject to Section 9785, the court may review the disposition or abandonment of the property upon the motion of a person described in subdivision (a) of Section 9782 who establishes that he or she did not actually receive notice of the proposed disposition or abandonment before the time to object expired.

9788. (a) Notwithstanding Sections 9783 and 9784, the personal representative may abandon or dispose of the property without court authorization if the person who made the objection or obtained the restraining order fails to take possession of the property at his or her expense within 10 days after the personal representative requests that the person do so.

(b) A person who takes possession of estate property pursuant to this section is liable for the safekeeping of the property until a court order is made relieving the person of this obligation.

Chapter 7. Borrowing, Refinancing, And Encumbering Property

9800. (a) Subject to subdivision (c), after authorization by order of court obtained under this chapter upon a showing that it would be to the advantage of the estate, the personal representative may borrow money on a note, either unsecured or to be secured by a security interest or other lien on the personal property of the estate, or any part thereof, or to be secured by a mortgage or deed of trust on the real property of the estate, or any part thereof, and may give a security interest or other lien on the personal property of the estate, or any part thereof, or a mortgage or deed of trust on the real property of the estate, or any part thereof, in order to do any one or more of the following:

(1) Pay the debts of the decedent or the estate, devises, expenses of administration, and charges against the estate.

(2) Pay, reduce, extend, or renew a security interest or lien or mortgage or deed of trust already existing on property of the estate.

(3) Improve, use, operate, or preserve property in the estate.

(b) The personal representative shall apply the money to the purpose specified in the order.

(c) Where the surviving spouse has elected to have his or her share of the community real property administered in the decedent's estate, the personal representative is authorized to borrow money to be secured by a mortgage or deed of trust on the community real property of the estate, or any part thereof, only with the written consent of the surviving spouse.

9801. If property of the estate consists of an undivided interest in real or personal property, or any other interest therein less than the entire ownership, upon a showing that it would be to the advantage of the estate to borrow money to improve, use, operate, or preserve the property jointly with the owners of the other interests therein, or to pay, reduce, extend, or renew a security interest, lien, mortgage, or deed of trust already existing on all of the property, the personal representative, after authorization by order of the court obtained under this chapter, may join with the owners of the other interests in borrowing money and the execution of a joint and several note and such security interest, lien, mortgage, or deed of trust as may be required to secure the payment of the note. The note may be for such sum as is required for the purpose.

9802. (a) The personal representative or any interested person may file a petition for an order under this chapter.

(b) The petition shall state the purpose for which the order is sought and the necessity for or the advantage to accrue from the order. If applicable, the petition shall also show the amount of money proposed to be borrowed, the rate of interest to be paid, the length of time the note is to run, and a general description of the property proposed to be mortgaged or subjected to the deed of trust, security interest, or other lien.

9803. Notice of the hearing on the petition shall be given as provided in Section 1220.

9804. (a) Subject to subdivision (c), if the court is satisfied that it will be to the advantage of the estate, the court shall make an order that authorizes or requires that the personal representative do any one or more of the following:

(1) Borrow money and execute a note.

(2) Execute a mortgage or deed of trust or give other security by security interest or other lien.

(3) Pay, reduce, extend, or renew a security interest or lien or mortgage or deed of trust already existing upon property of the estate.

(b) The court in its order may do any one or more of the following:

(1) Order that the amount specified in the petition, or a lesser amount, be borrowed.

(2) Prescribe the maximum rate of interest and the period of the loan.

(3) Require that the interest and the whole or any part of the principal be paid from time to time out of the whole estate or any part thereof.

(4) Require that the personal property used as security, or any buildings on real property to be mortgaged or subjected to the deed of trust, be insured for the further security of the lender and that the premiums be paid out of the estate.

(5) Specify the purpose for which the money to be borrowed is to be applied.

(6) Specify the terms and conditions of any extension or renewal agreement.

(7) Prescribe such other terms and conditions concerning the transaction as the court determines to be to the advantage of the estate.

(c) Where the surviving spouse has elected to have his or her share of the community real property administered in the decedent's estate, an order authorizing or requiring the personal representative to borrow money to be secured by a mortgage or deed of trust upon the community real property of the estate, or any part thereof, may be made only if the written consent of the surviving spouse has been filed with the court.

9805. (a) The personal representative shall execute and deliver the mortgage or deed of trust, or execute and deliver the instrument creating the security interest, setting forth therein that it is made by authority of the order, giving the date of the order.

(b) The note and the mortgage or deed

of trust or other instrument creating the security interest, if any, shall be signed by the personal representative and shall be acknowledged by the personal representative if the instrument creates a lien on real property.

9806. (a) Every mortgage, deed of trust, or security interest made pursuant to a court order obtained under this chapter is effectual to mortgage, or to subject to the deed of trust or security interest, all of the following:

(1) All right, title, and interest which the decedent had to the property described therein at the time of the decedent's death.

(2) Any right, title, or interest in the property acquired by the estate of the decedent, by operation of law or otherwise, since the time of the decedent's death.

(3) Any right, title, or interest in the community real property belonging to the decedent's surviving spouse whose written consent has been filed with the court and which is referred to in the court order obtained under this chapter.

(b) Jurisdiction of the court to administer the estate of the decedent vests the court with jurisdiction to make the order for the note and for the security interest, lien, mortgage, or deed of trust. This jurisdiction shall conclusively inure to the benefit of the owner of the security interest or lien, mortgagee named in the mortgage, or the trustee and beneficiary named in the deed of trust, and their heirs and assigns.

(c) No omission, error, or irregularity in the proceedings under this chapter shall impair or invalidate the proceedings or the note, security interest, lien, mortgage, or deed of trust given pursuant to an order under this chapter. Subject to Section 9807, the owner of the security interest or lien, the mortgagee named in the mortgage, or the trustee and beneficiary named in the deed of trust, and their heirs and assigns, have and possess the same rights and remedies on the note and the security interest or lien or mortgage or deed of trust as if it had been made by the decedent prior to his or her death.

9807. (a) Except as provided in subdivision (b), no judgment or claim for any deficiency shall be had or allowed against the personal representative or the estate if (1) there is a foreclosure or sale under a security interest, lien, mortgage, or deed of trust and (2) the proceeds of sale of the encumbered property are insufficient to pay the note, the security interest, lien, mortgage, or deed of trust, and the costs or expenses of sale.

(b) If the note, security interest, mortgage, or deed of trust was given to pay, reduce, extend, or renew a lien, security interest, mortgage, or deed of trust existing on property of the estate at the time of death of the decedent and the indebtedness secured thereby was a claim established under

Part 4 (commencing with Section 9000), the part of the indebtedness remaining unsatisfied shall be classed with other established claims.

Chapter 8. Actions And Proceedings By Or Against Personal Representative

9820. The personal representative may:

(a) Commence and maintain actions and proceedings for the benefit of the estate.

(b) Defend actions and proceedings against the decedent, the personal representative, or the estate.

9822. The personal representative may bring an action on the bond of any former personal representative of the same estate, for the use and benefit of all interested persons.

9823. (a) If the decedent leaves an undivided interest in any property, an action for partition of the property may be brought against the personal representative.

(b) The personal representative may bring an action against the other cotenants for partition of any property in which the decedent left an undivided interest.

Chapter 9. Compromise Of Claims And Actions; Extension, Renewal, Or Modification Of Obligations

9830. (a) Unless this chapter or some other applicable statute requires court authorization or approval, if it is to the advantage of the estate, the personal representative may do any of the following without court authorization, instruction, approval, or confirmation:

(1) Compromise or settle a claim, action, or proceeding by or for the benefit of, or against, the decedent, the personal representative, or the estate, including the giving of a covenant not to sue.

(2) Extend, renew, or in any manner modify the terms of an obligation owing to or in favor of the decedent or the estate.

(3) Release, in whole or in part, any claim belonging to the estate to the extent that the claim is uncollectible.

(b) Nothing in this section precludes the personal representative from seeking court authorization pursuant to the provisions of this chapter.

(c) Upon petition of an interested person or upon the court's own motion, the court may limit the authority of the personal representative under subdivision (a). Notice of the hearing on the petition shall be given as provided in Section 1220.

9831. Unless the time for filing creditor claims has expired, authorization by order of court is required for a compromise or settlement of a claim, action, or proceeding by or for the benefit of, or against, the decedent, the personal representative, or the estate.

9832. (a) Except as provided in subdivision (b), authorization by order of court is required for a compromise, settlement, extension, renewal, or modification which affects any of the following:

(1) Title to real property.

(2) An interest in real property or a lien or encumbrance on real property.

(3) An option to purchase real property or an interest in real property.

(b) If it is to the advantage of the estate, the personal representative without prior court authorization may extend, renew, or modify a lease of real property in either of the following cases:

(1) Where under the lease as extended, renewed, or modified the rental does not exceed five thousand dollars ($5,000) a month and the term does not exceed one year.

(2) Where the lease is from month to month, regardless of the amount of the rental.

(c) For the purposes of subdivision (b), if the lease as extended, renewed, or modified gives the lessee the right to extend the term of the lease, the length of the term shall be considered as though the right to extend had been exercised.

9833. Authorization by order of court is required for a compromise or settlement of a matter when the transaction requires the transfer or encumbrance of property of the estate, or the creation of an unsecured liability of the estate, or both, in an amount or value in excess of twenty-five thousand dollars ($25,000).

9834. Authorization by order of court is required for any of the following:

(a) A compromise or settlement of a claim by the estate against the personal representative or the personal representative's attorney, whether or not the claim arises out of the administration of the estate.

(b) An extension, renewal, or modification of the terms of a debt or similar obligation of the personal representative, or the personal representative's attorney, owing to, or in favor of, the estate.

9835. Authorization by order of court is required for the compromise or settlement of a claim or right of action given to the personal representative by any law for the wrongful death or injury of the decedent, including any action brought by the personal representative in attempting enforcement of the claim or right of action. Authorization to compromise or settle the claim or right of action includes authorization to give a covenant not to sue.

9836. The court authorization required by this chapter shall be obtained from the court in which the estate is being administered.

9837. (a) A petition for an order authorizing a compromise, settlement, extension, renewal, or modification under this chapter may be filed by any of the following:

(1) The personal representative.

(2) Any interested person who has obtained the written approval of the personal representative to file the petition.

(b) The petition shall show the terms of the compromise, settlement, extension, renewal, or modification and its advantage to the estate.

(c) Notice of the hearing on the petition shall be given as provided in Section 1220.

9838. (a) If an order made under Section 9837 authorizes a compromise or settlement that requires the transfer of real property of the estate, the personal representative shall execute a conveyance of the real property to the person entitled thereto under the compromise or settlement. The conveyance shall refer to the order authorizing the compromise or settlement and directing that the conveyance be executed. A certified copy of the order shall be recorded in the office of the county recorder in each county in which any portion of the real property is located.

(b) A conveyance made in compliance with the court order authorizing the compromise or settlement and directing the conveyance to be executed vests in the person to whom the property is transferred both of the following:

(1) All the right, title, and interest which the decedent had in the property at the time of the decedent's death.

(2) Any other or additional right, title, or interest in the property acquired by the estate of the decedent, by operation of law or otherwise, prior to the transfer.

9839. If the personal representative pays a claim for less than its full amount, the personal representative's accounts may be credited only for the amount actually paid.

Chapter 10. Acceptance Of Deed In Lieu Of Foreclosure Or Trustee's Sale; Grant Of Partial Satisfaction Or Partial Reconveyance

9850. (a) If it is to the advantage of the estate to accept a deed to property which is subject to a mortgage or deed of trust in lieu of foreclosure of the mortgage or sale under the deed of trust, the personal representative may, after authorization by order of the court and upon such terms and conditions as may be imposed by the court, accept a deed conveying the property to the heirs or devisees of the decedent, subject to administration.

(b) To obtain an order under this section, the personal representative or any interested person shall file a petition showing the advantage to the estate of accepting the deed. Notice of the hearing on the petition shall be given as provided in Section 1220.

(c) The court shall make an order under this section only if the advantage to the estate of accepting the deed is shown by clear and convincing evidence.

9851. (a) Except as provided in subdivision (c), if it is to the advantage of the estate for the personal representative to give a partial satisfaction of a mortgage or to cause a partial reconveyance to be executed by a trustee under a trust deed held by the estate, the personal representative may, after authorization by order of the court and upon such terms and conditions as may be imposed by the court, give the partial satisfaction or cause the partial reconveyance to be executed by the trustee.

(b) To obtain an order under this section, the personal representative or any interested person shall file a petition showing the advantage to the estate of giving the partial satisfaction or causing the partial reconveyance. Notice of the hearing on the petition shall be given as provided in Section 1220.

(c) No authorization by the court is necessary for the personal representative to give a partial satisfaction of a mortgage or to cause a partial reconveyance to be executed by a trustee under a deed of trust held by the estate if the partial satisfaction or partial reconveyance is executed pursuant to the terms of the mortgage or deed of trust held by the estate.

Chapter 12. Purchase Of Claims Or Estate Property By Personal Representative Or Personal Representative's Attorney

9880. Except as provided in this chapter, neither the personal representative nor the personal representative's attorney may do any of the following:

(a) Purchase any property of the estate or any claim against the estate, directly or indirectly.

(b) Be interested in any such purchase.

9881. Upon a petition filed under Section 9883, the court may make an order under this section authorizing the personal representative or the personal representative's attorney to purchase property of the estate if all of the following requirements are satisfied:

(a) Written consent to the purchase is signed by (1) each known heir whose interest in the estate would be affected by the proposed purchase and (2) each known devisee whose interest in the estate would be affected by the proposed purchase.

(b) The written consents are filed with the court.

(c) The purchase is shown to be to the advantage of the estate.

9882. Upon a petition filed under Section 9883, the court may make an order under this section authorizing the personal representative or the personal representative's attorney to purchase property of the estate if the will of the decedent authorizes the personal representative or the personal representative's attorney to purchase the property.

9883. (a) The personal representative may file a petition requesting that the court make an order under Section 9881 or 9882. The petition shall set forth the facts upon which the request for the order is based.

(b) If court confirmation of the sale is required, the court may make its order under Section 9881 or 9882 at the time of the confirmation.

(c) Notice of the hearing on the petition shall be given as provided in Section 1220 to all of the following persons:

(1) Each person listed in Section 1220.

(2) Each known heir whose interest in the estate would be affected by the proposed purchase.

(3) Each known devisee whose interest in the estate would be affected by the proposed purchase.

(d) If the court is satisfied that the purchase should be authorized, the court shall make an order authorizing the purchase upon the terms and conditions specified in the order, and the personal representative may execute a conveyance or transfer according to the terms of the order. Unless otherwise provided in the will or in the order of the court, the sale of the property shall be made in the same manner as the sale of other estate property of the same nature.

9884. This chapter does not prohibit the purchase of property of the estate by the personal representative or the personal representative's attorney pursuant to a contract in writing made during the lifetime of the decedent if the contract is one that can be specifically enforced and the requirements of Part 19 (commencing with Section 850) of Division 2 are satisfied.

9885. This chapter does not prevent the exercise by the personal representative or the personal representative's attorney of an option to purchase property of the estate given in the will of the decedent if the requirements of Chapter 17 (commencing with Section 9980) are satisfied.

Chapter 13. Dedication Or Conveyance To Governmental Entity; Easements And Access Rights

9900. If it is to the advantage of the estate and in the best interest of the interested persons, the personal representative, after authorization by order of the court obtained under this chapter and upon such terms and conditions as the court may prescribe, may do any of the following either with or without consideration:

(a) Dedicate or convey real property of the estate for any purpose to any of the following:

(1) This state or any public entity in this state.

(2) The United States or any agency or instrumentality of the United States.

(b) Dedicate or convey an easement over real property of the estate to any person for any purpose.

(c) Convey, release, or relinquish to this state or any public entity in this state any access rights to any street, highway, or freeway from any real property of the estate.

(d) Consent as a lienholder to a dedication, conveyance, release, or relinquishment under subdivision (a), (b), or (c) by the owner of property subject to the lien.

9901. (a) The personal representative or any interested person may file a petition for an order under this chapter.

(b) Notice of the hearing on the petition shall be given as provided in Section 1220.

Chapter 14. Exchange Of Property

9920. If it is to the advantage of the estate to exchange property of the estate for other property, the personal representative may, after authorization by order of court obtained under this chapter and upon such terms and conditions as may be prescribed by the court, exchange the property for the other property. The terms and conditions prescribed by the court may include the payment or receipt of part cash by the personal representative.

9921. To obtain an order under this chapter, the personal representative or any interested person shall file a petition containing all of the following:

(a) A description of the property.

(b) The terms and conditions of the proposed exchange.

(c) A showing that the proposed exchange is to the advantage of the estate.

9922. (a) Except as provided in subdivision (b), notice of the hearing on the petition shall be given as provided in Section 1220.

(b) If the petition is for authorization to exchange securities as defined in Section 10200 for different securities, the court, upon a showing of good cause, may order that the notice be given for a shorter period or that the notice be dispensed with. The order provided by this subdivision may be made ex parte.

9923. No omission, error, or irregularity in the proceedings under this chapter shall impair or invalidate the proceedings or the exchange made pursuant to an order made under this chapter.

Chapter 15. Leases8

9940. For the purpose of this chapter:

(a) "Lease" includes, without limitation, a lease that includes an option to purchase real propery of the estate.

(b) If a lease gives the lessee the right to extend the term of the lease, the length of the term shall be considered as though the right to extend had been exercised.

9941. If it is to the advantage of the estate, the personal representative may lease, as lessor, real property of the estate without authorization of the court in either of the following cases:

(a) Where the rental does not exceed five thousand dollars ($5,000) a month and the term does not exceed one year.

(b) Where the lease is from month to month, regardless of the amount of the rental.

9942. (a) The personal representative may lease, as lessor, real property of the estate after authorization by order of court obtained under this chapter upon a showing that the proposed lease is to the advantage of the estate.

(b) If the proposed lease includes an option to purchase real property of the estate, a petition for an order authorizing the lease shall be filed under this chapter but the applicable provisions for court approval both in this chapter and in Chapter 16 (commencing with Section 9960) apply to the execution of the lease.

9943. (a) To obtain an order under this chapter, the personal representative or any interested person shall file a petition containing all of the following:

(1) A general description of the real property proposed to be leased.

(2) The term, rental, and general conditions of the proposed lease.

(3) A showing that the proposed lease is to the advantage of the estate.

(b) If the lease is proposed to be for a term longer than 10 years, the petition shall also state facts showing the need for the longer lease and its advantage to the estate and its benefit to the interested persons.

9944. (a) Notice of the hearing on the petition shall be given as provided in Section 1220 and posted as provided in Section 1230.

(b) Notice of the hearing on the petition also shall be given as provided in Section 10300, but this notice is not required if the will authorizes or directs the personal representative to lease or sell property.

(c) If the lease is proposed to be for a term longer than 10 years, in addition to the notice required by subdivision (a), notice of the hearing shall be given as provided in Section 1220 to all of the following persons:

(1) Each known heir whose interest in the estate would be affected by the proposed lease.

(2) Each known devisee whose interest in the estate would be affected by the proposed lease.

9945. (a) At the hearing, the court shall entertain and consider any other offer made in good faith at the hearing to lease the same property on more favorable terms.

(b) If the court is satisfied that it will be

254

to the advantage of the estate, and, if the lease is for more than 10 years, that it is to the benefit of interested persons, the court shall make an order authorizing the personal representative to make the lease to the person on the terms and conditions stated in the order. The court shall not make an order authorizing the personal representative to make the lease to any person other than the lessee named in the petition unless the offer made at the hearing is acceptable to the personal representative.

9946. (a) Subject to Section 9947, an order authorizing the execution of a lease shall set forth the minimum rental or royalty or both and the period of the lease.

(b) The order may authorize other terms and conditions of the lease, including, with respect to a lease for the purpose of exploration for or production or removal of minerals, oil, gas, or other hydrocarbon substances, or geothermal energy, any one or more of the following provisions:

(1) A provision for the payment of rental and royalty to a depositary.

(2) A provision for the appointment of a common agent to represent the interests of all the lessors.

(3) A provision for the payment of a compensatory royalty in lieu of rental and in lieu of drilling and producing operations on the land covered by the lease.

(4) A provision empowering the lessee to enter into any agreement authorized by Section 3301 of the Public Resources Code with respect to the land covered by the lease.

(5) A provision for a community oil lease or a pooling or unitization by the lessee.

(c) If the lease covers additional property owned by other persons or an undivided or other interest of the decedent less than the entire ownership in the property, the order may authorize the lease to provide for division of rental and royalty in the proportion that the land or interest of each owner bears to the total area of the land or total interests covered by the lease.

9947. (a) Except as provided in this section, the term of the lease shall be for such period as the court may authorize.

(b) Except as provided in subdivision (c), the court shall not authorize a lease for longer than 10 years if any heir or devisee who has an interest in the property to be leased objects at the hearing.

(c) If the lease is for the purpose of exploration for or production or removal of minerals, oil, gas, or other hydrocarbon substances, or geothermal energy, the court may authorize that the lease be for a fixed period and any of the following:

(1) So long thereafter as minerals, oil, gas, or other hydrocarbon substances or geothermal energy are produced in paying quantities from the property leased or mining or drilling operations are conducted thereon.

(2) If the lease provides for the payment of a compensatory royalty, so long thereafter as such compensatory royalty is paid.

(3) If the land covered by the lease is included in an agreement authorized by Section 3301 of the Public Resources Code, so long thereafter as oil, gas, or other hydrocarbon substances are produced in paying quantities from any of the lands included in any such agreement or drilling operations are conducted thereon.

9948. (a) The personal representative shall execute, acknowledge, and deliver the lease as directed, setting forth therein that it is made by authority of the order, giving the date of the order.

(b) A lease made pursuant to an order obtained under this chapter is effectual to lease the premises described in the order at the rent, for the term, and upon the terms and conditions prescribed in the order.

(c) Jurisdiction of the court in proceedings under this code concerning the administration of the estate of the decedent vests the court with jurisdiction to make the order for the lease. This jurisdiction shall conclusively inure to the benefit of the lessee and the lessee's heirs and assigns.

(d) No omission, error, or irregularity in the proceedings under this chapter shall impair or invalidate the proceedings or the lease made pursuant to an order made under this chapter.

Chapter 16. Granting Option To Purchase Real Property

9960. After authorization by order of court obtained under this chapter, the personal representative may grant an option to purchase real property of the estate for a period within or beyond the period of administration.

9961. To obtain an order under this chapter, the personal representative shall file a petition containing all of the following:

(a) A description of the real property.

(b) The terms and conditions of the proposed option.

(c) A showing that granting the option is to the advantage of the estate.

9962. The purchase price of the real property subject to the option shall be at least 90 percent of the appraised value of the real property. The appraisal shall be made in the manner provided in subdivision (c) of Section 10309 within one year prior to the hearing of the petition.

9963. Notice of the hearing on the petition shall be posted as provided in Section 1230 and given as provided in Section 1220 to all of the following persons:

(a) Each person listed in Section 1220.

(b) Each known heir whose interest in the estate would be affected by the granting of the option.

(c) Each known devisee whose interest in the estate would be affected by the granting of the option.

9964. (a) The court shall make an order authorizing the personal representative to grant the option upon the terms and conditions stated in the order if the court is satisfied as to all of the following:

(1) Good reason exists to grant the option and granting the option will be to the advantage of the estate.

(2) It does not appear that a higher offer with respect to the purchase price of the real property subject to the option may be obtained. An offer is a higher offer with respect to purchase price only if the offer satisfies the requirements of Section 10311 governing increased bids in real property sales.

(3) It does not appear that a better offer with respect to the terms of the option may be obtained. An offer is a better offer with respect to the terms of the option only if the offer is materially more advantageous to the estate.

(b) A higher offer made either for cash or on credit, whether on the same or different credit terms, or a better offer, shall be considered only if the personal representative informs the court in person or by counsel, before the court makes its order authorizing the granting of the option, that the offer is acceptable.

9965. An option granted pursuant to an order made under this chapter, whether within or beyond the administration of the estate, is subject to Chapter 4 (commencing with Section 884.010) of Title 5 of Part 2 of Division 2 of the Civil Code.

9966. No omission, error, or irregularity in the proceedings under this chapter shall impair or invalidate the proceedings or the granting of an option pursuant to an order made under this chapter.

Chapter 17. Option To Purchase Given In Will

9980. (a) Where an option to purchase real or personal property is given in a will, the person given the option has the right to exercise the option at any time within the time limits provided by the will. For the purposes of this section, if a time limitation in the will is measured from the death of the testator, that time shall be extended by the period between the testator's death and the issuance of letters testamentary or of administration with the will annexed or by six months, whichever is the shorter period.

(b) If the will does not provide a time limit for exercise of the option, the time limit is one year from the death of the decedent.

(c) Subject to subdivision (b), if the option given in the will is exercisable under the terms of the will after the time that the estate would otherwise be closed, the property subject to the option shall be distributed subject to the option.

9981. (a) Where an option to purchase real or personal property is given in a will admitted to probate, the court may make an order under this chapter directing the personal representative to transfer or convey the property to the person given the option upon compliance with the terms and conditions stated in the will.

(b) The personal representative or the person given the option to purchase the property may file a petition for an order pursuant to this chapter.

(c) Notice of the hearing on the petition shall be given as provided in Section 1220.

9982. The court shall not make an order under this chapter unless one of the following requirements is satisfied:

(a) The court determines that the rights of creditors will not be impaired by the making of the order.

(b) The court requires a bond in an amount and with such surety as the court shall direct or approve.

9983. No omission, error, or irregularity in the proceedings under this chapter shall impair or invalidate the proceedings or the transfer or conveyance made pursuant to an order made under this chapter.

Chapter 18. Sales

Article 1. General Provisions

10000. Subject to the limitations, conditions, and requirements of this chapter, the personal representative may sell real or personal property of the estate in any of the following cases:

(a) Where the sale is necessary to pay debts, devises, family allowance, expenses of administration, or taxes.

(b) Where the sale is to the advantage of the estate and in the best interest of the interested persons.

(c) Where the property is directed by the will to be sold.

(d) Where authority is given in the will to sell the property.

10001. (a) If the personal representative neglects or refuses to sell the property, any interested person may petition the court for an order requiring the personal representative to sell real or personal property of the estate in any of the following cases:

(1) Where the sale is necessary to pay debts, devises, family allowance, expenses of administration, or taxes.

(2) Where the sale is to the advantage of the estate and in the best interest of the interested persons.

(3) Where the property is directed by the will to be sold.

(b) Notice of the hearing on the petition shall be given as provided in Section 1220.

(c) Notice of the hearing on the petition also shall be given to the personal representative by citation served at least five days before the hearing.

10002. (a) Subject to subdivision (b), if directions are given in the will as to the mode of selling or the particular property to be sold, the personal representative shall comply with those directions.

(b) If the court determines that it would be to the advantage of the estate and in the best interest of the interested persons, the court may make an order relieving the personal representative of the duty to comply with the directions in the will. The order shall specify the mode and the terms and conditions of selling or the particular property to be sold, or both. The personal representative or any interested person may file a petition for an order under this subdivision. Notice of the hearing on the petition shall be given as provided in Section 1220.

10003. Subject to Part 4 (commencing with Section 21400) of Division 11 and to Sections 10001 and 10002, if estate property is required or permitted to be sold, the personal representative may:

(a) Use discretion as to which property to sell first.

(b) Sell the entire interest of the estate in the property or any lesser interest therein.

(c) Sell the property either at public auction or private sale.

10004. (a) Where the personal representative determines in his or her discretion that, by use or relationship, any assets of the estate, whether real or personal, constitute a unit for purposes of sale, the personal representative may cause the property to be appraised as a unit.

(b) Whether or not the property is appraised as a unit, the personal representative may sell all the assets described in subdivision (a) as a unit and under one bid if the court finds the sale of the assets as a unit to be to the advantage of the estate.

(c) No private sale of the assets as a unit may be made for less than 90 percent of the sum of the appraised values of the personal property and the sum of the appraised values of the real property, appraised separately, or for less than 90 percent of the appraised value if appraised as a unit.

(d) If the assets to be sold as a unit include any real property, the sale shall be made in the manner provided for the sale of real property, and the bid and sale are subject to the limitations and restrictions established for the sale of real property. If the assets to be sold as a unit are entirely personal property, the property shall be sold in the manner provided for the sale of personal property.

10005. (a) If any property in the estate is sold for more than the appraised value, the personal representative shall account for the proceeds of sale, including the excess over the appraised value.

(b) If any property in the estate is sold for less than the appraised value and the sale has been made in accordance with law, the personal representative is not responsible for the loss.

10006. If property in the estate is to be sold as an undivided interest in a cotenancy, the other cotenants may file in the estate proceeding written consent to have their interests sold pursuant to this chapter. Thereafter, the court's orders made pursuant to this chapter are as binding on the consenting cotenants as on the personal representative.

Article 2. Contract With Agent, Broker, Or Auctioneer

10150. (a) The personal representative may enter into a written contract with either or both of the following:

(1) A licensed real estate broker to secure a purchaser for any real property of the estate. The broker may associate other licensed real estate brokers for this purpose, including use of a multiple listing service as defined in Section 1087 of the Civil Code.

(2) One or more agents or brokers to secure a purchaser for any personal property of the estate. If the particular property to be sold or the particular manner of sale requires that the agent or broker be licensed, the contract may be made only with an agent or broker that is so licensed.

(b) The contract may provide for payment of a fee, commission, or other compensation out of the proceeds of sale, but the contract is binding and valid as against the estate only for such amount as the court allows pursuant to Article 3 (commencing with Section 10160). No liability of any kind is incurred by the estate under the contract or a sale unless the sale is confirmed by the court, except for the obligations of the estate to the purchaser of personal property as to which title passes pursuant to Section 10259 without court confirmation or approval. The personal representative is not personally liable on the contract by reason of execution of the contract.

(c) The contract may grant an exclusive right to sell property for a period not in excess of 90 days if, prior to execution of the contract granting an exclusive right to sell, the personal representative obtains permission of the court to enter into the contract upon a showing of necessity and advantage to the estate. The court may grant the permission when the personal representative is appointed or at any subsequent time upon ex parte application. The personal representative may execute one or more extensions of the contract granting an exclusive right to sell property, each extension being for a period not to exceed 90 days, if for each extension the personal representative obtains permission of the court upon ex parte application to extend the contract upon a showing of necessity and advantage to the estate of the extension.

10151. (a) The personal representative may enter into a written contract with any of the following:

(1) Where the public auction sale will be held in this state, an auctioneer who is qualified to conduct business under Title 2.95 (commencing with Section 1812.600) of Part 4 of Division 3 of the Civil Code.

(2) Where the public auction sale will be held outside this state pursuant to an order made under Section 10254, an auctioneer who is legally permitted in the jurisdiction where the sale will be held to conduct a public auction sale and to secure purchasers by that method for the personal property authorized to be sold by public auction sale in that jurisdiction under the court order.

(b) The contract shall be one that is legally enforceable under the law of the jurisdiction where made.

(c) The contract may provide for payment to the auctioneer of a fee, commission, or other compensation out of the proceeds of sale and for reimbursement of expenses, but the contract is binding and valid as against the estate only for such amounts as the court allows pursuant to Section 10167. No liability of any kind is incurred by the estate under the contract or a sale unless the sale is approved by the court, except for the obligations of the estate to the purchaser of personal property as to which title passes pursuant to Section 10259 without court confirmation or approval. The personal representative is not personally liable on the contract by reason of execution of the contract.

(d) The contract may provide that personal property of two or more estates being administered by the same personal representative may be sold at the same public auction sale. Items of personal property may be sold separately or in a lot with other items from the same estate. A sale pursuant to the contract shall be with reserve. The auctioneer shall comply with the instructions of the personal representative with respect to withdrawal of items, risk of loss, place of delivery, warranties, and other matters.

Article 3. Compensation Of Agent, Broker, Or Auctioneer

10160. The estate is not liable to an agent, broker, or auctioneer under a contract for the sale of property or for any fee, commission, or other compensation or expenses in connection with a sale of property unless the following requirements are satisfied:

(a) An actual sale is made.

(b) If court confirmation or approval is required, the sale is confirmed or approved by the court as required.

(c) The sale is consummated.

10160.5. The estate is not liable to an agent or broker under a contract for the sale of property or for any fee, commission, or other compensation or expenses in connection with sale of the property in either of the following cases:

(a) Where the agent or broker, directly or indirectly, is the purchaser of the property.

(b) Where the agent or broker representing the purchaser to whom the sale is confirmed has any interest in the purchaser.

10161. (a) Subject to the provisions of this article, whether or not the agent or broker has a contract with the personal representative, the fee, commission, or other compensation of an agent or broker in connection with a sale of property shall be the amount the court, in its discretion, determines to be a reasonable compensation for the services of the agent or broker to the estate.

(b) Unless the agent or broker holds a contract granting an exclusive right to sell the property, an agent or broker is not entitled to any fee, commission, or other compensation for services to the estate in connection with a sale except in the following cases:

(1) Where the agent or broker produces the original bid which is returned to the court for confirmation.

(2) Where the property is sold on an increased bid, made at the time of the hearing on the petition for confirmation, to a purchaser procured by the agent or broker.

(c) If the agent or broker has a contract with the personal representative, the amount of the compensation of the agent or broker in connection with the sale of property shall not exceed the amount provided for in the contract.

10162. (a) Subject to subdivision (b), where the bid returned to the court for confirmation is made by a person who is not represented by an agent or broker and the successful bidder is represented by an agent or broker, the compensation of the agent or broker who procured the purchaser to whom the sale is confirmed shall not exceed one-half of the difference between the amount of the bid in the original return and the amount of the successful bid.

(b) This section does not limit the compensation of the agent or broker who holds a contract under Section 10150 granting him or her the exclusive right to sell the property.

10162.3. (a) This section applies if all of the following circumstances exist:

(1) There is no agent or broker holding a contract under Section 10150 granting the exclusive right to sell the property.

(2) The bid returned to court for confirmation is made by a purchaser represented by an agent or broker.

(3) The court confirms the sale to that purchaser either on the bid returned to court for confirmation or on an increased bid made at the time of the hearing on the petition for confirmation.

(b) If all the circumstances described in subdivision (a) exist, the court shall allow the agent or broker who procured the purchaser to whom the sale is confirmed the compensation determined under Section 10161 on the full amount for which the sale is confirmed.

10162.5. Subject to Section 10162.6, where an agent or broker holds a contract under Section 10150 granting the exclusive right to sell the property, the court shall allow to the agent or broker holding the contract the compensation determined under Section 10161 on:

(a) The full amount for which the sale is confirmed in either of the following circumstances:

(1) The bid returned to the court for confirmation is made by a purchaser who is not represented by an agent or broker and the court confirms the sale to that purchaser on that bid.

(2) The bid returned to the court for confirmation is made by a purchaser who is represented by the agent or broker holding the contract and the court confirms the sale to that purchaser on an increased bid made at the time of the hearing on the petition for confirmation.

(b) The amount of the original bid if both of the following circumstances exist:

(1) The bid returned to court for confirmation is made by a purchaser who is not represented by an agent or broker or who is represented by the agent or broker holding a contract under Section 10150 granting the exclusive right to sell the property.

(2) The court confirms the sale on an increased bid, made at the time of the hearing on the petition for confirmation, to a purchaser who was not procured by a bona fide agent or broker.

10162.6. (a) This section applies if both of the following circumstances exist:

(1) An agent or broker holds a contract under Section 10150 granting the exclusive right to sell the property.

(2) The contract provides that no compensation is payable to the agent or broker holding the contract if sale is confirmed to a particular purchaser named in the contract.

(b) If the court confirms the sale to the purchaser named in the contract, whether on an original bid returned to the court or on an increased bid made at the time of the hearing on the petition for confirmation, the compensation of any agents or brokers involved in the sale is determined as provided in this article, except that no compensation is payable to the agent or broker holding the contract.

(c) If the court confirms the sale to a purchaser other than the person named in the contract, whether on an original bid returned to the court or on an increased bid made at the time of the hearing on the petition for confirmation, the compensation of the agent or broker holding the contract, and of any other agents or brokers involved in the sale, is determined under this article as if the limitation in the contract did not exist.

10162.7. (a) Subject to Section 10162.6, this section applies if all of the following circumstances exist:

(1) There is an agent or broker holding a contract under Section 10150 granting the exclusive right to sell the property.

(2) The bid returned to court for confirmation is made by a purchaser procured by another agent or broker.

(3) The court confirms the sale to that purchaser either on the bid returned to court for confirmation or on an increased bid made at the time of the hearing on the petition for confirmation.

(b) If all the circumstances described in subdivision (a) exist, the court shall allow the compensation determined under Section 10161 on the full amount for which the sale is confirmed. The compensation allowed by the court shall be divided between the agent or broker holding the contract and the other agent or broker as is provided in any agreement between the agent or broker holding the contract and the other agent or broker. If there is no agreement, the compensation on the amount of the original bid returned to the court shall be divided equally between the agent or broker holding the contract and the other agent or broker and, if the sale is confirmed on an increased bid, the other agent or broker shall be paid all of the compensation on the difference between the original bid and the amount for which the sale is confirmed.

10163. Subject to Sections 10162 and 10162.6, where the original bid returned to the court for confirmation was made by a purchaser who was not procured by an agent or broker, the court shall allow the compensation determined under Section 10161 on the full amount for which the sale is confirmed to the agent or broker who procured the purchaser to whom the sale is confirmed if either of the following conditions is satisfied:

(a) The court confirms a sale on an increased bid, made at the time of the hearing on the petition for confirmation, to a purchaser procured by an agent or broker holding a contract under Section 10150 granting the exclusive right to sell the property.

(b) There is no agent or broker holding a contract under Section 10150 granting the exclusive right to sell the property and the court confirms a sale on an increased bid, made at the time of the hearing on the petition for confirmation, to a purchaser procured by a bona fide agent or broker.

10164. (a) This section applies only where the court confirms a sale on an increased bid, made at the time of the hearing on the petition for confirmation, to a purchaser who was not procured by a bona fide agent or broker.

(b) Except as provided in subdivision (c), the court shall allow the compensation determined under Section 10161 on the amount of the original bid to the agent or broker whose original bid was returned to the court.

(c) If an agent or broker holds a contract

under Section 10150 granting the exclusive right to sell the property and the original bid returned to the court is made by a purchaser who was procured by another agent or broker, the compensation determined under Section 10161 on the amount of the original bid shall be divided between the agent or broker holding the contract and the other agent or broker as is provided in any agreement between the agent or broker holding the contract and the other agent or broker. If there is no agreement, the compensation shall be divided equally between the agent or broker holding the contract and the other agent or broker.

10165. (a) Subject to Section 10162.6, where the court confirms a sale on an increased bid, made at the time of the hearing on the petition for confirmation, to a purchaser procured by a bona fide agent or broker, the court shall allow the compensation determined under Section 10161 on the full amount for which the sale is confirmed, as provided in this section, if either of the following conditions is satisfied:

(1) The original bid returned to the court for confirmation was made by a purchaser who was procured by another agent or broker.

(2) The original bid returned to the court for confirmation was made by a purchaser who was not represented by an agent or broker, and another agent or broker holds a contract under Section 10150 granting the exclusive right to sell the property.

(b) The agent or broker who procured the purchaser to whom the sale is confirmed shall be paid one-half of the compensation on the amount of the original bid and all of the compensation on the difference between the original bid and the amount for which the sale is confirmed.

(c) The other one-half of the compensation on the amount of the original bid shall be paid as follows:

(1) If the original bid returned to the court is made by a purchaser who was procured by the agent or broker holding a contract under Section 10150 granting the exclusive right to sell the property, the entire one-half of compensation on the original bid shall be paid to that agent or broker.

(2) If the original bid returned to the court is made by a purchaser who was procured by a bona fide agent or broker and there is no agent or broker holding a contract under Section 10150 granting the exclusive right to sell the property, the entire one-half of the compensation on the original bid shall be paid to that agent or broker.

(3) If there is an agent or broker who holds a contract under Section 10150 granting the exclusive right to sell the property and the original bid returned to the court is made by a purchaser who was procured by another agent or broker, the one-half of the compensation on the amount of the original bid

shall be divided between the agent or broker holding the contract granting the exclusive right to sell the property and the other agent or broker whose original bid was returned to the court for confirmation as is provided in any agreement between the agent or broker holding the contract and the other agent or broker. If there is no agreement, the one-half of the compensation on the amount of the original bid shall be divided equally between the agent or broker holding the contract and the other agent or broker whose original bid was returned to the court for confirmation.

(4) If there is an agent or broker who holds a contract under Section 10150 granting the exclusive right to sell the property and the original bid returned to the court is made by a purchaser who is not represented by an agent or broker and the court confirms the sale on an increased bid, made at the time of the hearing on the petition for confirmation, to a purchaser procured by another agent or broker, the entire one-half of the compensation on the original bid shall be paid to the agent or broker holding the contract.

(5) If the agent or broker compensated under subdivision (b) holds a contract under Section 10150 granting the exclusive right to sell the property, the entire one-half of the compensation on the original bid shall be paid to the other agent or broker who procured the original bid returned to the court.

10166. Notwithstanding that a bid contains a condition that a certain amount of the bid shall be paid to an agent or broker by the personal representative, only such compensation as is proper under this article shall be allowed. Acceptance of the bid by the court binds the bidder even though the compensation allowed by the court is less than that specified by the condition.

10167. (a) Subject to subdivision (b), whether or not the auctioneer has a contract with the personal representative, the fees, compensation, and expenses of an auctioneer in connection with a sale of property shall be the amount the court, in its discretion, determines to be a reasonable compensation for the services of the auctioneer to the estate.

(b) If the auctioneer has a contract with the personal representative, the amount of the compensation of the auctioneer in connection with the sale of property shall not exceed the amount provided for in the contract.

10168. This article does not supersede any agreement cooperating agents or brokers may have among themselves to divide the compensation payable under this article.

Article 4. Special Provisions Applicable To Particular Types Of Property

10200. (a) As used in this section, "securities" means "security" as defined in Section 70, land trust certificates, certificates of beneficial interest in trusts, investment trust certificates, mortgage participation certificates, or certificates of deposit for any of the foregoing, but does not include notes secured by a mortgage or deed of trust unless the note or notes have been authorized or permitted to be issued by the Commissioner of Corporations or have been made by a public utility subject to the Public Utilities Act (Part 1 (commencing with Section 201) of Division 1 of the Public Utilities Code).

(b) After authorization by order of court, securities may be sold or may be surrendered for redemption or conversion. Title to the securities sold or surrendered as authorized by an order obtained under this section passes without the need for subsequent court confirmation.

(c) To obtain an order under this section, the personal representative or any interested person shall file a petition stating the terms and conditions and the advantage to the estate of the proposed sale or redemption or conversion. If the court authorizes the sale, redemption, or conversion, the court's order shall fix the terms and conditions of sale, redemption, or conversion.

(d) Notice of the hearing on the petition shall be given as provided in Section 1220 and posted as provided in Section 1230, but the court may order that the notice be given for a shorter period or dispensed with.

(e) No notice of sale or of the redemption or conversion need be given if any of the following conditions are satisfied:

(1) The minimum selling price is fixed by the court.

(2) The securities are to be sold on an established stock or bond exchange.

(3) The securities to be sold are securities designated as a national market system security on an interdealer quotation system, or subsystem thereof, by the National Association of Securities Dealers, Inc., sold through a broker-dealer registered under the Securities Exchange Act of 1934 during the regular course of business of the broker-dealer.

(4) The securities are to be surrendered for redemption or conversion.

10201. (a) For purposes of this section:

(1) "Federal association" is defined in Section 5102 of the Financial Code.

(2) "Mutual capital certificate" is defined in Section 5111 of the Financial Code.

(3) "Savings account" is defined in Section 5116 of the Financial Code.

(4) "Savings association" is defined in Section 5102 of the Financial Code.

(5) "Withdrawal value" is defined in Section 5124 of the Financial Code.

(b) Notwithstanding Section 10200, savings accounts and mutual capital certificates of a savings association or federal association may be sold or surrendered for withdrawal by the personal representative, and title thereto passed, without notice of sale, prior order of court, or subsequent confirmation by the court, if an amount of money is obtained upon the sale or withdrawal not less than the withdrawal value of the savings account or the value of the mutual capital certificate.

(c) Notwithstanding Section 10200, credit union share accounts and certificates for funds may be sold or withdrawn by the personal representative, and title thereto passed, without notice of sale, prior order of court, or subsequent confirmation by the court, if an amount of money is obtained upon the sale or withdrawal not less than the withdrawal value of the share account or the value of the certificate for funds.

10202. Notwithstanding Section 10200, if an estate by reason of owning securities, also owns or receives subscription rights for the purchase of additional securities, the personal representative may sell all or part of the subscription rights without notice of sale, prior order of court, or subsequent confirmation by the court.

10203. (a) Except as provided in subdivision (b), where property to be sold consists of a leasehold interest, the sale shall be made as in the case of the sale of personal property of the estate.

(b) The sale of a leasehold interest shall be made as in the case of the sale of real property of the estate if the interest to be sold consists of any of the following:

(1) A leasehold interest in real property with an unexpired term of 10 years or longer. For this purpose, the leasehold interest shall be considered to have an unexpired term of 10 years or longer if the lessee has the right to extend the term and the term, if extended, would exceed 10 years.

(2) A leasehold interest in real property together with an option to purchase the leased property or some part thereof.

(3) A lease for the purpose of production of minerals, oil, gas, or other hydrocarbon substances, or geothermal energy.

10204. Property of the estate that consists of a partnership interest or an interest belonging to an estate by virtue of a partnership formerly existing may be sold in the same manner as other personal property.

10205. A chose in action belonging to the estate may be sold in the same manner as other personal property.

10206. (a) Except as otherwise provided in this section, if the decedent at the time of death was possessed of a contract for the purchase of real property and the decedent's interest in the property and under the contract is to be sold, the sale shall be made as in the case of the sale of real property of the estate.

(b) If the decedent's interest in the property and under the contract is sold, the sale shall be made subject to all payments which are due at the time of sale or which may thereafter become due on the contract.

Except as provided in subdivision (d), if there are any payments due or to become due, the court shall not confirm the sale until the purchaser executes a bond to the personal representative that satisfies the requirements of subdivision (c).

(c) The bond shall be for the benefit and indemnity of the personal representative and the persons entitled to the interest of the decedent in the real property contracted for. The amount of the bond shall be equal to the amount of payments then due and thereafter to become due on the contract, with such sureties as the court may approve. The bond shall be conditioned that the purchaser will (1) make all payments for the property which are then due or which become due after the date of the sale and (2) fully indemnify the personal representative and the person entitled to the interest of the decedent against all demands, costs, charges, and expenses, by reason of any covenant or agreement contained in the contract.

(d) The bond need not be given in either of the following cases:

(1) Where no claim has been made against the estate on the contract and the time for filing claims has expired.

(2) Where the person entitled to payment under the contract waives all recourse to the assets of the estate for payment and releases the estate and the personal representative from liability for payment.

10207. (a) Real property suitable for a shift-in-land-use loan to develop grazing or pasture facilities may be sold under this section by the personal representative to a grazing or pasture association in conformity with the federal Consolidated Farm and Rural Development Act (7 U.S.C. Sec. 1921, et seq.) after authorization by order of the court.

(b) The personal representative or any interested person may file a petition for an order under this section. Notice of the hearing on the petition shall be given as provided in Section 1220.

(c) An order for sale of property under this section may be made only if the court determines both of the following:

(1) Either the sale is made pursuant to the will of the decedent or all of the following have consented to the sale:

(A) Each known heir whose interest in the estate would be affected by the sale.

(B) Each known devisee who has an interest in the property under the decedent's will.

(2) The sale will not jeopardize the rights of creditors of the estate.

(d) If the court makes an order authorizing sale of the property, the personal representative may make the sale in accord with the terms and conditions set out in the order, subject to the following requirements:

(1) Except as provided in Sections 10002, 10301, 10303, and 10503, notice of the time

and place of the sale shall be published pursuant to Section 10300.

(2) The price of the sale made shall be not less than the value of the property as established by an independent and competent appraiser mutually acceptable to the federal government, the grazing or pasture association, and the personal representative.

(3) Except as provided in Sections 10002 and 10503, the sale shall be reported to and confirmed by the court as provided in Article 6 (commencing with Section 10300) before title to the property passes, but the sale may be made irrespective of whether a higher bid is made to the court at the hearing on the petition to confirm the sale.

Article 5. Sale Of Personal Property

10250. Subject to Sections 10251 and 10252 and except as otherwise provided by statute, personal property of the estate may be sold only after notice of sale is given by one or both of the following methods, as the personal representative may determine:

(a) Posting at the county courthouse of the county in which the proceedings are pending at least 15 days before:

(1) In the case of a private sale, the day specified in the notice of sale as the day on or after which the sale is to be made.

(2) In the case of a public auction sale, the day of the auction.

(b) Publication pursuant to Section 6063a of the Government Code in a newspaper in the county in which the proceedings are pending, such publication to be completed before:

(1) In the case of a private sale, the day specified in the notice of sale as the day on or after which the sale is to be made.

(2) In the case of a public auction sale, the day of the auction.

10251. (a) If it is shown that it will be to the advantage of the estate, the court or judge may by order shorten the time of notice of sale to not less than five days.

(b) If the court or judge makes an order under subdivision (a), notice of sale shall be given by one or both of the following methods, as the personal representative may determine:

(1) By posting as provided in Section 10250 except that the posting shall be for at least five days instead of 15 days as required by Section 10250.

(2) By publication as provided in Section 10250 except that the publication shall be pursuant to Section 6061 of the Government Code.

10252. Personal property may be sold with or without notice, as the personal representative may determine, in any of the following cases:

(a) Where the property is directed by the will to be sold.

(b) Where authority is given in the will to

sell the property.

(c) Where the property is perishable, will depreciate in value if not disposed of promptly, or will incur loss or expense by being kept.

(d) Where sale of the property is necessary to provide for the payment of a family allowance pending receipt of other sufficient funds.

10253. (a) The notice of sale given pursuant to Section 10250 shall state all of the following:

(1) Whether the sale is to be a private sale or a public auction sale.

(2) In the case of a private sale, the place at which bids or offers will be received and a day on or after which the sale will be made or, in the case of a public auction sale, the time and place of sale.

(3) A brief description of the personal property to be sold.

(b) The notice of sale may state other matters in addition to those required by subdivision (a), including terms and conditions of sale.

10254. (a) Unless the court orders otherwise pursuant to subdivision (b):

(1) A sale of personal property at a public auction sale shall be made within this state at the courthouse door, at the auction house, at some other public place, or at the residence of the decedent.

(2) No public auction sale shall be made of any tangible personal property that is not present at the time of sale.

(b) Upon petition of the personal representative or any interested person, the court may order either or both of the following:

(1) That a sale of personal property at public auction be made at any place within or without the United States.

(2) That tangible personal property need not be present at the time of sale.

(c) The personal representative may postpone a public auction sale of personal property from time to time if all of the following conditions are satisfied:

(1) The personal representative believes that the postponement is to the advantage of the estate.

(2) Notice of the postponement is given by public declaration at the time and place appointed for the sale.

(3) The postponement, together with previous postponements of sale of the property, does not exceed three months.

10255. (a) A private sale of personal property may not be made before the day stated in the notice of sale as the day on or after which the sale will be made, nor later than one year after that day.

(b) In the case of a private sale of personal property, the bids or offers shall be in writing and shall be left at the place designated in the notice of sale, or be delivered to the personal representative personally or to the person specified in the notice of sale, at any time after the first publication or posting of

notice of sale and before the making of the sale.

10256. Whether a sale of personal property is private or at public auction, bids shall substantially comply with any terms specified in the notice of sale.

10257. (a) Personal property may be sold for cash or on credit.

(b) Except as may otherwise be ordered by the court pursuant to Section 10258, if a sale is made on credit, not less than 25 percent of the purchase price shall be paid in cash at the time of sale, and the personal representative shall do one of the following:

(1) Take the note of the purchaser for the balance of the purchase money, with a security interest in the personal propery sold, to secure the payment of the balance.

(2) Enter into a conditional sale contract under which title is retained until the balance is paid.

(c) The terms of the note and security interest or conditional sale contract shall be approved by the court at the time of confirmation of sale.

(d) Where property sold by the personal representative for part cash and part deferred payments consists of an undivided interest in personal property or any other interest therein less than the entire ownership and the owner or owners of the remaining interests therein join in the sale, the note and security interest may be made to the personal representative and such others having an interest in the property. The interest of the personal representative in the note and security interest shall be in the same interest and in the same proportions as the estate's interest in the property prior to the sale.

10258. (a) On petition of the personal representative, the court may by order authorize a sale of personal property on credit on terms providing for less than 25 percent of the purchase price to be paid in cash at the time of sale, or may waive or modify the requirement that a security interest or other lien shall be retained or taken to secure payment of the balance of the purchase price, where it is shown that the terms are to the advantage of the estate and the property to be sold is of such a nature that it is impracticable to sell the property for a larger cash payment at the time of sale or to retain a security interest or other lien in the property. The order of the court shall fix the terms and conditions of the sale.

(b) Notice of the hearing on the petition shall be posted as provided in Section 1230 and given as provided in Section 1220 to all of the following persons:

(1) Each person listed in Section 1220.

(2) Each known heir whose interest in the estate would be affected by the sale.

(3) Each known devisee whose interest in the estate would be affected by the sale.

10259. (a) Title to the following personal property passes upon sale without the need for court confirmation or approval:

(1) Personal property which is perishable, which will depreciate in value if not disposed of promptly, or which will incur loss or expense by being kept.

(2) Personal property the sale of which is necessary to provide for the payment of a family allowance pending receipt of other sufficient funds.

(b) Title to personal property sold at public auction passes without the need for court confirmation or approval upon receipt of the purchase price and:

(1) In the case of tangible personal property, the delivery of the property to the purchaser.

(2) In the case of intangible personal property, the delivery to the purchaser of the instrument that transfers the title to the property to the purchaser.

(c) The personal representative is responsible for the actual value of the property described in subdivision (a) or (b) unless the sale is reported to and approved by the court.

10260. (a) Except as provided in Sections 10200, 10201, 10202, 10259, and 10503, all sales of personal property shall be reported to and be confirmed by the court before title to the property passes to the purchaser, notwithstanding that the property is directed by the will to be sold or authority is given in the will to sell the property.

(b) If the personal representative fails to file the report and a petition for confirmation of the sale within 30 days after the sale, the purchaser at the sale may file the report and petition for confirmation of the sale.

(c) Notice of the hearing on the petition for confirmation filed under subdivision (a) or (b) shall be given as provided in Section 1220 and posted as provided in Section 1230.

10261. (a) Except as provided in this subdivision, at the hearing on the petition for confirmation of the sale, the court shall examine into the necessity for the sale or the advantage to the estate and the benefit to the interested persons in making the sale. If the decedent's will authorizes or directs the property to be sold, there need be no showing of the necessity of the sale or the advantage to the estate and the benefit to the interested persons in making the sale.

(b) Any interested person may file written objections to the confirmation of the sale at or before the hearing and may testify and produce witnesses in support of the objections.

(c) Before confirming the sale of a partnership interest, whether made to the surviving partner or to any other person, the court shall do both of the following:

(1) Inquire into the condition of the partnership affairs.

(2) Examine any surviving partner if that surviving partner is a resident within the state at the time of the hearing and able to be present in court. The court may issue a citation to compel the surviving partner to attend the hearing.

(d) Upon its own motion or upon the request of the personal representative, the agent or broker, or any other interested person, made at the time of the confirmation hearing or at another time, the court shall fix the compensation of the agent or broker as provided in Article 3 (commencing with Section 10160).

10262. (a) Except as provided in subdivision (b), if a written offer to purchase the property is made to the court at the hearing on the petition for confirmation of the sale and the new bid is at least 10 percent more than the amount stated in the report made to the court, the court in its discretion may accept the new bid and confirm the sale to the offeror, or may order a new sale, if all of the following conditions are satisfied:

(1) The original bid as stated in the report to the court is more than one hundred dollars ($100) or, if the original bid is less than one hundred dollars ($100), the new bid is at least one hundred dollars ($100) more than the original bid.

(2) The new bid is made by a responsible person.

(3) The new bid complies with all provisions of law.

(b) If there is more than one offer that satisfies the requirements of subdivision (a), the court shall do one of the following:

(1) Accept the highest such offer and confirm the sale to the offeror.

(2) Order a new sale.

(c) This section does not apply to a sale of property described in Section 10259.

10263. If notice of the sale was required, before an order is made confirming the sale, it shall be proved to the satisfaction of the court that notice of the sale was given as required by this article, and the order of confirmation shall show that such proof was made.

10264. No omission, error, or irregularity in the proceedings under this article shall impair or invalidate the proceedings or the sale pursuant to an order made under this article.

Article 6. Sale Of Real Property

10300. (a) Except as provided in Sections 10301 to 10303, inclusive, and in Section 10503, real property of the estate may be sold only after notice of sale has been published pursuant to Section 6063a of the Government Code (1) in a newspaper published in the county in which the real property or some portion thereof is located or (2) if there is no such newspaper, in such newspaper as the court or judge may direct.

(b) The publication of notice of sale shall be completed before:

(1) In the case of a private sale, the day specified in the notice as the day on or after which the sale is to be made.

(2) In the case of a public auction sale, the day of the auction.

10301. (a) If it appears from the inventory and appraisal that the value of the real property to be sold does not exceed five thousand dollars ($5,000), the personal representative may in his or her discretion dispense with publication of notice of sale and, in lieu of publication, post the notice of sale at the courthouse of the county in which the real property or some portion thereof is located.

(b) Except as provided in Section 10302, posting pursuant to this section shall be for at least 15 days before:

(1) In the case of a private sale, the day specified in the notice of sale as the day on or after which the sale is to be made.

(2) In the case of a public auction sale, the day of the auction.

10302. (a) If it is shown that it will be to the advantage of the estate, the court or judge may by order shorten the time of notice of sale to not less than five days.

(b) Except as provided in subdivision (c), if the court or judge makes an order under subdivision (a), notice of sale shall be published as provided in Section 10300 except that the publication shall be pursuant to Section 6061 of the Government Code.

(c) In a case described in Section 10301, if the court makes an order under subdivision (a), notice of sale shall be posted as provided in Section 10301 except that the notice of sale shall be posted at least five days before the sale instead of 15 days as required by Section 10301.

10303. Real property may be sold with or without notice, as the personal representative may determine, in either of the following cases:

(a) Where the property is directed by the will to be sold.

(b) Where authority is given in the will to sell the property.

10304. (a) The notice of sale given pursuant to this article shall state all of the following:

(1) Whether the sale is to be a private sale or a public auction sale.

(2) In the case of a private sale, the place at which bids or offers will be received and a day on or after which the sale will be made or, in the case of a public auction sale, the time and place of sale.

(3) The street address or other common designation or, if none, a legal description of the real property to be sold.

(b) The notice of sale may state other matters in addition to those required by subdivision (a), including terms and conditions of sale.

10305. (a) A sale of real property at public auction shall be made in the county in which the property is located. If the property is located in two or more counties, it may be sold in any one of them.

(b) A sale of real property at public auc-

tion shall be made between 9 a.m. and 9 p.m., and the sale shall be made on the day specified in the notice of sale unless the sale is postponed.

(c) The personal representative may postpone a public auction sale of real property from time to time if all of the following conditions are satisfied:

(1) The personal representative believes that the postponement is to the advantage of the estate.

(2) Notice of the postponement is given by public declaration at the time and place appointed for the sale.

(3) The postponement, together with previous postponements of sale of the property, does not exceed three months in all.

10306. (a) A private sale of real property may not be made before the day stated in the notice of sale as the day on or after which the sale will be made, nor later than one year after that day.

(b) In the case of a private sale of real property, the bids or offers shall be in writing and shall be left at the place designated in the notice of sale, or be delivered to the personal representative personally or to the person specified in the notice of sale, at any time after the first publication or posting of notice of sale and before the making of the sale.

10307. Whether a sale of real property is private or at public auction, bids shall substantially comply with any terms specified in the notice of sale.

10308. (a) Except as provided in Section 10503, all sales of real property shall be reported to and be confirmed by the court before title to the property passes to the purchaser, whether the sale is a private sale or a public auction sale and notwithstanding that the property is directed by the will to be sold or authority is given in the will to sell the property.

(b) If the personal representative fails to file the report and a petition for confirmation of the sale within 30 days after the sale, the purchaser at the sale may file the report and petition for confirmation of the sale.

(c) Notice of the hearing on the petition for confirmation filed under subdivision (a) or (b) shall be given as provided in Section 1220 to the persons designated by that section and to the purchasers named in the petition, and posted as provided in Section 1230.

10309. (a) Except as provided in Section 10207, no sale of real property at private sale shall be confirmed by the court unless all of the following conditions are satisfied:

(1) The real property has been appraised within one year prior to the date of the confirmation hearing.

(2) The valuation date used in the appraisal described in paragraph (1) is within one year prior to the date of the confirmation hearing.

(3) The sum offered for the property is at least 90 percent of the appraised value of the property as determined by the appraisal described in paragraph (1).

(b) An appraisal of the property may be had at any time before the sale or the confirmation of sale in any of the following cases:

(1) Where the property has not been previously appraised.

(2) Where the property has not been appraised within one year before the date of the confirmation hearing.

(3) Where the valuation date used in the latest appraisal is more than one year before the date of the confirmation hearing.

(4) Where the court is satisfied that the latest appraisal is too high or too low.

(c) A new appraisal made pursuant to subdivision (b) need not be made by a probate referee if the original appraisal of the property was made by a person other than a probate referee. If the original appraisal of the property was made by a probate referee, the new appraisal may be made by the probate referee who made the original appraisal without further order of the court or further request for the appointment of a new probate referee. If appraisal by a probate referee is required, a new probate referee shall be appointed, using the same procedure as for the appointment of an original referee, to make the new appraisal if the original probate referee is dead, has been removed, or is otherwise unable to act, or if there is other reason to appoint another probate referee.

10310. (a) Except as provided in this subdivision, at the hearing on the petition for confirmation of the sale of the real property, the court shall examine into the necessity for the sale or the advantage to the estate and the benefit to the interested persons in making the sale. If the decedent's will authorizes or directs the property to be sold, there need be no showing of the necessity of the sale or the advantage to the estate and benefit to the interested persons in making the sale.

(b) The court shall examine into the efforts of the personal representative to obtain the highest and best price for the property reasonably attainable.

(c) Any interested person may file written objections to the confirmation of the sale at or before the hearing and may testify and produce witnesses in support of the objections.

10311. (a) Subject to subdivisions (b), (c), (d), and (e), and except as provided in Section 10207, if a written offer to purchase the real property is made to the court at the hearing on the petition for confirmation of the sale, the court shall accept the offer and confirm the sale to the offeror if all of the following conditions are satisfied:

(1) The offer is for an amount at least 10 percent more on the first ten thousand dollars ($10,000) of the original bid and 5 percent more on the amount of the original bid in excess of ten thousand dollars ($10,000).

(2) The offer is made by a responsible person.

(3) The offer complies with all provisions of law.

(b) Subject to subdivisions (c), (d), and (e), if there is more than one offer that satisfies the requirements of subdivision (a), the court shall accept the highest such offer and confirm the sale to the person making that offer.

(c) The court may, in its discretion, decline to accept the offer that satisfies the requirements of subdivisions (a) and (b); and, in such case, the court shall order a new sale.

(d) If the sale returned for confirmation is on credit and the higher offer is for cash or on credit, whether on the same or different credit terms, or the sale returned for confirmation is for cash and the higher offer is on credit, the court may not consider the higher offer unless the personal representative informs the court in person or by counsel prior to confirmation of sale that the higher offer is acceptable.

(e) For the purpose of this section, the amount of the original bid and any higher offer shall be determined by the court without regard to any of the following:

(1) Any commission on the amount of the bid to which an agent or broker may be entitled under a contract with the personal representative.

(2) Any condition of the bid that a certain amount of the bid be paid to an agent or broker by the personal representative.

10312. If notice of the sale was required, before an order is made confirming the sale it shall be proved to the satisfaction of the court that notice of the sale was given as required by this article, and the order of confirmation shall show that the proof was made.

10313. (a) The court shall make an order confirming the sale to the person making the highest offer that satisfies the requirements of this article, and directing conveyances or assignments or both to be executed, if it appears to the court that all of the following requirements are satisfied:

(1) Either the sale was authorized or directed to be made by the decedent's will or good reason existed for the sale.

(2) If notice of the sale was required, the proof required by Section 10312 has been made.

(3) The sale was legally made and fairly conducted.

(4) The amount for which the sale is to be confirmed is not disproportionate to the value of the property.

(5) In the case of a private sale, the sale complied with the requirements of Section 10309.

(6) If the sale is confirmed to the original bidder, it does not appear that a sum

exceeding the original bid by at least 10 percent more on the first ten thousand dollars ($10,000) of the original bid and 5 percent more on the amount of the original bid in excess of ten thousand dollars ($10,000), exclusive of the expenses of a new sale, may be obtained.

(b) Upon its own motion or upon the request of the personal representative, the agent or broker, or any other interested person, made at the time of the confirmation hearing or at another time, the court shall fix the compensation of the agent or broker as provided in Article 3 (commencing with Section 10160).

(c) If it appears to the court that the requirements of subdivision (a) are not satisfied, the court shall vacate the sale and order a new sale.

(d) If the court orders a new sale under subdivision (c) of this section or under subdivision (c) of Section 10311, notice of the new sale shall be given and the new sale shall in all respects be conducted as if no previous sale had taken place.

10314. (a) Except as provided in subdivision (b), upon confirmation of the sale, the personal representative shall execute a conveyance to the purchaser which shall refer to the order confirming the sale and directing the conveyance to be executed. A certified copy of the order shall be recorded in the office of the recorder of the county in which the real property or some portion thereof is located.

(b) Upon confirmation of a sale of the decedent's interest under a contract for the purchase of real property by the decedent and after the purchaser has given a bond if one is required under Section 10206, the personal representative shall execute an assignment of the contract to the purchaser.

(c) A conveyance made in compliance with the court order confirming the sale and directing the conveyance to be executed vests in the purchaser both of the following:

(1) All the right, title, and interest which the decedent had in the property at the time of the decedent's death.

(2) Any other or additional right, title, or interest in the property acquired by the estate of the decedent, by operation of law or otherwise, prior to the sale.

(d) An assignment made in compliance with the court order confirming the sale of the decedent's interest under a contract for the purchase of real property by the decedent vests in the purchaser all the right, title, and interest of the estate, or of the persons entitled to the interest of the decedent, at the time of sale in the property assigned. The purchaser of the decedent's interest under the contract for the purchase of the real property by the decedent has the same rights and remedies against the vendor of the property as the decedent would have had if living.

10315. (a) If a sale is made on credit, the personal representative shall take the note of the purchaser for the unpaid portion of the purchase money, with a mortgage or deed of trust on the property to secure payment of the note. The mortgage or deed of trust shall be subject only to encumbrances existing at the date of sale and such other encumbrances as the court may approve.

(b) Where property sold by the personal representative for part cash and part deferred payments consists of an undivided interest in real property or any other interest therein less than the entire ownership and the owner or owners of the remaining interests therein join in the sale, the note and deed of trust or mortgage may be made to the personal representative and such others having an interest in the property. The interest of the personal representative in the note and deed of trust or mortgage shall be in the same interest and in the same proportions as the estate's interest in the property prior to the sale.

10316. No omission, error, or irregularity in the proceedings under this article shall impair or invalidate the proceedings or the sale pursuant to an order made under this article.

Article 7. Vacating Sale For Purchaser's Default; Liability Of Defaulting Purchaser For Damages

10350. (a) If after court confirmation of sale of real or personal property the purchaser fails to comply with the terms of sale, the court may, on petition of the personal representative, vacate the order of confirmation, order a resale of the property, and award damages to the estate against the purchaser.

(b) Notice of the hearing on the petition shall be given as provided in Section 1220 to the persons designated by that section and the notice and a copy of the petition shall be given to the buyers and brokers named in the order confirming sale, except that notice need not be given to a defaulting purchaser whose written consent to the petition is filed with the court before the hearing.

(c) Notice of the resale of the property shall be given as provided in this chapter for a sale of the property in the first instance.

(d) Proceedings after notice of the resale shall be as provided in this chapter for a sale of the property in the first instance.

(e) If the property is resold, the defaulting purchaser is liable to the estate for damages equal to the sum of the following:

(1) The difference between the contract price of the first sale and the amount paid by the purchaser at the resale.

(2) Expenses made necessary by the purchaser's breach.

(3) Other consequential damages.

10351. (a) The court may vacate the order

of confirmation of a sale of real or personal property and make an order confirming the sale to the new high bidder if both of the following requirements are satisfied:

(1) A petition is filed within 60 days after confirmation of the sale showing that (A) the purchaser at the sale has failed to complete the purchase and (B) a bid has been made for the property in the same or a higher amount, on the same or better terms, and in the manner prescribed in the original notice of sale.

(2) The sale has not been vacated pursuant to Section 10350.

(b) Notice of the hearing on the petition shall be given as provided in Section 1220 to the persons designated by that section and the notice and a copy of the petition shall be given to the buyers and brokers named in the order confirming sale, except that notice need not be given to a defaulting purchaser whose written consent to the vacation of the order confirming the sale is filed with the court prior to the hearing.

(c) If the report and petition for confirmation of the second sale are not filed within 60 days of the confirmation of the first sale, the property may be resold only in the manner provided in Section 10350.

Article 8. Application Of Sale Proceeds Of Encumbered Property; Sale To Lienholder

10360. As used in this article:

(a) "Amount secured by the lien" includes interest and any costs and charges secured by the lien.

(b) "Encumbered property" means real or personal property that is subject to a lien for a secured debt which is a valid claim against the estate and which has been allowed or approved.

(c) "Lien" means a mortgage, deed of trust, or other lien.

10361. (a) If encumbered property is sold, the purchase money shall be applied in the following order:

(1) Expenses of administration which are reasonably related to the administration of the property sold as provided in paragraph (1) of subdivision (a) of Section 11420.

(2) The payment of the expenses of the sale.

(3) The payment and satisfaction of the amount secured by the lien on the property sold if payment and satisfaction of the lien is required under the terms of the sale.

(4) Application in the course of administration.

(b) The application of the purchase money, after the payment of those expenses set forth in paragraphs (1) and (2) of subdivision (a), to the payment and satisfaction of the amount secured by the lien on the property sold shall be made without delay; and, subject to Section 10362, the property sold remains subject to the lien until the purchase money has been actually so applied.

10361.5. The personal representative or any interested party may, at any time before payment is made to satisfy all liens on the encumbered property sold, petition for an order determining the amount of expenses of administration that are reasonably related to the administration of that encumbered property as provided in paragraph (1) of subdivision (a) of Section 11420. The petition may be heard as part of a petition for confirmation of sale of personal or real property as provided in Section 10260 or 10308, respectively or may be heard separately. If the petition is presented as part of a petition for confirmation of sale of real or personal property, the notice of hearing otherwise required by this code for a petition for confirmation of sale shall be given in addition to the notice requirements under Section 10361.6.

10361.6. (a) At least 30 days prior to the day of the hearing, the petitioner shall cause notice of the hearing and a copy of the petition to be served in the manner provided in Chapter 4 (commencing with Section 413.10) of Title 5 of Part 3 of the Code of Civil Procedure on all of the following persons:

(1) The personal representative, if the personal representative is not the petitioner.

(2) The holder of any mortgage or other lien secured by the property that is sold.

(3) All agents or brokers entitled to compensation from the proceeds of the property that is sold.

(b) Except for those persons given notice pursuant to subdivision (a), notice of the hearing, together with a copy of the petition, shall be given as provided in Section 1220 to all of the following persons:

(1) Each person listed in Section 1220.

(2) Each known heir whose interest in the estate would be affected by the petition.

(3) Each known devisee whose interest in the estate would be affected by the petition.

(4) The Attorney General, at the office of the Attorney General in Sacramento, if any portion of the estate is to escheat to the state and its interest in the estate would be affected by the petition.

(c) The court may not shorten the time for giving the notice of hearing under this section.

10362. (a) If encumbered property is sold, the purchase money, or so much of the purchase money as is sufficient to pay the amount secured by the lien on the property sold and the expenses of the sale, may be paid to the clerk of the court. Upon the payment being so made, the lien on the property sold ceases.

(b) The clerk of court without delay shall use the money paid to the clerk under this section to pay the expenses of the sale and to pay and satisfy the amount secured by the lien on the property sold. The clerk shall at once return the surplus, if any, to the personal representative unless the court, for good cause shown and after notice to the personal representative, otherwise orders.

10363. (a) At a sale of real or personal property subject to a lien, the lienholder may become the purchaser of the property, even though no claim for the amount secured by the lien on the property sold has been, or could have been, filed, allowed, or approved.

(b) Unless the property is sold subject to the lien:

(1) If the lienholder becomes the purchaser of the property and the amount secured by the lien on the property is a valid claim against the estate and has been allowed or approved, the receipt of the lienholder for the amount due the lienholder from the proceeds of the sale is a payment pro tanto.

(2) If the lienholder becomes the purchaser of the property and no claim for the amount secured by the lien on the property has been filed, allowed, or approved, the court may at the hearing on the petition for confirmation of the sale examine into the validity and enforceability of the lien and the amount secured by the lien, and the court may authorize the personal representative to accept the receipt of the lienholder for the amount secured by the lien as payment pro tanto.

(3) If the lienholder becomes the purchaser of the property and the amount for which the property is purchased is insufficient to pay the expenses of the sale and to discharge the lienholder's lien, whether or not a claim has been filed, allowed, or approved, the lienholder shall pay to the clerk of the court an amount sufficient to cover the expenses of the sale.

(c) Nothing permitted under this section shall be deemed to be an allowance or approval of a claim based upon the lien or the amount secured by the lien.

Article 9. Damages And Recovery Of Property

10380. The personal representative is liable to an interested person for damages suffered by the interested person by reason of the neglect or misconduct of the personal representative in the proceedings in relation to a sale.

10381. In addition to any other damages for which the personal representative is liable, if the personal representative fraudulently sells real property of the estate contrary to or otherwise than under the provisions of this chapter, the person having an estate of inheritance in the real property may recover from the personal representative, as liquidated damages, an amount equal to double the fair market value of the real property sold on the date of sale.

10382. (a) No action for the recovery of property sold by a personal representative on the claim that the sale is void may be maintained by an heir or other person claiming under the decedent unless the action is commenced within whichever of the following is the later time:

(1) Three years after the settlement of the final account of the personal representative.

(2) Three years after the discovery of any fraud upon which the action is based.

(b) The limitation established by subdivision (a) is not tolled for any reason.

Part 6. Independent Administration Of Estates

Chapter 1. General Provisions

10400. This part shall be known and may be cited as the Independent Administration of Estates Act.

10401. As used in this part, "court supervision" means the judicial order, authorization, approval, confirmation, or instructions that would be required if authority to administer the estate had not been granted under this part.

10402. As used in this part, "full authority" means authority to administer the estate under this part that includes all the powers granted under this part.

10403. As used in this part, "limited authority" means authority to administer the estate under this part that includes all the powers granted under this part except the power to do any of the following:

(a) Sell real property.

(b) Exchange real property.

(c) Grant an option to purchase real property.

(d) Borrow money with the loan secured by an encumbrance upon real property.

10404. The personal representative may not be granted authority to administer the estate under this part if the decedent's will provides that the estate shall not be administered under this part.

10405. A special administrator may be granted authority to administer the estate under this part if the special administrator is appointed with, or has been granted, the powers of a general personal representative.

10406. (a) Subject to subdivision (b), this part applies in any case where authority to administer the estate is granted under this part or where independent administration authority was granted under prior law.

(b) If the personal representative was granted independent administration authority prior to July 1, 1988, the personal representative may use that existing authority on and after July 1, 1988, to borrow money on a loan secured by an encumbrance upon real property, whether or not that existing authority includes the authority to sell real property.

Chapter 2. Granting Or Revoking Independent Administration Authority

10450. (a) To obtain authority to administer the estate under this part, the personal representative shall petition the court for that authority either in the petition for appointment of the personal representative or in a separate petition filed in the estate proceedings.

(b) The petition may request either of the following:

(1) Full authority to administer the estate under this part.

(2) Limited authority to administer the estate under this part.

10451. (a) If the authority to administer the estate under this part is requested in the petition for appointment of the personal representative, notice of the hearing on the petition shall be given for the period and in the manner applicable to the petition for appointment.

(b) Where proceedings for the administration of the estate are pending at the time a petition is filed under Section 10450, notice of the hearing on the petition shall be given as provided in Section 1220 to all of the following persons:

(1) Each person listed in Section 1220.

(2) Each known heir whose interest in the estate would be affected by the petition.

(3) Each known devisee whose interest in the estate would be affected by the petition.

(4) Each person named as executor in the will of the decedent.

(c) The notice of hearing of the petition for authority to administer the estate under this part, whether included in the petition for appointment or in a separate petition, shall include the substance of the following statement: "The petition requests authority to administer the estate under the Independent Administration of Estates Act. This will avoid the need to obtain court approval for many actions taken in connection with the estate. However, before taking certain actions, the personal representative will be required to give notice to interested persons unless they have waived notice or have consented to the proposed action. Independent administration authority will be granted unless good cause is shown why it should not be."

10452. Unless an interested person objects as provided in Section 1043 to the granting of authority to administer the estate under this part and the court determines that the objecting party has shown good cause why the authority to administer the estate under this part should not be granted, the court shall grant the requested authority. If the objecting party has shown good cause why only limited authority should be granted, the court shall grant only limited authority.

10453. (a) If the personal representative is otherwise required to file a bond and has full authority, the court, in its discretion, shall fix the amount of the bond at not more than the estimated value of the personal property, the estimated value of the decedent's interest in the real property authorized to be sold under this part, and the probable annual gross income of the estate, or, if the bond is to be given by personal sureties, at not less than twice that amount.

(b) If the personal representative is otherwise required to file a bond and has limited authority, the court, in its discretion, shall fix the amount of the bond at not more than the estimated value of the personal property and the probable annual gross income of the estate, or, if the bond is to be given by personal sureties, at not less than twice that amount.

10454. (a) Any interested person may file a petition requesting that the court make either of the following orders:

(1) An order revoking the authority of the personal representative to continue administration of the estate under this part.

(2) An order revoking the full authority of the personal representative to administer the estate under this part and granting the personal representative limited authority to administer the estate under this part.

(b) The petition shall set forth the basis for the requested order.

(c) Notice of the hearing on the petition shall be given as provided in Section 1220. In addition, the personal representative shall be served with a copy of the petition and a notice of the time and place of the hearing at least 15 days prior to the hearing. Service on the personal representative shall be made in the manner provided in Section 415.10 or 415.30 of the Code of Civil Procedure or in such manner as may be authorized by the court.

(d) If the court determines that good cause has been shown, the court shall make an order revoking the authority of the personal representative to continue administration of the estate under this part. Upon the making of the order, new letters shall be issued without the notation described in subdivision (c) of Section 8405.

(e) If the personal representative was granted full authority and the court determines that good cause has been shown, the court shall make an order revoking the full authority and granting the personal representative limited authority. Upon the making of the order, new letters shall be issued with the notation described in subdivision (c) of Section 8405 that is required where the authority granted is limited authority.

Chapter 3. Administration Under Independent Administration Authority

Article 1. General Provisions

10500. (a) Subject to the limitations and conditions of this part, a personal representative who has been granted authority to administer the estate under this part may administer the estate as provided in this part without court supervision, but in all other respects the personal representative shall administer the estate in the same manner as a personal representative who has not been granted authority to administer the estate under this part.

(b) Notwithstanding subdivision (a), the personal representative may obtain court supervision as provided in this code of any action to be taken by the personal representative during administration of the estate.

10501. (a) Notwithstanding any other provision of this part, whether the personal representative has been granted full authority or limited authority, a personal representative who has obtained authority to administer the estate under this part is required to obtain court supervision, in the manner provided in this code, for any of the following actions:

(1) Allowance of the personal representative's compensation.

(2) Allowance of compensation of the attorney for the personal representative.

(3) Settlement of accounts.

(4) Subject to Section 10520, preliminary and final distributions and discharge.

(5) Sale of property of the estate to the personal representative or to the attorney for the personal representative.

(6) Exchange of property of the estate for property of the personal representative or for property of the attorney for the personal representative.

(7) Grant of an option to purchase property of the estate to the personal representative or to the attorney for the personal representative.

(8) Allowance, payment, or compromise of a claim of the personal representative, or the attorney for the personal representative, against the estate.

(9) Compromise or settlement of a claim, action, or proceeding by the estate against the personal representative or against the attorney for the personal representative.

(10) Extension, renewal, or modification of the terms of a debt or other obligation of the personal representative, or the attorney for the personal representative, owing to or in favor of the decedent or the estate.

(b) Notwithstanding any other provision of this part, a personal representative who has obtained only limited authority to administer the estate under this part is required to obtain court supervision, in the manner provided in this code, for any of the following actions:

(1) Sale of real property.

(2) Exchange of real property.

(3) Grant of an option to purchase real property.

(4) Borrowing money with the loan secured by an encumbrance upon real property.

(c) Paragraphs (5) to (10), inclusive, of subdivision (a) do not apply to a transaction between the personal representative as such and the personal representative as an individual where all of the following requirements are satisfied:

(1) Either (A) the personal representative is the sole beneficiary of the estate or (B) all the known heirs or devisees have consented to the transaction.

(2) The period for filing creditor claims has expired.

(3) No request for special notice is on file or all persons who filed a request for special notice have consented to the transaction.

(4) The claim of each creditor who filed a claim has been paid, settled, or withdrawn, or the creditor has consented to the transaction.

10502. (a) Subject to the conditions and limitations of this part and to Section 9600, a personal representative who has been granted authority to administer the estate under this part has the powers described in Article 2 (commencing with Section 10510), Article 3 (commencing with Section 10530), and Article 4 (commencing with Section 10550).

(b) The will may restrict the powers that the personal representative may exercise under this part.

10503. Subject to the limitations and requirements of this part, when the personal representative exercises the authority to sell property of the estate under this part, the personal representative may sell the property either at public auction or private sale, and with or without notice, for such price, for cash or on credit, and upon such terms and conditions as the personal representative may determine, and the requirements applicable to court confirmation of sales of real property (including, but not limited to, publication of notice of sale, court approval of agents' and brokers' commissions, sale at not less than 90 percent of appraised value, and court examination into the necessity for the sale, advantage to the estate and benefit to interested persons, and efforts of the personal representative to obtain the highest and best price for the property reasonably attainable), and the requirements applicable to court confirmation of sales of personal property, do not apply to the sale.

Article 2. Powers Exercisable Only After Giving Notice Of Proposed Action

10510. The personal representative may exercise the powers described in this article only if the requirements of Chapter 4 (commencing with Section 10580) (notice of proposed action procedure) are satisfied.

10511. The personal representative who has full authority has the power to sell or exchange real property of the estate.

10512. The personal representative has the power to sell or incorporate any of the following:

(a) An unincorporated business or venture in which the decedent was engaged at the time of the decedent's death.

(b) An unincorporated business or venture which was wholly or partly owned by the decedent at the time of the decedent's death.

10513. The personal representative has the power to abandon tangible personal property where the cost of collecting, maintaining, and safeguarding the property would exceed its fair market value.

10514. (a) Subject to subdivision (b), the personal representative has the following powers:

(1) The power to borrow.

(2) The power to place, replace, renew, or extend any encumbrance upon any property of the estate.

(b) Only a personal representative who has full authority has the power to borrow money with the loan secured by an encumbrance upon real property.

10515. The personal representative who has full authority has the power to grant an option to purchase real property of the estate for a period within or beyond the period of administration.

10516. If the will gives a person the option to purchase real or personal property and the person has complied with the terms and conditions stated in the will, the personal representative has the power to convey or transfer the property to the person.

10517. The personal representative has the power to convey or transfer real or personal property to complete a contract entered into by the decedent to convey or transfer the property.

10518. The personal representative has the power to allow, compromise, or settle any of the following:

(a) A third-party claim to real or personal property if the decedent died in possession of, or holding title to, the property.

(b) The decedent's claim to real or personal property title to or possession of which is held by another.

10519. The personal representative has the power to make a disclaimer.

10520. If the time for filing claims has expired and it appears that the distribution may be made without loss to creditors or injury to the estate or any interested person, the personal representative has the power to make preliminary distributions of the following:

(a) Income received during administration to the persons entitled under Chapter 8 (commencing with Section 12000) of Part 10.

(b) Household furniture and furnishings, motor vehicles, clothing, jewelry, and other tangible articles of a personal nature to the persons entitled to the property under the decedent's will, not to exceed an aggregate fair market value to all persons of fifty thousand dollars ($50,000) computed cumulatively through the date of distribution. Fair market value shall be determined on the basis of the inventory and appraisal.

(c) Cash to general pecuniary devisees entitled to it under the decedent's will, not to exceed ten thousand dollars ($10,000) to any one person.

Article 3. Powers The Exercise Of Which Requires Giving Of Notice Of Proposed Action Under Some Circumstances

10530. Except to the extent that this article otherwise provides, the personal representative may exercise the powers described in this article without giving notice of proposed action under Chapter 4 (commencing with Section 10580).

10531. (a) The personal representative has the power to manage and control property of the estate, including making allocations and determinations under the Uniform Principal and Income Act, Chapter 3 (commencing with Section 16320) of Part 4 of Division 9. Except as provided in subdivision (b), the personal representative may exercise this power without giving notice of proposed action under Chapter 4 (commencing with Section 10580).

(b) The personal representative shall comply with the requirements of Chapter 4 (commencing with Section 10580) in any case where a provision of Chapter 3 (commencing with Section 10500) governing the exercise of a specific power so requires.

10532. (a) The personal representative has the power to enter into a contract in order to carry out the exercise of a specific power granted by this part, including, but not limited to, the powers granted by Sections 10531 and 10551. Except as provided in subdivision (b), the personal representative may exercise this power without giving notice of proposed action under Chapter 4 (commencing with Section 10580).

(b) The personal representative shall comply with the requirements of Chapter 4 (commencing with Section 10580) where the contract is one that by its provisions is not to be fully performed within two years, except that the personal representative is not required to comply with those requirements if the personal representative has the unrestricted right under the contract to terminate the contract within two years.

(c) Nothing in this section excuses compliance with the requirements of Chapter 4 (commencing with Section 10580) when the contract is made to carry out the exercise of a specific power and the provision that grants that power requires compliance with Chapter 4 (commencing with Section 10580) for the exercise of the power.

10533. (a) The personal representative has the power to do all of the following:

(1) Deposit money belonging to the estate in an insured account in a financial institution in this state.

(2) Invest money of the estate in any one or more of the following:

(A) Direct obligations of the United States, or of the State of California, maturing not later than one year from the date of making the investment.

(B) An interest in a money market mutual fund registered under the Investment Company Act of 1940 (15 U.S.C. Sec. 80a-1, et seq.) or an investment vehicle authorized for the collective investment of trust funds pursuant to Section 9.18 of Part 9 of Title 12 of the Code of Federal Regulations, the portfolios of which are limited to United States government obligations maturing not later than five years from the date of investment and to repurchase agreements fully collateralized by United States government obligations.

(C) Units of a common trust fund described in Section 1564 of the Financial Code. The common trust fund shall have as its objective investment primarily in short term fixed income obligations and shall be permitted to value investments at cost pursuant to regulations of the appropriate regulatory authority.

(D) Eligible securities for the investment of surplus state moneys as provided for in Section 16430 of the Government Code.

(3) Invest money of the estate in any manner provided by the will.

(b) Except as provided in subdivision (c), the personal representative may exercise the powers described in subdivision (a) without giving notice of proposed action under Chapter 4 (commencing with Section 10580).

(c) The personal representative shall comply with the requirements of Chapter 4 (commencing with Section 10580) where the personal representative exercises the power to make any investment pursuant to the power granted by subparagraph (D) of paragraph (2) of subdivision (a) or paragraph (3) of subdivision (a), except that the personal representative may invest in direct obligations of the United States, or of the State of California, maturing not later than one year from the date of making the investment without complying with the requirements of

Chapter 4 (commencing with Section 10580).

10534. (a) Subject to the partnership agreement and the provisions of the Uniform Partnership Act of 1994 (Chapter 5 (commencing with Section 16100) of Title 2 of the Corporations Code), the personal representative has the power to continue as a general partner in any partnership in which the decedent was a general partner at the time of death.

(b) The personal representative has the power to continue operation of any of the following:

(1) An unincorporated business or venture in which the decedent was engaged at the time of the decedent's death.

(2) An unincorporated business or venture which was wholly or partly owned by the decedent at the time of the decedent's death.

(c) Except as provided in subdivision (d), the personal representative may exercise the powers described in subdivisions (a) and (b) without giving notice of proposed action under Chapter 4 (commencing with Section 10580).

(d) The personal representative shall comply with the requirements of Chapter 4 (commencing with Section 10580) if the personal representative continues as a general partner under subdivision (a), or continues the operation of any unincorporated business or venture under subdivision (b), for a period of more than six months from the date letters are first issued to a personal representative.

10535. (a) The personal representative has the power to pay a reasonable family allowance. Except as provided in subdivision (b), the personal representative may exercise this power without giving notice of proposed action under Chapter 4 (commencing with Section 10580).

(b) The personal representative shall comply with the requirements of Chapter 4 (commencing with Section 10580) for all of the following:

(1) Making the first payment of a family allowance.

(2) Making the first payment of a family allowance for a period commencing more than 12 months after the death of the decedent.

(3) Making any increase in the amount of the payment of a family allowance.

10536. (a) The personal representative has the power to enter as lessor into a lease of property of the estate for any purpose (including, but not limited to, exploration for and production or removal of minerals, oil, gas, or other hydrocarbon substances or geothermal energy, including a community oil lease or a pooling or unitization agreement) for such period, within or beyond the period of administration, and for such rental or royalty or both, and upon such other terms and conditions as the personal representative may determine. Except as provided in subdivisions (b) and (c), the personal representative may exercise this power without giving notice of proposed action under Chapter 4 (commencing with Section 10580).

(b) The personal representative shall comply with the requirements of Chapter 4 (commencing with Section 10580) where the personal representative enters into a lease of real property for a term in excess of one year. If the lease gives the lessee the right to extend the term of the lease, the lease shall be considered as if the right to extend has been exercised.

(c) The personal representative shall comply with the requirements of Chapter 4 (commencing with Section 10580) where the personal representative enters into a lease of personal property and the lease is one described in subdivision (b) of Section 10532.

10537. (a) The personal representative has the power to sell personal property of the estate or to exchange personal property of the estate for other property upon such terms and conditions as the personal representative may determine. Except as provided in subdivision (b), the personal representative shall comply with the requirements of Chapter 4 (commencing with Section 10580) in exercising this power.

(b) The personal representative may exercise the power granted by subdivision (a) without giving notice of proposed action under Chapter 4 (commencing with Section 10580) in case of the sale or exchange of any of the following:

(1) A security sold on an established stock or bond exchange.

(2) A security designated as a national market system security on an interdealer quotation system, or subsystem thereof, by the National Association of Securities Dealers, Inc., sold through a broker-dealer registered under the Securities Exchange Act of 1934 during the regular course of business of the broker-dealer.

(3) Personal property referred to in Section 10202 or 10259 when sold for cash.

(4) A security described in Section 10200 surrendered for redemption or conversion.

10538. (a) The personal representative has the following powers:

(1) The power to grant an exclusive right to sell property for a period not to exceed 90 days.

(2) The power to grant to the same broker one or more extensions of an exclusive right to sell property, each extension being for a period not to exceed 90 days.

(b) Except as provided in subdivision (c), the personal representative may exercise the powers described in subdivision (a) without giving notice of proposed action under Chapter 4 (commencing with Section 10580).

(c) The personal representative shall comply with the requirements of Chapter 4 (commencing with Section 10580) where the personal representative grants to the same broker an extension of an exclusive right to sell property and the period of the extension, together with the periods of the original exclusive right to sell the property and any previous extensions of that right, is more than 270 days.

Article 4. Powers Exercisable Without Giving Notice Of Proposed Action

10550. The personal representative may exercise the powers described in this article without giving notice of proposed action under Chapter 4 (commencing with Section 10580).

10551. In addition to the powers granted to the personal representative by other sections of this chapter, the personal representative has all the powers that the personal representative could exercise without court supervision under this code if the personal representative had not been granted authority to administer the estate under this part.

10552. The personal representative has the power to do all of the following:

(a) Allow, pay, reject, or contest any claim by or against the estate.

(b) Compromise or settle a claim, action, or proceeding by or for the benefit of, or against, the decedent, the personal representative, or the estate.

(c) Release, in whole or in part, any claim belonging to the estate to the extent that the claim is uncollectible.

(d) Allow a claim to be filed after the expiration of the time for filing the claim.

10553. The personal representative has the power to do all of the following:

(a) Commence and maintain actions and proceedings for the benefit of the estate.

(b) Defend actions and proceedings against the decedent, the personal representative, or the estate.

10554. The personal representative has the power to extend, renew, or in any manner modify the terms of an obligation owing to or in favor of the decedent or the estate.

10555. The personal representative has the power to convey or transfer property in order to carry out the exercise of a specific power granted by this part.

10556. The personal representative has the power to pay all of the following:

(a) Taxes and assessments.

(b) Expenses incurred in the collection, care, and administration of the estate.

10557. The personal representative has the power to purchase an annuity from an insurer admitted to do business in this state to satisfy a devise of an annuity or other direction in the will for periodic payments to a devisee.

10558. The personal representative has the power to exercise an option right that is property of the estate.

10559. The personal representative has the power to purchase securities or commodities required to perform an incomplete contract of sale where the decedent died having sold but not delivered securities or commodities not owned by the decedent.

10560. The personal representative has the power to hold a security in the name of a nominee or in any other form without disclosure of the estate, so that title to the security may pass by delivery.

10561. The personal representative has the power to exercise security subscription or conversion rights.

10562. The personal representative has the power to make repairs and improvements to real and personal property of the estate.

10563. The personal representative has the power to accept a deed to property which is subject to a mortgage or deed of trust in lieu of foreclosure of the mortgage or sale under the deed of trust.

10564. The personal representative has the power to give a partial satisfaction of a mortgage or to cause a partial reconveyance to be executed by a trustee under a deed of trust held by the estate.

Chapter 4. Notice Of Proposed Action Procedure

10580. (a) A personal representative who has been granted authority to administer the estate under this part shall give notice of proposed action as provided in this chapter prior to the taking of the proposed action without court supervision if the provision of Chapter 3 (commencing with Section 10500) giving the personal representative the power to take the action so requires. Nothing in this subdivision authorizes a personal representative to take an action under this part if the personal representative does not have the power to take the action under this part.

(b) A personal representative who has been granted authority to administer the estate under this part may give notice of proposed action as provided in this chapter even if the provision of Chapter 3 (commencing with Section 10500) giving the personal representative the power to take the action permits the personal representative to take the action without giving notice of proposed action. Nothing in this subdivision requires the personal representative to give notice of proposed action where not required under subdivision (a) or authorizes a personal representative to take any action that the personal representative is not otherwise authorized to take.

10581. Except as provided in Sections 10582 and 10583, notice of proposed action shall be given to all of the following:

(a) Each known devisee whose interest in the estate would be affected by the proposed action.

(b) Each known heir whose interest in the estate would be affected by the proposed action.

(c) Each person who has filed a request under Chapter 6 (commencing with Section 1250) of Part 2, of Division 3 for special notice of petitions filed in the administration proceeding.

(d) The Attorney General, at the office of the Attorney General in Sacramento, if any portion of the estate is to escheat to the state and its interest in the estate would be affected by the proposed action.

10582. Notice of proposed action need not be given to any person who consents in writing to the proposed action. The consent may be executed at any time before or after the proposed action is taken.

10583. (a) Notice of proposed action need not be given to any person who, in writing, waives the right to notice of proposed action with respect to the particular proposed action. The waiver may be executed at any time before or after the proposed action is taken. The waiver shall describe the particular proposed action and may waive particular aspects of the notice, such as the delivery, mailing, or time requirements of Section 10586, or the giving of the notice in its entirety for the particular proposed action.

(b) Notice of proposed action need not be given to any person who has executed the Statutory Waiver of Notice of Proposed Action Form prescribed by the Judicial Council and in that form has made either of the following:

(1) A general waiver of the right to notice of proposed action.

(2) A waiver of the right to notice of proposed action for all transactions of a type which includes the particular proposed action.

10584. (a) A waiver or consent may be revoked only in writing and is effective only when the writing is received by the personal representative.

(b) A copy of the revocation may be filed with the court, but the effectiveness of the revocation is not dependent upon a copy being filed with the court.

10585. (a) The notice of proposed action shall state all of the following:

(1) The name and mailing address of the personal representative.

(2) The person and telephone number to call to get additional information.

(3) The action proposed to be taken, with a reasonably specific description of the action. Where the proposed action involves the sale or exchange of real property, or the granting of an option to purchase real property, the notice of proposed action shall state the material terms of the transaction, including, if applicable, the sale price and the amount of, or method of calculating, any commission or compensation paid or to be paid to an agent or broker in connection with the transaction.

(4) The date on or after which the proposed action is to be taken.

(b) The notice of proposed action may be given using the most current Notice of Proposed Action form prescribed by the Judicial Council.

(c) If the most current form prescribed by the Judicial Council is not used to give notice of proposed action, the notice of proposed action shall satisfy all of the following requirements:

(1) The notice of proposed action shall be in substantially the same form as the form prescribed by the Judicial Council.

(2) The notice of proposed action shall contain the statements described in subdivision (a).

(3) The notice of proposed action shall contain a form for objecting to the proposed action in substantially the form set out in the Judicial Council form.

10586. The notice of proposed action shall be mailed or personally delivered to each person required to be given notice of proposed action not less than 15 days before the date specified in the notice of proposed action on or after which the proposed action is to be taken. If mailed, the notice of proposed action shall be addressed to the person at the person's last known address. Sections 1215 and 1216 apply to the mailing or delivery of the notice of proposed action.

10587. (a) Any person entitled to notice of proposed action under Section 10581 may object to the proposed action as provided in this section.

(b) The objection to the proposed action is made by delivering or mailing a written objection to the proposed action to the personal representative at the address stated in the notice of proposed action. The person objecting to the proposed action either may use the Judicial Council form or may make the objection in any other writing that identifies the proposed action with reasonable certainty and indicates that the person objects to the taking of the proposed action.

(c) The personal representative is deemed to have notice of the objection to the proposed action if it is delivered or received at the address stated in the notice of proposed action before whichever of the following times is the later:

(1) The date specified in the notice of proposed action on or after which the proposed action is to be taken.

(2) The date the proposed action is actually taken.

10588. (a) Any person who is entitled to notice of proposed action for a proposed action described in subdivision (a) of Section 10580, or any person who is given notice of a proposed action described in subdivision (b) of Section 10580, may apply to the court having jurisdiction over the proceeding for an order restraining the personal representative from taking the proposed action without court supervision. The court shall grant the requested order without requiring notice to the personal representative and without cause being shown for the order.

(b) The personal representative is deemed to have notice of the restraining order if it is served upon the personal representative in the same manner as is provided for in Section 415.10 or 415.30 of the Code of Civil Procedure, or in the manner authorized by the court, before whichever of the following times is the later:

(1) The date specified in a notice of proposed action on or after which the proposed action is to be taken.

(2) The date the proposed action is actually taken.

10589. (a) If the proposed action is one that would require court supervision if the personal representative had not been granted authority to administer the estate under this part and the personal representative has notice of a written objection made under Section 10587 to the proposed action or a restraining order issued under Section 10588, the personal representative shall, if the personal representative desires to take the proposed action, take the proposed action under the provisions of this code dealing with court supervision of that kind of action.

(b) If the proposed action is one that would not require court supervision even if the personal representative had not been granted authority to administer the estate under this part but the personal representative has notice of the proposed action and has notice of a written objection made under Section 10587 to the proposed action or a restraining order issued under Section 10588, the personal representative shall, if he or she desires to take the proposed action, request instructions from the court concerning the proposed action. The personal representative may take the proposed action only under such order as may be entered by the court.

(c) A person who objects to a proposed action as provided in Section 10587 or serves a restraining order issued under Section 10588 in the manner provided in that section shall be given notice of any hearing on a petition for court authorization or confirmation of the proposed action.

10590. (a) Except as provided in subdivision (c), only a person described in Section 10581 has a right to have the court review the proposed action after it has been taken or otherwise to object to the proposed action after it has been taken. Except as provided in subdivisions (b) and (c), a person described in Section 10581 waives the right to have the court review the proposed action after it has been taken, or otherwise to object to the proposed action after it has been taken, if either of the following circumstances exists:

(1) The person has been given notice of a proposed action, as provided in Sections

10580 to 10586, inclusive, and fails to object as provided in subdivision (d).

(2) The person has waived notice of or consented to the proposed action as provided in Sections 10582 to 10584, inclusive.

(b) Unless the person has waived notice of or consented to the proposed action as provided in Sections 10582 to 10584, inclusive, the court may review the action taken upon motion of a person described in Section 10581 who establishes that he or she did not actually receive the notice of proposed action before the time to object under subdivision (d) expires.

(c) The court may review the action of the personal representative upon motion of an heir or devisee who establishes all of the following:

(1) At the time the notice was given, the heir or devisee lacked capacity to object to the proposed action or was a minor.

(2) No notice of proposed action was actually received by the guardian, conservator, or other legal representative of the heir or devisee.

(3) The guardian, conservator, or other legal representative did not waive notice of proposed action.

(4) The guardian, conservator, or other legal representative did not consent to the proposed action.

(d) For the purposes of this section, an objection to a proposed action is made only by one or both of the following methods:

(1) Delivering or mailing a written objection as provided in Section 10587 within the time specified in subdivision (c) of that section.

(2) Serving a restraining order obtained under Section 10588 in the manner prescribed and within the time specified in subdivision (b) of that section.

10591. (a) The failure of the personal representative to comply with subdivision (a) of Section 10580 and with Sections 10581, 10585, 10586, and 10589, and the taking of the action by the personal representative without such compliance, does not affect the validity of the action so taken or the title to any property conveyed or transferred to bona fide purchasers or the rights of third persons who, dealing in good faith with the personal representative, changed their position in reliance upon the action, conveyance, or transfer without actual notice of the failure of the personal representative to comply with those provisions.

(b) No person dealing with the personal representative has any duty to inquire or investigate whether or not the personal representative has complied with the provisions listed in subdivision (a).

10592. (a) In a case where notice of proposed action is required by this chapter, the court in its discretion may remove the personal representative from office unless the personal representative does one of the following:

(1) Gives notice of proposed action as provided in this chapter.

(2) Obtains a waiver of notice of proposed action as provided in this chapter.

(3) Obtains a consent to the proposed action as provided in this chapter.

(b) The court in its discretion may remove the personal representative from office if the personal representative takes a proposed action in violation of Section 10589.

Part 7. Compensation Of Personal Representative And Attorney For The Personal Representative

Chapter 1. Amount Of Compensation

Article 1. Compensation Of Personal Representative

10800. (a) Subject to the provisions of this part, for ordinary services the personal representative shall receive compensation based on the value of the estate accounted for by the personal representative, as follows

(1) Four percent on the first one hundred thousand dollars ($100,000).

(2) Three percent on the next one hundred thousand dollars ($100,000).

(3) Two percent on the next eight hundred thousand dollars ($800,000).

(4) One percent on the next nine million dollars ($9,000,000).

(5) One-half of one percent on the next fifteen million dollars ($15,000,000).

(6) For all amounts above twenty-five million dollars ($25,000,000), a reasonable amount to be determined by the court.

(b) For the purposes of this section, the value of the estate accounted for by the personal representative is the total amount of the appraisal value of property in the inventory, plus gains over the appraisal value on sales, plus receipts, less losses from the appraisal value on sales, without reference to encumbrances or other obligations on estate property.

10801. (a) Subject to the provisions of this part, in addition to the compensation provided by Section 10800, the court may allow additional compensation for extraordinary services by the personal representative in an amount the court determines is just and reasonable.

(b) The personal representative may also employ or retain tax counsel, tax auditors, accountants, or other tax experts for the performance of any action which such persons, respectively, may lawfully perform in the computation, reporting, or making of tax returns, or in negotiations or litigation which may be necessary for the final determination and payment of taxes, and pay from the funds of the estate for such services.

10802. (a) Except as otherwise provided in this section, if the decedent's will makes provision for the compensation of the personal representative, the compensation provided by the will shall be the full and only compensation for the services of the personal representative.

(b) The personal representative may petition the court to be relieved from a provision of the will that provides for the compensation of the personal representative.

(c) Notice of the hearing on the petition shall be given as provided in Section 1220 to all of the following persons:

(1) Each person listed in Section 1220.

(2) Each known heir whose interest in the estate would be affected by the petition.

(3) Each known devisee whose interest in the estate would be affected by the petition.

(4) The Attorney General, at the office of the Attorney General in Sacramento, if any portion of the estate is to escheat to the state and its interest in the estate would be affected by the petition.

(d) If the court determines that it is to the advantage of the estate and in the best interest of the persons interested in the estate, the court may make an order authorizing compensation for the personal representative in an amount greater than provided in the will.

10803. An agreement between the personal representative and an heir or devisee for higher compensation than that provided by this part is void.

10804. Notwithstanding any provision in the decedent's will, a personal representative who is an attorney shall be entitled to receive the personal representative's compensation as provided in this part, but shall not receive compensation for services as the attorney for the personal representative unless the court specifically approves the right to the compensation in advance and finds that the arrangement is to the advantage, benefit, and best interests of the decedent's estate.

10805. If there are two or more personal representatives, the personal representative's compensation shall be apportioned among the personal representatives by the court according to the services actually rendered by each personal representative or as agreed to by the personal representatives.

Article 2. Compensation Of Attorney For The Personal Representative

10810. (a) Subject to the provisions of this part, for ordinary services the attorney for the personal representative shall receive compensation based on the value of the estate accounted for by the personal representative, as follows:

(1) Four percent on the first one hundred thousand dollars ($100,000).

(2) Three percent on the next one hundred thousand dollars ($100,000).

(3) Two percent on the next eight hundred thousand dollars ($800,000).

(4) One percent on the next nine million dollars ($9,000,000).

(5) One-half of 1 percent on the next fifteen million dollars ($15,000,000).

(6) For all amounts above twenty-five million dollars ($25,000,000), a reasonable amount to be determined by the court.

(b) For the purposes of this section, the value of the estate accounted for by the personal representative is the total amount of the appraisal of property in the inventory, plus gains over the appraisal value on sales, plus receipts, less losses from the appraisal value on sales, without reference to encumbrances or other obligations on estate property.

10811. (a) Subject to the provisions of this part, in addition to the compensation provided by Section 10810, the court may allow additional compensation for extraordinary services by the attorney for the personal representative in an amount the court determines is just and reasonable.

(b) Extraordinary services by the attorney for which the court may allow compensation include services by a paralegal performing the extraordinary services under the direction and supervision of an attorney. The petition for compensation shall set forth the hours spent and services performed by the paralegal.

(c) An attorney for the personal representative may agree to perform extraordinary service on a contingent fee basis subject to the following conditions:

(1) The agreement is written and complies with all the requirements of Section 6147 of the Business and Professions Code.

(2) The agreement is approved by the court following a hearing noticed as provided in Section 10812.

(3) The court determines that the compensation provided in the agreement is just and reasonable and the agreement is to the advantage of the estate and in the best interests of the persons who are interested in the estate.

10812. (a) Except as otherwise provided in this section, if the decedent's will makes provision for the compensation of the attorney for the personal representative, the compensation provided by the will shall be the full and only compensation for the services of the attorney for the personal representative.

(b) The personal representative or the attorney for the personal representative may petition the court to be relieved from a provision of the will that provides for the compensation of the attorney for the personal representative.

(c) Notice of the hearing on the petition

shall be given as provided in Section 1220 to all of the following persons:

(1) Each person listed in Section 1220.

(2) Each known heir whose interest in the estate would be affected by the petition.

(3) Each known devisee whose interest in the estate would be affected by the petition.

(4) The Attorney General, at the office of the Attorney General in Sacramento, if any portion of the estate is to escheat to the state and its interest in the estate would be affected by the petition.

(5) If the court determines that it is to the advantage of the estate and in the best interest of the persons interested in the estate, the court may make an order authorizing compensation of the attorney for the personal representative in an amount greater than provided in the will.

10813. An agreement between the personal representative and the attorney for higher compensation for the attorney than that provided by this part is void.

10814. If there are two or more attorneys for the personal representative, the attorney's compensation shall be apportioned among the attorneys by the court according to the services actually rendered by each attorney or as agreed to by the attorneys.

Chapter 2. Allowance Of Compensation By Court

10830. (a) At any time after four months from the issuance of letters:

(1) The personal representative may file a petition requesting an allowance on the compensation of the personal representative.

(2) The personal representative or the attorney for the personal representative may file a petition requesting an allowance on the compensation of the attorney for the personal representative.

(b) Notice of the hearing on the petition shall be given as provided in Section 1220 to all of the following:

(1) Each person listed in Section 1220.

(2) Each known heir whose interest in the estate would be affected by the payment of the compensation.

(3) Each known devisee whose interest in the estate would be affected by the payment of the compensation.

(4) The Attorney General, at the office of the Attorney General in Sacramento, if any portion of the estate is to escheat to the state and its interest in the estate would be affected by the petition.

(c) On the hearing, the court may make an order allowing the portion of the compensation of the personal representative or the attorney for the personal representative, as the case may be, on account of services rendered up to that time, that the court determines is proper. The order shall authorize the personal representative to charge against the estate the amount allowed.

10831. (a) At the time of the filing of the final account and petition for an order for final distribution:

(1) The personal representative may petition the court for an order fixing and allowing the personal representative's compensation for all services rendered in the estate proceeding.

(2) The personal representative or the attorney for the personal representative may petition the court for an order fixing and allowing the compensation, of the attorney for all services rendered in the estate proceeding.

(b) The request for compensation may be included in the final account or the petition for final distribution or may be made in a separate petition.

(c) Notice of the hearing on the petition shall be given as provided in Section 1220 to all of the following:

(1) Each person listed in Section 1220.

(2) Each known heir whose interest in the estate would be affected by the payment of the compensation.

(3) Each known devisee whose interest in the estate would be affected by the payment of the compensation.

(4) The Attorney General, at the office of the Attorney General in Sacramento, if any portion of the estate is to escheat to the state and its interest in the estate would be affected by the petition.

(d) On the hearing, the court shall make an order fixing and allowing the compensation for all services rendered in the estate proceeding. In the case of an allowance to the personal representative, the order shall authorize the personal representative to charge against the estate the amount allowed, less any amount previously charged against the estate pursuant to Section 10830. In the case of the attorney's compensation the order shall require the personal representative to pay the attorney out of the estate the amount allowed, less any amount paid to the attorney out of the estate pursuant to Section 10830.

10832. Notwithstanding Sections 10830 and 10831, the court may allow compensation to the personal representative or to the attorney for the personal representative for extraordinary services before final distribution when any of the following requirements is satisfied:

(a) It appears likely that administration of the estate will continue, whether due to litigation or otherwise, for an unusually long time.

(b) Present payment will benefit the estate or the beneficiaries of the estate.

(c) Other good cause is shown.

Chapter 3. Application Of Part

10850. (a) This part does not apply in any proceeding for administration of a decedent's estate commenced before July 1, 1991.

(b) Notwithstanding its repeal, the applicable law in effect before July 1, 1991, governing the subject matter of this part continues to apply in any proceeding for administration of a decedent' s estate commenced before July 1, 1991.

Part 8. Accounts

Chapter 1. General Provisions

10900. (a) An account shall include both a financial statement and a report of administration as provided in Chapter 4 (commencing with Section 1060) of Part 1 of Division 3, and this section.

(b) The statement of liabilities in the report of administration shall include the following information:

(1) Whether notice to creditors was given under Section 9050.

(2) Creditor claims filed, including the date of filing the claim, the name of the claimant, the amount of the claim, and the action taken on the claim.

(3) Creditor claims not paid, satisfied, or adequately provided for. As to each such claim, the statement shall indicate whether the claim is due and the date due, the date any notice of rejection was given, and whether the creditor has brought an action on the claim. The statement shall identify any real or personal property that is security for the claim, whether by mortgage, deed of trust, lien, or other encumbrance.

(c) The amendments to this section made by Assembly Bill 2751 of the 1995-96 Regular Session shall become operative on July 1, 1997.

10901. On court order, or on request by an interested person filed with the clerk and a copy served on the personal representative, the personal representative shall produce for inspection and audit by the court or interested person the documents specified in the order or request that support an account.

10902. When a personal representative receives assets from the conservator of a deceased conservatee or the guardian of a deceased ward, the personal representative may incorporate by reference any accounting provided by the conservator or guardian for the decedent for the period subsequent to the date of death, and the personal representative is entitled to rely on the accounting by such other fiduciary, and shall not have a duty to independently investigate or verify the transactions reported in such an account.

Chapter 2. When Account Required

10950. (a) On its own motion or on petition of an interested person, the court may order an account at any time.

(b) The court shall order an account on petition of an interested person made more than one year after the last account was filed or, if no previous account has been filed, made more than one year after issuance of letters to the personal representative.

(c) The court order shall specify the time within which the personal representative must file an account.

10951. The personal representative shall file a final account and petition for an order for final distribution of the estate when the estate is in a condition to be closed.

10952. A personal representative who resigns or is removed from office or whose authority is otherwise terminated shall, unless the court extends the time, file an account not later than 60 days after termination of authority. If the personal representative fails to so file the account, the court may compel the account pursuant to Chapter 4 (commencing with Section 11050).

10953. (a) As used in this section:

(1) "Incapacitated" means lack of capacity to serve as personal representative.

(2) "Legal representative" means the personal representative of a deceased personal representative or the conservator of the estate of an incapacitated personal representative.

(b) If a personal representative dies or becomes incapacitated and a legal representative is appointed for the deceased or incapacitated personal representative, the legal representative shall not later than 60 days after appointment, unless the court extends the time, file an account of the administration of the deceased or incapacitated personal representative.

(c) If a personal representative dies or becomes incapacitated and no legal representative is appointed for the deceased or incapacitated personal representative, or if the personal representative absconds, the court may compel the attorney for the deceased, incapacitated, or absconding personal representative or attorney of record in the estate proceeding to file an account of the administration of the deceased, incapacitated, or absconding personal representative.

(d) The legal representative or attorney shall exercise reasonable diligence in preparing an account under this section. Verification of the account may be made on information and belief. The court shall settle the account as in other cases. The court shall allow reasonable compensation to the legal representative or the attorney for preparing the account. The amount allowed is a charge against the estate that was being administered by the deceased, incapacitated, or absconding personal representative. Legal services for which compensation shall be allowed to the attorney under this subdivision include those services rendered by any paralegal performing the services under the direction and supervision of an attorney. The petition or application for compensation shall set forth the hours spent and services performed by the paralegal.

10954. (a) Notwithstanding any other provision of this part, the personal representative is not required to file an account if any of the following conditions is satisfied as to each person entitled to distribution from the estate:

(1) The person has executed and filed a written waiver of account or a written acknowledgment that the person's interest has been satisfied.

(2) Adequate provision has been made for satisfaction in full of the person's interest. This paragraph does not apply to a residuary devisee or a devisee whose interest in the estate is subject to abatement, payment of expenses, or accrual of interest or income.

(b) A waiver or acknowledgment under subdivision (a) shall be executed as follows:

(1) If the person entitled to distribution is an adult and competent, by that person.

(2) If the person entitled to distribution is a minor, by a person authorized to receive money or property belonging to the minor. If the waiver or acknowledgment is executed by a guardian of the estate of the minor, the waiver or acknowledgment may be executed without the need to obtain approval of the court in which the guardianship proceeding is pending.

(3) If the person entitled to distribution is a conservatee, by the conservator of the estate of the conservatee. The waiver or acknowledgment may be executed without the need to obtain approval of the court in which the conservatorship proceeding is pending.

(4) If the person entitled to distribution is a trust, by the trustee, but only if the named trustee's written acceptance of the trust is filed with the court. In the case of a trust that is subject to the continuing jurisdiction of the court pursuant to Chapter 4 (commencing with Section 17300) of Part 5 of Division 9, the waiver or acknowledgment may be executed without the need to obtain approval of the court.

(5) If the person entitled to distribution is an estate, by the personal representative of the estate. The waiver or acknowledgment may be executed without the need to obtain approval of the court in which the estate is being administered.

(6) If the person entitled to distribution is incapacitated, unborn, unascertained, or is a person whose identity or address is unknown, or is a designated class of persons who are not ascertained or are not in being, and there is a guardian ad litem appointed to represent the person entitled to distribution, by the guardian ad litem.

(7) If the person entitled to distribution has designated an attorney in fact who has the power under the power of attorney to execute the waiver or acknowledgment, by either of the following:

(A) The person entitled to distribution if an adult and competent.

(B) The attorney in fact.

(c) Notwithstanding subdivision (a):

(1) The personal representative shall file a final report of administration at the time the final account would otherwise have been required. The final report shall include the amount of compensation paid or payable to the personal representative and to the attorney for the personal representative and shall set forth the basis for determining the amounts.

(2) A creditor whose interest has not been satisfied may petition under Section 10950 for an account.

Chapter 3. Settlement Of Account

11000. (a) The personal representative shall give notice of the hearing as provided in Section 1220 to all of the following persons:

(1) Each person listed in Section 1220.

(2) Each known heir whose interest in the estate would be affected by the account.

(3) Each known devisee whose interest in the estate would be affected by the account.

(4) The Attorney General, at the office of the Attorney General in Sacramento, if any portion of the estate is to escheat to the state and its interest would be affected by the account.

(5) If the estate is insolvent, each creditor who has filed a claim that is allowed or approved but is unpaid in whole or in part.

(b) If the petition for approval of the account requests allowance of all or a portion of the compensation of the personal representative or the attorney for the personal representative, the notice of hearing shall so state.

(c) If the account is a final account and is filed together with a petition for an order for final distribution of the estate, the notice of hearing shall so state.

11001. All matters relating to an account may be contested for cause shown, including, but not limited to:

(a) The validity of an allowed or approved claim not reported in a previous account and not established by judgment.

(b) The value of property for purposes of distribution.

(c) Actions taken by the personal representative not previously authorized or approved by the court, subject to Section 10590 (Independent Administration of Estates Act).

11002. (a) The court may conduct any hearing that may be necessary to settle the account, and may cite the personal representative to appear before the court for examination.

(b) The court may appoint one or more referees to examine the account and make a report on the account, subject to confirmation by the court. The court may allow a reasonable compensation to the referee to be paid out of the estate.

(c) The court may make any orders that the court deems necessary to effectuate the provisions of this section.

11003. (a) If the court determines that the contest was without reasonable cause and in bad faith, the court may award against the contestant the compensation and costs of the personal representative and other expenses and costs of litigation, including attorney's fees, incurred to defend the account. The amount awarded is a charge against any interest of the contestant in the estate and the contestant is personally liable for any amount that remains unsatisfied.

(b) If the court determines that the opposition to the contest was without reasonable cause and in bad faith, the court may award the contestant the costs of the contestant and other expenses and costs of litigation, including attorney's fees, incurred to contest the account. The amount awarded is a charge against the compensation or other interest of the personal representative in the estate and the personal representative is liable personally and on the bond, if any, for any amount that remains unsatisfied.

11004. The personal representative shall be allowed all necessary expenses in the administration of the estate, including, but not limited to, necessary expenses in the care, management, preservation, and settlement of the estate.

11005. If a debt has been paid within the time prescribed in Section 9154 but without a claim having been filed and established in the manner prescribed by statute, in settling the account the court shall allow the amount paid if all of the following are proven:

(a) The debt was justly due.

(b) The debt was paid in good faith.

(c) The amount paid did not exceed the amount reasonably necessary to satisfy the indebtedness.

(d) The estate is solvent.

Chapter 4. Compelling Account

11050. Subject to the provisions of this chapter, if the personal representative does not file a required account, the court shall compel the account by punishment for contempt.

11051. (a) A citation shall be issued, served, and returned, requiring a personal representative who does not file a required account to appear and show cause why the personal representative should not be punished for contempt.

(b) If the personal representative purposefully evades personal service of the citation, the personal representative shall be removed from office.

11052. If the personal representative does not appear and file a required account, after

having been duly cited, the personal representative may be punished for contempt or removed from office, or both, in the discretion of the court.

Part 9. Payment Of Debts

Chapter 1. Definitions And Preliminary Provisions

Article 1. Definitions

11400. Unless the provision or context otherwise requires, the definitions in this article govern the construction of this part.

11401. "Debt" means:

(a) A claim that is established under Part 4 (commencing with Section 9000) or that is otherwise payable in the course of administration.

(b) An expense of administration.

(c) A charge against the estate including, but not limited to, taxes, expenses of last illness, and family allowance.

11402. "Wage claim" means a claim for wages, not exceeding two thousand dollars ($2,000), of each employee of the decedent for work done or personal services rendered within 90 days before the death of the decedent.

Article 2. Proceedings Commenced Before July 1, 1988

11405. (a) This part does not apply in any proceeding for the administration of a decedent's estate commenced before July 1, 1988.

(b) The applicable law in effect before July 1, 1988, governing the subject matter of this part continues to apply in any proceeding for administration of a decedent's estate commenced before July 1, 1988, notwithstanding its repeal by Chapter 923 of the Statutes of 1987.

Chapter 2. General Provisions

11420. (a) Debts shall be paid in the following order of priority among classes of debts, except that debts owed to the United States or to this state that have preference under the laws of the United States or of this state shall be given the preference required by such laws:

(1) Expenses of administration. With respect to obligations secured by mortgage, deed of trust, or other lien, including, but not limited to, a judgment lien, only those expenses of administration incurred that are reasonably related to the administration of that property by which obligations are secured shall be given priority over these obligations.

(2) Obligations secured by a mortgage, deed of trust, or other lien, including, but not limited to, a judgment lien, in the order of their priority, so far as they may be paid out of the proceeds of the property subject to

the lien. If the proceeds are insufficient, the part of the obligation remaining unsatisfied shall be classed with general debts.

(3) Funeral expenses.

(4) Expenses of last illness.

(5) Family allowance.

(6) Wage claims.

(7) General debts, including judgments not secured by a lien and all other debts not included in a prior class.

(b) Except as otherwise provided by statute, the debts of each class are without preference or priority one over another. No debt of any class may be paid until all those of prior classes are paid in full. If property in the estate is insufficient to pay all debts of any class in full, each debt in that class shall be paid a proportionate share.

11421. Subject to Section 11420, as soon as the personal representative has sufficient funds, after retaining sufficient funds to pay expenses of administration, the personal representative shall pay the following:

(a) Funeral expenses.

(b) Expenses of last illness.

(c) Family allowance.

(d) Wage claims.

11422. (a) Except as provided in Section 11421, the personal representative is not required to pay a debt until payment has been ordered by the court.

(b) On the settlement of any account of the personal representative after the expiration of four months after the date letters are first issued to a general personal representative, the court shall order payment of debts, as the circumstances of the estate permit. If property in the estate is insufficient to pay all of the debts, the order shall specify the amount to be paid to each creditor.

(c) If the estate will be exhausted by the payment ordered, the account of the personal representative constitutes a final account, and notice of hearing shall be the notice given for the hearing of a final account. The personal representative is entitled to a discharge when the personal representative has complied with the terms of the order.

(d) Nothing in this section precludes settlement of an account of a personal representative for payment of a debt made without prior court authorization.

11423. (a) Interest accrues on a debt from the date the court orders payment of the debt until the date the debt is paid. Interest accrues at the legal rate on judgments.

(b) Notwithstanding subdivision (a), in the case of a debt based on a written contract, interest accrues at the rate and in accordance with the terms of the contract. The personal representative may, by order of the court, pay all or part of the interest accumulated and unpaid at any time when there are sufficient funds, whether the debt is then due or not.

(c) Notwithstanding subdivision (a), in the case of a debt for unpaid taxes or any other debt for which interest is expressly provided by statute, interest accrues at the rate and in accordance with the terms of the statute.

11424. The personal representative shall pay a debt to the extent of the order for payment of the debt, and is liable personally and on the bond, if any, for failure to make the payment.

11428. (a) If an estate is in all other respects ready to be closed, and it appears to the satisfaction of the court, on affidavit or evidence taken in open court, that a debt has not been and cannot be paid because the creditor cannot be found, the court or judge shall make an order fixing the amount of the payment and directing the personal representative to deposit the payment with the county treasurer of the county in which the proceeding is pending.

(b) The county treasurer shall give a receipt for the deposit, for which the county treasurer is liable on the official bond. The receipt shall be treated by the court or judge in favor of the personal representative with the same force and effect as if executed by the creditor.

(c) A deposit with the county treasurer under the provisions of this section shall be received, accounted for, and disposed of as provided by Section 1444 of the Code of Civil Procedure. A deposit in the State Treasury under the provisions of this section shall be deemed to be made under the provisions of Article 1 (commencing with Section 1440) of Chapter 6 of Title 10 of Part 3 of the Code of Civil Procedure.

11429. (a) Where the accounts of the personal representative have been settled and an order made for the payment of debts and distribution of the estate, a creditor who is not paid, whether or not included in the order for payment, has no right to require contribution from creditors who are paid or from distributees, except to the extent provided in Section 9392.

(b) Nothing in this section precludes recovery against the personal representative personally or on the bond, if any, by a creditor who is not paid, subject to Section 9053.

Chapter 3. Allocation Of Debts Between Estate And Surviving Spouse

11440. If it appears that a debt of the decedent has been paid or is payable in whole or in part by the surviving spouse, or that a debt of the surviving spouse has been paid or is payable in whole or in part from property in the decedent's estate, the personal representative, the surviving spouse, or a beneficiary may, at any time before an order for final distribution is made, petition for an order to allocate the debt.

11441. The petition shall include a statement of all of the following:

(a) All debts of the decedent and surviving spouse known to the petitioner that are alleged to be subject to allocation and whether paid in whole or part or unpaid.

(b) The reason why the debts should be allocated.

(c) The proposed allocation and the basis for allocation alleged by the petitioner.

11442. If it appears from the petition that allocation would be affected by the value of the separate property of the surviving spouse and any community property and quasi-community property not administered in the estate and if an inventory and appraisal of the property has not been provided by the surviving spouse, the court shall make an order to show cause why the information should not be provided.

11443. The petitioner shall give notice of the hearing as provided in Section 1220, together with a copy of the petition and the order to show cause, if any.

11444. (a) The personal representative and the surviving spouse may provide for allocation by agreement and, on a determination by the court that the agreement substantially protects the rights of interested persons, the allocation provided in the agreement shall be ordered by the court.

(b) In the absence of an agreement, each debt subject to allocation shall first be characterized by the court as separate or community, in accordance with the laws of the state applicable to marital dissolution proceedings. Following that characterization, the debt or debts shall be allocated as follows:

(1) Separate debts of either spouse shall be allocated to that spouse's separate property assets, and community debts shall be allocated to the spouses' community property assets.

(2) If a separate property asset of either spouse is subject to a secured debt that is characterized as that spouse's separate debt, and the net equity in that asset available to satisfy that secured debt is less than that secured debt, the unsatisfied portion of that secured debt shall be treated as an unsecured separate debt of that spouse and allocated to the net value of that spouse's other separate property assets.

(3) If the net value of either spouse's separate property assets is less than that spouse's unsecured separate debt or debts, the unsatisfied portion of the debt or debts shall be allocated to the net value of that spouse's one-half share of the community property assets. If the net value of that spouse's one-half share of the community property assets is less than that spouse's unsatisfied unsecured separate debt or debts, the remaining unsatisfied portion of the debt or debts shall be allocated to the net value of the other spouse's one-half share of the community property assets.

(4) If a community property asset is subject to a secured debt that is characterized as a community debt, and the net equity in that asset available to satisfy that secured debt is less than that secured debt, the unsatisfied portion of that secured debt shall be treated as an unsecured community debt and allocated to the net value of the other community property assets.

(5) If the net value of the community property assets is less than the unsecured community debt or debts, the unsatisfied portion of the debt or debts shall be allocated equally between the separate property assets of the decedent and the surviving spouse. If the net value of either spouse's separate property assets is less than that spouse's share of the unsatisfied portion of the unsecured community debt or debts, the remaining unsatisfied portion of the debt or debts shall be allocated to the net value of the other spouse's separate property assets.

(c) For purposes of this section:

(1) The net value of either spouse's separate property asset shall refer to its fair market value as of the date of the decedent's death, minus the date-of-death balance of any liens and encumbrances on that asset that have been characterized as that spouse's separate debts.

(2) The net value of a community property asset shall refer to its fair market value as of the date of the decedent's death, minus the date-of-death balance of any liens and encumbrances on that asset that have been characterized as community debts.

(3) In the case of a nonrecourse debt, the amount of that debt shall be limited to the net equity in the collateral, based on the fair market value of the collateral as of the date of the decedent's death, that is available to satisfy that debt. For the purposes of this paragraph, "nonrecourse debt" means a debt for which the debtor's obligation to repay is limited to the collateral securing the debt, and for which a deficiency judgment against the debtor is not permitted by law.

(d) Notwithstanding the foregoing provisions of this section, the court may order a different allocation of debts between the decedent's estate and the surviving spouse if the court finds a different allocation to be equitable under the circumstances.

(e) Nothing contained in this section is intended to impair or affect the rights of third parties. If a personal representative or the surviving spouse incurs any damages or expense, including attorney's fees, on account of the nonpayment of a debt that was allocated to the other party pursuant to subdivision (b), or as the result of a debt being misallocated due to fraud or intentional misrepresentation by the other party, the party incurring damages shall be entitled to recover from the other party for damages or expense deemed reasonable by the court that made the allocation.

11445. On making a determination as provided in this chapter, the court shall make an order that:

(a) Directs the personal representative to make payment of the amounts allocated to the estate by payment to the surviving spouse or creditors.

(b) Directs the personal representative to charge amounts allocated to the surviving spouse against any property or interests of the surviving spouse that are in the possession or control of the personal representative. To the extent that property or interests of the surviving spouse in the possession or control of the personal representative are insufficient to satisfy the allocation, the court order shall summarily direct the surviving spouse to pay the allocation to the personal representative.

11446. Notwithstanding any other statute, funeral expenses and expenses of last illness shall be charged against the estate of the decedent and shall not be allocated to, or charged against the community share of, the surviving spouse, whether or not the surviving spouse is financially able to pay the expenses and whether or not the surviving spouse or any other person is also liable for the expenses.

Chapter 4. Debts That Are Contingent, Disputed, Or Not Due

11460. As used in this chapter:

(a) A debt is "contingent" if it is established under Part 4 (commencing with Section 9000) in either a fixed or an uncertain amount and will become absolute on occurrence of a stated event other than the passage of time. The term includes a secured obligation for which there may be recourse against property in the estate, other than the property that is the security, if the security is insufficient.

(b) A debt is "disputed" if it is a claim rejected in whole or in part under Part 4 (commencing with Section 9000) and is not barred under Section 9353 as to the part rejected.

(c) A debt is "not due" if it is established under Part 4 (commencing with Section 9000) and will become due on the passage of time. The term includes a debt payable in installments.

11461. When all other debts have been paid and the estate is otherwise in a condition to be closed, on petition by an interested person, the court may make or modify an order or a combination of orders under this chapter that the court in its discretion determines is appropriate to provide adequately for a debt that is contingent, disputed, or not due, if the debt becomes absolute, established, or due. Notice of the hearing on the petition shall be given as provided in Section 1220 to the creditor whose debt is contingent, disputed, or not due, as well as to the persons provided in Section 11601.

11462. Notwithstanding any other provision of this chapter, if the court determines that all interested persons agree to the manner of providing for a debt that is contingent, disputed, or not due and that the agreement reasonably protects all interested persons and will not extend administration of the estate unreasonably, the court shall approve the agreement.

11463. The court may order an amount deposited in a financial institution, as provided in Chapter 3 (commencing with Section 9700) of Part 5, that would be payable if a debt that is contingent, disputed, or not due, were absolute, established, or due. The order shall provide that the amount deposited is subject to withdrawal only upon authorization of the court, to be paid to the creditor when the debt becomes absolute, established, or due, or to be distributed in the manner provided in Section 11642 if the debt does not become absolute or established.

11464. (a) The court may order property in the estate distributed to a person entitled to it under the final order for distribution, if the person files with the court an assumption of liability for a contingent or disputed debt as provided in subdivision (b). The court may impose any other conditions the court in its discretion determines are just, including that the distributee give a security interest in all or part of the property distributed or that the distributee give a bond in an amount determined by the court.

(b) As a condition for an order under subdivision (a), each distributee shall file with the court a signed and acknowledged agreement assuming personal liability for the contingent or disputed debt and consenting to jurisdiction within this state for the enforcement of the debt if it becomes absolute or established. The personal liability of each distributee shall not exceed the fair market value on the date of distribution of the property received by the distributee, less the amount of liens and encumbrances. If there is more than one distributee, the personal liability of the distributees is joint and several.

(c) If the debt becomes absolute or established, it may be enforced against each distributee in the same manner as it could have been enforced against the decedent if the decedent had not died. In an action based on the debt, the distributee may assert any defense, cross-complaint, or setoff that would have been available to the decedent if the decedent had not died.

(d) The statute of limitations applicable to a contingent debt is tolled from the time the creditor's claim is filed until 30 days after the order for distribution becomes final. The signing of an agreement under subdivision (b) neither extends nor revives any limitation period.

11465. (a) The court may order that a trustee be appointed to receive payment for a debt that is contingent, disputed, or not due. The court in determining the amount paid to the trustee shall compute the present value of the debt, giving consideration to a reasonable return on the amount to be invested. The trustee shall invest the payment in investments that would be proper for a personal representative or as authorized in the order.

(b) The trustee shall pay the debt as provided in the order. On completion of payment, any excess in possession of the trustee shall be distributed in the manner provided in Section 11642.

11466. The court may order property in the estate distributed to a person entitled to it under the final order for distribution, if the person gives a bond conditioned on payment by the person of the amount of a contingent or disputed debt that becomes absolute or established. The amount of the bond shall be determined by the court, not to exceed the fair market value on the date of distribution of the property received by the distributee, less the amount of liens and encumbrances. In the case of a disputed debt or in the case of a contingent debt where litigation is required to establish the contingency, the cost of the bond is recoverable from the unsuccessful party as a cost of litigation.

11467. The court may order that the administration of the estate continue until the contingency, dispute, or passage of time of a debt that is contingent, disputed, or not due is resolved.

Part 10. Distribution Of Estate

Chapter 1. Order For Distribution

Article 1. General Provisions

11600. The personal representative or an interested person may petition the court under this chapter for an order for preliminary or final distribution of the decedent's estate to the persons entitled thereto.

11601. Notice of the hearing on the petition shall be given as provided in Section 1220 to all of the following persons:

(a) Each person listed in Section 1220.

(b) Each known heir whose interest in the estate would be affected by the petition.

(c) Each known devisee whose interest in the estate would be affected by the petition.

(d) The Attorney General, at the office of the Attorney General in Sacramento, if any portion of the estate is to escheat to the state and its interest in the estate would be affected by the petition.

(e) The Controller, if property is to be distributed to the state because there is no known beneficiary or if property is to be distributed to a beneficiary whose whereabouts is unknown. A copy of the latest account filed with the court shall be served on the Controller with the notice.

11602. The personal representative or any interested person may oppose the petition.

11603. (a) If the court determines that the requirements for distribution are satisfied, the court shall order distribution of the decedent's estate, or such portion as the court directs, to the persons entitled thereto.

(b) The order shall:

(1) Name the distributees and the share to which each is entitled.

(2) Provide that property distributed subject to a limitation or condition, including, but not limited to, an option granted under Chapter 16 (commencing with Section 9960) of Part 5, is distributed to the distributees subject to the terms of the limitation or condition.

(c) If the whereabouts of a distributee named in the order is unknown, the order shall provide for alternate distributees and the share to which each is entitled. The alternate distributees shall be the persons, to the extent known or reasonably ascertainable, who would be entitled under the decedent's will or under the laws of intestate succession if the distributee named in the order had predeceased the decedent, or in the case of a devise for a charitable purpose, under the doctrine of cy pres. If the distributee named in the order does not claim the share to which the distributee is entitled within five years after the date of the order, the distributee is deemed to have predeceased the decedent for the purpose of this section and the alternate distributees are entitled to the share as provided in the order.

11604. (a) This section applies where distribution is to be made to any of the following persons:

(1) The transferee of a beneficiary.

(2) Any person other than a beneficiary under an agreement, request, or instructions of a beneficiary or the attorney in fact of a beneficiary.

(b) The court on its own motion, or on motion of the personal representative or other interested person or of the public administrator, may inquire into the circumstances surrounding the execution of, and the consideration for, the transfer, agreement, request, or instructions, and the amount of any fees, charges, or consideration paid or agreed to be paid by the beneficiary.

(c) The court may refuse to order distribution, or may order distribution on any terms that the court deems just and equitable, if the court finds either of the following:

(1) The fees, charges, or consideration paid or agreed to be paid by a beneficiary are grossly unreasonable.

(2) The transfer, agreement, request, or instructions were obtained by duress, fraud, or undue influence.

(d) Notice of the hearing on the motion

shall be served on the beneficiary and on the persons described in subdivision (a) at least 15 days before the hearing in the manner provided in Section 415.10 or 415.30 of the Code of Civil Procedure.

11604.5. (a) This section applies when distribution from a decedent' s estate is made to a transferee for value who acquires any interest of a beneficiary in exchange for cash or other consideration.

(b) For purposes of this section, a transferee for value is a person who satisfies both of the following criteria:

(1) He or she purchases the interest from a beneficiary for consideration pursuant to a written agreement.

(2) He or she, directly or indirectly, regularly engages in the purchase of beneficial interests in estates for consideration.

(c) This section does not apply to any of the following:

(1) A transferee who is a beneficiary of the estate or a person who has a claim to distribution from the estate under another instrument or by intestate succession.

(2) A transferee who is either the registered domestic partner of the beneficiary, or is related by blood, marriage, or adoption to the beneficiary or the decedent.

(3) A transaction made in conformity with the California Finance Lenders Law (Division 9 (commencing with Section 22000) of the Financial Code) and subject to regulation by the Department of Corporations.

(4) A transferee who is engaged in the business of locating missing or unknown heirs and who acquires an interest from a beneficiary solely in exchange for providing information or services associated with locating the heir or beneficiary.

(d) A written agreement is effective only if all of the following conditions are met:

(1) The executed written agreement is filed with the court not later than 30 days following the date of its execution or, if administration of the decedent's estate has not commenced, then within 30 days of issuance of the letters of administration or letters testamentary, but in no event later than 15 days prior to the hearing on the petition for final distribution. Prior to filing or serving that written agreement, the transferee for value shall redact any personally identifying information about the beneficiary, other than the name and address of the beneficiary, and any financial information provided by the beneficiary to the transferee for value on the application for cash or other consideration, from the agreement.

(2) If the negotiation or discussion between the beneficiary and the transferee for value leading to the execution of the written agreement by the beneficiary was conducted in a language other than English, the beneficiary shall receive the written agreement in English, together with a copy of the agreement translated into the language in which it was negotiated or discussed. The written agreement and the translated copy, if any, shall be provided to the beneficiary.

(3) The documents signed by, or provided to, the beneficiary are printed in at least 10-point type.

(4) The transferee for value executes a declaration or affidavit attesting that the requirements of this section have been satisfied, and the declaration or affidavit is filed with the court within 30 days of execution of the written agreement or, if administration of the decedent's estate has not commenced, then within 30 days of issuance of the letters of administration or letters testamentary, but in no event later than 15 days prior to the hearing on the petition for final distribution.

(5) Notice of the assignment is served on the personal representative or the attorney of record for the personal representative within 30 days of execution of the written agreement or, if general or special letters of administration or letters testamentary have not been issued, then within 30 days of issuance of the letters of administration or letters testamentary, but in no event later than 15 days prior to the hearing on the petition for final distribution.

(e) The written agreement shall include the following terms, in addition to any other terms:

(1) The amount of consideration paid to the beneficiary.

(2) A description of the transferred interest.

(3) If the written agreement so provides, the amount by which the transferee for value would have its distribution reduced if the beneficial interest assigned is distributed prior to a specified date.

(4) A statement of the total of all costs or fees charged to the beneficiary resulting from the transfer for value, including, but not limited to, transaction or processing fees, credit report costs, title search costs, due diligence fees, filing fees, bank or electronic transfer costs, or any other fees or costs. If all the costs and fees are paid by the transferee for value and are included in the amount of the transferred interest, then the statement of costs need not itemize any costs or fees. This subdivision shall not apply to costs, fees, or damages arising out of a material breach of the agreement or fraud by or on the part of the beneficiary.

(f) A written agreement shall not contain any of the following provisions and, if any such provision is included, that provision shall be null and void:

(1) A provision holding harmless the transferee for value, other than for liability arising out of fraud by the beneficiary.

(2) A provision granting to the transferee for value agency powers to represent the beneficiary's interest in the decedent's estate beyond the interest transferred.

(3) A provision requiring payment by the

beneficiary to the transferee for value for services not related to the written agreement or services other than the transfer of interest under the written agreement.

(4) A provision permitting the transferee for value to have recourse against the beneficiary if the distribution from the estate in satisfaction of the beneficial interest is less than the beneficial interest assigned to the transferee for value, other than recourse for any expense or damage arising out of the material breach of the agreement or fraud by the beneficiary.

(g) The court on its own motion, or on the motion of the personal representative or other interested person, may inquire into the circumstances surrounding the execution of, and the consideration for, the written agreement to determine that the requirements of this section have been satisfied.

(h) The court may refuse to order distribution under the written agreement, or may order distribution on any terms that the court considers equitable, if the court finds that the transferee for value did not substantially comply with the requirements of this section, or if the court finds that any of the following conditions existed at the time of transfer:

(1) The fees, charges, or consideration paid or agreed to be paid by the beneficiary were grossly unreasonable.

(2) The transfer of the beneficial interest was obtained by duress, fraud, or undue influence.

(i) In addition to any remedy specified in this section, for any willful violation of the requirements of this section found to be committed in bad faith, the court may require the transferee for value to pay to the beneficiary up to twice the value paid for the assignment.

(j) Notice of the hearing on any motion brought under this section shall be served on the beneficiary and on the transferee for value at least 15 days before the hearing in the manner provided in Section 415.10 or 415.30 of the Code of Civil Procedure.

(k) If the decedent's estate is not subject to a pending court proceeding under the Probate Code in California, but is the subject of a probate proceeding in another state, the transferee for value shall not be required to submit to the court a copy of the written agreement as required under paragraph (1) of subdivision (d). If the written agreement is entered into in California or if the beneficiary is domiciled in California, that written agreement shall otherwise conform to the provisions of subdivisions (d), (e), and (f) in order to be effective.

11605. When a court order made under this chapter becomes final, the order binds and is conclusive as to the rights of all interested persons.

Article 2. Preliminary Distribution

11620. A petition for an order for preliminary distribution of all, or a portion of, the share of a decedent's estate to which a beneficiary is entitled may not be filed unless at least two months have elapsed after letters are first issued to a general personal representative.

11621. (a) The court shall order distribution under this article if at the hearing it appears that the distribution may be made without loss to creditors or injury to the estate or any interested person.

(b) The order for distribution shall be stayed until any bond required by the court is filed.

11622. (a) If the court orders distribution before four months have elapsed after letters are first issued to a general personal representative, the court shall require a bond. The bond shall be in the amount of the distribution.

(b) If the court orders distribution after four months have elapsed after letters are first issued to a general personal representative, the court may require a bond. The bond shall be in the amount the court orders.

(c) Any bond required by the court shall be given by the distributee and filed with the court. The bond shall be conditioned on payment of the distributee's proper share of the debts of the estate, not exceeding the amount distributed.

11623. (a) Notwithstanding Section 11601, if authority is granted to administer the estate without court supervision under the Independent Administration of Estates Act, Part 6 (commencing with Section 10400):

(1) The personal representative may petition the court for an order for preliminary distribution on notice as provided in Section 1220. Notwithstanding subdivision (c) of Section 1220, the court may not dispense with notice unless the time for filing creditor claims has expired.

(2) The aggregate of all property distributed under this section shall not exceed 50 percent of the net value of the estate. For the purpose of this subdivision, "net value of the estate" means the excess of the value of the property in the estate, as determined by all inventories and appraisals on file with the court, over the total amount of all creditor claims and of all liens and encumbrances recorded or known to the personal representative not included in a creditor claim, excluding any estate tax lien occasioned by the decedent's death.

(b) Nothing in this section limits the authority of the personal representative to make preliminary distribution under other provisions of this chapter, whether or not authority is granted to administer the estate under the Independent Administration of Estates Act, Part 6 (commencing with Section 10400).

11624. The costs of a proceeding under this article shall be paid by the distributee or the estate in proportions determined by the court.

Article 3. Final Distribution

11640. (a) When all debts have been paid or adequately provided for, or if the estate is insolvent, and the estate is in a condition to be closed, the personal representative shall file a petition for, and the court shall make, an order for final distribution of the estate.

(b) The court shall hear and determine and resolve in the order all questions arising under Section 21135 (ademption by satisfaction) or Section 6409 (advancements).

(c) If debts remain unpaid or not adequately provided for or if, for other reasons, the estate is not in a condition to be closed, the administration may continue for a reasonable time, subject to Chapter 1 (commencing with Section 12200) of Part 11 (time for closing estate).

11641. When an order settling a final account and for final distribution is entered, the personal representative may immediately distribute the property in the estate to the persons entitled to distribution, without further notice or proceedings.

11642. Any property acquired or discovered after the court order for final distribution is made shall be distributed in the following manner:

(a) If the order disposes of the property, distribution shall be made in the manner provided in the order. The court may, in an appropriate case, require a supplemental account and make further instructions relating to the property.

(b) If the order does not dispose of the property, distribution shall be made either (1) in the manner ordered by the court on a petition for instructions or (2) under Section 12252 (administration after discharge) if the personal representative has been discharged.

Chapter 2. Determination Of Persons Entitled To Distribution

11700. At any time after letters are first issued to a general personal representative and before an order for final distribution is made, the personal representative, or any person claiming to be a beneficiary or otherwise entitled to distribution of a share of the estate, may file a petition for a court determination of the persons entitled to distribution of the decedent's estate. The petition shall include a statement of the basis for the petitioner's claim.

11701. Notice of the hearing on the petition shall be given as provided in Section 1220 to all of the following persons:

(a) Each person listed in Section 1220.

(b) Each known heir whose interest in the estate would be affected by the petition.

(c) Each known devisee whose interest in the estate would be affected by the petition.

(d) The Attorney General, at the office of the Attorney General in Sacramento, if any portion of the estate is to escheat to the state and its interest in the estate would be affected by the petition.

11702. (a) Any interested person may appear and, at or before the time of the hearing, file a written statement of the person's interest in the estate. The written statement may be in support of, or in opposition to, the petition. No other pleadings are necessary and the written statement of each claimant shall be deemed denied by each of the other claimants to the extent the written statements conflict.

(b) If a person fails timely to file a written statement:

(1) The case is at issue notwithstanding the failure and the case may proceed on the petition and written statements filed by the time of the hearing, and no further pleadings by other persons are necessary.

(2) The person may not participate further in the proceeding for determination of persons entitled to distribution, but the person's interest in the estate is not otherwise affected.

(3) The person is bound by the decision in the proceeding.

11703. The Attorney General shall be deemed to be a person entitled to distribution of the estate for purposes of this chapter if the estate involves or may involve any of the following:

(a) A charitable trust, other than a charitable trust with a designated trustee that may lawfully accept the trust.

(b) A devise for a charitable purpose without an identified beneficiary.

(c) An escheat to the State of California.

11704. (a) The court shall consider as evidence in the proceeding any statement made in a petition filed under Section 11700 and any statement of interest filed under Section 11702. The court shall not hear or consider a petition filed after the time prescribed in Section 11700.

(b) (1) The personal representative may petition the court for authorization to participate, as necessary to assist the court, in the proceeding. Notice of the hearing on the petition shall be given to the persons identified in Section 11701 in the manner provided in Section 1220.

(2) The court may grant or deny this petition, in whole or in part, on the pleadings, without an evidentiary hearing or further discovery. A petition filed pursuant to this subdivision may be granted only upon a showing of good cause. The court shall determine the manner and capacity in which the personal representative may provide as-

sistance in the proceeding. The court may direct the personal representative to file papers as a party to the proceeding, or to take other specified action, if deemed by the court to be necessary to assist the court.

11705. (a) The court shall make an order that determines the persons entitled to distribution of the decedent's estate and specifies their shares.

(b) When the court order becomes final it binds and is conclusive as to the rights of all interested persons.

Chapter 3. Distribution Of Property In Estate

11750. (a) The personal representative is responsible for distribution of the property in the estate in compliance with the terms of the court order for distribution.

(b) A distributee may demand, sue for, and recover from the personal representative or any person in possession, property to which the distributee is entitled.

(c) A distribution of property made in compliance with the terms of the court order for distribution is valid as to a person acting in good faith and for a valuable consideration.

11751. The personal representative shall obtain the receipt of the distributee for property in the estate distributed by the personal representative. In the case of real property, the personal representative shall record the court order for distribution or the personal representative's deed or both in the county in which the real property is located. Recordation of the order or deed is deemed to be a receipt of the distributee for the property.

11752. If personal property in the possession of a distributee is subject to possession by the distributee for life only, the personal representative shall demand an inventory of the property from the distributee. On receipt, the personal representative shall file the inventory with the court and deliver a copy to any distributee of the remainder.

11753. (a) Distribution in compliance with the court order entitles the personal representative to a full discharge with respect to property included in the order.

(b) The personal representative shall, before or at the time of the petition for discharge, file receipts for all property in the estate. In the case of real property, the personal representative shall file a statement that identifies the date and place of the recording and other appropriate recording information for the court order for distribution or the personal representative's deed.

(c) The court may excuse the filing of a receipt on a showing that the personal representative is unable, after reasonable effort, to obtain a receipt and that the property has been delivered to or is in the possession of the distributee.

11754. Expenses of administration of the estate shall include reasonable storage, delivery, and shipping costs for distribution of tangible personal property to a distributee.

Chapter 4. Deceased Distributee

11801. (a) Except as provided in subdivision (b), the share in a decedent's estate of a beneficiary who survives the decedent but who dies before distribution shall be distributed under this chapter with the same effect as though the distribution were made to the beneficiary while living.

(b) Subject to Section 21525, distribution may not be made under this chapter if the decedent's will provides that the beneficiary is entitled to take under the will only if the beneficiary survives the date of distribution or other period stated in the will and the beneficiary fails to survive the date of distribution or other period.

11802. If a beneficiary satisfies the requirement of Section 11801, the beneficiary's share in the decedent's estate shall be distributed as follows:

(a) Except as otherwise provided in this section, distribution shall be made to the personal representative of the estate of the beneficiary for the purpose of administration in the estate of the beneficiary.

(b) If the beneficiary was issue of the decedent and died intestate while under the age of majority and not having been emancipated, distribution shall be made directly to the heirs of the beneficiary without administration in the estate of the beneficiary.

(c) If a person entitled to the beneficiary's share proceeds under Division 8 (commencing with Section 13000) (disposition of estate without administration), distribution shall be made under Division 8.

Chapter 5. Deposit With County Treasurer

11850. Subject to Section 11851, the personal representative may deposit property to be distributed with the county treasurer of the county in which the proceedings are pending in the name of the distributee in any of the following cases:

(a) The property remains in the possession of the personal representative unclaimed or the whereabouts of the distributee is unknown.

(b) The distributee refuses to give a receipt for the property.

(c) The distributee is a minor or incompetent person who has no guardian, conservator, or other fiduciary to receive the property or person authorized to give a receipt for the property.

(d) For any other reason the property cannot be distributed, and the personal representative desires discharge. Notwithstanding Section 11851, deposit may not be made under this subdivision except on court order.

11851. (a) If property authorized by Section 11850 to be deposited with the county treasurer consists of money, the personal representative may deposit the money.

(b) If property authorized by Section 11850 to be deposited with the county treasurer consists of personal property other than money, the personal representative may not deposit the personal property except on court order. If it appears to the court that sale is for the benefit of interested persons, the court shall order the personal property sold, and the proceeds of sale, less expenses of sale allowed by the court, shall be deposited in the county treasury. If it appears to the court that sale is not for the benefit of interested persons, the court shall order the personal property deposited with the Controller, to be held subject to the provisions of Chapter 6 (commencing with Section 11900).

11852. The county treasurer shall give a receipt for a deposit made under this chapter and is liable on the official bond of the county treasurer for the money deposited. The receipt has the same effect as if executed by the distributee.

11853. If money is deposited or is already on deposit with the county treasurer, the personal representative shall deliver to the county treasurer a certified copy of the order for distribution.

11854. (a) A person may claim money on deposit in the county treasury by filing a petition with the court that made the order for distribution. The petition shall show the person's claim or right to the property. Unless the petition is filed by the person named in the decree for distribution of a decedent's estate, or the legal representative of the person or the person's estate, the petition shall state the facts required to be stated in a petition for escheated property filed under Section 1355 of the Code of Civil Procedure. On the filing of the petition, the same proceedings shall be had as are required by that section, except that the hearing shall be ex parte unless the court orders otherwise.

(b) If so ordered by the court, a copy of the petition shall be served on the Attorney General. The Attorney General may answer the petition, at the Attorney General's discretion.

(c) If the court is satisfied that the claimant has a right to the property claimed, the court shall make an order establishing the right. On presentation of a certified copy of the order, the county auditor shall draw a warrant on the county treasurer for the amount of money covered by the order.

(d) A claim for money distributed in the estate of a deceased person made after the deposit of the property in the State Treasury is governed by the provisions of Chapter 3 (commencing with Section 1335) of Title 10 of Part 3 of the Code of Civil Procedure.

Chapter 6. Distribution To State

11900. (a) The court shall order property that is not ordered distributed to known beneficiaries to be distributed to the state.

(b) Insofar as practicable, any real property or tangible personal property shall be converted to money before distribution to the state.

11901. If the court orders distribution of property in the decedent's estate to the state, and the order includes words that otherwise create a trust in favor of unknown or unidentified persons as a class, the distribution shall vest in the state both legal and equitable title to the property.

11902. (a) If the court orders distribution to the state, the personal representative shall promptly:

(1) Deliver any money to the State Treasurer.

(2) Deliver any personal property other than money to the Controller for deposit in the State Treasury.

(3) Cause a certified copy of the order to be recorded in the office of the county recorder of each county in which any real property is located.

(b) At the time of making a delivery of property or recordation under this section, the personal representative shall deliver to the Controller a certified copy of the order for distribution together with a statement of the date and place of each recording and other appropriate recording information.

11903. (a) Property distributed to the state shall be held by the Treasurer for a period of five years from the date of the order for distribution, within which time any person may claim the property in the manner provided by Title 10 (commencing with Section 1300) of Part 3 of the Code of Civil Procedure.

(b) A person who does not claim the property within the time prescribed in this section is forever barred, and the property vests absolutely in the state, subject to the provisions of Title 10 (commencing with Section 1300) of Part 3 of the Code of Civil Procedure.

11904. No deposit of property in an estate shall be made in the county treasury by a personal representative if any other property in the estate is to be or has been distributed to the state under this chapter, but the property that would otherwise be deposited in the county treasury shall be transmitted promptly to the State Treasurer or Controller as provided in this chapter.

Chapter 7. Partition Or Allotment Of Property

11950. (a) If two or more beneficiaries are entitled to the distribution of undivided interests in property and have not agreed among themselves to a partition, allotment, or other division of the property, any of them, or the personal representative at the request of any of them, may petition the court to make a partition, allotment, or other division of the property that will be equitable and will avoid the distribution of undivided interests.

(b) A proceeding under this chapter is limited to interests in the property that are subject to administration and does not include other interests except to the extent the owners of other interests in the property consent to be bound by the partition, allotment, or other division.

11951. (a) A petition under this chapter may be filed at any time before an order for distribution of the affected property becomes final.

(b) The petition shall:

(1) Describe the property.

(2) State the names of the persons having or claiming undivided interests.

(3) Describe the undivided interests, so far as known to the petitioner.

11952. (a) Notice of the hearing on the petition shall be given as provided in Section 1220 to the personal representative and to the persons entitled to distribution of the undivided interests.

(b) At the hearing the persons entitled to distribution of the undivided interests shall be considered the parties to the proceeding whether or not they have appeared or filed a responsive pleading. No one shall be considered as a plaintiff or as a defendant.

(c) Any objection to the jurisdiction of the court shall be made and resolved in the manner prescribed in Part 19 (commencing with Section 850) of Division 2.

11953. (a) The court shall partition, allot, or otherwise divide the property so that each party receives property with a value proportionate to the value of the party's interest in the whole.

(b) The court may direct the personal representative to sell property where, under the circumstances, sale would be more equitable than partition and where the property cannot conveniently be allotted to any one party. The sale shall be conducted in the same manner as other sales made during administration of an estate.

(c) Any two or more parties may agree to accept undivided interests.

11954. (a) The court, in its discretion, may appoint one or three referees to partition property capable of being partitioned, if requested to do so by a party. The number of referees appointed must conform to the request of at least one of the parties.

(b) The referees shall have the powers and perform the duties of referees in, and the court shall have the same powers with respect to their report as in, partition actions under Title 10.5 (commencing with Section 872.010) of Part 2 of the Code of Civil Procedure.

11955. The expenses of partition shall be equitably apportioned by the court among the parties, but each party must pay the party's own attorney's fees. The amount charged to each party shall be included and specified in the order and, to the extent unpaid, constitutes a lien on the property allotted to the party.

11956. (a) The partition, allotment, or other division made by the court shall control in proceedings for distribution, unless modified for good cause on reasonable notice.

(b) The proceedings leading to the partition, allotment, or other division may be reviewed on appeal from the order for distribution.

Chapter 8. Interest And Income Accruing During Administration

12000. The provisions of this chapter apply where the intention of the testator is not otherwise indicated by the will.

12001. If interest is payable under this chapter, the rate of interest is three percentage points less than the legal rate on judgments in effect one year after the date of the testator's death and shall not be recomputed in the event of a change in the applicable rate thereafter.

12002. (a) Except as provided in this section, a specific devise does not bear interest.

(b) A specific devise carries with it income on the devised property from the date of death, less expenses attributable to the devised property during administration of the estate. For purposes of this section, expenses attributable to property are expenses that result directly from the use or ownership of the property, including property tax and tax on the income from the property, but excluding estate and generation-skipping transfer taxes.

(c) If income of specifically devised property is not sufficient to pay expenses attributable to the property, the deficiency shall be paid out of the estate until the property is distributed to the devisee or the devisee takes possession of or occupies the property, whichever occurs first. To the extent a deficiency paid out of the estate is attributable to the period that commences one year after the testator's death, whether paid during or after expiration of the one year period following the date of death, the amount paid is a charge against the share of the devisee, and the personal representative has an equitable lien on the specifically devised property as against the devisee in the amount paid.

(d) If specifically devised property is sold during administration of the estate, the devisee is entitled to the net income from the property until the date of sale, and to interest on the net sale proceeds thereafter, but no interest accrues during the first year after the testator's death.

12003. If a general pecuniary devise, including a general pecuniary devise in trust, is not distributed within one year after the testator's death, the devise bears interest thereafter.

12004. (a) An annuity commences at the testator's death and shall be paid at the end of the annual, monthly, or other specified period.

(b) If an annuity is not paid at the end of the specified period, it bears interest thereafter, but no interest accrues during the first year after the testator's death.

12005. A devisee of a devise for maintenance is entitled to interest on the amount of any unpaid accumulations of the payments held by the personal representative on each anniversary of the testator's death, computed from the date of the anniversary.

12006. Net income received during administration not paid under other provisions of this chapter and not otherwise devised shall be distributed pro rata as income among all distributees who receive either residuary or intestate property. If a distributee takes for life or for a term of years, the pro rata share of income belongs to the tenant for life or for the term of years.

12007. This chapter does not apply in cases where the decedent died before July 1, 1989. In cases where the decedent died before July 1, 1989, the applicable law in effect before July 1, 1989, continues to apply.

Part 11. Closing Estate Administration

Chapter 1. Time For Closing Estate

12200. The personal representative shall either petition for an order for final distribution of the estate or make a report of status of administration not later than the following times:

(a) In an estate for which a federal estate tax return is not required, within one year after the date of issuance of letters.

(b) In an estate for which a federal estate tax return is required, within 18 months after the date of issuance of letters.

12201. If a report of status of administration is made under Section 12200:

(a) The report shall show the condition of the estate, the reasons why the estate cannot be distributed and closed, and an estimate of the time needed to close administration of the estate.

(b) The report shall be filed with the court. Notice of hearing of the report shall be given as provided in Section 1220 to persons then interested in the estate, and shall include a statement in not less than 10-point boldface type or a reasonable equivalent thereof if printed, or in all capital letters if not printed, in substantially the following words:

"YOU HAVE THE RIGHT TO PETITION FOR AN ACCOUNT UNDER SECTION 10950 OF THE CALIFORNIA PROBATE CODE."

(c) On the hearing of the report, the court may order either of the following:

(1) That the administration of the estate continue for the time and on the terms and conditions that appear reasonable, including an account under Section 10950, if the court determines that continuation of administration is in the best interests of the estate or of interested persons.

(2) That the personal representative shall petition for final distribution.

12202. (a) The court may, on petition of any interested person or on its own motion, for good cause shown on the record, cite the personal representative to appear before the court and show the condition of the estate and the reasons why the estate cannot be distributed and closed.

(b) On the hearing of the citation, the court may either order the administration of the estate to continue or order the personal representative to petition for final distribution, as provided in Section 12201.

12203. (a) For purposes of this chapter, continuation of the administration of the estate in order to pay a family allowance is not in the best interests of the estate or interested persons unless the court determines both of the following:

(1) The family allowance is needed by the recipient to pay for necessaries of life, including education so long as pursued to advantage.

(2) The needs of the recipient for continued family allowance outweigh the needs of the decedent's beneficiaries whose interests would be adversely affected by continuing the administration of the estate for this purpose.

(b) Nothing in this section shall be construed to authorize continuation of a family allowance beyond the time prescribed in Section 6543.

(c) Nothing in this section limits the power of the court to order a preliminary distribution of the estate.

12204. Failure of the personal representative to comply with an order made under this chapter is grounds for removal from office.

12205. (a) The court may reduce the compensation of the personal representative or the attorney for the personal representative by an amount the court determines to be appropriate if the court makes all of the following determinations:

(1) The time taken for administration of the estate exceeds the time required by this chapter or prescribed by the court.

(2) The time taken was within the control of the personal representative or attorney

whose compensation is being reduced.

(3) The delay was not in the best interest of the estate or interested persons.

(b) An order under this section reducing compensation may be made regardless of whether the compensation otherwise allowable under Part 7 (commencing with Section 10800) would be reasonable compensation for the services rendered by the personal representative or attorney.

(c) An order under this section may be made at any of the following hearings:

(1) The hearing for final distribution.

(2) The hearing for an allowance on the compensation of the personal representative or attorney.

(d) In making a determination under this section, the court shall take into account any action taken under Section 12202 as a result of a previous delay.

12206. A limitation in a will of the time for administration of an estate is directory only and does not limit the power of the personal representative or the court to continue administration of the estate beyond the time limitation in the will if the continuation is necessary.

Chapter 2. Discharge Of Personal Representative

12250. (a) When the personal representative has complied with the terms of the order for final distribution and has filed the appropriate receipts or the court has excused the filing of a receipt as provided in Section 11753, the court shall, on ex parte petition, make an order discharging the personal representative from all liability incurred thereafter.

(b) Nothing in this section precludes discharge of the personal representative for distribution made without prior court order, so long as the terms of the order for final distribution are satisfied.

12251. (a) At any time after appointment of a personal representative and whether or not letters have been issued, if it appears there is no property of any kind belonging to the estate and subject to administration, the personal representative may petition for the termination of further proceedings and for discharge of the personal representative. The petition shall state the facts required by this subdivision.

(b) Notice of the hearing on the petition shall be given as provided in Section 1220 to all interested persons.

(c) If it appears to the satisfaction of the court on the hearing that the facts stated in the petition are true, the court shall make an order terminating the proceeding and discharging the personal representative.

12252. If subsequent administration of an estate is necessary after the personal representative has been discharged because other property is discovered or because it becomes necessary or proper for any other cause, both

of the following shall apply:

(a) The court shall appoint as personal representative the person entitled to appointment in the same order as is directed in relation to an original appointment, except that the person who served as personal representative at the time of the order of discharge has priority.

(b) Notice of hearing of the appointment shall be given as provided in Section 1220 to the person who served as personal representative at the time of the order of discharge and to other interested persons. If property has been distributed to the State of California, a copy of any petition for subsequent appointment of a personal representative and the notice of hearing shall be given as provided in Section 1220 to the Controller.

Part 12. Administration Of Estates Of Missing Persons Presumed Dead

12400. Unless the provision or context otherwise requires, as used in this part, "missing person" means a person who is presumed to be dead under Section 12401.

12401. In proceedings under this part, a person who has not been seen or heard from for a continuous period of five years by those who are likely to have seen or heard from that person, and whose absence is not satisfactorily explained after diligent search or inquiry, is presumed to be dead. The person's death is presumed to have occurred at the end of the period unless there is sufficient evidence to establish that death occurred earlier.

12402. Subject to the provisions of this part, the estate of a missing person may be administered in the manner provided generally for the administration of estates of deceased persons.

12403. (a) If the missing person was a resident of this state when last seen or heard from, the superior court of the county of the person's last known place of residence has jurisdiction for the purposes of this part.

(b) If the missing person was a nonresident of this state when last seen or heard from, the superior court of a county where real property of the missing person is located, or of a county where personal property is located if the missing person has no real property in this state, has jurisdiction for the purposes of this part.

12404. (a) A petition may be filed in the court having jurisdiction under Section 12403 for the administration of the estate of a missing person.

(b) The petition may be filed by any person who may be appointed as a personal representative, other than a person described in subdivision (r) of Section 8461.

(c) In addition to the matters otherwise required in a petition for administration of the estate, the petition shall state all of the following:

(1) The last known place of residence and the last known address of the missing person.

(2) The time and circumstances when the missing person was last seen or heard from.

(3) That the missing person has not been seen or heard from for a continuous period of five years by the persons likely to have seen or heard from the missing person (naming them and their relationship to the missing person) and that the whereabouts of the missing person is unknown to those persons and to the petitioner.

(4) A description of the search or the inquiry made concerning the whereabouts of the missing person.

12405. Notice of hearing shall be served and published, and proof made, in the same manner as in proceedings for administration of the estate of a decedent, except that notice of hearing on the petition shall also be sent by registered mail to the missing person at his or her last known address.

12406. (a) At the hearing, the court shall determine whether the alleged missing person is a person who is presumed to be dead under Section 12401. The court may receive evidence and consider the affidavits and depositions of persons likely to have seen or heard from or know the whereabouts of the alleged missing person.

(b) If the court is not satisfied that a diligent search or inquiry has been made for the missing person, the court may order the petitioner to conduct a diligent search or inquiry and to report the results. The court may order the search or inquiry to be made in any manner that the court determines to be advisable, including any or all of the following methods:

(1) Inserting in one or more suitable newspapers or other periodicals a notice requesting information from any person having knowledge of the whereabouts of the missing person.

(2) Notifying law enforcement officials and public welfare agencies in appropriate locations of the disappearance of the missing person.

(3) Engaging the services of an investigator.

(c) The costs of a search ordered by the court pursuant to subdivision (b) shall be paid by the estate of the missing person, but if there is no administration, the court in its discretion may order the petitioner to pay the costs.

12407. (a) If the court finds that the alleged missing person is a person presumed to be dead under Section 12401, the court shall do both of the following:

(1) Appoint a personal representative for the estate of the missing person in the manner provided for the estates of deceased persons.

(2) Determine the date of the missing person's death.

(b) The personal representative shall administer the estate of the missing person in the same general manner and method of procedure, and with the same force and effect, as provided for the administration of the estates of deceased persons, except as otherwise provided in this part.

12408. (a) If the missing person reappears:

(1) The missing person may recover property of the missing person's estate in the possession of the personal representative, less fees, costs, and expenses thus far incurred.

(2) The missing person may recover from distributees any property of the missing person's estate that is in their possession, or the value of distributions received by them, to the extent that recovery from distributees is equitable in view of all the circumstances, but an action under this paragraph is forever barred five years after the time the distribution was made.

(b) The remedies available to the missing person under subdivision (a) are exclusive, except for any remedy the missing person may have by reason of fraud or intentional wrongdoing.

(c) Except as provided in subdivisions (a) and (b), the order for final distribution, when it becomes final, is conclusive as to the rights of the missing person, the rights of the beneficiaries of the missing person, and the rights of all other persons interested in the estate.

(d) If a dispute arises as to the identity of a person claiming to be a reappearing missing person, the person making the claim or any other interested person may file a petition under Section 11700, notwithstanding the limitations of time prescribed in Section 11700, for the determination of the identity of the person claiming to be the reappearing missing person.

Part 13. Nondomiciliary Decedents

Chapter 1. Definitions

12500. Unless the provision or context otherwise requires, the definitions in this chapter govern the construction of this part.

12501. "Ancillary administration" means proceedings in this state for administration of the estate of a nondomiciliary decedent.

12502. "Foreign nation" means a jurisdiction other than a state of the United States.

12503. "Foreign nation personal representative" means a personal representative appointed in a jurisdiction other than a state of the United States.

12504. "Local personal representative" means a nondomiciliary decedent's personal representative appointed in this state.

12505. "Nondomiciliary decedent" means a person who dies domiciled in a sister state or foreign nation.

12506. "Sister state" means a state other than this state.

12507. "Sister state personal representative" means a personal representative appointed in a sister state.

Chapter 2. Ancillary Administration

Article 1. Opening Ancillary Administration

12510. Any interested person, or a sister state or foreign nation personal representative, may commence an ancillary administration proceeding by a petition to the court for either or both of the following:

(a) Probate of the nondomiciliary decedent's will.

(b) Appointment of a local personal representative.

12511. The proper county for an ancillary administration proceeding under this chapter is the county determined pursuant to Section 7052.

12512. Notice of an ancillary administration proceeding shall be given and, except as provided in Article 2 (commencing with Section 12520), the same proceedings had as in the case of a petition for probate of a will or appointment of a personal representative of a person who dies domiciled in this state.

12513. If the decedent dies while domiciled in a sister state, a personal representative appointed by a court of the decedent's domicile has priority over all other persons except where the decedent's will nominates a different person to be the personal representative in this state. The sister state personal representative may nominate another person as personal representative and the nominee has the same priority as the sister state personal representative.

Article 2. Probate Of Nondomiciliary Decedent's Will Admitted To Probate In Sister State Or Foreign Nation

12520. (a) If a nondomiciliary decedent's will has been admitted to probate in a sister state or foreign nation and satisfies the requirements of this article, probate of the will in an ancillary administration proceeding is governed by this article.

(b) If a nondomiciliary decedent's will has been admitted to probate in a sister state or foreign nation, but does not satisfy the requirements of this article, the will may be probated in an ancillary administration proceeding pursuant to Part 2 (commencing with Section 8000).

12521. (a) A petition for probate of a nondomiciliary decedent's will under this article shall include both of the following:

(1) The will or an authenticated copy of the will.

(2) An authenticated copy of the order admitting the will to probate in the sister state or foreign nation or other evidence of the establishment or proof of the will in accordance with the law of the sister state or foreign nation.

(b) As used in this section, "authenticated copy" means a copy that satisfies the requirements of Article 2 (commencing with Section 1530) of Chapter 2 of Division 11 of the Evidence Code.

12522. If a will of a nondomiciliary decedent was admitted to probate, or established or proved, in accordance with the laws of a sister state, the court shall admit the will to probate in this state, and may not permit a contest or revocation of probate, unless one or more of the following are shown:

(a) The determination in the sister state is not based on a finding that at the time of death the decedent was domiciled in the sister state.

(b) One or more interested parties were not given notice and an opportunity for contest in the proceedings in the sister state.

(c) The determination in the sister state is not final.

12523. (a) Except as provided in subdivision (b), if a will of a nondomiciliary decedent was admitted to probate, or established or proved, in accordance with the laws of a foreign nation, the court shall admit the will to probate in this state, and may not permit a contest or revocation of probate, if it appears from the order admitting the will to probate in the foreign nation, or otherwise appears, that all of the following conditions are satisfied:

(1) The determination in the foreign nation is based on a finding that at the time of death the decedent was domiciled in the foreign nation.

(2) All interested parties were given notice and an opportunity for contest in the proceedings in the foreign nation.

(3) The determination in the foreign nation is final.

(b) The court may refuse to admit the will, even though it is shown to satisfy the conditions provided in subdivision (a), where the order admitting the will was made under a judicial system that does not provide impartial tribunals or procedures compatible with the requirements of due process of law.

12524. A nondomiciliary decedent's will admitted to probate under this article has the same force and effect as the will of a person who dies while domiciled in this state that is admitted to probate in this state.

Article 3. Application Of General Provisions

12530. Except to the extent otherwise provided in this chapter, ancillary administration of a decedent's estate is subject to all other provisions of this code concerning the administration of the decedent's estate, including, but not limited to, opening estate administration, inventory and appraisal, creditor claims, estate management, independent administration, compensation, accounts, payment of debts, distribution, and closing estate administration.

Article 4. Distribution Of Property To Sister State Personal Representative

12540. (a) If a person dies while domiciled in a sister state, the court in an ancillary administration proceeding may make an order for preliminary or final distribution of all or part of the decedent's personal property in this state to the sister state personal representative if distribution is in the best interest of the estate or interested persons.

(b) The court order shall be made in the manner and pursuant to the procedure provided in, and is subject to the provisions of, Chapter 1 (commencing with Section 11600) of Part 10.

12541. If necessary to make distribution pursuant to this article, real property in the nondomiciliary decedent's estate may be sold and the court may order the proceeds to be distributed to the sister state personal representative. The sale shall be made in the same manner as other sales of real property of a decedent.

12542. If the nondomiciliary decedent's estate in the sister state where the decedent was domiciled is insolvent, distribution may be made only to the sister state personal representative and not to the beneficiaries.

Chapter 3. Collection Of Personal Property Of Small Estate By Sister State Personal Representative Without Ancillary Administration

12570. If a nondomiciliary decedent's property in this state satisfies the requirements of Section 13100, a sister state personal representative may, without petitioning for ancillary administration, use the affidavit procedure provided by Chapter 3 (commencing with Section 13100) of Part 1 of Division 8 to collect personal property of the decedent.

12571. The effect of payment, delivery, or transfer of personal property to the sister state personal representative pursuant to this chapter, and the effect of failure to do so, are governed by Chapter 3 (commencing with Section 13100) of Part 1 of Division 8.

12572. The sister state personal representative may bring an action against a holder of the decedent's property, and may be awarded attorney's fees, as provided in subdivision (b) of Section 13105.

12573. A sister state personal representa-

tative who takes property by affidavit under this chapter is not liable as a person to whom payment, delivery, or transfer of the decedent's property is made under Section 13109 or 13110 to the extent that the sister state personal representative restores the property to the nondomiciliary decedent's estate in the sister state in compliance with Section 13111.

Chapter 4. Jurisdiction Over Foreign Personal Representative

12590. A sister state personal representative or foreign nation personal representative submits personally in a representative capacity to the jurisdiction of the courts of this state in any proceeding relating to the estate by any of the following actions:

(a) Filing a petition for ancillary administration.

(b) Receiving money or other personal property pursuant to Chapter 3 (commencing with Section 12570). Jurisdiction under this subdivision is limited to the amount of money and the value of personal property received.

(c) Doing any act in this state as a personal representative that would have given this state jurisdiction over the personal representative as an individual.

12591. A sister state personal representative or foreign nation personal representative is subject to the jurisdiction of the courts of this state in a representative capacity to the same extent that the nondomiciliary decedent was subject to jurisdiction at the time of death.

Division 8. Disposition Of Estate Without Administration

Part 1. Collection Or Transfer Of Small Estate Without Administration

Chapter 1. Definitions

13000. Unless the provision or context otherwise requires, the definitions in this chapter govern the construction of this part.

13002. "Holder of the decedent's property" or "holder" means, with respect to any particular item of property of the decedent, the person owing money to the decedent, having custody of tangible personal property of the decedent, or acting as registrar or transfer agent of the evidences of a debt, obligation, interest, right, security, or chose in action belonging to the decedent.

13004. (a) "Particular item of property" means:

(1) Particular personal property of the decedent which is sought to be collected, received, or transferred by the successor of the decedent under Chapter 3 (commencing with Section 13100).

(2) Particular real property of the decedent, or particular real and personal property of the decedent, for which the successor of the decedent seeks a court order determining succession under Chapter 4 (commencing with Section 13150).

(3) Particular real property of the decedent with respect to which the successor of the decedent files an affidavit of succession under Chapter 5 (commencing with Section 13200).

(b) Subject to subdivision (a), "particular item of property" includes all interests specified in Section 62.

13005. "Property of the decedent," "decedent's property," "money due the decedent," and similar phrases, include property that becomes part of the decedent's estate on the decedent's death, whether by designation of the estate as beneficiary under an insurance policy on the decedent's life or under the decedent's retirement plan, or otherwise.

13006. "Successor of the decedent" means:

(a) If the decedent died leaving a will, the sole beneficiary or all of the beneficiaries who succeeded to a particular item of property of the decedent under the decedent's will. For the purposes of this part, a trust is a beneficiary under the decedent's will if the trust succeeds to the particular item of property under the decedent's will.

(b) If the decedent died without a will, the sole person or all of the persons who succeeded to the particular item of property of the decedent under Sections 6401 and 6402 or, if the law of a sister state or foreign nation governs succession to the particular item of property, under the law of the sister state or foreign nation.

13007. "Proceeding" means either that a petition is currently pending in this state for administration of a decedent's estate under Division 7 (commencing with Section 7000), a special administrator for the decedent's estate has been appointed in this state and is now serving, or a personal representative for the decedent's estate has been appointed in this state with general powers. "Proceeding" does not include a petition for administration which was dismissed without the appointment of a personal representative, any proceeding under Division 8 (commencing with Section 13000), or any action or proceeding in another state.

Chapter 2. General Provisions

13050. (a) For the purposes of this part:

(1) Any property or interest or lien thereon which, at the time of the decedent's death, was held by the decedent as a joint tenant, or in which the decedent had a life or other interest terminable upon the decedent's death, or which was held by the decedent and passed to the decedent's surviving spouse pursuant to Section 13500, shall be excluded in determining the property or estate of the decedent or its value. This excluded property shall include, but not be limited to, property in a trust revocable by the decedent during his or her lifetime.

(2) A multiple-party account to which the decedent was a party at the time of the decedent's death shall be excluded in determining the property or estate of the decedent or its value, whether or not all or a portion of the sums on deposit are community property, to the extent that the sums on deposit belong after the death of the decedent to a surviving party, P.O.D. payee, or beneficiary. For the purposes of this paragraph, the terms "multiple-party account," "party," "P.O.D. payee," and "beneficiary" are defined in Article 2 (commencing with Section 5120) of Chapter 1 of Part 2 of Division 5.

(b) For the purposes of this part, all of the following property shall be excluded in determining the property or estate of the decedent or its value:

(1) Any vehicle registered under Division 3 (commencing with Section 4000) of the Vehicle Code or titled under Division 16.5 (commencing with Section 38000) of the Vehicle Code.

(2) Any vessel numbered under Division 3.5 (commencing with Section 9840) of the Vehicle Code.

(3) Any manufactured home, mobilehome, commercial coach, truck camper, or floating home registered under Part 2 (commencing with Section 18000) of Division 13 of the Health and Safety Code.

(c) For the purposes of this part, the value

of the following property shall be excluded in determining the value of the decedent's property in this state:

(1) Any amounts due to the decedent for services in the Armed Forces of the United States.

(2) The amount, not exceeding fifteen thousand dollars ($15,000), of salary or other compensation, including compensation for unused vacation, owing to the decedent for personal services from any employment.

13051. For the purposes of this part:

(a) The guardian or conservator of the estate of a person entitled to any of the decedent's property may act on behalf of the person without authorization or approval of the court in which the guardianship or conservatorship proceeding is pending.

(b) The trustee of a trust may act on behalf of the trust. In the case of a trust that is subject to continuing jurisdiction of the court pursuant to Chapter 4 (commencing with Section 17300) of Part 5 of Division 9, the trustee may act on behalf of the trust without the need to obtain approval of the court.

(c) If the decedent's will authorizes a custodian under the Uniform Gifts to Minors Act or the Uniform Transfers to Minors Act of any state to receive a devise to a beneficiary, the custodian may act on behalf of the beneficiary until such time as the custodianship terminates.

(d) A sister state personal representative may act on behalf of the beneficiaries as provided in Chapter 3 (commencing with Section 12570) of Part 13 of Division 7.

(e) The attorney in fact authorized under a durable power of attorney may act on behalf of the beneficiary giving the power of attorney.

13052. In making an appraisal for the purposes of this part, the probate referee shall use the date of the decedent's death as the date of valuation of the property.

13053. (a) Except as provided in subdivision (b), this part applies whether the decedent died before, on, or after July 1, 1987.

(b) This part does not apply and the law in effect at the time of payment, delivery, or transfer shall apply if the payment, delivery, or transfer was made prior to July 1, 1987, pursuant to former Probate Code Sections 630 to 632, inclusive, repealed by Chapter 783 of the Statutes of 1986.

13054. A reference in any statute of this state or in a written instrument, including a will or trust, to a provision of former Sections 630 to 632, inclusive, repealed by Chapter 783, Statutes of 1986, shall be deemed to be a reference to the comparable provisions of Chapter 3 (commencing with Section 13100).

Chapter 3. Affidavit Procedure For Collection Or Transfer Of Personal Property

13100. Excluding the property described in Section 13050, if the gross value of the decedent's real and personal property in this state does not exceed one hundred fifty thousand dollars ($150,000) and if 40 days have elapsed since the death of the decedent, the successor of the decedent may, without procuring letters of administration or awaiting probate of the will, do any of the following with respect to one or more particular items of property:

(a) Collect any particular item of property that is money due the decedent.

(b) Receive any particular item of property that is tangible personal property of the decedent.

(c) Have any particular item of property that is evidence of a debt, obligation, interest, right, security, or chose in action belonging to the decedent transferred, whether or not secured by a lien on real property.

13101. (a) To collect money, receive tangible personal property, or have evidences of a debt, obligation, interest, right, security, or chose in action transferred under this chapter, an affidavit or a declaration under penalty of perjury under the laws of this state shall be furnished to the holder of the decedent's property stating all of the following:

(1) The decedent's name.

(2) The date and place of the decedent's death.

(3) "At least 40 days have elapsed since the death of the decedent, as shown in a certified copy of the decedent's death certificate attached to this affidavit or declaration."

(4) Either of the following, as appropriate:

(A) "No proceeding is now being or has been conducted in California for administration of the decedent's estate."

(B) "The decedent's personal representative has consented in writing to the payment, transfer, or delivery to the affiant or declarant of the property described in the affidavit or declaration."

(5) "The current gross fair market value of the decedent's real and personal property in California, excluding the property described in Section 13050 of the California Probate Code, does not exceed one hundred fifty thousand dollars ($150,000)."

(6) A description of the property of the decedent that is to be paid, transferred, or delivered to the affiant or declarant.

(7) The name of the successor of the decedent (as defined in Section 13006 of the California Probate Code) to the described property.

(8) Either of the following, as appropriate:

(A) "The affiant or declarant is the successor of the decedent (as defined in Section 13006 of the California Probate Code) to the decedent's interest in the described property."

(B) "The affiant or declarant is authorized under Section 13051 of the California Probate Code to act on behalf of the successor of the decedent (as defined in Section 13006 of the California Probate Code) with respect to the decedent's interest in the described property."

(9) "No other person has a superior right to the interest of the decedent in the described property."

(10) "The affiant or declarant requests that the described property be paid, delivered, or transferred to the affiant or declarant."

(11) "The affiant or declarant affirms or declares under penalty of perjury under the laws of the State of California that the foregoing is true and correct."

(b) Where more than one person executes the affidavit or declaration under this section, the statements required by subdivision (a) shall be modified as appropriate to reflect that fact.

(c) If the particular item of property to be transferred under this chapter is a debt or other obligation secured by a lien on real property and the instrument creating the lien has been recorded in the office of the county recorder of the county where the real property is located, the affidavit or declaration shall satisfy the requirements both of this section and of Section 13106.5.

(d) A certified copy of the decedent's death certificate shall be attached to the affidavit or declaration.

(e) If the decedent's personal representative has consented to the payment, transfer, or delivery of the described property to the affiant or declarant, a copy of the consent and of the personal representative's letters shall be attached to the affidavit or declaration.

13102. (a) If the decedent had evidence of ownership of the property described in the affidavit or declaration and the holder of the property would have had the right to require presentation of the evidence of ownership before the duty of the holder to pay, deliver, or transfer the property to the decedent would have arisen, the evidence of ownership, if available, shall be presented with the affidavit or declaration to the holder of the decedent's property.

(b) If the evidence of ownership is not presented to the holder pursuant to subdivision (a), the holder may require, as a condition for the payment, delivery, or transfer of the property, that the person presenting the affidavit or declaration provide the holder with a bond or undertaking in a reasonable amount determined by the holder to be sufficient to indemnify the holder against all liability, claims, demands, loss, damages, costs, and expenses that the holder may incur or suffer by reason of the payment, delivery, or transfer of the property. Nothing in this subdivision precludes the holder and the person presenting the affidavit or declaration from dispensing with the requirement that a bond or undertaking be provided and instead entering into an agreement satisfactory to the holder concerning the duty of the person presenting the affidavit or declaration to indemnify the holder.

13103. If the estate of the decedent includes any real property in this state, the affidavit or declaration shall be accompanied by an inventory and appraisal of the real property. The inventory and appraisal of the real property shall be made as provided in Part 3 (commencing with Section 8800) of Division 7. The appraisal shall be made by a probate referee selected by the affiant or declarant from those probate referees appointed by the Controller under Section 400 to appraise property in the county where the real property is located.

13104. (a) Reasonable proof of the identity of each person executing the affidavit or declaration shall be provided to the holder of the decedent's property.

(b) Reasonable proof of identity is provided for the purposes of this section if both of the following requirements are satisfied:

(1) The person executing the affidavit or declaration is personally known to the holder.

(2) The person executes the affidavit or declaration in the presence of the holder.

(c) If the affidavit or declaration is executed in the presence of the holder, a written statement under penalty of perjury by a person personally known to the holder affirming the identity of the person executing the affidavit or declaration is reasonable proof of identity for the purposes of this section.

(d) If the affidavit or declaration is executed in the presence of the holder, the holder may reasonably rely on any of the following as reasonable proof of identity for the purposes of this section:

(1) An identification card or driver's license issued by the Department of Motor Vehicles of this state that is current or was issued during the preceding five years.

(2) A passport issued by the Department of State of the United States that is current or was issued during the preceding five years.

(3) Any of the following documents if the document is current or was issued during the preceding five years and contains a photograph and description of the person named on it, is signed by the person, and bears a serial or other identifying number:

(A) A passport issued by a foreign government that has been stamped by the United States Immigration and Naturalization Service.

(B) A driver's license issued by a state other than California.

(C) An identification card issued by a state other than California.

(D) An identification card issued by any

branch of the armed forces of the United States.

(e) For the purposes of this section, a notary public's certificate of acknowledgment identifying the person executing the affidavit or declaration is reasonable proof of identity of the person executing the affidavit or declaration.

(f) Unless the affidavit or declaration contains a notary public's certificate of acknowledgment of the identity of the person, the holder shall note on the affidavit or declaration either that the person executing the affidavit or declaration is personally known or a description of the identification provided by the person executing the affidavit or declaration.

13105. (a) If the requirements of Sections 13100 to 13104, inclusive, are satisfied:

(1) The person or persons executing the affidavit or declaration as successor of the decedent are entitled to have the property described in the affidavit or declaration paid, delivered, or transferred to them.

(2) A transfer agent of a security described in the affidavit or declaration shall change the registered ownership on the books of the corporation from the decedent to the person or persons executing the affidavit or declaration as successor of the decedent.

(b) If the holder of the decedent's property refuses to pay, deliver, or transfer any personal property or evidence thereof to the successor of the decedent within a reasonable time, the successor may recover the property or compel its payment, delivery, or transfer in an action brought for that purpose against the holder of the property. If an action is brought against the holder under this section, the court shall award reasonable attorney's fees to the person or persons bringing the action if the court finds that the holder of the decedent's property acted unreasonably in refusing to pay, deliver, or transfer the property to them as required by subdivision (a).

13106. (a) If the requirements of Sections 13100 to 13104, inclusive, are satisfied, receipt by the holder of the decedent's property of the affidavit or declaration constitutes sufficient acquittance for the payment of money, delivery of property, or changing registered ownership of property pursuant to this chapter and discharges the holder from any further liability with respect to the money or property. The holder may rely in good faith on the statements in the affidavit or declaration and has no duty to inquire into the truth of any statement in the affidavit or declaration.

(b) If the requirements of Sections 13100 to 13104, inclusive, are satisfied, the holder of the decedent's property is not liable for any taxes due to this state by reason of paying money, delivering property, or changing registered ownership of property pursuant to this chapter.

13106.5. (a) If the particular item of property transferred under this chapter is a debt or other obligation secured by a lien on real property and the instrument creating the lien has been recorded in the office of the county recorder of the county where the real property is located, the affidavit or declaration described in Section 13101 shall be recorded in the office of the county recorder of that county and, in addition to the contents required by Section 13101, shall include both of the following:

(1) The recording reference of the instrument creating the lien.

(2) A notary public's certificate of acknowledgment identifying each person executing the affidavit or declaration.

(b) The transfer under this chapter of the debt or obligation secured by a lien on real property has the same effect as would be given to an assignment of the right to collect the debt or enforce the obligation. The recording of the affidavit or declaration under subdivision (a) shall be given the same effect as is given under Sections 2934 and 2935 of the Civil Code to recording an assignment of a mortgage and an assignment of the beneficial interest under a deed of trust.

(c) If a deed of trust upon the real property was given to secure the debt and the requirements of subdivision (a) and of Sections 13100 to 13103, inclusive, are satisfied:

(1) The trustee under the deed of trust may rely in good faith on the statements made in the affidavit or declaration and has no duty to inquire into the truth of any statement in the affidavit or declaration.

(2) A person acting in good faith and for a valuable consideration may rely upon a recorded reconveyance of the trustee under the deed of trust.

(d) If a mortgage upon the real property was given to secure the debt and the requirements of subdivision (a) and of Sections 13100 to 13103, inclusive, are satisfied, a person acting in good faith and for a valuable consideration may rely upon a recorded discharge of the mortgage executed by the person or persons executing the affidavit or declaration as successor of the decedent or by their successors in interest.

13107. Where the money or property claimed in an affidavit or declaration presented under this chapter is that of a deceased heir or devisee of a deceased person whose estate is being administered in this state, the personal representative of the person whose estate is being administered shall present the affidavit or declaration to the court in which the estate is being administered. The court shall direct the personal representative to pay the money or deliver the property to the person or persons identified by the affidavit or declaration as the successor of the decedent to the extent that the order for distribution determines that the deceased heir or devisee was entitled to the money or property under the will or the laws of succession.

13107.5. Where the money or property claimed in an affidavit or declaration executed under this chapter is the subject of a pending action or proceeding in which the decedent was a party, the successor of the decedent shall, without procuring letters of administration or awaiting probate of the will, be substituted as a party in place of the decedent by making a motion under Article 3 (commencing with Section 377.30) of Chapter 4 of Title 2 of Part 2 of the Code of Civil Procedure. The successor of the decedent shall file the affidavit or declaration with the court when the motion is made. For the purpose of Article 3 (commencing with Section 377.30) of Chapter 4 of Title 2 of Part 2 of the Code of Civil Procedure, a successor of the decedent who complies with this chapter shall be considered as a successor in interest of the decedent.

13108. (a) The procedure provided by this chapter may be used only if one of the following requirements is satisfied:

(1) No proceeding for the administration of the decedent's estate is pending or has been conducted in this state.

(2) The decedent's personal representative consents in writing to the payment, transfer, or delivery of the property described in the affidavit or declaration pursuant to this chapter.

(b) Payment, delivery, or transfer of a decedent's property pursuant to this chapter does not preclude later proceedings for administration of the decedent's estate.

13109. A person to whom payment, delivery, or transfer of the decedent's property is made under this chapter is personally liable, to the extent provided in Section 13112, for the unsecured debts of the decedent. Any such debt may be enforced against the person in the same manner as it could have been enforced against the decedent if the decedent had not died. In any action based upon the debt, the person may assert any defenses, cross-complaints, or setoffs that would have been available to the decedent if the decedent had not died. Nothing in this section permits enforcement of a claim that is barred under Part 4 (commencing with Section 9000) of Division 7. Section 366.2 of the Code of Civil Procedure applies in an action under this section.

13110. (a) Except as provided in subdivision (b), each person to whom payment, delivery, or transfer of the decedent's property is made under this chapter is personally liable to the extent provided in Section 13112 to any person having a superior right by testate or intestate succession from the decedent.

(b) In addition to any other liability the person has under this section and Sections 13109, 13111, and 13112, any person who fraudulently secures the payment, delivery,

or transfer of the decedent's property under this chapter is liable to the person having such a superior right for three times the fair market value of the property. For the purposes of this subdivision, the "fair market value of the property" is the fair market value of the property paid, delivered, or transferred to the person liable under this subdivision, valued as of the time the person liable under this subdivision presents the affidavit or declaration under this chapter to the holder of the decedent's property, less any liens and encumbrances on that property at that time.

(c) An action to impose liability under this section is forever barred three years after the affidavit or declaration is presented under this chapter to the holder of the decedent's property, or three years after the discovery of the fraud, whichever is later. The three-year period specified in this subdivision is not tolled for any reason.

13111. (a) Subject to the provisions of this section, if proceedings for the administration of the decedent's estate are commenced in this state, or if the decedent's personal representative has consented to the payment, transfer, or delivery of the decedent's property under this chapter and the personal representative later requests that the property be restored to the estate, each person to whom payment, delivery, or transfer of the decedent's property is made under this chapter is liable for:

(1) The restitution of the property to the estate if the person still has the property, together with (A) the net income the person received from the property and (B) if the person encumbered the property after it was delivered or transferred to the person, the amount necessary to satisfy the balance of the encumbrance as of the date the property is restored to the estate.

(2) The restitution to the estate of the fair market value of the property if the person no longer has the property, together with (A) the net income the person received from the property and (B) interest on the fair market value of the property from the date of disposition at the rate payable on a money judgment. For the purposes of this subdivision, the "fair market value of the property" is the fair market value, determined as of the time of the disposition of the property, of the property paid, delivered, or transferred to the person under this chapter, less any liens and encumbrances on the property at that time.

(b) Subject to subdivision (c) and subject to any additional liability the person has under Sections 13109 to 13112, inclusive, if the person fraudulently secured the payment, delivery, or transfer of the decedent's property under this chapter, the person is liable under this section for restitution to the decedent's estate of three times the fair market value of the property. For the purposes of this subdivision, the "fair market value of the property" is the fair market value, determined as of the time the person liable under this subdivision presents the affidavit or declaration under this chapter, of the property paid, delivered, or transferred to the person under this chapter, less the amount of any liens and encumbrances on the property at that time.

(c) The property and amount required to be restored to the estate under this section shall be reduced by any property or amount paid by the person to satisfy a liability under Section 13109 or 13110.

(d) An action to enforce the liability under this section may be brought only by the personal representative of the estate of the decedent. In an action to enforce the liability under this section, the court's judgment may enforce the liability only to the extent necessary to protect the interests of the heirs, devisees, and creditors of the decedent.

(e) An action to enforce the liability under this section is forever barred three years after presentation of the affidavit or declaration under this chapter to the holder of the decedent's property, or three years after the discovery of the fraud, whichever is later. The three-year period specified in this subdivision is not tolled for any reason.

(f) In the case of a nondomiciliary decedent, restitution under this section shall be made to the estate in an ancillary administration proceeding.

13112. (a) A person to whom payment, delivery, or transfer of the decedent's property has been made under this chapter is not liable under Section 13109 or 13110 if proceedings for the administration of the decedent's estate are commenced in this state, and the person satisfies the requirements of Section 13101.

(b) Except as provided in subdivision (b) of Section 13110, the aggregate of the personal liability of a person under Sections 13109 and 13110 shall not exceed the fair market value, valued as of the time the affidavit or declaration is presented under this chapter, of the property paid, delivered, or transferred to the person under this chapter, less the amount of any liens and encumbrances on that property at that time, together with the net income the person received from the property and, if the property has been disposed of, interest on the fair market value of the property accruing from the date of disposition at the rate payable on a money judgment. For the purposes of this subdivision, "fair market value of the property" has the same meaning as defined in paragraph (2) of subdivision (a) of Section 13111. |

13113. The remedies available under Sections 13109 to 13112, inclusive, are in addition to any remedies available by reason of any fraud or intentional wrongdoing.

13114. (a) A public administrator who has taken possession or control of property of a decedent under Article 1 (commencing with Section 7600) of Chapter 4 of Part 1 of Division 7 may refuse to pay money or deliver property pursuant to this chapter if payment of the costs and fees described in Section 7604 has not first been made or adequately assured to the satisfaction of the public administrator.

(b) A coroner who has property found upon the body of a decedent, or who has taken charge of property of the decedent pursuant to Section 27491.3 of the Government Code, may refuse to pay or deliver the property pursuant to this chapter if payment of the reasonable costs of holding or safeguarding the property has not first been made or adequately assured to the satisfaction of the coroner.

13115. The procedure provided in this chapter may not be used to obtain possession or the transfer of real property.

13116. The procedure provided in this chapter is in addition to and supplemental to any other procedure for (1) collecting money due to a decedent, (2) receiving tangible personal property of a decedent, or (3) having evidence of ownership of property of a decedent transferred. Nothing in this chapter restricts or limits the release of tangible personal property of a decedent pursuant to any other provision of law. This section is declaratory of existing law.

Chapter 4. Court Order Determining Succession To Property

13150. The procedure provided by this chapter may be used only if one of the following requirements is satisfied:

(a) No proceeding is being or has been conducted in this state for administration of the decedent's estate.

(b) The decedent's personal representative consents in writing to use of the procedure provided by this chapter to determine that real property of the decedent is property passing to the petitioners.

13151. Exclusive of the property described in Section 13050, if a decedent dies leaving real property in this state and the gross value of the decedent's real and personal property in this state does not exceed one hundred fifty thousand dollars ($150,000) and 40 days have elapsed since the death of the decedent, the successor of the decedent to an interest in a particular item of property that is real property, without procuring letters of administration or awaiting the probate of the will, may file a petition in the superior court of the county in which the estate of the decedent may be administered requesting a court order determining that the petitioner has succeeded to that real property. A petition under this chapter may include an additional request that the court make an order determining that the petitioner has succeeded to personal property described in the petition.

13152. (a) The petition shall be verified by each petitioner, shall contain a request that the court make an order under this chapter determining that the property described in the petition is property passing to the petitioner, and shall state all of the following:

(1) The facts necessary to determine that the petition is filed in the proper county.

(2) The gross value of the decedent's real and personal property in this state, excluding the property described in Section 13050, as shown by the inventory and appraisal attached to the petition, does not exceed one hundred fifty thousand dollars ($150,000).

(3) A description of the particular item of real property in this state which the petitioner alleges is property of the decedent passing to the petitioner, and a description of the personal property which the petitioner alleges is property of the decedent passing to the petitioner if the requested order also is to include a determination that the described personal property is property passing to the petitioner.

(4) The facts upon which the petitioner bases the allegation that the described property is property passing to the petitioner.

(5) Either of the following, as appropriate:

(A) A statement that no proceeding is being or has been conducted in this state for administration of the decedent's estate.

(B) A statement that the decedent's personal representative has consented in writing to use of the procedure provided by this chapter.

(6) Whether estate proceedings for the decedent have been commenced in any other jurisdiction and, if so, where those proceedings are pending or were conducted.

(7) The name, age, address, and relation to the decedent of each heir and devisee of the decedent, the names and addresses of all persons named as executors of the will of the decedent, and, if the petitioner is the trustee of a trust that is a devisee under the will of the decedent, the names and addresses of all persons interested in the trust, as determined in cases of future interests pursuant to paragraph (1), (2), or (3) of subdivision (a) of Section 15804, so far as known to any petitioner.

(8) The name and address of each person serving as guardian or conservator of the estate of the decedent at the time of the decedent's death, so far as known to any petitioner.

(b) There shall be attached to the petition an inventory and appraisal in the form set forth in Section 8802 of the decedent's real and personal property in this state, excluding the property described in Section 13050. The appraisal shall be made by a probate referee selected by the petitioner from those probate referees appointed by the Controller under Section 400 to appraise property in the county where the real property is located. The appraisal shall be made as provided in Part 3 (commencing with Section 8800) of

Division 7. The petitioner may appraise the assets which a personal representative could appraise under Section 8901.

(c) If the petitioner bases his or her claim to the described property upon the will of the decedent, a copy of the will shall be attached to the petition.

(d) If the decedent's personal representative has consented to use of the procedure provided by this chapter, a copy of the consent shall be attached to the petition.

13153. Notice of the hearing shall be given as provided in Section 1220 to each of the persons named in the petition pursuant to Section 13152.

13154. (a) If the court makes the determinations required under subdivision (b), the court shall issue an order determining (1) that real property, to be described in the order, of the decedent is property passing to the petitioners and the specific property interest of each petitioner in the described property and (2) if the petition so requests, that personal property, to be described in the order, of the decedent is property passing to the petitioners and the specific property interest of each petitioner in the described property.

(b) The court may make an order under this section only if the court makes all of the following determinations:

(1) The gross value of the decedent's real and personal property in this state, excluding the property described in Section 13050, does not exceed one hundred fifty thousand dollars ($150,000).

(2) Not less than 40 days have elapsed since the death of the decedent.

(3) Whichever of the following is appropriate:

(A) No proceeding is being or has been conducted in this state for administration of the decedent's estate.

(B) The decedent's personal representative has consented in writing to use of the procedure provided by this chapter.

(4) The property described in the order is property of the decedent passing to the petitioner.

(c) If the petition has attached an inventory and appraisal that satisfies the requirements of subdivision (b) of Section 13152, the determination required by paragraph (1) of subdivision (b) of this section shall be made on the basis of the verified petition and the attached inventory and appraisal, unless evidence is offered by a person opposing the petition that the gross value of the decedent's real and personal property in this state, excluding the property described in Section 13050, exceeds one hundred fifty thousand dollars ($150,000).

13155. Upon becoming final, an order under this chapter determining that property is property passing to the petitioner is conclusive on all persons, whether or not they are in being.

13156. (a) Subject to subdivisions (b), (c), and (d), the petitioner who receives the decedent's property pursuant to an order under this chapter is personally liable for the unsecured debts of the decedent.

(b) The personal liability of any petitioner shall not exceed the fair market value at the date of the decedent's death of the property received by that petitioner pursuant to an order under this chapter, less the amount of any liens and encumbrances on the property.

(c) In any action or proceeding based upon an unsecured debt of the decedent, the petitioner may assert any defense, cross-complaint, or setoff which would have been available to the decedent if the decedent had not died.

(d) Nothing in this section permits enforcement of a claim that is barred under Part 4 (commencing with Section 9000) of Division 7.

(e) Section 366.2 of the Code of Civil Procedure applies in an action under this section.

13157. The attorney's fees for services performed in connection with the filing of a petition and obtaining a court order under this chapter shall be determined by private agreement between the attorney and the client and are not subject to approval by the court. If there is no agreement between the attorney and the client concerning the attorney's fees for services performed in connection with the filing of a petition and obtaining of a court order under this chapter and there is a dispute concerning the reasonableness of the attorney's fees for those services, a petition may be filed with the court in the same proceeding requesting that the court determine the reasonableness of the attorney's fees for those services. If there is an agreement between the attorney and the client concerning the attorney's fees for services performed in connection with the filing of a petition and obtaining a court order under this chapter and there is a dispute concerning the meaning of the agreement, a petition may be filed with the court in the same proceeding requesting that the court determine the dispute.

13158. Nothing in this chapter excuses compliance with Chapter 3 (commencing with Section 13100) by the holder of the decedent's personal property if an affidavit or declaration is furnished as provided in that chapter.

Chapter 5. Affidavit Procedure For Real Property Of Small Value

13200. (a) No sooner than six months from the death of a decedent, a person or persons claiming as successor of the decedent to a particular item of property that is real property may file in the superior court in the county in which the decedent was domi-

ciled at the time of death, or if the decedent was not domiciled in this state at the time of death, then in any county in which real property of the decedent is located, an affidavit in the form prescribed by the Judicial Council pursuant to Section 1001 stating all of the following:

(1) The name of the decedent.

(2) The date and place of the decedent's death.

(3) A legal description of the real property and the interest of the decedent therein.

(4) The name and address of each person serving as guardian or conservator of the estate of the decedent at the time of the decedent's death, so far as known to the affiant.

(5) "The gross value of all real property in the decedent's estate located in California, as shown by the inventory and appraisal attached to this affidavit, excluding the real property described in Section 13050 of the California Probate Code, does not exceed fifty thousand dollars ($50,000)."

(6) "At least six months have elapsed since the death of the decedent as shown in a certified copy of decedent's death certificate attached to this affidavit."

(7) Either of the following, as appropriate:

(A) "No proceeding is now being or has been conducted in California for administration of the decedent's estate."

(B) "The decedent's personal representative has consented in writing to use of the procedure provided by this chapter."

(8) "Funeral expenses, expenses of last illness, and all unsecured debts of the decedent have been paid."

(9) "The affiant is the successor of the decedent (as defined in Section 13006 of the Probate Code) and to the decedent's interest in the described property, and no other person has a superior right to the interest of the decedent in the described property."

(10) "The affiant declares under penalty of perjury under the laws of the State of California that the foregoing is true and correct."

(b) For each person executing the affidavit, the affidavit shall contain a notary public's certificate of acknowledgment identifying the person.

(c) There shall be attached to the affidavit an inventory and appraisal of the decedent's real property in this state, excluding the real property described in Section 13050. The inventory and appraisal of the real property shall be made as provided in Part 3 (commencing with Section 8800) of Division 7. The appraisal shall be made by a probate referee selected by the affiant from those probate referees appointed by the Controller under Section 400 to appraise property in the county where the real property is located.

(d) If the affiant claims under the decedent's will and no estate proceeding is pending or has been conducted in California, a copy of the will shall be attached to the affidavit.

(e) A certified copy of the decedent's death certificate shall be attached to the affidavit. If the decedent's personal representative has consented to the use of the procedure provided by this chapter, a copy of the consent and of the personal representative's letters shall be attached to the affidavit.

(f) The affiant shall mail a copy of the affidavit and attachments to any person identified in paragraph (4) of subdivision (a).

13201. Notwithstanding any other provision of law, the total fee for the filing of an affidavit under Section 13200 and the issuance of one certified copy of the affidavit under Section 13202 is as provided in subdivision (b) of Section 70626 of the Government Code.

13202. Upon receipt of the affidavit and the required fee, the court clerk, upon determining that the affidavit is complete and has the required attachments, shall file the affidavit and attachments and shall issue a certified copy of the affidavit without the attachments. The certified copy shall be recorded in the office of the county recorder of the county where the real property is located. The county recorder shall index the certified copy in the index of grantors and grantees. The decedent shall be indexed as the grantor and each person designated as a successor to the property in the certified copy shall be indexed as a grantee.

13203. (a) A person acting in good faith and for a valuable consideration with a person designated as a successor of the decedent to a particular item of property in a certified copy of an affidavit issued under Section 13202 and recorded in the county in which the real property is located has the same rights and protections as the person would have if each person designated as a successor in the recorded certified copy of the affidavit had been named as a distributee of the real property in an order for distribution that had become final.

(b) The issuance and recording of a certified copy of an affidavit under this chapter does not preclude later proceedings for administration of the decedent's estate.

13204. Each person who is designated as a successor of the decedent in a certified copy of an affidavit issued under Section 13202 is personally liable to the extent provided in Section 13207 for the unsecured debts of the decedent. Any such debt may be enforced against the person in the same manner as it could have been enforced against the decedent if the decedent had not died. In any action based upon the debt, the person may assert any defense, cross-complaint, or setoff that would have been available to the decedent if the decedent had not died. Nothing in this section permits enforcement of a claim that is barred under Part 4 (commencing with Section 9000) of Division 7. Section 366.2 of the Code of Civil Procedure applies in an action under this section.

13205. (a) Except as provided in subdivision (b), each person who is designated as a successor of the decedent in a certified copy of any affidavit issued under Section 13202 is personally liable to the extent provided in Section 13207 to any person having a superior right by testate or intestate succession from the decedent.

(b) In addition to any other liability the person has under this section and Sections 13204, 13206, and 13207, if the person fraudulently executed or filed the affidavit under this chapter, the person is liable to the person having a superior right for three times the fair market value of the property. For the purposes of this subdivision, the "fair market value of the property" is the fair market value, determined as of the time the certified copy of the affidavit was issued under Section 13202, of the property the person liable took under the certified copy of the affidavit to which the other person has a superior right, less any liens and encumbrances on the property at that time.

(c) An action to impose liability under this section is forever barred three years after the certified copy of the affidavit is issued under Section 13202, or three years after the discovery of the fraud, whichever is later. The three-year period specified in this subdivision is not tolled for any reason.

13206. (a) Subject to subdivisions (b), (c), (d), and (e), if proceedings for the administration of the decedent's estate are commenced, or if the decedent's personal representative has consented to use of the procedure provided by this chapter and the personal representative later requests that the property be restored to the estate, each person who is designated as a successor of the decedent in a certified copy of an affidavit issued under Section 13202 is liable for:

(1) The restitution to the decedent's estate of the property the person took under the certified copy of the affidavit if the person still has the property, together with (A) the net income the person received from the property and (B) if the person encumbered the property after the certified copy of the affidavit was issued, the amount necessary to satisfy the balance of the encumbrance as of the date the property is restored to the estate.

(2) The restitution to the decedent's estate of the fair market value of the property if the person no longer has the property, together with (A) the net income the person received from the property prior to disposing of it and (B) interest from the date of disposition at the rate payable on a money judgment on the fair market value of the property. For the purposes of this paragraph, the "fair market value of the property" is the fair market value, determined as of the time of the disposition of the property, of the property the person took under the certified copy of the affidavit, less the amount of any liens and

encumbrances on the property at the time the certified copy of the affidavit was issued.

(b) Subject to subdivision (d), if the person fraudulently executed or filed the affidavit under this chapter, the person is liable under this section for restitution to the decedent's estate of three times the fair market value of the property. For the purposes of this subdivision, the "fair market value of the property" is the fair market value, determined as of the time the certified copy of the affidavit was issued, of the property the person took under the certified copy of the affidavit, less the amount of any liens and encumbrances on the property at that time.

(c) Subject to subdivision (d), if proceedings for the administration of the decedent's estate are commenced and a person designated as a successor of the decedent in a certified copy of an affidavit issued under Section 13202 made a significant improvement to the property taken by the person under the certified copy of the affidavit in the good faith belief that the person was the successor of the decedent to that property, the person is liable for whichever of the following the decedent's estate elects:

(1) The restitution of the property, as improved, to the estate of the decedent upon the condition that the estate reimburse the person making restitution for (A) the amount by which the improvement increases the fair market value of the property restored, determined as of the time of restitution, and (B) the amount paid by the person for principal and interest on any liens or encumbrances that were on the property at the time the certified copy of the affidavit was issued.

(2) The restoration to the decedent's estate of the fair market value of the property, determined as of the time of the issuance of the certified copy of the affidavit under Section 13202, less the amount of any liens and encumbrances on the property at that time, together with interest on the net amount at the rate payable on a money judgment running from the date of the issuance of the certified copy of the affidavit.

(d) The property and amount required to be restored to the estate under this section shall be reduced by any property or amount paid by the person to satisfy a liability under Section 13204 or 13205.

(e) An action to enforce the liability under this section may be brought only by the personal representative of the estate of the decedent. In an action to enforce the liability under this section, the court's judgment may enforce the liability only to the extent necessary to protect the interests of the heirs, devisees, and creditors of the decedent.

(f) An action to enforce the liability under this section is forever barred three years after the certified copy of the affidavit is issued under Section 13202, or three years after the discovery of the fraud, whichever is later. The three-year period specified in this subdivision is not tolled for any reason.

13207. (a) A person designated as a successor of the decedent in a certified copy of an affidavit issued under Section 13202 is not liable under Section 13204 or 13205 if proceedings for the administration of the decedent's estate are commenced, or if the decedent's personal representative has consented to use of the procedure provided by this chapter and the personal representative later requests that the property be restored to the estate, and the person satisfies the requirements of Section 13206.

(b) Except as provided in subdivision (b) of Section 13205, the aggregate of the personal liability of a person under Sections 13204 and 13205 shall not exceed the sum of the following:

(1) The fair market value at the time of the issuance of the certified copy of the affidavit under Section 13202 of the decedent's property received by that person under this chapter, less the amount of any liens and encumbrances on the property at that time.

(2) The net income the person received from the property.

(3) If the property has been disposed of, interest on the fair market value of the property from the date of disposition at the rate payable on a money judgment. For the purposes of this paragraph, "fair market value of the property" has the same meaning as defined in paragraph (2) of subdivision (a) of Section 13206.

13208. The remedies available under Sections 13204 to 13207, inclusive, are in addition to any remedies available by reason of any fraud or intentional wrongdoing.

13210. The procedure provided by this chapter may be used only if one of the following requirements is satisfied:

(a) No proceeding for the administration of the decedent's estate is pending or has been conducted in this state.

(b) The decedent's personal representative consents in writing to use of the procedure provided by this chapter.

Part 2. Passage Of Property To Surviving Spouse Without Administration

Chapter 1. General Provisions

13500. Except as provided in this chapter, when a husband or wife dies intestate leaving property that passes to the surviving spouse under Section 6401, or dies testate and by his or her will devises all or a part of his or her property to the surviving spouse, the property passes to the survivor subject to the provisions of Chapter 2 (commencing with Section 13540) and Chapter 3 (commencing with Section 13550), and no administration is necessary.

13501. Except as provided in Chapter 6 (commencing with Section 6600) of Division 6 and in Part 1 (commencing with Section 13000) of this division, the following property of the decedent is subject to administration under this code:

(a) Property passing to someone other than the surviving spouse under the decedent's will or by intestate succession.

(b) Property disposed of in trust under the decedent's will.

(c) Property in which the decedent's will limits the surviving spouse to a qualified ownership. For the purposes of this subdivision, a devise to the surviving spouse that is conditioned on the spouse surviving the decedent by a specified period of time is not a "qualified ownership" interest if the specified period of time has expired.

13502. (a) Upon the election of the surviving spouse or the personal representative, guardian of the estate, or conservator of the estate of the surviving spouse, all or a portion of the following property may be administered under this code:

(1) The one-half of the community property that belongs to the decedent under Section 100, the one-half of the quasi-community property that belongs to the decedent under Section 101, and the separate property of the decedent.

(2) The one-half of the community property that belongs to the surviving spouse under Section 100 and the one-half of the quasi-community property that belongs to the surviving spouse under Section 101.

(b) The election shall be made by a writing specifically evidencing the election filed in the proceedings for the administration of the estate of the deceased spouse within four months after the issuance of letters, or within any further time that the court may allow upon a showing of good cause, and before entry of an order under Section 13656.

13502.5. (a) Upon a petition by the personal representative of a decedent and a showing of good cause, the court may order that a pecuniary devise to the surviving spouse, or a fractional interest passing to the surviving spouse in any property in which the remaining fraction is subject to the administration, may be administered under this code, except to the extent that it has passed by inheritance as determined by an order pursuant to Chapter 5 (commencing with Section 13650).

(b) Notice of this petition shall be given as provided in Section 1220 to the person designated in that section and to the surviving spouse.

13503. (a) The surviving spouse or the personal representative, guardian of the estate, or conservator of the estate of the surviving spouse may file an election and agreement to have all or part of the one-half of the community property that belongs to the surviving spouse under Section 100 and the one-half of the quasi-community property that belongs to the surviving spouse under Section 101 transferred by the surviving spouse or the surviving spouse's personal representative, guardian, or conservator to the trustee under the will of the deceased spouse or the trustee of an existing trust identified by the will of the deceased spouse, to be administered and distributed by the trustee.

(b) The election and agreement shall be filed in the proceedings for the administration of the estate of the deceased spouse and before the entry of the order for final distribution in the proceedings.

13504. Notwithstanding the provisions of this part, community property held in a revocable trust described in Section 761 of the Family Code is governed by the provisions, if any, in the trust for disposition in the event of death.

13505. This part applies whether the deceased spouse died before, on, or after July 1, 1987.

13506. A reference in any statute of this state or in a written instrument, including a will or trust, to a provision of former Sections 202 to 206, inclusive, of the Probate Code (as repealed by Chapter 527 of the Statutes of 1984) or former Sections 649.1 to 649.5, inclusive, or Sections 650 to 658, inclusive, of the Probate Code (as repealed by Chapter 783 of the Statutes of 1986) shall be deemed to be a reference to the comparable provision of this part.

Chapter 2. Right Of Surviving Spouse To Dispose Of Property

13540. (a) Except as provided in Section 13541, after 40 days from the death of a spouse, the surviving spouse or the personal representative, guardian of the estate, or conservator of the estate of the surviving spouse has full power to sell, convey, lease, mortgage, or otherwise deal with and dispose of the community or quasi-community real property, and the right, title, and interest of any grantee, purchaser, encumbrancer, or lessee shall be free of rights of the estate of the deceased spouse or of devisees or creditors of the deceased spouse to the same extent as if the property had been owned as the separate property of the surviving spouse.

(b) The surviving spouse or the personal representative, guardian of the estate, or conservator of the estate of the surviving spouse may record, prior to or together with the instrument that makes a disposition of property under this section, an affidavit of the facts that establish the right of the surviving spouse to make the disposition.

(c) Nothing in this section affects or limits the liability of the surviving spouse under Sections 13550 to 13553, inclusive, and Chapter 3.5 (commencing with Section 13560).

13541. (a) Section 13540 does not apply to a sale, conveyance, lease, mortgage, or other disposition that takes place after a notice that satisfies the requirements of this section is recorded in the office of the county recorder of the county in which real property is located.

(b) The notice shall contain all of the following:

(1) A description of the real property in which an interest is claimed.

(2) A statement that an interest in the property is claimed by a named person under the will of the deceased spouse.

(3) The name or names of the owner or owners of the record title to the property.

(c) There shall be endorsed on the notice instructions that it shall be indexed by the recorder in the name or names of the owner or owners of record title to the property, as grantor or grantors, and in the name of the person claiming an interest in the property, as grantee.

(d) A person shall not record a notice under this section for the purpose of slandering title to the property. If the court in an action or proceeding relating to the rights of the parties determines that a person recorded a notice under this section for the purpose of slandering title, the court shall award against the person the cost of the action or proceeding, including a reasonable attorney's fee, and the damages caused by the recording.

13542. The repeal of former Section 649.2 by Chapter 783 of the Statutes of 1986 does not affect any sale, lease, mortgage, or other transaction or disposition of real property made prior to July 1, 1987, to which that section applied, and such a sale, lease, mortgage, or other transaction or disposition shall continue to be governed by the provisions of former Section 649.2 notwithstanding the repeal of that section.

13545. (a) After the death of a spouse, the surviving spouse, or the personal representative, guardian of the estate, or conservator of the estate of the surviving spouse has full power to sell, assign, pledge, or otherwise deal with and dispose of community or quasi-community property securities registered in the name of the surviving spouse alone, and the right, title, and interest of any purchaser, assignee, encumbrancer, or other transferee shall be free of the rights of the estate of the deceased spouse or of devisees or creditors of the deceased spouse to the same extent as if the deceased spouse had not died.

(b) Nothing in this section affects or limits the liability of a surviving spouse under Sections 13550 to 13553, inclusive, and Chapter 3.5 (commencing with Section 13560).

Chapter 3. Liability For Debts Of Deceased Spouse

13550. Except as provided in Sections 11446, 13552, 13553, and 13554, upon the death of a married person, the surviving spouse is personally liable for the debts of the deceased spouse chargeable against the property described in Section 13551 to the extent provided in Section 13551.

13551. The liability imposed by Section 13550 shall not exceed the fair market value at the date of the decedent's death, less the amount of any liens and encumbrances, of the total of the following:

(a) The portion of the one-half of the community and quasi-community property belonging to the surviving spouse under Sections 100 and 101 that is not exempt from enforcement of a money judgment and is not administered in the estate of the deceased spouse.

(b) The portion of the one-half of the community and quasi-community property belonging to the decedent under Sections 100 and 101 that passes to the surviving spouse without administration.

(c) The separate property of the decedent that passes to the surviving spouse without administration.

13552. If proceedings are commenced in this state for the administration of the estate of the deceased spouse and the time for filing claims has commenced, any action upon the liability of the surviving spouse pursuant to Section 13550 is barred to the same extent as provided for claims under Part 4 (commencing with Section 9000) of Division 7, except as to the following:

(a) Creditors who commence judicial proceedings for the enforcement of the debt and serve the surviving spouse with the complaint therein prior to the expiration of the time for filing claims.

(b) Creditors who have or who secure the surviving spouse's acknowledgment in writing of the liability of the surviving spouse for the debts.

(c) Creditors who file a timely claim in the proceedings for the administration of the estate of the deceased spouse.

13553. The surviving spouse is not liable under this chapter if all the property described in paragraphs (1) and (2) of subdivision (a) of Section 13502 is administered under this code.

13554. (a) Except as otherwise provided in this chapter, any debt described in Section 13550 may be enforced against the surviving spouse in the same manner as it could have been enforced against the deceased spouse if the deceased spouse had not died.

(b) In any action or proceeding based upon the debt, the surviving spouse may assert any defense, cross-complaint, or setoff which would have been available to the deceased spouse if the deceased spouse had not died.

(c) Section 366.2 of the Code of Civil Procedure applies in an action under this section.

Chapter 3.5. Liability For Decedent's Property

13560. For the purposes of this chapter, "decedent's property" means the one-half of the community property that belongs to the decedent under Section 100 and the one-half of the quasi-community property that belongs to the decedent under Section 101.

13561. (a) If the decedent's property is in the possession or control of the surviving spouse at the time of the decedent's death, the surviving spouse is personally liable to the extent provided in Section 13563 to any person having a superior right by testate succession from the decedent.

(b) An action to impose liability under this section is forever barred three years after the death of the decedent. The three-year period specified in this subdivision is not tolled for any reason.

13562. (a) Subject to subdivisions (b), (c), and (d), if proceedings for the administration of the decedent's estate are commenced, the surviving spouse is liable for:

(1) The restitution to the decedent's estate of the decedent's property if the surviving spouse still has the decedent's property, together with (A) the net income the surviving spouse received from the decedent's property and (B) if the surviving spouse encumbered the decedent's property after the date of death, the amount necessary to satisfy the balance of the encumbrance as of the date the decedent's property is restored to the estate.

(2) The restitution to the decedent's estate of the fair market value of the decedent's property if the surviving spouse no longer has the decedent's property, together with (A) the net income the surviving spouse received from the decedent's property prior to disposing of it and (B) interest from the date of disposition at the rate payable on a money judgment on the fair market value of the decedent's property. For the purposes of this paragraph, the "fair market value of the decedent's property" is the fair market value of the decedent's property, determined as of the time of the disposition of the decedent's property, less the amount of any liens and encumbrances on the decedent's property at the time of the decedent's death.

(b) Subject to subdivision (c), if proceedings for the administration of the decedent's estate are commenced and the surviving spouse made a significant improvement to the decedent's property in the good faith belief that the surviving spouse was the successor of the decedent to the decedent's property, the surviving spouse is liable for whichever of the following the decedent's estate elects:

(1) The restitution of the decedent's property, as improved, to the estate of the decedent upon the condition that the estate reimburse the surviving spouse for (A) the amount by which the improvement increases the fair market value of the decedent's property restored, valued as of the time of restitution, and (B) the amount paid by the surviving spouse for principal and interest on any liens or encumbrances that were on the decedent's property at the time of the decedent's death.

(2) The restoration to the decedent's estate of the fair market value of the decedent's property, valued as of the time of the decedent's death, excluding the amount of any liens and encumbrances on the decedent's property at that time, together with interest on the net amount at the rate payable on a money judgment running from the date of the decedent's death.

(c) The property and amount required to be restored to the estate under this section shall be reduced by any property or amount paid by the surviving spouse to satisfy a liability under Chapter 3 (commencing with Section 13550).

(d) An action to enforce the liability under this section may be brought only by the personal representative of the estate of the decedent. In an action to enforce the liability under this section, the court's judgment may enforce the liability only to the extent necessary to protect the interests of the heirs, devisees, and creditors of the decedent.

(e) An action to enforce the liability under this section is forever barred three years after the death of the decedent. The three-year period specified in this subdivision is not tolled for any reason.

13563. (a) The surviving spouse is not liable under Section 13561 if proceedings for the administration of the decedent's estate are commenced and the surviving spouse satisfies the requirements of Section 13562.

(b) The aggregate of the personal liability of the surviving spouse under Section 13561 shall not exceed the sum of the following:

(1) The fair market value at the time of the decedent's death, less the amount of any liens and encumbrances on the decedent's property at that time, of the portion of the decedent's property that passes to any person having a superior right by testate succession from the decedent.

(2) The net income the surviving spouse received from the portion of the decedent's property that passes to any person having a superior right by testate succession from the decedent.

(3) If the decedent's property has been disposed of, interest on the fair market value of the portion of the decedent's property that passes to any person having a superior right by testate succession from the decedent from the date of disposition at the rate payable on a money judgment. For the purposes

of this paragraph, "fair market value" is fair market value, determined as of the time of disposition of the decedent's property, less the amount of any liens and encumbrances on the decedent's property at the time of the decedent's death.

13564. The remedies available under Sections 13561 to 13563, inclusive, are in addition to any remedies available by reason of any fraud or intentional wrongdoing.

Chapter 4. Collection By Affidavit Of Compensation Owed To Deceased Spouse

13600. (a) At any time after a husband or wife dies, the surviving spouse or the guardian or conservator of the estate of the surviving spouse may, without procuring letters of administration or awaiting probate of the will, collect salary or other compensation owed by an employer for personal services of the deceased spouse, including compensation for unused vacation, not in excess of fifteen thousand dollars ($15,000) net.

(b) Not more than fifteen thousand dollars ($15,000) net in the aggregate may be collected by or for the surviving spouse under this chapter from all of the employers of the decedent.

(c) For the purposes of this chapter, a guardian or conservator of the estate of the surviving spouse may act on behalf of the surviving spouse without authorization or approval of the court in which the guardianship or conservatorship proceeding is pending.

(d) The fifteen-thousand-dollar ($15,000) net limitation set forth in subdivisions (a) and (b) does not apply to the surviving spouse or the guardian or conservator of the estate of the surviving spouse of a firefighter or peace officer described in subdivision (a) of Section 22820 of the Government Code.

(e) On January 1, 2003, and on January 1 of each year thereafter, the maximum net amount of salary or compensation payable under subdivisions (a) and (b) to the surviving spouse or the guardian or conservator of the estate of the surviving spouse may be adjusted to reflect any increase in the cost of living occurring after January 1 of the immediately preceding year. The United States city average of the "Consumer Price Index for All Urban Consumers," as published by the United States Bureau of Labor Statistics, shall be used as the basis for determining the changes in the cost of living. The cost-of-living increase shall equal or exceed 1 percent before any adjustment is made. The net amount payable may not be decreased as a result of the cost-of-living adjustment.

13601. (a) To collect salary or other compensation under this chapter, an affidavit or a declaration under penalty of perjury under the laws of this state shall be furnished to the employer of the deceased spouse stating all of the following:

(1) The name of the decedent.

(2) The date and place of the decedent's death.

(3) Either of the following, as appropriate:

(A) "The affiant or declarant is the surviving spouse of the decedent."

(B) "The affiant or declarant is the guardian or conservator of the estate of the surviving spouse of the decedent."

(4) "The surviving spouse of the decedent is entitled to the earnings of the decedent under the decedent's will or by intestate succession and no one else has a superior right to the earnings."

(5) "No proceeding is now being or has been conducted in California for administration of the decedent's estate."

(6) "Sections 13600 to 13605, inclusive, of the California Probate Code require that the earnings of the decedent, including compensation for unused vacation, not in excess of fifteen thousand dollars ($15,000) net, be paid promptly to the affiant or declarant."

(7) "Neither the surviving spouse, nor anyone acting on behalf of the surviving spouse, has a pending request to collect compensation owed by another employer for personal services of the decedent under Sections 13600 to 13605, inclusive, of the California Probate Code."

(8) "Neither the surviving spouse, nor anyone acting on behalf of the surviving spouse, has collected any compensation owed by an employer for personal services of the decedent under Sections 13600 to 13605, inclusive, of the California Probate Code except the sum of ____ dollars ($____) which was collected from ____."

(9) "The affiant or declarant requests that he or she be paid the salary or other compensation owed by you for personal services of the decedent, including compensation for unused vacation, not to exceed fifteen thousand dollars ($15,000) net, less the amount of ____ dollars ($____) which was previously collected."

(10) "The affiant or declarant affirms or declares under penalty of perjury under the laws of the State of California that the foregoing is true and correct."

(b) Reasonable proof of the identity of the surviving spouse shall be provided to the employer. If a guardian or conservator is acting for the surviving spouse, reasonable proof of the identity of the guardian or conservator shall also be provided to the employer. Proof of identity that is sufficient under Section 13104 is sufficient proof of identity for the purposes of this subdivision.

(c) If a person presenting the affidavit or declaration is a person claiming to be the guardian or conservator of the estate of the surviving spouse, the employer shall be provided with reasonable proof, satisfactory to the employer, of the appointment of the person to act as guardian or conservator of the estate of the surviving spouse.

13602. If the requirements of Section 13600 are satisfied, the employer to whom the affidavit or declaration is presented shall promptly pay the earnings of the decedent, including compensation for unused vacation, not in excess of fifteen thousand dollars ($15,000) net, to the person presenting the affidavit or declaration.

13603. If the requirements of Section 13601 are satisfied, receipt by the employer of the affidavit or declaration constitutes sufficient acquittance for the compensation paid pursuant to this chapter and discharges the employer from any further liability with respect to the compensation paid. The employer may rely in good faith on the statements in the affidavit or declaration and has no duty to inquire into the truth of any statement in the affidavit or declaration.

13604. (a) If the employer refuses to pay as required by this chapter, the surviving spouse may recover the amount the surviving spouse is entitled to receive under this chapter in an action brought for that purpose against the employer.

(b) If an action is brought against the employer under this section, the court shall award reasonable attorney's fees to the surviving spouse if the court finds that the employer acted unreasonably in refusing to pay as required by this chapter.

13605. (a) Nothing in this chapter limits the rights of the heirs or devisees of the deceased spouse. Payment of a decedent's compensation pursuant to this chapter does not preclude later proceedings for administration of the decedent's estate.

(b) Any person to whom payment is made under this chapter is answerable and accountable therefor to the personal representative of the decedent's estate and is liable for the amount of the payment to any other person having a superior right to the payment received. In addition to any other liability the person has under this section, a person who fraudulently secures a payment under this chapter is liable to a person having a superior right to the payment for three times the amount of the payment.

13606. The procedure provided in this chapter is in addition to, and not in lieu of, any other method of collecting compensation owed to a decedent.

Chapter 5. Determination Or Confirmation Of Property Passing Or Belonging To Surviving Spouse

13650. (a) A surviving spouse or the personal representative, guardian of the estate, or conservator of the estate of the surviving spouse may file a petition in the superior court of the county in which the estate of the deceased spouse may be administered requesting an order that administration of all or part of the estate is not necessary for the reason that all or part of the estate is property passing to the surviving spouse. The petition may also request an order confirming the ownership of the surviving spouse of property belonging to the surviving spouse under Section 100 or 101.

(b) To the extent of the election, this section does not apply to property that the petitioner has elected, as provided in Section 13502, to have administered under this code.

(c) A guardian or conservator may file a petition under this section without authorization or approval of the court in which the guardianship or conservatorship proceeding is pending.

13651. (a) A petition filed pursuant to Section 13650 shall allege that administration of all or a part of the estate of the deceased spouse is not necessary for the reason that all or a part of the estate is property passing to the surviving spouse, and shall set forth all of the following information:

(1) If proceedings for the administration of the estate are not pending, the facts necessary to determine the county in which the estate of the deceased spouse may be administered.

(2) A description of the property of the deceased spouse which the petitioner alleges is property passing to the surviving spouse, including the trade or business name of any property passing to the surviving spouse that consists of an unincorporated business or an interest in an unincorporated business which the deceased spouse was operating or managing at the time of death, subject to any written agreement between the deceased spouse and the surviving spouse providing for a non pro rata division of the aggregate value of the community property assets or quasi-community assets, or both.

(3) The facts upon which the petitioner bases the allegation that all or a part of the estate of the deceased spouse is property passing to the surviving spouse.

(4) A description of any interest in the community property or quasi-community property, or both, which the petitioner requests the court to confirm to the surviving spouse as belonging to the surviving spouse pursuant to Section 100 or 101, subject to any written agreement between the deceased spouse and the surviving spouse providing for a non pro rata division of the aggregate value of the community property assets or quasi-community assets, or both.

(5) The name, age, address, and relation to the deceased spouse of each heir and devisee of the deceased spouse, the names and addresses of all persons named as executors of the will of the deceased spouse, and the names and addresses of all persons appointed as personal representatives of the deceased spouse, which are known to the petitioner.

Disclosure of any written agreement between the deceased spouse and the surviving spouse providing for a non pro rata division of the aggregate value of the community property assets or quasi-community property assets, or both, or the affirmative statement that this agreement does not exist. If a dispute arises as to the division of the community property assets or quasi-community property assets, or both, pursuant to this agreement, the court shall determine the division subject to terms and conditions or other remedies that appear equitable under the circumstances of the case, taking into account the rights of all interested persons.

(b) If the petitioner bases the allegation that all or part of the estate of the deceased spouse is property passing to the surviving spouse upon the will of the deceased spouse, a copy of the will shall be attached to the petition.

(c) If the petitioner bases the description of the property of the deceased spouse passing to the surviving spouse or the property to be confirmed to the surviving spouse, or both, upon a written agreement between the deceased spouse and the surviving spouse providing for a non pro rata division of the aggregate value of the community property assets or quasi-community assets, or both, a copy of the agreement shall be attached to the petition.

13652. If proceedings for the administration of the estate of the deceased spouse are pending, a petition under this chapter shall be filed in those proceedings without the payment of an additional fee.

13653. If proceedings for the administration of the estate of the deceased spouse are not pending, a petition under this chapter may, but need not, be filed with a petition for probate of the will of the deceased spouse or for administration of the estate of the deceased spouse.

13654. The filing of a petition under this chapter does not preclude the court from admitting the will of the deceased spouse to probate or appointing a personal representative of the estate of the deceased spouse upon the petition of any person legally entitled, including any petition for probate of the will or for administration of the estate which is filed with a petition filed under this chapter.

13655. (a) If proceedings for the administration of the estate of the deceased spouse are pending at the time a petition is filed under this chapter, or if the proceedings are not pending and if the petition filed under this chapter is not filed with a petition for probate of the deceased spouse's will or for administration of the estate of the deceased spouse, notice of the hearing on the petition filed under this chapter shall be given as provided in Section 1220 to all of the following persons:

(1) Each person listed in Section 1220 and each person named as executor in any will of the deceased spouse.

(2) All devisees and known heirs of the deceased spouse and, if the petitioner is the trustee of a trust that is a devisee under the will of the decedent, all persons interested in the trust, as determined in cases of future interests pursuant to paragraph (1), (2), or (3) of subdivision (a) of Section 15804.

(b) The notice specified in subdivision (a) shall also be mailed as provided in subdivision (a) to the Attorney General, addressed to the office of the Attorney General at Sacramento, if the petitioner bases the allegation that all or part of the estate of the deceased spouse is property passing to the surviving spouse upon the will of the deceased spouse and the will involves or may involve either of the following:

(1) A testamentary trust of property for charitable purposes other than a charitable trust with a designated trustee, resident in this state.

(2) A devise for a charitable purpose without an identified devisee or beneficiary

13656. (a) If the court finds that all of the estate of the deceased spouse is property passing to the surviving spouse, the court shall issue an order describing the property, determining that the property is property passing to the surviving spouse, and determining that no administration is necessary. The court may issue any further orders which may be necessary to cause delivery of the property or its proceeds to the surviving spouse.

(b) If the court finds that all or part of the estate of the deceased spouse is not property passing to the surviving spouse, the court shall issue an order (1) describing any property which is not property passing to the surviving spouse, determining that that property does not pass to the surviving spouse and determining that that property is subject to administration under this code and (2) describing the property, if any, which is property passing to the surviving spouse, determining that that property passes to the surviving spouse, and determining that no administration of that property is necessary. If the court determines that property passes to the surviving spouse, the court may issue any further orders which may be necessary to cause delivery of that property or its proceeds to the surviving spouse.

(c) If the petition filed under this chapter includes a description of the interest of the surviving spouse in the community or quasi-community property, or both, which belongs to the surviving spouse pursuant to Section 100 or 101 and the court finds that the interest belongs to the surviving spouse, the court shall issue an order describing the property and confirming the ownership of the surviving spouse and may issue any further orders which may be necessary to cause ownership of the property to be confirmed in the surviving spouse.

13657. Upon becoming final, an order under Section 13656 (1) determining that property is property passing to the surviving spouse or (2) confirming the ownership of the surviving spouse of property belonging to the surviving spouse under Section 100 or 101 shall be conclusive on all persons, whether or not they are in being.

13658. If the court determines that all or a part of the property passing to the surviving spouse consists of an unincorporated business or an interest in an unincorporated business which the deceased spouse was operating or managing at the time of death, the court shall require the surviving spouse to file a list of all of the known creditors of the business and the amounts owing to each of them. The court may issue any order necessary to protect the interests of the creditors of the business, including, but not limited to, the filing of (1) an undertaking and (2) an inventory and appraisal in the form provided in Section 8802 and made as provided in Part 3 (commencing with Section 8800) of Division 7.

13659. Except as provided in Section 13658, no inventory and appraisal of the estate of the deceased spouse is required in a proceeding under this chapter. However, within three months after the filing of a petition under this chapter, or within such further time as the court or judge for reasonable cause may allow, the petitioner may file with the clerk of the court an inventory and appraisal made as provided in Part 3 (commencing with Section 8800) of Division 7. The petitioner may appraise the assets which a personal representative could appraise under Section 8901.

13660. The attorney's fees for services performed in connection with the filing of a petition and obtaining of a court order under this chapter shall be determined by private agreement between the attorney and the client and are not subject to approval by the court. If there is no agreement between the attorney and the client concerning the attorney's fees for services performed in connection with the filing of a petition and obtaining of a court order under this chapter and there is a dispute concerning the reasonableness of the attorney's fees for those services, a petition may be filed with the court in the same proceeding requesting that the court determine the reasonableness of the attorney's fees for those services. If there is an agreement between the attorney and the client concerning the attorney's fees for services performed in connection with the filing of a petition and obtaining a court order under this chapter and there is a dispute concerning the meaning of the agreement, a petition may be filed with the court in the same proceeding requesting that the court determine the dispute.

Division 9. Trust Law

Part 1. General Provisions

15000. This division shall be known and may be cited as the Trust Law.

15001. Except as otherwise provided by statute:

(a) This division applies to all trusts regardless of whether they were created before, on, or after July 1, 1987.

(b) This division applies to all proceedings concerning trusts commenced on or after July 1, 1987.

(c) This division applies to all proceedings concerning trusts commenced before July 1, 1987, unless in the opinion of the court application of a particular provision of this division would substantially interfere with the effective conduct of the proceedings or the rights of the parties and other interested persons, in which case the particular provision of this division does not apply and prior law applies.

15002. Except to the extent that the common law rules governing trusts are modified by statute, the common law as to trusts is the law of this state.

15003. (a) Nothing in this division affects the substantive law relating to constructive or resulting trusts.

(b) The repeal of Title 8 (commencing with Section 2215) of Part 4 of Division 3 of the Civil Code by Chapter 820 of the Statutes of 1986 was not intended to alter the rules applied by the courts to fiduciary and confidential relationships, except as to express trusts governed by this division.

(c) Nothing in this division or in Section 82 is intended to prevent the application of all or part of the principles or procedures of this division to an entity or relationship that is excluded from the definition of "trust" provided by Section 82 where these principles or procedures are applied pursuant to statutory or common law principles, by court order or rule, or by contract.

15004. Unless otherwise provided by statute, this division applies to charitable trusts that are subject to the jurisdiction of the Attorney General to the extent that the application of the provision is not in conflict with the Uniform Supervision of Trustees for Charitable Purposes Act, Article 7 (commencing with Section 12580) of Chapter 6 of Part 2 of Division 3 of Title 2 of the Government Code.

Part 2. Creation, Validity, Modification, And Termination Of Trusts

Chapter 1. Creation And Validity Of Trusts

15200. Subject to other provisions of this chapter, a trust may be created by any of the following methods:

(a) A declaration by the owner of property that the owner holds the property as trustee.

(b) A transfer of property by the owner during the owner's lifetime to another person as trustee.

(c) A transfer of property by the owner, by will or by other instrument taking effect upon the death of the owner, to another person as trustee.

(d) An exercise of a power of appointment to another person as trustee.

(e) An enforceable promise to create a trust.

15201. A trust is created only if the settlor properly manifests an intention to create a trust.

15202. A trust is created only if there is trust property.

15203. A trust may be created for any purpose that is not illegal or against public policy.

15204. A trust created for an indefinite or general purpose is not invalid for that reason if it can be determined with reasonable certainty that a particular use of the trust property comes within that purpose.

15205. (a) A trust, other than a charitable trust, is created only if there is a beneficiary.

(b) The requirement of subdivision (a) is satisfied if the trust instrument provides for either of the following:

(1) A beneficiary or class of beneficiaries that is ascertainable with reasonable certainty or that is sufficiently described so it can be determined that some person meets the description or is within the class.

(2) A grant of a power to the trustee or some other person to select the beneficiaries based on a standard or in the discretion of the trustee or other person.

15206. A trust in relation to real property is not valid unless evidenced by one of the following methods:

(a) By a written instrument signed by the trustee, or by the trustee's agent if authorized in writing to do so.

(b) By a written instrument conveying the trust property signed by the settlor, or by the settlor's agent if authorized in writing to do so.

(c) By operation of law.

15207. (a) The existence and terms of an oral trust of personal property may be established only by clear and convincing evidence.

(b) The oral declaration of the settlor, standing alone, is not sufficient evidence of the creation of a trust of personal property.

(c) In the case of an oral trust, a reference in this division or elsewhere to a trust instrument or declaration means the terms of the trust as established pursuant to subdivision (a).

15208. Consideration is not required to create a trust, but a promise to create a trust in the future is enforceable only if the requirements for an enforceable contract are satisfied.

15209. If a trust provides for one or more successor beneficiaries after the death of the settlor, the trust is not invalid, merged, or terminated in either of the following circumstances:

(a) Where there is one settlor who is the sole trustee and the sole beneficiary during the settlor's lifetime.

(b) Where there are two or more settlors, one or more of whom are trustees, and the beneficial interest in the trust is in one or more of the settlors during the lifetime of the settlors.

15210. A trust created pursuant to this chapter which relates to real property may be recorded in the office of the county recorder in the county where all or a portion of the real property is located.

15211. A trust for a noncharitable corporation or unincorporated society or for a lawful noncharitable purpose may be performed by the trustee for only 21 years, whether or not there is a beneficiary who can seek enforcement or termination of the trust and whether or not the terms of the trust contemplate a longer duration.

15212. (a) Subject to the requirements of this section, a trust for the care of an animal is a trust for a lawful noncharitable purpose. Unless expressly provided in the trust, the trust terminates when no animal living on the date of the settlor's death remains alive. The governing instrument of the animal trust shall be liberally construed to bring the trust within this section, to presume against the merely precatory or honorary nature of the disposition, and to carry out the general intent of the settlor. Extrinsic evidence is admissible in determining the settlor's intent.

(b) A trust for the care of an animal is subject to the following requirements:

(1) Except as expressly provided otherwise in the trust instrument, the principal or income shall not be converted to the use of the trustee or to any use other than for the benefit of the animal.

(2) Upon termination of the trust, the trustee shall distribute the unexpended trust property in the following order:

(A) As directed in the trust instrument.

(B) If the trust was created in a nonresiduary clause in the settlor's will or in a codicil to the settlor's will, under the residuary clause in the settlor's will.

(C) If the application of subparagraph (A) or (B) does not result in distribution of unexpended trust property, to the settlor's heirs under Section 21114.

(3) For the purposes of Section 21110, the residuary clause described in subparagraph (B) of paragraph (2) shall be treated as creating a future interest under the terms of a trust.

(c) The intended use of the principal or income may be enforced by a person designated for that purpose in the trust instrument or, if none is designated, by a person appointed by a court. In addition to a person identified in subdivision (a) of Section 17200, any person interested in the welfare of the animal or any nonprofit charitable organization that has as its principal activity the care of animals may petition the court regarding the trust as provided in Chapter 3 (commencing with Section 17200) of Part 5.

(d) If a trustee is not designated or no designated or successor trustee is willing or able to serve, a court shall name a trustee. A court may order the transfer of the trust property to a court-appointed trustee, if it is required to ensure that the intended use is carried out and if a successor trustee is not designated in the trust instrument or if no designated successor trustee agrees to serve or is able to serve. A court may also make all other orders and determinations as it shall deem advisable to carry out the intent of the settlor and the purpose of this section.

(e) The accountings required by Section 16062 shall be provided to the beneficiaries who would be entitled to distribution if the animal were then deceased and to any nonprofit charitable corporation that has as its principal activity the care of animals and that has requested these accountings in writing. However, if the value of the assets in the trust does not exceed forty thousand dollars ($40,000), no filing, report, registration, periodic accounting, separate maintenance of funds, appointment, or fee is required by reason of the existence of the fiduciary relationship of the trustee, unless ordered by the court or required by the trust instrument.

(f) Any beneficiary, any person designated by the trust instrument or the court to enforce the trust, or any nonprofit charitable corporation that has as its principal activity the care of animals may, upon reasonable request, inspect the animal, the premises where the animal is maintained, or the books and records of the trust.

(g) A trust governed by this section is not subject to termination pursuant to subdivision (b) of Section 15408.

(h) Section 15211 does not apply to a trust governed by this section.

(i) For purposes of this section, "animal" means a domestic or pet animal for the benefit of which a trust has been established.

Chapter 2. Restrictions On Voluntary And Involuntary Transfers

15300. Except as provided in Sections 15304 to 15307, inclusive, if the trust instrument provides that a beneficiary's interest in income is not subject to voluntary or involuntary transfer, the beneficiary's interest in income under the trust may not be transferred and is not subject to enforcement of a money judgment until paid to the beneficiary.

15301. (a) Except as provided in subdivision (b) and in Sections 15304 to 15307, inclusive, if the trust instrument provides that a beneficiary's interest in principal is not subject to voluntary or involuntary transfer, the beneficiary's interest in principal may not be transferred and is not subject to enforcement of a money judgment until paid to the beneficiary.

(b) After an amount of principal has become due and payable to the beneficiary under the trust instrument, upon petition to the court under Section 709.010 of the Code of Civil Procedure by a judgment creditor, the court may make an order directing the trustee to satisfy the money judgment out of that principal amount. The court in its discretion may issue an order directing the trustee to satisfy all or part of the judgment out of that principal amount.

15302. Except as provided in Sections 15304 to 15307, inclusive, if the trust instrument provides that the trustee shall pay income or principal or both for the education or support of a beneficiary, the beneficiary's interest in income or principal or both under the trust, to the extent the income or principal or both is necessary for the education or support of the beneficiary, may not be transferred and is not subject to the enforcement of a money judgment until paid to the beneficiary.

15303. (a) If the trust instrument provides that the trustee shall pay to or for the benefit of a beneficiary so much of the income or principal or both as the trustee in the trustee's discretion sees fit to pay, a transferee or creditor of the beneficiary may not compel the trustee to pay any amount that may be paid only in the exercise of the trustee's discretion.

(b) If the trustee has knowledge of the transfer of the beneficiary's interest or has been served with process in a proceeding under Section 709.010 of the Code of Civil Procedure by a judgment creditor seeking to reach the beneficiary's interest, and the trustee pays to or for the benefit of the beneficiary any part of the income or principal that may be paid only in the exercise of the trustee's discretion, the trustee is liable to the transferee or creditor to the extent that the payment to or for the benefit of the beneficiary impairs the right of the transferee or creditor. This subdivision does not apply if the beneficiary's interest in the trust is subject to a restraint on transfer that is valid under Section 15300 or 15301.

(c) This section applies regardless of whether the trust instrument provides a standard for the exercise of the trustee's discretion.

(d) Nothing in this section limits any right the beneficiary may have to compel the trustee to pay to or for the benefit of the beneficiary all or part of the income or principal.

15304. (a) If the settlor is a beneficiary of a trust created by the settlor and the settlor's interest is subject to a provision restraining the voluntary or involuntary transfer of the settlor's interest, the restraint is invalid against transferees or creditors of the settlor. The invalidity of the restraint on transfer does not affect the validity of the trust.

(b) If the settlor is the beneficiary of a trust created by the settlor and the trust instrument provides that the trustee shall pay income or principal or both for the education or support of the beneficiary or gives the trustee discretion to determine the amount of income or principal or both to be paid to or for the benefit of the settlor, a transferee or creditor of the settlor may reach the maximum amount that the trustee could pay to or for the benefit of the settlor under the trust instrument, not exceeding the amount of the settlor's proportionate contribution to the trust.

15305. (a) As used in this section, "support judgment" means a money judgment for support of the trust beneficiary's spouse or former spouse or minor child.

(b) If the beneficiary has the right under the trust to compel the trustee to pay income or principal or both to or for the benefit of the beneficiary, the court may, to the extent that the court determines it is equitable and reasonable under the circumstances of the particular case, order the trustee to satisfy all or part of the support judgment out of all or part of those payments as they become due and payable, presently or in the future.

(c) Whether or not the beneficiary has the right under the trust to compel the trustee to pay income or principal or both to or for the benefit of the beneficiary, the court may, to the extent that the court determines it is equitable and reasonable under the circumstances of the particular case, order the trustee to satisfy all or part of the support judgment out of all or part of future payments that the trustee, pursuant to the exercise of the trustee's discretion, determines to make to or for the benefit of the beneficiary.

(d) This section applies to a support judgment notwithstanding any provision in the trust instrument.

15305.5. (a) As used in this section, "restitution judgment" means a judgment awarding restitution for the commission of a felony or a money judgment for damages incurred as a result of conduct for which the defendant was convicted of a felony.

(b) If the beneficiary has the right under the trust to compel the trustee to pay income or principal or both to or for the benefit of the beneficiary, the court may, to the extent that the court determines it is equitable and reasonable under the circumstances of the particular case, order the trustee to satisfy all or part of the restitution judgment out of all or part of those payments as they become due and payable, presently or in the future.

(c) Whether or not the beneficiary has the right under the trust to compel the trustee to pay income or principal or both to or for the benefit of the beneficiary, the court may, to the extent that the court determines it is equitable and reasonable under the circumstances of the particular case, order the trustee to satisfy all or part of the restitution judgment out of all or part of future payments that the trustee, pursuant to the exercise of the trustee's discretion, determines to make to or for the benefit of the beneficiary.

(d) This section applies to a restitution judgment notwithstanding any provision in the trust instrument.

15306. (a) Notwithstanding any provision in the trust instrument, if a statute of this state makes the beneficiary liable for reimbursement of this state or a local public entity in this state for public support furnished to the beneficiary or to the beneficiary' s spouse or minor child, upon petition to the court under Section 709.010 of the Code of Civil Procedure by the appropriate state or local public entity or public official, to the extent the court determines it is equitable and reasonable under the circumstances of the particular case, the court may do the following:

(1) If the beneficiary has the right under the trust to compel the trustee to pay income or principal or both to or for the benefit of the beneficiary, order the trustee to satisfy all or part of the liability out of all or part of the payments as they become due, presently or in the future.

(2) Whether or not the beneficiary has the right under the trust to compel the trustee to pay income or principal or both to or for the benefit of the beneficiary, order the trustee to satisfy all or part of the liability out of all or part of the future payments that the trustee, pursuant to the exercise of the trustee's discretion, determines to make to or for the benefit of the beneficiary.

(3) If the beneficiary is a settlor or the spouse or minor child of the settlor and the beneficiary does not have the right under the trust to compel the trustee to pay income or principal or both to or for the benefit of the beneficiary, to the extent that the trustee has the right to make payments of income or principal or both to or for the beneficiary pursuant to the exercise of the trustee's discretion, order the trustee to satisfy all or

part of the liability without regard to whether the trustee has then exercised or may thereafter exercise the discretion in favor of the beneficiary.

(b) Subdivision (a) does not apply to any trust that is established for the benefit of an individual who has a disability that substantially impairs the individual's ability to provide for his or her own care or custody and constitutes a substantial handicap. If, however, the trust results in the individual being ineligible for needed public social services under Division 9 (commencing With Section 10000) of the Welfare and Institutions Code, this subdivision is not applicable and the provisions of subdivision (a) are to be applied.

15306.5. (a) Notwithstanding a restraint on transfer of the beneficiary's interest in the trust under Section 15300 or 15301, and subject to the limitations of this section, upon a judgment creditor' s petition under Section 709.010 of the Code of Civil Procedure, the court may make an order directing the trustee to satisfy all or part of the judgment out of the payments to which the beneficiary is entitled under the trust instrument or that the trustee, in the exercise of the trustee's discretion, has determined or determines in the future to pay to the beneficiary.

(b) An order under this section may not require that the trustee pay in satisfaction of the judgment an amount exceeding 25 percent of the payment that otherwise would be made to, or for the benefit of, the beneficiary.

(c) An order under this section may not require that the trustee pay in satisfaction of the judgment any amount that the court determines is necessary for the support of the beneficiary and all the persons the beneficiary is required to support.

(d) An order for satisfaction of a support judgment, as defined in Section 15305, has priority over an order to satisfy a judgment under this section. Any amount ordered to be applied to the satisfaction of a judgment under this section shall be reduced by the amount of an order for satisfaction of a support judgment under Section 15305, regardless of whether the order for satisfaction of the support judgment was made before or after the order under this section.

(e) If the trust gives the trustee discretion over the payment of either principal or income of a trust, or both, nothing in this section affects or limits that discretion in any manner. The trustee has no duty to oppose a petition to satisfy a judgment under this section or to make any claim for exemption on behalf of the beneficiary. The trustee is not liable for any action taken, or omitted to be taken, in compliance with any court order made under this section.

(f) Subject to subdivision (d), the aggregate of all orders for satisfaction of money judgments against the beneficiary's interest in the trust may not exceed 25 percent of the payment that otherwise would be made to, or for the benefit of, the beneficiary.

15307. Notwithstanding a restraint on transfer of a beneficiary's interest in the trust under Section 15300 or 15301, any amount to which the beneficiary is entitled under the trust instrument or that the trustee, in the exercise of the trustee's discretion, has determined to pay to the beneficiary in excess of the amount that is or will be necessary for the education and support of the beneficiary may be applied to the satisfaction of a money judgment against the beneficiary. Upon the judgment creditor's petition under Section 709.010 of the Code of Civil Procedure, the court may make an order directing the trustee to satisfy all or part of the judgment out of the beneficiary's interest in the trust.

15308. Any order entered by a court under Section 15305, 15306, 15306.5, or 15307 is subject to modification upon petition of an interested person filed in the court where the order was made.

15309. A disclaimer or renunciation by a beneficiary of all or part of his or her interest under a trust shall not be considered a transfer under Section 15300 or 15301.

Chapter 3. Modification And Termination Of Trusts

15400. Unless a trust is expressly made irrevocable by the trust instrument, the trust is revocable by the settlor. This section applies only where the settlor is domiciled in this state when the trust is created, where the trust instrument is executed in this state, or where the trust instrument provides that the law of this state governs the trust.

15401. (a) A trust that is revocable by the settlor or any other person may be revoked in whole or in part by any of the following methods:

(1) By compliance with any method of revocation provided in the trust instrument.

(2) By a writing, other than a will, signed by the settlor or any other person holding the power of revocation and delivered to the trustee during the lifetime of the settlor or the person holding the power of revocation. If the trust instrument explicitly makes the method of revocation provided in the trust instrument the exclusive method of revocation, the trust may not be revoked pursuant to this paragraph.

(b) (1) Unless otherwise provided in the instrument, if a trust is created by more than one settlor, each settlor may revoke the trust as to the portion of the trust contributed by that settlor, except as provided in Section 761 of the Family Code.

(2) Notwithstanding paragraph (1), a settlor may grant to another person, including,

but not limited to, his or her spouse, a power to revoke all or part of that portion of the trust contributed by that settlor, regardless of whether that portion was separate property or community property of that settlor, and regardless of whether that power to revoke is exercisable during the lifetime of that settlor or continues after the death of that settlor, or both.

(c) A trust may not be modified or revoked by an attorney in fact under a power of attorney unless it is expressly permitted by the trust instrument.

(d) This section shall not limit the authority to modify or terminate a trust pursuant to Section 15403 or 15404 in an appropriate case.

(e) The manner of revocation of a trust revocable by the settlor or any other person that was created by an instrument executed before July 1, 1987, is governed by prior law and not by this section.

15402. Unless the trust instrument provides otherwise, if a trust is revocable by the settlor, the settlor may modify the trust by the procedure for revocation.

15403. (a) Except as provided in subdivision (b), if all beneficiaries of an irrevocable trust consent, they may compel modification or termination of the trust upon petition to the court.

(b) If the continuance of the trust is necessary to carry out a material purpose of the trust, the trust cannot be modified or terminated unless the court, in its discretion, determines that the reason for doing so under the circumstances outweighs the interest in accomplishing a material purpose of the trust. Under this section the court does not have discretion to permit termination of a trust that is subject to a valid restraint on transfer of the beneficiary's interest as provided in Chapter 2 (commencing with Section 15300).

15404. (a) If the settlor and all beneficiaries of a trust consent, they may compel the modification or termination of the trust.

(b) If any beneficiary does not consent to the modification or termination of the trust, upon petition to the court, the other beneficiaries, with the consent of the settlor, may compel a modification or a partial termination of the trust if the interests of the beneficiaries who do not consent are not substantially impaired.

(c) If the trust provides for the disposition of principal to a class of persons described only as "heirs" or "next of kin" of the settlor, or using other words that describe the class of all persons who would take under the rules of intestacy, the court may limit the class of beneficiaries whose consent is needed to compel the modification or termination of the trust to the beneficiaries who are reasonably likely to take under the circumstances.

15405. For the purposes of Sections 15403

and 15404, the consent of a beneficiary who lacks legal capacity, including a minor, or who is an unascertained or unborn person may be given in proceedings before the court by a guardian ad litem, if it would be appropriate to do so. In determining whether to give consent, the guardian ad litem may rely on general family benefit accruing to living members of the beneficiary's family as a basis for approving a modification or termination of the trust.

15406. In determining the class of beneficiaries whose consent is necessary to modify or terminate a trust pursuant to Section 15403 or 15404, the presumption of fertility is rebuttable.

15407. (a) A trust terminates when any of the following occurs:

(1) The term of the trust expires.

(2) The trust purpose is fulfilled.

(3) The trust purpose becomes unlawful.

(4) The trust purpose becomes impossible to fulfill.

(5) The trust is revoked.

(b) On termination of the trust, the trustee continues to have the powers reasonably necessary under the circumstances to wind up the affairs of the trust.

15408. (a) On petition by a trustee or beneficiary, if the court determines that the fair market value of the principal of a trust has become so low in relation to the cost of administration that continuation of the trust under its existing terms will defeat or substantially impair the accomplishment of its purposes, the court may, in its discretion and in a manner that conforms as nearly as possible to the intention of the settlor, order any of the following:

(1) Termination of the trust.

(2) Modification of the trust.

(3) Appointment of a new trustee.

(b) Notwithstanding subdivision (a), if the trust principal does not exceed forty thousand dollars ($40,000) in value, the trustee has the power to terminate the trust.

(c) The existence of a trust provision restraining transfer of the beneficiary's interest does not prevent application of this section.

15409. (a) On petition by a trustee or beneficiary, the court may modify the administrative or dispositive provisions of the trust or terminate the trust if, owing to circumstances not known to the settlor and not anticipated by the settlor, the continuation of the trust under its terms would defeat or substantially impair the accomplishment of the purposes of the trust. In this case, if necessary to carry out the purposes of the trust, the court may order the trustee to do acts that are not authorized or are forbidden by the trust instrument.

(b) The court shall consider a trust provision restraining transfer of the beneficiary's interest as a factor in making its decision whether to modify or terminate the trust, but the court is not precluded from exercising its discretion to modify or terminate the trust solely because of a restraint on transfer.

15410. At the termination of a trust, the trust property shall be disposed of as follows:

(a) In the case of a trust that is revoked by the settlor, the trust property shall be disposed of in the following order of priority:

(1) As directed by the settlor.

(2) As provided in the trust instrument.

(3) To the extent that there is no direction by the settlor or in the trust instrument, to the settlor, or his or her estate, as the case may be.

(b) In the case of a trust that is revoked by any person holding a power of revocation other than the settlor, the trust property shall be disposed of in the following order of priority:

(1) As provided in the trust instrument.

(2) As directed by the person exercising the power of revocation.

(3) To the extent that there is no direction in the trust instrument or by the person exercising the power of revocation, to the person exercising the power of revocation, or his or her estate, as the case may be.

(c) In the case of a trust that is terminated by the consent of the settlor and all beneficiaries, as agreed by the settlor and all beneficiaries.

(d) In any other case, as provided in the trust instrument or in a manner directed by the court that conforms as nearly as possible to the intention of the settlor as expressed in the trust instrument.

(e) If a trust is terminated by the trustee pursuant to subdivision (b) of Section 15408, the trust property may be distributed as determined by the trustee pursuant to the standard provided in subdivision (d) without the need for a court order. If the trust instrument does not provide a manner of distribution at termination and the settlor's intent is not adequately expressed in the trust instrument, the trustee may distribute the trust property to the living beneficiaries on an actuarial basis.

15411. If the terms of two or more trusts are substantially similar, on petition by a trustee or beneficiary, the court, for good cause shown, may combine the trusts if the court determines that administration as a single trust will not defeat or substantially impair the accomplishment of the trust purposes or the interests of the beneficiaries.

15412. On petition by a trustee or beneficiary, the court, for good cause shown, may divide a trust into two or more separate trusts, if the court determines that dividing the trust will not defeat or substantially impair the accomplishment of the trust purposes or the interests of the beneficiaries.

15413. A trust provision, express or implied, that the trust may not be terminated is ineffective insofar as it purports to be applicable after the expiration of the longer of the periods provided by the statutory rule against perpetuities, Article 2 (commencing with Section 21205) of Chapter 1 of Part 2 of Division 11.

15414. Notwithstanding any other provision in this chapter, if a trust continues in existence after the expiration of the longer of the periods provided by the statutory rule against perpetuities, Article 2 (commencing with Section 21205) of Chapter 1 of Part 2 of Division 11, the trust may be terminated in either of the following manners:

(a) On petition by a majority of the beneficiaries.

(b) On petition by the Attorney General or by any person who would be affected by the termination, if the court finds that the termination would be in the public interest or in the best interest of a majority of the persons who would be affected by the termination.

Part 3. Trustees And Beneficiaries

Chapter 1. Trustees

Article 1. General Provisions

15600. (a) The person named as trustee may accept the trust, or a modification of the trust, by one of the following methods:

(1) Signing the trust instrument or the trust instrument as modified, or signing a separate written acceptance.

(2) Knowingly exercising powers or performing duties under the trust instrument or the trust instrument as modified, except as provided in subdivision (b).

(b) In a case where there is an immediate risk of damage to the trust property, the person named as trustee may act to preserve the trust property without accepting the trust or a modification of the trust, if within a reasonable time after acting the person delivers a written rejection of the trust or the modification of the trust to the settlor or, if the settlor is dead or incompetent, to a beneficiary. This subdivision does not impose a duty on the person named as trustee to act.

15601. (a) A person named as trustee may in writing reject the trust or a modification of the trust.

(b) If the person named as trustee does not accept the trust or a modification of the trust by a method provided in subdivision (a) of Section 15600 within a reasonable time after learning of being named as trustee or of the modification, the person has rejected the trust or the modification.

(c) A person named as trustee who rejects the trust or a modification of the trust is not liable with respect to the rejected trust or modification.

15602. (a) A trustee is not required to give a bond to secure performance of the trustee's duties, unless any of the following circumstances occurs:

(1) A bond is required by the trust instrument.

(2) Notwithstanding a waiver of a bond in the trust instrument, a bond is found by the court to be necessary to protect the interests of beneficiaries or other persons having an interest in the trust.

(3) An individual who is not named as a trustee in the trust instrument is appointed as a trustee by the court.

(b) Notwithstanding paragraphs (1) and (3) of subdivision (a), the court may excuse a requirement of a bond, reduce or increase the amount of a bond, release a surety, or permit the substitution of another bond with the same or different sureties. The court may not, however, excuse the requirement of a bond for an individual described in paragraph (3) of subdivision (a), except under compelling circumstances. For the purposes of this section, a request by all the adult beneficiaries of a trust that bond be waived for an individual described in paragraph (3) of subdivision (a) for their trust is deemed to constitute a compelling circumstance.

(c) If a bond is required, it shall be filed or served and shall be in the amount and with sureties and liabilities ordered by the court.

(d) Except as otherwise provided in the trust instrument or ordered by the court, the cost of the bond shall be charged against the trust.

(e) A trust company may not be required to give a bond, notwithstanding a contrary provision in the trust instrument.

15603. On application by the trustee, the court clerk shall issue a certificate that the trustee is a duly appointed and acting trustee under the trust if the court file shows the incumbency of the trustee.

15604. (a) Notwithstanding any other provision of law, a nonprofit charitable corporation may be appointed as trustee of a trust created pursuant to this division, if all of the following conditions are met:

(1) The corporation is incorporated in this state.

(2) The articles of incorporation specifically authorize the corporation to accept appointments as trustee.

(3) For the three years prior to the filing of a petition under this section, the nonprofit charitable corporation has been exempt from payment of income taxes pursuant to Section 501(c)(3) of the Internal Revenue Code and has served as a private professional conservator in the state.

(4) The settlor or an existing trustee consents to the appointment of the nonprofit corporation as trustee or successor trustee, either in the petition or in a writing signed either before or after the petition is filed.

(5) The court determines the trust to be in the best interest of the settlor.

(6) The court determines that the appointment of the nonprofit corporation as trustee is in the best interest of the settlor and the trust estate.

(b) A petition for appointment of a nonprofit corporation as trustee under this section may be filed by any of the following:

(1) The settlor or the spouse of the settlor.

(2) The nonprofit charitable corporation.

(3) An existing trustee.

(c) The petition shall include in the caption the name of a responsible corporate officer who shall act for the corporation for purposes of this section. If, for any reason, the officer so named ceases to act as the responsible corporate officer for purposes of this section, the corporation shall file with the court a notice containing (1) the name of the successor responsible corporate officer and (2) the date the successor becomes the responsible corporate officer.

(d) The petition shall request that a trustee be appointed for the estate, shall specify the name, address, and telephone number of the proposed trustee and the name, address, and telephone number of the settlor or proposed settlor, and state the reasons why the appointment of the trustee is necessary.

(e) The petition shall set forth, so far as the information is known to the petitioner, the names and addresses of all persons entitled to notice of a conservatorship petition, as specified in subdivision (b) of Section 1821.

(f) Notice of the hearing on the petition shall be given in the same manner as provided in Sections 1822 and 1824.

(g) The trustee appointed by the court pursuant to this section shall do all of the following:

(1) File the required bond for the benefit of the trust estate in the same manner provided for conservators of the estate as set forth in Section 2320. This bond may not be waived, but the court may, in its discretion, permit the filing of a bond in an amount less than would otherwise be required under Section 2320.

(2) Comply with the requirements for registration and filing of annual statements pursuant to Article 4 (commencing with Section 2340) of Chapter 4 of Part 4 of Division 4.

(3) File with the court inventories and appraisals of the trust estate and present its accounts of the trust estate in the manner provided for conservators of the estate set forth in Chapter 7 (commencing with Section 2600) of Part 4 of Division 4.

(4) Be reimbursed for expenses and compensated as trustee in the manner provided for conservators of the estate as described in Chapter 8 (commencing with Section 2640) of Part 4 of Division 4. However, compensation as trustee appointed under this section shall be allowed only for services actually rendered.

(5) Be represented by counsel in all proceedings before the court. Any fee allowed

for an attorney for the nonprofit charitable corporation shall be for services actually rendered.

(h) The trustee appointed by the court under this section may be removed by the court, or may resign in accordance with Chapter 9 (commencing with Section 2650) of Part 4 of Division 4. If the nonprofit charitable corporation resigns or is removed by the court, the settlor may appoint another person as successor trustee, or another nonprofit charitable corporation as trustee under this section.

(i) The trustee appointed by the court under this section is bound by the trust instrument created by the settlor, and shall be subject to the duties and responsibilities of a trustee as provided in this code.

Article 2. Cotrustees

15620. Unless otherwise provided in the trust instrument, a power vested in two or more trustees may only be exercised by their unanimous action.

15621. Unless otherwise provided in the trust instrument, if a vacancy occurs in the office of a cotrustee, the remaining cotrustee or cotrustees may act for the trust as if they are the only trustees.

15622. Unless otherwise provided in the trust instrument, if a cotrustee is unavailable to perform the duties of the cotrustee because of absence, illness, or other temporary incapacity, the remaining cotrustee or cotrustees may act for the trust, as if they are the only trustees, where necessary to accomplish the purposes of the trust or to avoid irreparable injury to the trust property.

Article 3. Resignation And Removal Of Trustees

15640. A trustee who has accepted the trust may resign only by one of the following methods:

(a) As provided in the trust instrument.

(b) In the case of a revocable trust, with the consent of the person holding the power to revoke the trust.

(c) In the case of a trust that is not revocable, with the consent of all adult beneficiaries who are receiving or are entitled to receive income under the trust or to receive a distribution of principal if the trust were terminated at the time consent is sought. If a beneficiary has a conservator, the conservator may consent to the trustee's resignation on behalf of the conservatee without obtaining court approval. Without limiting the power of the beneficiary to consent to the trustee's resignation, if the beneficiary has designated an attorney in fact who has the power under the power of attorney to consent to the trustee's resignation, the attorney in fact may consent to the resignation.

(d) Pursuant to a court order obtained on petition by the trustee under Section 17200. The court shall accept the trustee's resig-

nation and may make any orders necessary for the preservation of the trust property, including the appointment of a receiver or a temporary trustee.

15641. The liability for acts or omissions of a resigning trustee or of the sureties on the trustee's bond, if any, is not released or affected in any manner by the trustee's resignation.

15642. (a) A trustee may be removed in accordance with the trust instrument, by the court on its own motion, or on petition of a settlor, cotrustee, or beneficiary under Section 17200.

(b) The grounds for removal of a trustee by the court include the following:

(1) Where the trustee has committed a breach of the trust.

(2) Where the trustee is insolvent or otherwise unfit to administer the trust.

(3) Where hostility or lack of cooperation among cotrustees impairs the administration of the trust.

(4) Where the trustee fails or declines to act.

(5) Where the trustee's compensation is excessive under the circumstances.

(6) Where the sole trustee is a person described in subdivision (a) of Section 21350 or subdivision (a) of Section 21380, whether or not the person is the transferee of a donative transfer by the transferor, unless, based upon any evidence of the intent of the settlor and all other facts and circumstances, which shall be made known to the court, the court finds that it is consistent with the settlor's intent that the trustee continue to serve and that this intent was not the product of fraud or undue influence. Any waiver by the settlor of this provision is against public policy and shall be void. This paragraph shall not apply to instruments that became irrevocable on or before January 1, 1994. This paragraph shall not apply if any of the following conditions are met:

(A) The settlor is related by blood or marriage to, or is a cohabitant with, any one or more of the trustees, the person who drafted or transcribed the instrument, or the person who caused the instrument to be transcribed.

(B) The instrument is reviewed by an independent attorney who (1) counsels the settlor about the nature of his or her intended trustee designation and (2) signs and delivers to the settlor and the designated trustee a certificate in substantially the following form:

PLEASE SEE THE APPENDIX

This independent review and certification may occur either before or after the instrument has been executed, and if it occurs after the date of execution, the named trustee shall not be subject to removal under this paragraph. Any attorney whose written engagement signed by the client is expressly limited to the preparation of a certificate under this subdivision, including the prior counseling, shall not be considered to otherwise represent the client.

(C) After full disclosure of the relationships of the persons involved, the instrument is approved pursuant to an order under Article 10 (commencing with Section 2580) of Chapter 6 of Part 4 of Division 4.

(7) If, as determined under Part 17 (commencing with Section 810) of Division 2, the trustee is substantially unable to manage the trust's financial resources or is otherwise substantially unable to execute properly the duties of the office. When the trustee holds the power to revoke the trust, substantial inability to manage the trust's financial resources or otherwise execute properly the duties of the office may not be proved solely by isolated incidents of negligence or improvidence.

(8) If the trustee is substantially unable to resist fraud or undue influence. When the trustee holds the power to revoke the trust, substantial inability to resist fraud or undue influence may not be proved solely by isolated incidents of negligence or improvidence.

(9) For other good cause.

(c) If, pursuant to paragraph (6) of subdivision (b), the court finds that the designation of the trustee was not consistent with the intent of the settlor or was the product of fraud or undue influence, the person being removed as trustee shall bear all costs of the proceeding, including reasonable attorney's fees.

(d) If the court finds that the petition for removal of the trustee was filed in bad faith and that removal would be contrary to the settlor's intent, the court may order that the person or persons seeking the removal of the trustee bear all or any part of the costs of the proceeding, including reasonable attorney's fees.

(e) If it appears to the court that trust property or the interests of a beneficiary may suffer loss or injury pending a decision on a petition for removal of a trustee and any appellate review, the court may, on its own motion or on petition of a cotrustee or beneficiary, compel the trustee whose removal is sought to surrender trust property to a cotrustee or to a receiver or temporary trustee. The court may also suspend the powers of the trustee to the extent the court deems necessary.

(f) For purposes of this section, the term "related by blood or marriage" shall include persons within the seventh degree.

15643. There is a vacancy in the office of trustee in any of the following circumstances:

(a) The person named as trustee rejects the trust.

(b) The person named as trustee cannot be identified or does not exist.

(c) The trustee resigns or is removed.

(d) The trustee dies.

(e) A conservator or guardian of the person or estate of an individual trustee is appointed.

(f) The trustee is the subject of an order for relief in bankruptcy.

(g) A trust company's charter is revoked or powers are suspended, if the revocation or suspension is to be in effect for a period of 30 days or more.

(h) A receiver is appointed for a trust company if the appointment is not vacated within a period of 30 days.

15644. When a vacancy has occurred in the office of trustee, the former trustee who holds property of the trust shall deliver the trust property to the successor trustee or a person appointed by the court to receive the property and remains responsible for the trust property until it is delivered. A trustee who has resigned or is removed has the powers reasonably necessary under the circumstances to preserve the trust property until it is delivered to the successor trustee and to perform actions necessary to complete the resigning or removed trustee's administration of the trust.

15645. If the trustee of a trust that is not revocable has refused to transfer administration of the trust to a successor trust company on request of the beneficiaries described in subdivision (c) of Section 15640 and the court in subsequent proceedings under Section 17200 makes an order removing the existing trustee and appointing a trust company as successor trustee, the court may, in its discretion, award costs and reasonable attorney's fees incurred by the petitioner in the proceeding to be paid by the trustee or from the trust as ordered by the court.

Article 4. Appointment Of Trustees

15660. (a) If the trust has no trustee or if the trust instrument requires a vacancy in the office of a cotrustee to be filled, the vacancy shall be filled as provided in this section.

(b) If the trust instrument provides a practical method of appointing a trustee or names the person to fill the vacancy, the vacancy shall be filled as provided in the trust instrument.

(c) If the vacancy in the office of trustee is not filled as provided in subdivision (b), the vacancy may be filled by a trust company that has agreed to accept the trust on agreement of all adult beneficiaries who are receiving or are entitled to receive income under the trust or to receive a distribution of principal if the trust were terminated at the time the agreement is made. If a beneficiary has a conservator, the conservator may agree to the successor trustee on behalf of the conservatee without obtaining court approval. Without limiting the power of the beneficiary to agree to the successor trustee, if the beneficiary has designated an attorney in fact who has the power under the power of attorney to agree to the successor trustee, the attorney in fact may agree to the successor trustee.

(d) If the vacancy in the office of trustee is not filled as provided in subdivision (b) or (c), on petition of any interested person or any person named as trustee in the trust instrument, the court may, in its discretion, appoint a trustee to fill the vacancy. If the trust provides for more than one trustee, the court may, in its discretion, appoint the original number or any lesser number of trustees. In selecting a trustee, the court shall give consideration to any nomination by the beneficiaries who are 14 years of age or older.

15660.5. (a) The court may appoint as trustee of a trust the public guardian or public administrator of the county in which the matter is pending subject to the following requirements:

(1) Neither the public guardian nor the public administrator shall be appointed as trustee unless the court finds, after reasonable inquiry, that no other qualified person is willing to act as trustee or the public guardian, public administrator, or his or her representative consents.

(2) The public administrator shall not be appointed as trustee unless either of the following is true:

(A) At the time of the appointment and pursuant to the terms of the trust, the entire trust is then to be distributed outright. For purposes of this paragraph, a trust that is "then to be distributed outright" does not include a trust pursuant to which payments to, or on behalf of, a beneficiary or beneficiaries are to be made from the trust on an ongoing basis for more than six months after the date of distribution.

(B) The public administrator consents.

(3) Neither the public guardian nor the public administrator shall be appointed as a cotrustee unless the public guardian, public administrator, or his or her representative consents.

(4) Neither the public guardian nor the public administrator shall be appointed as general trustee without a hearing and notice to the public guardian or public administrator, or his or her representative, and other interested persons as provided in Section 17203.

(5) Neither the public guardian nor the public administrator shall be appointed as temporary trustee without receiving notice of hearing as provided in Section 1220. The court shall not waive this notice of hearing, but may shorten the time for notice upon a finding of good cause.

(b) (1) If the public guardian or the public administrator consents to the appointment as trustee under this section, he or she shall submit a written certification of the consent to the court no later than two court days

after the noticed hearing date described in paragraph (4) or (5) of subdivision (a). The public administrator shall not be appointed as trustee under subparagraph (A) of paragraph (2) of subdivision (a) if, after receiving notice as required by this section, the public administrator files a written certification with the court that the public administrator is unable to provide the level of services needed to properly fulfill the obligations of a trustee of the trust.

(2) If the public administrator has been appointed as trustee without notice as required in paragraph (4) or (5) of subdivision (a), and the public administrator files a written certification with the court that he or she is unable to provide the level of services needed to properly fulfill the obligations of a trustee of the trust, this shall be good cause for the public administrator to be relieved as trustee.

(c) The order of appointment shall provide for an annual bond fee as described in Section 15688.

Article 5. Compensation And Indemnification Of Trustees

15680. (a) Subject to subdivision (b), and except as provided in Section 15688, if the trust instrument provides for the trustee's compensation, the trustee is entitled to be compensated in accordance with the trust instrument.

(b) Upon proper showing, the court may fix or allow greater or lesser compensation than could be allowed under the terms of the trust in any of the following circumstances:

(1) Where the duties of the trustee are substantially different from those contemplated when the trust was created.

(2) Where the compensation in accordance with the terms of the trust would be inequitable or unreasonably low or high.

(3) In extraordinary circumstances calling for equitable relief.

(c) An order fixing or allowing greater or lesser compensation under subdivision (b) applies only prospectively to actions taken in administration of the trust after the order is made.

15681. If the trust instrument does not specify the trustee's compensation, the trustee is entitled to reasonable compensation under the circumstances.

15682. The court may fix an amount of periodic compensation under Sections 15680 and 15681 to continue for as long as the court determines is proper.

15683. Unless the trust instrument otherwise provides or the trustees otherwise agree, if the trust has two or more trustees, the compensation shall be apportioned among the cotrustees according to the services rendered by them.

15684. A trustee is entitled to the repayment out of the trust property for the following:

(a) Expenditures that were properly incurred in the administration of the trust.

(b) To the extent that they benefited the trust, expenditures that were not properly incurred in the administration of the trust.

15685. The trustee has an equitable lien on the trust property as against the beneficiary in the amount of advances, with any interest, made for the protection of the trust, and for expenses, losses, and liabilities sustained in the administration of the trust or because of ownership or control of any trust property.

15686. (a) As used in this section, "trustee's fee" includes, but is not limited to, the trustee's periodic base fee, rate of percentage compensation, minimum fee, hourly rate, and transaction charge, but does not include fees for extraordinary services.

(b) A trustee may not charge an increased trustee's fee for administration of a particular trust unless the trustee first gives at least 60 days' written notice of that increased fee to all of the following persons:

(1) Each beneficiary who is entitled to an account under Section 16062.

(2) Each beneficiary who was given the last preceding account.

(3) Each beneficiary who has made a written request to the trustee for notice of an increased trustee's fee and has given an address for receiving notice by mail.

(c) If a beneficiary files a petition under Section 17200 for review of the increased trustee's fee or for removal of the trustee and serves a copy of the petition on the trustee before the expiration of the 60-day period, the increased trustee's fee does not take effect as to that trust until otherwise ordered by the court or the petition is dismissed.

15687. (a) Notwithstanding any provision of a trust to the contrary, a trustee who is an attorney may receive only (1) the trustee's compensation provided in the trust or otherwise provided in this article or (2) compensation for legal services performed for the trustee, unless the trustee obtains approval for the right to dual compensation as provided in subdivision (d).

(b) No parent, child, sibling, or spouse of a person who is a trustee, and no law partnership or corporation whose partner, shareholder, or employee is serving as a trustee shall receive any compensation for legal services performed for the trustee unless the trustee waives trustee compensation or unless the trustee obtains approval for the right to dual compensation as provided in subdivision (d).

(c) This section shall not apply if the trustee is related by blood or marriage to, or is a cohabitant with, the settlor.

(d) After full disclosure of the nature of the compensation and relationship of the trustee to all persons receiving compensation under this section, the trustee may obtain approval for dual compensation by either of the following:

(1) An order pursuant to paragraph (21) of subdivision (b) of Section 17200.

(2) Giving 30 days' advance written notice to the persons entitled to notice under Section 17203. Within that 30-day period, any person entitled to notice may object to the proposed action by written notice to the trustee or by filing a petition pursuant to paragraph (21) of subdivision (b) of Section 17200. If the trustee receives this objection during that 30-day period and if the trustee wishes dual compensation, the trustee shall file a petition for approval pursuant to paragraph (21) of subdivision (b) of Section 17200.

(e) Any waiver of the requirements of this section is against public policy and shall be void.

(f) This section applies to services rendered on or after January 1, 1994.

15688. Notwithstanding any other provision of this article and the terms of the trust, a public guardian or public administrator who is appointed as a trustee of a trust pursuant to Section 15660.5 shall be paid from the trust property for all of the following:

(a) Reasonable expenses incurred in the administration of the trust.

(b) Compensation for services of the public guardian or public administrator and the attorney of the public guardian or public administrator, as follows:

(1) If the public guardian or public administrator is appointed as trustee of a trust that provides for the outright distribution of the entire trust estate, compensation for the public guardian or public administrator, and any attorney for the public guardian or public administrator, shall be calculated as that provided to a personal representative and attorney pursuant to Part 7 (commencing with Section 10800) of Division 7, based on the fair market value of the assets as of the date of the appointment, provided that the minimum amount of compensation for the public guardian or the public administrator shall be one thousand dollars ($1,000). Additionally, the minimum amount of compensation for the attorney for the public guardian or the public administrator, if any, shall be one thousand dollars ($1,000).

(2) For a trust other than that described in paragraph (1), the public guardian or public administrator shall be compensated as provided in Section 15680. Compensation shall be consistent with compensation allowed for professional fiduciaries or corporate fiduciaries providing comparable services.

(3) Except as provided in paragraph (1), reasonable compensation for the attorney for the public guardian or public administrator.

(c) An annual bond fee in the amount of twenty-five dollars ($25) plus one-fourth of 1 percent of the amount of the trust assets greater than ten thousand dollars ($10,000). The amount charged shall be deposited in the county treasury.

Chapter 2. Beneficiaries

15800. Except to the extent that the trust instrument otherwise provides or where the joint action of the settlor and all beneficiaries is required, during the time that a trust is revocable and the person holding the power to revoke the trust is competent:

(a) The person holding the power to revoke, and not the beneficiary, has the rights afforded beneficiaries under this division.

(b) The duties of the trustee are owed to the person holding the power to revoke.

15801. (a) In any case where the consent of a beneficiary may be given or is required to be given before an action may be taken, during the time that a trust is revocable and the person holding the power to revoke the trust is competent, the person holding the power to revoke, and not the beneficiary, has the power to consent or withhold consent.

(b) This section does not apply where the joint consent of the settlor and all beneficiaries is required by statute.

15802. Notwithstanding any other statute, during the time that a trust is revocable and the person holding the power to revoke the trust is competent, a notice that is to be given to a beneficiary shall be given to the person holding the power to revoke and not to the beneficiary.

15803. The holder of a presently exercisable general power of appointment or power to withdraw property from the trust has the rights of a person holding the power to revoke the trust that are provided by Sections 15800 to 15802, inclusive, to the extent of the holder's power over the trust property.

15804. (a) Subject to subdivisions (b) and (c), it is sufficient compliance with a requirement in this division that notice be given to a beneficiary, or to a person interested in the trust, if notice is given as follows:

(1) Where an interest has been limited on any future contingency to persons who will compose a certain class upon the happening of a certain event without further limitation, notice shall be given to the persons in being who would constitute the class if the event had happened immediately before the commencement of the proceeding or if there is no proceeding, if the event had happened immediately before notice is given.

(2) Where an interest has been limited to a living person and the same interest, or a share therein, has been further limited upon the happening of a future event to the surviving spouse or to persons who are or may be the distributees, heirs, issue, or other kindred of the living person, notice shall be given to the living person.

(3) Where an interest has been limited upon the happening of any future event to a person, or a class of persons, or both, and the interest, or a share of the interest, has been further limited upon the happening of an additional future event to another person, or a class of persons, or both, notice shall be given to the person or persons in being who would take the interest upon the happening of the first of these events.

(b) If a conflict of interest involving the subject matter of the trust proceeding exists between a person to whom notice is required to be given and a person to whom notice is not otherwise required to be given under subdivision (a), notice shall also be given to persons not otherwise entitled to notice under subdivision (a) with respect to whom the conflict of interest exists.

(c) Nothing in this section affects any of the following:

(1) Requirements for notice to a person who has requested special notice, a person who has filed notice of appearance, or a particular person or entity required by statute to be given notice.

(2) Availability of a guardian ad litem pursuant to Section 1003.

(d) As used in this section, "notice" includes other papers.

15805. Notwithstanding any other provision of law, the Attorney General is subject to the limitations on the rights of beneficiaries of revocable trusts provided by Sections 15800 to 15802, inclusive.

Part 4. Trust Administration

Chapter 1. Duties Of Trustees

Article 1. Trustee's Duties In General

16000. On acceptance of the trust, the trustee has a duty to administer the trust according to the trust instrument and, except to the extent the trust instrument provides otherwise, according to this division.

16001. (a) Except as provided in subdivision (b), the trustee of a revocable trust shall follow any written direction acceptable to the trustee given from time to time (1) by the person then having the power to revoke the trust or the part thereof with respect to which the direction is given or (2) by the person to whom the settlor delegates the right to direct the trustee.

(b) If a written direction given under subdivision (a) would have the effect of modifying the trust, the trustee has no duty to follow the direction unless it complies with the requirements for modifying the trust.

16002. (a) The trustee has a duty to administer the trust solely in the interest of the beneficiaries.

(b) It is not a violation of the duty provided in subdivision (a) for a trustee who administers two trusts to sell, exchange, or participate in the sale or exchange of trust property between the trusts, if both of the following requirements are met:

(1) The sale or exchange is fair and reasonable with respect to the beneficiaries of both trusts.

(2) The trustee gives to the beneficiaries of both trusts notice of all material facts related to the sale or exchange that the trustee knows or should know.

16003. If a trust has two or more beneficiaries, the trustee has a duty to deal impartially with them and shall act impartially in investing and managing the trust property, taking into account any differing interests of the beneficiaries.

16004. (a) The trustee has a duty not to use or deal with trust property for the trustee's own profit or for any other purpose unconnected with the trust, nor to take part in any transaction in which the trustee has an interest adverse to the beneficiary.

(b) The trustee may not enforce any claim against the trust property that the trustee purchased after or in contemplation of appointment as trustee, but the court may allow the trustee to be reimbursed from trust property the amount that the trustee paid in good faith for the claim.

(c) A transaction between the trustee and a beneficiary which occurs during the existence of the trust or while the trustee's influence with the beneficiary remains and by which the trustee obtains an advantage from the beneficiary is presumed to be a violation of the trustee's fiduciary duties. This presumption is a presumption affecting the burden of proof. This subdivision does not apply to the provisions of an agreement between a trustee and a beneficiary relating to the hiring or compensation of the trustee.

16004.5. (a) A trustee may not require a beneficiary to relieve the trustee of liability as a condition for making a distribution or payment to, or for the benefit of, the beneficiary, if the distribution or payment is required by the trust instrument.

(b) This section may not be construed as affecting the trustee's right to:

(1) Maintain a reserve for reasonably anticipated expenses, including, but not limited to, taxes, debts, trustee and accounting fees, and costs and expenses of administration.

(2) Seek a voluntary release or discharge of a trustee's liability from the beneficiary.

(3) Require indemnification against a claim by a person or entity, other than a beneficiary referred to in subdivision (a), which may reasonably arise as a result of the distribution.

(4) Withhold any portion of an otherwise required distribution that is reasonably in dispute.

(5) Seek court or beneficiary approval of an accounting of trust activities.

16005. The trustee of one trust has a duty not to knowingly become a trustee of another trust adverse in its nature to the interest of the beneficiary of the first trust, and a duty to eliminate the conflict or resign as trustee when the conflict is discovered.

16006. The trustee has a duty to take reasonable steps under the circumstances to take and keep control of and to preserve the trust property.

16007. The trustee has a duty to make the trust property productive under the circumstances and in furtherance of the purposes of the trust.

16009. The trustee has a duty to do the following:

(a) To keep the trust property separate from other property not subject to the trust.

(b) To see that the trust property is designated as property of the trust.

16010. The trustee has a duty to take reasonable steps to enforce claims that are part of the trust property.

16011. The trustee has a duty to take reasonable steps to defend actions that may result in a loss to the trust.

16012. (a) The trustee has a duty not to delegate to others the performance of acts that the trustee can reasonably be required personally to perform and may not transfer the office of trustee to another person nor delegate the entire administration of the trust to a cotrustee or other person.

(b) In a case where a trustee has properly delegated a matter to an agent, cotrustee, or other person, the trustee has a duty to exercise general supervision over the person performing the delegated matter.

(c) This section does not apply to investment and management functions under Section 16052.

16013. If a trust has more than one trustee, each trustee has a duty to do the following:

(a) To participate in the administration of the trust.

(b) To take reasonable steps to prevent a cotrustee from committing a breach of trust or to compel a cotrustee to redress a breach of trust.

16014. (a) The trustee has a duty to apply the full extent of the trustee's skills.

(b) If the settlor, in selecting the trustee, has relied on the trustee's representation of having special skills, the trustee is held to the standard of the skills represented.

16015. The provision of services for compensation by a regulated financial institution or its affiliates in the ordinary course of business either to a trust of which it also acts as trustee or to a person dealing with the trust is not a violation of the duty provided in Section 16002 or 16004. For the purposes of this section, "affiliate" means a corporation that directly or indirectly through one or more intermediaries controls, is controlled by, or is under common control with another domestic or foreign corporation.

Article 2. Trustee's Standard Of Care

16040. (a) The trustee shall administer the trust with reasonable care, skill, and caution under the circumstances then prevailing that a prudent person acting in a like capacity would use in the conduct of an enterprise of like character and with like aims to accomplish the purposes of the trust as determined from the trust instrument.

(b) The settlor may expand or restrict the standard provided in subdivision (a) by express provisions in the trust instrument. A trustee is not liable to a beneficiary for the trustee's good faith reliance on these express provisions.

(c) This section does not apply to investment and management functions governed by the Uniform Prudent Investor Act, Article 2.5 (commencing with Section 16045).

16041. A trustee's standard of care and performance in administering the trust is not affected by whether or not the trustee receives any compensation.

16042. (a) Notwithstanding the requirements of this article, Article 2.5 (commencing with Section 16045), and the terms of the trust, all trust funds that come within the custody of the public guardian who is appointed as trustee of the trust pursuant to Section 15660.5 may be deposited or invested in the same manner, and would be subject to the same terms and conditions, as a deposit or investment by the public administrator of funds in the estate of a decedent pursuant to Article 3 (commencing with Section 7640) of Chapter 4 of Part 1 of Division 7.

(b) Upon the deposit or investment of trust property pursuant to subdivision (a), the public guardian shall be deemed to have met the standard of care specified in this article and Article 2.5 (commencing with Section 16045) with respect to this trust property.

Article 2.5. Uniform Prudent Investor Act

16045. This article, together with subdivision (a) of Section 16002 and Section 16003, constitutes the prudent investor rule and may be cited as the Uniform Prudent Investor Act.

16046. (a) Except as provided in subdivision (b), a trustee who invests and manages trust assets owes a duty to the beneficiaries of the trust to comply with the prudent investor rule.

(b) The settlor may expand or restrict the prudent investor rule by express provisions in the trust instrument. A trustee is not liable to a beneficiary for the trustee's good faith reliance on these express provisions.

16047. (a) A trustee shall invest and manage trust assets as a prudent investor would, by considering the purposes, terms, distribution requirements, and other circumstances of the trust. In satisfying this standard, the trustee shall exercise reasonable care, skill, and caution.

(b) A trustee's investment and management decisions respecting individual assets and courses of action must be evaluated not in isolation, but in the context of the trust portfolio as a whole and as a part of an overall investment strategy having risk and return objectives reasonably suited to the trust.

(c) Among circumstances that are appropriate to consider in investing and managing trust assets are the following, to the extent relevant to the trust or its beneficiaries:

(1) General economic conditions.

(2) The possible effect of inflation or deflation.

(3) The expected tax consequences of investment decisions or strategies.

(4) The role that each investment or course of action plays within the overall trust portfolio.

(5) The expected total return from income and the appreciation of capital.

(6) Other resources of the beneficiaries known to the trustee as determined from information provided by the beneficiaries.

(7) Needs for liquidity, regularity of income, and preservation or appreciation of capital.

(8) An asset's special relationship or special value, if any, to the purposes of the trust or to one or more of the beneficiaries.

(d) A trustee shall make a reasonable effort to ascertain facts relevant to the investment and management of trust assets.

(e) A trustee may invest in any kind of property or type of investment or engage in any course of action or investment strategy consistent with the standards of this chapter.

16048. In making and implementing investment decisions, the trustee has a duty to diversify the investments of the trust unless, under the circumstances, it is prudent not to do so.

16049. Within a reasonable time after accepting a trusteeship or receiving trust assets, a trustee shall review the trust assets and make and implement decisions concerning the retention and disposition of assets, in order to bring the trust portfolio into compliance with the purposes, terms, distribution requirements, and other circumstances of the trust, and with the requirements of this chapter.

16050. In investing and managing trust assets, a trustee may only incur costs that are appropriate and reasonable in relation to the assets, overall investment strategy, purposes, and other circumstances of the trust.

16051. Compliance with the prudent investor rule is determined in light of the facts and circumstances existing at the time of a trustee's decision or action and not by hindsight.

16052. (a) A trustee may delegate investment and management functions as prudent under the circumstances. The trustee shall exercise prudence in the following:

(1) Selecting an agent.

(2) Establishing the scope and terms of the delegation, consistent with the purposes and terms of the trust.

(3) Periodically reviewing the agent's overall performance and compliance with the terms of the delegation.

(b) In performing a delegated function, an agent has a duty to exercise reasonable care to comply with the terms of the delegation.

(c) Except as otherwise provided in Section 16401, a trustee who complies with the requirements of subdivision (a) is not liable to the beneficiaries or to the trust for the decisions or actions of the agent to whom the function was delegated.

(d) By accepting the delegation of a trust function from the trustee of a trust that is subject to the law of this state, an agent submits to the jurisdiction of the courts of this state.

16053. The following terms or comparable language in the provisions of a trust, unless otherwise limited or modified, authorizes any investment or strategy permitted under this chapter: "investments permissible by law for investment of trust funds," "legal investments," "authorized investments," "using the judgment and care under the circumstances then prevailing that persons of prudence, discretion, and intelligence exercise in the management of their own affairs, not in regard to speculation but in regard to the permanent disposition of their funds, considering the probable income as well as the probable safety of their capital," "prudent man rule," "prudent trustee rule," "prudent person rule," and "prudent investor rule."

16054. This article applies to trusts existing on and created after its effective date. As applied to trusts existing on its effective date, this article governs only decisions or actions occurring after that date.

Article 3. Trustee's Duty To Report Information And Account To Beneficiaries

16060. The trustee has a duty to keep the beneficiaries of the trust reasonably informed of the trust and its administration.

16060.5. As used in this article, "terms of the trust" means the written trust instrument of an irrevocable trust or those provisions of a written trust instrument in effect at the settlor's death that describe or affect that portion of a trust that has become irrevocable at the death of the settlor. In addition, "terms of the trust" includes, but is not limited to, signatures, amendments, disclaimers, and any directions or instructions to the trustee that affect the disposition of the trust. "Terms of the trust" does not include documents which were intended to affect disposition only while the trust was revocable. If a trust has been completely restated, "terms of the trust" does not include trust instruments or amendments which are superseded by the last restatement before the settlor's death, but it does include amendments executed after the restatement. "Terms of the trust" also includes any document irrevocably exercising a power of appointment over the trust or over any portion of the trust which has become irrevocable.

16060.7. On the request of a beneficiary, the trustee shall provide the terms of the trust to the beneficiary unless the trustee is not required to provide the terms of the trust to the beneficiary in accordance with Section 16069.

16061. Except as provided in Section 16069, on reasonable request by a beneficiary, the trustee shall report to the beneficiary by providing requested information to the beneficiary relating to the administration of the trust relevant to the beneficiary's interest.

16061.5. (a) A trustee shall provide a true and complete copy of the terms of the irrevocable trust, or irrevocable portion of the trust, to each of the following:

(1) Any beneficiary of the trust who requests it, and to any heir of a deceased settlor who requests it, when a revocable trust or any portion of a revocable trust becomes irrevocable because of the death of one or more of the settlors of the trust, when a power of appointment is effective or lapses upon the death of a settlor under the circumstances described in paragraph (3) of subdivision (a) of Section 16061.7, or because, by the express terms of the trust, the trust becomes irrevocable within one year of the death of a settlor because of a contingency related to the death of one or more of the settlors of the trust.

(2) Any beneficiary of the trust who requests it, whenever there is a change of trustee of an irrevocable trust.

(3) If the trust is a charitable trust subject to the supervision of the Attorney General, to the Attorney General, if requested, when a revocable trust or any portion of a revocable trust becomes irrevocable because of the death of one or more of the settlors of the trust, when a power of appointment is effective or lapses upon the death of a settlor under the circumstances described in paragraph (3) of subdivision (a) of Section 16061.7, or because, by the express terms of the trust, the trust becomes irrevocable within one year of the death of a settlor because of a contingency related to the death of one or more of the settlors of the trust, and whenever there is a change of trustee of an irrevocable trust.

(b) The trustee shall, for purposes of this section, rely upon any final judicial determination of heirship. However, the trustee shall have discretion to make a good faith determination by any reasonable means of the heirs of a deceased settlor in the absence of a final judicial determination of heirship known to the trustee.

16061.7. (a) A trustee shall serve a notification by the trustee as described in this section in the following events:

(1) When a revocable trust or any portion thereof becomes irrevocable because of the death of one or more of the settlors of the trust, or because, by the express terms of the trust, the trust becomes irrevocable within one year of the death of a settlor because of a contingency related to the death of one or more of the settlors of the trust.

(2) Whenever there is a change of trustee of an irrevocable trust.

(3) Whenever a power of appointment retained by a settlor is effective or lapses upon death of the settlor with respect to an inter vivos trust which was, or was purported to be, irrevocable upon its creation. This paragraph shall not apply to a charitable remainder trust. For purposes of this paragraph, "charitable remainder trust" means a charitable remainder annuity trust or charitable remainder unitrust as defined in Section 664(d) of the Internal Revenue Code.

(4) The duty to serve the notification by the trustee pursuant to this subdivision is the duty of the continuing or successor trustee, and any one cotrustee may serve the notification.

(b) The notification by the trustee required by subdivision (a) shall be served on each of the following:

(1) Each beneficiary of the irrevocable trust or irrevocable portion of the trust, subject to the limitations of Section 15804.

(2) Each heir of the deceased settlor, if the event that requires notification is the death of a settlor or irrevocability within one year of the death of the settlor of the trust by the express terms of the trust because of a contingency related to the death of a settlor.

(3) If the trust is a charitable trust subject to the supervision of the Attorney General, to the Attorney General.

(c) A trustee shall, for purposes of this section, rely upon any final judicial determination of heirship, known to the trustee, but the trustee shall have discretion to make a good faith determination by any reasonable means of the heirs of a deceased settlor in the absence of a final judicial determination of heirship known to the trustee.

(d) The trustee need not provide a copy of the notification by trustee to any beneficiary or heir (1) known to the trustee but who cannot be located by the trustee after reasonable diligence or (2) unknown to the trustee.

(e) The notification by trustee shall be served by mail to the last known address, pursuant to Section 1215, or by personal delivery.

(f) The notification by trustee shall be served not later than 60 days following the occurrence of the event requiring service of the notification by trustee, or 60 days after the trustee became aware of the existence of a person entitled to receive notification by trustee, if that person was not known to the trustee on the occurrence of the event requiring service of the notification. If there is a vacancy in the office of the trustee on the date of the occurrence of the event requiring service of the notification by trustee, or if that event causes a vacancy, then the 60-day period for service of the notification by trustee commences on the date the new trustee commences to serve as trustee.

(g) The notification by trustee shall contain the following information:

(1) The identity of the settlor or settlors of the trust and the date of execution of the trust instrument.

(2) The name, mailing address and telephone number of each trustee of the trust.

(3) The address of the physical location where the principal place of administration of the trust is located, pursuant to Section 17002.

(4) Any additional information that may be expressly required by the terms of the trust instrument.

(5) A notification that the recipient is entitled, upon reasonable request to the trustee, to receive from the trustee a true and complete copy of the terms of the trust.

(h) If the notification by the trustee is served because a revocable trust or any portion of it has become irrevocable because of the death of one or more settlors of the trust, or because, by the express terms of the trust, the trust becomes irrevocable within one year of the death of a settlor because of a contingency related to the death of one or more of the settlors of the trust, the notification by the trustee shall also include a warning, set out in a separate paragraph in not less than 10-point boldface type, or a reasonable equivalent thereof, that states as follows:

"You may not bring an action to contest the trust more than 120 days from the date this notification by the trustee is served upon you or 60 days from the date on which a copy of the terms of the trust is mailed or personally delivered to you during that 120-day period, whichever is later."

(i) Any waiver by a settlor of the requirement of serving the notification by trustee required by this section is against public policy and shall be void.

(j) A trustee may serve a notification by trustee in the form required by this section on any person in addition to those on whom the notification by trustee is required to be served. A trustee is not liable to any person for serving or for not serving the notice on any person in addition to those on whom the notice is required to be served. A trustee is not required to serve a notification by trustee if the event that otherwise requires service of the notification by trustee occurs before January 1, 1998.

16061.8. No person upon whom the notification by the trustee is served pursuant to this chapter, whether the notice is served on him or her within or after the time period set forth in subdivision (f) of Section 16061.7, may bring an action to contest the trust more than 120 days from the date the notification by the trustee is served upon him or her, or 60 days from the day on which a copy of the terms of the trust is mailed or personally delivered to him or her during that 120-day period, whichever is later.

16061.9. (a) A trustee who fails to serve the notification by trustee as required by Section 16061.7 on a beneficiary shall be responsible for all damages, attorney's fees, and costs caused by the failure unless the trustee makes a reasonably diligent effort to comply with that section.

(b) A trustee who fails to serve the notification by trustee as required by Section 16061.7 on an heir who is not a beneficiary and whose identity is known to the trustee shall be responsible for all damages caused to the heir by the failure unless the trustee shows that the trustee made a reasonably diligent effort to comply with that section. For purposes of this subdivision, "reasonably diligent effort" means that the trustee has sent notice by first-class mail to the heir at the heir's last mailing address actually known to the trustee.

(c) A trustee, in exercising discretion with respect to the timing and nature of distributions of trust assets, may consider the fact that the period in which a beneficiary or heir could bring an action to contest the trust has not expired.

16062. (a) Except as otherwise provided in this section and in Section 16064, the trustee shall account at least annually, at the termination of the trust, and upon a change of trustee, to each beneficiary to whom income or principal is required or authorized in the trustee's discretion to be currently distributed.

(b) A trustee of a living trust created by an instrument executed before July 1, 1987, is not subject to the duty to account provided by subdivision (a).

(c) A trustee of a trust created by a will executed before July 1, 1987, is not subject to the duty to account provided by subdivision (a), except that if the trust is removed from continuing court jurisdiction pursuant to Article 2 (commencing with Section 17350) of Chapter 4 of Part 5, the duty to account provided by subdivision (a) applies to the trustee.

(d) Except as provided in Section 16064, the duty of a trustee to account pursuant to former Section 1120.1a of the Probate Code (as repealed by Chapter 820 of the Statutes of 1986), under a trust created by a will executed before July 1, 1977, which has been removed from continuing court jurisdiction pursuant to former Section 1120.1a, contin-

ues to apply after July 1, 1987. The duty to account under former Section 1120.1a may be satisfied by furnishing an account that satisfies the requirements of Section 16063.

(e) Any limitation or waiver in a trust instrument of the obligation to account is against public policy and shall be void as to any sole trustee who is either of the following:

(1) A disqualified person as defined in Section 21350.5.

(2) Described in subdivision (a) of Section 21380, but not described in Section 21382.

16063. (a) An account furnished pursuant to Section 16062 shall contain the following information:

(1) A statement of receipts and disbursements of principal and income that have occurred during the last complete fiscal year of the trust or since the last account.

(2) A statement of the assets and liabilities of the trust as of the end of the last complete fiscal year of the trust or as of the end of the period covered by the account.

(3) The trustee's compensation for the last complete fiscal year of the trust or since the last account.

(4) The agents hired by the trustee, their relationship to the trustee, if any, and their compensation, for the last complete fiscal year of the trust or since the last account.

(5) A statement that the recipient of the account may petition the court pursuant to Section 17200 to obtain a court review of the account and of the acts of the trustee.

(6) A statement that claims against the trustee for breach of trust may not be made after the expiration of three years from the date the beneficiary receives an account or report disclosing facts giving rise to the claim.

(b) All accounts filed to be approved by a court shall be presented in the manner provided in Chapter 4 (commencing with Section 1060) of Part 1 of Division 3.

16064. The trustee is not required to account to a beneficiary as described in subdivision (a) of Section 16062, in any of the following circumstances:

(a) To the extent the trust instrument waives the account, except that no waiver described in subdivision (e) of Section 16062 shall be valid or enforceable. Regardless of a waiver of accounting in the trust instrument, upon a showing that it is reasonably likely that a material breach of the trust has occurred, the court may compel the trustee to account.

(b) As to a beneficiary who has waived in writing the right to an account. A waiver of rights under this subdivision may be withdrawn in writing at any time as to accounts for transactions occurring after the date of the written withdrawal. Regardless of a waiver of accounting by a beneficiary, upon a showing that is reasonably likely that a material breach of the trust has occurred, the court may compel the trustee to account.

(c) In any of the circumstances set forth in Section 16069.

16068. Any waiver by a settlor of the obligation of the trustee of either of the following is against public policy and shall be void:

(a) To provide the terms of the trust to the beneficiary as required by Sections 16060.7 and 16061.5.

(b) To provide requested information to the beneficiary as required by Section 16061.

16069. The trustee is not required to account to the beneficiary, provide the terms of the trust to a beneficiary, or provide requested information to the beneficiary pursuant to Section 16061, in any of the following circumstances:

(a) In the case of a beneficiary of a revocable trust, as provided in Section 15800, for the period when the trust may be revoked.

(b) If the beneficiary and the trustee are the same person.

Article 4. Duties With Regard To Discretionary Powers

16080. Except as provided in Section 16081, a discretionary power conferred upon a trustee is not left to the trustee's arbitrary discretion, but shall be exercised reasonably.

16081. (a) Subject to the additional requirements of subdivisions (b), (c), and (d), if a trust instrument confers "absolute," "sole," or "uncontrolled" discretion on a trustee, the trustee shall act in accordance with fiduciary principles and shall not act in bad faith or in disregard of the purposes of the trust.

(b) Notwithstanding the use of terms like "absolute," "sole," or "uncontrolled" by a settlor or a testator, a person who is a beneficiary of a trust that permits the person, either individually or as trustee or cotrustee, to make discretionary distributions of income or principal to or for the benefit of himself or herself pursuant to a standard, shall exercise that power reasonably and in accordance with the standard.

(c) Unless a settlor or a testator clearly indicates that a broader power is intended by express reference to this subdivision, a person who is a beneficiary of a trust that permits the person, as trustee or cotrustee, to make discretionary distributions of income or principal to or for the benefit of himself or herself may exercise that power in his or her favor only for his or her health, education, support, or maintenance within the meaning of Sections 2041 and 2514 of the Internal Revenue Code. Notwithstanding the foregoing and the provisions of Section 15620, if a power to make discretionary distributions of income or principal is conferred upon two or more trustees, the power may be exercised by any trustee who is not a current permissible beneficiary of that power ; and provided further that if there is no trustee who is not a current permissible beneficiary of that power, any party in interest may apply to a court of competent jurisdiction to appoint a trustee who is not a current permissible beneficiary of that power, and the power may be exercised by the trustee appointed by the court.

(d) Subdivision (c) does not apply to either of the following:

(1) Any power held by the settlor of a revocable or amendable trust.

(2) Any power held by a settlor's spouse or a testator's spouse who is the trustee of a trust for which a marital deduction, as defined in Section 21520, has been allowed.

(e) Subdivision (c) applies to any of the following:

(1) Any trust executed on or after January 1, 1997.

(2) Any testamentary trust created under a will executed on or after January 1, 1997.

(3) Any irrevocable trust created under a document executed before January 1, 1997, or any revocable trust executed before that date if the settlor was incapacitated as of that date, unless all parties in interest elect affirmatively not to be subject to the application of subdivision (c) through a written instrument delivered to the trustee. That election shall be made on or before the latest of January 1, 1998, three years after the date on which the trust became irrevocable, or, in the case of a revocable trust where the settlor was incapacitated, three years after the date on which the settlor became incapacitated.

(f) Notwithstanding the foregoing, the provisions of subdivision (c) neither create a new cause of action nor impair an existing cause of action that, in either case, relates to any power limited by subdivision (c) that was exercised before January 1, 1997.

(g) For purposes of this section, the term "party in interest" means any of the following persons:

(1) If the trust is revocable and the settlor is incapacitated, the settlor's legal representative under applicable law, or the settlor's attorney-in-fact under a durable power of attorney that is sufficient to grant the authority required under subdivision (c) or (e), as applicable.

(2) If the trust is irrevocable, each trustee, each beneficiary then entitled or authorized to receive income distributions from the trust, or each remainder beneficiary who would be entitled to receive notice of a trust proceeding under Section 15804. Any beneficiary who lacks legal capacity may be represented by the beneficiary's legal representative, attorney-in-fact under a durable power of attorney that is sufficient to grant the authority required under subdivision (c) or (e), as applicable, or in the absence of a legal representative or attorney-in-fact, a guardian ad litem appointed for that purpose.

16082. Except as otherwise specifically provided in the trust instrument, a person who holds a power to appoint or distribute income or principal to or for the benefit of others, either as an individual or as trustee, may not use the power to discharge the legal obligations of the person holding the power.

Article 5. Duties Of Trustees Of Private Foundations, Charitable Trusts, And Split-Interest Trusts

16100. As used in this article, the following definitions shall control:

(a) "Charitable trust" means a charitable trust as described in Section 4947(a)(1) of the Internal Revenue Code.

(b) "Private foundation" means a private foundation as defined in Section 509 of the Internal Revenue Code.

(c) "Split-interest trust" means a split-interest trust as described in Section 4947(a)(2) of the Internal Revenue Code.

16101. During any period when a trust is deemed to be a charitable trust or a private foundation, the trustee shall distribute its income for each taxable year (and principal if necessary) at a time and in a manner that will not subject the property of the trust to tax under Section 4942 of the Internal Revenue Code.

16102. During any period when a trust is deemed to be a charitable trust, a private foundation, or a split-interest trust, the trustee shall not do any of the following:

(a) Engage in any act of self-dealing as defined in Section 4941 (d) of the Internal Revenue Code.

(b) Retain any excess business holdings as defined in Section 4943 (c) of the Internal Revenue Code.

(c) Make any investments in such manner as to subject the property of the trust to tax under Section 4944 of the Internal Revenue Code.

(d) Make any taxable expenditure as defined in Section 4945(d) of the Internal Revenue Code.

16103. With respect to split-interest trusts:

(a) Subdivisions (b) and (c) of Section 16102 do not apply to any trust described in Section 4947(b)(3) of the Internal Revenue Code.

(b) Section 16102 does not apply with respect to any of the following:

(1) Any amounts payable under the terms of such trust to income beneficiaries, unless a deduction was allowed under Section 170(f)(2) (B), 2055(e)(2)(B), or 2522(c)(2)(B) of the Internal Revenue Code.

(2) Any amounts in trust other than amounts for which a deduction was allowed under Section 170, 545(b)(2), 556(b)(2), 642(c), 2055, 2106(a)(2), or 2522 of the Internal Revenue Code, if the amounts are segregated, as that term is defined in Section 4947(a)(3) of the Internal Revenue Code, from amounts for which no deduction was allowable.

(3) Any amounts irrevocably transferred in trust before May 27, 1969.

16104. The provisions of Sections 16101, 16102, and 16103 shall be deemed to be contained in the instrument creating every trust to which this article applies. Any provision of the instrument inconsistent with or contrary to this article is without effect.

16105. (a) A proceeding contemplated by Section 101(l)(3) of the federal Tax Reform Act of 1969 (Public Law 91-172) may be commenced pursuant to Section 17200 by the organization involved. All specifically named beneficiaries of the organization and the Attorney General shall be parties to the proceedings. Notwithstanding Section 17000, this provision is not exclusive and does not limit any jurisdiction that otherwise exists.

(b) If an instrument creating a trust affected by this section has been recorded, a notice of pendency of judicial proceedings under this section shall be recorded in a similar manner within 10 days from the commencement of the proceedings. A duly certified copy of any final judgment or decree in the proceedings shall be similarly recorded.

Chapter 2. Powers Of Trustees

Article 1. General Provisions

16200. A trustee has the following powers without the need to obtain court authorization:

(a) The powers conferred by the trust instrument.

(b) Except as limited in the trust instrument, the powers conferred by statute.

(c) Except as limited in the trust instrument, the power to perform any act that a trustee would perform for the purposes of the trust under the standard of care provided in Section 16040 or 16047.

16201. This chapter does not affect the power of a court to relieve a trustee from restrictions on the exercise of powers under the trust instrument.

16202. The grant of a power to a trustee, whether by the trust instrument, by statute, or by the court, does not in itself require or permit the exercise of the power. The exercise of a power by a trustee is subject to the trustee's fiduciary duties.

16203. An instrument that incorporates the powers provided in former Section 1120.2 (repealed by Chapter 820 of the Statutes of 1986) shall be deemed to refer to the powers provided in Article 2 (commencing with Section 16220). For this purpose, the trustee's powers under former Section 1120.2 are not diminished and the trustee is not required to obtain court approval for exercise of a power for which court approval was not required by former law.

Article 2. Specific Powers Of Trustees

16220. The trustee has the power to collect, hold, and retain trust property received from a settlor or any other person until, in the judgment of the trustee, disposition of the property should be made. The property may be retained even though it includes property in which the trustee is personally interested.

16221. The trustee has the power to accept additions to the property of the trust from a settlor or any other person.

16222. (a) Subject to subdivision (b), the trustee has the power to continue or participate in the operation of any business or other enterprise that is part of the trust property and may effect incorporation, dissolution, or other change in the form of the organization of the business or enterprise.

(b) Except as provided in subdivision (c), the trustee may continue the operation of a business or other enterprise only as authorized by the trust instrument or by the court. For the purpose of this subdivision, the lease of four or fewer residential units is not considered to be the operation of a business or other enterprise.

(c) The trustee may continue the operation of a business or other enterprise for a reasonable time pending a court hearing on the matter or pending a sale of the business or other enterprise.

(d) The limitation provided in subdivision (b) does not affect any power to continue or participate in the operation of a business or other enterprise that the trustee has under a trust created by an instrument executed before July 1, 1987.

16224. (a) In the absence of an express provision to the contrary in a trust instrument, where the instrument directs or permits investment in obligations of the United States government, the trustee has the power to invest in those obligations directly or in the form of an interest in a money market mutual fund registered under the Investment Company Act of 1940 (15 U.S.C. Sec. 80a-1 et seq.) or an investment vehicle authorized for the collective investment of trust funds pursuant to Section 9.18 of Part 9 of Title 12 of the Code of Federal Regulations, the portfolios of which are limited to United States government obligations maturing not later than five years from the date of investment or reinvestment and to repurchase agreements fully collateralized by United States government obligations.

(b) This section applies only to trusts created on or after January 1, 1985.

16225. (a) The trustee has the power to deposit trust funds at reasonable interest in any of the following accounts:

(1) An insured account in a financial institution.

(2) To the extent that the account is collateralized, an account in a bank, an account in an insured savings and loan association, or an account in an insured credit union.

(b) A trustee may deposit trust funds pursuant to subdivision (a) in a financial institution operated by, or that is an affiliate of, the trustee. For the purpose of this subdivision, "affiliate" means a corporation that directly or indirectly through one or more intermediaries controls, is controlled by, or is under common control with another domestic or foreign corporation.

(c) This section does not limit the power of a trustee in a proper case to deposit trust funds in an account described in subdivision (a) that is subject to notice or other conditions respecting withdrawal prescribed by law or governmental regulation.

(d) The court may authorize the deposit of trust funds in an account described in subdivision (a) in an amount greater than the maximum insured or collateralized amount.

(e) Nothing in this section prevents the trustee from holding an amount of trust property reasonably necessary for the orderly administration of the trust in the form of cash or in a checking account without interest.

16226. The trustee has the power to acquire or dispose of property, for cash or on credit, at public or private sale, or by exchange.

16227. The trustee has the power to manage, control, divide, develop, improve, exchange, partition, change the character of, or abandon trust property or any interest therein.

16228. The trustee has the power to encumber, mortgage, or pledge trust property for a term within or extending beyond the term of the trust in connection with the exercise of any power vested in the trustee.

16229. The trustee has the power to do any of the following:

(a) Make ordinary or extraordinary repairs, alterations, or improvements in buildings or other trust property.

(b) Demolish any improvements.

(c) Raze existing or erect new party walls or buildings.

16230. The trustee has the power to do any of the following:

(a) Subdivide or develop land.

(b) Dedicate land to public use.

(c) Make or obtain the vacation of plats and adjust boundaries.

(d) Adjust differences in valuation on exchange or partition by giving or receiving consideration.

(e) Dedicate easements to public use without consideration.

16231. The trustee has the power to enter into a lease for any purpose as lessor or lessee with or without the option to purchase or renew and for a term within or extending beyond the term of the trust.

16232. The trustee has the power to enter into a lease or arrangement for exploration and removal of gas, oil, or other minerals or geothermal energy, and to enter into a community oil lease or a pooling or unitization agreement, and for a term within or extending beyond the term of the trust.

16233. The trustee has the power to grant an option involving disposition of trust property or to take an option for the acquisition of any property, and an option may be granted or taken that is exercisable beyond the term of the trust.

16234. With respect to any shares of stock of a domestic or foreign corporation, any membership in a nonprofit corporation, or any other property, a trustee has the power to do any of the following:

(a) Vote in person, and give proxies to exercise, any voting rights with respect to the shares, memberships, or property.

(b) Waive notice of a meeting or give consent to the holding of a meeting.

(c) Authorize, ratify, approve, or confirm any action that could be taken by shareholders, members, or property owners.

16235. The trustee has the power to pay calls, assessments, and any other sums chargeable or accruing against or on account of securities.

16236. The trustee has the power to sell or exercise stock subscription or conversion rights.

16237. The trustee has the power to consent, directly or through a committee or other agent, to the reorganization, consolidation, merger, dissolution, or liquidation of a corporation or other business enterprise, and to participate in voting trusts, pooling arrangements, and foreclosures, and in connection therewith, to deposit securities with and transfer title and delegate discretion to any protective or other committee as the trustee may deem advisable.

16238. The trustee has the power to hold a security in the name of a nominee or in other form without disclosure of the trust so that title to the security may pass by delivery.

16239. The trustee has the power to deposit securities in a securities depository, as defined in Section 30004 of the Financial Code, which is licensed under Section 30200 of the Financial Code or is exempt from licensing by Section 30005 or 30006 of the Financial Code. The securities may be held by the securities depository in the manner authorized by Section 775 of the Financial Code.

16240. The trustee has the power to insure the property of the trust against damage or loss and to insure the trustee against liability with respect to third persons.

16241. The trustee has the power to borrow money for any trust purpose to be repaid from trust property. The lender may include, but is not limited to, a bank holding company, affiliate, or subsidiary of the trustee.

16242. The trustee has the power to do any of the following:

(a) Pay or contest any claim.

(b) Settle a claim by or against the trust by compromise, arbitration, or otherwise.

(c) Release, in whole or in part, any claim belonging to the trust.

16243. The trustee has the power to pay taxes, assessments, reasonable compensation of the trustee and of employees and agents of the trust, and other expenses incurred in the collection, care, administration, and protection of the trust.

16244. The trustee has the following powers:

(a) To make loans out of trust property to the beneficiary on terms and conditions that the trustee determines are fair and reasonable under the circumstances.

(b) To guarantee loans to the beneficiary by encumbrances on trust property.

16245. The trustee has the power to pay any sum of principal or income distributable to a beneficiary, without regard to whether the beneficiary is under a legal disability, by paying the sum to the beneficiary or by paying the sum to another person for the use or benefit of the beneficiary. Any sum distributable under this section to a custodian under the California Uniform Transfers to Minors Act (Part 9 (commencing with Section 3900)) shall be subject to Section 3906.

16246. The trustee has the power to effect distribution of property and money in divided or undivided interests and to adjust resulting differences in valuation. A distribution in kind may be made pro rata or non pro rata, and may be made pursuant to any written agreement providing for a non pro rata division of the aggregate value of the community property assets or quasi-community property assets, or both.

16247. The trustee has the power to hire persons, including accountants, attorneys, auditors, investment advisers, appraisers (including probate referees appointed pursuant to Section 400), or other agents, even if they are associated or affiliated with the trustee, to advise or assist the trustee in the performance of administrative duties.

16248. The trustee has the power to execute and deliver all instruments which are needed to accomplish or facilitate the exercise of the powers vested in the trustee.

16249. The trustee has the power to prosecute or defend actions, claims, or proceedings for the protection of trust property and of the trustee in the performance of the trustee's duties.

Chapter 3. Uniform Principal And Income Act

Article 1. Short Title And Definitions

16320. This chapter may be cited as the Uniform Principal and Income Act.

16321. The definitions in this article govern the construction of this chapter.

16322. "Accounting period" means a calendar year unless another 12-month period is selected by a fiduciary. The term includes a portion of a calendar year or other 12-month period that begins when an income interest begins or ends when an income interest ends.

16323. "Fiduciary" means a personal representative or a trustee.

16324. "Income" means money or property that a fiduciary receives as current return from a principal asset. The term includes a portion of receipts from a sale, exchange, or liquidation of a principal asset, to the extent provided in Article 5.1 (commencing with Section 16350), 5.2 (commencing with Section 16355), or 5.3 (commencing with Section 16360).

16325. "Income beneficiary" means a person to whom net income of a trust is or may be payable.

16326. "Income interest" means the right of an income beneficiary to receive all or part of net income, whether the trust requires it to be distributed or authorizes it to be distributed in the trustee's discretion.

16327. "Mandatory income interest" means the right of an income beneficiary to receive net income that the trust requires the fiduciary to distribute.

16328. "Net income" means the total receipts allocated to income during an accounting period minus the disbursements made from income during the accounting period, plus or minus transfers under this chapter to or from income during the accounting period. During any period in which the trust is being administered as a unitrust, either pursuant to the powers conferred by Sections 16336.4 to 16336.6, inclusive, or pursuant to the terms of the governing instrument, "net income" means the unitrust amount, if the unitrust amount is no less than 3 percent and no more than 5 percent of the fair market value of the trust assets, whether determined annually or averaged on a multiple year basis.

Article 2. General Provisions And Fiduciary Duties

16335. (a) In allocating receipts and disbursements to or between principal and income, and with respect to any other matter within the scope of this chapter, a fiduciary:

(1) Shall administer a trust or decedent's estate in accordance with the trust or the will, even if there is a different provision in this chapter.

(2) May administer a trust or decedent's estate by the exercise of a discretionary power of administration given to the fiduciary by the trust or the will, even if the exercise of the power produces a result different from a result required or permitted by this chapter, and no inference that the fiduciary has improperly exercised the discretion arises from the fact that the fiduciary has made an allocation contrary to a provision of this chapter.

(3) Shall administer a trust or decedent's estate in accordance with this chapter if the trust or the will does not contain a different provision or does not give the fiduciary a discretionary power of administration.

(4) Shall add a receipt or charge a disbursement to principal to the extent that the trust or the will and this chapter do not provide a rule for allocating the receipt or disbursement to or between principal and income.

(b) In exercising a discretionary power of administration regarding a matter within the scope of this chapter, whether granted by a trust, a will, or this chapter, including the trustee's power to adjust under subdivision (a) of Section 16336, and the trustee's power to convert into a unitrust or reconvert or change the unitrust payout percentage pursuant to Sections 16336.4 to 16336.6, inclusive, the fiduciary shall administer the trust or decedent's estate impartially, except to the extent that the trust or the will expresses an intention that the fiduciary shall or may favor one or more of the beneficiaries. The exercise of discretion in accordance with this chapter is presumed to be fair and reasonable to all beneficiaries.

16336. (a) Subject to subdivision (b), a trustee may make an adjustment between principal and income to the extent the trustee considers necessary if all of the following conditions are satisfied:

(1) The trustee invests and manages trust assets under the prudent investor rule.

(2) The trust describes the amount that shall or may be distributed to a beneficiary by referring to the trust's income.

(3) The trustee determines, after applying the rules in subdivision (a) of Section 16335, and considering any power the trustee may have under the trust to invade principal or accumulate income, that the trustee is unable to comply with subdivision (b) of Section 16335.

(b) A trustee may not make an adjustment between principal and income in any of the following circumstances:

(1) Where it would diminish the income interest in a trust (A) that requires all of the income to be paid at least annually to a spouse and (B) for which, if the trustee did not have the power to make the adjustment, an estate tax or gift tax marital deduction would be allowed, in whole or in part.

(2) Where it would reduce the actuarial value of the income interest in a trust to which a person transfers property with the intent to qualify for a gift tax exclusion.

(3) Where it would change the amount payable to a beneficiary as a fixed annuity or a fixed fraction of the value of the trust assets.

(4) Where it would be made from any amount that is permanently set aside for charitable purposes under a will or trust, unless both income and principal are so set aside.

(5) Where possessing or exercising the power to make an adjustment would cause an individual to be treated as the owner of all or part of the trust for income tax purposes, and the individual would not be treated as the owner if the trustee did not possess the power to make an adjustment.

(6) Where possessing or exercising the power to make an adjustment would cause all or part of the trust assets to be included for estate tax purposes in the estate of an individual who has the power to remove a trustee or appoint a trustee, or both, and the assets would not be included in the estate of the individual if the trustee did not possess the power to make an adjustment.

(7) Where the trustee is a beneficiary of the trust.

(8) During any period in which the trust is being administered as a unitrust pursuant to the trustee's exercise of the power to convert provided in Section 16336.4 or 16336.5, or pursuant to the terms of the governing instrument.

(c) Notwithstanding Section 15620, if paragraph (5), (6), or (7) of subdivision (b) applies to a trustee and there is more than one trustee, a cotrustee to whom the provision does not apply may make the adjustment unless the exercise of the power by the remaining trustee or trustees is not permitted by the trust.

(d) A trustee may release the entire power conferred by subdivision (a) or may release only the power to adjust from income to principal or the power to adjust from principal to income in either of the following circumstances:

(1) If the trustee is uncertain about whether possessing or exercising the power will cause a result described in paragraphs (1) to (6), inclusive, of subdivision (b).

(2) If the trustee determines that possessing or exercising the power will or may deprive the trust of a tax benefit or impose a tax burden not described in subdivision (b).

(e) A release under subdivision (d) may be permanent or for a specified period, including a period measured by the life of an individual.

(f) A trust that limits the power of a trustee to make an adjustment between principal and income does not affect the application of this section unless it is clear from the trust that it is intended to deny the trustee the

power of adjustment provided by subdivision (a).

(g) In deciding whether and to what extent to exercise the power to make adjustments under this section, the trustee may consider, but is not limited to, any of the following:

(1) The nature, purpose, and expected duration of the trust.

(2) The intent of the settlor.

(3) The identity and circumstances of the beneficiaries.

(4) The needs for liquidity, regularity of income, and preservation and appreciation of capital.

(5) The assets held in the trust; the extent to which they consist of financial assets, interests in closely held enterprises, tangible and intangible personal property, or real property; the extent to which an asset is used by a beneficiary; and whether an asset was purchased by the trustee or received from the settlor.

(6) The net amount allocated to income under other statutes and the increase or decrease in the value of the principal assets, which the trustee may estimate as to assets for which market values are not readily available.

(7) Whether and to what extent the trust gives the trustee the power to invade principal or accumulate income or prohibit the trustee from invading principal or accumulating income, and the extent to which the trustee has exercised a power from time to time to invade principal or accumulate income.

(8) The actual and anticipated effect of economic conditions on principal and income and effects of inflation and deflation.

(9) The anticipated tax consequences of an adjustment.

(h) Nothing in this section or in this chapter is intended to create or imply a duty to make an adjustment, and a trustee is not liable for not considering whether to make an adjustment or for choosing not to make an adjustment.

16336.4. (a) Unless expressly prohibited by the governing instrument, a trustee may convert a trust into a unitrust, as described in this section. A trust that limits the power of the trustee to make an adjustment between principal and income or modify the trust does not affect the application of this section unless it is clear from the governing instrument that it is intended to deny the trustee the power to convert into a unitrust.

(b) The trustee may convert a trust into a unitrust without a court order if all of the following apply:

(1) The conditions set forth in subdivision (a) of Section 16336 are satisfied.

(2) The unitrust proposed by the trustee conforms to the provisions of paragraphs (1) to (8), inclusive, of subdivision (e).

(3) The trustee gives written notice of the

trustee's intention to convert the trust into a unitrust and furnishes the information required by subdivision (c). The notice shall comply with the requirements of Chapter 5 (commencing with Section 16500), including notice to a beneficiary who is a minor and to the minor's guardian, if any.

(4) No beneficiary objects to the proposed action in a writing delivered to the trustee within the period prescribed by subdivision (d) of Section 16502 or a longer period as is specified in the notice described in subdivision (c).

(c) The notice described in paragraph (3) of subdivision (b) shall include a copy of Sections 16336.4 to 16336.7, inclusive, and all of the following additional information:

(1) A statement that the trust shall be administered in accordance with the provisions of subdivision (e) and the effective date of the conversion.

(2) A description of the method to be used for determining the fair market value of trust assets.

(3) The amount actually distributed to the income beneficiary during the previous accounting year of the trust.

(4) The amount that would have been distributed to the income beneficiary during the previous accounting year of the trust had the trustee's proposed changes been in effect during that entire year.

(5) The discretionary decisions the trustee proposes to make as of the conversion date pursuant to subdivision (f).

(d) In deciding whether to exercise the power conferred by this section, a trustee may consider, among other things, the factors set forth in subdivision (g) of Section 16336.

(e) Except to the extent that the court orders otherwise or the parties agree otherwise pursuant to Section 16336.5 after a trust is converted to a unitrust, all of the following shall apply:

(1) The trustee shall make regular distributions in accordance with the governing instrument construed in accordance with the provisions of this section.

(2) The term "income" in the governing instrument shall mean an annual distribution, the unitrust amount, equal to 4 percent, which is the payout percentage, of the net fair market value of the trust's assets, whether those assets would be considered income or principal under other provisions of this chapter, averaged over the lesser of the following:

(A) The three preceding years.

(B) The period during which the trust has been in existence.

(3) During each accounting year of the trust following its conversion into a unitrust, the trustee shall, as early in the year as is practicable, furnish each income beneficiary with a statement describing the computation of the unitrust amount for that accounting year.

(4) The trustee shall determine the net fair market value of each asset held in the trust no less often than annually. However, the following property shall not be included in determining the unitrust amount:

(A) Any residential property or any tangible personal property that, as of the first business day of the current accounting year, one or more current beneficiaries of the trust have or have had the right to occupy, or have or have had the right to possess or control, other than in his or her capacity as trustee of the trust, which property shall be administered according to other provisions of this chapter as though no conversion to a unitrust had occurred.

(B) Any asset specifically devised to a beneficiary to the extent necessary, in the trustee's reasonable judgment, to avoid a material risk of exhausting other trust assets prior to termination of the trust. All net income generated by a specifically devised asset excluded from the unitrust computation pursuant to this subdivision shall be accumulated or distributed by the trustee according to the rules otherwise applicable to that net income pursuant to other provisions of this chapter.

(C) Any asset while held in a testator's estate or a terminating trust.

(5) The unitrust amount, as otherwise computed pursuant to this subdivision, shall be reduced proportionally for any material distribution made to accomplish a partial termination of the trust required by the governing instrument or made as a result of the exercise of a power of appointment or withdrawal, other than distributions of the unitrust amount, and shall be increased proportionately for the receipt of any material addition to the trust, other than a receipt that represents a return on investment, during the period considered in paragraph (2) in computing the unitrust amount. For the purpose of this paragraph, a distribution or an addition shall be "material" if the net value of the distribution or addition, when combined with all prior distributions made or additions received during the same accounting year, exceeds 10 percent of the value of the assets used to compute the unitrust amount as of the most recent prior valuation date. The trustee may, in the reasonable exercise of his or her discretion, adjust the unitrust amount pursuant to this subdivision even if the distributions or additions are not sufficient to meet the definition of materiality set forth in the preceding sentence.

(6) In the case of a short year in which a beneficiary's right to payments commences or ceases, the trustee shall prorate the unitrust amount on a daily basis.

(7) Unless otherwise provided by the governing instrument or determined by the trustee, the unitrust amount shall be considered paid in the following order from the following sources:

(A) From the net taxable income, other than capital gains, determined as if the trust were other than a unitrust.

(B) From net realized short-term capital gains.

(C) From net realized long-term capital gains.

(D) From tax-exempt and other income.

(E) From principal of the trust.

(8) Expenses that would be deducted from income if the trust were not a unitrust may not be deducted from the unitrust amount.

(f) The trustee shall determine, in the trustee's discretion, all of the following matters relating to administration of a unitrust created pursuant to this section:

(1) The effective date of a conversion to a unitrust.

(2) The frequency of payments in satisfaction of the unitrust amount.

(3) Whether to value the trust's assets annually or more frequently.

(4) What valuation dates to use.

(5) How to value nonliquid assets.

(6) The characterization of the unitrust payout for income tax reporting purposes. However, the trustee's characterization shall be consistent.

(7) Any other matters that the trustee deems appropriate for the proper functioning of the unitrust.

(g) A conversion into a unitrust does not affect a provision in the governing instrument directing or authorizing the trustee to distribute principal or authorizing the exercise of a power of appointment over or withdrawal of all or a portion of the principal.

(h) A trustee may not convert a trust into a unitrust in any of the following circumstances:

(1) If payment of the unitrust amount would change the amount payable to a beneficiary as a fixed annuity or a fixed fraction of the value of the trust assets.

(2) If the unitrust distribution would be made from any amount that is permanently set aside for charitable purposes under the governing instrument and for which a federal estate or gift tax deduction has been taken, unless both income and principal are set aside.

(3) If possessing or exercising the power to convert would cause an individual to be treated as the owner of all or part of the trust for federal income tax purposes, and the individual would not be treated as the owner if the trustee did not possess the power to convert.

(4) If possessing or exercising the power to convert would cause all or part of the trust assets to be subject to federal estate or gift tax with respect to an individual, and the assets would not be subject to federal estate or gift tax with respect to the individual if the trustee did not possess the power to convert.

(5) If the conversion would result in the disallowance of a federal estate tax or gift tax marital deduction that would be allowed if the trustee did not have the power to convert.

(i) If paragraph (3) or (4) of subdivision (h) applies to a trustee and there is more than one trustee, a cotrustee to whom the provision does not apply may convert the trust unless the exercise of the power by the remaining trustee or trustees is prohibited by the governing instrument. If paragraph (3) or (4) of subdivision (h) applies to all of the trustees, the court may order the conversion as provided in subdivision (b) of Section 16336.5.

(j) (1) A trustee may release the power conferred by this section to convert to a unitrust if either of the following circumstances exist:

(A) The trustee is uncertain about whether possessing or experiencing the power will cause a result described in paragraph (3), (4), or (5) of subdivision (h).

(B) The trustee determines that possessing or exercising the power will or may deprive the trust of a tax benefit or impose a tax burden not described in subdivision (h).

(2) A release pursuant to paragraph (1) may be permanent or for a specified period, including a period measured by the life of an individual.

16336.5. (a) The trustee may convert a trust into a unitrust upon terms other than those set forth in subdivision (e) of Section 16336.4, without court order, if all of the following apply:

(1) The conditions set forth in subdivision (a) of Section 16336 are satisfied.

(2) The trustee gives written notice of the trustee's intention to convert the trust into a unitrust and furnishes the information required by subdivision (c) of Section 16336.4. The notice shall comply with the requirements of Chapter 5 (commencing with Section 16500), including notice to a beneficiary who is a minor and to the minor's guardian, if any.

(3) The payout percentage to be adopted is at least 3 percent and no greater than 5 percent.

(4) All beneficiaries entitled to notice under Section 16501 consent in writing to the proposed conversion after having been furnished with the notice described in subdivision (c) of Section 16336.4.

(b) The court may order the conversion of a trust into a unitrust as provided in this subdivision.

(1) (A) The trustee may petition the court to approve the conversion to a unitrust for any one of the following reasons:

(i) A beneficiary timely objects to a proposed conversion to a unitrust.

(ii) The trustee proposes to make the conversion upon terms other than those described in subdivision (e) of Section 16336.4.

(iii) Paragraph (3) or (4) of subdivision (h) of Section 16336.4 applies to all currently acting trustees.

(iv) If the trustee determines, in its discretion, that a petition is advisable.

(B) In no event, however, may the court authorize conversion to a unitrust with a payout percentage of less than 3 percent or greater than 5 percent of the fair market value of the trust assets.

(2) A beneficiary may petition the court to order the conversion.

(3) The court shall approve the conversion proposed by the trustee or direct the conversion requested by the beneficiary if the conditions set forth in subdivision (a) of Section 16336 are satisfied and the court concludes that conversion of the trust on the terms proposed will enable the trustee to better comply with the provisions of subdivision (b) of Section 16335.

(4) In deciding whether to approve a proposed conversion or direct a requested conversion, the court may consider, among other factors, those described in subdivision (g) of Section 16336.

16336.6. Unless expressly prohibited by the governing instrument, a trustee may reconvert the trust from a unitrust or change the payout percentage of a unitrust.

(a) The trustee may make the reconversion or change in payout percentage without a court order if all of the following conditions are satisfied:

(1) At least three years have elapsed since the most recent conversion to a unitrust.

(2) The trustee determines that reconversion or change in payout percentage would enable the trustee to better comply with the provisions of subdivision (b) of Section 16335.

(3) One of the following notice requirements is satisfied:

(A) In the case of a proposed reconversion, the trustee gives written notice of the trustee's intention to convert that complies with the requirements of Chapter 5 (commencing with Section 16500) and no beneficiary objects to the proposed action in a writing delivered to the trustee within the period prescribed by subdivision (d) of Section 16502. The trustee's notice shall include the information described in subdivision (3) and (4) of subdivision (c) of Section 16336.4.

(B) In the case of a proposed change in payout percentage, the trustee gives written notice stating the new payout percentage that the trustee proposes to adopt, which notice shall comply with the requirements of Chapter 5 (commencing with Section 16500), and no beneficiary objects to the proposed action in a writing delivered to the trustee within the period prescribed by subdivision (d) of Section 16502.

(b) The trustee may make the reconversion or change in payout percentage at any time pursuant to court order provided that: (1) the court determines that reconversion or change in payout percentage will enable the trustee to better comply with the provisions of subdivision (b) of Section 16335, and (2)

in the case of a change in payout percentage, the new payout percentage is at least 3 percent and no greater than 5 percent. The court may enter an order pursuant to this subdivision upon the petition of the trustee or any beneficiary.

16336.7. (a) Sections 16336.4 to 16336.6, inclusive, shall not impose any duty on the trustee to convert or reconvert a trust or to consider a conversion or reconversion.

(b) Subdivision (b) of Section 16503 applies to all actions pursuant to Sections 16336.4 to 16336.6, inclusive, for which notice of proposed action is given in compliance with Chapter 5 (commencing with Section 16500), including notice to a beneficiary who is a minor and to the minor's guardian, if any.

16337. A trustee may give a notice of proposed action regarding a matter governed by this chapter as provided in Chapter 5 (commencing with Section 16500). For the purpose of this section, a proposed action includes a course of action and a decision not to take action.

16338. In a proceeding with respect to a trustee's exercise or nonexercise of the power to make an adjustment under Section 16336, the sole remedy is to direct, deny, or revise an adjustment between principal and income. In a proceeding with respect to a trustee's exercise or nonexercise of a power conferred by Sections 16336.4 to 16336.6, inclusive, the sole remedy is to obtain an order directing the trustee to convert the trust to a unitrust, to reconvert from a unitrust, to change the distribution percentage, or to order any administrative procedures the court determines to be necessary or helpful for the proper functioning of the trust.

16339. This chapter applies to every trust or decedent's estate existing on or after January 1, 2000, except as otherwise expressly provided in the trust or will or in this chapter.

Article 3. Decedent's Estate Or Terminating Income Interest

16340. After the decedent's death, in the case of a decedent's estate, or after an income interest in a trust ends, the following rules apply:

(a) If property is specifically given to a beneficiary, by will or trust, the fiduciary of the estate or of the terminating income interest shall distribute the net income and principal receipts to the beneficiary who is to receive the property, subject to the following rules:

(1) The net income and principal receipts from the specifically given property are determined by including all of the amounts the fiduciary receives or pays with respect to the property, whether the amounts accrued or became due before, on, or after the decedent's death or an income interest in a trust ends, and by making a reasonable provision

for amounts the fiduciary believes the estate or terminating income interest may become obligated to pay after the property is distributed.

(2) The fiduciary may not reduce income and principal receipts from the specifically given property on account of a payment described in Section 16370 or 16371, to the extent that the will, the trust, or Section 12002 requires payment from other property or to the extent that the fiduciary recovers the payment from a third person.

(3) A specific gift distributable under a trust shall carry with it the same benefits and burdens as a specific devise under a will, as set forth in Chapter 8 (commencing with Section 12000) of Part 10 of Division 7.

(b) A general pecuniary gift, an annuity, or a gift of maintenance distributable under a trust carries with it income and bears interest in the same manner as a general pecuniary devise, an annuity, or a gift of maintenance under a will, as set forth in Chapter 8 (commencing with Section 12000) of Part 10 of Division 7. The fiduciary shall distribute to a beneficiary who receives a pecuniary amount, whether outright or in trust, the interest or any other amount provided by the will, the trust, this subdivision, or Chapter 8 (commencing with Section 12000) of Part 10 of Division 7, from the remaining net income determined under subdivision (c) or from principal to the extent that net income is insufficient.

(c) The fiduciary shall determine the remaining net income of the decedent's estate or terminating income interest as provided in this chapter and by doing the following:

(1) Including in net income all income from property used to discharge liabilities.

(2) Paying from income or principal, in the fiduciary's discretion, fees of attorneys, accountants, and fiduciaries, court costs and other expenses of administration, and interest on death taxes, except that the fiduciary may pay these expenses from income of property passing to a trust for which the fiduciary claims an estate tax marital or charitable deduction only to the extent that the payment of these expenses from income will not cause the reduction or loss of the deduction.

(3) Paying from principal all other disbursements made or incurred in connection with the settlement of a decedent's estate or the winding up of a terminating income interest, including debts, funeral expenses, disposition of remains, family allowances, and death taxes and related penalties that are apportioned to the estate or terminating income interest by the will, the trust, or Division 10 (commencing with Section 20100).

(d) After distributions required by subdivision (b), the fiduciary shall distribute the remaining net income determined under subdivision (c) in the manner provided in Section 16341 to all other beneficiaries.

(e) For purposes of this section, a reference in Chapter 8 (commencing with Section 12000) of Part 10 of Division 7 to the date of the testator's death means the date of the settlor's death or of the occurrence of some other event on which the distributee's right to receive the gift depends.

(f) If a trustee has distributed a specific gift or a general pecuniary gift before January 1, 2007, the trustee may allocate income and principal as set forth in this chapter or in any other manner permissible under the law in effect at the time of the distribution. If the trustee distributes a specific gift or a general pecuniary gift after December 31, 2006, then the trustee shall allocate income and principal as provided in this chapter.

16341. (a) Each beneficiary described in subdivision (d) of Section 16340 is entitled to receive a portion of the net income equal to the beneficiary's fractional interest in undistributed principal assets, using values as of the distribution dates and without reducing the values by any unpaid principal obligations.

(b) If a fiduciary does not distribute all of the collected but undistributed net income to each beneficiary as of a distribution date, the fiduciary shall maintain appropriate records showing the interest of each beneficiary in that net income.

(c) The distribution date for purposes of this section may be the date as of which the fiduciary calculates the value of the assets if that date is reasonably near the date on which assets are actually distributed.

Article 4. Apportionment At Beginning And End Of Income Interest

16345. (a) An income beneficiary is entitled to net income from the date on which the income interest begins. An income interest begins on the date specified in the trust or, if no date is specified, on the date an asset becomes subject to a trust or successive income interest.

(b) An asset becomes subject to a trust at the following times:

(1) In the case of an asset that is transferred to a trust during the transferor's life, on the date it is transferred to the trust.

(2) In the case of an asset that becomes subject to a trust by reason of a will, even if there is an intervening period of administration of the testator's estate, on the date of the testator's death.

(3) In the case of an asset that is transferred to a fiduciary by a third party because of the individual's death, on the date of the individual's death.

(c) An asset becomes subject to a successive income interest on the day after the preceding income interest ends, as determined under subdivision (d), even if there is an intervening period of administration to wind up the preceding income interest.

(d) An income interest ends on the day before an income beneficiary dies, or another terminating event occurs, or on the last day of a period during which there is no beneficiary to whom a trustee may distribute income.

16346. (a) A trustee shall allocate an income receipt or disbursement other than one to which subdivision (a) of Section 16340 applies to principal if its due date occurs before a decedent dies in the case of an estate or before an income interest begins in the case of a trust or successive income interest.

(b) A trustee shall allocate an income receipt or disbursement to income if its due date occurs on or after the date on which a decedent dies or an income interest begins and it is a periodic due date. An income receipt or disbursement shall be treated as accruing from day to day if its due date is not periodic or it has no due date. The portion of the receipt or disbursement accruing before the date on which a decedent dies or an income interest begins shall be allocated to principal and the balance shall be allocated to income.

(c) An item of income or an obligation is due on the date the payer is required to make a payment. If a payment date is not stated, there is no due date for the purposes of this chapter. Distributions to shareholders or other owners from an entity to which Section 16350 applies are deemed to be due on the date fixed by the entity for determining who is entitled to receive the distribution or, if no date is fixed, on the declaration date for the distribution. A due date is periodic for receipts or disbursements that must be paid at regular intervals under a lease or an obligation to pay interest or if an entity customarily makes distributions at regular intervals.

16347. (a) For the purposes of this section, "undistributed income" means net income received before the date on which an income interest ends. The term does not include an item of income or expense that is due or accrued or net income that has been added or is required to be added to principal by the trust.

(b) Except as provided in subdivision (c), on the date when a mandatory income interest ends, the trustee shall pay to a mandatory income beneficiary who survives that date, or to the estate of a deceased mandatory income beneficiary whose death causes the interest to end, the beneficiary's share of the undistributed income that is not disposed of under the trust.

(c) If immediately before the income interest ends, the beneficiary under subdivision (b) has an unqualified power to revoke more than 5 percent of the trust, the undistributed income from the portion of the trust that may be revoked shall be added to principal.

(d) When a trustee's obligation to pay a fixed annuity or a fixed fraction of the value of the trust's assets ends, the trustee shall prorate the final payment.

Article 5.1. Allocation Of Receipts During Administration Of Trust: Receipts From Entities

16350. (a) For the purposes of this section:

(1) "Entity" means a corporation, partnership, limited liability company, regulated investment company, real estate investment trust, common trust fund, or any other organization in which a trustee has an interest other than a trust or decedent's estate to which Section 16351 applies, a business or activity to which Section 16352 applies, or an asset-backed security to which Section 16367 applies.

(2) "Capital asset" means a capital asset as defined in Section 1221 of the Internal Revenue Code.

(b) Except as otherwise provided in this section, a trustee shall allocate to income money received from an entity.

(c) A trustee shall allocate to principal the following receipts from an entity:

(1) Property other than money.

(2) Money received in one distribution or a series of related distributions in exchange for part or all of a trust's interest in the entity.

(3) Money received in total liquidation of the entity or in partial liquidation of the entity, as defined in subdivision (d).

(4) Money received from an entity that is a regulated investment company or a real estate investment trust if the money distributed is a capital gain dividend for federal income tax purposes.

(d) For purposes of paragraph (3) of subdivision (c), money shall be treated as received in partial liquidation to the extent the amount received from the distributing entity is attributable to the proceeds from a sale by the distributing entity, or by the distributing entity's subsidiary or affiliate, of a capital asset. The following shall apply to determine whether money is received in partial liquidation:

(1) A trustee may rely without investigation on a written statement made by the distributing entity regarding the receipt.

(2) A trustee may rely without investigation on other information actually known by the trustee regarding whether the receipt is attributable to the proceeds from a sale by the distributing entity, or by the distributing entity's subsidiary or affiliate, of a capital asset.

(3) With regard to each receipt from a distributing entity, if within 30 days from the date of the receipt the distributing entity provides no written statement to the trustee that the receipt is a distribution attributable to the proceeds from a sale of a capital asset by the distributing entity or by the distributing entity's subsidiary or affiliate and the

trustee has no actual knowledge that the receipt is a distribution attributable to the proceeds from a sale of a capital asset by the distributing entity or by the distributing entity's subsidiary or affiliate, then the following shall apply:

(A) The trustee shall have no duty to investigate whether the receipt from the distributing entity is in partial liquidation of the entity.

(B) If, on the date of receipt, the receipt from the distributing entity is in excess of 10 percent of the value of the trust's interest in the distributing entity, then the receipt shall be deemed to be received in partial liquidation of the distributing entity, and the trustee shall allocate all of the receipt to principal. For purposes of this subparagraph, the value of the trust's interest in the distributing entity shall be determined as follows:

(i) In the case of an interest that is a security regularly traded on a public exchange or market, the closing price of the security on the public exchange or market occurring on the last business day before the date of the receipt.

(ii) In the case of an interest that is not a security regularly traded on a public exchange or market, the trust's proportionate share of the value of the distributing entity as set forth in the most recent appraisal, if any, actually received by the trustee and prepared by a professional appraiser with a valuation date within three years of the date of the receipt. The trustee shall have no duty to investigate the existence of the appraisal or to obtain an appraisal nor shall the trustee have any liability for relying upon an appraisal prepared by a professional appraiser. The term "professional appraiser" shall refer to an appraiser who has earned an appraisal designation for valuing the type of property subject to the appraisal from a recognized professional appraiser organization.

(iii) If the trust's interest in the distributing entity cannot be valued under clause (i) or clause (ii), the trust's proportionate share of the distributing entity's net assets, to be calculated as gross assets minus liabilities, as shown in the distributing entity's yearend financial statements immediately preceding the receipt.

(iv) If the trust's interest in the distributing entity cannot be valued under clause (i), (ii), or (iii), the federal cost basis of the trust's interest in the distributing entity on the date immediately before the date of the receipt.

(e) If a trustee allocates a receipt to principal in accordance with subdivision (d), or allocates a receipt to income because the receipt is not determined to be in partial liquidation under subdivision (d), the trustee shall not be liable for any claim of improper allocation of the receipt that is based on information that was not received or actually known by the trustee as of the date of allocation.

(f) (1) Notwithstanding anything to the contrary in subdivision (d), if the receipt was allocated between December 2, 2004, and July 18, 2005, a trustee shall not be liable for allocating the receipt to income if the amount received by the trustee, when considered together with the amount received by all owners, collectively, exceeded 20 percent of the entity's gross assets, but the amount received by the trustee did not exceed 20 percent of the entity's gross assets.

(2) Money is not received in partial liquidation, nor may it be taken into account under subdivision (d), to the extent that it does not exceed the amount of income tax that a trustee or beneficiary is required to pay on taxable income of the entity that distributes the money.

16351. A trustee shall allocate to income an amount received as a distribution of income from a trust or a decedent's estate (other than an interest in an investment entity) in which the trust has an interest other than a purchased interest, and shall allocate to principal an amount received as a distribution of principal from the trust or estate.

16352. (a) If a trustee who conducts a business or other activity determines that it is in the best interest of all the beneficiaries to account separately for the business or other activity instead of accounting for it as part of the trust's general accounting records, the trustee may maintain separate accounting records for its transactions, whether or not its assets are segregated from other trust assets.

(b) A trustee who accounts separately for a business or other activity may determine the extent to which its net cash receipts must be retained for working capital, the acquisition or replacement of fixed assets, and its other reasonably foreseeable needs, and the extent to which the remaining net cash receipts are accounted for as principal or income in the trust's general accounting records. If a trustee sells assets of the business or other activity, other than in the ordinary course of the business or other activity, the trustee shall account for the net amount received as principal in the trust's general accounting records to the extent the trustee determines that the amount received is no longer required in the conduct of the business or other activity.

(c) Businesses and other activities for which a trustee may maintain separate accounting records may include the following:

(1) Retail, manufacturing, service, and other traditional business activities.

(2) Farming.

(3) Raising and selling livestock and other animals.

(4) Managing rental properties.

(5) Extracting minerals and other natural resources.

(6) Timber operations.

(7) Activities to which Section 16366 applies.

Article 5.2. Allocation Of Receipts During Administration Of Trust: Receipts Not Normally Apportioned

16355. A trustee shall allocate to principal:

(a) To the extent not allocated to income under this chapter, assets received from a transferor during the transferor's lifetime, a decedent's estate, a trust with a terminating income interest, or a payer under a contract naming the trust or its trustee as beneficiary.

(b) Subject to any contrary rules in this article and in Articles 5.1 (commencing with Section 16350) and 5.3 (commencing with Section 16360), money or other property received from the sale, exchange, liquidation, or change in form of a principal asset, including realized profit.

(c) Amounts recovered from third parties to reimburse the trust because of disbursements described in paragraph (7) of subdivision (a) of Section 16371 or for other reasons to the extent not based on the loss of income.

(d) Proceeds of property taken by eminent domain, but a separate award made for the loss of income with respect to an accounting period during which a current income beneficiary had a mandatory income interest is income.

(e) Net income received in an accounting period during which there is no beneficiary to whom a trustee may or must distribute income.

(f) Other receipts allocated to principal as provided in Article 5.3 (commencing with Section 16360).

16356. Unless the trustee accounts for receipts from rental property pursuant to Section 16352, the trustee shall allocate to income an amount received as rent of real or personal property, including an amount received for cancellation or renewal of a lease. An amount received as a refundable deposit, including a security deposit or a deposit that is to be applied as rent for future periods, shall be added to principal and held subject to the terms of the lease, and is not available for distribution to a beneficiary until the trustee's contractual obligations have been satisfied with respect to that amount.

16357. (a) An amount received as interest, whether determined at a fixed, variable, or floating rate, on an obligation to pay money to the trustee, including an amount received as consideration for prepaying principal, shall be allocated to income without any provision for amortization of premium.

(b) An amount received from the sale, redemption, or other disposition of an obligation to pay money to the trustee more than one year after it is purchased or acquired by the trustee, including an obligation whose purchase price, or its value when it is otherwise acquired, is less than its value at

maturity, shall be allocated to principal. If the obligation matures within one year after it is purchased or acquired by the trustee, an amount received in excess of its purchase price, or its value when it is otherwise acquired, shall be allocated to income.

(c) This section does not apply to an obligation to which Section 16361, 16362, 16363, 16364, 16366, or 16367 applies.

16358. (a) Except as otherwise provided in subdivision (b), a trustee shall allocate to principal the proceeds of a life insurance policy or other contract in which the trust or its trustee is named as beneficiary, including a contract that insures the trust or its trustee against loss for damage to, destruction of, or loss of title to a trust asset. The trustee shall allocate dividends on an insurance policy to income if the premiums on the policy are paid from income, and to principal if the premiums are paid from principal.

(b) A trustee shall allocate to income proceeds of a contract that insures the trustee against loss of occupancy or other use by an income beneficiary, loss of income, or, subject to Section 16352, loss of profits from a business.

(c) This section does not apply to a contract to which Section 16361 applies.

Article 5.3. Allocation Of Receipts During Administration Of Trust: Receipts Normally Apportioned

16360. (a) If a trustee determines that an allocation between principal and income required by Section 16361, 16362, 16363, 16364, or 16367 is insubstantial, the trustee may allocate the entire amount to principal unless one of the circumstances described in subdivision (b) of Section 16336 applies to the allocation. This power may be exercised by a cotrustee in the circumstances described in subdivision (c) of Section 16336 and may be released for the reasons and in the manner provided in subdivisions (d) and (e) of Section 16336.

(b) An allocation is presumed to be insubstantial in either of the following cases:

(1) Where the amount of the allocation would increase or decrease net income in an accounting period, as determined before the allocation, by less than 10 percent.

(2) Where the value of the asset producing the receipt for which the allocation would be made is less than 10 percent of the total value of the trust's assets at the beginning of the accounting period.

(c) Nothing in this section imposes a duty on the trustee to make an allocation under this section, and the trustee is not liable for failure to make an allocation under this section.

16361. (a) For purposes of this section, the following terms have the following meanings:

(1) "Payment" means a payment that a

trustee may receive over a fixed number of years or during the life of an individual because of services rendered or property transferred to the payer in exchange for future payments. The term also includes a payment made in money or property from the payer's general assets or from a separate fund created by the payer. For purposes of subdivisions (d), (e), (f), and (g), "payment" also includes any payment from a separate fund, regardless of the reason for the payment.

(2) "Separate fund" includes a private or commercial annuity, an individual retirement account, and a pension, profit-sharing, stock bonus, or stock ownership plan.

(b) To the extent that any portion of the payment is characterized by the payer as interest, a dividend, or a payment made in lieu of interest or a dividend, a trustee shall allocate that portion of the payment to income. The trustee shall allocate to principal the balance of the payment.

(c) If no part of a payment is characterized as interest, a dividend, or an equivalent payment, and all or part of the payment is required to be made, a trustee shall allocate to income 10 percent of the part that is required to be made during the accounting period and the balance to principal. If no part of a payment is required to be made or the payment received is the entire amount to which the trustee is entitled, the trustee shall allocate the entire payment to principal. For purposes of this subdivision, a payment is not "required to be made" to the extent that it is made because the trustee exercises a right of withdrawal.

(d) Subdivisions (f) and (g) shall apply, except as provided in subdivision (e), and subdivisions (b) and (c) shall not apply, in determining the allocation of a payment made from a separate fund to either of the following:

(1) A trust to which an election to qualify for a marital deduction is made under Section 2056(b)(7) of the Internal Revenue Code.

(2) A trust that qualifies for the marital deduction under Section 2056(b)(5) of the Internal Revenue Code.

(e) Subdivisions (d), (f), and (g) shall not apply if the series of payments would, without the application of subdivision (d), qualify for the marital deduction under Section 2056(b)(7)(C) of the Internal Revenue Code.

(f) If the separate fund payer provides documentation reflecting the internal income of the separate fund to the trustee, the trustee shall allocate the internal income of each separate fund for the accounting period as if the separate fund were a trust subject to this act. Upon request of the surviving spouse, the trustee shall require that the person administering the separate fund distribute this internal income to the trust. The trustee shall allocate a payment from the separate fund to income to the extent of the internal income of the separate fund

and distribute that amount to the surviving spouse. The trustee shall allocate the balance to principal. Upon request of the surviving spouse, the trustee shall allocate principal to income to the extent the internal income of the separate fund exceeds payments made from the separate fund to the trust during the accounting period.

(g) If the separate fund payer does not provide documentation reflecting the internal income of the separate fund to the trustee, but the trustee can determine the value of the separate fund, the internal income of the separate fund is deemed to equal 4 percent of the fund's value, according to the most recent statement of value preceding the beginning of the accounting period. If the separate fund payer does not provide documentation reflecting the internal income of the separate fund to the trustee and the trustee cannot determine the value of the separate fund, the internal income of the fund is deemed to equal the product of the interest rate and the present value of the expected future payments, as determined under Section 7520 of the Internal Revenue Code for the month preceding the accounting period for which the computation is made.

(h) This section does not apply to a payment to which Section 16362 applies.

16361.1. Section 16361, as amended by the act adding this section, applies to a trust described in subdivision (d) of Section 16361, on and after the following dates:

(a) If the trust is not funded as of January 1, 2010, the date of the decedent's death.

(b) If the trust is initially funded in the calendar year beginning January 1, 2010, the date of the decedent's death.

(c) If the trust is not described in subdivision (a) or (b), on January 1, 2010.

16362. (a) In this section, "liquidating asset" means an asset whose value will diminish or terminate because the asset is expected to produce receipts for a period of limited duration. The term includes a leasehold, patent, copyright, royalty right, and right to receive payments under an arrangement that does not provide for the payment of interest on the unpaid balance. The term does not include a payment subject to Section 16361, resources subject to Section 16363, timber subject to Section 16364, an activity subject to Section 16366, an asset subject to Section 16367, or any asset for which the trustee establishes a reserve for depreciation under Section 16372.

(b) A trustee shall allocate to income 10 percent of the receipts from a liquidating asset and the balance to principal.

16363. (a) To the extent that a trustee accounts for receipts from an interest in minerals, water, or other natural resources pursuant to this section, the trustee shall allocate them as follows:

(1) If received as a nominal bonus, nominal delay rental, or nominal annual rent on a

lease, a receipt shall be allocated to income.

(2) If received from a production payment, a receipt shall be allocated to income if and to the extent that the agreement creating the production payment provides a factor for interest or its equivalent. The balance shall be allocated to principal.

(3) If an amount received as a royalty, shut-in-well payment, take-or-pay payment, bonus, or delay rental is more than nominal, 90 percent shall be allocated to principal and the balance to income.

(4) If an amount is received from a working interest or any other interest in mineral or other natural resources not described in paragraph (1), (2), or (3), 90 percent of the net amount received shall be allocated to principal and the balance to income.

(b) An amount received on account of an interest in water that is renewable shall be allocated to income. If the water is not renewable, 90 percent of the amount shall be allocated to principal and the balance to income.

(c) This chapter applies whether or not a decedent or donor was extracting minerals, water, or other natural resources before the interest became subject to the trust.

(d) If a trust owned an interest in minerals, water, or other natural resources on January 1, 2000, the trustee may at all times allocate receipts from the interest as provided in this chapter or in the manner reasonably used by the trustee prior to that date. Receipts from an interest in minerals, water, or other natural resources acquired after January 1, 2000, shall be allocated by the trustee as provided in this chapter. If the interest was owned by the trust on January 1, 2000, a trustee that allocated receipts from the interest between January 1, 2000, and December 31, 2006, as provided in this chapter shall not have a duty to review that allocation and shall not have liability arising from the allocation. Nothing in this section is intended to create or imply a duty to allocate in a manner used by the trustee prior to January 1, 2000, and a trustee is not liable for not considering whether to make such an allocation or for choosing not to make such an allocation.

16364. (a) To the extent that a trustee accounts for receipts from the sale of timber and related products pursuant to this section, the trustee shall allocate the net receipts as follows:

(1) To income to the extent that the amount of timber removed from the land does not exceed the rate of growth of the timber during the accounting periods in which a beneficiary has a mandatory income interest.

(2) To principal to the extent that the amount of timber removed from the land exceeds the rate of growth of the timber or the net receipts are from the sale of standing timber.

(3) To or between income and principal if the net receipts are from the lease of timberland or from a contract to cut timber from land owned by a trust, by determining the amount of timber removed from the land under the lease or contract and applying the rules in paragraphs (1) and (2).

(4) To principal to the extent that advance payments, bonuses, and other payments are not allocated pursuant to paragraph (1), (2), or (3).

(b) In determining net receipts to be allocated under subdivision (a), a trustee shall deduct and transfer to principal a reasonable amount for depletion.

(c) This chapter applies whether or not a decedent or transferor was harvesting timber from the property before it became subject to the trust.

(d) If a trust owned an interest in timberland on January 1, 2000, the trustee may at all times allocate net receipts from the sale of timber and related products as provided in this chapter or in the manner reasonably used by the trustee prior to that date. Net receipts from an interest in timberland acquired after January 1, 2000, shall be allocated by the trustee as provided in this chapter. If the interest was owned by the trust on January 1, 2000, a trustee that allocated net receipts from the interest between January 1, 2000, and December 31, 2006, as provided in this chapter shall not have a duty to review that allocation and shall not have liability arising from the allocation. Nothing in this section is intended to create or imply a duty to allocate in a manner used by the trustee prior to January 1, 2000, and a trustee is not liable for not considering whether to make such an allocation or for choosing not to make such an allocation.

16365. (a) If a marital deduction is allowed for all or part of a trust whose assets consist substantially of property that does not provide the spouse with sufficient income from or use of the trust assets, and if the amounts that the trustee transfers from principal to income under Section 16336 and distributes to the spouse from principal pursuant to the terms of the trust are insufficient to provide the spouse with the beneficial enjoyment required to obtain the marital deduction, the spouse may require the trustee to make property productive of income or convert it into productive property or exercise the power under subdivision (a) of Section 16336 within a reasonable time. The trustee may decide which action or combination of actions to take.

(b) In cases not governed by subdivision (a), proceeds from the sale or other disposition of a trust asset are principal without regard to the amount of income the asset produces during any accounting period.

16366. (a) In this section, "derivative" means a contract or financial instrument or a combination of contracts and financial instruments that gives a trust the right or obligation to participate in some or all changes in the price of a tangible or intangible asset or group of assets, or changes in a rate, an index of prices or rates, or other market indicator for an asset or a group of assets.

(b) To the extent that a trustee does not account under Section 16352 for transactions in derivatives, the trustee shall allocate to principal receipts from and disbursements made in connection with those transactions.

(c) If a trustee grants an option to buy property from the trust, whether or not the trust owns the property when the option is granted, grants an option that permits another person to sell property to the trust, or acquires an option to buy property for the trust or an option to sell an asset owned by the trust, and the trustee or other owner of the asset is required to deliver the asset if the option is exercised, an amount received for granting the option shall be allocated to principal. An amount paid to acquire the option shall be paid from principal. A gain or loss realized upon the exercise of an option, including an option granted to a settlor of the trust for services rendered, shall be allocated to principal.

16367. (a) In this section, "asset-backed security" means an asset whose value is based upon the right it gives the owner to receive distributions from the proceeds of financial assets that provide collateral for the security. The term includes an asset that gives the owner the right to receive from the collateral financial assets only the interest or other current return or only the proceeds other than interest or current return. The term does not include an asset to which Section 16350 or 16361 applies.

(b) If a trust receives a payment from interest or other current return and from other proceeds of the collateral financial assets, the trustee shall allocate to income the portion of the payment which the payer identifies as being from interest or other current return and shall allocate the balance of the payment to principal.

(c) If a trust receives one or more payments in exchange for the trust's entire interest in an asset-backed security in one accounting period, the trustee shall allocate the payments to principal. If a payment is one of a series of payments that will result in the liquidation of the trust's interest in the security over more than one accounting period, the trustee shall allocate 10 percent of the payment to income and the balance to principal.

Article 6. Allocation Of Disbursements During Administration Of Trust

16370. A trustee shall make the following disbursements from income to the extent that they are not disbursements to which paragraph (2) or (3) of subdivision (c) of Section 16340 applies:

(a) Except as otherwise ordered by the court, one-half of the regular compensation of the trustee and of any person providing investment advisory or custodial services to the trustee.

(b) Except as otherwise ordered by the court, one-half of all expenses for accountings, judicial proceedings, or other matters that involve both the income and remainder interests.

(c) All of the other ordinary expenses incurred in connection with the administration, management, or preservation of trust property and the distribution of income, including interest, ordinary repairs, regularly recurring taxes assessed against principal, and expenses of a proceeding or other matter that concerns primarily the income interest.

(d) All recurring premiums on insurance covering the loss of a principal asset or the loss of income from or use of the asset.

16371. (a) A trustee shall make the following disbursements from principal:

(1) Except as otherwise ordered by the court, the remaining one-half of the disbursements described in subdivisions (a) and (b) of Section 16370.

(2) Except as otherwise ordered by the court, all of the trustee's compensation calculated on principal as a fee for acceptance, distribution, or termination, and disbursements made to prepare property for sale.

(3) Payments on the principal of a trust debt.

(4) Expenses of a proceeding that concerns primarily principal, including a proceeding to construe the trust or to protect the trust or its property.

(5) Premiums paid on a policy of insurance not described in subdivision (d) of Section 16370 of which the trust is the owner and beneficiary.

(6) Estate, inheritance, and other transfer taxes, including penalties, apportioned to the trust.

(7) Disbursements related to environmental matters, including reclamation, assessing environmental conditions, remedying and removing environmental contamination, monitoring remedial activities and the release of substances, preventing future releases of substances, collecting amounts from persons liable or potentially liable for the costs of those activities, penalties imposed under environmental laws or regulations and other payments made to comply with those laws or regulations, statutory or common law claims by third parties, and defending claims based on environmental matters.

(b) If a principal asset is encumbered with an obligation that requires income from that asset to be paid directly to the creditor, the trustee shall transfer from principal to income an amount equal to the income paid to the creditor in reduction of the principal balance of the obligation.

16372. (a) For purposes of this section, "depreciation" means a reduction in value due to wear, tear, decay, corrosion, or gradual obsolescence of a fixed asset having a useful life of more than one year.

(b) A trustee may transfer from income to principal a reasonable amount of the net cash receipts from a principal asset that is subject to depreciation, under generally accepted accounting principles, but may not transfer any amount for depreciation under this section in any of the following circumstances:

(1) As to the portion of real property used or available for use by a beneficiary as a residence or of tangible personal property held or made available for the personal use or enjoyment of a beneficiary.

(2) During the administration of a decedent's estate.

(3) If the trustee is accounting under Section 16352 for the business or activity in which the asset is used.

(c) An amount transferred from income to principal need not be held as a separate fund.

16373. (a) If a trustee makes or expects to make a principal disbursement described in this section, the trustee may transfer an appropriate amount from income to principal in one or more accounting periods to reimburse principal or to provide a reserve for future principal disbursements.

(b) Principal disbursements to which subdivision (a) applies include the following, but only to the extent that the trustee has not been and does not expect to be reimbursed by a third party:

(1) An amount chargeable to income but paid from principal because it is unusually large, including extraordinary repairs.

(2) A capital improvement to a principal asset, whether in the form of changes to an existing asset or the construction of a new asset, including special assessments.

(3) Disbursements made to prepare property for rental, including tenant allowances, leasehold improvements, and broker's commissions.

(4) Periodic payments on an obligation secured by a principal asset to the extent that the amount transferred from income to principal for depreciation is less than the periodic payments.

(5) Disbursements described in paragraph (7) of subdivision (a) of Section 16371.

(c) If the asset whose ownership gives rise to the disbursements becomes subject to a successive income interest after an income interest ends, a trustee may continue to transfer amounts from income to principal as provided in subdivision (a).

16374. (a) A tax required to be paid by a trustee based on receipts allocated to income shall be paid from income.

(b) A tax required to be paid by a trustee based on receipts allocated to principal shall be paid from principal, even if the tax is called an income tax by the taxing authority.

(c) A tax required to be paid by a trustee on the trust's share of an entity's taxable income shall be paid as follows:

(1) From income to the extent that receipts from the entity are allocated only to income.

(2) From principal to the extent that receipts from the entity are allocated only to principal.

(3) Proportionately from principal and income to the extent that receipts from the entity are allocated to both income and principal.

(4) From principal to the extent that the tax exceeds the total receipts from the entity.

(d) After applying subdivisions (a), (b), and (c), the trustee shall adjust income or principal receipts to the extent that the trust's taxes are reduced because the trust receives a deduction for payments made to a beneficiary.

16374.5. Unless otherwise provided by the governing instrument, determined by the trustee, or ordered by the court, distributions to beneficiaries shall be considered paid in the following order from the following sources:

(a) From net taxable income other than capital gains.

(b) From net realized short-term capital gains.

(c) From net realized long-term capitalized gains.

(d) From tax-exempt and other income.

(e) From principal of the trust.

16375. (a) A fiduciary may make adjustments between principal and income to offset the shifting of economic interests or tax benefits between income beneficiaries and remainder beneficiaries that arise from any of the following:

(1) Elections and decisions, other than those described in subdivision (b), that the fiduciary makes from time to time regarding tax matters.

(2) An income tax or any other tax that is imposed upon the fiduciary or a beneficiary as a result of a transaction involving or a distribution from the estate or trust.

(3) The ownership by a decedent's estate or trust of an interest in an entity whose taxable income, whether or not distributed, is includable in the taxable income of the estate, trust, or a beneficiary.

(b) If the amount of an estate tax marital deduction or charitable contribution deduction is reduced because a fiduciary deducts an amount paid from principal for income tax purposes instead of deducting it for estate tax purposes, and as a result estate taxes paid from principal are increased and income taxes paid by a decedent's estate, trust, or beneficiary are decreased, each estate, trust, or beneficiary that benefits from the decrease in income tax shall reimburse the principal from which the increase in estate tax is paid. The total reimbursement must equal the increase in the estate tax to the extent that the principal used to pay the increase would have qualified for a marital deduction or charitable contribution deduction but for the payment. The proportionate share of the reimbursement for each estate, trust, or beneficiary whose income taxes are reduced must be the same as its proportionate share of the total decrease in income tax. An estate or trust shall reimburse principal from income.

Chapter 4. Liability Of Trustees To Beneficiaries

Article 1. Liability For Breach Of Trust

16400. A violation by the trustee of any duty that the trustee owes the beneficiary is a breach of trust.

16401. (a) Except as provided in subdivision (b), the trustee is not liable to the beneficiary for the acts or omissions of an agent.

(b) Under any of the circumstances described in this subdivision, the trustee is liable to the beneficiary for an act or omission of an agent employed by the trustee in the administration of the trust that would be a breach of the trust if committed by the trustee:

(1) Where the trustee directs the act of the agent.

(2) Where the trustee delegates to the agent the authority to perform an act that the trustee is under a duty not to delegate.

(3) Where the trustee does not use reasonable prudence in the selection of the agent or the retention of the agent selected by the trustee.

(4) Where the trustee does not periodically review the agent's overall performance and compliance with the terms of the delegation.

(5) Where the trustee conceals the act of the agent.

(6) Where the trustee neglects to take reasonable steps to compel the agent to redress the wrong in a case where the trustee knows of the agent's acts or omissions.

(c) The liability of a trustee for acts or omissions of agents that occurred before July 1, 1987, is governed by prior law and not by this section.

16402. (a) Except as provided in subdivision (b), a trustee is not liable to the beneficiary for a breach of trust committed by a cotrustee.

(b) A trustee is liable to the beneficiary for a breach committed by a cotrustee under any of the following circumstances:

(1) Where the trustee participates in a breach of trust committed by the cotrustee.

(2) Where the trustee improperly delegates the administration of the trust to the cotrustee.

(3) Where the trustee approves, knowingly acquiesces in, or conceals a breach of trust committed by the cotrustee.

(4) Where the trustee negligently enables the cotrustee to commit a breach of trust.

(5) Where the trustee neglects to take reasonable steps to compel the cotrustee to redress a breach of trust in a case where the trustee knows or has information from which the trustee reasonably should have known of the breach.

(c) The liability of a trustee for acts or omissions of a cotrustee that occurred before July 1, 1987, is governed by prior law and not by this section.

16403. (a) Except as provided in subdivision (b), a successor trustee is not liable to the beneficiary for a breach of trust committed by a predecessor trustee.

(b) A successor trustee is liable to the beneficiary for breach of trust involving acts or omissions of a predecessor trustee in any of the following circumstances:

(1) Where the successor trustee knows or has information from which the successor trustee reasonably should have known of a situation constituting a breach of trust committed by the predecessor trustee and the successor trustee improperly permits it to continue.

(2) Where the successor trustee neglects to take reasonable steps to compel the predecessor trustee to deliver the trust property to the successor trustee.

(3) Where the successor trustee neglects to take reasonable steps to redress a breach of trust committed by the predecessor trustee in a case where the successor trustee knows or has information from which the successor trustee reasonably should have known of the predecessor trustee's breach.

(c) The liability of a trustee for acts or omissions of a predecessor trustee that occurred before July 1, 1987, is governed by prior law and not by this section.

Article 2. Remedies For Breach Of Trust

16420. (a) If a trustee commits a breach of trust, or threatens to commit a breach of trust, a beneficiary or cotrustee of the trust may commence a proceeding for any of the following purposes that is appropriate:

(1) To compel the trustee to perform the trustee's duties.

(2) To enjoin the trustee from committing a breach of trust.

(3) To compel the trustee to redress a breach of trust by payment of money or otherwise.

(4) To appoint a receiver or temporary trustee to take possession of the trust property and administer the trust.

(5) To remove the trustee.

(6) Subject to Section 18100, to set aside acts of the trustee.

(7) To reduce or deny compensation of the trustee.

(8) Subject to Section 18100, to impose an equitable lien or a constructive trust on trust property.

(9) Subject to Section 18100, to trace trust property that has been wrongfully disposed of and recover the property or its proceeds.

(b) The provision of remedies for breach of trust in subdivision (a) does not prevent resort to any other appropriate remedy provided by statute or the common law.

16421. The remedies of a beneficiary against the trustee are exclusively in equity.

Article 3. Measure Of Liability For Breach Of Trust

16440. (a) If the trustee commits a breach of trust, the trustee is chargeable with any of the following that is appropriate under the circumstances:

(1) Any loss or depreciation in value of the trust estate resulting from the breach of trust, with interest.

(2) Any profit made by the trustee through the breach of trust, with interest.

(3) Any profit that would have accrued to the trust estate if the loss of profit is the result of the breach of trust.

(b) If the trustee has acted reasonably and in good faith under the circumstances as known to the trustee, the court, in its discretion, may excuse the trustee in whole or in part from liability under subdivision (a) if it would be equitable to do so.

16441. (a) If the trustee is liable for interest pursuant to Section 16440, the trustee is liable for the greater of the following amounts:

(1) The amount of interest that accrues at the legal rate on judgments in effect during the period when the interest accrued.

(2) The amount of interest actually received.

(b) If the trustee has acted reasonably and in good faith under the circumstances as known to the trustee, the court, in its discretion, may excuse the trustee in whole or in part from liability under subdivision (a) if it would be equitable to do so.

16442. The provisions in this article for liability of a trustee for breach of trust do not prevent resort to any other remedy available under the statutory or common law.

Article 4. Limitations And Exculpation

16460. (a) Unless a claim is previously barred by adjudication, consent, limitation, or otherwise:

(1) If a beneficiary has received an interim or final account in writing, or other written report, that adequately discloses the existence of a claim against the trustee for breach of trust, the claim is barred as to that beneficiary unless a proceeding to assert the claim is commenced within three years after receipt of the account or report. An account or report adequately discloses existence of a claim if it provides sufficient information so that the beneficiary knows of the claim or reasonably should have inquired into the existence of the claim.

(2) If an interim or final account in writing or other written report does not adequately disclose the existence of a claim against the trustee for breach of trust or if a beneficiary does not receive any written account or report, the claim is barred as to that beneficiary unless a proceeding to assert the claim is commenced within three years after the beneficiary discovered, or reasonably should have discovered, the subject of the claim.

(b) For the purpose of subdivision (a), a beneficiary is deemed to have received an account or report, as follows:

(1) In the case of an adult who is reasonably capable of understanding the account or report, if it is received by the adult personally.

(2) In the case of an adult who is not reasonably capable of understanding the account or report, if it is received by the person's legal representative, including a guardian ad litem or other person appointed for this purpose.

(3) In the case of a minor, if it is received by the minor's guardian or, if the minor does not have a guardian, if it is received by the minor's parent so long as the parent does not have a conflict of interest.

(c) A written account or report under this section may, but need not, satisfy the requirements of Section 16061 or 16063 or any other provision.

16461. (a) Except as provided in subdivision (b), (c), or (d), the trustee can be relieved of liability for breach of trust by provisions in the trust instrument.

(b) A provision in the trust instrument is not effective to relieve the trustee of liability (1) for breach of trust committed intentionally, with gross negligence, in bad faith, or with reckless indifference to the interest of the beneficiary, or (2) for any profit that the trustee derives from a breach of trust.

(c) Subject to subdivision (b), a provision in a trust instrument that releases the trustee from liability if a beneficiary fails to object to an item in an interim or final account or other written report within a specified time period is effective only if all of the following conditions are met:

(1) The account or report sets forth the item.

(2) The period specified in the trust instrument for the beneficiary to object is not less than 180 days, or the trustee elects to follow the procedure provided in subdivision (d).

(3) Written notice in 12-point boldface type is provided to a beneficiary with the account or report in the following form:

350

NOTICE TO BENEFICIARIES
YOU HAVE [insert "180 days" or the period specified in the trust instrument, whichever is longer] FROM YOUR RECEIPT OF THIS ACCOUNT OR REPORT TO MAKE AN OBJECTION TO ANY ITEM SET FORTH IN THIS ACCOUNT OR REPORT. ANY OBJECTION YOU MAKE MUST BE IN WRITING; IT MUST BE DELIVERED TO THE TRUSTEE WITHIN THE PERIOD STATED ABOVE; AND IT MUST STATE YOUR OBJECTION. YOUR FAILURE TO DELIVER A WRITTEN OBJECTION TO THE TRUSTEE WITHIN THE PERIOD STATED ABOVE WILL PERMANENTLY PREVENT YOU FROM LATER ASSERTING THIS OBJECTION AGAINST THE TRUSTEE. IF YOU DO MAKE AN OBJECTION TO THE TRUSTEE, THE THREE-YEAR PERIOD PROVIDED IN SECTION 16460 OF THE PROBATE CODE FOR COMMENCEMENT OF LITIGATION WILL APPLY TO CLAIMS BASED ON YOUR OBJECTION AND WILL BEGIN TO RUN ON THE DATE THAT YOU RECEIVE THIS ACCOUNT OR REPORT.

(d) A provision in a trust instrument that provides for a period less than 180 days to object to an item in an account or report shall be ineffective to release the trustee from liability. A trustee of a trust created by an instrument with an ineffective period may elect to be governed by the provisions of subdivision (c) by complying with the requirements of subdivision (c), except that "180 days" shall be substituted in the notice form for the ineffective period.

(e) Subject to subdivision (b), a beneficiary who fails to object in writing to an account or report that complies with the requirements of subdivision (c) within the specified, valid period shall be barred from asserting any claim against the trustee regarding an item that is adequately disclosed in the account or report. An item is adequately disclosed if the disclosure regarding the item meets the requirements of paragraph (1) of subdivision (a) of Section 16460.

(f) Except as provided in subdivision (a) of Section 16460, the trustee may not be released from liability as to any claim based on a written objection made by a beneficiary if the objection is delivered to the trustee within the specified, effective period. If a beneficiary has filed a written objection to an account or report that complies with the requirements of subdivision (c) within the specified, valid period that concerns an item that affects any other beneficiary of the trust, any affected beneficiary may join in the objection anytime within the specified, valid period or while the resolution of the objection is pending, whichever is later. This section is not intended to establish a class of beneficiaries for actions on an account and report or provide that the action of one beneficiary is for the benefit of all beneficiaries. This section does not create a duty for any trustee to notify beneficiaries of objections or resolution of objections.

(g) Provided that a beneficiary has filed a written objection to an account or report that complies with the requirements of subdivision (c) within the specified, valid period, a supplemental written objection may be delivered in the same manner as the objection not later than 180 days after the receipt of the account or report or no later than the period specified in the trust instrument, whichever is longer.

(h) Compliance with subdivision (c) excuses compliance with paragraph (6) of subdivision (a) of Section 16063 for the account or report to which that notice relates.

(i) Subject to subdivision (b), if proper notice has been given and a beneficiary has not made a timely objection, the trustee is not liable for any other claims adequately disclosed by any item in the account or report.

(j) Subdivisions (c) to (i), inclusive, apply to all accounts and reports submitted after the effective date of the act adding these subdivisions.

16462. (a) Notwithstanding Section 16461, a trustee of a revocable trust is not liable to a beneficiary for any act performed or omitted pursuant to written directions from the person holding the power to revoke, including a person to whom the power to direct the trustee is delegated.

(b) Subdivision (a) applies to a trust that is revocable in part with respect to the interest of the beneficiary in that part of the trust property.

16463. (a) Except as provided in subdivisions (b) and (c), a beneficiary may not hold the trustee liable for an act or omission of the trustee as a breach of trust if the beneficiary consented to the act or omission before or at the time of the act or omission.

(b) The consent of the beneficiary does not preclude the beneficiary from holding the trustee liable for a breach of trust in any of the following circumstances:

(1) Where the beneficiary was under an incapacity at the time of the consent or of the act or omission.

(2) Where the beneficiary at the time consent was given did not know of his or her rights and of the material facts (A) that the trustee knew or should have known and (B) that the trustee did not reasonably believe that the beneficiary knew.

(3) Where the consent of the beneficiary was induced by improper conduct of the trustee.

(c) Where the trustee has an interest in the transaction adverse to the interest of the beneficiary, the consent of the beneficiary does not preclude the beneficiary from holding the trustee liable for a breach of trust under any of the circumstances described in subdivision (b) or where the transaction to which the beneficiary consented was not fair and reasonable to the beneficiary.

16464. (a) Except as provided in subdivision (b), a beneficiary may be precluded from holding the trustee liable for a breach of trust by the beneficiary's release or contract effective to discharge the trustee's liability to the beneficiary for that breach.

(b) A release or contract is not effective to discharge the trustee's liability for a breach of trust in any of the following circumstances:

(1) Where the beneficiary was under an incapacity at the time of making the release or contract.

(2) Where the beneficiary did not know of his or her rights and of the material facts (A) that the trustee knew or reasonably should have known and (B) that the trustee did not reasonably believe that the beneficiary knew.

(3) Where the release or contract of the beneficiary was induced by improper conduct of the trustee.

(4) Where the transaction involved a bargain with the trustee that was not fair and reasonable.

16465. (a) Except as provided in subdivision (b), if the trustee, in breach of trust, enters into a transaction that the beneficiary may at his or her option reject or affirm, and the beneficiary affirms the transaction, the beneficiary shall not thereafter reject it and hold the trustee liable for any loss occurring after the trustee entered into the transaction.

(b) The affirmance of a transaction by the beneficiary does not preclude the beneficiary from holding a trustee liable for a breach of trust if, at the time of the affirmance, any of the following circumstances existed:

(1) The beneficiary was under an incapacity.

(2) The beneficiary did not know of his or her rights and of the material facts (A) that the trustee knew or reasonably should have known and (B) that the trustee did not reasonably believe that the beneficiary knew.

(3) The affirmance was induced by improper conduct of the trustee.

(4) The transaction involved a bargain with the trustee that was not fair and reasonable.

Chapter 5. Notice Of Proposed Action By Trustee

16500. Subject to subdivision (d) of Section 16501, a trustee may give a notice of proposed action regarding a matter governed by Chapter 2 (commencing with Section 16200) or Chapter 3 (commencing with Section 16320) as provided in this chapter. For the purpose of this chapter, a proposed action includes a course of action or a decision not to take action. This chapter does not preclude an application or assertion of any other rights or remedies available to an interested party as otherwise provided in this part regarding an action to be taken or not to be taken by the trustee.

16501. (a) The trustee who elects to provide notice pursuant to this chapter shall mail notice of the proposed action to each of the following:

(1) A beneficiary who is receiving, or is entitled to receive, income under the trust, including a beneficiary who is entitled to receive income at the discretion of the trustee.

(2) A beneficiary who would receive a distribution of principal if the trust were terminated at the time the notice is given.

(b) Notice of proposed action is not required to be given to a person who consents in writing to the proposed action. The consent may be executed at any time before or after the proposed action is taken.

(c) A trustee is not required to provide a copy of the notice of proposed action to a beneficiary who is known to the trustee but who cannot be located by the trustee after reasonable diligence or who is unknown to the trustee.

(d) Notwithstanding any other provision of this chapter, the trustee may not use a notice of proposed action in any of the following actions:

(1) Allowance of the trustee's compensation.

(2) Allowance of compensation of the attorney for the trustee.

(3) Settlement of accounts.

(4) Preliminary and final distributions and discharge.

(5) Sale of property of the trust to the trustee or to the attorney for the trustee.

(6) Exchange of property of the trust for property of the trustee or for property of the attorney for the trustee.

(7) Grant of an option to purchase property of the trust to the trustee or to the attorney for the trustee.

(8) Allowance, payment, or compromise of a claim of the trustee, or the attorney for the trustee, against the trust.

(9) Compromise or settlement of a claim, action, or proceeding by the trust against the trustee or against the attorney for the trust.

(10) Extension, renewal, or modification of the terms of a debt or other obligation of the trustee, or the attorney for the trustee, owing to or in favor of the trust.

16502. The notice of proposed action shall state that it is given pursuant to this section and shall include all of the following:

(a) The name and mailing address of the trustee.

(b) The name and telephone number of a person who may be contacted for additional information.

(c) A description of the action proposed to be taken and an explanation of the reasons for the action.

(d) The time within which objections to the proposed action can be made, which shall be at least 45 days from the mailing of the notice of proposed action.

(e) The date on or after which the proposed action may be taken or is effective.

16503. (a) A beneficiary may object to the proposed action by mailing a written objection to the trustee at the address stated in the notice of proposed action within the time period specified in the notice of proposed action.

(b) A trustee is not liable to a beneficiary for an action regarding a matter governed by this part if the trustee does not receive a written objection to the proposed action from a beneficiary within the applicable period and the other requirements of this section are satisfied. If no beneficiary entitled to notice objects under this section, the trustee is not liable to any current or future beneficiary with respect to the proposed action. This subdivision does not apply to a person who is a minor or an incompetent adult at the time of receiving the notice of proposed action unless the notice is served on a guardian or conservator of the estate of the person.

(c) If the trustee receives a written objection within the applicable period, either the trustee or a beneficiary may petition the court to have the proposed action taken as proposed, taken with modifications, or denied. In the proceeding, a beneficiary objecting to the proposed action has the burden of proving that the trustee's proposed action should not be taken. A beneficiary who has not objected is not estopped from opposing the proposed action in the proceeding.

(d) If the trustee decides not to implement the proposed action, the trustee shall notify the beneficiaries of the decision not to take the action and the reasons for the decision, and the trustee's decision not to implement the proposed action does not itself give rise to liability to any current or future beneficiary. A beneficiary may petition the court to have the action taken, and has the burden of proving that it should be taken.

16504. This chapter does not require a trustee to use these procedures prior to taking any action.

Part 5. Judicial Proceedings Concerning Trusts

Chapter 1. Jurisdiction And Venue

17000. (a) The superior court having jurisdiction over the trust pursuant to this part has exclusive jurisdiction of proceedings concerning the internal affairs of trusts.

(b) The superior court having jurisdiction over the trust pursuant to this part has concurrent jurisdiction of the following:

(1) Actions and proceedings to determine the existence of trusts.

(2) Actions and proceedings by or against creditors or debtors of trusts.

(3) Other actions and proceedings involving trustees and third persons.

17001. In proceedings commenced pursuant to this division, the court is a court of general jurisdiction and has all the powers of the superior court.

17002. (a) The principal place of administration of the trust is the usual place where the day-to-day activity of the trust is carried on by the trustee or its representative who is primarily responsible for the administration of the trust.

(b) If the principal place of administration of the trust cannot be determined under subdivision (a), it shall be determined as follows:

(1) If the trust has a single trustee, the principal place of administration of the trust is the trustee's residence or usual place of business.

(2) If the trust has more than one trustee, the principal place of administration of the trust is the residence or usual place of business of any of the cotrustees as agreed upon by them or, if not, the residence or usual place of business of any of the cotrustees.

17003. Subject to Section 17004:

(a) By accepting the trusteeship of a trust having its principal place of administration in this state the trustee submits personally to the jurisdiction of the court under this division.

(b) To the extent of their interests in the trust, all beneficiaries of a trust having its principal place of administration in this state are subject to the jurisdiction of the court under this division.

17004. The court may exercise jurisdiction in proceedings under this division on any basis permitted by Section 410.10 of the Code of Civil Procedure.

17005. (a) The proper county for commencement of a proceeding pursuant to this division is either of the following:

(1) In the case of a living trust, the county where the principal place of administration of the trust is located.

(2) In the case of a testamentary trust, either the county where the decedent's estate is administered or where the principal place of administration of the trust is located.

(b) If a living trust has no trustee, the proper county for commencement of a proceeding for appointing a trustee is the county where the trust property, or some portion of the trust property, is located.

(c) Except as otherwise provided in subdivisions (a) and (b), the proper county for commencement of a proceeding pursuant to this division is determined by the rules applicable to civil actions generally.

17006. There is no right to a jury trial in proceedings under this division concerning the internal affairs of trusts.

Chapter 2. Notice

17100. Except as otherwise provided in this division, notice in proceedings commenced pursuant to this division, or notice otherwise required by this division, is governed by Part 2 (commencing with Section 1200) of Division 3.

17105. A petitioner or other person required to give notice may cause notice to be given to any person interested in the trust without the need for a court order.

Chapter 3. Proceedings Concerning Trusts

17200. (a) Except as provided in Section 15800, a trustee or beneficiary of a trust may petition the court under this chapter concerning the internal affairs of the trust or to determine the existence of the trust.

(b) Proceedings concerning the internal affairs of a trust include, but are not limited to, proceedings for any of the following purposes:

(1) Determining questions of construction of a trust instrument.

(2) Determining the existence or nonexistence of any immunity, power, privilege, duty, or right.

(3) Determining the validity of a trust provision.

(4) Ascertaining beneficiaries and determining to whom property shall pass or be delivered upon final or partial termination of the trust, to the extent the determination is not made by the trust instrument.

(5) Settling the accounts and passing upon the acts of the trustee, including the exercise of discretionary powers.

(6) Instructing the trustee.

(7) Compelling the trustee to do any of the following:

(A) Provide a copy of the terms of the trust.

(B) Provide information about the trust under Section 16061 if the trustee has failed to provide the requested information within 60 days after the beneficiary's reasonable written request, and the beneficiary has not received the requested information from the trustee within the six months preceding the request.

(C) Account to the beneficiary, subject to the provisions of Section 16064, if the trustee has failed to submit a requested account within 60 days after written request of the beneficiary and no account has been made within six months preceding the request.

(8) Granting powers to the trustee.

(9) Fixing or allowing payment of the trustee's compensation or reviewing the reasonableness of the trustee's compensation.

(10) Appointing or removing a trustee.

(11) Accepting the resignation of a trustee.

(12) Compelling redress of a breach of the trust by any available remedy.

(13) Approving or directing the modification or termination of the trust.

(14) Approving or directing the combination or division of trusts.

(15) Amending or conforming the trust instrument in the manner required to qualify a decedent's estate for the charitable estate tax deduction under federal law, including the addition of mandatory governing instrument requirements for a charitable remainder trust as required by final regulations and rulings of the United States Internal Revenue Service.

(16) Authorizing or directing transfer of a trust or trust property to or from another jurisdiction.

(17) Directing transfer of a testamentary trust subject to continuing court jurisdiction from one county to another.

(18) Approving removal of a testamentary trust from continuing court jurisdiction.

(19) Reforming or excusing compliance with the governing instrument of an organization pursuant to Section 16105.

(20) Determining the liability of the trust for any debts of a deceased settlor. However, nothing in this paragraph shall provide standing to bring an action concerning the internal affairs of the trust to a person whose only claim to the assets of the decedent is as a creditor.

(21) Determining petitions filed pursuant to Section 15687 and reviewing the reasonableness of compensation for legal services authorized under that section. In determining the reasonableness of compensation under this paragraph, the court may consider, together with all other relevant circumstances, whether prior approval was obtained pursuant to Section 15687.

(22) If a member of the State Bar of California has transferred the economic interest of his or her practice to a trustee and if the member is a deceased member under Section 9764, a petition may be brought to appoint a practice administrator. The procedures, including, but not limited to, notice requirements, that apply to the appointment of a practice administrator for a deceased member shall apply to the petition brought under this section.

(23) If a member of the State Bar of California has transferred the economic interest of his or her practice to a trustee and if the member is a disabled member under Section 2468, a petition may be brought to appoint a practice administrator. The procedures, including, but not limited to, notice requirements, that apply to the appointment of a practice administrator for a disabled member shall apply to the petition brought under this section.

(c) The court may, on its own motion, set and give notice of an order to show cause why a trustee who is a professional fiduciary, and who is required to be licensed under Chapter 6 (commencing with Section 6500) of Division 3 of the Business and Professions

Code, should not be removed for failing to hold a valid, unexpired, unsuspended license.

17200.1. All proceedings concerning the transfer of property of the trust shall be conducted pursuant to the provisions of Part 19 (commencing with Section 850) of Division 2.

17201. A proceeding under this chapter is commenced by filing a petition stating facts showing that the petition is authorized under this chapter. The petition shall also state the grounds of the petition and the names and addresses of each person entitled to notice of the petition.

17202. The court may dismiss a petition if it appears that the proceeding is not reasonably necessary for the protection of the interests of the trustee or beneficiary.

17203. (a) At least 30 days before the time set for the hearing on the petition, the petitioner shall cause notice of hearing to be mailed to all of the following persons:

(1) All trustees.

(2) All beneficiaries, subject to Chapter 2 (commencing with Section 15800) of Part 3.

(3) The Attorney General, if the petition relates to a charitable trust subject to the jurisdiction of the Attorney General.

(b) At least 30 days before the time set for hearing on the petition, the petitioner shall cause notice of the hearing and a copy of the petition to be served in the manner provided in Chapter 4 (commencing with Section 413.10) of Title 5 of Part 2 of the Code of Civil Procedure on any person, other than a trustee or beneficiary, whose right, title, or interest would be affected by the petition and who does not receive notice pursuant to subdivision (a). The court may not shorten the time for giving notice under this subdivision.

(c) If a person to whom notice otherwise would be given has been deceased for at least 40 days, and no personal representative has been appointed for the estate of that person, and the deceased person' s right, title, or interest has not passed to any other person pursuant to Division 8 (commencing with Section 13000) or otherwise, notice may instead be given to the following persons:

(1) Each heir and devisee of the decedent, and all persons named as executors of the will of the decedent, so far as known to the petitioner.

(2) Each person serving as guardian or conservator of the decedent at the time of the decedent's death, so far as known to the petitioner.

17204. (a) If proceedings involving a trust are pending, a beneficiary of the trust may, in person or by attorney, file with the court clerk where the proceedings are pending a written request stating that the beneficiary desires special notice of the filing of petitions in the proceeding relating to any or all of the purposes described in Section 17200

and giving an address for receiving notice by mail. A copy of the request shall be personally delivered or mailed to the trustee or the trustee's attorney. If personally delivered, the request is effective when it is delivered. If mailed, the request is effective when it is received. When the original of the request is filed with the court clerk, it shall be accompanied by a written admission or proof of service. A request for special notice may be modified or withdrawn in the same manner as provided for the making of the initial request.

(b) (1) An interested person may request special notice in the same manner as a beneficiary under subdivision (a), for the purpose set forth in paragraph (9) of subdivision (b) of Section 17200. The request for special notice shall be accompanied by a verified statement of the person's interest.

(2) For purposes set forth in paragraphs (2), (4) to (6), inclusive, (8), (12), (16), (20), and (21) of subdivision (b) of Section 17200, an interested person may petition the court for an order for special notice of proceedings involving a trust. The petition shall include a verified statement of the creditor's interest and may be served on the trustee or the trustee's attorney by personal delivery or in the manner required by Section 1215. The petition may be made by ex parte application.

(3) For purposes of this subdivision, an "interested person" means only a creditor of a trust or, if the trust has become irrevocable upon the death of a trustor, a creditor of the trustor.

(4) This section does not confer standing on an interested person if standing does not otherwise exist.

(c) Except as provided in subdivision (d), after serving and filing a request and proof of service pursuant to subdivision (a) or paragraph (1) of subdivision (b), the beneficiary or the interested person is entitled to notice pursuant to Section 17203. If the petition of an interested person filed pursuant to paragraph (2) of subdivision (b) is granted by the court, the interested person is entitled to notice pursuant to Section 17203.

(d) A request for special notice made by a beneficiary whose right to notice is restricted by Section 15802 is not effective.

17205. If a trustee or beneficiary has served and filed either a notice of appearance, in person or by counsel, directed to the petitioner or the petitioner's counsel in connection with a particular petition and proceeding or a written request for a copy of the petition, and has given an address to which notice or a copy of the petition may be mailed or delivered, the petitioner shall cause a copy of the petition to be mailed to that person within five days after service of the notice of appearance or receipt of the request.

17206. The court in its discretion may make any orders and take any other action necessary or proper to dispose of the matters presented by the petition, including appointment of a temporary trustee to administer the trust in whole or in part.

17209. The administration of trusts is intended to proceed expeditiously and free of judicial intervention, subject to the jurisdiction of the court.

17210. In a case involving a charitable trust subject to the jurisdiction of the Attorney General, the Attorney General may petition under this chapter.

17211. (a) If a beneficiary contests the trustee's account and the court determines that the contest was without reasonable cause and in bad faith, the court may award against the contestant the compensation and costs of the trustee and other expenses and costs of litigation, including attorney's fees, incurred to defend the account. The amount awarded shall be a charge against any interest of the beneficiary in the trust. The contestant shall be personally liable for any amount that remains unsatisfied.

(b) If a beneficiary contests the trustee's account and the court determines that the trustee's opposition to the contest was without reasonable cause and in bad faith, the court may award the contestant the costs of the contestant and other expenses and costs of litigation, including attorney's fees, incurred to contest the account. The amount awarded shall be a charge against the compensation or other interest of the trustee in the trust. The trustee shall be personally liable and on the bond, if any, for any amount that remains unsatisfied.

Chapter 4. Testamentary Trusts Subject To Continuing Court Jurisdiction

Article 1. Administration Of Testamentary Trusts Subject To Continuing Court Jurisdiction

17300. This article applies only to the following:

(a) A trust created by a will executed before July 1, 1977, and not incorporated by reference in a will on or after July 1, 1977.

(b) A trust created by a will which provides that the trust is subject to the continuing jurisdiction of the superior court.

17301. If a trust described in Section 17300 continues after distribution of the decedent's estate, the court in which the decedent's estate was administered retains jurisdiction over the trust for any of the purposes specified in Section 17200.

17302. Except as otherwise provided in this article, proceedings relating to trusts under continuing court jurisdiction are governed by this part.

17303. This article does not apply to a trust described in Section 17300 that has been removed from continuing court jurisdiction.

17304. (a) At any time after final distribution of the decedent's estate, a trust described in Section 17300 may be transferred to a different county in this state as provided in this section.

(b) The petition for transfer shall set forth all of the following:

(1) The name of the county to which jurisdiction over the trust is sought to be transferred.

(2) The names, ages, and places of residence of the trustees and all beneficiaries of the trust, so far as known to the petitioner.

(3) A brief description of the character, condition, value, and location of property of the trust.

(4) A brief statement of the reasons for transfer.

(c) If, after hearing, it appears to the court that the transfer of jurisdiction to the county designated in the petition or to any other county in this state will be in the best interests of the estate, or that economical and convenient administration of the trust will be facilitated by the transfer, the court shall make an order transferring jurisdiction over the trust. Upon such order, the court clerk shall certify a copy of the order of transfer to the clerk of the court to which jurisdiction is transferred, together with copies of the instrument creating the trust, the decree of distribution, and any other documents or matters of record the court determines by order to be necessary to define the powers and duties of the trustee, or otherwise to be necessary in connection with further administration of the trust.

(d) The court to which jurisdiction is transferred may from time to time require by order the filing of certified copies of additional papers or matters of record from the court in which the decedent's estate was administered as are required.

(e) Upon the filing of a certified copy of the order of transfer, together with supporting documents, the court to which jurisdiction is transferred has the same jurisdiction over the trust as the court in which the decedent's estate was administered but for the transfer.

Article 2. Removal Of Trusts From Continuing Court Jurisdiction

17350. This article applies only to trusts created by will executed before July 1, 1977, and not incorporated by reference in a will on or after July 1, 1977.

17351. (a) If any of the trustees of a trust described in Section 17350 is a trust company, the trust shall be removed from continuing court jurisdiction as provided in this section. Within six months after the initial funding of the trust, the trustee shall give a notice of removal of the trust from continuing court jurisdiction to each beneficiary. Notice of removal shall be sent by registered or certified mail or by first-class mail, but notice sent by first-class mail is effective only if an acknowledgment of receipt of notice is signed by the beneficiary and returned to the trustee.

(b) The notice of removal of the trust from continuing court jurisdiction shall contain the following:

(1) A statement that as of January 1, 1983, the law was changed to remove the necessity for continuing court jurisdiction over the trust.

(2) A statement that Section 17200 of the Probate Code gives any beneficiary the right to petition a court to determine important matters relating to the administration of the trust.

(3) A copy of the text of Sections 17200 and 17201.

(4) A statement that each income beneficiary, as defined in Section 16325, is entitled to an annual statement of the principal and income receipts and disbursements of the trust and that any other beneficiary is entitled to such information upon written request to the trustee.

(5) The name and location of the court in the county in which it is appropriate to file a petition pursuant to Section 17200, the name and location of the court that had jurisdiction over the administration of the decedent's estate, and a statement that it is appropriate to file a petition pursuant to Section 17200 with either court.

(c) The trustee shall file with the court that had jurisdiction over the administration of the decedent's estate proof of giving notice under this section within seven months after the initial funding of the trust.

17352. (a) If none of the trustees of a trust described in Section 17350 is a trust company, the trust may be removed from continuing court jurisdiction only with approval of the court. The trustee may petition for court approval at any time, and from time to time, in the trustee's discretion.

(b) The petition for removal shall set forth the trust accounts in detail, report the trustee's acts, and show the condition of the trust estate. A copy of the trust instrument shall be attached to the petition.

(c) At the hearing the court may receive testimony from any interested person and may grant or deny the petition, or may grant the petition on such conditions as the court in its discretion deems proper.

(d) If the petition is granted, the trustee shall send the notice of removal of the trust provided in subdivision (b) of Section 17351 and file proof of service as required by subdivision (c) of Section 17351 within six months and seven months, respectively, from the date the petition is granted. A copy of the court order granting the petition shall be attached to the notice.

(e) If the petition is not granted, the trust

shall continue to be administered under Article 1 (commencing with Section 17300) as if the settlor had provided in the will that the court does not lose jurisdiction of the estate by final distribution.

17353. If a trust company is appointed as a successor trustee of a trust which, at the time of the appointment, is subject to continuing court jurisdiction because it was not removed pursuant to Section 17352, the successor trustee shall comply with Section 17351. For the purpose of complying with Section 17351, the date of appointment of the successor trustee shall be treated as the date of initial funding of the trust.

17354. After a trust is removed from continuing court jurisdiction pursuant to this article, neither a change in trustees nor any other event causes the trust to be subject to continuing court jurisdiction under Article 1 (commencing with Section 17300).

Chapter 5. Transfer Of Trust To Another Jurisdiction

17400. (a) This chapter applies to all of the following:

(1) A trust that is subject to this division.

(2) A trust subject to Chapter 8 (commencing with Section 6320) of Part 1 of Division 6.

(3) Any other trust to which the provisions of this chapter are made applicable by statute or trust instrument.

(b) This chapter does not prevent the transfer of the place of administration of a trust or of trust property to another jurisdiction by any other available means.

17401. (a) The court may make an order for the transfer of the place of administration of a trust or the transfer of some or all of the trust property to a jurisdiction outside this state as provided in this chapter.

(b) Except as otherwise provided in this chapter, proceedings under this chapter are governed by this part.

17402. The petition for transfer shall set forth all of the following:

(a) The names and places of residence of the following:

(1) The trustee administering the trust in this state.

(2) The trustee, including any domiciliary trustee, who will administer the trust or trust property in the other jurisdiction.

(b) The names, ages, and places of residence of the living beneficiaries, as far as known to the petitioner.

(c) Whether the trustee who will administer the trust in the other jurisdiction has agreed to accept the trust. If so, the acceptance or a copy shall be attached as an exhibit to the petition or otherwise filed with the court.

(d) A general statement of the qualifications of the trustee who will administer the trust in the other jurisdiction and the amount of fiduciary bond, if any. If the trustee is an individual, the statement shall include the trustee's age.

(e) A general statement of the nature and value of the property of any trust of the same settlor being administered in the other jurisdiction by the trustee who will administer the trust in the other jurisdiction.

(f) The name of the court, if any, having jurisdiction of the trustee in the other jurisdiction or of its accounts or in which a proceeding may be had with respect to administration of the trust or the trustee's accounts.

(g) A statement of the character, condition, location, and value of the trust property sought to be transferred.

(h) Whether there is any pending civil action in this state against the trustee arising out of the administration of the trust sought to be transferred.

(i) A statement of the reasons for the transfer.

17403. (a) At least 30 days before the time set for the hearing on the petition, the petitioner shall cause notice of the time and place of the hearing to be mailed to each of the persons named in the petition at their respective addresses as stated in the petition.

(b) Any person interested in the trust, as trustee, beneficiary, or otherwise, may appear and file written grounds in opposition to the petition.

17404. The court may, in its discretion, grant the petition and order the trustee to transfer the trust property or to transfer the place of administration of the trust to the other jurisdiction if, after hearing, all of the following appear to the court:

(a) The transfer of the trust property to a trustee in another jurisdiction, or the transfer of the place of administration of the trust to another jurisdiction, will promote the best interests of the trust and those interested in it, taking into account the interest in the economical and convenient administration of the trust.

(b) The transfer will not violate the trust instrument.

(c) Any new trustee to whom the trust property is to be transferred is qualified, willing, and able to administer the trust or trust property under the trust instrument.

17405. If a transfer is ordered under this chapter, the court may direct the manner of transfer and impose terms and conditions as may be just, including, but not limited to, a requirement for the substitution of a successor trustee in any pending litigation in this state. The delivery of property in accordance with the order of the court is a full discharge of the trustee in relation to all property embraced in the order.

Chapter 6. Transfer Of Trust From Another Jurisdiction

17450. (a) This chapter applies to a trust, or portion thereof, administered in a jurisdiction outside this state.

(b) This chapter does not prevent the transfer of the place of administration of a trust or of trust property to this state by any other available means.

17451. (a) The court may make an order accepting the transfer of the place of administration of a trust from another jurisdiction to this state or the transfer of some or all of the trust property in another jurisdiction to a trustee in this state as provided in this chapter.

(b) Except as otherwise provided in this chapter, proceedings under this chapter are governed by this part.

17452. (a) If the petition requests that a resident of this state be appointed trustee, the petition shall be filed in the court of the county where the proposed principal place of administration of the trust pursuant to Section 17002 is located.

(b) If the petition requests that only a nonresident of this state be appointed trustee, the petition shall be filed in the court of the county where either (1) any beneficiary resides or (2) a substantial portion of the trust property to be transferred is located or will be located.

17453. The petition for transfer shall set forth all of the following:

(a) The names and places of residence of the following:

(1) The trustee administering the trust in the other jurisdiction.

(2) The proposed trustee to whom administration of the trust or trust property will be transferred.

(b) The names, ages, and places of residence of all living beneficiaries, as far as known to the petitioner.

(c) Whether administration of the trust has been subject to supervision in a jurisdiction outside this state. If so, the petition shall state whether a petition or appropriate request for transfer of place of administration of the trust or trust property to this state has been filed, if necessary, with the court in the other jurisdiction, and the status of the petition or request.

(d) Whether the trustee proposed to administer the trust in this state has agreed to accept the trust in this state. If the trustee has agreed, the acceptance shall be attached as an exhibit to the petition or otherwise filed with the court.

(e) A general statement of the qualifications of the trustee proposed to administer the trust in this state and the amount of any bond to be requested. If the trustee is an individual, the statement shall include the trustee's age.

(f) A copy of the trust instrument or a

statement of the terms of the trust instrument in effect at the time the petition is filed, including all amendments thereto.

(g) A statement of the character, condition, location, and value of the trust property sought to be transferred.

(h) A statement of the reasons for the transfer.

17454. (a) At least 30 days before the time set for the hearing on the petition, the petitioner shall cause notice of the time and place of the hearing to be mailed to each of the persons named in the petition at their respective addresses as stated in the petition.

(b) Any person interested in the trust, as trustee, beneficiary, or otherwise, may appear and file written grounds in opposition to the petition.

17455. (a) The court may, in its discretion, grant the petition and issue an order accepting transfer of trust property or the place of administration of the trust to this state and appoint a trustee to administer the trust in this state, if, after hearing, all of the following appear to the court:

(1) The transfer of the trust property to a trustee in this state, or the transfer of the place of administration of the trust to this state, will promote the best interests of the trust and those interested in it, taking into account the interest in the economical and convenient administration of the trust.

(2) The transfer will not violate the trust instrument.

(3) The trustee appointed by the court to administer the trust in this state, and to whom the trust property is to be transferred, is qualified, willing, and able to administer the trust or trust property under the trust instrument.

(4) The proper court in the other jurisdiction has approved the transfer if approval is necessary under the law of the other jurisdiction.

(b) If the court grants the petition under subdivision (a), the court shall require the trustee to give a bond, if necessary under the law of the other jurisdiction or of this state, and may require bond as provided in Section 15602.

17456. If appropriate to facilitate transfer of the trust property or the place of administration of a trust to this state, the court may issue a conditional order appointing a trustee to administer the trust in this state and indicating that transfer to this state will be accepted if transfer is approved by the proper court of the other jurisdiction.

17457. A trust transferred to this state pursuant to this chapter shall be administered in the same manner as a trust of that type created in this state. The validity of a trust and the construction of the beneficial provisions of a trust transferred to this state are not affected by this section.

Part 6. Rights Of Third Persons

Chapter 1. Liability Of Trustee To Third Persons

18000. (a) Unless otherwise provided in the contract or in this chapter, a trustee is not personally liable on a contract properly entered into in the trustee's fiduciary capacity in the course of administration of the trust unless the trustee fails to reveal the trustee's representative capacity or identify the trust in the contract.

(b) The personal liability of a trustee on a contract entered into before July 1, 1987, is governed by prior law and not by this section.

18001. A trustee is personally liable for obligations arising from ownership or control of trust property only if the trustee is personally at fault.

18002. A trustee is personally liable for torts committed in the course of administration of the trust only if the trustee is personally at fault.

18003. (a) A cotrustee who does not join in exercising a power held by three or more cotrustees is not liable to third persons for the consequences of the exercise of the power.

(b) A dissenting cotrustee who joins in an action at the direction of the majority cotrustees is not liable to third persons for the action if the dissenting cotrustee expresses the dissent in writing to any other cotrustee at or before the time the action is taken.

(c) This section does not excuse a cotrustee from liability for failure to discharge the cotrustee's duties as a trustee.

18004. A claim based on a contract entered into by a trustee in the trustee's representative capacity, on an obligation arising from ownership or control of trust property, or on a tort committed in the course of administration of the trust may be asserted against the trust by proceeding against the trustee in the trustee's representative capacity, whether or not the trustee is personally liable on the claim.

18005. The question of liability as between the trust estate and the trustee personally may be determined in a proceeding under Section 17200.

Chapter 2. Protection Of Third Persons

18100. With respect to a third person dealing with a trustee or assisting a trustee in the conduct of a transaction, if the third person acts in good faith and for a valuable consideration and without actual knowledge that the trustee is exceeding the trustee's powers or improperly exercising them:

(a) The third person is not bound to inquire whether the trustee has power to act or is properly exercising a power and may assume without inquiry the existence of a trust power and its proper exercise.

(b) The third person is fully protected in dealing with or assisting the trustee just as if the trustee has and is properly exercising the power the trustee purports to exercise.

18100.5. (a) The trustee may present a certification of trust to any person in lieu of providing a copy of the trust instrument to establish the existence or terms of the trust. A certification of trust may be executed by the trustee voluntarily or at the request of the person with whom the trustee is dealing.

(b) The certification of trust may confirm the following facts or contain the following information:

(1) The existence of the trust and date of execution of the trust instrument.

(2) The identity of the settlor or settlors and the currently acting trustee or trustees of the trust.

(3) The powers of the trustee.

(4) The revocability or irrevocability of the trust and the identity of any person holding any power to revoke the trust.

(5) When there are multiple trustees, the signature authority of the trustees, indicating whether all, or less than all, of the currently acting trustees are required to sign in order to exercise various powers of the trustee.

(6) The trust identification number, whether a social security number or an employer identification number.

(7) The manner in which title to trust assets should be taken.

(8) The legal description of any interest in real property held in the trust.

(c) The certification shall contain a statement that the trust has not been revoked, modified, or amended in any manner which would cause the representations contained in the certification of trust to be incorrect and shall contain a statement that it is being signed by all of the currently acting trustees of the trust. The certification shall be in the form of an acknowledged declaration signed by all currently acting trustees of the trust. The certification signed by the currently acting trustee may be recorded in the office of the county recorder in the county where all or a portion of the real property is located.

(d) The certification of trust may, but is not required to, include excerpts from the original trust documents, any amendments thereto, and any other documents evidencing or pertaining to the succession of successor trustees. The certification of trust shall not be required to contain the dispositive provisions of the trust which set forth the distribution of the trust estate.

(e) A person whose interest is, or may be, affected by the certification of trust may require that the trustee offering or recording the certification of trust provide copies of those excerpts from the original trust documents, any amendments thereto, and any other documents which designate, evidence, or pertain to the succession of the trustee or confer upon the trustee the power to act in the pending transaction, or both. Nothing in this section is intended to require or imply an obligation to provide the dispositive provisions of the trust or the entire trust and amendments thereto.

(f) A person who acts in reliance upon a certification of trust without actual knowledge that the representations contained therein are incorrect is not liable to any person for so acting. A person who does not have actual knowledge that the facts contained in the certification of trust are incorrect may assume without inquiry the existence of the facts contained in the certification of trust. Actual knowledge shall not be inferred solely from the fact that a copy of all or part of the trust instrument is held by the person relying upon the trust certification. Any transaction, and any lien created thereby, entered into by the trustee and a person acting in reliance upon a certification of trust shall be enforceable against the trust assets. However, if the person has actual knowledge that the trustee is acting outside the scope of the trust, then the transaction is not enforceable against the trust assets. Nothing contained herein shall limit the rights of the beneficiaries of the trust against the trustee.

(g) A person's failure to demand a certification of trust does not affect the protection provided that person by Section 18100, and no inference as to whether that person has acted in good faith may be drawn from the failure to demand a certification of trust. Nothing in this section is intended to create an implication that a person is liable for acting in reliance upon a certification of trust under circumstances where the requirements of this section are not satisfied.

(h) Except when requested by a beneficiary or in the context of litigation concerning a trust and subject to the provisions of subdivision (e), any person making a demand for the trust documents in addition to a certification of trust to prove facts set forth in the certification of trust acceptable to the third party shall be liable for damages, including attorney's fees, incurred as a result of the refusal to accept the certification of trust in lieu of the requested documents if the court determines that the person acted in bad faith in requesting the trust documents.

(i) Any person may record a certification of trust that relates to an interest in real property in the office of the county recorder in any county in which all or a portion of the real property is located. The county recorder shall impose any fee prescribed by law for recording that document sufficient to cover all costs incurred by the county in recording the document. The recorded certification of trust shall be a public record of the real property involved. This subdivision does not create a requirement to record a certification of trust in conjunction with the recordation of a transfer of title of real property involving a trust.

18101. A third person who acts in good faith is not bound to ensure the proper application of trust property paid or delivered to the trustee.

18102. If a third person acting in good faith and for a valuable consideration enters into a transaction with a former trustee without knowledge that the person is no longer a trustee, the third person is fully protected just as if the former trustee were still a trustee.

18103. If an express trust relating to real property is not contained or declared in the grant to the trustee, or in an instrument signed by the trustee and recorded in the same office with the grant to the trustee, the grant shall be deemed absolute in favor of a person dealing with the trustee in good faith and for a valuable consideration.

18104. (a) If an interest in or lien or encumbrance on real property is conveyed, created, or affected by an instrument in favor of a person in trust but no beneficiary is indicated in the instrument, it is presumed that the person holds the interest, lien, or encumbrance absolutely and free of the trust. This is a presumption affecting the burden of proof. In an action or proceeding involving the interest, lien, or encumbrance instituted against the person, the person shall be deemed the only necessary representative of the undisclosed beneficiary and of the original grantor or settlor and anyone claiming under them. A judgment is binding upon and conclusive against these persons as to all matters finally adjudicated in the judgment.

(b) An instrument executed by the person holding an interest, lien, or encumbrance described in subdivision (a), whether purporting to be the act of that person in his or her own right or in the capacity of a trustee, is presumed to affect the interest, lien, or encumbrance according to the tenor of the instrument. This is a presumption affecting the burden of proof. Upon the recording of the instrument in the county where the land affected by the instrument is located, the presumption is conclusive in favor of a person acting in good faith and for valuable consideration.

18105. If title to an interest in real property is affected by a change of trustee, the successor trustee may execute and record in the county in which the property is located an affidavit of change of trustee. The county recorder shall impose any fee prescribed by law for recording that document in an amount sufficient to cover all costs incurred by the county in recording the document. The affidavit shall include the legal description of the real property, the name of the former trustee or trustees and the name of the successor trustee or trustees. The affida-

vit may also, but is not required to, include excerpts from the original trust documents, any amendments thereto, and any other documents evidencing or pertaining to the succession of the successor trustee or trustees.

18106. (a) A document establishing the fact of change of trustee recorded pursuant to this chapter is subject to all statutory requirements for recorded documents.

(b) The county recorder shall index a document establishing the fact of change of a trustee recorded pursuant to this section in the index of grantors and grantees. The index entry shall be for the grantor, and for the purpose of this index, the person who has been succeeded as trustee shall be deemed to be the grantor. The county recorder shall impose any fee prescribed by law for indexing that document in an amount sufficient to cover all costs incurred by the county in indexing the document.

18107. A document establishing the change of a trustee recorded pursuant to this chapter is prima facie evidence of the change of trustee insofar as the document identifies an interest in real property located in the county, title to which is affected by the change of trustee. The presumption established by this section is a presumption affecting the burden of producing evidence.

18108. Any person whose interest is, or may be, affected by the recordation of an affidavit of change of trustee pursuant to this chapter may require that the successor trustee provide copies of those excerpts from the original trust documents, any amendments thereto, and any other documents which evidence or pertain to the succession of the successor trustee or trustees. Nothing in this section is intended to require or imply an obligation to provide the dispositive provisions of the trust or the entire trust and any amendments thereto.

Chapter 3. Rights Of Creditors Of Settlor

18200. If the settlor retains the power to revoke the trust in whole or in part, the trust property is subject to the claims of creditors of the settlor to the extent of the power of revocation during the lifetime of the settlor.

18201. Any settlor whose trust property is subject to the claims of creditors pursuant to Section 18200 shall be entitled to all exemptions as provided in Chapter 4 (commencing with Section 703.010) of Division 2 of Title 9 of Part 2 of the Code of Civil Procedure.

Part 7. Uniform Prudent Management Of Institutional Funds Act

18501. This part may be cited as the Uniform Prudent Management of Institutional Funds Act.

18502. As used in this part, the following

terms shall have the following meanings:

(a) "Charitable purpose" means the relief of poverty, the advancement of education or religion, the promotion of health, the promotion of a governmental purpose, or any other purpose the achievement of which is beneficial to the community.

(b) "Endowment fund" means an institutional fund or part thereof that, under the terms of a gift instrument, is not wholly expendable by the institution on a current basis. The term does not include assets that an institution designates as an endowment fund for its own use.

(c) "Gift instrument" means a record or records, including an institutional solicitation, under which property is granted to, transferred to, or held by an institution as an institutional fund.

(d) "Institution" means any of the following:

(1) A person, other than an individual, organized and operated exclusively for charitable purposes.

(2) A government or governmental subdivision, agency, or instrumentality, to the extent that it holds funds exclusively for a charitable purpose.

(3) A trust that had both charitable and noncharitable interests, after all noncharitable interests have terminated.

(e) "Institutional fund" means a fund held by an institution exclusively for charitable purposes. The term does not include any of the following:

(1) Program-related assets.

(2) A fund held for an institution by a trustee that is not an institution.

(3) A fund in which a beneficiary that is not an institution has an interest, other than an interest that could arise upon violation or failure of the purposes of the fund.

(f) "Person" means an individual, corporation, business trust, estate, trust, partnership, limited liability company, association, joint venture, public corporation, government or governmental subdivision, agency, or instrumentality, or any other legal or commercial entity.

(g) "Program-related asset" means an asset held by an institution primarily to accomplish a charitable purpose of the institution and not primarily for investment.

(h) "Record" means information that is inscribed on a tangible medium or that is stored in an electronic or other medium and is retrievable in perceivable form.

18503. (a) Subject to the intent of a donor expressed in a gift instrument, an institution, in managing and investing an institutional fund, shall consider the charitable purposes of the institution and the purposes of the institutional fund.

(b) In addition to complying with the duty of loyalty imposed by law other than this part, each person responsible for managing and investing an institutional fund shall manage and invest the fund in good faith and with the care an ordinarily prudent person in a like position would exercise under similar circumstances.

(c) In managing and investing an institutional fund, an institution is subject to both of the following:

(1) It may incur only costs that are appropriate and reasonable in relation to the assets, the purposes of the institution, and the skills available to the institution.

(2) It shall make a reasonable effort to verify facts relevant to the management and investment of the fund.

(d) An institution may pool two or more institutional funds for purposes of management and investment.

(e) Except as otherwise provided by a gift instrument, the following rules apply:

(1) In managing and investing an institutional fund, all of the following factors, if relevant, must be considered:

(A) General economic conditions.

(B) The possible effect of inflation or deflation.

(C) The expected tax consequences, if any, of investment decisions or strategies.

(D) The role that each investment or course of action plays within the overall investment portfolio of the fund.

(E) The expected total return from income and the appreciation of investments.

(F) Other resources of the institution.

(G) The needs of the institution and the fund to make distributions and to preserve capital.

(H) An asset's special relationship or special value, if any, to the charitable purposes of the institution.

(2) Management and investment decisions about an individual asset must be made not in isolation but rather in the context of the institutional fund's portfolio of investments as a whole and as a part of an overall investment strategy having risk and return objectives reasonably suited to the fund and to the institution.

(3) Except as otherwise provided by law other than this part, an institution may invest in any kind of property or type of investment consistent with this section.

(4) An institution shall diversify the investments of an institutional fund unless the institution reasonably determines that, because of special circumstances, the purposes of the fund are better served without diversification.

(5) Within a reasonable time after receiving property, an institution shall make and carry out decisions concerning the retention or disposition of the property or to rebalance a portfolio, in order to bring the institutional fund into compliance with the purposes, terms, and distribution requirements of the institution as necessary to meet other circumstances of the institution and the requirements of this part.

(6) A person that has special skills or ex-

pertise, or is selected in reliance upon the person's representation that the person has special skills or expertise, has a duty to use those skills or that expertise in managing and investing institutional funds.

(f) Nothing in this section alters the duties and liabilities of a director of a nonprofit public benefit corporation under Section 5240 of the Corporations Code.

18504. (a) Subject to the intent of a donor expressed in the gift instrument, an institution may appropriate for expenditure or accumulate so much of an endowment fund as the institution determines is prudent for the uses, benefits, purposes, and duration for which the endowment fund is established. Unless stated otherwise in the gift instrument, the assets in an endowment fund are donor-restricted assets until appropriated for expenditure by the institution. In making a determination to appropriate or accumulate, the institution shall act in good faith, with the care that an ordinarily prudent person in a like position would exercise under similar circumstances, and shall consider, if relevant, all of the following factors:

(1) The duration and preservation of the endowment fund.

(2) The purposes of the institution and the endowment fund.

(3) General economic conditions.

(4) The possible effect of inflation or deflation.

(5) The expected total return from income and the appreciation of investments.

(6) Other resources of the institution.

(7) The investment policy of the institution.

(b) To limit the authority to appropriate for expenditure or accumulate under subdivision (a), a gift instrument must specifically state the limitation.

(c) Terms in a gift instrument designating a gift as an endowment, or a direction or authorization in the gift instrument to use only "income," "interest," "dividends," or "rents, issues, or profits," or "to preserve the principal intact," or words of similar import have both of the following effects:

(1) To create an endowment fund of permanent duration unless other language in the gift instrument limits the duration or purpose of the fund.

(2) To not otherwise limit the authority to appropriate for expenditure or accumulate under subdivision (a).

(d) The appropriation for expenditure in any year of an amount greater than 7 percent of the fair market value of an endowment fund, calculated on the basis of market values determined at least quarterly and averaged over a period of not less than three years immediately preceding the year in which the appropriation for expenditure is made, creates a rebuttable presumption of imprudence. For an endowment fund in existence for fewer than three years, the fair

market value of the endowment fund shall be calculated for the period the endowment fund has been in existence. This subdivision does not do any of the following:

(1) Apply to an appropriation for expenditure permitted under law other than this part or by the gift instrument.

(2) Apply to a private or public postsecondary educational institution, or to a campus foundation established by and operated under the auspices of such an educational institution.

(3) Create a presumption of prudence for an appropriation for expenditure of an amount less than or equal to 7 percent of the fair market value of the endowment fund.

18505. (a) Subject to any specific limitation set forth in a gift instrument or in law other than this part, an institution may delegate to an external agent the management and investment of an institutional fund to the extent that an institution could prudently delegate under the circumstances. An institution shall act in good faith, with the care that an ordinarily prudent person in a like position would exercise under similar circumstances, in all of the following:

(1) Selecting an agent.

(2) Establishing the scope and terms of the delegation, consistent with the purposes of the institution and the institutional fund.

(3) Periodically reviewing the agent's actions in order to monitor the agent's performance and compliance with the scope and terms of the delegation.

(b) In performing a delegated function, an agent owes a duty to the institution to exercise reasonable care to comply with the scope and terms of the delegation.

(c) An institution that complies with subdivision (a) is not liable for the decisions or actions of an agent to which the function was delegated except to the extent a trustee would be liable for those actions or decisions under Sections 16052 and 16401.

(d) By accepting delegation of a management or investment function from an institution that is subject to the laws of this state, an agent submits to the jurisdiction of the courts of this state in all proceedings arising from or related to the delegation or the performance of the delegated function.

(e) An institution may delegate management and investment functions to its committees, officers, or employees as authorized by law of this state other than this part.

18506. (a) If the donor consents in a record, an institution may release or modify, in whole or in part, a restriction contained in a gift instrument on the management, investment, or purpose of an institutional fund. A release or modification may not allow a fund to be used for a purpose other than a charitable purpose of the institution.

(b) The court, upon application of an institution, may modify a restriction contained in a gift instrument regarding the management or investment of an institutional fund if the restriction has become impracticable or wasteful, if it impairs the management or investment of the fund, or if, because of circumstances not anticipated by the donor, a modification of a restriction will further the purposes of the fund. The institution shall notify the Attorney General of the application, and the Attorney General must be given an opportunity to be heard. To the extent practicable, any modification must be made in accordance with the donor's probable intention.

(c) If a particular charitable purpose or a restriction contained in a gift instrument on the use of an institutional fund becomes unlawful, impracticable, impossible to achieve, or wasteful, the court, upon application of an institution, may modify the purpose of the fund or the restriction on the use of the fund in a manner consistent with the charitable purposes expressed in the gift instrument. The institution shall notify the Attorney General of the application, and the Attorney General must be given an opportunity to be heard.

(d) If an institution determines that a restriction contained in a gift instrument on the management, investment, or purpose of an institutional fund is unlawful, impracticable, impossible to achieve, or wasteful, the institution, 60 days after notification to the Attorney General and to the donor at the donor's last known address in the records of the institution, may release or modify the restriction, in whole or part, if all of the following apply:

(1) The institutional fund subject to the restriction has a total value of less than one hundred thousand dollars ($100,000).

(2) More than 20 years have elapsed since the fund was established.

(3) The institution uses the property in a manner consistent with the charitable purposes expressed in the gift instrument. An institution that releases or modifies a restriction under this subdivision may, if appropriate circumstances arise thereafter, use the property in accordance with the restriction notwithstanding its release or modification, and that use is deemed to satisfy the consistency requirement of this paragraph.

18507. Compliance with this part is determined in light of the facts and circumstances existing at the time a decision is made or action is taken, and not by hindsight.

18508. This part applies to institutional funds existing on or established after January 1, 2009. As applied to institutional funds existing on January 1, 2009, this part governs only decisions made or actions taken on or after that date.

18509. This part modifies, limits, and supersedes the Electronic Signatures in Global and National Commerce Act (15 U.S.C. Sec. 7001 et seq.), but does not modify, limit, or supersede Section 101 of that act (15 U.S.C. Sec. 7001(a)), or authorize electronic delivery of any of the notices described in Section 103 of that act (15 U.S.C. Sec. 7003(b)).

18510. In applying and construing this uniform act, consideration must be given to the need to promote uniformity of the law with respect to its subject matter among states that enact it.

Part 8. Payment Of Claims, Debts, And Expenses From Revocable Trust Of Deceased Settlor

Chapter 1. General Provisions

19000. As used in this part:

(a) "Claim" means a demand for payment for any of the following, whether due, not due, accrued or not accrued, or contingent, and whether liquidated or unliquidated:

(1) Liability of the deceased settlor, whether arising in contract, tort, or otherwise.

(2) Liability for taxes incurred before the deceased settlor's death, whether assessed before or after the deceased settlor's death, other than property taxes and assessments secured by real property liens.

(3) Liability for the funeral expenses of the deceased settlor.

(b) "Claim" does not include a dispute regarding title to specific property alleged to be included in the trust estate.

(c) "Creditor" means a person who may have a claim against the trust property.

(d) "Trust" means a trust described in Section 18200, or, if a portion of a trust, that portion that remained subject to the power of revocation at the deceased settlor's death.

(e) "Deceased settlor" means a deceased person who, at the time of his or her death, held the power to revoke the trust in whole or in part.

(f) "Debts" means all claims, as defined in subdivision (a), all expenses of administration, and all other proper charges against the trust estate, including taxes.

19001. (a) Upon the death of a settlor, the property of the deceased settlor that was subject to the power of revocation at the time of the settlor's death is subject to the claims of creditors of the deceased settlor's estate and to the expenses of administration of the estate to the extent that the deceased settlor's estate is inadequate to satisfy those claims and expenses.

(b) The deceased settlor, by appropriate direction in the trust instrument, may direct the priority of sources of payment of debts among subtrusts or other gifts established by the trust at the deceased settlor's death. Notwithstanding this subdivision, no direction by the settlor shall alter the priority of payment, from whatever source, of the matters set forth in Section 11420 which shall be applied to the trust as it applies to a probate estate.

19002. (a) Except as expressly provided, this part shall not be construed to affect the right of any creditor to recover from any revocable trust established by the deceased settlor.

(b) Nothing in this part shall be construed as a construction or alteration of any claims procedure set forth under Part 4 (commencing with Section 9000) of Division 7.

19003. (a) At any time following the death of the settlor, and during the time that there has been no filing of a petition to administer the estate of the deceased settlor in this state of which the trustee has actual knowledge, the trustee may file with the court a proposed notice to creditors. Upon the court's assignment of a proceeding number to the proposed notice, the trustee shall publish and serve notice to creditors of the deceased settlor in the form and within the time prescribed in Chapters 3 (commencing with Section 19040) and 4 (commencing with Section 19050). That action shall constitute notice to creditors of the requirements of this part.

(b) The filing shall be made with the superior court for the county in this state where the deceased settlor resided at the time of death, or if none, in any county in this state in which trust property was located at the time of the settlor's death, or if none, in the county in this state that was the principal place of administration of the trust at the time of the settlor's death.

(c) Nothing in subdivision (a) affects a notice or request to a public entity required by Chapter 7 (commencing with Section 19200).

19004. If the trustee files, publishes, and serves notice as set forth in Section 19003, then:

(a) All claims against the trust shall be filed in the manner and within the time provided in this part.

(b) A claim that is not filed as provided in this part is barred from collection from trust assets.

(c) The holder of a claim may not maintain an action on the claim against the trust unless the claim is first filed as provided in this part.

19005. The trustee may at any time pay, reject, or contest any claim against the deceased settlor or settle any claim by compromise, arbitration, or otherwise. The trustee may also file a petition in the manner set forth in Chapter 2 (commencing with Section 19020) to settle any claim.

19006. (a) If a trustee of a trust established by the deceased settlor files, publishes, and serves notice as provided in Section 19003 the protection from creditors afforded that trustee and trust shall also be afforded to any other trusts established by the de-

ceased settlor and the trustees and beneficiaries of those trusts.

(b) If the personal representative of the deceased settlor's estate has published notice under Section 8120 and given notice of administration of the estate of the deceased settlor under Chapter 2 (commencing with Section 9050) of Part 4 of Division 7, the protection from creditors afforded the personal representative of the deceased settlor's estate shall be afforded to the trustee and to the beneficiaries of the trust.

(c) In the event that, following the filing and publication of the notice set forth in Section 19003, there shall be commenced any proceeding under which a notice pursuant to Section 8120 is required to be published, then the trustee shall have a right of collection against that estate to recover the amount of any debts paid from trust assets that would otherwise have been satisfied (whether by law or by direction in the deceased settlor's will or trust) by the property subject to probate proceedings.

19007. Nothing in this part shall determine the liability of any trust established by the deceased settlor as against any other trust established by that settlor, except to the extent that the trustee of the other trust shall file, publish, and serve the notice specified in Section 19003 and thereafter seek a determination of relative liability pursuant to Chapter 2 (commencing with Section 19020).

19008. If there is no proceeding to administer the estate of the deceased settlor, and if the trustee does not file a proposed notice to creditors pursuant to Section 19003 and does not publish notice to creditors pursuant to Chapter 3 (commencing with Section 19040), then the liability of the trust to any creditor of the deceased settlor shall be as otherwise provided by law.

19009. Nothing in this part shall be construed to permit or require disclosure of the existence of the trust or the contents of any of its provisions to any creditor or beneficiary except as that creditor or beneficiary may otherwise be entitled to that information.

19010. Nothing in this part imposes any duty on the trustee to initiate the notice proceeding set forth in Section 19003, and the trustee is not liable for failure to initiate the proceeding under this part.

19011. (a) The Judicial Council may prescribe the form and contents of the petition, notice, claim form, and allowance or rejection form to be used pursuant to this part. The allowance or rejection form may be part of the claim form.

(b) Any claim form adopted by the Judicial Council shall inform the creditor that the claim must be filed with the court and a copy mailed or delivered to the trustee. The claim form shall include a proof of mailing or delivery of a copy of the claim to the trustee, which may be completed by the claimant.

19012. (a) This part applies to claims against any deceased settlor who dies on or after January 1, 1992.

(b) The applicable law in effect before January 1, 1992, continues to apply to claims against any deceased settlor who dies before January 1, 1992.

Chapter 2. Petition For Approval And Settlement Of Claims Against Deceased Settlor

19020. At any time after the filing and first publication of notice pursuant to Chapter 3 (commencing with Section 19040), and after expiration of the time to file claims provided in that chapter, a trustee or beneficiary may petition the court under this chapter to approve either of the following:

(a) Allowance, compromise, or settlement of any claims that have not been rejected by the trustee under the procedure provided in this part and for which trust property may be liable.

(b) An allocation of any amounts due by reason of an action described in subdivision (a) to two or more trusts which may be liable for the claims.

19021. The petition shall be filed in that county as may be determined pursuant to Section 19003. In the event this action seeks approval of allocation to two or more trusts for which the notice proceeding in Section 19003 would prescribe superior courts for more than one county, the court located in the county so prescribed for the trustee initiating the proceeding under this chapter shall have jurisdiction.

19022. (a) A proceeding under this chapter is commenced by filing a verified petition stating facts showing that the petition is authorized under this chapter and the grounds of the petition.

(b) The petition shall set forth a description of the trust and the names of creditors with respect to which action is requested and a description of each claim, together with the requested determination by the court with respect to the claims, provided, however, that this section does not require the filing of a copy of the trust or disclosure of the beneficial interests of the trust. That petition shall also set forth the beneficiaries of the trust, those claimants whose interest in the trust may be affected by the petition, and the trustees of any other trust to which an allocation of liability may be approved by the court pursuant to the petition.

(c) The clerk shall set the matter for hearing.

19023. At least 30 days before the time set for the hearing on the petition, the petitioner shall cause notice of the time and place of the hearing and a copy of the petition to be served on each of the creditors whose interests in the estate may be affected by the petition in the manner provided in Chapter 4 (commencing with Section 413.10) of Title 5 of Part 2 of the Code of Civil Procedure.

19024. At least 30 days before the time set for the hearing on the petition, the petitioner shall cause notice of the time and place of the hearing, together with a copy of the petition, to be mailed to each of the following persons who is not a petitioner:

(a) All trustees of the trust and of any other trusts to which an allocation of liability may be approved by the court pursuant to the petition.

(b) All beneficiaries affected.

(c) The personal representative of the deceased settlor's estate, if any is known to the trustee.

(d) The Attorney General, if the petition relates to a charitable trust subject to the jurisdiction of the Attorney General, unless the Attorney General waives notice.

19025. (a) If any creditor, beneficiary, or trustee fails timely to file a written pleading upon notice, then the case is at issue, notwithstanding the failure. The case may proceed on the petition and written statements filed by the time of the hearing, and no further pleadings by other persons are necessary. The creditor, beneficiary, or trustee who failed timely to file a written pleading upon notice may not participate further in the proceeding for the determination requested, and that creditor, beneficiary, or trustee shall be bound by the decision in the proceeding.

(b) The court's order, when final, shall be conclusive as to the liability of the trust property with respect to the claims at issue in the petition. In the event of a subsequent administration of the estate of the deceased settlor, that order shall be binding on the personal representative of the estate of the deceased settlor as well as all creditors and beneficiaries who had notice of the petition.

19026. The court may dismiss a petition if it appears that the proceeding is not reasonably necessary for the protection of the interests of the trustee or any beneficiary of the trust.

19027. (a) The court in its discretion may make any orders and take any other action necessary or proper to dispose of the matters presented by the petition.

(b) If the court determines that the assets of the trust estate are insufficient to pay all debts, then the court shall order payment in the manner specified by Section 11420.

19029. The court may, on its own motion or on request of a trustee or other person interested in the trust, appoint a guardian ad litem in accordance with Section 1003.

19030. In a case involving a charitable trust subject to the jurisdiction of the Attorney General, the Attorney General may petition under this chapter.

Chapter 3. Publication Of Notice

19040. (a) Publication of notice pursuant to this section shall be for at least 15 days. Three publications in a newspaper published once a week or more often, with at least five days intervening between the first and last publication dates, not counting the first and last publication dates as part of the five-day period, are sufficient. Notice shall be published in a newspaper of general circulation in the city, county, or city and county in this state where the deceased settlor resided at the time of death, or if none, in the city, county, or city and county in this state wherein trust property was located at the time of the settlor's death, or if none, in the city, county, or city and county in this state wherein the principal place of administration of the trust was located at the time of the settlor's death. If there is no newspaper of general circulation published in the applicable city, county, or city and county, notice shall be published in a newspaper of general circulation published in this state nearest to the applicable city, county, or city and county seat, and which is circulated within the applicable city, county, or city and county. If there is no such newspaper, notice shall be given in written or printed form, posted at three of the most public places within the community. For purposes of this section, "city" means a charter city as defined in Section 34101 of the Government Code or a general law city as defined in Section 34102 of the Government Code.

(b) The caption of the notice, the deceased settlor's name, and the name of the trustee shall be in at least 8-point type, the text of the notice shall be in at least 7-point type, and the notice shall state substantially as follows:

PLEASE SEE THE APPENDIX

(c) An affidavit showing due publication of notice shall be filed with the clerk upon completion of the publication. The affidavit shall contain a copy of the notice, and state the date of its first publication.

19041. The Legislature finds and declares that to be most effective, notice to creditors should be published in compliance with the procedures specified in Section 19040. However, the Legislature recognizes the possibility that in unusual cases due to confusion over jurisdictional boundaries or oversights the notice may inadvertently be published in a newspaper which does not meet these requirements. Therefore, to prevent a minor error in publication from invalidating what would otherwise be a proper proceeding, the Legislature further finds and declares that notice published in a good faith attempt to comply with Section 19040 shall be sufficient to provide notice to creditors and establish jurisdiction if the court expressly finds that the notice was published in a newspaper of general circulation published within the city, county, or city and county and widely circulated within a true cross section of the community in which the deceased settlor resided or wherein the principal place of administration of the trust was located or the property was located in substantial compliance with Section 19040.

Chapter 4. Actual Notice To Creditors

19050. Except as provided in Section 19054, if the trustee has knowledge of a creditor of the deceased settlor, the trustee shall give notice to the creditor. The notice shall be given as provided in Section 1215. For the purpose of this section, a trustee has knowledge of a creditor of the deceased settlor if the trustee is aware that the creditor has demanded payment from the deceased settlor or the trust estate.

19051. The notice shall be given before expiration of the later of the following times:

(a) Four months after the first publication of notice under Section 19040.

(b) Thirty days after the trustee first has knowledge of the creditor.

19052. The notice shall be in substantially the following form:

PLEASE SEE THE APPENDIX

19053. (a) If the trustee believes that notice to a particular creditor is or may be required by this chapter and gives notice based on that belief, the trustee is not liable to any person for giving the notice, whether or not required by this chapter.

(b) If the trustee fails to give notice required by this chapter, the trustee is not liable to any person for that failure, unless a creditor establishes all of the following:

(1) The failure was in bad faith.

(2) The creditor did not have actual knowledge of the proceedings under Chapter 1 (commencing with Section 19000) sooner than one year after publication of notice to creditors under Section 19040, and payment would have been made on the creditor's claim if the claim had been properly filed.

(3) Within 16 months after the first publication of notice under Section 19040, the creditor did both of the following:

(A) Filed a petition requesting that the court in which the proceedings under Chapter 1 (commencing with Section 19000) were initiated make an order determining the liability of the trustee under this subdivision.

(B) At least 30 days before the hearing on the petition, caused notice of the hearing and a copy of the petition to be served on the trustee in the manner provided in Chapter 4 (commencing with Section 413.10) of Title 5 of Part 2 of the Code of Civil Procedure.

(c) Nothing in this section affects the liability of the trust estate, if any, for the claim of a creditor, and the trustee is not liable to the extent the claim is paid out of the trust estate.

(d) Nothing in this chapter imposes a duty on the trustee to make a search for creditors of the deceased settlor.

19054. Notwithstanding Section 19050, the trustee need not give notice to a creditor even though the trustee has knowledge of the creditor if either of the following conditions is satisfied:

(a) The creditor has filed a claim as provided in this part.

(b) The creditor has demanded payment and the trustee elects to treat the demand as a claim under Section 19154.

Chapter 5. Time For Filing Claims

19100. (a) A creditor shall file a claim before expiration of the later of the following times:

(1) Four months after the first publication of notice to creditors under Section 19040.

(2) Sixty days after the date actual notice is mailed or personally delivered to the creditor. This paragraph does not extend the time provided in Section 366.2 of the Code of Civil Procedure.

(b) A reference in another statute to the time for filing a claim means the time provided in paragraph (1) of subdivision (a).

(c) This section shall not be interpreted to extend or toll any other statute of limitations, including that provided by Section 366.2 of the Code of Civil Procedure.

19101. A vacancy in the office of the trustee that occurs before expiration of the time for filing a claim does not extend the time.

19102. A claim that is filed before expiration of the time for filing the claim is timely even if acted on by the trustee or the court after expiration of the time for filing claims.

19103. (a) Except as provided in subdivision (b), upon petition by a creditor or a trustee, the court may allow a claim to be filed after expiration of the time for filing a claim provided in Section 19100 if either of the following conditions are satisfied:

(1) The trustee failed to send proper and timely notice to the creditor and the petition is filed within 60 days after the creditor has actual knowledge of the administration of the trust.

(2) The creditor did not have knowledge of the facts giving rise to the existence of the claim more than 30 days prior to the time for filing a claim as provided in Section 19100, and the petition is filed within 60 days after the creditor has actual knowledge of both of the following:

(A) The existence of the facts reasonably giving rise to the existence of the claim.

(B) The administration of the trust.

(b) Notwithstanding subdivision (a), the court shall not allow a claim to be filed under this section more than one year after the date of first publication of notice to creditors under Section 19040. Nothing in this subdivision authorizes allowance or approval of a claim barred by, or extends the time provided in, Section 366.2 of the Code of Civil Procedure.

(c) The court may condition the claim on terms that are just and equitable. The court may deny the claimant's petition if a distribution to trust beneficiaries or payment to general creditors has been made and it appears the filing or establishment of the claim would cause or tend to cause unequal treatment among beneficiaries or creditors.

(d) Regardless of whether the claim is later established in whole or in part, property distributed under the terms of the trust subsequent to an order settling claims under Chapter 2 (commencing with Section 19020) and payments otherwise properly made before a claim is filed under this section are not subject to the claim. Except to the extent provided in Chapter 12 (commencing with Section 19400) and subject to Section 19053, the trustee, distributee, or payee is not liable on account of the prior distribution or payment. This subdivision does not limit the liability of a person who receives a preliminary distribution of property to restore to the trust an amount sufficient for payment of the beneficiary's proper share of the claim, not exceeding the amount distributed.

19104. (a) Subject to subdivision (b), if a claim is filed within the time provided in this chapter, the creditor may later amend or revise the claim. The amendment or revision shall be filed in the same manner as the claim.

(b) An amendment or revision may not be made to increase the amount of the claim after the time for filing a claim has expired. An amendment or revision to specify the amount of a claim that, at the time of filing, was not due, was contingent, or was not yet ascertainable, is not an increase in the amount of the claim within the meaning of this subdivision. An amendment or revision of a claim may not be made for any purpose after the earlier of the following times:

(1) The time the court makes an order approving settlement of the claim against the deceased settlor under Chapter 2 (commencing with Section 19020).

(2) One year after the date of the first publication of notice to creditors under Section 19040. Nothing in this paragraph authorizes allowance or approval of a claim barred by, or extends the time provided in, Section 366.2 of the Code of Civil Procedure.

Chapter 6. Filing Of Claims

19150. (a) A claim may be filed by the creditor or a person acting on behalf of the claimant.

(b) A claim shall be filed with the court

and a copy shall be mailed to the trustee. Failure to mail a copy to the trustee does not invalidate a properly filed claim, but any loss that results from the failure shall be borne by the creditor.

19151. (a) A claim shall be supported by the affidavit of the creditor or the person on behalf of the claimant stating:

(1) The claim is a just claim.

(2) If the claim is due, the facts supporting the claim, the amount of the claim, and that all payments on and offsets to the claim have been credited.

(3) If the claim is not due or contingent, or the amount is not yet ascertainable, the facts supporting the claim.

(4) If the affidavit is made by a person other than the creditor, the reason it is not made by the creditor.

(b) The trustee may require satisfactory vouchers or proof to be produced to support the claim. An original voucher may be withdrawn after a copy is provided. If a copy is provided, the copy shall be attached to the claim.

19152. (a) If a claim is based on a written instrument, either the original or a copy of the original with all endorsements shall be attached to the claim. If a copy is attached, the original instrument shall be exhibited to the trustee on demand unless it is lost or destroyed, in which case the fact that it is lost or destroyed shall be stated in the claim.

(b) If the claim or a part of the claim is secured by a mortgage, deed of trust, or other lien that is recorded in the office of the recorder of the county in which the property subject to the lien is located, it is sufficient to describe the mortgage, deed of trust, or lien and the recording reference for the instrument that created the mortgage, deed of trust, or other lien.

19153. The Judicial Council may adopt a claim form which shall inform the creditor that the claim must be filed with the court and a copy mailed or delivered to the trustee. Any such claim form shall include a proof of mailing or delivery of a copy of the claim to the trustee which may be completed by the creditor.

19154. (a) Notwithstanding any other provision of this part, if a creditor makes a written demand for payment within the time specified in Section 19100, the trustee may waive formal defects and elect to treat the demand as a claim that is filed and established under this part by paying the amount demanded.

(b) Nothing in this section limits application of the doctrines of waiver, estoppel, laches, or detrimental reliance or any other equitable principle.

Chapter 7. Claims By Public Entities

19200. (a) Except as provided in this chapter, a claim by a public entity shall be filed within the time otherwise provided in this part. A claim not so filed is barred, including any lien imposed for the claim

(b) As used in this chapter, "public entity" has the meaning provided in Section 811.2 of the Government Code, and includes an officer authorized to act on behalf of the public entity.

19201. (a) Notwithstanding any other statute, if a claim of a public entity arises under a law, act, or code listed in subdivision (b):

(1) The public entity may provide a form to be used for the written notice or request to the public entity required by this chapter. Where appropriate, the form may require the decedent's social security number, if known.

(2) The claim is barred only after written notice or request to the public entity and expiration of the period provided in the applicable section. If no written notice or request is made, the claim is enforceable by the remedies, and is barred at the time, otherwise provided in the law, act, or code.

(b)

LAW, ACT, OR CODE	APPLICABLE SECTION
Sales and Use Tax Law (commencing with Section 6001 of the Revenue and Taxation Code)	Section 6487.1 of the Revenue and Taxation Code
Bradley-Burns Uniform Local Sales and Use Tax Law (commencing with Section 7200 of the Revenue and Taxation Code)	Section 6487.1 of the Revenue and Taxation Code
Transactions and Use Tax Law (commencing with Section 7251 of the Revenue and Taxation Code)	Section 6487.1 of the Revenue and Taxation Code
Motor Vehicle Fuel License Tax Law (commencing with Section 7301 of the Revenue and Taxation Code)	Section 7675.1 of the Revenue and Taxation Code

Law, Act, or Code	Applicable Section
Use Fuel Tax Law (commencing with Section 8601 of the Revenue and Taxation Code)	Section 8782.1 of the Revenue and Taxation Code
Administration of Franchise and Income Tax Law (commencing with Section 18401 of the Revenue and Taxation Code)	Section 19517 of the Revenue and Taxation Code
Cigarette Tax Law (commencing with Section 30001 of the Revenue and Taxation Code)	Section 30207.1 of the Revenue and Taxation Code
Alcoholic Beverage Tax Law (commencing with Section 32001 of the Revenue and Taxation Code)	Section 32272.1 of the Revenue and Taxation Code
Unemployment Insurance Code	Section 1090 of the Unemployment Insurance Code
State Hospitals for the Mentally Disordered (commencing with Section 7200 of the Welfare and Institutions Code)	Section 7277.1 of the Welfare and Institutions Code
Medi-Cal Act (commencing with Section 14000 of the Welfare and Institutions Code)	Section 9202 of the Probate Code
Waxman-Duffy Prepaid Health Plan Act (commencing with Section 14200 of the Welfare and Institutions Code)	Section 9202 of the Probate Code

19202. (a) If the trustee knows or has reason to believe that the deceased settlor received health care under Chapter 7 (commencing with Section 14000) or Chapter 8 (commencing with Section 14200) of Part 3 of Division 9 of the Welfare and Institutions Code, or was the surviving spouse of a person who received that health care, the trustee shall give the State Director of Health

Services notice of the death of the deceased settlor or surviving spouse in the manner provided in Section 215.

(b) The director has four months after notice is given in which to file a claim.

19203. If property in the trust is distributed before expiration of the time allowed a public entity to file a claim, the public entity has a claim against the distributees to the full extent of the public entity's claim or each distributee's share of the distributed property, as set forth in Section 19402, whichever is less. The public entity's claim against distributees includes interest at a rate equal to that specified in Section 19521 of the Revenue and Taxation Code, from the date of distribution or the date of filing the claim by the public entity, whichever is later, plus other accruing costs as in the case of enforcement of a money judgment.

19204. Nothing in this chapter shall be construed to affect the order of priority of debts provided for under other provisions of law.

19205. This chapter does not apply to liability for the restitution of amounts illegally acquired through the means of a fraudulent, false, or incorrect representation, or a forged or unauthorized endorsement.

Chapter 8. Allowance And Rejection Of Claims

19250. When a claim is filed, the trustee shall allow or reject the claim in whole or in part.

19251. (a) Any allowance or rejection shall be in writing. The trustee shall file the allowance or rejection with the court clerk and give notice to the claimant, together with a copy of the allowance or rejection, as provided in Section 1215.

(b) The allowance or rejection shall contain the following information:

(1) The name of the claimant.

(2) The date of the settlor's death.

(3) The total amount of the claim.

(4) The amount allowed or rejected by the trustee.

(5) A statement that the claimant has 90 days from the time the notice of rejection is given, or 90 days after the claim becomes due, whichever is later, in which to bring an action on a claim rejected in whole or in part.

(c) The Judicial Council shall prescribe an allowance or rejection form, which may be part of the claim form. Use of a form prescribed by the Judicial Council is deemed to satisfy the requirements.

(d) This section does not apply to a demand the trustee elects to treat as a claim under Section 19154.

19252. The trustee shall have the power to pay any claim or portion of a claim and payment shall constitute allowance of the claim to the extent of the payment. The trustee shall have the power to compromise any claim or portion of a claim. If the trustee or the attorney for the trustee is a creditor of the deceased settlor, the trustee shall have the same powers regarding allowance, rejection, payment, or compromise set forth in this chapter.

19253. (a) A claim barred by the statute of limitations may not be allowed by the trustee.

(b) The filing of a claim tolls the statute of limitations otherwise applicable to the claim until the trustee gives notice of allowance or rejection.

(c) The allowance of a claim further tolls the statute of limitations as to the part of the claim allowed until the allowed portion of the claim is paid.

(d) Notwithstanding the statute of limitations otherwise applicable to a claim, if an action on a rejected claim is not commenced or if the matter is not referred to a referee or to arbitration within the time prescribed in Section 19255, it is forever barred.

19254. If within 30 days after a claim is filed the trustee has refused or neglected to act on the claim, the refusal or neglect may, at the option of the claimant, be deemed equivalent to the giving of a notice of rejection on the 30th day.

19255. (a) A rejected claim is barred as to the part rejected unless the creditor brings an action on the claim or the matter is referred to a referee or to arbitration within the following times, excluding any time during which there is a vacancy in the office of the trustee:

(1) If the claim is due at the time of giving the notice of rejection, 90 days after the notice is given.

(2) If the claim is not due at the time of giving the notice of rejection, 90 days after the claim becomes due.

(b) In addition to any other county in which an action on a rejected claim may be commenced, the action may be commenced in the county or city and county wherein the principal place of administration of the trust is located.

(c) The creditor shall file a notice of the pendency of the action or the referral to a referee or to arbitration with the court clerk in the trust proceeding, together with proof of giving a copy of the notice to the trustee as provided in Section 1215. Personal service of a copy of the summons and complaint on the trustee is equivalent to the filing and giving of the notice.

(d) Any property distributed by the trustee under the terms of the trust after 120 days from the later of the time the notice of rejection is given or the claim is due and before the notice of pendency of action or referral or arbitration is filed and given, excluding therefrom any time during which there is a vacancy in the office of the trustee, is not subject to the claim. Neither the trustee nor the distributee is liable on account of the distribution.

(e) The prevailing party in the action shall be awarded court costs and, if the court determines that the prosecution or defense of the action against the prevailing party was unreasonable, the prevailing party shall be awarded reasonable litigation expenses, including attorney's fees. For the purpose of this subdivision, the prevailing party shall be the trustee if the creditor recovers an amount equal to or less than the amount of the claim allowed by the trustee, and shall be the creditor if the creditor recovers an amount greater than the amount of the claim allowed by the trustee.

Chapter 9. Claims Established By Judgment

19300. (a) Except as provided in Section 19303, after the death of the settlor all money judgments against the deceased settlor on a claim against the deceased settlor or against the trustee on a claim against the decedent or the trust estate are payable in the course of administration and are not enforceable against property in the trust estate of the deceased settlor under the Enforcement of Judgments Law (Title 9 (commencing with Section 680.010) of Part 2 of the Code of Civil Procedure).

(b) Subject to Section 19301, a judgment referred to in subdivision (a) shall be filed in the same manner as other claims.

19301. When a money judgment against a trustee in a representative capacity becomes final, it conclusively establishes the validity of the claim for the amount of the judgment. The judgment shall provide that it is payable out of property in the deceased settlor's trust estate in the course of administration. An abstract of the judgment shall be filed in the trust administration proceedings.

19302. (a) Notwithstanding the death of the settlor, a judgment for possession of trust property or a judgment for sale of trust property may be enforced under the Enforcement of Judgments Law (Title 9 (commencing with Section 680.010) of Part 2 of the Code of Civil Procedure). Nothing in this subdivision authorizes enforcement under the Enforcement of Judgments Law against any property in the trust estate of the deceased settlor other than the property described in the judgment for possession or sale.

(b) After the death of the settlor, a demand for money that is not satisfied from the trust property described in a judgment for sale of property shall be filed as a claim in the same manner as other claims and is payable in the course of administration.

19303. If trust property of the deceased settlor is subject to an execution lien at the time of the settlor's death, enforcement against the property may proceed under the Enforcement of Judgments Law (Title 9 (commencing with Section 680.010) of Part 2 of the Code of Civil Procedure) to satisfy the judgment. The levying officer, as defined in Section 680.260 of the Code of Civil Procedure, shall account to the trustee for any surplus. If the judgment is not satisfied, the balance of the judgment remaining unsatisfied is payable in the course of administration.

19304. (a) An attachment lien may be converted into a judgment lien on property in the trust estate subject to the attachment lien, with the same priority as the attachment lien, in either of the following cases:

(1) Where the judgment debtor dies after entry of judgment in an action in which the property was attached.

(2) Where a judgment is entered after the death of the defendant in an action in which the property was attached.

(b) To convert the attachment lien into a judgment lien, the levying officer shall, after entry of judgment in the action in which the property was attached and before the expiration of the attachment lien, do one of the following:

(1) Serve an abstract of the judgment, and a notice that the attachment lien has become a judgment lien, on the trustee or other person holding property subject to the attachment lien.

(2) Record or file in any office where the writ of attachment and notice of attachment are recorded or filed an abstract of the judgment and a notice that the attachment lien has become a judgment lien. If the attached property is real property, the plaintiff or the plaintiff's attorney may record the required abstract and notice with the same effect as if recorded by the levying officer.

(c) After the death of the settlor, any members of the deceased settlor's family who were supported in whole or in part by the deceased settlor may claim an exemption provided in Section 487.020 of the Code of Civil Procedure for property levied on under the writ of attachment if the right to the exemption exists at the time the exemption is claimed. The trustee may claim the exemption on behalf of members of the deceased settlor's family. The claim of exemption may be made at any time before the time the abstract and notice are served, recorded, or filed under subdivision (b) with respect to the property claimed to be exempt. The claim of exemption shall be made in the same manner as an exemption is claimed under Section 482.100 of the Code of Civil Procedure.

Chapter 10. Allocation Of Debts Between Trust And Surviving Spouse

19320. If it appears that a debt of the deceased settlor has been paid or is payable in whole or in part from property in the deceased settlor's trust, then the trustee, the surviving spouse, the personal representative, if any, or a deceased settlor's probate estate, or a beneficiary may petition for an order to allocate the debt.

19321. A petition under Section 19320 shall include a statement of all of the following:

(a) All debts of the deceased settlor and surviving spouse known to the petitioner that are alleged to be subject to allocation and whether paid in whole or in part or unpaid.

(b) The reason why the debts should be allocated.

(c) The proposed allocation and the basis for allocation alleged by the petitioner.

19322. If it appears from the petition under Section 19320 that allocation would be affected by the value of the separate property of the surviving spouse and any community property and quasi-community property not administered in the trust, and if an inventory and appraisal of the property has not been provided by the surviving spouse, the court shall make an order to show cause why the information should not be provided.

19323. (a) At least 30 days before the time set for the hearing on the petition, the petitioner shall cause notice of the time and place of the hearing and a copy of the petition to be served on the surviving spouse in the manner provided in Chapter 4 (commencing with Section 413.10) of Title 5 of Part 2 of the Code of Civil Procedure.

(b) At least 30 days before the time set for the hearing on the petition, the petitioner shall cause notice of the time and place of hearing, together with a copy of the petition, to be mailed to each of the following persons who are not petitioners:

(1) All trustees of the trust and of any trusts to which an allocation of liability may be approved by the court pursuant to the petition.

(2) All beneficiaries affected.

(3) The personal representative of the deceased settlor's estate, if any is known to the trustee.

(4) The Attorney General, if the petition relates to a charitable trust subject to the jurisdiction of the Attorney General, unless the Attorney General waives notice.

19324. (a) The trustee, the personal representative, if any, of a deceased settlor's probate estate, and the surviving spouse may provide for allocation of debts by agreement so long as the agreement substantially protects the rights of other interested persons. The trustee, the personal representative, or the spouse may request and obtain court approval of the allocation provided in the agreement.

(b) In the absence of an agreement, each debt subject to allocation shall first be characterized by the court as separate or community, in accordance with the laws of the state applicable to marital dissolution proceedings. Following that characterization, the debt or debts shall be allocated as follows:

(1) Separate debts of either spouse shall be allocated to that spouse's separate property assets, and community debts shall be allocated to the spouses' community property assets.

(2) If a separate property asset of either spouse is subject to a secured debt that is characterized as that spouse's separate debt, and the net equity in that asset available to satisfy that secured debt is less than that secured debt, the unsatisfied portion of that secured debt shall be treated as an unsecured separate debt of that spouse and allocated to the net value of that spouse's other separate property assets.

(3) If the net value of either spouse's separate property assets is less than that spouse's unsecured separate debt or debts, the unsatisfied portion of the debt or debts shall be allocated to the net value of that spouse's one-half share of the community property assets. If the net value of that spouse's one-half share of the community property assets is less than that spouse's unsatisfied unsecured separate debt or debts, the remaining unsatisfied portion of the debt or debts shall be allocated to the net value of the other spouse's one-half share of the community property assets.

(4) If a community property asset is subject to a secured debt that is characterized as a community debt, and the net equity in that asset available to satisfy that secured debt is less than that secured debt, the unsatisfied portion of that secured debt shall be treated as an unsecured community debt and allocated to the net value of the other community property assets.

(5) If the net value of the community property assets is less than the unsecured community debt or debts, the unsatisfied portion of the debt or debts shall be allocated equally between the separate property assets of the deceased settlor and the surviving spouse. If the net value of either spouse's separate property assets is less than that spouse's share of the unsatisfied portion of the unsecured community debt or debts, the remaining unsatisfied portion of the debt or debts shall be allocated to the net value of the other spouse's separate property assets.

(c) For purposes of this section:

(1) The net value of either spouse's separate property asset shall refer to its fair market value as of the date of the deceased settlor's death, minus the date-of-death balance of any liens and encumbrances on that asset that have been characterized as that spouse's separate debts.

(2) The net value of a community property asset shall refer to its fair market value as of the date of the deceased settlor's death, minus the date-of-death balance of any liens and encumbrances on that asset that have been characterized as community debts.

(3) In the case of a nonrecourse debt, the amount of that debt shall be limited to the net equity in the collateral, based on the fair market value of the collateral as of the date of the decedent's death, that is available to satisfy that debt. For the purposes of this paragraph, "nonrecourse debt" means a debt for which the debtor's obligation to repay is limited to the collateral securing the debt, and for which a deficiency judgment against the debtor is not permitted by law.

(d) Notwithstanding the foregoing provisions of this section, the court may order a different allocation of debts between the deceased settlor's probate estate, trust, and the surviving spouse if the court finds a different allocation to be equitable under the circumstances.

(e) Nothing contained in this section is intended to impair or affect the rights of third parties. If a trustee, a personal representative, if any, of a deceased settlor's probate estate, or the surviving spouse incurs any damages or expense, including attorney's fees, on account of the nonpayment of a debt that was allocated to the other party pursuant to subdivision (b), or as the result of a debt being misallocated due to fraud or intentional misrepresentation by the other party, the party incurring damages shall be entitled to recover from the other party for damages or expense deemed reasonable by the court that made the allocation.

19325. On making a determination as provided in this chapter, the court shall make an order that:

(a) Directs the trustee to make payment of the amounts allocated to the trust by payment to the surviving spouse or creditors.

(b) Directs the trustee to charge amounts allocated to the surviving spouse against any property or interests of the surviving spouse that are in the possession or control of the trustee. To the extent that property or interests of the surviving spouse in the possession or control of the trustee are insufficient to satisfy the allocation, the court order shall summarily direct the surviving spouse to pay the allocation to the trustee.

19326. Notwithstanding any other statute, funeral expenses and expenses of last illness, in the absence of specific provisions in a will or trust to the contrary, shall be charged against the deceased settlor's probate estate and thereafter, against the deceased settlor's share of the trust and shall not be allocated to or charged against, the community share of the surviving spouse, whether or not the surviving spouse is financially able to pay the expenses and whether or not the surviving spouse or any other person is also liable for the expenses.

Chapter 11. Liability Of Settlor's Surviving Spouse

19330. If proceedings are commenced under this part for the settlement of claims against the trust, and the time for filing claims has commenced, any action upon the liability of the surviving spouse under

Chapter 3 (commencing with Section 13550) is barred to the same extent as provided for claims under this part, except as to the following:

(a) Any creditor who commences judicial proceedings to enforce a claim and serves the surviving spouse with the complaint prior to the expiration of the time for filing claims.

(b) Any creditor who has or who secures the surviving spouse's acknowledgment in writing of the liability of the surviving spouse for the claim.

(c) Any creditor who files a timely claim in the proceedings for the administration of the estate of the deceased spouse.

Chapter 12. Distributee Liability

19400. Subject to Section 366.2 of the Code of Civil Procedure, if there is no proceeding to administer the estate of the deceased settlor, and if the trustee does not file a proposed notice to creditors pursuant to Section 19003 and does not publish notice to creditors pursuant to Chapter 3 (commencing with Section 19040), then a beneficiary of the trust to whom payment, delivery, or transfer of the deceased settlor's property is made pursuant to the terms of the trust is personally liable, to the extent provided in Section 19402, for the unsecured claims of the creditors of the deceased settlor's estate.

19401. Subject to Section 19402, if the trustee filed a proposed notice to creditors pursuant to Section 19003 and published notice to creditors pursuant to Section 19040, and if the identity of the creditor was known to, or reasonably ascertainable by, the trustee within four months of the first publication of notice pursuant to Section 19040, then a person to whom property is distributed is personally liable for the claim of the creditor, without a claim first having been filed, if all of the following conditions are satisfied:

(a) The claim of the creditor was not merely conjectural.

(b) Notice to the creditor was not given to the creditor under Chapter 4 (commencing with Section 19050) and neither the creditor nor the attorney representing the creditor in the matter had actual knowledge of the administration of the trust estate sooner than one year after the date of first publication of notice pursuant to Section 19040.

(c) The statute of limitations applicable to the claim under Section 366.2 of the Code of Civil Procedure has not expired at the time of commencement of an action under this section.

19402. (a) In any action under this chapter, subject to Section 366.2 of the Code of Civil Procedure, the distributee may assert any defenses, cross-complaints, or setoffs that would have been available to the deceased settlor if the settlor had not died.

(b) Personal liability under this chapter is applicable only to the extent the claim of the creditor cannot be satisfied out of the trust estate of the deceased settlor and is limited to a pro rata portion of the claim of the creditor, based on the proportion that the value of the property distributed to the person out of the trust estate bears to the total value of all property distributed to all persons out of the trust estate. Personal liability under this chapter for all claims of all creditors shall not exceed the value of the property distributed to the person out of the trust estate. As used in this chapter, the value of the property is the fair market value of the property on the date of its distribution, less the amount of any liens and encumbrances on the property at that time.

19403. Nothing in this chapter affects the rights of a purchaser or encumbrancer of property in good faith and for value from a person who is personally liable under this section.

Division 10. Proration Of Taxes

Chapter 1. Proration Of Estate Taxes

Article 1. General Provisions

20100. Except where the context otherwise requires, the following definitions shall govern the construction of this chapter:

(a) "Estate tax" means a tax imposed by any federal or California estate tax law, now existing or hereafter enacted, and includes interest and penalties on any deficiency.

(b) "Person interested in the estate" means any person, including a personal representative, entitled to receive, or who has received, from a decedent while alive or by reason of the death of the decedent any property or interest therein.

(c) "Personal representative" includes a guardian, conservator, trustee, or other person charged with the responsibility of paying the estate tax.

(d) "Property" means property included in the gross estate for federal estate tax purposes.

(e) "Value" means fair market value as determined for federal estate tax purposes.

20101. (a) This chapter does not apply to persons interested in the estate of a decedent who died before January 1, 1987.

(b) Notwithstanding the repeal of former Article 4a (commencing with Section 970) of Chapter 15 of Division 3 of the Probate Code by Chapter 783 of the Statutes of 1986, the provisions of that former article remain applicable where the decedent died before January 1, 1987. No inference as to the applicable law in effect before January 1, 1987, shall be drawn from the enactment of this chapter.

Article 2. Proration

20110. (a) Except as provided in subdivision (b), any estate tax shall be equitably prorated among the persons interested in the estate in the manner prescribed in this article.

(b) This section does not apply:

(1) To the extent the decedent in a written inter vivos or testamentary instrument disposing of property specifically directs that the property be applied to the satisfaction of an estate tax or that an estate tax be prorated to the property in the manner provided in the instrument. As used in this paragraph, an "instrument disposing of property" includes an instrument that creates an interest in property or an amendment to an instrument that disposes of property or creates an interest in property.

(2) Where federal law directs otherwise. If federal law directs the manner of proration of the federal estate tax, the California estate tax shall be prorated in the same manner.

20111. The proration required by this article shall be made in the proportion that the value of the property received by each person interested in the estate bears to the total value of all property received by all persons interested in the estate, subject to the provisions of this article.

20112. (a) In making a proration of the federal estate tax, allowances shall be made for credits allowed for state or foreign death taxes in determining the federal tax payable and for exemptions and deductions allowed for the purpose of determining the taxable estate.

(b) In making a proration of the California estate tax, allowances shall be made for (1) credits (other than the credit for state death taxes paid) allowed by the federal estate tax law and attributable to property located in this state, and (2) exemptions and deductions allowed by the federal estate tax law for the purpose of determining the taxable estate attributable to property located in this state.

(c) In making a proration of an estate tax, interest on extension of taxes and interest and penalties on any deficiency shall be charged to equitably reflect the benefits and burdens of the extension or deficiency and of any tax deductions associated with the interest and penalties.

20113. If a trust is created, or other provision made whereby a person is given an interest in the income of, an estate for years or for life in, or other temporary interest in, any property, the estate tax on both the temporary interest and on the remainder thereafter shall be charged against and paid out of the corpus of the property without apportionment between remainders and temporary estates.

20114. (a) As used in this section, 'qualified real property" means qualified real property as defined in Section 2032A of the Internal Revenue Code (26 U.S.C. Sec. 2032A).

(b) If an election is made pursuant to Section 2032A of the Internal Revenue Code (26 U.S.C. Sec. 2032A), the proration shall be based upon the amount of federal estate tax that would be payable but for the election. The amount of the reduction in federal estate tax resulting from an election pursuant to Section 2032A of the Internal Revenue Code (26 U.S.C. Sec. 2032A) shall reduce the tax that is otherwise attributable to the qualified real property that is the subject of the election. If the tax that is otherwise attributable to the qualified real property is reduced to zero pursuant to this subdivision, any excess amount of reduction shall reduce the tax otherwise payable with respect to the other property, this amount to be equitably prorated in accordance with Section 20111.

(c) If additional federal estate tax is imposed under subsection (c) of Section 2032A of the Internal Revenue Code (26 U.S.C. Sec. 2032A) by reason of early disposition or cessation of qualified use, the additional tax shall be a charge against the portion of the qualified real property to which the additional tax is attributable, and shall be equitably prorated among the persons interested in that portion of the qualified real property in proportion to their interests.

20114.5. (a) As used in this section:

(1) A reference to Section 4980A of the Internal Revenue Code means Section 4980A of the federal Internal Revenue Code of 1986 as amended (26 U.S.C. Sec. 4980A) and also means former Section 4981A of the federal Internal Revenue Code of 1986.

(2) "Excess retirement accumulation" has the meaning given it in paragraph (3) of subsection (d) of Section 4980A.

(b) If the federal estate tax is increased under subsection (d) of Section 4980A of the Internal Revenue Code, the amount of the increase shall be a charge against the persons who receive the excess retirement accumulation that gives rise to the increase, and shall be equitably prorated among all persons who receive interests in qualified employer plans and individual retirement plans to which the excess retirement accumulation is attributable.

20115. Where the payment of any portion of the federal estate tax is extended under the provisions of the federal estate tax law, the amount of extended tax shall be a charge against the persons who receive the specific property that gives rise to the extension.

20116. (a) If all property does not come into the possession of the personal representative, the personal representative is entitled, and has the duty, to recover from the persons interested in the estate the proportionate amount of the estate tax with which the persons are chargeable under this chapter.

(b) If the personal representative cannot collect from any person interested in the estate the amount of an estate tax apportioned to the person, the amount not recoverable shall be equitably prorated among the other persons interested in the estate who are subject to proration.

20117. (a) If a person is charged with or required to pay an estate tax greater than the amount prorated to that person because another person does not pay the amount of estate tax prorated to the other person, the person charged with or required to pay the greater amount has a right of reimbursement against the other person.

(b) The right of reimbursement may be enforced through the personal representative in the discretion of the personal representative, or may be enforced directly by the person charged with or required to pay the greater amount, and for the purpose of direct enforcement the person is subrogated to the position of the personal representative.

(c) The personal representative or person who has a right of reimbursement may commence a proceeding to have a court determine the right of reimbursement. The provisions of Article 3 (commencing with Section 20120) shall govern the proceeding, with changes necessary to make the provisions appropriate for application to the proceeding, and the court order determining the right of reimbursement is an enforceable judgment.

Article 3. Judicial Proceedings

20120. (a) The personal representative or any person interested in the estate may commence a proceeding to have a court determine the proration pursuant to this chapter.

(b) A proceeding under this article shall be commenced in the court in which the estate of the decedent was administered or, if no administration proceedings have been commmenced, in the superior court of any county in which the estate of the decedent may be administered.

(c) If proceedings for the administration of the decedent's estate are pending, a proceeding under this article shall be combined with the administration proceedings. If a proceeding is commenced at any time before final distribution, there shall be no additional filing fee.

20121. A proceeding under this article shall be commenced by filing a petition that sets forth all of the following information:

(a) The jurisdictional facts.

(b) Other facts necessary for the court to determine the proration of estate taxes.

20122. Not less than 30 days before the hearing, the petitioner shall do both of the following:

(a) Cause notice of the hearing and a copy of the petition to be mailed to the personal representative and to each person interested in the estate against whom prorated amounts may be charged pursuant to paragraph (1) of subdivision (a) of Section 20123.

(b) Cause a summons and a copy of the petition to be served on each person interested in the estate who may be directed to make payment of prorated amounts pursuant to paragraph (2) of subdivision (a) of Section 20123. The summons shall be in the form and shall be served in the manner prescribed in Title 5 (commencing with Section 410.10) of Part 2 of the Code of Civil Procedure.

20123. (a) The court, upon making a determination as provided in this article, shall make an order:

(1) Directing the personal representative to charge the prorated amounts against the persons against whom an estate tax has been prorated insofar as the personal representative is in possession of any property or interests of the persons against whom the charge may be made.

(2) Summarily directing all other persons against whom an estate tax has been prorated to make payment of the prorated amounts to the personal representative.

(b) A court order made under this section is a judgment that may be enforced against the persons against whom an estate tax has been prorated.

20124. Upon petition by the personal representative or any person interested in the estate, the court shall modify an order made pursuant to this article whenever it appears that the amount of estate tax as actually determined is different from the amount of estate tax on which the court based the order.

20125. (a) A personal representative acting or resident in another state may commence an action in this state to recover from a person interested in the estate, who either is resident in this state or owns property in this state, the amount of the federal estate tax, or an estate tax or death duty payable to another state, apportioned to the person.

(b) The action shall be commenced in the superior court of any county in which administration of the estate of the decedent would be proper or, if none, in which any defendant resides.

(c) For purposes of the action the apportionment by the court having jurisdiction of the administration of the decedent's estate in the other state is prima facie correct.

Chapter 2. Proration Of Taxes On Generation-Skipping Transfer

Article 1. General Provisions

20200. Except where the context otherwise requires, the following definitions shall govern the construction of this chapter:

(a) "Generation-skipping transfer tax" means a tax imposed by any federal or California generation-skipping transfer tax law, now existing or hereafter enacted, and includes interest and penalties on any deficiency.

(b) "Property" means property on which a generation-skipping transfer tax is imposed.

(c) "Transferee" means any person who receives, who is deemed to receive, or who is the beneficiary of, any property.

(d) "Trustee" means any person who is a trustee within the meaning of the federal generation-skipping transfer tax law, or who is otherwise required to pay a generation-skipping transfer tax.

(e) "Value" means fair market value as determined for generation-skipping transfer tax purposes.

20201. (a) This chapter does not apply to transferees of property of a decedent who died before January 1, 1987.

(b) No inference as to the applicable law in effect before January 1, 1987, shall be drawn from the enactment of this chapter.

Article 2. Proration

20210. (a) Except as provided in subdivision (b), any generation-skipping transfer tax shall be equitably prorated among the transferees in the manner prescribed in this article.

(b) This section does not apply:

(1) To the extent the transferor in a written instrument transferring property specifically directs that the property be applied to the satisfaction of a generation-skipping transfer tax or that a generation-skipping transfer tax be prorated to the property in the manner provided in the instrument.

(2) Where federal law directs otherwise. If federal law directs the manner of proration of the federal generation-skipping transfer tax, the California generation-skipping transfer tax shall be prorated in the same manner.

20211. The proration required by this article shall be made in the proportion that the value of the property received by each transferee bears to the total value of all property received by all transferees, subject to the provisions of this article.

20212. In making a proration required by this article:

(a) Allowances shall be made for credits, exemptions, and deductions allowed for the purpose of determining the tax payable.

(b) Interest and penalties on any deficiency shall be charged to equitably reflect the benefits and burdens of the deficiency and of any tax deductions associated with the interest and penalties.

20213. If a trust is created or other provision made whereby a transferee is given an interest in income, or an estate for years or for life, or another temporary interest in property, the tax on both the temporary interest and other interests in the property shall be charged against, and paid out of, the corpus of the property without apportionment between the temporary and other interests.

20214. (a) If all property does not come into the possession of the trustee, the trustee is entitled, and has the duty, to recover from the transferees, the proportionate amount of the tax with which the transferees are chargeable under this chapter.

(b) If the trustee cannot collect from any transferee the amount of tax apportioned to the transferee, the amount not recoverable shall be equitably prorated among the other transferees who are subject to proration.

20215. (a) If a person is charged with, or required to pay, a generation-skipping transfer tax greater than the amount prorated to that person because another person does not pay the amount of generation-skipping transfer tax prorated to the other person, the person charged with or required to pay the greater amount has a right of reimbursement against the other person.

(b) The right of reimbursement may be enforced through the trustee in the discretion of the trustee, or may be enforced directly by the person charged with, or required to pay, the greater amount and, for the purpose of direct enforcement, the person is subrogated to the position of the trustee.

(c) The trustee or person who has a right of reimbursement may commence a proceeding to have a court determine the right of reimbursement. The provisions of Article 3 (commencing with Section 20220) shall govern the proceeding, with changes necessary to make the provisions appropriate for application to the proceeding, and the court order determining the right of reimbursement is an enforceable judgment.

Article 3. Judicial Proceedings

20220. (a) The trustee or any transferee may commence a proceeding to have a court determine the proration pursuant to this chapter.

(b) A proceeding under this article shall be commenced in the court in which the estate of the decedent was administered or, if no administration proceedings have been commenced, in the superior court of any county in which the estate of the decedent may be administered.

(c) If proceedings for the administration of the decedent's estate are pending, a proceeding under this article shall be combined with the administration proceedings. If a proceeding is commenced at any time before final distribution, there shall be no additional filing fee.

20221. A proceeding under this article shall be commenced by filing a petition that sets forth all of the following information:

(a) The jurisdictional facts.

(b) Other facts necessary for the court to determine the proration of the generation-skipping transfer tax.

20222. Not less than 30 days before the hearing the petitioner shall do both of the following:

(a) Cause notice of the hearing and a copy of the petition to be mailed to the trustee and each transferee against whom prorated amounts may be charged pursuant to paragraph (1) of subdivision (a) of Section 20223.

(b) Cause a summons and a copy of the petition to be served on each transferee who may be directed to make payment of prorated amounts pursuant to paragraph (2) of subdivision (a) of Section 20223. The summons shall be in the form and shall be served in the manner prescribed in Title 5 (commencing with Section 410.10) of Part 2 of the Code of Civil Procedure.

20223. (a) The court, upon making a determination as provided in this article, shall make an order:

(1) Directing the trustee to charge the prorated amounts against the transferees against whom the generation-skipping transfer tax has been prorated insofar as the trustee is in possession of any property or interests of the transferees against whom the charge may be made.

(2) Summarily directing all other transferees against whom the generation-skipping transfer tax has been prorated to make payment of the prorated amounts to the trustee.

(b) A court order made under this section is a judgment that may be enforced against the persons against whom a generation-skipping transfer tax has been prorated.

20224. Upon petition by the trustee or any transferee, the court shall modify an order made pursuant to this article whenever it appears that the amount of generation-skipping transfer tax as actually determined is different from the amount of tax on which the court based the order.

20225. (a) A trustee acting or resident in another state may commence an action in this state to recover from a transferee, who either is resident in this state or owns property in this state, the amount of the federal generation-skipping transfer tax, or a generation-skipping transfer tax payable to another state, apportioned to the person.

(b) The action shall be commenced in the superior court of any county in which administration of the estate of the decedent would be proper or, if none, in which any defendant resides.

(c) For purposes of the action an apportionment by the court having jurisdiction of the administration of the decedent's estate in the other state is prima facie correct.

Division 11. Construction Of Wills, Trusts, And Other Instruments

Part 1. Rules For Interpretation Of Instruments

Chapter 1. General Provisions

21101. Unless the provision or context otherwise requires, this part applies to a will, trust, deed, and any other instrument.

21102. (a) The intention of the transferor as expressed in the instrument controls the legal effect of the dispositions made in the instrument.

(b) The rules of construction in this part apply where the intention of the transferor is not indicated by the instrument.

(c) Nothing in this section limits the use of extrinsic evidence, to the extent otherwise authorized by law, to determine the intention of the transferor.

21103. The meaning and legal effect of a disposition in an instrument is determined by the local law of a particular state selected by the transferor in the instrument unless the application of that law is contrary to the rights of the surviving spouse to community and quasi-community property, to any other public policy of this state applicable to the disposition, or, in the case of a will, to Part 3 (commencing with Section 6500) of Division 6.

21104. As used in this part, "at-death transfer" means a transfer that is revocable during the lifetime of the transferor, but does not include a joint tenancy or joint account with right of survivorship.

21105. Except as otherwise provided in Sections 641 and 642, a will passes all property the testator owns at death, including property acquired after execution of the will.

21107. If an instrument directs the conversion of real property into money at the transferor's death, the real property and its proceeds shall be deemed personal property from the time of the transferor's death.

21108. The law of this state does not include (a) the common law rule of worthier title that a transferor cannot devise an interest to his or her own heirs or (b) a presumption or rule of interpretation that a transferor does not intend, by a transfer to his or her own heirs or next of kin, to transfer an interest to them. The meaning of a transfer of a legal or equitable interest to a transferor's own heirs or next of kin, however designated, shall be determined by the general rules applicable to the interpretation of instruments.

21109. (a) A transferee who fails to survive the transferor of an at-death transfer or until any future time required by the instrument does not take under the instrument.

(b) If it cannot be determined by clear and convincing evidence that the transferee survived until a future time required by the instrument, it is deemed that the transferee did not survive until the required future time.

21110. (a) Subject to subdivision (b), if a transferee is dead when the instrument is executed, or fails or is treated as failing to survive the transferor or until a future time required by the instrument, the issue of the deceased transferee take in the transferee's place in the manner provided in Section 240. A transferee under a class gift shall be a transferee for the purpose of this subdivision unless the transferee's death occurred before the execution of the instrument and that fact was known to the transferor when the instrument was executed.

(b) The issue of a deceased transferee do not take in the transferee's place if the instrument expresses a contrary intention or a substitute disposition. A requirement that the initial transferee survive the transferor or survive for a specified period of time after the death of the transferor constitutes a contrary intention. A requirement that the initial transferee survive until a future time that is related to the probate of the transferor's will or administration of the estate of the transferor constitutes a contrary intention.

(c) As used in this section, "transferee" means a person who is kindred of the transferor or kindred of a surviving, deceased, or former spouse of the transferor.

21111. (a) Except as provided in subdivision (b) and subject to Section 21110, if a transfer fails for any reason, the property is transferred as follows:

(1) If the transferring instrument provides for an alternative disposition in the event the transfer fails, the property is transferred according to the terms of the instrument.

(2) If the transferring instrument does not provide for an alternative disposition but does provide for the transfer of a residue, the property becomes a part of the residue transferred under the instrument.

(3) If the transferring instrument does not provide for an alternative disposition and does not provide for the transfer of a residue, or if the transfer is itself a residuary gift, the property is transferred to the decedent's estate.

(b) Subject to Section 21110, if a residuary gift or a future interest is transferred to two or more persons and the share of a transferee fails for any reason, and no alternative disposition is provided, the share passes to the other transferees in proportion to their other interest in the residuary gift or the future interest.

(c) A transfer of "all my estate" or words of similar import is a residuary gift for purposes of this section.

(d) If failure of a future interest results in an intestacy, the property passes to the heirs of the transferor determined pursuant to Section 21114.

21112. A condition in a transfer of a present or future interest that refers to a person's death "with" or "without" issue, or to a person's "having" or "leaving" issue or no issue, or a condition based on words of similar import, is construed to refer to that person's being dead at the time the transfer takes effect in enjoyment and to that person either having or not having, as the case may be, issue who are alive at the time of enjoyment.

21114. (a) If a statute or an instrument provides for transfer of a present or future interest to, or creates a present or future interest in, a designated person's "heirs," "heirs at law," "next of kin," "relatives," or "family," or words of similar import, the transfer is to the persons, including the state under Section 6800, and in the shares that would succeed to the designated person's intestate estate under the intestate succession law of the transferor's domicile, if the designated person died when the transfer is to take effect in enjoyment. If the designated person's surviving spouse is living but is remarried at the time the transfer is to take effect in enjoyment, the surviving spouse is not an heir of the designated person for purposes of this section.

(b) As used in this section, "designated person" includes the transferor.

21115. (a) Except as provided in subdivision (b), halfbloods, adopted persons, persons born out of wedlock, stepchildren, foster children, and the issue of these persons when appropriate to the class, are included in terms of class gift or relationship in accordance with the rules for determining relationship and inheritance rights for purposes of intestate succession.

(b) In construing a transfer by a transferor who is not the natural parent, a person born to the natural parent shall not be considered the child of that parent unless the person lived while a minor as a regular member of the household of the natural parent or of that parent's parent, brother, sister, spouse, or surviving spouse. In construing a transfer by a transferor who is not the adoptive parent, a person adopted by the adoptive parent shall not be considered the child of that parent unless the person lived while a minor (either before or after the adoption) as a regular member of the household of the adopting parent or of that parent's parent, brother, sister, or surviving spouse.

(c) Subdivisions (a) and (b) shall also apply in determining:

(1) Persons who would be kindred of the transferor or kindred of a surviving, deceased, or former spouse of the transferor under Section 21110.

(2) Persons to be included as issue of a deceased transferee under Section 21110.

(3) Persons who would be the transferor's or other designated person's heirs under Section 21114.

(d) The rules for determining intestate succession under this section are those in effect at the time the transfer is to take effect in enjoyment.

21117. At-death transfers are classified as follows:

(a) A specific gift is a transfer of specifically identifiable property.

(b) A general gift is a transfer from the general assets of the transferor that does not give specific property.

(c) A demonstrative gift is a general gift that specifies the fund or property from which the transfer is primarily to be made.

(d) A general pecuniary gift is a pecuniary gift within the meaning of Section 21118.

(e) An annuity is a general pecuniary gift that is payable periodically.

(f) A residuary gift is a transfer of property that remains after all specific and general gifts have been satisfied.

21118. (a) If an instrument authorizes a fiduciary to satisfy a pecuniary gift wholly or partly by distribution of property other than money, property selected for that purpose shall be valued at its fair market value on the date of distribution, unless the instrument expressly provides otherwise. If the instrument permits the fiduciary to value the property selected for distribution as of a date other than the date of distribution, then, unless the instrument expressly provides otherwise, the property selected by the fiduciary for that purpose shall fairly reflect net appreciation and depreciation (occurring between the valuation date and the date of distribution) in all of the assets from which the distribution could have been made.

(b) As used in this section, "pecuniary gift" means a transfer of property made in an instrument that either is expressly stated as a fixed dollar amount or is a dollar amount determinable by the provisions of the instrument.

Chapter 2. Ascertaining Meaning Of Language Used In The Instrument

21120. The words of an instrument are to receive an interpretation that will give every expression some effect, rather than one that will render any of the expressions inoperative. Preference is to be given to an interpretation of an instrument that will prevent intestacy or failure of a transfer, rather than one that will result in an intestacy or failure of a transfer.

21121. All parts of an instrument are to be construed in relation to each other and so as, if possible, to form a consistent whole. If the meaning of any part of an instrument is ambiguous or doubtful, it may be explained by any reference to or recital of that part in another part of the instrument.

21122. The words of an instrument are to be given their ordinary and grammatical meaning unless the intention to use them in another sense is clear and their intended meaning can be ascertained. Technical words are not necessary to give effect to a disposition in an instrument. Technical words are to be considered as having been used in their technical sense unless (a) the context clearly indicates a contrary intention or (b) it satisfactorily appears that the instrument was drawn solely by the transferor and that the transferor was unacquainted with the technical sense.

Chapter 3. Exoneration; Ademption

21131. A specific gift passes the property transferred subject to any mortgage, deed of trust, or other lien existing at the date of death, without right of exoneration, regardless of a general directive to pay debts contained in the instrument.

21132. (a) If a transferor executes an instrument that makes an at-death transfer of securities and the transferor then owned securities that meet the description in the instrument, the transfer includes additional securities owned by the transferor at death to the extent the additional securities were acquired by the transferor after the instrument was executed as a result of the transferor's ownership of the described securities and are securities of any of the following types:

(1) Securities of the same organization acquired by reason of action initiated by the organization or any successor, related, or acquiring organization, excluding any acquired by exercise of purchase options.

(2) Securities of another organization acquired as a result of a merger, consolidation, reorganization, or other distribution by the organization or any successor, related, or acquiring organization.

(3) Securities of the same organization acquired as a result of a plan of reinvestment.

(b) Distributions in cash before death with respect to a described security are not part of the transfer.

21133. A recipient of an at-death transfer of a specific gift has a right to the property specifically given, to the extent the property is owned by the transferor at the time the gift takes effect in possession or enjoyment, and all of the following:

(a) Any balance of the purchase price (together with any security agreement) owing from a purchaser to the transferor at the time the gift takes effect in possession or enjoyment by reason of sale of the property.

(b) Any amount of an eminent domain award for the taking of the property unpaid at the time the gift takes effect in possession or enjoyment.

(c) Any proceeds unpaid at the time the gift takes effect in possession or enjoyment on fire or casualty insurance on or other recovery for injury to the property.

(d) Property owned by the transferor at the time the gift takes effect in possession or enjoyment and acquired as a result of foreclosure, or obtained in lieu of foreclosure, of the security interest for a specifically given obligation.

21134. (a) Except as otherwise provided in this section, if, after the execution of the instrument of gift, specifically given property is sold, or encumbered by a deed of trust, mortgage, or other instrument, by a conservator, by an agent acting within the authority of a durable power of attorney for an incapacitated principal, or by a trustee acting for an incapacitated settlor of a trust established by the settlor as a revocable trust, the transferee of the specific gift has the right to a general pecuniary gift equal to the net sale price of the property unreduced by the payoff of any such encumbrance, or the amount of the unpaid encumbrance on the property as well as the property itself.

(b) Except as otherwise provided in this section, if an eminent domain award for the taking of specifically given property is paid to a conservator, to an agent acting within the authority of a durable power of attorney for an incapacitated principal, or to a trustee acting for an incapacitated settlor of a trust established by the settlor as a revocable trust, or if the proceeds on fire or casualty insurance on, or recovery for injury to, specifically gifted property are paid to a conservator, to an agent acting within the authority of a durable power of attorney for an incapacitated principal, or to a trustee acting for an incapacitated settlor of a trust established by the settlor as a revocable trust, the recipient of the specific gift has the right to a general pecuniary gift equal to the eminent domain award or the insurance proceeds or recovery unreduced by the payoff of any encumbrance placed on the property by the conservator, agent, or trustee, after the execution of the instrument of gift.

(c) For the purpose of the references in this section to a conservator, this section does not apply if, after the sale, mortgage, condemnation, fire, or casualty, or recovery, the conservatorship is terminated and the transferor survives the termination by one year.

(d) For the purpose of the references in this section to an agent acting with the authority of a durable power of attorney for an incapacitated principal, or to a trustee acting for an incapacitated settlor of a trust established by the settlor as a revocable trust, (1) "incapacitated principal" or "incapacitated settlor" means a principal or settlor who is an incapacitated person, (2) no adjudication of incapacity before death is necessary, and (3) the acts of an agent within the authority of a durable power of attorney are presumed to be for an incapacitated principal. However, there shall be no presumption of a settlor's incapacity concerning the acts of a trustee.

(e) The right of the transferee of the specific gift under this section shall be reduced by any right the transferee has under Section 21133.

21135. (a) Property given by a transferor during his or her lifetime to a person is treated as a satisfaction of an at-death transfer to that person in whole or in part only if one of the following conditions is satisfied:

(1) The instrument provides for deduction of the lifetime gift from the at-death transfer.

(2) The transferor declares in a contemporaneous writing that the gift is in satisfaction of the at-death transfer or that its value is to be deducted from the value of the at-death transfer.

(3) The transferee acknowledges in writing that the gift is in satisfaction of the at-death transfer or that its value is to be deducted from the value of the at-death transfer.

(4) The property given is the same property that is the subject of a specific gift to that person.

(b) Subject to subdivision (c), for the purpose of partial satisfaction, property given during lifetime is valued as of the time the transferee came into possession or enjoyment of the property or as of the time of death of the transferor, whichever occurs first.

(c) If the value of the gift is expressed in the contemporaneous writing of the transferor, or in an acknowledgment of the transferee made contemporaneously with the gift, that value is conclusive in the division and distribution of the estate.

(d) If the transferee fails to survive the transferor, the gift is treated as a full or partial satisfaction of the gift, as the case may be, in applying Sections 21110 and 21111 unless the transferor's contemporaneous writing provides otherwise.

21139. The rules stated in Sections 21133 to 21135, inclusive, are not exhaustive, and nothing in those sections is intended to increase the incidence of ademption under the law of this state.

Chapter 4. Effective Dates

21140. This part applies to all instruments, regardless of when they were executed.

Part 2. Perpetuities

Chapter 1. Uniform Statutory Rule Against Perpetuities

Article 1. General Provisions

21200. This chapter shall be known and may be cited as the Uniform Statutory Rule Against Perpetuities.

21201. This chapter supersedes the common law rule against perpetuities.

21202. (a) Except as provided in subdivision (b), this part applies to nonvested property interests and unexercised powers of appointment regardless of whether they were created before, on, or after January 1, 1992.

(b) This part does not apply to any property interest or power of appointment the validity of which has been determined in a judicial proceeding or by a settlement among interested persons.

Article 2. Statutory Rule Against Perpetuities

21205. A nonvested property interest is invalid unless one of the following conditions is satisfied:

(a) When the interest is created, it is certain to vest or terminate no later than 21 years after the death of an individual then alive.

(b) The interest either vests or terminates within 90 years after its creation.

21206. A general power of appointment not presently exercisable because of a condition precedent is invalid unless one of the following conditions is satisfied:

(a) When the power is created, the condition precedent is certain to be satisfied or become impossible to satisfy no later than 21 years after the death of an individual then alive.

(b) The condition precedent either is satisfied or becomes impossible to satisfy within 90 years after its creation.

21207. A nongeneral power of appointment or a general testamentary power of appointment is invalid unless one of the following conditions is satisfied:

(a) When the power is created, it is certain to be irrevocably exercised or otherwise to terminate no later than 21 years after the death of an individual then alive.

(b) The power is irrevocably exercised or otherwise terminates within 90 years after its creation.

21208. In determining whether a nonvested property interest or a power of appointment is valid under this article, the possibility that a child will be born to an individual after the individual's death is disregarded.

21209. (a) If, in measuring a period from the creation of a trust or other property arrangement, language in a governing instrument (1) seeks to disallow the vesting or termination of any interest or trust beyond, (2) seeks to postpone the vesting or termination of any interest or trust until, or (3) seeks to operate in effect in any similar fashion upon, the later of (A) the expiration of a period of time not exceeding 21 years after the death of the survivor of specified lives in being at the creation of the trust or other property arrangement or (B) the expiration of a period of time that exceeds or might exceed 21 years after the death of the survivor of lives in being at the creation of the trust or other property arrangement, that language is inoperative to the extent it produces a period that exceeds 21 years after the death of the survivor of the specified lives.

(b) Notwithstanding Section 21202, this section applies only to governing instruments, including instruments exercising powers of appointment, executed on or after January 1, 1992.

Article 3. Time Of Creation Of Interest

21210. Except as provided in Sections 21211 and 21212, the time of creation of a nonvested property interest or a power of appointment is determined by other applicable statutes or, if none, under general principles of property law.

21211. For purposes of this chapter:

(a) If there is a person who alone can exercise a power created by a governing instrument to become the unqualified beneficial owner of (1) a nonvested property interest or (2) a property interest subject to a power of appointment described in Section 21206 or 21207, the nonvested property interest or power of appointment is created when the power to become the unqualified beneficial owner terminates.

(b) A joint power with respect to community property held by individuals married to each other is a power exercisable by one person alone.

21212. For purposes of this chapter, a nonvested property interest or a power of appointment arising from a transfer of property to a previously funded trust or other existing property arrangement is created when the nonvested property interest or power of appointment in the original contribution was created.

Article 4. Reformation

21220. On petition of an interested person, a court shall reform a disposition in the manner that most closely approximates the transferor's manifested plan of distribution and is within the 90 years allowed by the applicable provision in Article 2 (commencing with Section 21205), if any of the following conditions is satisfied:

(a) A nonvested property interest or a power of appointment becomes invalid under the statutory rule against perpetuities provided in Article 2 (commencing with Section 21205).

(b) A class gift is not but might become invalid under the statutory rule against perpetuities provided in Article 2 (commencing with Section 21205), and the time has arrived when the share of any class member is to take effect in possession or enjoyment.

(c) A nonvested property interest that is not validated by subdivision (a) of Section 21205 can vest but not within 90 years after its creation.

Article 5. Exclusions From Statutory Rule Against Perpetuities

21225. Article 2 (commencing with Section 21205) does not apply to any of the following:

(a) A nonvested property interest or a power of appointment arising out of a nondonative transfer, except a nonvested property interest or a power of appointment arising out of (1) a premarital or postmarital agreement, (2) a separation or divorce settlement, (3) a spouse's election, (4) or a similar arrangement arising out of a prospective, existing, or previous marital relationship between the parties, (5) a contract to make or not to revoke a will or trust, (6) a contract to exercise or not to exercise a power of appointment, (7) a transfer in satisfaction of a duty of support, or (8) a reciprocal transfer.

(b) A fiduciary's power relating to the administration or management of assets, including the power of a fiduciary to sell, lease, or mortgage property, and the power of a fiduciary to determine principal and income.

(c) A power to appoint a fiduciary.

(d) A discretionary power of a trustee to distribute principal before termination of a trust to a beneficiary having an indefeasibly vested interest in the income and principal.

(e) A nonvested property interest held by a charity, government, or governmental agency or subdivision, if the nonvested property interest is preceded by an interest held by another charity, government, or governmental agency or subdivision.

(f) A nonvested property interest in or a power of appointment with respect to a trust or other property arrangement forming part of a pension, profit-sharing, stock bonus, health, disability, death benefit, income deferral, or other current or deferred benefit plan for one or more employees, independent contractors, or their beneficiaries or spouses, to which contributions are made for the purpose of distributing to or for the benefit of the participants or their beneficiaries or spouses the property, income, or principal in the trust or other property arrangement, except a nonvested property interest or a power of appointment that is created by an election of a participant or a beneficiary or spouse.

(g) A property interest, power of appointment, or arrangement that was not subject to the common law rule against perpetuities or is excluded by another statute of this state.

(h) A trust created for the purpose of providing for its beneficiaries under hospital service contracts, group life insurance, group disability insurance, group annuities, or any combination of such insurance, as defined in the Insurance Code.

Chapter 2. Related Provisions

21230. The lives of individuals selected to govern the time of vesting pursuant to Article 2 (commencing with Section 21205) of Chapter 1 may not be so numerous or so situated that evidence of their deaths is likely to be unreasonably difficult to obtain.

21231. In determining the validity of a nonvested property interest pursuant to Article 2 (commencing with Section 21205) of Chapter 1, an individual described as the spouse of an individual alive at the commencement of the perpetuities period shall be deemed to be an individual alive when the interest is created, whether or not the individual so described was then alive.

Part 3. No Contest Clause

21310. As used in this part:

(a) "Contest" means a pleading filed with the court by a beneficiary that would result in a penalty under a no contest clause, if the no contest clause is enforced.

(b) "Direct contest" means a contest that alleges the invalidity of a protected instrument or one or more of its terms, based on one or more of the following grounds:

(1) Forgery.

(2) Lack of due execution.

(3) Lack of capacity.

(4) Menace, duress, fraud, or undue influence.

(5) Revocation of a will pursuant to Section 6120, revocation of a trust pursuant to Section 15401, or revocation of an instrument other than a will or trust pursuant to the procedure for revocation that is provided by statute or by the instrument.

(6) Disqualification of a beneficiary under Section 6112, 21350, or 21380.

(c) "No contest clause" means a provision in an otherwise valid instrument that, if enforced, would penalize a beneficiary for filing a pleading in any court.

(d) "Pleading" means a petition, complaint, cross-complaint, objection, answer, response, or claim.

(e) "Protected instrument" means all of the following instruments:

(1) The instrument that contains the no contest clause.

(2) An instrument that is in existence on the date that the instrument containing the no contest clause is executed and is express-ly identified in the no contest clause, either individually or as part of an identifiable class of instruments, as being governed by the no contest clause.

21311. (a) A no contest clause shall only be enforced against the following types of contests:

(1) A direct contest that is brought without probable cause.

(2) A pleading to challenge a transfer of property on the grounds that it was not the transferor's property at the time of the transfer. A no contest clause shall only be enforced under this paragraph if the no contest clause expressly provides for that application.

(3) The filing of a creditor's claim or prosecution of an action based on it. A no contest clause shall only be enforced under this paragraph if the no contest clause expressly provides for that application.

(b) For the purposes of this section, probable cause exists if, at the time of filing a contest, the facts known to the contestant would cause a reasonable person to believe that there is a reasonable likelihood that the requested relief will be granted after an opportunity for further investigation or discovery.

21312. In determining the intent of the transferor, a no contest clause shall be strictly construed.

21313. This part is not intended as a complete codification of the law governing enforcement of a no contest clause. The common law governs enforcement of a no contest clause to the extent this part does not apply.

21314. This part applies notwithstanding a contrary provision in the instrument.

21315. (a) This part applies to any instrument, whenever executed, that became irrevocable on or after January 1, 2001.

(b) This part does not apply to an instrument that became irrevocable before January 1, 2001.

Part 3.7. Presumption Of Fraud Or Undue Influence

Chapter 1. Definitions

21360. The definitions in this chapter govern the construction of this part.

21362. (a) "Care custodian" means a person who provides health or social services to a dependent adult, except that "care custodian" does not include a person who provided services without remuneration if the person had a personal relationship with the dependent adult (1) at least 90 days before providing those services, (2) at least six months before the dependent adult's death, and (3) before the dependant adult was admitted to hospice care, if the dependent adult was admitted to hospice care. As used in this subdivision, "remuneration" does not include the donative transfer at issue under this chapter or the reimbursement of expenses.

(b) For the purposes of this section, "health and social services" means services provided to a dependent adult because of the person's dependent condition, including, but not limited to, the administration of medicine, medical testing, wound care, assistance with hygiene, companionship, housekeeping, shopping, cooking, and assistance with finances.

21364. "Cohabitant" has the meaning provided in Section 13700 of the Penal Code.

21366. "Dependent adult" means a person who, at the time of executing the instrument at issue under this part, was a person described in either of the following:

(a) The person was 65 years of age or older and satisfied one or both of the following criteria:

(1) The person was unable to provide properly for his or her personal needs for physical health, food, clothing, or shelter.

(2) Due to one or more deficits in the mental functions listed in paragraphs (1) to (4), inclusive, of subdivision (a) of Section 811, the person had difficulty managing his or her own financial resources or resisting fraud or undue influence.

(b) The person was 18 years of age or older and satisfied one or both of the following criteria:

(1) The person was unable to provide properly for his or her personal needs for physical health, food, clothing, or shelter.

(2) Due to one or more deficits in the mental functions listed in paragraphs (1) to (4), inclusive, of subdivision (a) of Section 811, the person had substantial difficulty managing his or her own financial resources or resisting fraud or undue influence.

21368. "Domestic partner" has the meaning provided in Section 297 of the Family Code.

21370. "Independent attorney" means an attorney who has no legal, business, financial, professional, or personal relationship with the beneficiary of a donative transfer at issue under this part, and who would not be appointed as a fiduciary or receive any pecuniary benefit as a result of the operation of the instrument containing the donative transfer at issue under this part.

21374. (a) A person who is "related by blood or affinity" to a specified person means any of the following persons:

(1) A spouse or domestic partner of the specified person.

(2) A relative within a specified degree of kinship to the specified person or within a specified degree of kinship to the spouse or domestic partner of the specified person.

(3) The spouse or domestic partner of a person described in paragraph (2).

(b) For the purposes of this section, "spouse or domestic partner" includes a predeceased spouse or predeceased domestic partner.

(c) In determining a relationship under this section, Sections 6406 and 6407, and Chapter 2 (commencing with Section 6450) of Part 2 of Division 6, are applicable.

Chapter 2. Operation And Effect Of Presumption

21380. (a) A provision of an instrument making a donative transfer to any of the following persons is presumed to be the product of fraud or undue influence:

(1) The person who drafted the instrument.

(2) A person in a fiduciary relationship with the transferor who transcribed the instrument or caused it to be transcribed.

(3) A care custodian of a transferor who is a dependent adult, but only if the instrument was executed during the period in which the care custodian provided services to the transferor, or within 90 days before or after that period.

(4) A person who is related by blood or affinity, within the third degree, to any person described in paragraphs (1) to (3), inclusive.

(5) A cohabitant or employee of any person described in paragraphs (1) to (3), inclusive.

(6) A partner, shareholder, or employee of a law firm in which a person described in paragraph (1) or (2) has an ownership interest.

(b) The presumption created by this section is a presumption affecting the burden of proof. The presumption may be rebutted by proving, by clear and convincing evidence, that the donative transfer was not the product of fraud or undue influence.

(c) Notwithstanding subdivision (b), with respect to a donative transfer to the person who drafted the donative instrument, or to a person who is related to, or associated with, the drafter as described in paragraph (4), (5), or (6) of subdivision (a), the presumption created by this section is conclusive.

(d) If a beneficiary is unsuccessful in rebutting the presumption, the beneficiary shall bear all costs of the proceeding, including reasonable attorney's fees.

21382. Section 21380 does not apply to any of the following instruments or transfers:

(a) A donative transfer to a person who is related by blood or affinity, within the fourth degree, to the transferor or is the cohabitant of the transferor.

(b) An instrument that is drafted or transcribed by a person who is related by blood or affinity, within the fourth degree, to the transferor or is the cohabitant of the transferor.

(c) An instrument that is approved pursuant to an order under Article 10 (commencing with Section 2580) of Chapter 6 of Part 4 of Division 4, after full disclosure of the relationships of the persons involved.

(d) A donative transfer to a federal, state, or local public entity, an entity that qualifies for an exemption from taxation under Section 501(c)(3) or 501(c)(19) of the Internal Revenue Code, or a trust holding the transferred property for the entity.

(e) A donative transfer of property valued at five thousand dollars ($5,000) or less, if the total value of the transferor's estate equals or exceeds the amount stated in Section 13100.

(f) An instrument executed outside of California by a transferor who was not a resident of California when the instrument was executed.

21384. (a) A gift is not subject to Section 21380 if the instrument is reviewed by an independent attorney who counsels the transferor, out of the presence of any heir or proposed beneficiary, about the nature and consequences of the intended transfer, including the effect of the intended transfer on the transferor's heirs and on any beneficiary of a prior donative instrument, attempts to determine if the intended transfer is the result of fraud or undue influence, and signs and delivers to the transferor an original certificate in substantially the following form:

PLEASE SEE THE APPENDIX

(b) An attorney whose written engagement, signed by the transferor, is expressly limited solely to compliance with the requirements of this section, shall not be considered to otherwise represent the transferor as a client.

(c) An attorney who drafts an instrument can review and certify the same instrument pursuant to this section, but only as to a gift to a care custodian. In all other circumstances, an attorney who drafts an instrument may not review and certify the instrument.

(d) If the certificate is prepared by an attorney other than the attorney who drafted the instrument that is under review, a copy of the signed certification shall be provided to the drafting attorney.

21386. If a gift fails under this part, the instrument making the gift shall operate as if the beneficiary had predeceased the transferor without spouse, domestic partner, or issue.

21388. (a) A person is not liable for transferring property pursuant to an instrument that is subject to the presumption created under this part, unless the person is served with notice, prior to transferring the property, that the instrument has been contested under this part.

(b) A person who is served with notice that an instrument has been contested under this part is not liable for failing to transfer property pursuant to the instrument, unless the person is served with notice that the validity of the transfer has been conclusively determined by a court.

21390. This part applies notwithstanding a contrary provision in an instrument.

21392. (a) This part shall apply to instruments that become irrevocable on or after January 1, 2011. For the purposes of this section, an instrument that is otherwise revocable or amendable shall be deemed to be irrevocable if, on or after January 1, 2011, the transferor by reason of incapacity was unable to change the disposition of the transferor's property and did not regain capacity before the date of the transferor's death.

(b) It is the intent of the Legislature that this part supplement the common law on undue influence, without superseding or interfering in the operation of that law. Nothing in this part precludes an action to contest a donative transfer under the common law or under any other applicable law. This subdivision is declarative of existing law.

Part 4. Abatement

21400. Notwithstanding any other provision of this part, if the instrument provides for abatement, or if the transferor's plan or if the purpose of the transfer would be defeated by abatement as provided in this part, the shares of beneficiaries abate as is necessary to effectuate the instrument, plan, or purpose.

21401. Except as provided in Sections 21612 (omitted spouse) and 21623 (omitted children) and in Division 10 (commencing with Section 20100) (proration of taxes), shares of beneficiaries abate as provided in this part for all purposes, including payment of the debts, expenses, and charges specified in Section 11420, satisfaction of gifts, and payment of expenses on specifically devised property pursuant to Section 12002, and without any priority as between real and personal property.

21402. (a) Shares of beneficiaries abate in the following order:

(1) Property not disposed of by the instrument.

(2) Residuary gifts.

(3) General gifts to persons other than the transferor's relatives.

(4) General gifts to the transferor's relatives.

(5) Specific gifts to persons other than the transferor's relatives.

(6) Specific gifts to the transferor's relatives.

(b) For purposes of this section, a "relative" of the transferor is a person to whom property would pass from the transferor under Section 6401 or 6402 (intestate succession) if the transferor died intestate and there were no other person having priority.

21403. (a) Subject to subdivision (b), shares of beneficiaries abate pro rata within each class specified in Section 21402.

(b) Gifts of annuities and demonstrative gifts are treated as specific gifts to the extent they are satisfied out of the fund or property specified in the gift and as general gifts to the extent they are satisfied out of property other than the fund or property specified in the gift.

21404. If an instrument requires property that is the subject of a specific gift to be exonerated from a mortgage, deed of trust, or other lien, a specific gift of other property does not abate for the purpose of exonerating the encumbered property.

21405. (a) In any case in which there is abatement when a distribution is made during estate administration, the court shall fix the amount each distributee must contribute for abatement. The personal representative shall reduce the distributee's share by that amount.

(b) If a specific gift must be abated, the beneficiary of the specific gift may satisfy the contribution for abatement out of the beneficiary's property other than the property that is the subject of the specific gift.

21406. (a) This part does not apply to a gift made before July 1, 1989. In the case of a gift made before July 1, 1989, the law that would have applied had this part not been enacted shall apply.

(b) For purposes of this section a gift by will is made on the date of the decedent's death.

Part 5. Compliance With Internal Revenue Code

Chapter 1. General Provisions

21500. As used in this part, "Internal Revenue Code" means the Internal Revenue Code of 1986, as amended from time to time. A reference to a provision of the Internal Revenue Code includes any subsequent provision of law enacted in its place.

21501. (a) This part applies to a distribution made on or after January 1, 1988, whether the transferor died before, on, or after that date.

(b) A distribution made on or after January 1, 1983, and before January 1, 1988, is governed by the applicable law in effect before January 1, 1988.

21502. (a) This part does not apply to an instrument the terms of which expressly or by necessary implication make this part inapplicable.

(b) By an appropriate statement made in an instrument, the transferor may incorporate by reference any or all of the provisions of this part. The effect of incorporating a provision of this part in an instrument is to make the incorporated provision a part of the instrument as though the language of the incorporated provision were set forth verbatim in the instrument. Unless an instrument incorporating a provision of this part provides otherwise, the instrument automatically incorporates the provision's amendments.

21503. (a) If an instrument includes a formula intended to eliminate the federal estate tax, the formula shall be applied to eliminate or to reduce to the maximum extent possible the federal estate tax.

(b) If an instrument includes a formula that refers to a maximum fraction or amount that will not result in a federal estate tax, the formula shall be construed to refer to the maximum fraction or amount that will not result in or increase the federal estate tax.

Chapter 2. Marital Deduction Gifts

21520. As used in this chapter:

(a) "Marital deduction" means the federal estate tax deduction allowed for transfers under Section 2056 of the Internal Revenue Code or the federal gift tax deduction allowed for transfers under Section 2523 of the Internal Revenue Code.

(b) "Marital deduction gift" means a transfer of property that is intended to qualify for the marital deduction.

21521. Sections 21524 and 21526 do not apply to a trust that qualifies for the marital deduction under Section 20.2056(e)-2(b) of the Code of Federal Regulations (commonly referred to as the "estate trust").

21522. If an instrument contains a marital deduction gift:

(a) The provisions of the instrument, including any power, duty, or discretionary authority given to a fiduciary, shall be construed to comply with the marital deduction provisions of the Internal Revenue Code.

(b) The fiduciary shall not take any action or have any power that impairs the deduction as applied to the marital deduction gift.

(c) The marital deduction gift may be satisfied only with property that qualifies for the marital deduction.

21523. (a) The Economic Recovery Tax Act of 1981 was enacted August 13, 1981. This section applies to an instrument executed before September 12, 1981 (before 30 days after enactment of the Economic Recovery Tax Act of 1981).

(b) If an instrument described in subdivision (a) indicates the transferor's intention to make a gift that will provide the maximum allowable marital deduction, the instrument passes to the recipient an amount equal to the maximum amount of the marital deduction that would have been allowed as of the date of the gift under federal law as it existed before enactment of the Economic Recovery Tax Act of 1981, with adjustments for the following, if applicable:

(1) The provisions of Section 2056(c)(1) (B) and (C) of the Internal Revenue Code in effect immediately before enactment of the Economic Recovery Tax Act of 1981.

(2) To reduce the amount passing under the gift by the final federal estate tax values of any other property that passes under or outside of the instrument and qualifies

for the marital deduction. This subdivision does not apply to qualified terminable interest property under Section 2056(b)(7) of the Internal Revenue Code.

21524. If a marital deduction gift is made in trust, in addition to the other provisions of this chapter, each of the following provisions also applies to the marital deduction trust:

(a) The transferor's spouse is the only beneficiary of income or principal of the marital deduction property as long as the spouse is alive. Nothing in this subdivision precludes exercise by the transferor's spouse of a power of appointment included in a trust that qualifies as a general power of appointment marital deduction trust.

(b) Subject to subdivision (d), the transferor's spouse is entitled to all of the income of the marital deduction property not less frequently than annually, as long as the spouse is alive.

(c) The transferor's spouse has the right to require that the trustee of the trust make unproductive marital deduction property productive or to convert it into productive property within a reasonable time.

(d) Notwithstanding Section 16347, in the case of qualified terminable interest property under Section 2056(b)(7) or Section 2523 (f) of the Internal Revenue Code, on termination of the interest of the transferor's spouse in the trust all of the remaining accrued or undistributed income shall pass to the estate of the transferor's spouse, unless the instrument provides a different disposition that qualifies for the marital deduction.

21525. (a) If an instrument that makes a marital deduction gift includes a condition that the transferor's spouse survive the transferor by a period that exceeds or may exceed six months, other than a condition described in subdivision (b), the condition shall be limited to six months as applied to the marital deduction gift.

(b) If an instrument that makes a marital deduction gift includes a condition that the transferor's spouse survive a common disaster that results in the death of the transferor, the condition shall be limited to the time of the final audit of the federal estate tax return for the transferor's estate, if any, as applied to the marital deduction gift.

(c) The amendment of subdivision (a) made by Chapter 113 of the Statutes of 1988 is declaratory of, and not a change in, either existing law or former Section 1036 (repealed by Chapter 923 of the Statutes of 1987).

21526. A fiduciary is not liable for a good faith decision to make any election, or not to make any election, referred to in Section 2056(b)(7) or Section 2523(f) of the Internal Revenue Code.

Chapter 3. Charitable Gifts

21540. If an instrument indicates the transferor's intention to comply with the Internal Revenue Code requirements for a charitable remainder unitrust or a charitable remainder annuity trust as each is defined in Section 664 of the Internal Revenue Code, the provisions of the instrument, including any power, duty, or discretionary authority given to a fiduciary, shall be construed to comply with the charitable deduction provisions of Section 2055 or Section 2522 of the Internal Revenue Code and the charitable remainder trust provisions of Section 664 of the Internal Revenue Code in order to conform to that intent. In no event shall the fiduciary take an action or have a power that impairs the charitable deduction. The provisions of the instrument may be augmented in any manner consistent with Section 2055(e) or Section 2522(c) of the Internal Revenue Code on a petition provided for in Section 17200.

21541. If an instrument indicates the transferor's intention to comply with the requirements for a charitable lead trust as described in Section 170(f)(2)(B) and Section 2055(e)(2) or Section 2522(c)(2) of the Internal Revenue Code, the provisions of the instrument, including any power, duty, or discretionary authority given to a fiduciary, shall be construed to comply with the provisions of that section in order to conform to that intent. In no event shall the fiduciary take any action or have any power that impairs the charitable deduction. The provisions of the instrument may be augmented in any manner consistent with that intent upon a petition provided for in Section 17200.

Part 6. Family Protection: Omitted Spouses And Children

Chapter 1. General Provisions

21600. This part shall apply to property passing by will through a decedent's estate or by a trust, as defined in Section 82, that becomes irrevocable only on the death of the settlor.

21601. (a) For purposes of this part, "decedent's testamentary instruments" means the decedent's will or revocable trust.

(b) "Estate" as used in this part shall include a decedent's probate estate and all property held in any revocable trust that becomes irrevocable on the death of the decedent.

Chapter 2. Omitted Spouses

21610. Except as provided in Section 21611, if a decedent fails to provide in a testamentary instrument for the decedent's surviving spouse who married the decedent after the execution of all of the decedent's testamentary instruments, the omitted spouse shall receive a share in the decedent's estate, consisting of the following property in said estate:

(a) The one-half of the community property that belongs to the decedent under Section 100.

(b) The one-half of the quasi-community property that belongs to the decedent under Section 101.

(c) A share of the separate property of the decedent equal in value to that which the spouse would have received if the decedent had died without having executed a testamentary instrument, but in no event is the share to be more than one-half the value of the separate property in the estate.

21611. The spouse shall not receive a share of the estate under Section 21610 if any of the following is established:

(a) The decedent's failure to provide for the spouse in the decedent's testamentary instruments was intentional and that intention appears from the testamentary instruments.

(b) The decedent provided for the spouse by transfer outside of the estate passing by the decedent's testamentary instruments and the intention that the transfer be in lieu of a provision in said instruments is shown by statements of the decedent or from the amount of the transfer or by other evidence.

(c) The spouse made a valid agreement waiving the right to share in the decedent's estate.

21612. (a) Except as provided in subdivision (b), in satisfying a share provided by this chapter:

(1) The share will first be taken from the decedent's estate not disposed of by will or trust, if any.

(2) If that is not sufficient, so much as may be necessary to satisfy the share shall be taken from all beneficiaries of decedent's testamentary instruments in proportion to the value they may respectively receive. The proportion of each beneficiary's share that may be taken pursuant to this subdivision shall be determined based on values as of the date of the decedent's death.

(b) If the obvious intention of the decedent in relation to some specific gift or devise or other provision of a testamentary instrument would be defeated by the application of subdivision (a), the specific devise or gift or provision may be exempted from the apportionment under subdivision (a), and a different apportionment, consistent with the intention of the decedent, may be adopted.

Chapter 3. Omitted Children

21620. Except as provided in Section 21621, if a decedent fails to provide in a testamentary instrument for a child of decedent born or adopted after the execution of all of the decedent's testamentary instruments, the omitted child shall receive a share in the decedent' s estate equal in value to that which the child would have received if the decedent had died without having executed any testamentary instrument.

21621. A child shall not receive a share of the estate under Section 21620 if any of the following is established:

(a) The decedent's failure to provide for the child in the decedent's testamentary instruments was intentional and that intention appears from the testamentary instruments.

(b) The decedent had one or more children and devised or otherwise directed the disposition of substantially all the estate to the other parent of the omitted child.

(c) The decedent provided for the child by transfer outside of the estate passing by the decedent's testamentary instruments and the intention that the transfer be in lieu of a provision in said instruments is show by statements of the decedent or from the amount of the transfer or by other evidence.

21622. If, at the time of the execution of all of decedent's testamentary instruments effective at the time of decedent's death, the decedent failed to provide for a living child solely because the decedent believed the child to be dead or was unaware of the birth of the child, the child shall receive a share in the estate equal in value to that which the child would have received if the decedent had died without having executed any testamentary instruments.

21623. (a) Except as provided in subdivision (b), in satisfying a share provided by this chapter:

(1) The share will first be taken from the decedent's estate not disposed of by will or trust, if any.

(2) If that is not sufficient, so much as may be necessary to satisfy the share shall be taken from all beneficiaries of decedent's testamentary instruments in proportion to the value they may respectively receive. The proportion of each beneficiary's share that may be taken pursuant to this subdivision shall be determined based on values as of the date of the decedent's death.

(b) If the obvious intention of the decedent in relation to some specific gift or devise or other provision of a testamentary instrument would be defeated by the application of subdivision (a), the specific devise or gift or provision of a testamentary instrument may be exempted from the apportionment under subdivision (a), and a different apportionment, consistent with the intention of the decedent, may be adopted.

Chapter 4. Applicability

21630. This part does not apply if the decedent died before January 1, 1998. The law applicable prior to January 1, 1998, applies if the decedent died before January 1, 1998.

Part 7. Contracts Regarding Testamentary Or Intestate Succession

21700. (a) A contract to make a will or devise or other instrument, or not to revoke a will or devise or other instrument, or to die intestate, if made after the effective date of this statute, can be established only by one of the following:

(1) Provisions of a will or other instrument stating the material provisions of the contract.

(2) An expressed reference in a will or other instrument to a contract and extrinsic evidence proving the terms of the contract.

(3) A writing signed by the decedent evidencing the contract.

(4) Clear and convincing evidence of an agreement between the decedent and the claimant or a promise by the decedent to the claimant that is enforceable in equity.

(5) Clear and convincing evidence of an agreement between the decedent and another person for the benefit of the claimant or a promise by the decedent to another person for the benefit of the claimant that is enforceable in equity.

(b) The execution of a joint will or mutual wills does not create a presumption of a contract not to revoke the will or wills.

(c) A contract to make a will or devise or other instrument, or not to revoke a will or devise or other instrument, or to die intestate, if made prior to the effective date of this section, shall be construed under the law applicable to the contract prior to the effective date of this section.

Appendix: Forms Referenced in Code

§ 715 Form

NOTICE AND ACKNOWLEDGMENT

To: _____ (Name of depositor)

_____ (Address)

_____ (City, state, and ZIP)

I have accepted your will or other estate planning document for safekeeping. I must use ordinary care for preservation of the document.

You must keep me advised of any change in your address shown above. If you do not and I cannot return this document to you when necessary, I will no longer be required to use ordinary care for preservation of the document, and I may transfer it to another attorney, or I may transfer it to the clerk of the superior court of the county of your last known domicile, and give notice of the transfer to the State Bar of California.

_____

(Signature of attorney)

_____

(Address of attorney)

_____

(City, state, ZIP)

My address shown above is correct. I understand that I must keep you advised of any change in this address.

Dated: _____

_____

(Signature of depositor)

§ 1061 Form

SUMMARY OF ACCOUNT

CHARGES:

Property on hand at beginning of account (or Inventories) $ _____

Additional property received (or Supplemental Inventories)   _____

Receipts (Schedule _____)   _____

Gains on Sale or Other Disposition (Schedule _____)   _____

Net income from trade or business (Schedule _____)   _____

Total Charges: $ _____

CREDITS:

Disbursements (Schedule _____)   _____

Losses on Sale or Other Disposition (Schedule _____)   _____

Net loss from trade or business (Schedule _____)   _____

Distributions (Schedule _____)   _____

Property on hand at close of account (Schedule _____)   _____

Total Credits: $_____

❦ ～ ❧

§ 1211 Form

SUPERIOR
COURT
OF THE STATE OF
CALIFORNIA
FOR THE (CITY AND) COUNTY OF _____

Estate of   No. _____

_____

NOTICE OF HEARING

(If to be published, describe purport or character of the notice to be given.)

Notice is hereby given that (name of petitioner and representative capacity, if any) has filed   herein a (nature of petition, application, report, or account), reference to which is made for further particulars, and that the time and place of hearing the same has been set for _____ (date) _____, at _____.m., in the courtroom (of Department No. _____, if any) of said court, at (the courthouse, or state other location of the court), in the City of _____, California.

Dated _____

_____, Clerk

By _____, Deputy Clerk

§ 2901 Form

CERTIFICATE OF AUTHORITY

THIS IS AN OFFICIAL CERTIFICATE ENTITLING THE PUBLIC GUARDIAN
TO TAKE POSSESSION OF ANY AND ALL PROPERTY BELONGING TO THE
FOLLOWING INDIVIDUAL:

(Name of Individual) _____

This Certificate of Authority has been issued by the Public Guardian pursuant to and in compliance with Chapter 1 (commencing with Section 2900) of Part 5 of Division 4 of the California Probate Code. Under California law, this Certificate of Authority authorizes the Public Guardian to take possession or control of property belonging to the above-named individual.

SPECIAL NOTE TO FINANCIAL INSTITUTIONS:

State law requires that upon receiving a copy of this Certificate of Authority, financial institutions shall provide the public guardian with information concerning property held by the above-named individual and surrender the property to the Public Guardian if requested.

This Certificate of Authority shall only be valid when signed and dated by the Public Guardian or a deputy Public Guardian of the County of _____ and affixed with the official seal of the Public Guardian below.

This Certificate of Authority expires 30 days after the date of issuance.

Signature of Public Guardian: _____

Date: _____

Official Seal

❦ ⁓ ❦

§ 2901.5 Form

CERTIFICATE OF AUTHORITY

THIS IS AN OFFICIAL CERTIFICATE ENTITLING THE PUBLIC GUARDIAN/
PUBLIC CONSERVATOR TO RESTRAIN ANY PERSON FROM TRANSFERRING,
ENCUMBERING, OR IN ANY WAY DISPOSING OF ANY REAL OR PERSONAL
PROPERTY HELD IN THE FOLLOWING TRUST:

(Name of Trust) _____

THE PUBLIC GUARDIAN/PUBLIC CONSERVATOR HAS DETERMINED THAT
IT HAS AUTHORITY TO ISSUE THIS CERTIFICATE WITH RESPECT TO THE
ABOVE-NAMED TRUST AND IN CONNECTION WITH PROCEEDINGS THAT ARE
OR WILL BE PENDING RELATED TO THE FOLLOWING INDIVIDUAL:

(Name of Individual) _____

This Certificate of Authority has been issued by the Public Guardian/Public Conservator pursuant to and in compliance with Chapter 1 (commencing with Section 2900) of Part 5 of Division 4 of the California Probate Code. Under California law, this Certificate of Authority authorizes the Public Guardian/Public Conservator to restrain any person from transferring, encumbering, or in any way disposing of any real or personal property held in the above-named trust.

SPECIAL NOTE TO FINANCIAL INSTITUTIONS:

State law requires that, upon receiving a copy of this Certificate of Authority, financial institutions shall provide the public guardian/public conservator with information concerning property held in the above-named trust and shall restrain any person from transferring, encumbering, or in any way disposing of any real or personal property held in the above-named trust.

This Certificate of Authority shall only be valid when signed and dated by the Public Guardian/Public Conservator or a deputy Public Guardian/Public Conservator of the County of _____ and affixed with the official seal of the Public Guardian/Public Conservator below.

This Certificate of Authority expires 30 days after the date of issuance.

Signature of Public Guardian/Public Conservator: _____

Date: _____

Official Seal

§ 2952 Form

CERTIFICATE OF AUTHORITY

THIS IS AN OFFICIAL CERTIFICATE ENTITLING THE PUBLIC GUARDIAN TO TAKE POSSESSION OF ANY AND ALL PROPERTY BELONGING TO THE FOLLOWING INDIVIDUAL:

(Name of Victim) _____

This Certificate of Authority has been issued by the Public Guardian pursuant to and in compliance with the Financial Abuse of Mentally Impaired Elders statute, Chapter 4 (commencing with Section 2950) of Part 5 of Division 4 of the California Probate Code. Under California law, this Certificate of Authority authorizes the Public Guardian to take possession or control of property belonging to the above-named individual.

SPECIAL NOTE TO FINANCIAL INSTITUTIONS:

State law requires that upon receiving a copy of this Certificate of Authority, financial institutions shall provide the public guardian with information concerning property held by the above-named individual and surrender the property to the Public Guardian if requested.

This Certificate of Authority shall only be valid when signed and dated by the Public Guardian or a deputy Public Guardian of the County of _____ and affixed with the official seal of the Public Guardian below.

Signature of Public Guardian: _____

Date: _____

Official Seal

§ 2954 Form

DECLARATION
PRINT OR TYPE

1. My name is: _____. My badge number is: _____. My office address and telephone number are: _____

2. I am a duly sworn peace officer presently employed by _____, in the County of _____, in the State of California. On _____ (date) I personally interviewed _____ (victim) at _____ a.m./p.m. at __ _____ (address).

3. The victim resides at _____ (address, telephone number, and name of facility, if applicable).

There is probable cause to believe that:

(a) _____ (Victim) is substantially unable to manage his or her financial resources or to resist fraud or undue influence, and (b) There exists a significant danger the victim will lose all or a portion of his or her property as a result of fraud or misrepresentations or the mental incapacity of the victim, and

4. (c) There is probable cause to believe that a crime is being committed against the victim, and (d) The crime is connected to the victim's inability to manage his or her financial resources or to resist fraud or undue influence, and (e) The victim suffers from that inability as a result of deficits in one or more of the following mental functions:

INSTRUCTIONS TO PEACE OFFICER: CHECK ALL BLOCKS THAT APPLY:

(A) ALERTNESS AND ATTENTION

( ) 1. Levels of arousal. (Lethargic, responds only to vigorous and persistent stimulation, stupor.)

( ) 2. Orientation. Person _____ Time _____ (day, date, month, season, year), Place _____ (address, town, state), Situation _____ (why am I here?).

( ) 3. Ability to attend and concentrate. (Give detailed answers from memory, mental ability required to thread a needle.)

(B) INFORMATION PROCESSING

( ) 1. Ability to: Remember, i.e., short- and long-term memory, immediate recall. (Deficits reflected by: forgets question before answering, cannot recall names, relatives, past presidents, events of past 24 hours.)

( ) 2. Understand and communicate either verbally or otherwise. (Deficits reflected by: inability to comprehend questions, follow instructions, use words correctly or name objects; nonsense words.)

( ) 3. Recognize familiar objects and persons. (Deficits reflected by: inability to recognize familiar faces, objects, etc.)

( ) 4. Understand and appreciate quantities. (Perform simple calculations.)

( ) 5. Reason using abstract concepts. (Grasp abstract aspects of his or her situation;

interpret idiomatic expressions or proverbs.)

( ) 6. Plan, organize, and carry out actions (assuming physical ability) in one's own rational self-interest. (Break complex tasks down into simple steps and carry them out.)

( ) 7. Reason logically.

(C) THOUGHT DISORDERS

( ) 1. Severely disorganized thinking. (Rambling, nonsensical, incoherent, or nonlinear thinking.)

( ) 2. Hallucinations. (Auditory, visual, olfactory.)

( ) 3. Delusions. (Demonstrably false belief maintained without or against reason or evidence.)

( ) 4. Uncontrollable or intrusive thoughts. (Unwanted compulsive thoughts, compulsive behavior.)

(D) ABILITY TO MODULATE MOOD AND AFFECT

Pervasive and persistent or recurrent emotional state which appears severely inappropriate in degree to the patient's circumstances. Encircle the inappropriate mood(s):

Anger	Euphoria	Helplessness
Anxiety	Depression	Apathy
Fear	Hopelessness	Indifference
Panic	Despair	

5. The property at risk is identified as, but not limited to, the following:
Bank account located at: _____ (name, telephone number, and address of the bank branch) Account number(s):_____
Securities/other funds located at:_____ (name, telephone number, and address of financial institution) Account number(s):_____
Real property located at:_____ (address)
Automobile described as:_____ (make, model/color)
_____ (license plate number and state)
Other property described as:_____
Other property located at:_____
6. A criminal investigation will ( ) will not ( ) be commenced against: _____
_____ (name, address, and telephone number) for alleged financial abuse.

BLOCKS 1, 2, AND 3 MUST BE CHECKED IN ORDER FOR THIS DECLARATION TO BE VALID:

( ) 1. I am a peace officer in the county identified above. I have consulted concerning this case with a supervisor in the county's adult protective services agency who has signed below, indicating that he or she concurs that,

( ) 2. based on the information I provided to him or her, or based on information he or she obtained independently, this declaration is warranted under the circumstances.

( ) 3. I have consulted concerning this case with an individual qualified to perform a mental status examination.

_____
Signature of Declarant Peace Officer

_____
Date

_____
Signature of Concurring Adult
Protective Services Supervisor

§ 3909 Form

TRANSFER UNDER THE CALIFORNIA UNIFORM TRANSFERS TO MINORS ACT

I,_____ (Name of Transferor or Name and Representative Capacity if a Fiduciary) hereby transfer to _____ , (Name of Custodian) as custodian for _____ (Name of Minor) under the California Uniform Transfers to Minors Act, the following:
  (insert a description of the custodial property sufficient to identify it).

Dated: _____

_____
(Signature)

_____ acknowledges (Name of Custodian) receipt of the property described above as custodian for the minor named above under the California Uniform Transfers to Minors Act.

Dated: _____

_____
(Signature of Custodian)

§ 3914 Form

DECLARATION UNDER THE CALIFORNIA UNIFORM TRANSFERS TO MINORS ACT

I, _____, (Name of Transferor-Custodian) as custodian for _____ (Name of Minor) under the California Uniform Transfers to Minors Act, hereby irrevocably elect to be governed under subdivision (d) of Section 3914 of the Probate Code in my custodial capacity over the following described property _____. (Description of Custodial Property)
  I declare under penalty of perjury that the foregoing is true and correct.

Dated: _____, 19___

_____
(Signature of Transferor-Custodian)

NOTICE TO PERSON EXECUTING DURABLE POWER OF ATTORNEY

A durable power of attorney is an important legal document. By signing the durable power of attorney, you are authorizing another person to act for you, the principal. Before you sign this durable power of attorney, you should know these important facts:

Your agent (attorney-in-fact) has no duty to act unless you and your agent agree otherwise in writing.

This document gives your agent the powers to manage, dispose of, sell, and convey your real and personal property, and to use your property as security if your agent borrows money on your behalf. This document does not give your agent the power to accept or receive any of your property, in trust or otherwise, as a gift, unless you specifically authorize the agent to accept or receive a gift.

Your agent will have the right to receive reasonable payment for services provided under this durable power of attorney unless you provide otherwise in this power of attorney.

The powers you give your agent will continue to exist for your entire lifetime, unless you state that the durable power of attorney will last for a shorter period of time or unless you otherwise terminate the durable power of attorney. The powers you give your agent in this durable power of attorney will continue to exist even if you can no longer make your own decisions respecting the management of your property.

You can amend or change this durable power of attorney only by executing a new durable power of attorney or by executing an amendment through the same formalities as an original. You have the right to revoke or terminate this durable power of attorney at any time, so long as you are competent.

This durable power of attorney must be dated and must be acknowledged before a notary public or signed by two witnesses. If it is signed by two witnesses, they must witness either (1) the signing of the power of attorney or (2) the principal's signing or acknowledgment of his or her signature. A durable power of attorney that may affect real property should be acknowledged before a notary public so that it may easily be recorded.

You should read this durable power of attorney carefully. When effective, this durable power of attorney will give your agent the right to deal with property that you now have or might acquire in the future. The durable power of attorney is important to you. If you do not understand the durable power of attorney, or any provision of it, then you should obtain the assistance of an attorney or other qualified person.

Notice to Person Accepting the Appointment as Attorney-in-Fact

By acting or agreeing to act as the agent (attorney-in-fact) under this power of attorney you assume the fiduciary and other legal responsibilities of an agent. These responsibilities include:

1. The legal duty to act solely in the interest of the principal and to avoid conflicts of interest.

2. The legal duty to keep the principal's property separate and distinct from any other property owned or controlled by you.

You may not transfer the principal's property to yourself without full and adequate consideration or accept a gift of the principal's property unless this power of attorney specifically authorizes you to transfer property to yourself or accept a gift of the principal's property. If you transfer the principal's property to yourself without specific authorization in the power of attorney, you may be prosecuted for fraud and/or embezzlement. If the principal is 65 years of age or older at the time that the property is transferred to you without authority, you may also be prosecuted for elder abuse under Penal Code Section 368. In addition to criminal prosecution, you may also be sued in civil court.

I have read the foregoing notice and I understand the legal and fiduciary duties that I assume by acting or agreeing to act as the agent (attorney-in-fact) under the terms of this power of attorney.

Date:

_____
(Signature of agent)

_____
(Print name of agent)

§ 4401 Form

UNIFORM STATUTORY FORM POWER OF ATTORNEY

(California Probate Code Section 4401)

NOTICE: THE POWERS GRANTED BY THIS DOCUMENT ARE BROAD AND SWEEPING. THEY ARE EXPLAINED IN THE UNIFORM STATUTORY FORM POWER OF ATTORNEY ACT (CALIFORNIA PROBATE CODE SECTIONS 4400-4465). THE POWERS LISTED IN THIS DOCUMENT DO NOT INCLUDE ALL POWERS THAT ARE AVAILABLE UNDER THE PROBATE CODE. ADDITIONAL POWERS AVAILABLE UNDER THE PROBATE CODE MAY BE ADDED BY SPECIFICALLY LISTING THEM UNDER THE SPECIAL INSTRUCTIONS SECTION OF THIS DOCUMENT. IF YOU HAVE ANY QUESTIONS ABOUT THESE POWERS, OBTAIN COMPETENT LEGAL ADVICE. THIS DOCUMENT DOES NOT AUTHORIZE ANYONE TO MAKE MEDICAL AND OTHER HEALTH-CARE DECISIONS FOR YOU. YOU MAY REVOKE THIS POWER OF ATTORNEY IF YOU LATER WISH TO DO SO.

ALL POWERS CONFERRED UPON THE AGENT in this UNIFORM STATUTORY FORM POWER OF ATTORNEY shall also function completely as a DURABLE POWER OF ATTORNEY within all circumstances set forth herein:

I, _____, (PRINCIPAL)
APPOINT:

_____ (NAME)

_____ (ADDRESS)

_____

_____ (PHONE NUMBER[s])

_____

[name and address of the person appointed, or of each person appointed if you want to designate more than one] as my AGENT (attorney-in-fact) to act for me in any lawful way with respect to the following initialed subjects:

TO GRANT ALL OF THE FOLLOWING POWERS, INITIAL THE LINE IN FRONT OF (N) AND IGNORE THE LINES IN FRONT OF THE OTHER POWERS.

TO GRANT ONE OR MORE, BUT FEWER THAN ALL, OF THE FOLLOWING POWERS, INITIAL THE LINE IN FRONT OF EACH POWER YOU ARE GRANTING.

TO WITHHOLD A POWER, DO NOT INITIAL THE LINE IN FRONT OF IT. YOU MAY, BUT NEED NOT, CROSS OUT EACH POWER WITHHELD.

INITIAL:

_____ (A) Real property transactions.
_____ (B) Tangible personal property transactions.
_____ (C) Stock and bond transactions.
_____ (D) Commodity and option transactions.
_____ (E) Banking and other financial institution transactions.
_____ (F) Business operating transactions.
_____ (G) Insurance and annuity transactions.
_____ (H) Estate, trust, and other beneficiary transactions.
_____ (I) Claims and litigation.
_____ (J) Personal and family maintenance.
_____ (K) Benefits from the Social Security Administration, Medicare, Medicaid, or other governmental programs, or civil or military service.
_____ (L) Retirement plan transactions.
_____ (M) Tax matters.
_____ (N) ALL OF THE POWERS LISTED ABOVE.

YOU NEED NOT INITIAL ANY OTHER LINES IF YOU INITIAL LINE (N).

SPECIAL INSTRUCTIONS:

ON THE FOLLOWING LINES YOU MAY GIVE SPECIAL INSTRUCTIONS LIMITING OR EXTENDING THE POWERS GRANTED TO YOUR AGENT.

(A) _____
_____
_____
_____

(B)   DURABLE POWER OF ATTORNEY

1.   This Uniform Statutory Form Power of Attorney shall at all times be legally interpreted and relied upon as a Durable Power of Attorney (also known herein as a "Power of Attorney") for all reasons set forth within the entirety of this document. Any provision of this document which is challenged by a third party as ineffective shall not affect the remaining provisions herein; all remaining provisions shall remain in full force and effect, within all governing periods of this document.

(C)   AUTHORIZATION TO USE PHOTOCOPIES:

1.   Only ONE ORIGINAL of this Uniform Statutory Form Power of Attorney has been executed. The Agent specified in this instrument is authorized to make photocopies of this instrument and any attached documents (such as certificates of incapacity, attached as necessary) as frequently and in such quantities as the Agent deems appropriate. Each photocopy shall have the same force and effect as the original, and all parties dealing with the Agent herein are authorized to rely fully on any such photocopy showing the Principal's signature thereon.

2.   A copy of a Uniform Statutory Form Power of Attorney, setting forth specifically within, a Durable Power of Attorney, shall be certified in accordance with California Probate Code Section 4307; and shall have the same force and effect as the original, so long as the attached certification is effectuated by 1), an authorized notary public in California; 2) an attorney authorized to practice law in California; and 3) an official of the state or of a political subdivision who is authorized to make such certification, who states that the certifying person has examined the original Uniform Statutory Form Power of Attorney and that the copy is a true and correct copy of the original Uniform Statutory Form Power of Attorney. CA Probate Code Section 4307(c); see CA Govt. Code Section 8205(a)(2) and (4).

(D)   ADDITIONAL POWERS APPLICABLE HEREIN:

1.   An Agent under a Uniform Statutory Form Power of Attorney, on the date executed or upon a subsequent date which adheres to all legal formalities under California law, can modify, revoke, or terminate a trust as provided for in the Principal's trust document only with express authority granted in this Uniform Statutory Form Power of Attorney instrument;

2.   The Agent designated in this Uniform Statutory Form Power of Attorney may reject, disclaim, or make payment from, an estate, a trust or another fund only with the express consent of the Principal herein;

3.   The power of an Agent under this Uniform Statutory Form Power of Attorney with regard to insurance, annuity, and retirement plan transactions; and other beneficiary transactions, can be changed only by the express consent of the Principal herein;

4.   This Uniform Statutory Form Power of Attorney requires notification to the Principal herein that this Uniform Statutory Form Power of Attorney does not include all of the powers under the California Probate Code; and

5.   This Uniform Statutory Form Power of Attorney provides that the authority of an Agent with respect to family maintenance is not dependent on any other grant of authority for the Agent herein to make gifts on the Principal's behalf, and is also not limited by any limitation placed on the Agent's authority to make gifts on the Principal's behalf.

_____

UNLESS YOU DIRECT OTHERWISE ON THE LINE ABOVE, THIS POWER OF ATTORNEY IS EFFECTIVE IMMEDIATELY AND WILL CONTINUE UNTIL IT IS REVOKED.

This Power of Attorney will continue to be effective even though I become incapacitated.

STRIKE THE PRECEDING SENTENCE IF YOU DO NOT WANT THIS POWER OF ATTORNEY TO CONTINUE IF YOU BECOME INCAPACITATED.

(E)   EXERCISE OF POWER OF ATTORNEY WHERE MORE THAN ONE AGENT IS

DESIGNATED

If I have designated more than one agent, the agents are to act_____.
                                                    ["separately" or "jointly"]
INITIAL: _____
IF YOU APPOINTED MORE THAN ONE AGENT AND YOU WANT EACH AGENT TO

BE ABLE TO ACT ALONE WITHOUT THE OTHER AGENT JOINING, WRITE THE
WORD "SEPARATELY" IN THE BLANK SPACE ABOVE. IF YOU DO NOT INSERT
ANY WORD IN THE BLANK SPACE, OR IF YOU INSERT THE WORD "JOINTLY,"
THEN ALL OF YOUR AGENTS MUST ACT OR SIGN TOGETHER.

I agree that any third party who receives a copy of this document may act under it according to the specific provisions set forth in the Special Instructions section herein, above. A
third party may seek identification. Revocation of this Power of Attorney is not effective
as to a third party until the third party has actual knowledge of the revocation. I agree
to indemnify the third party for any claims that arise against the third party because of
reliance on this Power of Attorney.

Signed on _____, 2013 at _____,
California.

_____
[signature]

_____,
PRINCIPAL [print name]

BY ACCEPTING OR ACTING UNDER THE APPOINTMENT, THE AGENT
(ATTORNEY-IN-FACT) ASSUMES THE FIDUCIARY AND OTHER LEGAL
RESPONSIBILITIES OF AN AGENT UNDER THIS UNIFORM STATUTORY FORM
POWER OF ATTORNEY.

STATE OF CALIFORIA   )

)

COUNTY OF _____)

On _____, 2013, before me _____,
Notary Public [name and title of officer], personally appeared _____
_____ _____ who proved to me on the basis of satisfactory evidence
to be the person(s) whose name(s) is/are subscribed to the within instrument and acknowledged to me that he/she/they executed the same in his/her/their authorized capacity(ies),
and that by his/her signature(s) on the instrument the person(s), or the entity upon behalf
of which the person(s) acted, executed the instrument.

I certify under PENALTY OF PERJURY under the laws of the State of California that the
foregoing paragraph is true and correct.

WITNESS my hand and official seal.

_____
[Signature of Officer]

[Officer's Seal]

ADVANCE HEALTH CARE DIRECTIVE
(California Probate Code Section 4701)

Explanation

You have the right to give instructions about your own health care. You also have the right to name someone else to make health care decisions for you. This form lets you do either or both of these things. It also lets you express your wishes regarding donation of organs and the designation of your primary physician. If you use this form, you may complete or modify all or any part of it. You are free to use a different form.

Part 1 of this form is a power of attorney for health care. Part 1 lets you name another individual as agent to make health care decisions for you if you become incapable of making your own decisions or if you want someone else to make those decisions for you now even though you are still capable. You may also name an alternate agent to act for you if your first choice is not willing, able, or reasonably available to make decisions for you. (Your agent may not be an operator or employee of a community care facility or a residential care facility where you are receiving care, or your supervising health care provider or employee of the health care institution where you are receiving care, unless your agent is related to you or is a coworker.)

Unless the form you sign limits the authority of your agent, your agent may make all health care decisions for you. This form has a place for you to limit the authority of your agent. You need not limit the authority of your agent if you wish to rely on your agent for all health care decisions that may have to be made. If you choose not to limit the authority of your agent, your agent will have the right to:

(a) Consent or refuse consent to any care, treatment, service, or procedure to maintain, diagnose, or otherwise affect a physical or mental condition.

(b) Select or discharge health care providers and institutions.

(c) Approve or disapprove diagnostic tests, surgical procedures, and programs of medication.

(d) Direct the provision, withholding, or withdrawal of artificial nutrition and hydration and all other forms of health care, including cardiopulmonary resuscitation.

(e) Make anatomical gifts, authorize an autopsy, and direct disposition of remains.

Part 2 of this form lets you give specific instructions about any aspect of your health care, whether or not you appoint an agent. Choices are provided for you to express your wishes regarding the provision, withholding, or withdrawal of treatment to keep you alive, as well as the provision of pain relief. Space is also provided for you to add to the choices you have made or for you to write out any additional wishes. If you are satisfied to allow your agent to determine what is best for you in making end-of-life decisions, you need not fill out Part 2 of this form.

Part 3 of this form lets you express an intention to donate your bodily organs and tissues following your death.

Part 4 of this form lets you designate a physician to have primary responsibility for your health care.

After completing this form, sign and date the form at the end. The form must be signed by two qualified witnesses or acknowledged before a notary public. Give a copy of the signed and completed form to your physician, to any other health care providers you may have, to any health care institution at which you are receiving care, and to any health care agents you have named. You should talk to the person you have named as agent to make sure that he or she understands your wishes and is willing to take the responsibility. You have the right to revoke this advance health care directive or replace this form at any time.

∼

PART 1
POWER OF ATTORNEY FOR HEALTH CARE

(1.1) DESIGNATION OF AGENT: I designate the   following individual as my agent to make health care decisions for me:

_____
(name of individual you choose as agent)

_____
(address)   (city)   (state) (ZIP Code)

_____
(home phone)   (work phone)

OPTIONAL: If I revoke my agent's authority or if   my agent is not willing, able, or reasonably available to make a health care decision for me, I designate as my first alternate agent:

_____
(name of individual you choose as first alternate agent)

_____
(address) (city) (state) (ZIP Code)

_____
(home phone)   (work phone)

OPTIONAL: If I revoke the authority of my agent and first alternate agent or if neither is willing, able, or reasonably available to make a health care decision for me, I designate as my second alternate agent:

_____
(name of individual you choose as second alternate agent)

_____
(address) (city) (state) (ZIP Code)

_____
(home phone)   (work phone)

(1.2) AGENT'S   AUTHORITY: My agent is authorized to make all health care decisions for me, including decisions to provide, withhold, or withdraw artificial nutrition and hydration and all other forms of health care to keep me alive, except as I state here:

_____
_____
_____
(Add additional sheets if needed.)

(1.3) WHEN AGENT'S AUTHORITY BECOMES EFFECTIVE:
My agent's authority becomes effective when my primary physician determines that I am unable to make my own health care decisions unless I mark the following box. If I mark this box ( ), my agent's authority to make health care decisions for me takes effect immediately.

(1.4) AGENT'S OBLIGATION: My agent shall make health care decisions for me in accordance with this power of attorney for health care, any instructions I give in Part 2 of this form, and my other wishes to the extent known to my agent.

To the extent my wishes are unknown, my agent shall make health care decisions for me in accordance with what my agent determines to be in my best interest. In determining my best interest, my agent shall consider my personal values to the extent known to my agent.

(1.5) AGENT'S POSTDEATH AUTHORITY: My agent is authorized to make anatomical gifts, authorize an autopsy, and direct disposition of my remains, except as I state here or in Part 3 of this form:

_____
_____
_____
(Add additional sheets if needed.)

(1.6) NOMINATION OF CONSERVATOR: If a conservator of my person needs to be appointed for me by a court, I nominate the agent designated in this form. If that agent is not willing, able, or reasonably available to act as conservator, I nominate the alternate agents whom I have named, in the order designated.

~

PART 2
INSTRUCTIONS FOR HEALTH CARE

If you fill out this part of the form, you may strike any wording you do not want.

(2.1) END-OF-LIFE DECISIONS: I direct that my health care providers and others involved in my care provide, withhold, or withdraw treatment in accordance with the choice I have marked below:

( ) (a) Choice Not To Prolong Life

I do not want my life to be prolonged if (1) I have an incurable and irreversible condition that will result in my death within a relatively short time, (2) I become unconscious and, to a reasonable degree of medical certainty, I will not regain consciousness, or (3) the likely risks and burdens of treatment would outweigh the expected benefits, OR

( ) (b) Choice To Prolong Life

I want my life to be prolonged as long as possible within the limits of generally accepted health care standards.

402

(2.2) RELIEF FROM PAIN: Except as I state in the following space, I direct that treatment for alleviation of pain or discomfort be provided at all times, even if it hastens my death:

_____

_____

(Add additional sheets if needed.)

(2.3) OTHER WISHES: (If you do not agree with any of the optional choices above and wish to write your own, or if you wish to add to the instructions you have given above, you may do so here.)

I direct that:

_____

_____

(Add additional sheets if needed.)

~

PART 3
DONATION OF ORGANS AT DEATH
(OPTIONAL)

(3.1) Upon my death (mark applicable box):

( ) (a) I give any needed organs, tissues, or parts, OR

( ) (b) I give the following organs, tissues, or parts only.

_____

(c) My gift is for the following purposes (strike any of the following you do not want):

(1) Transplant

(2) Therapy

(3) Research

(4) Education

~

PART 4
PRIMARY PHYSICIAN
(OPTIONAL)

(4.1) I designate the following physician as my primary physician:

_____

(name of physician)

_____

(address)   (city) (state) (ZIP Code)

_____

(phone)

OPTIONAL: If the physician I have designated above is not willing, able, or reasonably available to act as my primary physician, I designate the following physician as my primary physician:

_____

(name of physician)

_____

(address)   (city) (state) (ZIP Code)

_____

(phone)

~

PART 5

(5.1) EFFECT OF COPY: A copy of this form has the same effect as the original.

(5.2) SIGNATURE: Sign and date the form here:

_____   _____

(date)   (sign your name)

_____   _____

(address)   (print your name)

_____
(city)   (state)

(5.3) STATEMENT OF WITNESSES: I declare under penalty of perjury under the laws of California (1) that the individual who signed or acknowledged this advance health care directive is personally known to me, or that the individual's identity was proven to me by convincing evidence, (2) that the individual signed or acknowledged this advance directive in my presence, (3) that the individual appears to be of sound mind and under no duress, fraud, or undue influence, (4) that I am not a person appointed as agent by this advance directive, and (5) that I am not the individual's health care provider, an employee of the individual's health care provider, the operator of a community care facility, an employee of an operator of a community care facility, the operator of a residential care facility for   the elderly, nor an employee of an operator of a residential care facility for the elderly.

First witness   Second witness

_____   _____
(print name)   (print name)

_____   _____
(address)   (address)

_____   _____
(city)   (state)   (city)   (state)

_____   _____
(signature of witness)   (signature of witness)

_____   _____
(date)   (date)

(5.4) ADDITIONAL STATEMENT OF   WITNESSES: At least one of the above witnesses must also sign the following declaration:

I further declare under penalty of perjury under the laws of California that I am not related to the individual executing this advance health care directive by blood, marriage, or adoption, and to the best of my knowledge, I am not entitled to any part of the individual's estate upon his or her death under a will now existing or by operation of law.

_____   _____
(signature of witness)   (signature of witness)

~

PART 6
SPECIAL WITNESS REQUIREMENT

(6.1) The following statement is required only if you are a patient in a skilled nursing facility--a health care facility that provides the following basic services: skilled nursing care and supportive care to patients whose primary need is for availability of skilled nursing care on an extended basis. The patient advocate or ombudsman must sign the following statement:

STATEMENT OF PATIENT ADVOCATE OR OMBUDSMAN

I declare under penalty of perjury under the laws of California that I am a patient advocate or ombudsman as designated by the State Department of Aging and that I am serving as a witness as required by Section 4675 of the Probate Code.

_____   _____
(date)   (sign your name)

_____   _____
(address)   (print your name)

_____
(city)   (state)

404

QUESTIONS AND ANSWERS ABOUT THIS CALIFORNIA
STATUTORY WILL

The following information, in question and answer form, is not a part of the California Statutory Will. It is designed to help you understand about Wills and to decide if this Will meets your needs. This Will is in a simple form. The complete text of each paragraph of this Will is printed at the end of the Will.

1. What happens if I die without a Will? If you die without a Will, what you own (your "assets") in your name alone will be divided among your spouse, domestic partner, children, or other relatives according to state law. The court will appoint a relative to collect and distribute your assets.

2. What can a Will do for me? In a Will you may designate who will receive your assets at your death. You may designate someone (called an "executor") to appear before the court, collect your assets, pay your debts and taxes, and distribute your assets as you specify. You may nominate someone (called a "guardian") to raise your children who are under age 18. You may designate someone (called a "custodian") to manage assets for your children until they reach any age from 18 to 25.

3. Does a Will avoid probate? No. With or without a Will, assets in your name alone usually go through the court probate process. The court's first job is to determine if your Will is valid.

4. What is community property? Can I give away my share in my Will? If you are married and you or your spouse earned money during your marriage from work and wages, that money (and the assets bought with it) is community property. Your Will can only give away your one-half of community property. Your Will cannot give away your spouse's one-half of community property.

5. Does my Will give away all of my assets? Do all assets go through probate? No. Money in a joint tenancy bank account automatically belongs to the other named owner without probate. If your spouse, domestic partner, or child is on the deed to your house as a joint tenant, the house automatically passes to him or her. Life insurance and retirement plan benefits may pass directly to the named beneficiary. A Will does not necessarily control how these types of "nonprobate" assets pass at your death.

6. Are there different kinds of Wills? Yes. There are handwritten Wills, typewritten Wills, attorney-prepared Wills, and statutory Wills. All are valid if done precisely as the law requires. You should see a lawyer if you do not want to use this Statutory Will or if you do not understand this form.

7. Who may use this Will? This Will is based on California law. It is designed only for California residents. You may use this form if you are single, married, a member of a domestic partnership, or divorced. You must be age 18 or older and of sound mind.

8. Are there any reasons why I should NOT use this Statutory Will?
Yes. This is a simple Will. It is not designed to reduce death taxes or other taxes. Talk to a lawyer to do tax planning, especially if (i) your assets will be worth more than $600,000 or the current amount excluded from estate tax under federal law at your death, (ii) you own business-related assets, (iii) you want to create a trust fund for your children's education or other purposes, (iv) you own assets in some other state, (v) you want to disinherit your spouse, domestic partner, or descendants, or (vi) you have valuable interests in pension or profit-sharing plans. You should talk to a lawyer who knows about estate planning if this Will does not meet your needs. This Will treats most adopted children like natural children. You should talk to a lawyer if you have stepchildren or foster children whom you have not adopted.

9. May I add or cross out any words on this Will? No. If you do, the Will may be invalid or the court may ignore the crossed out or added words. You may only fill in the blanks. You may amend this Will by a separate document (called a codicil). Talk to a lawyer if you want to do something with your assets which is not allowed in this form.

10. May I change my Will? Yes. A Will is not effective until you die. You may make and sign a new Will. You may change your Will at any time, but only by an amendment (called a codicil). You can give away or sell your assets before your death. Your Will only acts on what you own at death.

11. Where should I keep my Will? After you and the witnesses sign the Will, keep your Will in your safe deposit box or other safe place. You should tell trusted family members where your Will is kept.

12. When should I change my Will? You should make and sign a new Will if you marry, divorce, or terminate your domestic partnership after you sign this Will. Divorce, annulment, or termination of a domestic partnership automatically cancels all property stated to pass to a former husband, wife, or domestic partner under this Will, and revokes the designation

of a former spouse or domestic partner as executor, custodian, or guardian. You should sign a new Will when you have more children, or if your spouse or a child dies, or a domestic partner dies or marries. You may want to change your Will if there is a large change in the value of your assets. You may also want to change your Will if you enter a domestic partnership or your domestic partnership has been terminated after you sign this Will.

13. What can I do if I do not understand something in this Will? If there is anything in this Will you do not understand, ask a lawyer to explain it to you.

14. What is an executor? An "executor" is the person you name to collect your assets, pay your debts and taxes, and distribute your assets as the court directs. It may be a person or it may be a qualified bank or trust company.

15. Should I require a bond? You may require that an executor post a "bond." A bond is a form of insurance to replace assets that may be mismanaged or stolen by the executor. The cost of the bond is paid from the estate's assets.

16. What is a guardian? Do I need to designate one? If you have children under age 18, you should designate a guardian of their "persons" to raise them.

17. What is a custodian? Do I need to designate one? A "custodian" is a person you may designate to manage assets for someone (including a child) who is under the age of 25 and who receives assets under your Will. The custodian manages the assets and pays as much as the custodian determines is proper for health, support, maintenance, and education. The custodian delivers what is left to the person when the person reaches the age you choose (from 18 to 25). No bond is required of a custodian.

18. Should I ask people if they are willing to serve before I designate them as executor, guardian, or custodian? Probably yes. Some people and banks and trust companies may not consent to serve or may not be qualified to act.

19. What happens if I make a gift in this Will to someone and that person dies before I do? A person must survive you by 120 hours to take a gift under this Will. If that person does not, then the gift fails and goes with the rest of your assets. If the person who does not survive you is a relative of yours or your spouse, then certain assets may go to the relative's descendants.

20. What is a trust? There are many kinds of trusts, including trusts created by Wills (called "testamentary trusts") and trusts created during your lifetime (called "revocable living trusts"). Both kinds of trusts are long-term arrangements in which a manager (called a "trustee") invests and manages assets for someone (called a "beneficiary") on the terms you specify. Trusts are too complicated to be used in this Statutory Will. You should see a lawyer if you want to create a trust.

21. What is a domestic partner? You have a domestic partner if you have met certain legal requirements and filed a form entitled "Declaration of Domestic Partnership" with the Secretary of State. Notwithstanding Section 299.6 of the Family Code, if you have not filed a Declaration of Domestic Partnership with the Secretary of State, you do not meet the required definition and should not use the section of the Statutory Will form that refers to domestic partners even if you have registered your domestic partnership with another governmental entity. If you are unsure if you have a domestic partner or if your domestic partnership meets the required definition, please contact the Secretary of State's office.

INSTRUCTIONS

1. READ THE WILL. Read the whole Will first. If you do not understand something, ask a lawyer to explain it to you.

2. FILL IN THE BLANKS. Fill in the blanks. Follow the instructions in the form carefully. Do not add any words to the Will (except for filling in blanks) or cross out any words.

3. DATE AND SIGN THE WILL AND HAVE TWO WITNESSES SIGN IT. Date and sign the Will and have two witnesses sign it. You and the witnesses should read and follow the Notice to Witnesses found at the end of this Will.

*You do not need to have this document notarized. Notarization will not fulfill the witness requirement.

California Statutory Will
California Probate Code, Section 6240

INSTRUCTIONS

1. READ THE WILL. Read the whole Will first. If you do not understand something, ask a lawyer to explain it to you.

2. FILL IN THE BLANKS. Fill in the blanks. Follow the instructions in the form carefully. Do not add any words to the Will (except for filling in blanks) or cross out any words.

3. DATE AND SIGN THE WILL AND HAVE TWO WITNESSES SIGN IT. Date and sign the Will and have two witnesses sign it. You and the witnesses should read and follow the Notice to Witnesses found at the end of this Will.

CALIFORNIA STATUTORY WILL OF

> Print Your Full Name

1. <u>Will.</u> This is my Will. I revoke all prior Wills and codicils.

2. <u>Specific Gift of Personal Residence.</u> (Optional-use only if you want to give your personal residence to a different person or persons than you give the balance of your assets to under paragraph 5 below.) I give my interest in my principal personal residence at the time of my death (subject to mortgages and liens) as follows:

(Select one choice only and sign in the box after your choice.)

a. <u>Choice One:</u> All to my spouse or domestic partner, registered with the California Secretary of State, if my spouse or domestic partner, registered with the California Secretary of State, survives me; otherwise to my descendants (my children and the descendants of my children) who survive me.

b. <u>Choice Two:</u> Nothing to my spouse or domestic partner, registered with the California Secretary of State; all to my descendants (my children and the descendants of my children) who survive me.

c. <u>Choice Three</u>: All to the following person if he or she survives me (Insert the name of the person.):

_____

d. <u>Choice Four</u>: Equally among the following persons who survive me (Insert the names of two or more persons.):

_____
_____
_____

3. <u>Specific Gift of Automobiles, Household and Personal Effects.</u> (Optional—use only if you want to give automobiles and household and personal effects to a different person or persons than you give the balance of your assets to under paragraph 5 below.) I give all of my automobiles (subject to loans), furniture, furnishings, household items, clothing, jewelry, and other tangible articles of a personal nature at the time of my death as follows:

(Select one choice only and sign in the box after your choice.)

a. <u>Choice One</u>: All to my spouse or domestic partner, registered with the California Secretary of State, if my spouse or domestic partner, registered with the California Secretary of State, survives me; otherwise to my descendants (my children and the descendants of my children) who survive me.

b. <u>Choice Two</u>: Nothing to my spouse or domestic partner, registered with the California Secretary of State; all to my descendants (my children and the descendants of my children) who survive me.

c. <u>Choice Three</u>: All to the following person if he or she survives me (Insert the name of the person.):

_____

d. <u>Choice Four</u>: Equally among the following persons who survive me (Insert the names of two or more persons.):

_____
_____
_____
_____

4. <u>Specific Gifts of Cash.</u> (Optional) I make the following cash gifts to the persons named below who survive me, or to the named charity, and I sign my name in the box after each gift. If I do not sign in the box, I do not make a gift. (Sign in the box after each gift you make.)

Name of Person or Charity to receive gift (*name one only – please print*)	Amount of Cash Gift _____ *Sign your name in this box to make this gift*
Name of Person or Charity to receive gift (*name one only – please print*)	Amount of Cash Gift _____ *Sign your name in this box to make this gift*
Name of Person or Charity to receive gift (*name one only – please print*)	Amount of Cash Gift _____ *Sign your name in this box to make this gift*
Name of Person or Charity to receive gift (*name one only – please print*)	Amount of Cash Gift _____ *Sign your name in this box to make this gift*
Name of Person or Charity to receive gift (*name one only – please print*)	Amount of Cash Gift _____ *Sign your name in this box to make this gift*

5. <u>Balance of My Assets</u>. Except for the specific gifts made in paragraphs 2, 3 and 4 above, I give the balance of my assets as follows:

(Select <u>one</u> choice only and sign in the box after your choice. If I sign in more than one box or if I do not sign in any box, the court will distribute my assets as if I did not make a Will.)

a. <u>Choice One</u>: All to my spouse or domestic partner, registered with the California Secretary of State, if my spouse or domestic partner, registered with the California Secretary of State, survives me; otherwise to my descendants (my children and the descendants of my children) who survive me.

408

b. <u>Choice Two</u>: Nothing to my spouse or domestic partner, registered with the California Secretary of State; all to my descendants (my children and the descendants of my children) who survive me.

c. <u>Choice Three</u>: All to the following person if he or she survives me (Insert the name of the person.):

_____

d. <u>Choice Four</u>: Equally among the following persons who survive me (Insert the names of two or more persons.):

_____
_____
_____
_____

6. <u>Guardian of the Child's Person.</u> If I have a child under age 18 and the child does not have a living parent at my death, I nominate the individual named below as First Choice as guardian of the person of that child (to raise the child). If the First Choice does not serve, then I nominate the Second Choice, and then the Third Choice, to serve. Only an individual (not a bank or trust company) may serve.

Name of First Choice for Guardian of the Person

Name of Second Choice for Guardian of the Person

Name of Third Choice for Guardian of the Person

7. <u>Special Provision for Property of Persons Under Age 25.</u> (Optional—unless you use this paragraph, assets that go to a child or other person who is <u>under</u> age 18 may be given to the parent of the person, or to the Guardian named in paragraph 6 above as guardian of the person until age 18, and the court will require a bond, and assets that go to a child or other person who is age 18 or older will be given outright to the person. By using this paragraph you may provide that a custodian will hold the assets for the person until the person reaches any age from 18 to 25 which you choose.) If a beneficiary of this Will is under the age chosen below, I nominate the individual or bank or trust company named below as First Choice as custodian of the property. If the First Choice does not serve, then I nominate the Second Choice, and then the Third Choice, to serve.

Name of First Choice for Custodian of Assets

Name of Second Choice for Custodian of Assets

Name of Third Choice for Custodian of Assets

Insert any age from 18 to 25 as the age for the person to receive the property:
(If you do not choose an age, age 18 will apply.)

8. <u>Executor.</u> I nominate the individual or bank or trust company named below as First Choice as executor. If the First Choice does not serve, then I nominate the Second Choice, and then the Third Choice, to serve.

Name of First Choice for Executor

Name of Second Choice for Executor

Name of Third Choice for Executor

9. Bond. My signature in this box means a bond is not required for any person named as executor. A bond may be required if I do not sign in this box:

No bond shall be required.

(Notice: You must sign this Will in the presence of two (2) adult witnesses. The witnesses must sign their names in your presence and in each other's presence. You must first read to them the following sentence.)

This is my Will: I ask the persons who sign below to be my witnesses.

Signed on_____ at _____, California.
              (date)   (city)

Signature of Maker of Will

(Notice to Witnesses: Two (2) adults must sign as witnesses. Each witness must read the following clause before signing. The witnesses should not receive assets under this Will.)

Each of us declares under penalty of perjury under the laws of the State of California that the following is true and correct:

       a. On the date written below the maker of this Will declared to us that this instrument was the maker's Will and requested us to act as witnesses to it;

b. We understand this is the maker's Will;

c. The maker signed this Will in our presence, all of us being present at the same time;

d. We now, at the maker's request, and in the maker's and each other's presence, sign below as witnesses;

e. We believe the maker is of sound mind and memory;

f. We believe that this Will was not procured by duress, menace, fraud or undue influence;

g. The maker is age 18 or older; and

h. Each of us is now age 18 or older, is a competent witness, and resides at the address set forth after his or her name.

Dated: _____, _____

Signature of witness	Signature of witness

Print name here: Print name here:

_____   _____

Residence address: Residence address

_____   _____

_____   _____

AT LEAST TWO WITNESSES <u>MUST</u> SIGN
NOTARIZATION ALONE IS NOT SUFFICIENT

❧ ～ ☙

§ 6384 Form

CERTIFICATE

(Convention of October 26, 1973)

1. I, _____ (name, address, and capacity)
a person authorized to act in connection with international wills,

2. certify that on _____ (date) at _____ (place)

3. _____ (testator) _____
(name, address, date and place of birth)
in my presence and that of the witnesses

4. (a) _____ (name, address, date and place of
birth)

(b) _____ (name, address, date and place of birth)
has declared that the attached document is his will and that he knows the contents thereof.

5. I furthermore certify that:

6. (a) in my presence and in that of the witnesses

(1) the testator has signed the will or has acknowledged his signature previously affixed.

(2) following a declaration of the testator stating that he was unable to sign his will for the
following reason _____, I
have mentioned this declaration on the will,* and the signature has been affixed by
_____ (name and address)*

7. (b) the witnesses and I have signed the will;

8. (c) each page of the will has been signed by

_____ and numbered;*

9. (d) I have satisfied myself as to the identity of the testator and of the witnesses as designated above;

10. (e) the witnesses met the conditions requisite to act as such according to the law under
which I am acting;

11. (f) the testator has requested me to include the following statement concerning the
safekeeping of this will:*

_____

12. PLACE OF EXECUTION
13. DATE
14. SIGNATURE and, if necessary, SEAL

_____

*to be completed if appropriate

§ 8100 Form

NOTICE OF PETITION TO ADMINISTER

ESTATE OF _____,
ESTATE NO. _____

To all heirs, beneficiaries, creditors, and contingent creditors of _____ and persons who may be otherwise interested in the will or estate, or both:

A petition has been filed by _____ in the Superior Court of California, County of _____, requesting that _____ be appointed as personal representative to administer the estate of _____ (and for probate of the decedent's will, which is available for examination in the court file).

(The petition requests authority to administer the estate under the Independent Administration of Estates Act. This will avoid the need to obtain court approval for many actions taken in connection with the estate. However, before taking certain actions, the personal representative will be required to give notice to interested persons unless they have waived notice or have consented to the proposed action. The petition will be granted unless good cause is shown why it should not be.)

The petition is set for hearing in Dept. No. _____ at _____ _____ (Address) on _____ (Date of hearing) at _____ (Time of hearing)

IF YOU OBJECT to the granting of the petition, you should appear at the hearing and state your objections or file written objections with the court before the hearing. Your appearance may be in person or by your attorney.

IF YOU ARE A CREDITOR or a contingent creditor of the deceased, you must file your claim with the court and mail a copy to the personal representative appointed by the court within the later of either (1) four months from the date of first issuance of letters to a general personal representative, as defined in subdivision (b) of Section 58 of the California Probate Code, or (2) 60 days from the date of mailing or personal delivery of the notice to you under Section 9052 of the California Probate Code.

YOU MAY EXAMINE the file kept by the court. If you are interested in the estate, you may request special notice of the filing of an inventory and appraisal of estate assets or of any petition or account as provided in Section 1250 of the California Probate Code.

_____
(Name and address of petitioner or petitioner's attorney)

❖～❖

§ 9052 Form

NOTICE OF ADMINISTRATION

OF

ESTATE OF _____, DECEDENT

Notice to creditors:

Administration of the estate of _____ (deceased) has been commenced by _____ (personal representative) in Estate No. _____ in the Superior Court of California, County of _____. You must file your claim with the court and mail or deliver a copy to the personal representative within the last to occur of four months after _____ (the date letters were first issued to a general personal representative, as defined in subdivision (b) of Section 58 of the California Probate Code), or 60 days after the date this notice was mailed to you or, in the case of personal delivery, 60 days after the date this notice was delivered to you, or you must petition to file a late claim as provided in Section 9103 of the California Probate Code. Failure to file a claim with the court and serve a copy of the claim on the personal representative will, in most instances, invalidate your claim. A claim form may be obtained from the court clerk. For your protection, you are encouraged to file your claim by certified mail, with return receipt requested.

_____
(Date of mailing
this notice)

_____
(Name and address of
personal
representative or attorney)

§ 15642 Form

CERTIFICATE OF INDEPENDENT REVIEW

I, _____ (attorney's name), have reviewed _____ (name of instrument) and have counseled my client, _____ (name of client) fully and privately on the nature and legal effect of the designation as trustee of _____ (name of trustee) contained in that instrument. I am so disassociated from the interest of the person named as trustee as to be in a position to advise my client impartially and confidentially as to the consequences of the designation. On the basis of this counsel, I conclude that the designation of a person who would otherwise be subject to removal under paragraph (6) of subdivision (b) of Section 15642 of the Probate Code is clearly the settlor's intent and that intent is not the product of fraud, menace, duress, or undue influence.

_____   _____ "
(Name of Attorney)   (Date)

❧ ∼ ☙

§ 19040 Form

NOTICE TO CREDITORS
OF _____

_____
SUPERIOR COURT OF CALIFORNIA COUNTY OF _____
Notice is hereby given to the creditors and contingent creditors of the above-named decedent, that all persons having claims against the decedent are required to file them with the Superior Court, at _____, and mail a copy to _____, as trustee of the trust dated _____ wherein the decedent was the settlor, at _____, within the later of four months after ____ (the date of the first publication of notice to creditors) or, if notice is mailed or personally delivered to you, 60 days after the date this notice is mailed or personally delivered to you. A claim form may be obtained from the court clerk. For your protection, you are encouraged to file your claim by certified mail, with return receipt requested.

(name and address of trustee or attorney)

❧ ∼ ☙

§ 19052 Form

NOTICE TO CREDITORS
OF _____

_____
SUPERIOR COURT OF CALIFORNIA COUNTY OF _____

Notice is hereby given to the creditors and contingent creditors of the above-named decedent, that all persons having claims against the decedent are required to file them with the Superior Court, at _____, and mail or deliver a copy to _____, as trustee of the trust dated _____ wherein the decedent was the settlor, at _____, within the later of four months after _____ (the date of the first publication of notice to creditors) or, if notice is mailed or personally delivered to you, 60 days after the date this notice is mailed or personally delivered to you, or you must petition to file a late claim as provided in Section 19103 of the Probate Code. A claim form may be obtained from the court clerk. For your protection, you are encouraged to file your claim by certified mail, with return receipt requested.

_____
(Date of mailing this
  notice if applicable)

_____
(name and address of
  trustee or attorney)

CERTIFICATE OF INDEPENDENT REVIEW

I, _____, (attorney's name) have reviewed _____ (name of instrument) and have counseled the transferor, _____, (name of transferor) on the nature and consequences of any transfers of property to _____ (name of person described in Section 21380 of the Probate Code) that would be made by the instrument.

I am an "independent attorney" as defined in Section 21370 of the Probate Code and am in a position to advise the transferor independently, impartially, and confidentially as to the consequences of the transfer.

On the basis of this counsel, I conclude that the transfers to _____ (name of person described in Section 21380 of the Probate Code) that would be made by the instrument are not the product of fraud or undue influence.

_____   _____
(Name of Attorney)   (Date)